CBT: Science Into Practice

Series Editor

Nikolaos Kazantzis, Cognitive Behavior Therapy Research Unit
Melbourne, VIC, Australia

This series addresses topics that reflect current thinking in the field of cognitive behavior therapy, the most widely accepted form of therapy across mental health disciplines. Despite the consensus that CBT is an effective treatment modality, much of the existing clinical literature focuses on single facets, such as specific disorders or populations. Mostly it does not take into account the latest evidence for transdiagnostic change mechanisms and processes. This series provides guidance on how the latest evidence can be translated into practice. Volumes focus on enhancing flexibility in both the selection and delivery of techniques tailored to individual clients. Each provides clinical insights enhanced by case studies and vignettes to ensure relevance for the practicing professional.

Jennifer S. Wachen • Tara E. Galovski
Editors

Cognitive Processing Therapy for Complex Cases

Evidence-based Strategies

Springer

Editors
Jennifer S. Wachen
Women's Health Sciences Division, National Center for PTSD
VA Boston Healthcare System and Boston University Chobanian and Avedesian School of Medicine
Boston, MA, USA

Tara E. Galovski
Women's Health Sciences Division, National Center for PTSD
VA Boston Healthcare System and Boston University Chobanian and Avedesian School of Medicine
Boston, MA, USA

ISSN 2946-5419 ISSN 2946-5427 (electronic)
CBT: Science Into Practice
ISBN 978-3-031-87355-3 ISBN 978-3-031-87356-0 (eBook)
https://doi.org/10.1007/978-3-031-87356-0

This Springer imprint is published by the registered company Springer Nature Switzerland AG
The registered company address is: Gewerbestrasse 11, 6330 Cham, Switzerland

Jennifer Wachen: To Matt, Will, and Ollie, who fill my life with love, support, and so much happiness. And to my parents, John and Jan, who always believed in me and supported me along this journey.

Tara Galovski: To Jim, Saige, Hope, and Sam who are my well of love, laughter, strength, and light. To all those who have suffered through the sorrow and pain of trauma, I hope that this work helps to pave your path toward recovery and well-being. It has been an honor and privilege to have walked this journey with so many who have suffered so much. I hold you in my heart.

Foreword

The practice of cognitive-behavioral therapy (CBT) is ever-evolving, with evidence-based interventions continually refined to address the complexity of mental health challenges. Among these, Cognitive Processing Therapy (CPT) has emerged as a cornerstone treatment for posttraumatic stress disorder (PTSD), offering a structured, effective approach for addressing the multifaceted impacts of trauma. Yet, as PTSD presentations become increasingly complex, influenced by comorbid conditions, diverse sociocultural factors, and resource disparities, clinicians face the challenge of adapting CPT to meet the needs of a broader range of patients and treatment settings.

It is with great enthusiasm that I introduce *Cognitive Processing Therapy for Complex Cases: Evidence-Based Strategies*, part of the **CBT: Science into Practice** book series, edited by Dr. Jennifer Schuster Wachen and Dr. Tara E. Galovski. This volume provides an essential, practical guide for clinicians, educators, and researchers seeking to enhance their delivery of CPT. By integrating the latest empirical findings with actionable clinical strategies, this book equips readers to navigate the complexities of trauma treatment with precision and confidence.

The opening chapter offers a compelling overview of the evolution of CPT, tracing its development from foundational cognitive theories to its current, evidence-based applications. It underscores the flexibility of the CPT framework in addressing the cognitive, emotional, and behavioral sequelae of trauma. At the same time, the chapter highlights the significant gaps in practical guidance for applying CPT in real-world settings where complex clinical presentations are the norm. This volume bridges those gaps, providing readers with a roadmap for effectively tailoring CPT to the unique challenges faced by their patients.

The book is thoughtfully organized into sections addressing key dimensions of CPT delivery. The initial chapters focus on integrating CPT with interventions for common comorbid conditions such as depression, substance use, and chronic pain, offering clinicians insights into how these conditions intersect with PTSD and how CPT can be modified to address these overlaps. Subsequent sections delve into culturally attuned applications of CPT for diverse populations, including minoritized and underserved communities, as well as the adaptation of CPT for alternative formats such as massed sessions and telehealth delivery.

What sets this volume apart is its combination of research-informed guidance and clinical practicality. Each chapter includes a synthesis of the latest empirical findings, followed by detailed case examples that bring theoretical concepts to life. This dual emphasis ensures that readers not only understand the science behind CPT but also have the tools to translate this knowledge into actionable steps in their own practice.

Dr. Wachen and Dr. Galovski bring an impressive depth of expertise to this volume. A Clinical Research Psychologist in the Women's Health Sciences Division at the VA Boston Healthcare System and an Associate Professor of Psychiatry at Boston University Chobanian and Avedesian School of Medicine, Dr. Wachen has dedicated her career to advancing the treatment of PTSD, particularly among veterans and active-duty military populations. Her federally funded research focuses on improving the efficiency and effectiveness of CPT to address PTSD and psychosocial functioning, as well as novel delivery modalities such as massed treatment. Dr. Galovski is the Director of the Women's Health Sciences Division of the National Center for PTSD and a Professor in the Department of Psychiatry at Boston University Chobanian and Avedesian School of Medicine. She has conducted numerous clinical trials within a variety of populations exposed to different types of trauma including combat, sexual trauma, domestic violence, community violence, and motor vehicle accidents. Dr. Galovski's research interests center around improving interventions by testing modifications to protocols designed to enhance effectiveness and increase reach. Drs. Wachen and Galovski are trainers and consultants in CPT and have trained over 1000 mental health providers nationwide. With a strong foundation in both clinical practice and research, they are uniquely positioned to guide clinicians through the complexities of delivering CPT in diverse and challenging contexts.

This book is more than a practical guide—it is a testament to the adaptability and continued relevance of CPT as a treatment modality. By addressing the complexities of PTSD through a research-informed lens, this volume demonstrates how CPT can evolve to meet the diverse needs of patients and clinical settings. Its emphasis on culturally responsive care, innovative delivery methods, and integration with broader systems of health care ensures that CPT remains a dynamic and accessible intervention for trauma survivors worldwide.

The contributions in this volume advance the field by offering new perspectives on how CPT can be adapted and applied without compromising its core principles. It sets a high standard for integrating research into practice, fostering a dialogue between empirical evidence and clinical expertise that will inspire future innovations in trauma-focused care.

I commend Dr. Wachen and Dr. Galovski and their contributors for producing a work that is as rigorous as it is practical. *Cognitive Processing Therapy for Complex*

Cases: Evidence-Based Strategies is an invaluable resource for clinicians committed to improving the lives of trauma survivors. It is a vital addition to the literature on PTSD and a significant step forward in the evolution of CBT.

Cognitive Behavior Therapy Research Unit
Melbourne, VIC, Australia
Beck Institute for Cognitive Behavior Therapy
Philadelphia, PA, USA

Nikolaos Kazantzis

Acknowledgments

We first want to thank Dr. Patricia Resick for working tirelessly to develop and study cognitive processing therapy and for her guidance to us and so many of the authors who have contributed to this work. We also would like to thank all the authors who contributed their time, effort, and expertise to this book. We are confident that their wisdom will have far-reaching impact. We would especially like to thank the brave trauma survivors from all walks of life, cultures, and experiences who found the courage to engage in the arduous process of recovery from PTSD. Survivors will forever continue to benefit from your willingness to share your journey.

Conflicts of Interest Kazantzis disclosed his royalties from the Guilford Press (Therapeutic Relationship in Cognitive Behavior Therapy; Cognitive and Behavior Theories in Clinical Practice), Routledge (Using Homework Assignments in Cognitive Behavior Therapy); SpringerNature publishers (CBT: Science into Practice Book Series; Handbook of Homework Assignments in Psychotherapy: Research, Practice, & Prevention). He also disclosed editor stipend from the Association for Behavioral and Cognitive Therapies for his role as Editor-in-Chief for Cognitive and Behavioral Practice (Elsevier).

Competing Interests Jennifer Wachen has received research grants to study cognitive processing therapy from the U.S. Department of Defense and receives honoraria for training and consulting in CPT. Tara Galovski has received research grants to study cognitive processing therapy from the U.S. Department of Defense, National Institutes of Health, Veterans Health Administration, Substance Abuse and Mental Health Service Administration, and foundation support and receives honoraria for training and consulting in CPT.

Contents

About the Editors and Contributors

About the Editors

Jennifer S. Wachen, Ph.D. is a Clinical Research Psychologist in the Women's Health Sciences Division of the National Center for PTSD and an Associate Professor in the Department of Psychiatry at Boston University Chobanian and Avedesian School of Medicine. She is a trainer and consultant in Cognitive Processing Therapy (CPT) and has trained numerous providers to implement CPT across a range of treatment settings including military facilities, the Department of Veterans Affairs, and community-based medical centers. Dr. Wachen's research focuses on improving the efficiency and effectiveness of CPT, including novel delivery modalities such as massed treatment. Other research interests include examining the effect of PTSD treatment on physical health and psychosocial functioning outcomes. Dr. Wachen has conducted several Department of Defense-funded clinical trials investigating CPT in military and veteran populations and serves as a consultant on a number of research studies and dissemination initiatives implementing CPT in diverse healthcare settings. She is the author of over 70 peer-reviewed publications and has co-authored over one dozen invited book chapters. She serves on the Editorial Boards of *Psychological Trauma: Theory, Research, Practice, and Policy; Cognitive and Behavioral Practice;* and *Contemporary Clinical Trials.*

Tara E. Galovski, Ph.D. is the Director of the Women's Health Sciences Division of the National Center for PTSD and a Professor in the Department of Psychiatry at Boston University Chobanian and Avedesian School of Medicine. Her research examines the effects of exposure to traumatic events and the development of psychological interventions designed to treat PTSD and comorbid psychiatric disorders. She has conducted federally funded clinical trials within a variety of populations exposed to different trauma types including combat, sexual trauma, domestic violence, community violence, and motor vehicle accidents. The results of Dr. Galovski's program of research have been published in over 100 peer-reviewed publications and book chapters. She has also written two books on related topics. More specific areas of interest include investigations into the role of sleep impairment in recovery from trauma, anger, and physical health complications in the maintenance of and recovery from PTSD. Dr. Galovski is a national trainer of Cognitive Processing Therapy (CPT) and has disseminated the intervention across numerous patient populations and healthcare systems. Over the last decade, she has personally trained over 1100 mental health providers nationwide in CPT. Finally, Dr. Galovski continues to investigate gender differences in PTSD clinical presentations and treatment outcomes. She served as an Associate Editor of one of the top trauma journals, *Journal of Traumatic Stress*, for a decade.

Contributors

Sebastian Bliss, PhD U.S. Department of Veteran Affairs, VA Boston Healthcare System, Boston, MA, USA

Kathleen M. Chard, PhD Cincinnati VA Medical Center, Cincinnati, OH, USA

Department of Psychiatry and Behavioral Neuroscience, University of Cincinnati School of Medicine, Cincinnati, OH, USA

Nicole Christ, PhD Center for Care Delivery & Outcomes Research, Minneapolis VA Healthcare System, Minneapolis, MN, USA

Elizabeth N. Collazo, PhD U.S. Department of Veteran Affairs, VA Boston Healthcare System, Boston, MA, USA

Department of Psychiatry, Boston University Chobanian & Avedisian School of Medicine, Boston, MA, USA

National Center for PTSD, Behavioral Science Division, Boston, MA, USA

Brittany C. Davis, PhD James A. Haley Veteran's Hospital, Tampa, FL, USA

Kristine Dell, PhD VA San Diego Healthcare System and University of California San Diego Department of Psychiatry, San Diego, CA, USA

Marja Elizabeth, PhD Flinders University, College of Education, Psychology and Social Work, Flinders Institute for Mental Health and Wellbeing, Adelaide, SA, Australia

Tara E. Galovski, PhD Women's Health Sciences Division, National Center for PTSD, Boston, MA, USA

Chobanian and Avedisian School of Medicine at Boston University, Boston, MA, USA

VA Boston Healthcare System, Boston, MA, USA

Saige E. Galovski, MA University of Vermont, Burlington, VT, USA

Lisa Glassman, PhD Naval Health Research Center, San Diego, CA, USA

Rosalba M. Gomez, BA Durham VA Medical Center, Durham, NC, USA

Ellen T. Healy, PhD Office of Mental Health, VA Central Office, Washington, DC, USA

Department of Psychiatry, Boston University Chobanian & Avedisian School of Medicine, Boston, MA, USA

Philip Held, PhD Department of Psychiatry and Behavioral Sciences, Rush University Medical Center, Chicago, IL, USA

Cara Herbitter, PhD, MPH U.S. Department of Veteran Affairs, VA Boston Healthcare System, Boston, MA, USA

Department of Psychiatry, Boston University Chobanian & Avedisian School of Medicine, Boston, MA, USA

Nicholas Holder, PhD San Francisco Veterans Affairs Health Care System, San Francisco, CA, USA

University of California, San Francisco School of Medicine, San Francisco, CA, USA

Center for Data to Discovery and Delivery Innovation (3DI COIN), San Francisco, CA, USA

Ryan Holliday, PhD Rocky Mountain Mental Illness Research, Education, and Clinical Center for Suicide Prevention, Aurora, CO, USA

University of Colorado Anschutz Medical Campus, Aurora, CO, USA

VA Pacific Islands Health Care System, Honolulu, USA

Amy Jak, PhD VA San Diego Healthcare System, San Diego, CA, USA

University of California San Diego Department of Psychiatry, San Diego, CA, USA

Debra L. Kaysen, PhD Department of Psychiatry & Behavioral Sciences, Stanford University, Palo Alto, CA, USA

Shannon M. Kehle-Forbes, PhD Women's Health Sciences Division, National Center for PTSD, Department of Veterans Affairs, Boston, MA, USA

Center for Care Delivery & Outcomes Research, Minneapolis VA Healthcare System, Minneapolis, MN, USA

Brian J. Klassen, PhD Department of Psychiatry and Behavioral Sciences, Rush University Medical Center, Chicago, IL, USA

Julie Klunk-Gillis, PhD U.S. Department of Veteran Affairs, VA Boston Healthcare System, Boston, MA, USA

Department of Psychiatry, Boston University Chobanian & Avedisian School of Medicine, Boston, MA, USA

Nicholas A. Livingston, PhD U.S. Department of Veteran Affairs, VA Boston Healthcare System, Boston, MA, USA

Department of Psychiatry, Boston University Chobanian & Avedisian School of Medicine, Boston, MA, USA

National Center for PTSD, Behavioral Science Division, Boston, MA, USA

Stefanie T. LoSavio, PhD Department of Psychiatry and Behavioral Sciences, University of Texas Health Science Center at San Antonio, San Antonio, TX, USA

Kelly P. Maieritsch, PhD National Center for PTSD, Executive Division, White River Junction, VT, USA

Colleen Martin, PhD Cincinnati VA Medical Center, Trauma Recovery Center, Cincinnati, OH, USA

Lauren B. McSweeney, PhD Women's Health Sciences Division, National Center for PTSD, Boston, MA, USA

Chobanian and Avedisian School of Medicine at Boston University, Boston, MA, USA

VA Boston Healthcare System, Boston, MA, USA

John C. Moring, PhD Department of Psychiatry and Behavioral Sciences, The University of Texas Health Science Center at San Antonio, San Antonio, TX, USA

Leslie A. Morland, PsyD National Center for PTSD, Women's Health Science Division, Boston, VA, USA

John Nanney, PhD Private Practice, St. Louis, MO, USA

Reginald D. V. Nixon, PhD Flinders University, College of Education, Psychology and Social Work, Flinders Institute for Mental Health and Wellbeing, Adelaide, SA, Australia

Julia Richardson, MA Department of Psychological Sciences, University of Missouri—St. Louis, St. Louis, MO, USA

Stephanie A. Sacks, PhD Cognitive Behavioral Therapy Center of the Palm Beaches, Boca Raton, FL, USA

Nova Southeastern University, Fort Lauderdale, FL, USA

University of Southern California, Los Angeles, CA, USA

Caroline R. Scheid, PhD Cincinnati VA Medical Center, Trauma Recovery Center, Cincinnati, OH, USA

Christine Serpe, PhD U.S. Department of Veteran Affairs, VA Boston Healthcare System, Boston, MA, USA

Department of Psychiatry, Boston University Chobanian & Avedisian School of Medicine, Boston, MA, USA

Luzimar Vega, PsyD James A. Haley Veterans' Hospital, Department of Veteran Affairs, Tampa, FL, USA

Jennifer S. Wachen, PhD Women's Health Sciences Division, National Center for PTSD, VA Boston Healthcare System, Boston, MA, USA

Boston University Chobanian and Avedisian School of Medicine, Boston, MA, USA

Tamara R. Wachsman, BA VA San Diego Healthcare System, San Diego, CA, USA

Hannah E. Walker, PhD Durham VA Medical Center, Durham, NC, USA

Kristen H. Walter, PhD Psychological Health & Readiness, Naval Health Research Center, San Diego, CA, USA

School of Public Health, San Diego State University, San Diego, CA, USA

Rachel A. Wamser, PhD Department of Psychological Sciences, University of Missouri—St. Louis, St. Louis, MO, USA

Stephanie Y. Wells, PhD Durham Center of Innovation to Accelerate Discovery and Practice Transformation (ADAPT), Durham VA Health Care System, Durham, NC, USA

VA Mid-Atlantic Mental Illness Research, Education, and Clinical Center, Durham, NC, USA

Kimberly B. Werner, PhD College of Nursing, University of Missouri–St. Louis, St. Louis, MO, USA

Amy M. Williams, PhD The Headstrong Project, New York, NY, USA

Part I
Introduction

Chapter 1
The Development and Evolution of Cognitive Processing Therapy

Jennifer S. Wachen and Tara E. Galovski

Most individuals will encounter a traumatic event at some point during their lives, such as a natural disaster, physical or sexual assault, or the sudden unexpected death of a loved one (Kessler et al., 2017). Immediately following such an event, it is common for people to experience a range of symptoms in reaction to experiencing a trauma. They may have recurring thoughts or images of the event, difficulty sleeping or nightmares, or may feel irritable or emotionally numb. In the weeks and months following the traumatic event, most individuals will recover naturally from the distress and symptoms that occur immediately following the trauma, but some will go on to develop more significant mental health conditions such as posttraumatic stress disorder (PTSD).

The diagnostic criteria for PTSD include 20 symptoms distributed across four clusters: intrusions, avoidance, negative alterations in cognitions and mood, and hyperarousal (American Psychiatric Association, 2022). While individuals need to demonstrate symptoms in each of the four clusters to meet full criteria for a PTSD diagnosis, the myriad number of symptom combinations that can contribute to the diagnosis speaks to the significant variability of clinical presentations associated with PTSD (Galatzer-Levy & Bryant, 2013). Additionally, PTSD rarely occurs in isolation and the clinical presentation is often complex, with high rates of comorbidities with other mental health conditions including depression, anxiety, and substance use disorders (e.g., Brady et al., 2000). Clinical presentations of PTSD are often further complicated by a wide range of physical health conditions such as the residual effects of traumatic brain injuries or chronic pain (e.g., Lew et al., 2009).

J. S. Wachen (✉) · T. E. Galovski
Women's Health Sciences Division, National Center for PTSD, VA Boston Healthcare System and Boston University Chobanian and Avedesian School of Medicine, Boston, MA, USA
e-mail: Jennifer.Wachen@va.gov

J. S. Wachen, T. E. Galovski (eds.), *Cognitive Processing Therapy for Complex Cases*, CBT: Science Into Practice,
https://doi.org/10.1007/978-3-031-87356-0_1

Impairment across major domains of psychosocial functioning, including occupational, recreational, and relational, may be substantial as the disorder progresses (e.g., Fang et al., 2015). The impact of PTSD may be even greater for those survivors of trauma who identify as members of minoritized communities or who exist in low resource environments (e.g., Hoppen et al., 2021; Williams et al., 2021). Related stressors may contribute to symptoms and complicate treatment. Furthermore, the definition of what constitutes a traumatic stressor has evolved over time and may impact the implementation of treatments for PTSD.

Fortunately, there are evidence-based psychotherapies shown to be effective in the treatment of PTSD. One such treatment, cognitive processing therapy (CPT; Resick et al., 2024b), is a manualized, trauma-focused, cognitive behavioral therapy that is listed as one of the first-line recommended treatments for PTSD in current clinical practice guidelines including American Psychological Association (APA; 2017), the International Society for Traumatic Stress Studies (ISTSS; 2018), the National Institute for Health and Care Excellence (NICE; 2018), the Phoenix Australia Centre for Posttraumatic Mental Health (Phoenix Australia Centre for Posttraumatic Mental Health, 2013), and the U.S. Departments of Veterans Affairs and Defense (VA/DoD; 2023). These guidelines, developed by prominent professional associations and national organizations spanning three continents, include treatment recommendations based on the strength of the empirical evidence for each treatment including randomized controlled trials and meta-analyses. Indeed, decades of research support the effectiveness of CPT with a range of patient populations (see Resick, LoSavio, et al., 2024a for details about the current state of the science). However, there is little concrete and practical guidance for addressing the full range of PTSD's complex clinical presentations within the CPT protocol and the published extant literature. The primary aim of this book is to provide evidence-based and in-depth clinical guidance on the implementation of CPT across a wide range of patient populations and treatment settings. Special attention is devoted to using the framework of CPT to address the complexities of PTSD as it manifests within the larger context of individuals' comorbid presenting problems and psychosocial environmental influences.

This chapter reviews the historical context regarding the development and evolution of CPT over the years. We briefly discuss the theoretical background that influenced the development of the therapy and provide an overview of the course of treatment. Additionally, we review the various iterations and evolution of the therapy, from the original treatment developed by Resick and Schnicke (1993) to the most recent version of the comprehensive therapist manual (Resick, Monson, et al., 2024b), including changes to the protocol over time and a review of the rationale for those changes. Finally, we provide an overview of the clinical and psychosocial complexities associated with PTSD and highlight how each section of the book will illustrate how these factors can be addressed within the context of CPT.

Theoretical Background

The CPT protocol was developed as a result of Resick's early work with survivors of rape beginning in the 1980s. Although at this time most researchers were focusing on applying treatments to PTSD that had been developed for anxiety disorders, such as exposure therapy (Keane & Kaloupek, 1982), Resick and colleagues noted that trauma responses were frequently accompanied by depressive symptoms, as well as guilt and anger, suggesting that PTSD after rape differed from fear/anxiety disorders in important ways. In their early research on trauma, Resick and colleagues also found that the *perception of danger* was a more important predictor of later symptoms than was the *actual, objective danger* of the situation (Girelli, Resick, Marhoefer-Dvorak, & Hutter, 1986). This suggested that the interpretation of the traumatic event was an important contributor to the traumatic response. As a result, Resick began to explore the application of cognitive theory to explain the development and maintenance of PTSD and inform an intervention focused on survivors' perceptions and cognitive processing of traumatic events.

The development of CPT was informed by several theoretical models of PTSD that explain the impact of traumatic events on existing beliefs and cognitions and the role that inaccurate or distorted cognitions have on emotional responses and behavior. One major influence was Beck's cognitive theory (Beck et al., 1979), which posits that the way in which individuals interpret events influences their reactions to those events, and that these interpretations are based on cognitive schemas. Schemas are deeply held beliefs about the self and the world that are used to help people interpret or make sense of life experiences and inform choices that enable them to navigate their environment. Traumatic events can disrupt schemas and drastically alter the way people view the world, themselves, and others. Therefore, in order to recover from the trauma, individuals need to make sense of the traumatic event in relation to their existing schemas. Another influence was the work of McCann et al. (1988), who proposed a constructivist theory of trauma in which people integrate traumatic events into their overall conceptual systems either by interpreting the event in a way that is consistent with their existing schemas or by altering their existing schemas to be more consistent with the traumatic experience. They also proposed that beliefs about self and others develop in five major areas of psychological and interpersonal functioning that have particular relevance for survivors of trauma: safety, trust, power, esteem, and intimacy. These themes were incorporated into CPT as key areas to address in the latter part of treatment.

The terminology from these cognitive theories is central to the proposed mechanism of CPT. *Assimilation* occurs when new information, including information related to traumatic events, is incorporated into prior beliefs about oneself or the world, whether positive or negative. New information that is congruent with prior beliefs about self or world is integrated quickly because the information matches the prior schemas, or core beliefs. However, if these preexisting beliefs were negative, assimilation may serve to reinforce maladaptive cognitions following a trauma. For example, a woman with a history of childhood abuse may quickly assimilate later intimate partner violence without effort because the information matches her previous schemas (e.g., "I deserve to have bad things happen to me"). Assimilation can also occur when individuals' memories or their causal appraisals of the traumatic event are altered to be more congruent with their prior beliefs. For example, if a woman previously believed that she could keep herself safe and then experiences a rape, she might conclude that the rape was her fault and that she *should* have been able to prevent the event, in order to maintain a sense of safety and control. Similarly, if a servicemember believes that everyone in the unit will be safe if everyone performs their duties correctly, then they may blame themself or others around them if an unforeseen event (e.g., an explosive device killing soldiers on a convoy) happens. Conversely, *accommodation* occurs when individuals reconcile the event with their preexisting beliefs or modify their beliefs in order to incorporate the new information in a realistic way (e.g., "I was harmed that night, but nothing I did caused the event"). Accommodation represents balanced thinking and acceptance of the facts of the traumatic event, and is a primary goal of CPT. CPT also added the notion of *overaccommodation*, which occurs when individuals extremely alter their existing belief structure about the world, self and others in an attempt to make sense of the trauma. For instance, someone who believed that the world was a safe place prior to the trauma and then was assaulted may develop a new belief that "*Nowhere is safe.*" Prior traumatic events or negative preexisting beliefs may further reinforce that these extreme statements are true.

A primary focus of CPT is the identification of "stuck points," or maladaptive beliefs resulting from the trauma that keep the individual "stuck" in their recovery from the event. *Assimilated* stuck points are problematic beliefs about the event itself (e.g., "why" the event happened). Assimilated stuck points are often related to self-blame or hindsight bias or contradict the "just-world" belief that the world is fundamentally fair and just (Resick et al., 2024b). *Overaccommodated* stuck points reflect how the individual's beliefs about themselves, others, or the world have changed as a result of the traumatic experience (e.g., "I am unworthy of love" or "No one can be trusted"). In treatment, it is important to focus on addressing assimilated stuck points prior to overaccommodated stuck points, as assimilated stuck points may serve to reinforce the overaccommodated beliefs. Indeed, prioritization of assimilation before overaccommodation is associated with greater PTSD symptom improvement (Farmer et al., 2017).

In addition to a focus on cognitive change, emotions play a large role in recovering from trauma using CPT (Resick et al., 2024b). *Natural emotions*, such as fear, anger, or sadness, may result directly from the trauma. For instance, significant loss or death of a loved one is universally experienced with sadness. CPT postulates that the intensity of natural emotions diminishes over time when survivors stop avoiding the memory of the traumatic event and allow themselves to experience those emotions. Alternatively, *manufactured emotions* such as guilt and shame result directly from thoughts and interpretations about the cause of the event and beliefs about the meaningfulness of the trauma on the world, self, and others, rather than the facts of the event itself. These manufactured emotions will persist as long as the individual continues to hold the inaccurate, maladaptive beliefs that are fueling them.

Therefore, it is important to identify, challenge, and modify the underlying trauma-related beliefs (or stuck points) that contribute to manufactured emotions in order to reduce the associated negative emotions and lead to symptom improvement.

Another notion underlying CPT is that the expression of natural emotions is also necessary to facilitate recovery from PTSD. Because individuals with PTSD may avoid experiencing the strong affect related to the natural emotions stemming from the trauma, they remain stuck in their recovery. Further, because this avoidance prevents cognitive processing from occurring, the trauma memories continue to emerge through intrusive reminders. The emotional responses and arousal that are part of the trauma memory also emerge, which triggers further avoidance. Therefore, CPT suggests that it is important for individuals to experience their natural emotions in order for the trauma memory to be fully examined. It is assumed that the natural affect, once accessed, will dissipate rather quickly, and that the work of examining beliefs about the trauma and accommodating the trauma memory continues. Once assimilated beliefs regarding the event (e.g., self-blame) and overaccommodated beliefs about self, others, and the world (e.g., safety, trust, control, esteem, intimacy) are examined and modified, then the manufactured emotions will diminish along with PTSD symptoms.

Treatment Overview

CPT is a manualized therapy originally developed as a 12-session protocol, although the most recent version of the treatment manual allows for early termination or additional sessions based on the degree of symptom improvement (Resick et al., 2024b). In the early phase of treatment (Sessions 1–3), clients are educated about the symptoms of PTSD, the rationale behind CPT, and understanding the connection between thoughts and feelings. Clients write an Impact Statement about why they believe the traumatic event occurred and its impact on their current and future beliefs about themselves, others, and the world. This assignment is used to begin to identify stuck points that are tracked throughout treatment on a Stuck Point Log. Clients then are taught to identify the connection between events, thoughts, and feelings using an ABC worksheet. This assignment helps clients learn to identify a range of emotions and to recognize the underlying thoughts contributing to each emotion. The ABC worksheets can be used to identify stuck points to be examined as a focus of treatment and to begin to facilitate cognitive restructuring of these inaccurate and maladaptive thoughts. The therapist uses Socratic dialogue to facilitate uncovering alternative beliefs to the client's current way of thinking. This in turn teaches the client the skill of cognitive flexibility that will be enlisted throughout the remainder of the treatment.

In the middle phase of treatment (Sessions 4–7), sessions focus on processing the experience of the trauma through more direct examination of stuck points related to the event. First using ABC worksheets, assimilated stuck points (focused on beliefs related to self-blame, erroneous other-blame, or the just-world belief) are identified and initially targeted using Socratic questioning to help the client reappraise the stuck points. An optional written account, in which the client writes the details of the traumatic event and associated emotions, also may be assigned to elicit additional emotional processing. Worksheets are introduced to assist the client in examining their thinking about the traumatic event independent of their therapist. The Examining Questions (previously Challenging Questions) Worksheet helps the client examine individual stuck points, starting with assimilated stuck points that typically include self- and other-blame, undoing and hindsight bias about the cause of the event. The Thinking Patterns (previously Problematic Patterns of Thinking) worksheet helps clients identify habitual and frequently unproductive ways in which they tend to respond to situations, such as jumping to conclusions, mind reading, and emotional reasoning. This helps clients to become more aware of their typical (and sometimes automatic) thought processes and work to identify and modify these types of patterns in their thinking in the future. The Alternative Thoughts (previously Challenging Beliefs) worksheet is a culmination of the previous worksheets that enables clients to identify stuck points that emerge in response to trauma- and non-trauma-related events, identify emotions caused by the stuck point, challenge the accuracy of the assumptions behind the thoughts, and generate alternative beliefs (and experience-related emotions) that are more accurate and reflective of all aspects relevant to the situation.

In the final phase of treatment (Sessions 8–12), the therapist and client work together to help the client further challenge their stuck points, including any remaining assimilated stuck points and also considering beliefs that have overgeneralized from the events (overaccommodated stuck points). Overaccommodated stuck points in five areas—safety, trust, power/control, esteem, and intimacy—are specifically highlighted and examined, particularly as they relate to self, others, and the world. The goal of this phase of treatment is to generate healthier, and more accurate, beliefs in relation to the event(s) based on real evidence. Lastly, clients rewrite a final Impact Statement for discussion in the last treatment session in which they describe their thoughts and feelings about the meaning of the event upon treatment completion.

Evolution of the CPT Protocol

The first CPT manual (Resick & Schnicke, 1993) was developed from Resick's early work studying this newly developed treatment in a weekly group format with survivors of rape (Resick & Schnicke, 1992). This version of the manual was used in the first large-scale randomized clinical trials (RCTs) of CPT. The first trial (Resick et al., 2002) compared CPT to prolonged exposure (PE) and a minimal attention waitlist in a sample of women who had been raped and found that both CPT and PE were highly efficacious and superior to the minimal attention group. The second study (Resick et al., 2008) broadened the sample to include women who had experienced any type of interpersonal violence in childhood or adulthood. This trial was a dismantling study designed to compare the full protocol of CPT with its constituent components—cognitive therapy only (CPT-C) and written accounts (WA). The results showed that participants in all three groups showed significant reductions in PTSD and depressive symptoms, and that the CPT-C condition reported greater improvement than the WA condition, suggesting that CPT is effective without the written account component. Additionally, the CPT condition had a dropout rate of 22%, compared to 34% in CPT + A, suggesting that offering CPT without the account may improve treatment retention. These findings would greatly influence subsequent versions of the treatment manual.

During the time of the dismantling study, Monson conducted the first trial of CPT in a primarily male veteran population and found significant improvements in PTSD and related symptoms (Monson et al., 2006). This study provided the first evidence that CPT could be used effectively for chronic military-related PTSD. Resick received funding from the U.S. Department of Veterans Affairs (VA) to further develop materials for the dissemination of CPT throughout VA (see Chap. 17 for a detailed description of the implementation of CPT within VA). The result was a Military/Veteran version of the CPT treatment manual (Resick et al., 2007). This version of the manual offered two versions of the CPT protocol—a version that included the use of the written account (CPT) and a cognitive-only version (CPT-C) that omitted the written account and instead spent an additional session focused on cognitive work using ABC worksheets. Because the dismantling study (Resick et al., 2008) had shown that CPT-C was as effective as CPT with the account (and showed faster symptom improvement in the early phase of treatment), clinicians were advised to offer a choice to patients about which version of the treatment they would prefer. It was suggested that patients who are reluctant to engage in the written account and may otherwise drop out of treatment prematurely may be more amenable to engaging in CPT-C.

A major shift in terminology occurred when Resick, Monson, and Chard published the first CPT manual outside of VA (Resick et al., 2017a). Again based on the findings of the dismantling study (Resick et al., 2008) that found that CPT with the written account did not provide superior benefits to CPT without the account and may reduce dropout, the authors decided that CPT-C would now be the primary version of the treatment, and would thereby be referred to as CPT. The version of CPT that includes the written account would now be called CPT + A (CPT + Account).

The authors recently released a second edition of the CPT manual (Resick et al., 2024b) that contains some additional changes to the protocol. Specifically, there was a shift in the tone of the language used throughout the treatment. The wording of the worksheets was softened, such that Challenging Questions was changed to Exploring Questions, Patterns of Problematic Thinking became Thinking Patterns, and the Challenging Beliefs Worksheet was changed to the Alternate Thoughts Worksheet. Of note, because at the time of the writing of our book the new treatment manual had not yet been published, and because some case examples describe treatment using an earlier version of the manual, some of the chapters refer to the worksheets by their former names. In those cases, we have added the new names of the worksheets in parentheses to clarify how the examples would translate to the new treatment materials. Other changes to the manual include the addition of a case conceptualization form for use by the therapist, a reduced number of questions on the Exploring Questions and Thinking Patterns worksheets, and an additional handout for tracking the behavioral assignments in the last few sessions of the protocol.

From Research to Practice

Currently, the CPT manual has been translated into 15 languages, and its reach continues to grow. Since the first open trial of CPT (Resick & Schnicke, 1992) there have been 44 published RCTs to date, conducted across eight countries and with a range of populations and traumatic events. CPT has been studied in community samples (e.g., Galovski et al., 2012) and with veterans (e.g., Schnurr et al., 2022) and servicemembers (e.g., Resick et al., 2017b), in outpatient and residential settings (e.g., Walter et al., 2014), in groups and individually (e.g., Resick et al., 2015), delivered in-home and via telehealth (e.g., Peterson et al., 2022), and modified for delivery in under-resourced countries (e.g., Bass et al., 2013). The extant research demonstrates that CPT is used successfully with clinically complex patients, including those with comorbidities such as depression (e.g., Angelakis et al., 2020), substance use (Simpson et al., 2022), emotion dysregulation (e.g., Holder et al., 2017), and physical health concerns such as sleep disturbance (e.g., Galovski et al., 2016; Pigeon et al., 2022) and postconcussive symptoms from a traumatic brain injury (e.g., Jak et al., 2019). CPT is shown to be effective across a range of traumas, including physical and sexual assault (e.g., Resick et al., 2008), combat (e.g., Resick et al., 2017b), and multiple repeated lifetime traumas (e.g., Weiss et al., 2015). Recent research also highlights novel delivery modalities of CPT, including massed delivery (e.g., Held, 2023; Wachen et al., 2024) and the incorporation of case formulation throughout treatment (e.g., Galovski et al., 2024). Additionally, through the use of national rollouts (Karlin & Cross, 2014) and learning collaborative models (LoSavio et al., 2019), CPT has been disseminated in large healthcare systems and community practices, further extending the reach of trained providers.

These decades of extensive research provide a multitude of insights on how to deliver CPT most effectively across a range of complex clinical presentations and treatment settings. Each of the chapters in this book will review the relevant literature in each topic area and present the clinical implications of the research findings that may be incorporated into clinical practice. The first chapters are devoted to addressing comorbid mental and physical health conditions within the context of CPT. The next section addresses the implementation of CPT in specific patient populations and identities. Then, the delivery of CPT in alternative formats is presented, and finally, the dissemination efforts of CPT in large healthcare systems and community settings are described. Each chapter highlights the unique clinical considerations for each topic area and includes specific case examples to provide practical guidance to clinicians delivering CPT in these contexts. A discussion of the future direction of CPT in each topic area is also provided.

The contributors to this book are leading researchers and clinicians in the field of PTSD research, and in CPT specifically. We hope that this compilation of their expertise will be of great value to clinicians who hope to put the results of cutting-edge research into practice and are interested in learning how to effectively provide CPT across a range of complex patient populations in diverse treatment environments.

Competing Interests Jennifer Wachen has received research grants to study cognitive processing therapy from the U.S. Department of Defense and receives honoraria for training and consulting in CPT. Tara Galovski has received research grants to study cognitive processing therapy from the U.S. Department of Defense, National Institutes of Health, Veterans Health Administration, Substance Abuse and Mental Health Service Administration, and foundation support and receives honoraria for training and consulting in CPT.

References

American Psychiatric Association. (2022). *Diagnostic and statistical manual of mental disorders* (5th ed., text rev.). https://doi.org/10.1176/appi.books.9780890425787.

American Psychological Association. (2017). *Clinical practice guideline for the treatment of posttraumatic stress disorder (PTSD) in adults*. Author.

Angelakis, S., Weber, N., & Nixon, R. D. V. (2020). Comorbid posttraumatic stress disorder and major depressive disorder: The usefulness of a sequential treatment approach within a randomised design. *Journal of Anxiety Disorders, 76*, 102324.

Bass, J. K., Annan, J., McIvor Murray, S., Kaysen, D., Griffiths, S., Cetinoglu, T., Wachter, K., Murray, L. K., & Bolton, P. A. (2013). Controlled trial of psychotherapy for Congolese survivors of sexual violence. *New England Journal of Medicine, 368*, 2182–2191.

Beck, A. T., Rush, A. J., Shaw, B. F., & Emery, G. (1979). *Cognitive therapy of depression*. Guilford.

Brady, K. T., Killeen, T. K., Brewerton, T., & Lucerini, S. (2000). Comorbidity of psychiatric disorders and posttraumatic stress disorder. *Journal of Clinical Psychiatry, 61*, 22–32.

Department of Veterans Affairs and Department of Defense (VA/DoD). (2023). *VA/DoD clinical practice guideline for the management of posttraumatic stress disorder and acute stress disorder*. Author.

Farmer, C. C., Mitchell, K. S., Parker-Guilbert, K., & Galovski, T. E. (2017). Fidelity to the cognitive processing therapy protocol: Evaluation of critical elements. *Behavior Therapy, 48*(2), 195–206.

Fang, S. C., Schnurr, P. P., Kulish, A. L., Holowka, D. W., Marx, B. P., Keane, T. M., & Rosen, R. (2015). Psychosocial functioning and health-related quality of life associated with posttraumatic stress disorder in male and female Iraq and Afghanistan war veterans: The VALOR registry. *Journal of Women's Health, 24*, 1038–1046. https://doi.org/10.1089/jwh.2014.5096

Galatzer-Levy, I. R., & Bryant, R. A. (2013). 636,120 ways to have posttraumatic stress disorder. *Perspectives on Psychological Science, 8*(6), 651–662.

Galovski, T. E., Blain, L., Mott, J., Elwood, L., & Houle, T. (2012). Manualized therapy for PTSD: Flexing the structure of cognitive processing therapy. *Journal of Consulting and Clinical Psychology, 80*(6), 968–981.

Galovski, T. E., Harik, J. M., Blain, L. M., Elwood, L., Gloth, C., & Fletcher, T. D. (2016). Augmenting cognitive processing therapy to improve sleep impairment in PTSD: A randomized controlled trial. *Journal of Consulting and Clinical Psychology, 84*(2), 167.

Galovski, T. E., McSweeney, L. B., Nixon, R. D. V., Wachen, J. S., Smith, B. N., Noorbaloochi, S., et al. (2024). Personalizing cognitive processing therapy with a case formulation approach to intentionally target impairment in psychosocial functioning associated with PTSD. *Contemporary Clinical Trials Communications, 42*, 101385.

Girelli, S. A., Resick, P. A., Marhoefer-Dvorak, S., & Hutter, C. K. (1986). Subjective distress and violence during rape: Their effects on long-term fear. *Violence and Victims, 1*, 35–46.

Held, P., Smith, D. L., Pridgen, S., Coleman, J. A., & Klassen, B. J. (2023). More is not always better: 2 weeks of intensive cognitive processing therapy-based treatment are noninferior to 3 weeks. *Psychological Trauma: Theory, Research, Practice, and Policy, 15*(1), 100.

Holder, N., Holliday, R., Pai, A., & Surís, A. (2017). Role of borderline personality disorder in the treatment of military sexual trauma-related posttraumatic stress disorder with cognitive processing therapy. *Behavioral Medicine, 43*, 184–190.

Hoppen, T. H., Priebe, S., Vetter, I., & Morina, N. (2021). Global burden of post-traumatic stress disorder and major depression in countries affected by war between 1989 and 2019: A systematic review and meta-analysis. *BMJ Global Health, 6*(7), 1–13.

International Society for Traumatic Stress Studies (ISTSS). (2018). *ISTSS PTSD prevention and treatment guidelines: Methodology and recommendations*. Retrieved from http://www.istss.org/getattachment/Treating-Trauma/New-ISTSS-Prevention-and-Treatment-Guidelines/ISTSS_PreventionTreatmentGuidelines_FNL-March-19-2019.pdf.aspx

Jak, A. J., Jurick, S., Crocker, L. D., Sanderson-Cimino, M., Aupperle, R., Rodgers, C. S., et al. (2019). SMART-CPT for veterans with comorbid post-traumatic stress disorder and history of traumatic brain injury: A randomised controlled trial. *Journal of Neurology, Neurosurgery & Psychiatry, 90*(3), 333–341.

Karlin, B. E., & Cross, G. (2014). From the laboratory to the therapy room: National dissemination and implementation of evidence-based psychotherapies in the US Department of Veterans Affairs Health Care System. *American Psychologist, 69*(1), 19–33.

Keane, T. M., & Kaloupek, D. G. (1982). Imaginal flooding in the treatment of a posttraumatic stress disorder. *Journal of Consulting and Clinical Psychology, 50*, 138–140.

Kessler, R. C., Aguilar-Gaxiola, S., Alonso, J., Benjet, C., Bromet, E. J., Cardoso, G., et al. (2017). Trauma and PTSD in the WHO world mental health surveys. *European Journal of Psychotraumatology, 8*(sup5), 1353383.

Lew, H. L., Otis, J. D., Tun, C., Kerns, R. D., Clark, M. E., & Cifu, D. X. (2009). Prevalence of chronic pain, posttraumatic stress disorder, and persistent postconcussive symptoms in OIF/OEF veterans: Polytrauma clinical triad. *Journal of Rehabilitation Research & Development, 46*(6), 697–702.

LoSavio, S. T., Dillon, K. H., Murphy, R. A., Goetz, K., Houston, F., & Resick, P. A. (2019). Using a learning collaborative model to disseminate cognitive processing therapy to community-based agencies. *Behavior Therapy, 50*(1), 36–49.

McCann, I. L., Sakheim, D. K., & Abrahamson, D. J. (1988). Trauma and victimization: A model of psychological adaptation. *The Counseling Psychologist, 16*(4), 531–594.

Monson, C. M., Schnurr, P. P., Resick, P. A., Friedman, M. J., Young-Xu, Y., & Stevens, S. P. (2006). Cognitive processing therapy for veterans with military-related posttraumatic stress disorder. *Journal of Consulting and Clinical Psychology, 74*, 898–907.

National Institute for Health and Care Excellence (NICE). (2018). *Guideline for post-traumatic stress disorder*. National Institute for Health and Clinical Practice.

Phoenix Australia Centre for Posttraumatic Mental Health. (2013). *Australian guidelines for the treatment of acute stress disorder and posttraumatic stress disorder*. Author.

Peterson, A. L., Mintz, J., Moring, J. C., Straud, C. L., Young-McCaughan, S., McGeary, C. A., McGeary, D. D., Litz, B. T., Velligan, D. I., Macdonald, A., Mata-Galan, E., Holliday, S. L., Dillon, K. H., Roache, J. D., Bira, L. M., Nabity, P. S., Medellin, E. M., Hale, W. J., Resick, P. A., & for the STRONG STAR Consortium. (2022). In-office, in-home, and telehealth cognitive processing therapy for posttraumatic stress disorder in veterans: A randomized clinical trial. *BMC Psychiatry, 22*, 41.

Pigeon, W. R., Crean, H. F., Cerulli, C., Gallegos, A. M., Bishop, T. M., & Heffner, K. L. (2022). A randomized clinical trial of cognitive-behavioral therapy for insomnia to augment PTSD treatment in survivors of interpersonal violence. *Psychotherapy and Psychosomatics, 91*(1), 50.

Resick, P. A., Galovski, T. E., Uhlmansiek, M. O., Scher, C. D., Clum, G., & Young-Xu, Y. (2008). A randomized clinical trial to dismantle components of cognitive processing therapy for posttraumatic stress disorder in female victims of interpersonal violence. *Journal of Consulting & Clinical Psychology, 76*, 243–258.

Resick, P. A., LoSavio, S. T., Monson, C. M., Kaysen, D. L., Wachen, J. S., Galovski, T. E., et al. (2024a). State of the science of cognitive processing therapy. *Behavior Therapy, 55*, 1205–1221.

Resick, P. A. Monson, C. M., & Chard, K. M. (2024b). Cognitive processing therapy for PTSD: *A Comprehensive Manual. 2nd editio*n. New York, NY: Guilford.

Resick, P. A., Monson, C. M., & Chard, K. M. (2007). *Cognitive processing therapy: Veteran/military version: Therapist's manual.* Department of Veterans' Affairs.

Resick, P. A., Monson, C. M., & Chard, K. M. (2017a). *Cognitive processing therapy for PTSD: A comprehensive manual.* Guilford.

Resick, P. A., Nishith, P., Weaver, T. L., Astin, M. C., & Feuer, C. A. (2002). A comparison of cognitive processing therapy, prolonged exposure and a waiting condition for the treatment of posttraumatic stress disorder in female rape victims. *Journal of Consulting and Clinical Psychology, 70*, 867–879.

Resick, P. A., & Schnicke, M. K. (1992). Cognitive processing therapy for sexual assault victims. *Journal of Consulting and Clinical Psychology, 60*(5), 748–756.

Resick, P. A., & Schnicke, M. K. (1993). *Cognitive processing therapy for rape victims: A treatment manual.* Sage.

Resick, P. A., Wachen, J. S., Mintz, J., Young-McCaughan, S., Roache, J. D., Borah, A. M., Borah, E. V., Dondanville, K. A., Hembree, E. A., Litz, B. T., Peterson, A. L., & On behalf of the STRONG STAR Consortium. (2015). A randomized clinical trial of group cognitive processing therapy compared with group present-centered therapy for PTSD among active duty military personnel. *Journal of Consulting and Clinical Psychology, 83*, 1058–1068.

Resick, P. A., Wachen, J. S., Dondanville, K. A., Pruiksma, K. E., Yarvis, J. S., Mintz, J., Peterson, A. L., & the STRONG STAR Consortium. (2017b). Effect of group vs. individual cognitive processing therapy in active-duty military seeking treatment for posttraumatic stress disorder: A randomized clinical trial. *JAMA Psychiatry, 74*, 28–36.

Schnurr, P. P., Chard, K. M., Ruzek, J. I., Chow, B. K., Resick, P. A., Foa, E. B., et al. (2022). Comparison of prolonged exposure vs cognitive processing therapy for treatment of posttraumatic stress disorder among US veterans: A randomized clinical trial. *JAMA Network Open, 5*(1), e2136921–e2136921.

Simpson, T. L., Kaysen, D. L., Fleming, C. B., Rhew, I. C., Jaffe, A. E., Desai, S., Hien, D. A., Berliner, L., Donovan, D., & Resick, P. A. (2022). Cognitive processing therapy or relapse prevention for comorbid posttraumatic stress disorder and alcohol use disorder: A randomized clinical trial. *PLoS One, 17*(11), e0276111.

Wachen, J. S., Morris, K. L., Galovski, T. E., Dondanville, K. A., Resick, P. A., & Schwartz, C. (2024). Massed cognitive processing therapy for combat-related posttraumatic stress disorder: Study design and methodology of a non-inferiority randomized controlled trial. *Contemporary Clinical Trials, 107405*, 107405.

Walter, K. H., Varkovitzky, R. L., Owens, G. P., Lewis, J., & Chard, K. M. (2014). Cognitive processing therapy for veterans with posttraumatic stress disorder: A comparison between outpatient and residential treatment. *Journal of Consulting and Clinical Psychology, 82*(4), 551–561. https://doi.org/10.1037/a0037075

Weiss, W. M., Murray, L. K., Zangana, G. A. S., Mahmooth, Z., Kaysen, D., Dorsey, S., Lindgren, K., Gross, A., Murray, S. M., Bass, J. K., & Bolton, P. (2015). Community-based mental health treatments for survivors of torture and militant attacks in southern Iraq: A randomized control trial. *BMC Psychiatry, 15*, 1–16.

Williams, M. T., Osman, M., Gran-Ruaz, S., & Lopez, J. (2021). Intersection of racism and PTSD: Assessment and treatment of racial stress and trauma. *Current Treatment Options in Psychiatry, 8*(4), 167–185.

Part II
Addressing Comorbidities with Cognitive Processing Therapy

Chapter 2
Delivering CPT in the Context of Depression

Reginald D. V. Nixon and Marja Elizabeth

Scope of Problem

As often said with PTSD, comorbidity[1] is the norm, not the exception. Over a number of years and despite changes in diagnostic criteria, a consistent finding is that between 30% and 50% of individuals with PTSD are also diagnosed with a comorbid depressive disorder, typically defined as major depression (MDD) or persistent depressive disorder (PDD, previously dysthymia) (Kessler et al., 2005; Rytwinski et al., 2013; Walter et al., 2018b). In some trauma populations (e.g., intimate partner violence), this comorbidity is higher (e.g., >60%; Nixon et al., 2004) and in randomized trials of CPT, up to 70% suffer from this comorbidity (Galovski et al., 2020). This comorbidity has significant clinical and functional ramifications across a number of important domains, with impacted individuals more likely to have greater health issues, more severe symptoms, increased suicide risk, poorer quality of life and social functioning, and a more chronic course of impairment than those with either disorder alone (Bedard-Gilligan et al., 2015; Ikin et al., 2010; Nichter et al., 2019a, 2019b; Oquendo et al., 2005; Post et al., 2011). PTSD is routinely underdiagnosed in health settings (Cusack et al., 2006; Lewis et al., 2017; Shannon et al., 2011) and relatedly, possibly due to some shared symptoms, therapists may

[1] We use the term comorbidity (not co-occurring) to reflect PTSD and depressive disorders are strongly linked, mutually influence each other, and can complicate an individual's treatment, versus co-occurrence which refers to conditions that are present simultaneously, but without the conditions necessarily having strong interactive or exacerbating effects on each other.

R. D. V. Nixon (✉) · M. Elizabeth
Flinders University, College of Education, Psychology and Social Work, Flinders Institute for Mental Health and Wellbeing, Adelaide, South Australia, Australia
e-mail: reg.nixon@flinders.edu.au

J. S. Wachen, T. E. Galovski (eds.), *Cognitive Processing Therapy for Complex Cases*, CBT: Science Into Practice,
https://doi.org/10.1007/978-3-031-87356-0_2

be more likely to diagnose and treat depression without identifying or at least screening for PTSD (Basco et al., 2000; Liebschutz et al., 2007; Meltzer et al., 2012).

There is an abundance of literature demonstrating MDD or depressive symptoms are associated with attenuated treatment response in psychological interventions for PTSD (see Kline et al., 2021). PTSD and depression have similar cognitive and memorial processes hypothesized to contribute to both the development and maintenance of the respective disorders, such as overgeneralized autobiographical memory retrieval, rumination, and maladaptive cognitions (Angelakis & Nixon, 2015). These and other factors (e.g., emotional numbing) are thought to interfere with optimal outcomes in the context of PTSD therapy (Angelakis et al., 2020; Galovski et al., 2020). We now discuss relevant key CPT findings that will in part inform later strategies for managing this comorbidity.

Research Overview

Although CPT[2] is a therapy designed to treat PTSD, it has regularly demonstrated its impact on successfully reducing depressive symptoms. It is beyond the scope of this chapter to extensively detail this research, but in both randomized and open trials across a range of trauma types and clinical settings, clinically significant reductions have been consistently achieved without needing to modify the standard CPT approach. In clinical trials of CPT, approximately 40–70% of clients have formally diagnosed depression (Galovski et al., 2020) with 20–60% no longer having the diagnosis by follow-up (e.g., Angelakis et al., 2020; Resick et al., 2002, 2008). These trials and other CPT studies have also shown that problems that frequently accompany depression (e.g., suicidal ideation, alexithymia, interpersonal difficulties) also significantly improve following CPT (Galovski et al., 2020; see also Angelakis et al., 2020; Monson et al., 2006; Rozek et al., 2022). When it comes to PTSD in the presence of comorbid depression, with some qualification, the general recommendation is that therapists treat PTSD first (Rosen et al., 2020). The evidence to support this recommendation in relation to CPT is now discussed, as well as selected relevant research that offers alternative guidance when addressing depression in the context of CPT.

The evidence that initial depression severity is associated with smaller PTSD treatment effects (Kline et al., 2021) is often seen in CPT findings (e.g., Galovski et al., 2016; Schumm et al., 2013; Stein et al., 2012). In Galovski et al., while PTSD and depression changed in a similar fashion for two thirds of the sample, this was not the case for the remainder; that is, PTSD symptoms might reduce but not necessarily depression. Examining varying forms of CPT (i.e., with and without use of a

[2] Where we use "CPT" we refer to CPT in its standard form in that it does not include use of the trauma account (in line with the recent treatment manuals, Resick et al., 2017, 2024). CPT + A or "CPT with a trauma account" is used when this component was utilized, typically in earlier research.

trauma account, the written account only, as well as Prolonged Exposure [PE]), Stein and colleagues observed that the majority of individuals identified as nonresponders had MDD at pretreatment. They concluded that while most clients responded to the different therapies under examination, clients with certain risk factors, including depression, might need fuller (or more comprehensive) treatment packages such as PE and CPT (including use of a trauma account) and/or additional treatment to achieve good outcomes. Consistent with this, the suggestion that the inclusion of a trauma account in CPT has benefits for depression was seen in the outcomes of veterans in a PTSD residential program, 73% of whom had comorbid MDD (Walter et al., 2014), with veterans who received the trauma account showing larger reductions in depressive symptoms at posttreatment than those receiving standard CPT.

In the military and veteran context, the nature of the traumatic event may play a role in PTSD and depression outcomes. In Schumm et al. (2013) discussed above, individuals who showed an attenuated response to CPT not only had higher baseline depression severity, but they were also more likely to report their worst trauma being combat-related. This dovetails with the findings of the impact of traumatic loss in a CPT study with active-duty military personnel (Jacoby et al., 2019). Noting the strong relationship between grief and depression, they observed that smaller depression change mediated the relationship between trauma type (traumatic loss versus other trauma type) and PTSD outcome.

The above findings represent a snapshot of the impact of depression on PTSD outcomes when CPT is delivered in a relatively standard fashion and with samples with high levels of depression or MDD comorbidity—nonetheless, not all individuals in these studies had *both* PTSD and MDD. Although there are theoretical and empirical arguments to suggest depression needs to be explicitly targeted as part of PTSD treatment to improve outcomes for those with this comorbidity (see, for discussion, Angelakis & Nixon, 2015; Rosen et al., 2020; Schumm et al., 2013), there is relatively little research as to how this is optimally implemented with CPT. We do have, however, two methodologically rigorous studies that provide some caution against assuming that depression should always be the first target.

The first study by Angelakis et al. (2020) examined this issue using a sequential therapy approach as part of a randomized design. All clients ($N = 52$) had PTSD and MDD, with PTSD caused primarily by interpersonal trauma. Clients received either five sessions of Behavioral Activation (BA) before CPT (BA/CPT), after CPT (CPT/BA), or received standard CPT. In this study BA was adapted from previous BA interventions (Addis & Martell, 2004; Martell et al., 2001) and involved psychoeducation, activity monitoring, mastery and pleasant event scheduling, and explicit discussion of the role of avoidance behaviors on mood. When combined with BA, CPT comprised of ten sessions (6×60 min, 4×90 min) to minimize length of therapy (in weeks). Although all three groups demonstrated substantial reductions in PTSD and depression severity that was maintained at 6-month follow-up, contrary to expectations, targeting depression first (BA/CPT) did not result in the best outcomes. Instead, the overall results in terms of remission, session attendance, and effect sizes suggested that the CPT/BA group showed the strongest outcomes. For example, at the 6-month follow-up, 50% of this group had remission of both PTSD and depression vs. 18% and 11% of CPT only and BA/CPT individuals, respectively. The CPT/BA group generally had substantially lower symptom scores on PTSD and depression outcomes relative to the other groups, especially compared with BA/CPT. The conclusions were that, in general, starting with a depression focus was not optimal for this group, and in some cases, might have inadvertently resulted in colluding with client avoidance of addressing key traumatic material that was maintaining both their PTSD and depression. Because CPT was made more intensive in the CPT/BA group (i.e., covered more CPT content in a 10-week interval than in standard weekly CPT sessions), it is possible this allowed faster gains to be realized in this group, which could have fostered greater engagement, self-efficacy, and trust in the therapeutic process. This is not dissimilar to studies of intensively delivered CPT (delivered over 1–4 weeks) which report comparable outcomes to standard weekly therapy but with substantially higher completion rates, typically over 85% (e.g., Bryan et al., 2022; Galovski et al., 2022; Goetter et al., 2021; Yamokoski et al., 2023).

Using a slightly different design and sample, Walter et al. (2023) found that the addition of BA did not improve outcomes above and beyond standard CPT. This randomized trial of active-duty military participants with both PTSD and MDD ($N = 94$; 55% female, 48.9% of the total sample had sexual trauma as index event) used what was described as an integrated BA + CPT approach. This comprised 14 sessions with the first two sessions focused on BA, with BA techniques integrated through the remainder of CPT. In regard to this integration, subsequent CPT sessions involved reviewing BA content and between session exercises, then setting new behavioral goals for the subsequent session. The remainder of the session was spent on CPT content (see Walter et al., 2018a, for more detail). CPT alone consisted of the usual CPT content delivered over 12 sessions. Overall, there were almost no clinically meaningful differences in outcomes between the groups. At 3-month follow-up, 30% of those receiving CPT no longer had PTSD or MDD, with a rate of 25.9% in the BA + CPT condition. Like Angelakis et al. (2020), superior outcomes were not observed with an approach that started with BA. A difference was that in Walter et al. (2023), when CPT sessions were delivered, they accommodated the integration of BA components. This might have meant a slight dilution of CPT content in those sessions, whereas with Angelakis et al., BA was primarily administered in the sessions preceding CPT. Regardless of this difference, both studies found that *starting* with BA did not confer an advantage over and above standard CPT.

It should be recognized that the presence of comorbid depression does not automatically mean a nonresponse to CPT is guaranteed and the findings of the last two studies indicate the importance of considering carefully why and how one would deviate from the normal delivery of CPT. We next discuss judicious deviations or modifications to CPT and the introduction of non-CPT techniques that nonetheless might be considered with the goal of providing optimal care to individuals with comorbid presentations.

Clinical Application

We preface this section with the assumption that it is appropriate to begin treating PTSD with the individual. That is, no other urgent clinical issues need to be first addressed (i.e., depression severity is so severe a person requires electroconvulsive therapy, or imminent risk of harm that is a clinical priority). Complementing this is the importance of good clinical assessment, including psychosocial history (in particular, current social support), depression severity (using a valid self-report measure at a minimum), and assessment of both past trauma and details of the index trauma. This provides critical information that can alert the therapist to the *possibility* that depression might need to be watched closely in CPT.

We divide this next section into two components. First, we highlight and show that CPT alone is a powerful intervention, and that many existing CPT strategies and techniques can be leveraged in a targeted fashion to address depression. Next, we give examples of evidence-based, but non-CPT methods and techniques that could be brought into play when existing CPT methods need further augmentation. Guiding both approaches is of course good initial assessment and ongoing case formulation, which we emphasize throughout.

The early sessions of CPT offer multiple opportunities to address the challenge that depression can pose to successful treatment. The therapist should be mindful of these challenges if the client has a comorbid depressive disorder or has reported moderate-to-high depression levels. These challenges include difficulties with *motivation* and *engagement*, with depression imposing an added layer to the PTSD-related *avoidance* that has typically maintained a person's difficulties. Avoidance of potentially rewarding and reinforcing activity is common in depression, thus these clients may have pervasive avoidance of not only trauma-related stimuli but life in general. So how should this be addressed? This should start in Session 1 with the psychoeducation piece, when explaining not only how and why PTSD occurs and what may have hindered the client's natural recovery process, but in relation to the role of avoidance. The therapist can personalize this to the client's situation. For some clients, when discussing PTSD avoidance symptoms, it is useful to highlight the vicious cycle that avoidance has not only on maintaining PTSD symptoms, but also its broader impact on mood and activity. For others, when discussing cognitions and the therapy rationale, possible depressogenic-type stuck points [SPs] (e.g., "It's hopeless", "I don't think I can change after so many years like this") might arise. This provides an opportunity to not only foster some hope (remember, the therapist often has to be the cheerleader initially to engender optimism in the client) but also an opportunity to discuss why the client is in treatment in the first place. This could involve a mild challenging of the SP—"I'm curious, why are you here then if you think there is no way you can ever get better?"—followed by a conversation that incorporates what is a realistic expectation of therapy (that CPT is a very effective therapy so we do have good cause to expect positive change for the client).

For motivation, reduced energy, and concentration reasons, clients with significant depression might experience challenges completing assignments. These challenges are typically readily apparent early on in CPT. Thus, breaking down of tasks or focusing on completion of fewer worksheets (but of high quality) may help, although the expectation should always be that the number of worksheets will be increased as therapy progresses (and mood lifts). Occasionally scheduling out-of-session contact (e.g., brief phone call, text, or emails) might be helpful to support and motivate clients (see Chapter 10 in Galovski et al., 2020, for further discussion).

Although we do not have definitive evidence to support this as a standard recommendation, data from studies discussed earlier tentatively suggest that the use of a trauma account (CPT + A) could be considered when clients present with comorbid depression. We certainly endorse the current recommendation of giving clients a choice between CPT and CPT + A as per the manual (Resick et al., 2024). However, we have found with some clients with significant numbing in the context of depression that it has been useful to circle back to a conversation about using a trauma account, even when initially the plan was to follow the standard CPT protocol. We have done this when it was identified that clients have had difficulty feeling strong affect around their index trauma(s), when there has been a general flattening of affect, or when on discussion with the client we have observed that there has been what we call "avoidance by cognitive therapy"—clients completing excellent worksheets *on paper* but not letting their emotions seep through. Thus, we have at times introduced a trauma account later in the CPT process (e.g., Sessions 6–7, or even later) when expected changes were not being observed and formulation suggested the utility of this approach. Of course, standard CPT processes around affect should not be forgotten (e.g., good use of the emotion identification handout, examining stuck points in relation to allowing one to feel feelings, etc.).

Before discussing CPT techniques that can be augmented later in the CPT process, we encourage therapists not to forget other factors that influence depression and the extent to which brief psychoeducation early in CPT is effective. Sleep and alcohol use are good examples. Again, this should be personalized as part of early formulation, but the depressant effects of alcohol are well established, as well as the importance of obtaining high quality sleep. While we tend to find clients are aware of health issues associated with heavy or hazardous drinking, they are not always as aware of its impact on mood (and sleep quality). Thus, in some cases brief psychoeducation and tips around these issues, accompanied by easy-to-complete weekly monitoring might be indicated. We know that just monitoring behavior can change it somewhat; thus in these cases we have seen reductions in alcohol use and/or improvements around sleep hygiene without impacting routine delivery of CPT, with concurrent positive impacts on mood. This type of monitoring also gathers useful information if mood does not improve as therapy progresses.

In later stages of CPT there are several critical opportunities to address factors that contribute to significant depression, especially when addressing over-accommodation SPs and related themes. We illustrate next where specific beliefs and behaviors contributing to depression can be worked on across the five CPT themes.

Safety

Addressing unhelpful beliefs regarding the inability to keep oneself safe from harm is a critical foundational goal of CPT. This is particularly important in the context of depression. If a client's SPs include strong beliefs that other people are trying to hurt them, or that they can't take care of themselves, it is likely to result in avoidance behaviors (not going out alone or at all), which leads to increased isolation and in turn, increased depressive symptoms. It's that vicious cycle again! It is important to clarify when discussing safety that you are not suggesting that the world is *completely* safe and that the client discard *all* safety strategies, but to instead highlight behaviors and strategies that are resulting in overestimating risk and contributing to fear-based avoidance and withdrawal from others and the world.

Trust

Unsurprisingly, clients' SPs in this domain set up barriers to social engagement and support. Expectations that people will always take advantage of you or are out to betray you is pretty depressing in and of itself. We sometimes find therapists new to CPT underestimate the importance and value of exercises like the Trust Star, which can help clients see the clear social benefits of learning to judiciously become balanced in their beliefs in trusting others. One of our client's depression had significantly worsened when they moved to a new city with no social support. Addressing trust and using the Trust Star in light of their situational context led them to appropriately lower their guard when meeting new people in their neighborhood, which subsequently resulted in social invitations and marked improvement in mood. This client noted previously they would have simply remained at home (and endured months in a depressive episode).

Power and Control

SPs associated with a lack of control or powerlessness can be quite marked in clients with significant depression. This can also be seen in clients who may struggle to be assertive in their lives. Although not restricted to those who have experienced repeated trauma, some of these beliefs are likely to reflect learned helplessness. Thus, in the face of repeated stressful experiences over which clients believe they have had little control, SPs such as "I have no control" or "There is no point in trying" may be present. These likely reinforce strong feelings of hopelessness, which in turn, interferes with beliefs and behaviors that could counter this way of thinking. Again, the CPT process addresses these SPs very effectively and the therapist, with an awareness of the role of depression, can greatly assist clients to target beliefs in a way that changes this cycle. For example, by helping clients see the many ways they do have control over their lives and situations, encouraging them to assert positive control (e.g., appropriately asking for time off at a job where a client might ordinarily avoid making such a request) can lead to more hope and optimism for the future, increasing the likelihood clients will continue behaviors in accordance with their goals.

It is also worth noting that hopelessness and helplessness associated with comorbid depression means clients can come across as passive and unassertive, and in some cases, be taken advantage of. Developing strong beliefs about having a sense of control and power is important not just for these domains, but also in relation to safety and interpersonal relationships. We often see that as clients develop healthy beliefs and behaviors around power/control, they appear more engaged and active in their lives, and appear more self-confident, which complements both earlier work on safety and trust as well as laying a strong foundation for upcoming work in esteem and intimacy.

Esteem

CPT does well at addressing both self-esteem and esteem of others. Indeed, sometimes it is very hard to resist jumping straight to addressing SPs in this area early in CPT at the expense of self-blame and related assimilation SPs. We remind people to trust the CPT process and the research about the importance of addressing assimilation SPs prior to over-accommodation SPs (Farmer et al., 2017). We provide a rationale in our case example that you can adopt with clients for why the sequencing is important. That said, individuals with comorbid depression frequently need some extra attention in the esteem department. There are different ways this can be achieved. If our initial assessment and formulation of a client with comorbid PTSD and depression highlights significant restrictions of activity and reinforcement, we might introduce some of the behavioral activation tasks earlier than usual that are normally reserved for later in CPT (i.e., doing a nice thing for oneself each day or identifying a small mastery task). While not allowing this discussion to dominate early sessions, it is important to briefly check-in with how this activity has gone each week. Thus, as the client begins to reengage in their life, with hopefully small but incremental changes to mood, they (and the therapist) will begin to accumulate valuable information that can then provide evidence against esteem-related SPs. For example, esteem SPs such as being "hopeless" are harder to hold if there is now documented evidence of completing tasks around the house.

When the esteem module is introduced as per standard delivery of CPT, we can still flex its power more strongly for clients with depression. Here, it is critical to understand not only the relevant SP, but also to use our best Socratic dialogue to better understand how and where these SPs originated. We often observe these SPs are an unfortunate perfect storm of not only traumatic events, but other distressing and adverse life experiences. For example, we had a client whose belief was, "I am a total failure in life". This, in part, was not only due to their belief they should have been able to prevent a fatal accident from happening (don't worry, that self-blame was targeted early in therapy!), but was also the result of years of parental belittling and bullying at school. For this client, time spent on the giving and receiving compliments component of the esteem session was particularly fruitful. This cognitive work helped emphasize the important link between feeling valued and their mood, served as a counterpoint to their lack of reinforcement in childhood, and allowed insightful discussions about SPs that got in the way of the client fully accepting genuine compliments and praise from people.

Intimacy and Connection with Others

With respect to self-intimacy, the importance of being alone without feeling lonely or empty, and having the ability to self-soothe and calm oneself in the presence of stress or distress are important factors for healthy functioning. Clients with depressive symptoms often struggle with internal soothing and self-validation without resorting to self-criticism and rumination. As noted earlier, it is not uncommon that clients with negative intimacy beliefs will look to external sources of comfort such as food, substance use, spending money, or sex to meet these intimacy deficits. This often sets up a vicious cycle with respect to intimacy, given that none of these external comforts tend to have long-lasting effects and their use often leads to more negative cognitions as a result ("I'm drinking again, I'm a failure"). One of the cornerstones of CPT is the expression of natural emotions and the increased knowledge that feelings are transient. For clients with intimacy deficits, who may have little experience that "riding the wave" of emotions will see their natural dissipation, the course of therapy can provide them with alternatives to manage emotional distress and replace intimacy-related SPs of "If I get emotional, I'll be out of control" with more balanced cognitions of "This feeling will pass. I can take care of myself and use the skills I have learned to cope".

In addition, the formation and maintenance of relationships requires a level of emotional vulnerability often lacking in clients with PTSD symptoms, with past experiences of intimate connectedness often associated with being physically or emotionally hurt and a loss of power and/or agency in relationships. An inability to trust other people or even one's own decisions about the safety, authenticity or motivations of other people results in clients operating from a position of "no trust", rather than a position of "no information" about others. As such, withdrawal from others is an understandable option; however, the resultant effect is that one of the fundamental human needs of emotional connections with others is not able to be met. Here also, the esteem-related exercise of "giving and receiving compliments" has a secondary function in those individuals whose depressive symptoms have kept them from emotionally connecting with others. Needing to notice and remark upon something that another person, even a stranger, is doing requires human interaction and, even if brief, human connection. More experiences of positive outcomes of this type (e.g., logging the responses of those to whom compliments were directed) serves to provide more positive evidence to the client that at least *some* human beings are worth engaging with or don't treat them badly. The more of these experiences a person has, the narrower the gap between self and others.

Flexing the power of CPT in modules such as trust, esteem, and intimacy can have a significant impact for clients with comorbid depression. Keeping this in mind, the reader hopefully can see that when we have a "depression awareness hat" on with our clients, we can identify multiple opportunities to address SPs that contribute to this presentation.

Traumatic Loss

Given the intersection between grief and loss with depressive symptoms, when a client's trauma involves traumatic loss or violent death of someone close to them, certain SPs may interfere with CPT. The CPT manual has a small section with good guidance of these issues (and a handout on common grief-related SPs in Resick et al., 2017). CPT as a rule addresses these issues very well. By removing SPs associated with self-blame in relation to the person's death (if relevant) and by reducing avoidance of traumatic memories and reminders, the therapist helps pave the way for the experience of natural emotions (including grief and sadness). Stuck points that get in the way of this processing can be addressed (e.g., "If I get over this trauma/my son's death, it means I have stopped caring as much about him" or "If I don't grieve this way, his memory will fade"). We have found that little tasks may also be helpful with this process that are not strictly parts of CPT. For example, having clients visit the avoided gravesite with a view to not only address SPs about not being able to cope with the emotions elicited by such a visit, but to also have the opportunity to engage in mourning, a process that might have been put off in the struggle to accept the loved one's death. We had one of our adolescent clients write a letter to their mother who was murdered, telling her what they were now doing in their life and what they most wanted her to know. This served as a reminder that the client still had a relationship and connection with their mother, albeit different to the nature of a relationship with a living person, and gave the client an opportunity to say things they wished they had said to their mother before her death.

The above highlights how CPT in its standard form can be used in a strategic fashion to address depression in the context of PTSD. However, there are times when the use of additional evidence-based but non-CPT techniques could be considered to augment CPT. It is beyond the scope of this chapter to detail every possible method (see Chap. 15 for more detail in diverging from the protocol to best meet client needs), but we highlight several approaches and when they might be introduced. We also point the reader to important treatment manuals or "how to" resources as well as chapters within this book that not only suggest how to use case formulation to guide deviations from CPT (Chap. 15) but also address issues that impact on mood (e.g., sleep, Chap. 7; substance abuse, Chap. 5).

Behavioral Experiments

We have found the use of behavioral experiments (BEs) to be a powerful tool that nicely complements CPT. BEs, a technique that tests the accuracy of a targeted unhelpful cognition and, usually, the predicted negative consequence of that belief, has similar goals and outcomes of challenging belief worksheets in CPT. The BE technique subtly differs from the standard cognitive work in CPT in that it has a more experiential aspect to the process and usually involves explicit behavioral actions in its execution (the client is asked to *do* something to test their belief). We detail later how a BE might work in a case example. We typically incorporate BEs when a SP appears particularly "sticky". Specifically, this may be useful when despite client and therapist's best efforts, over multiple worksheets and good Socratic Dialogue, a SP refuses to budge, or a client remains stuck in the "I know this isn't true, but…" cycle. It can also be helpful when clients intellectualize or complete "perfect" worksheets but do not truly believe or allow themselves to engage emotionally in the process. An excellent resource is Bennett-Levy et al. (2004), which outlines the use of BEs for not only PTSD and depression, but also for low self-esteem and in the context of interpersonal difficulties (see also Greenberger & Padesky, 2015).

As an example, a combat medic client of ours who experienced overwhelming guilt and depression from their trauma struggled with the SP, "I should have been able to save him [a seriously injured comrade]". He and his therapist tested this SP using cognitive processing techniques such as Socratic Questions and the use of worksheets and were not able to arrive at a more balanced alternative explanation (i.e., "I couldn't have done any more, I gave him optimal care, and nothing would have been able to save him"). Instead, they agreed on a behavioral experiment to help the client gather real evidence against his SP. The experiment involved the client surveying several trauma surgeons about what was required to save someone as seriously injured as this person. The results of this experiment were that the client had done everything humanly possible, with one surgeon noting that even if the comrade had been injured next to a Level 1 trauma center and put on an operating table within minutes, the injured soldier sadly would still have died. As a result, the client found they were able to genuinely *believe* what they intellectually knew, but had difficulty accepting, and now took comfort in that their comrade was cared for right to the end of their life.

Core Beliefs

Like the use of BEs, sometimes clients with comorbid depression will need extra help developing more balanced, alternative ways of thinking, especially when their SPs are a culmination of years of rehearsal and repetitive trauma. Clients with such histories might struggle with accepting or believing a new way of looking at themselves. Thus, after challenging a SP about being a "bad" person, they may find it difficult to fully believe they are a "worthy" or "lovable" person. Complementing challenging belief worksheets with the use of a positive data log or similar record of evidence (past and current) to support a new core belief (Greenberger & Padesky, 1995, 2015) can be useful. Thus, a client can create a "historical record" by looking over their lifetime for the evidence and examples that show they were a worthwhile person (e.g., an aunt giving them a toy for their birthday early in childhood, comments from friends or teachers during their school years that showed positive regard or interest in them, documenting little wins and achievements over their life). This process of gathering evidence from across the lifespan helps clients bring information and experiences to memory that might not always be easily and spontaneously retrieved. Ongoing collection and reviewing of such information can give a boost to the usual CPT worksheets that might be used to address esteem and related SPs.

Rumination

Maladaptive ruminative or repetitive negative thinking is a transdiagnostic process and particularly evident in both PTSD and depression (Ehring & Watkins, 2008; Kubota & Nixon, 2017). In some instances, future-oriented concerns (e.g., excessive worry) can be addressed with techniques such as worry-postponement (scheduling worry time for a discrete period of time). Although the CPT process can address unhelpful ruminative thinking styles (e.g., when a client accepts that an accident or trauma occurred because sometimes these events just happen without real reason), at times rumination is less amenable to change. Components of Rumination-Focused Cognitive Behavioral Therapy (RF-CBT; Watkins, 2016, 2022) can be helpful in these instances. Discussing helpful versus unhelpful ruminative styles is important. Thinking through a problem in a focused, concrete, and problem-solving fashion is adaptive (concrete processing), especially if it can result in a useful decision or plan. Abstract and vague stewing over questions that cannot be answered or problems that cannot be solved, is not fruitful. We find clients often respond well to *concreteness training*. Rather than being evaluative or judgmental of the incident or situation that has led to the ruminative thinking, clients practice being active in thinking about the specifics, with a solution-focused mindset. Learning ways of thinking that are opposite to abstract or vague processes prevents clients getting stuck in ruminative cycles.

Another technique, labeled *absorption training*, using imagery and visualization, involves learning to get into the "flow" of activities. For example, a client learned to become absorbed in his physical movements when doing daily tasks, which reduced the "space" in his mind for ruminative thoughts to enter. This just represents a snapshot of possible intervention points for when clients struggle with excessive rumination. A final tip is that we often find these clients will write excessively on worksheets, almost transcribing their ruminative thinking on paper. In these instances, we adopt the "short is sweet" principle, only allowing a single, one-line, sentence to be used in the relevant part of the sheet (e.g., the SP), one word for an emotion description. In a few cases, we have had to initially restrict clients to only use a few key challenging questions until they learned not to write a comprehensive ruminative essay under each question or had them restrict the amount of time spent on a sheet (e.g., 20 min) so that they did not excessively ruminate by working on the sheet for hours. We find that, in most cases, we can integrate the above strategies briefly in the course of a normal CPT session when rumination is not a major impediment to progress; however, when it is causing marked interference, thoughtful and time-limited divergence to address rumination with more intense use of these techniques might be considered.

Interpersonal Issues

Interpersonal Psychotherapy (IPT), originally developed to treat depressive disorders, is accumulating evidence as a potential therapy for significant trauma symptoms and/or PTSD with or without comorbid depression (see Althobaiti et al., 2020; Duberstein et al., 2018; Markowitz, 2016, 2021; Pickover et al., 2021). Although we share valid cautions about over-complicating or diluting effective protocols with additional methods (Bleiberg & Markowitz, 2019) and are not aware of research integrating IPT with CPT, from both a formulation and treatment component view, we believe elements of IPT can be useful adjuncts to CPT. For example, IPT specifically targets social and interpersonal influences on depression (e.g., grief, role transition, conflict, social isolation). These topics are particularly relevant to those who have experienced trauma, which we illustrate further in one of the case examples. As a further example, one of the modifications of IPT by Duberstein and colleagues (IPT for trauma; IPT-T) addresses “interpersonal patterns”—long-standing problems that stem from developmental trauma that undermine healthy interpersonal effectiveness. Thus, for clients where depression appears to be related to social and interpersonal issues, the social component of IPT theory is a nice fit with the socio-cognitive model of CPT. IPT theory generates a useful framework to discuss with clients how their traumatic (and possibly early life) experiences influence their thoughts (SPs) and behaviors (e.g., withdrawing from support or excessively seeking it), which leads to maladaptive or unsatisfactory interpersonal interactions, resulting in symptoms of depression, feelings of isolation, loneliness, etc. Techniques within IPT can assist in these and related domains. For example, in addition to standard CPT work addressing SPs about expectations of others (which could be underpinned by a trust, power/control, or intimacy type SP), IPT methods such as problem-solving and role playing on how to improve interpersonal communication are effective strategies which can be practiced in future situations. Thus, many elements of the IPT approach can complement the CPT therapist’s toolkit when tackling depression. We typically use such methods when working on over-accommodated SPs in CPT, that is, *not* while assimilation SPs (e.g., self-blame) need to be the focus of attention.

Behavioral Activation

As highlighted earlier, BA is one of the few methods to have been explicitly studied as a potential augmentation of CPT for those with comorbid depression. Although preliminary, it was seen to be most effective when sequenced *after* CPT (Angelakis et al., 2020). Less clear is optimal methods for its *integrated* use throughout CPT (see Walter et al., 2023), however we highlight several considerations in this context. Where there is a significant absence of reinforcement or marked isolation in a client's life, where a client is having significant difficulty in achieving any tasks (both in life in general and in CPT), more than the "light touch" BA described previously might be required and introduced earlier in the therapeutic process. If this is to be a more central focus early in CPT, it needs to be prefaced by discussing with the client the purpose of this deviation, setting a time limit on this divergence (e.g., 2–3 sessions), and being explicit that this is not to avoid or put off trauma work per se. Alternatively, if logistics and resources allow it, serious consideration should be made for several 90-min sessions that comprise a standard CPT session with 30 min added to incorporate BA techniques and/or twice-weekly sessions. We do repeat the importance of good case formulation in these decision processes (see Chap. 15 for elaboration).

Related to improving positive reinforcement, BA is not only useful for increasing social engagement but also a means for gradual skill development or refinement. For example, if clients either have lost confidence in, or never had the opportunity to develop good social skills, looking for activities that involve "side by side" interaction rather than extensive direct conversations, can be handy. Thus, a one-to-one coffee catch up might be too challenging for some, whereas we've had clients join a painting class or bushwalking club, where the nature of the activity removed sustained attention on the client (e.g., the walking group talked with one another, but they also had to watch their feet!). It is important to remember the fundamental aspects of BA for those with comorbid PTSD and depression. This includes encouraging clients to attempt action and behavior change regardless of current low mood state and being aware that clients often will want to wait until they are "feeling up" to doing things. Therapists also need to let clients know that activity and mastery will lead to pleasure and improved mood, but that it can take time and repetition. The therapist must bring extra energy to the session and initially provide the beacon of hope for clients experiencing significant depression. That said, at some point, we would want the client to become their own beacon. On some occasions, certain activities (especially excessive exercise) can constitute avoidance behaviors. In these cases, we ask clients to remain active, but in a healthier way. CPT work complements this. For example, one client agreed to replace one of their many frenetic gym sessions with going on a leisurely walk.

BA is also often an explicit treatment component in CBT protocols for those experiencing traumatic bereavement (e.g., Lenferink et al., 2023), and its use has been suggested in the context of CPT when trauma loss is the index or primary trauma (see Jacoby et al., 2019). As such, we have used it to help bereaved clients reengage in their social worlds. For example, we had our adolescent client mentioned earlier return to attending extended family events, which gradually resulted in improved mood as he increasingly spent time with his cousins.

Case Examples

Following are two case examples to illustrate how CPT can be flexibly adapted to address symptoms of depression during therapy or, with reference to good formulation and in accordance with outcome measures,[3] outline where we might deviate from CPT to introduce a different technique to specifically target depression before returning to standard CPT.

A cautionary note—as mentioned earlier, it is not uncommon for clients with depression to want to address beliefs that are likely to have been with them for a long time and may even predate the index trauma, given that those beliefs are often ruminative in nature and are genuinely unhelpful and causing low mood. Targeting those beliefs which are characteristic of depression (e.g., "I'm stupid", "I'm worthless", "If I get close to people they'll find out the real me and won't like me") is often difficult and requires significant changes in thinking. Being sidetracked into targeting esteem or intimacy-related SPs too early in therapy or thinking that it would be more beneficial for the client to address these first to raise their motivation for therapy is, in most cases, unlikely to result in quick treatment gains. Instead, being able to make small changes in thinking earlier on in therapy, with SPs which are less ingrained, provides evidence that the client *can* shift their thinking on some thoughts, which engenders hope that they can also shift their thinking on other beliefs. This also allows the therapist to refer back to these examples when the going gets tough (e.g., "You used to believe people couldn't be trusted, but now you think differently on that; is it possible then that you might not always believe that you are not deserving of love?").

For the client who is insistent on tackling these more difficult SPs first, there may be times the therapist needs to explain the rationale behind the sequencing of CPT in a way that shares understanding and does not minimize the client's concerns. Take for example our client "Leanne". Aged 58, she reported a long history of domestic violence commencing with her first marriage which ended in an incident of rape when she was 35. Following this, she reported a pattern of physical violence and abuse in successive relationships, the last of which ended 12 months before coming to see us. Leanne described an unstable childhood environment; her parents had divorced when she was 12 with her mother becomingly increasingly depressed and critical after her father left. Both parents had high expectations of Leanne and her siblings, with Leanne noting she was constantly worried about making mistakes

[3] A valid PTSD symptom measure such as the PTSD Checklist for DSM-5 (PCL-5) should be used routinely at each session. In addition, at each session we also use a measure of depression (e.g., the Depression, Anxiety and Stress Scale [DASS-21], or the Patient Health Questionnaire [PHQ-9]).

and was very self-critical as a result. Many of her assimilated SPs were also linked to her esteem ("I stayed because I'm stupid"; "If I was smarter, I would have seen the signs"). Reading the impact statement and creating the SP log were powerful for Leanne as she started to see the links between her symptoms of depression, her experience during her marriage and her experiences as a child. In Sessions 3 and 4, we focused on her assimilated SPs through Socratic questioning, just as good CPT therapists should! At the beginning of the fifth session however, Leanne said she didn't think CPT was for her and that she wasn't sure she wanted to continue.

Leanne: *I think those early sessions were good and I thought getting those stuck points out was useful, but I'm a bit disappointed by our last couple of sessions if I'm really honest.*

Therapist: *I'm glad you are telling me that; are you happy to let me know what you would have preferred we discussed? It's important that we don't skip over things that you know are causing you to feel badly.*

Leanne: *I really wanted to talk about the thoughts I've had around "I didn't deserve any better because I'm not good enough". This is what is making me feel badly and I feel like we aren't getting into it. When we put this stuck point on the log it was a revelation, and I think that everything that happened in my marriage to Peter is related to this and why I have felt depressed for years. It didn't matter if I did well at school or if I won an award for sport, it was never enough for my parents—they always treated me like everything I did was just not good enough.*

Therapist: *It's a great stuck point and one that is really tied into your sense of worth and value. When we added it to the log, I remember you saying how awful this has made you feel for such a long time. I can understand why you would have wanted to explore it straight away. I'm sorry that I wasn't as clear as I could have been in explaining the process in which we will be tackling the stuck points. Is it okay if I explain that a little more so that it might make more sense as to why we might be focusing on this a little later in therapy, rather than straight away?*

Leanne: *That would be helpful, yes.*

Therapist: *Thank you for that. I just want to start by saying that we will have plenty of time together over the course of therapy to address the stuck points that you can recognize have caused you a lot of issues over the years. It's wonderful that you can see where this one came from and how it makes you feel. It's very tied to your esteem and sounds deeply ingrained—which is why it might be just a little more "stuck" than some other thoughts that are on the log and why it makes you feel really down.*

Leanne: *Yes that makes sense. I was never good enough with Peter either—I couldn't even cook eggs properly without making him mad.*

Therapist: *I can hear that your experience with Peter ties in to how you felt when you were younger, and that no matter how much you tried it didn't seem to be enough. In CPT there is a sequence to what we are doing together, so that we first address those stuck points that are tied to thoughts of self-blame and guilt that we spoke about last session, such as when you said; "If I would have spoken up for myself, the abuse wouldn't have happened". These thoughts really lie at the core of PTSD, so by starting with them, we start at the heart of the story. Then we move to* *looking at the effects of the trauma on your life, including how these thoughts are linked to your depression. Given they have been with you a long time, they can take some more time and effort to challenge and shift. If we tried to start with them before learning all of the skills needed to challenge them, then it's a bit like trying to run before we learn to walk.*

Leanne: *So you are saying that we need to get through some top layers first, before we get to some of these deeper layers?*

Therapist: *Yes that's a nice way of looking at it—the modules done in the order we do them have a logical sequence. For example, it is hard to have intimacy with other people if at first we don't feel safe, distrust others, feel like we are powerless in relationships and generally don't feel good about ourselves. Which is why intimacy is the last aspect that we will look at.*

Leanne: *Okay that makes sense now. I feel better knowing that we are going to get to those things at some stage and they won't be forgotten about.*

In some cases, presenting the rationale for sequencing the CPT modules in a particular way and delaying processing of SPs that are more likely linked to depressive symptoms may not be an effective strategy. In situations where depression is causing a barrier to therapy (as evidenced by little to no change in the overall PCL as therapy progresses, consistently high scores in the negative cognitions symptom cluster, high depression symptoms on the specific depression measure used, and/or clinical observations and client self-report), consideration should be given to either "flexing" the standard CPT protocol, or briefly deviating from CPT to address the issues.

Early Wins

Before deviating from CPT, the first approach should be how best to flex sessions using the CPT material to address SPs which may be related to depression. Indicators of this may be present very early in therapy. For example, if a client comes to Session 3 having completed no ABC sheets, there may be a range of reasons, *other than avoidance,* which need to be explored. For example, esteem related SPs such as "I am stupid" can result in resistance to completing worksheets or even attempting practice assignments altogether and, as we know, without doing any work outside of sessions, it is unlikely that a client is going to get better! In contrast to the situation with Leanne where we delayed addressing over-accommodated SPs, dealing with this esteem related SP immediately assists in providing both the evidence and the motivation to complete the worksheets and engage in therapy. Without spending time on this SP, therapy may be stalled with clients repeatedly coming to sessions having done no work outside of the session and being reliant on the therapist to assist them with worksheets. Just a tip—don't be tempted to switch to the modified or simplified CPT worksheets too soon as a solution—we don't want to contribute to a client's belief that they are stupid and can't manage the worksheets! Instead, reinforcing that worksheets take practice is far more helpful. Almost all clients will be able to identify something that they weren't good at in the beginning, whether it be learning a musical instrument, playing a sport, starting a craft, cooking, cleaning ... the list is endless! Learning how to do CPT worksheets is no different, and with repetition and encouragement, most clients should be able to manage the standard worksheets with no issues.

Regular Outcome Monitoring and Targeting What Drives the Depression

As discussed, the usual CPT approaches and techniques (Socratic questioning, worksheets, trust star, giving and taking power, giving and receiving compliments log), when presented in the usual sequence, have been shown to be effective in reducing over-accommodated SPs, even in clients with depressive symptoms. Sometimes however, where symptoms of depression are not shifting, consideration might be given to changing the order of therapy so that the cognitions related to the depression are tackled earlier. These decisions should always be based on what we are seeing at each session on our symptom measures. The PCL is not only useful (and essential!) in tracking the overall trajectory of PTSD symptoms, but also enables us to identify and target those symptoms which are more intractable. In our work, we always ask ourselves two questions about the PCL: (1) *What is the client's total score*? and (2) *Which symptoms are most endorsed by the client*? To illustrate, let's consider Leanne at Session 6 and consider how we might approach future sessions depending on her PCL.

In Scenario 1, midway through CPT, Leanne had made good progress with her assimilated SPs, with a total PCL score of 37,[4] however a detailed look is required to give us a clearer picture of what is going on. Although many symptoms of PTSD had reduced, with scores of "1" in the intrusion and avoidance symptom clusters (i.e., low levels in these domains) and no endorsement of self-blame or guilt, Leanne had endorsed most of the symptoms related to depression at the extreme range, including having difficulty concentrating and sleep issues which are also often attributable to low mood. Of the total PCL score, these items accounted for well over half.

When faced with a situation like this, a useful strategy is to flex the order of CPT to address the symptoms of depression. We already know from our earlier sessions that Leanne's long-standing depression was related to her esteem and self-criticism, so bringing forward aspects of the esteem module from Session 10 and its associated behavioral components (giving and receiving compliments log and doing nice things daily) makes good sense here (while still expecting Leanne to continue to

[4] Leanne's pretreatment PCL-5 was 55, well above the clinical cut-off for this self-report measure (i.e., scores of ≥31–33 representing probable-PTSD, Blevins et al., 2015). Each of the 20 PTSD symptoms is scored on a 0–4 scale.

work on residual trauma-SPs). For some clients this work may be challenging as they are so accustomed and/or attuned to hearing criticism that they behave like a "compliments deflector" (i.e., they either don't hear any compliments received, or when they do hear them—they don't believe them and reject them). For clients with depression, we find giving a more detailed explanation for the giving and receiving compliments exercise, helpful.

Therapist: *Your assignment is to practice giving one compliment and receiving one compliment every day, and to log it down on this sheet. Logging it is important as it will help you take notice of it, and you can look back over the week and remember the compliments.*

A compliment is different from gratitude. For example, if someone cooks you dinner or helps you with something, it's customary to thank them for doing that. A compliment however is a bit more like a gift you are offering someone else, which says "I noticed that you do this (whatever that thing is) really well and I wanted to let you know that".

Now when we give someone a gift—we wouldn't really expect them to just look at the gift and not take it from us would we? Or we wouldn't expect them to take the gift—then hand it back to us saying—"oh that's not really anything much". We have chosen the gift carefully because we want the other person to acknowledge and enjoy receiving the gift as much as we liked picking it out and giving it to them. We aren't giving gifts to just anyone are we?! We are choosy with our gifts and who we give them to. But sometimes people aren't used to receiving the gift of a compliment, so they will treat it with suspicion, or will deflect it quickly without even taking a good look at the gift. When that happens, it can force the person giving the gift to give it again, until it is accepted.

Instead of this to and fro—the only real way to respond when you receive the gift of a compliment is to say, "Thank you". Take the gift, tuck it away somewhere close; take it out on occasion and look at it again, and believe that the person who gave you the gift saw something in you that was worthy of it.

So, when you are doing this exercise and giving a compliment, I would like you to write down not just who you gave it to, but what they did with it. Treat it like an experiment to see what people do with compliments. Do they accept it with a "thank you", or do they reject or deflect it? Remember too that the most valuable compliments people give and receive are about things that a person does, rather than on how they look or what they wear or how they style their hair.

In the second part of the exercise, where you are writing down compliments you receive, I would like you to do the same—treat these compliments as gifts; acknowledge them; take them without suspicion or deflection; tuck them away and notice and log how they make you feel.

What to do if clients return from doing this exercise not having logged any compliments? A simple, yet effective, technique is to start the session with giving the client a compliment. This can be anything relevant to the client ("I never have to wonder if you will be on time because you're so reliable"; "You always put so much thought into your worksheets, I'm looking forward to seeing them"). If faced with a blank log, ask the client if they have received a compliment *that day* (knowing full well that they did because it came from you!). This allows you to raise the very real possibility that if they missed that one, it may be possible they are missing others. It's a simple way to illustrate the point in a very behavioral way!

For Leanne, completing the behavioral exercises became "homework for life" and the log was completed and discussed every session through to the end of therapy alongside the usual completion of the Challenging Beliefs Worksheets, resulting in improved mood as she engaged more positively with the world, slowly built her esteem of self and others, and learned to challenge her self-critical voice.

But what if at Session 6 the symptoms contributing to Leanne's overall total PCL of 37 included elevated symptoms of intrusions, self-blame, arousal, and avoidance, alongside marked depressive symptoms? In this case, we might hypothesize it is possible that the symptoms of depression are getting in the way of therapy and preventing change in PTSD. For some SPs, the therapist and client might be finding that they are too difficult or entrenched to resolve by CPT techniques alone, and consideration could be given to the use of adjunct techniques to complement CPT to address the depression which is holding up assimilated SPs. This of course is only done when careful reformulation of the client's progress and presentation indicates this focus might help nudge depression sufficiently to allow CPT to do its work.

There Is Something Wrong with Me

In clients with experiences such as Leanne's, where they have been subjected to violence in several successive relationships, it is not uncommon to have assimilated SPs which are linked to these repeat exposures (e.g., "There is something wrong with me that this keeps happening"). These beliefs can contribute to high levels of self-blame and feelings of low self-worth (and depression) which can be difficult to shift. This is because repeated interpersonal abuse appears to give the client a significant amount of "evidence for" that that there is indeed something wrong with them—in the client's mind, if there *wasn't* something wrong with them, then it wouldn't keep happening to them. Leanne might have found it easier to accept that one abusive relationship was not her fault, but what if, as in her case, *most or every* relationship was abusive? Research indicates that women who have experienced early childhood abuse are more likely to be victimized in adulthood (Classen et al., 2005). Good Socratic questioning in CPT can certainly challenge clients' SPs about the likelihood of future abusive relationships, but this is easier to do when clients now have the skills (or maturity) to minimize these risks. But this was not the case for Leanne. This is where the concept of "The Shark Cage" helped. Developed by Australian psychologist Ursula Benstead (2011), the metaphor was designed to assist women to understand reasons for the revictimization they were experiencing, and to develop strategies to prevent it into the future. The metaphor likens the world to an ocean, filled with both harmless fish and sharks. For protection we learn from caregivers, schools, friends, etc. how to develop bars on our "shark cage", i.e., boundaries, which allow access to the harmless fish, but keep out the sharks. However not everyone builds these bars early in childhood, or some people may have been exposed to sharks when very young or had caregivers who didn't have well developed shark cages themselves to teach us these boundaries.

The metaphor is clear that there is nothing wrong with us and we aren't asking to be abused, but we do need to learn and use the skills to build or repair our shark cages. For Leanne, the metaphor helped address her assimilated SPs in a way that didn't blame her for the abuse (that blame still belongs to the sharks!) but acknowledged that she *was* responsible for building the boundaries to create and maintain a robust cage, without creating an impenetrable barrier so that no one can get through (which can be typical of survivors of repeated domestic violence and sexual assault, e.g., "If I let anyone get close to me, they will hurt me") and which can contribute to withdrawal from other people.

A Behavioral Experiment

But how do we start to build these boundaries and let others get closer to us in a very real and practical sense? Given her domestic violence and abuse history, Leanne had a SP of "If I say no to other people, they will think badly of me or verbally abuse me" which was getting in the way of maintaining healthy relationships and forming new ones. We already noted how Leanne's difficulty in creating boundaries can be seen to contribute to her vulnerability in relationships—using Socratic questioning and the metaphor of the shark cage, she was ready to try something different. During therapy, Leanne was introduced to the concept of more healthy ways of giving and taking power in relationships and identified that she generally did this in ways that were less healthy than she would like. For example, she would often place other people's needs above her own but then become resentful and either gave ultimatums (that she generally wouldn't follow through with, leaving her more vulnerable to boundary violations) or would end the relationship at a moment's notice. Although Leanne had a great alternative thought for her SP about saying "no" ("Even though I can't always get everything I want, I can influence others by being assertive about my needs and wants"), she found it difficult to do this in practice and was worried about how others would react. This is where the use of a behavioral experiment can nicely supplement CPT.

The first step was to formulate Leanne's SP in less global terms and focus on what she predicted would happen if she set a boundary, and which person or people she could test this notion with. For Leanne, her prediction was that if she said no to someone, they would think she was rude and would get angry at her and not speak to her again. Leanne also knew, however, that if she continued to struggle to learn to say no and set boundaries, this would keep her vulnerable to abuse and being taken advantage of. Leanne decided to use the experiment with a friend of her daughter's mother, Jill. Jill would expect that the girls meet up at Leanne's house with Jill dropping off her daughter, saying a quick hello and then leaving the girls there to play (and be supervised) by Leanne. We planned an experiment in which Leanne would speak to Jill the next time she was doing a dash and drop and ask that they take turns in having the girls at each other's houses, which would be a good change of environment for the girls and give the mothers a well-deserved break. The result was that Jill took this well and was a bit surprised she hadn't thought of it first. Contrary to Leanne's prediction, Jill did not get upset or angry and refuse to speak to Leanne. This provided her with some great evidence that setting a boundary can have very beneficial results and encouraged her to repeat boundary setting with others.

Keeping in mind that the reactions of other people are unpredictable, it is important to prepare the client that not everyone may like a boundary. But that doesn't mean that the boundary is unfair or unreasonable or shouldn't be drawn. For clients such as Leanne who have limited experience with boundary setting, role-playing assertive communication and encouraging repeat performances of the behavioral experiments (with different people or different boundaries with the same people) is the key to increasing success and confidence.

When Social or Interpersonal Context Is Contributing to Depression: Interpersonal Psychotherapy (IPT) Techniques

As noted above, for clients with significant depressive symptoms or comorbid depression, it is not uncommon for them to present with few interpersonal relationships and deficits in interpersonal skills and a lack of resources or willingness to form new relationships. It can be difficult to connect with others when we are feeling depressed and low, and SPs can serve to reinforce this withdrawal from others ("They won't like me"; "They're too busy"; "People think I'm boring or stupid"). Although CPT can go a long way in challenging these beliefs, it can be difficult to truly internalize changes in thinking when a person's experience remains the same, for example, continued high levels of conflict in interpersonal relationships, limited friendships, and few social activities, with these issues often the interpersonal consequences of the trauma rather than the trauma itself. In these cases, deviating from CPT to spend time on skills development to resolve interpersonal conflicts and decrease social isolation may assist in reducing the symptoms of depression associated with these issues.

We find that difficulties in interpersonal relationships are particularly pertinent for veterans and first responders, given that the transition from military or emergency services to civilian life is often accompanied by the loss of a well-established social identity and the formation of a new post-service identity. This can be exacerbated by PTSD symptoms themselves, including withdrawing from people and activities, irritability, hypervigilance, and negative cognitions about self and others. This withdrawal both reduces social support (which we know is a protective factor) and perpetuates a view that people can't be trusted, want something from you, or are unsafe. In these cases, we might consider a more substantial divergence from CPT in order to address the impact of the trauma on a client's interpersonal relationships.

Take for example our client James. A career soldier with 40 years of service having joined at the age of 18, he retired as a senior officer because he had "had enough". James came to therapy describing feeling guilty about the suicide of his best mate. James had encouraged his friend to take up an overseas deployment opportunity alongside him, and although he could see his friend's declining mental health upon his return, wasn't sure what to do or how to help. After his friend's death, his widow made some comments to James about her husband only having accepted the deployment to make James happy, and that this deployment had significantly contributed to his death.

James said that he thought retirement would make everything better—but instead he felt a lot worse. Drinking secretively alone, reporting no real friends and fractured relationships with his children from a previous marriage and, with little purpose or motivation, James reported he felt numb and had little emotion to events that he knew he should have feelings to. He felt distant and cut off from everyone, including his wife, and was going to bed before 7:30 in the evening so that he could be by himself in the dark; however, he experienced broken sleep and was often tired.

Processing assimilated SPs made sense to James, and with good Socratic dialogue and challenging of hindsight bias he made treatment gains in respect to his assimilated SPs very quickly. Despite this, he continued to think badly about himself and other people (e.g., "Civilians can never understand me"; "People are idiots") and remained withdrawn and isolated. James came to session wanting to talk about a recent argument he'd had with his wife and questioned whether he should leave the marriage. He described being angry and frustrated, with his wife accusing him of barking orders at her and treating her like one of his soldiers—"*She had the audacity to tell me that I don't listen to her and that I just wait till she's finished speaking so that I can tell her what to do*", he said. *"That's complete nonsense. I listen to her complaining about everything but then she does nothing to fix it. I just want her to DO something about it instead of always telling me about it*".

James' relationship with his wife was a protective factor for him. At his assessment, he stated that he had thoughts of suicide, but that he couldn't do that to his wife given his own experience of his friend. For James, dealing with how he was managing the conflict in his relationship became critical, given that his social isolation and lack of support outside of his marriage meant that if this imploded, he would be more at risk. Given the importance of James' relationship with his wife in maintaining his safety, the decision was made to diverge from the CPT protocol to address this issue in the context of IPT.

Of the four IPT problem areas which typically trigger and maintain depression, James was experiencing issues in each: grief (over the suicide of his best friend); role transition (from military to civilian life); role dispute (conflict in his relationships); and interpersonal deficits (social isolation and loneliness). Focusing first on the relationship with his wife, our goals were to help him understand what he and his wife expected from the relationship and to learn a new way of communicating which relied less on the style he would have become accustomed to using in military service and to practice a new way. Using questioning techniques about the value of the relationship and what needed to change, perspective taking about his wife's opinion, reactions and feelings and role-playing, James started to practice a different communication style to use with his wife. This included listening before collaboratively problem solving, expressing his deeper feelings of hurt or fear rather than anger and defensiveness, and focusing on "I statements" rather than "You statements". Changing the communication style which had served him while in the military but was not serving him in civilian life (and certainly not in his marriage!) took time and practice for James. On reverting back to the standard protocol, we continued to check his progress with communication briefly at the beginning of each CPT session. By the end of treatment, not only were James's symptoms of PTSD no longer a problem, but he reported far less conflict in his marriage and starting to engage in other activities within his community.

Future Directions

We could write another chapter on the research that is required to understand how best to optimize the treatment of comorbid PTSD and depression! Although we have some good evidence as to what works to treat PTSD and depression independently, we still have too few well-powered randomized trials examining "what works best for whom". This includes how best to sequence specific treatments and what elements or dosage of evidence-based treatments such as BA or IPT could be incorporated into CPT.

Relatedly, we lack a nuanced understanding of the complex relationships between PTSD and depression symptoms, their underlying mechanisms, and what are the optimal techniques to employ at the *individual* level throughout therapy. We have the statistical and methodological means to do this better, moving beyond week-to-week measurement studies examining how changes in PTSD and depression reciprocally influence PTSD treatment outcomes to using experience sampling methods (ESM) with multiple *daily* measurements of both symptoms and relevant variables (e.g., responses to relationship stressors, level of social contact, influence of grief, etc.). Additionally, although we know that emotional numbing and alexithymia can improve following standard PTSD treatments including CPT (see Angelakis et al., 2020; Galovski et al., 2020), we lack good guidance on how to best address these in therapy. Examining the application of new approaches to targeting anhedonia to PTSD (e.g., Craske et al., 2022) is likely to be fruitful. When it comes to the role of psychopharmacology, studies have compared antidepressant medication against or in combination with Prolonged Exposure (e.g., Rauch et al., 2019) and CPT and medication for dual PTSD and substance abuse (Elbarazi et al., 2022; Petrakis et al., 2020); however, there do not appear to be any specifically involving CPT and comorbid depression. New methods or adjunctive interventions have been proposed for PTSD treatments that have relevance to CPT and comorbid depression (e.g., use of exercise, McKeon et al., 2021; processing of positive memories, Contractor et al., 2021), yet work in this area is in its infancy. Finally, research suggests more frequent CPT sessions are associated with better PTSD outcomes (Gutner et al., 2016) and for depression, biweekly sessions of IPT or CBT resulted in better depression outcomes than weekly therapy (Bruijniks et al., 2020). Studies of varying treatment intensity in comorbid PTSD and depression samples are needed.

Summary

We hope this chapter provides helpful guidance for therapists using CPT when comorbid depression is present. We end with what we believe are the key take-home messages.

- A proper initial assessment and consideration of a client's depression at the very beginning of CPT sets the framework for effective therapy.
- Standard CPT is highly effective in reducing depression. Thus, divergences or additions need to be defensible and guided by good case formulation and routine outcome monitoring. See Chap. 15 for more information on diverging from the CPT protocol without compromising efficacy.
- If divergence is required, it is critical to return to trauma-focused CPT work. Remember, if you have diverged, it was because depression was getting in way of PTSD treatment, but you need to come back to the CPT if PTSD is still a problem.
- Repetition of skills is important. SP work, worksheets, behavioral experiments—often these are being used to target what are likely to be core beliefs and ingrained patterns of behavior. Therapists need to be clear with clients that this work needs repetition and practice.
- Many of the non-CPT techniques and adjunctive treatments require good case formulation and functional analysis skills. We are strong advocates of professional development and supervision for all therapists, no matter how experienced.
- Our work with clients is both extremely rewarding but challenging. It is critically important for therapists to adopt good self-care when working with clients with complex and challenging comorbidities, and to practice the very skills we impart to them.

Competing Interests
Reginald D.V. Nixon receives royalties from the book *Flexible applications of cognitive processing therapy: Evidence-based treatment methods* and has received speaker and consultant honoraria related to CPT workshops and training. Marja Elizabeth has received speaker and consultant honoraria related to CPT workshops and training.

References

Clinical Guides, Manuals, or "How to" Resources

Addis, M. E., & Martell, C. R. (2004). *Overcoming depression one step at a time: The new behavioral activation approach to getting your life back*. New Harbinger Publications.

Bennett-Levy, J., Butler, G., Fennell, M., Hackman, A., Mueller, M., & Westbrook, D. (Eds.). (2004). *Oxford guide to behavioural experiments in cognitive therapy*. Oxford University Press.

Benstead, U. (2011). 'The shark cage': The use of metaphor with women who have experienced abuse. *Psychotherapy in Australia, 17*, 70–76.

Greenberger, D., & Padesky, C. A. (1995). *Mind over mood: A cognitive therapy treatment manual for clients*. Guilford Press.

Greenberger, D., & Padesky, C. A. (2015). *Mind over mood: Change how you feel by changing the way you think* (2nd ed.). Guilford Publications.

Galovski, T. E., Nixon, R. D., & Kaysen, D. (2020). *Flexible applications of cognitive processing therapy: Evidence-based treatment methods*. Academic Press.

Markowitz, J. C. (2016). *Interpersonal psychotherapy for posttraumatic stress disorder*. Oxford University Press.

Markowitz, J. C. (2021). *In the aftermath of the pandemic: Interpersonal psychotherapy for anxiety, depression, and PTSD*. Oxford University Press.

Martell, C. R., Addis, M. E., & Jacobson, N. S. (2001). *Depression in context: Strategies for guided action*. WW Norton & Co.

Resick, P. A., Monson, C. M., & Chard, K. M. (2017). Cognitive processing therapy for PTSD: A comprehensive manual. .

Resick, P. A., Monson, C. M., & Chard, K. M. (2024). *Cognitive processing therapy for PTSD: A comprehensive therapist manual* (2nd ed.).

Watkins, E. R. (2016). *Rumination-focused cognitive-behavioral therapy for depression*. Guilford Press.

Watkins, E. R. (2022). Rumination-focused cognitive behavioral therapy. In G. Todd & R. Branch (Eds.), *Evidence-based treatment for anxiety disorders and depression: A cognitive behavioral therapy compendium* (pp. 402–417). Cambridge University Press.

Other References

Althobaiti, S., Kazantzis, N., Ofori-Asenso, R., Romero, L., Fisher, J., Mills, K. E., & Liew, D. (2020). Efficacy of interpersonal psychotherapy for post-traumatic stress disorder: A systematic review and meta-analysis. *Journal of Affective Disorders, 264*, 286–294.

Angelakis, S., & Nixon, R. D. (2015). The comorbidity of PTSD and MDD: Implications for clinical practice and future research. *Behaviour Change, 32*(1), 1–25.

Angelakis, S., Weber, N., & Nixon, R. D. (2020). Comorbid posttraumatic stress disorder and major depressive disorder: The usefulness of a sequential treatment approach within a randomised design. *Journal of Anxiety Disorders, 76*, 1–12.

Basco, M. R., Bostic, J. Q., Davies, D., Rush, A. J., Witte, B., Hendrickse, W., & Barnett, V. (2000). Methods to improve diagnostic accuracy in a community mental health setting. *The American Journal of Psychiatry, 157*(10), 1599–1605.

Bedard-Gilligan, M., Duax Jakob, J. M., Doane, L. S., Jaeger, J., Eftekhari, A., Feeny, N., & Zoellner, L. A. (2015). An investigation of depression, trauma history, and symptom severity in individuals enrolled in a treatment trial for chronic PTSD. *Journal of Clinical Psychology, 71*(7), 725–740.

Bleiberg, K. L., & Markowitz, J. C. (2019). Interpersonal psychotherapy for PTSD: Treating trauma without exposure. *Journal of Psychotherapy Integration, 29*(1), 15–22.

Blevins, C. A., Weathers, F. W., Davis, M. T., Witte, T. K., & Domino, J. L. (2015). The post-traumatic stress disorder checklist for DSM-5 (PCL-5): Development and initial psychometric evaluation. *Journal of Traumatic Stress, 28*(6), 489–498.

Bruijniks, S. J. E., Lemmens, L., Hollon, S. D., Peeters, F., Cuijpers, P., Arntz, A., Dingemanse, P., Willems, L., van Oppen, P., Twisk, J. W. R., van den Boogaard, M., Spijker, J., Bosmans, J., & Huibers, M. J. H. (2020). The effects of once- versus twice-weekly sessions on psychotherapy outcomes in depressed patients. *The British Journal of Psychiatry, 216*(4), 222–230.

Bryan, C. J., Russell, H. A., Bryan, A. O., Rozek, D. C., Leifker, F. R., Rugo, K. F., Baker, J. C., Khazem, L. R., Roberge, E. M., Shirley, D. M., & Asnaani, A. (2022). Impact of treatment setting and format on symptom severity following cognitive processing therapy for posttraumatic stress disorder. *Behavior Therapy, 53*(4), 673–685.

Classen, C. C., Palesh, O. G., & Aggarwal, R. (2005). Sexual revictimization: A review of the empirical literature. *Trauma Violence & Abuse, 6*(2), 103–129.

Contractor, A. A., Weiss, N. H., & Shea, M. T. (2021). Processing of positive memories technique (PPMT) for posttraumatic stress disorder: A primer. *Journal of Psychotherapy Integration, 31*(2), 195–207.

Craske, M. G., Dour, H. J., Treanor, M., & Meuret, A. E. (2022). *Positive affect treatment for depression and anxiety: Therapist guide*. Oxford University Press.

Cusack, K. J., Grubaugh, A. L., Knapp, R. G., & Frueh, B. C. (2006). Unrecognized trauma and PTSD among public mental health consumers with chronic and severe mental illness. *Community Mental Health Journal, 42*(5), 487–500.

Duberstein, P. R., Ward, E. A., Chaudron, L. H., He, H., Toth, S. L., Wang, W., Van Orden, K. A., Gamble, S. A., & Talbot, N. L. (2018). Effectiveness of interpersonal psychotherapy-trauma for depressed women with childhood abuse histories. *Journal of Consulting and Clinical Psychology, 86*(10), 868–878.

Ehring, T., & Watkins, E. R. (2008). Repetitive negative thinking as a Transdiagnostic process. *International Journal of Cognitive Therapy, 1*(3), 192–205.

ElBarazi, A., Badary, O. A., Elmazar, M. M., & Elrassas, H. (2022). Cognitive processing therapy versus medication for the treatment of comorbid substance use disorder and Post-traumatic stress disorder in Egyptian patients (randomized clinical trial). *Journal of Evidence-Based Psychotherapies, 22*(2), 63.

Farmer, C. C., Mitchell, K. S., Parker-Guilbert, K., & Galovski, T. E. (2017). Fidelity to the cognitive processing therapy protocol: Evaluation of critical elements. *Behavior Therapy, 48*(2), 195–206.

Galovski, T. E., Harik, J. M., Blain, L. M., Farmer, C., Turner, D., & Houle, T. (2016). Identifying patterns and predictors of PTSD and depressive symptom change during cognitive processing therapy. *Cognitive Therapy and Research, 40*(5), 617–626.

Galovski, T. E., Werner, K. B., Weaver, T. L., Morris, K. L., Dondanville, K. A., Nanney, J., Wamser-Nanney, R., McGlinchey, G., Fortier, C. B., & Iverson, K. M. (2022). Massed cognitive processing therapy for posttraumatic stress disorder in women survivors of intimate partner violence. *Psychological Trauma: Theory, Research, Practice, and Policy, 14*(5), 769–779.

Goetter, E. M., Blackburn, A. M., Stasko, C., Han, Y., Brenner, L. H., Lejeune, S., Tanev, K. S., Spencer, T. J., & Wright, E. C. (2021). Comparative effectiveness of prolonged exposure and cognitive processing therapy for military service members in an intensive treatment program. *Psychological Trauma: Theory, Research, Practice, and Policy, 13*(6), 632–640.

Gutner, C. A., Suvak, M. K., Sloan, D. M., & Resick, P. A. (2016). Does timing matter? Examining the impact of session timing on outcome. *Journal of Consulting and Clinical Psychology, 84*(12), 1108–1115.

Ikin, J. F., Creamer, M. C., Sim, M. R., & McKenzie, D. P. (2010). Comorbidity of PTSD and depression in Korean war veterans: Prevalence, predictors, and impairment. *Journal of Affective Disorders, 125*(1–3), 279–286.

Jacoby, V. M., Hale, W., Dillon, K., Dondanville, K. A., Wachen, J. S., Yarvis, J. S., Litz, B. T., Mintz, J., Young-McCaughan, S., Peterson, A. L., Resick, P. A., & Consortium, S. S. (2019).

Depression suppresses treatment response for traumatic loss-related posttraumatic stress disorder in active duty military personnel. *Journal of Traumatic Stress, 32*(5), 774–783.

Kessler, R. C., Berglund, P., Demler, O., Jin, R., Merikangas, K. R., & Walters, E. E. (2005). Lifetime prevalence and age-of-onset distributions of DSM-IV disorders in the National Comorbidity Survey Replication. *Archives of General Psychiatry, 62*(6), 593–602.

Kline, A. C., Cooper, A. A., Rytwinski, N. K., & Feeny, N. C. (2021). The effect of concurrent depression on PTSD outcomes in trauma-focused psychotherapy: A meta-analysis of randomized controlled trials. *Behavior Therapy, 52*(1), 250–266.

Kubota, R., & Nixon, R. D. V. (2017). An analogue investigation into the effect of trauma-related rumination on trauma intrusions and the moderating role of trait rumination and depression. *Journal of Experimental Psychopathology, 8*(4), 413–442.

Lenferink, L. I. M., Eisma, M. C., Buiter, M. Y., de Keijser, J., & Boelen, P. A. (2023). Online cognitive behavioral therapy for prolonged grief after traumatic loss: A randomized waitlist-controlled trial. *Cognitive Behaviour Therapy, 52*(5), 508–522.

Lewis, C., Raisanen, L., Bisson, J. I., Jones, I., & Zammit, S. (2017). Trauma exposure and undetected posttraumatic stress disorder among adults with a mental disorder. *Depression & Anxiety, 35*(2), 178–184.

Liebschutz, J., Saitz, R., Brower, V., Keane, T. M., Lloyd-Travaglini, C., Averbuch, T., & Samet, J. H. (2007). PTSD in urban primary care: High prevalence and low physician recognition. *Journal of General Internal Medicine, 22*(6), 719–726.

McKeon, G., Steel, Z., Wells, R., Newby, J., Hadzi-Pavlovic, D., Vancampfort, D., & Rosenbaum, S. (2021). A mental health-informed physical activity intervention for first responders and their partners delivered using Facebook: Mixed methods pilot study. *JMIR Formative Research, 5*(4), 1–18.

Meltzer, E. C., Averbuch, T., Samet, J. H., Saitz, R., Jabbar, K., Lloyd-Travaglini, C., & Liebschutz, J. M. (2012). Discrepancy in diagnosis and treatment of Post-traumatic stress disorder (PTSD): Treatment for the wrong reason. *The Journal of Behavioral Health Services & Research, 39*, 190–201.

Monson, C. M., Schnurr, P. P., Resick, P. A., Friedman, M. J., Young-Xu, Y., & Stevens, S. P. (2006). Cognitive processing therapy for veterans with military-related posttraumatic stress disorder. *Journal of Consulting and Clinical Psychology, 74*(5), 898–907.

Nichter, B., Norman, S., Haller, M., & Pietrzak, R. H. (2019a). Physical health burden of PTSD, depression, and their comorbidity in the U.S. veteran population: Morbidity, functioning, and disability. *Journal of Psychosomatic Research, 124*, 1–7.

Nichter, B., Norman, S., Haller, M., & Pietrzak, R. H. (2019b). Psychological burden of PTSD, depression, and their comorbidity in the U.S. veteran population: Suicidality, functioning, and service utilization. *Journal of Affective Disorders, 256*, 633–640.

Nixon, R. D., Resick, P. A., & Nishith, P. (2004). An exploration of comorbid depression among female victims of intimate partner violence with posttraumatic stress disorder. *Journal of Affective Disorders, 82*(2), 315–320.

Oquendo, M., Brent, D. A., Birmaher, B., Greenhill, L., Kolko, D., Stanley, B., Zelazny, J., Burke, A., Firinciogullari, S., & Mann, J. J. (2005). Posttraumatic stress disorder comorbid with major depression: Factors mediating the association with suicidal behavior. *American Journal of Psychiatry, 162*(3), 560–566.

Petrakis, I., Ralevski, E., Arias, A. J., DeNegre, D., Newcomb, J., Gianoli, M., McCarthy, E., Meshberg-Cohen, S., & Yoon, G. (2020). Zonisamide as an adjunctive treatment to cognitive processing therapy for veterans with posttraumatic stress disorder and comorbid alcohol use disorder: A pilot study. *The American Journal on Addictions, 29*(6), 515–524.

Pickover, A., Lowell, A., Lazarov, A., Lopez-Yianilos, A., Sanchez-Lacay, A., Ryba, M., Such, S., Arnon, S., Amsalem, D., Neria, Y., & Markowitz, J. C. (2021). Interpersonal psychotherapy of posttraumatic stress disorder for veterans and family members: An open trial. *Psychiatric Services, 72*(8), 866–873.

Post, L. M., Zoellner, L. A., Youngstrom, E., & Feeny, N. C. (2011). Understanding the relationship between co-occurring PTSD and MDD: Symptom severity and affect. *Journal of Anxiety Disorders, 25*(8), 1123–1130.

Rauch, S. A. M., Kim, H. M., Powell, C., Tuerk, P. W., Simon, N. M., Acierno, R., Allard, C. B., Norman, S. B., Venners, M. R., Rothbaum, B. O., Stein, M. B., Porter, K., Martis, B., King, A. P., Liberzon, I., Phan, K. L., & Hoge, C. W. (2019). Efficacy of prolonged exposure therapy, sertraline hydrochloride, and their combination among combat veterans with posttraumatic stress disorder: A randomized clinical trial. *JAMA Psychiatry, 76*(2), 117–126.

Resick, P. A., Galovski, T. E., Uhlmansiek, M. O. B., Scher, C. D., Clum, G. A., & Young-Xu, Y. (2008). A randomized clinical trial to dismantle components of cognitive processing therapy for posttraumatic stress disorder in female victims of interpersonal violence. *Journal of Consulting and Clinical Psychology, 76*(2), 243.

Resick, P. A., Nishith, P., Weaver, T. L., Astin, M. C., & Feuer, C. A. (2002). A comparison of cognitive-processing therapy with prolonged exposure and a waiting condition for the treatment of chronic posttraumatic stress disorder in female rape victims. *Journal of Consulting and Clinical Psychology, 70*(4), 867.

Rosen, V., Ortiz, N. F., & Nemeroff, C. B. (2020). Double trouble: Treatment considerations for patients with comorbid PTSD and depression. *Current Treatment Options in Psychiatry, 7*(3), 258–274.

Rozek, D. C., Baker, S. N., Rugo, K. F., Steigerwald, V. L., Sippel, L. M., Holliday, R., Roberge, E. M., Held, P., Mota, N., & Smith, N. B. (2022). Addressing co-occurring suicidal thoughts and behaviors and posttraumatic stress disorder in evidence-based psychotherapies for adults: A systematic review. *Journal of Traumatic Stress, 35*(2), 729–745.

Rytwinski, N. K., Scur, M. D., Feeny, N. C., & Youngstrom, E. A. (2013). The co-occurrence of major depressive disorder among individuals with posttraumatic stress disorder: A meta-analysis. *Journal of Traumatic Stress, 26*(3), 299–309.

Schumm, J. A., Walter, K. H., & Chard, K. M. (2013). Latent class differences explain variability in PTSD symptom changes during cognitive processing therapy for veterans. *Psychological Trauma: Theory, Research, Practice, and Policy, 5*(6), 536–544.

Shannon, C., Maguire, C., Anderson, J., Meenagh, C., & Mulholland, C. (2011). Enquiring about traumatic experiences in bipolar disorder: A case note and self-report comparison. *Journal of Affective Disorders, 133*(2), 352–355.

Stein, N. R., Dickstein, B. D., Schuster, J., Litz, B. T., & Resick, P. A. (2012). Trajectories of response to treatment for posttraumatic stress disorder. *Behavior Therapy, 43*(4), 790–800.

Walter, K. H., Dickstein, B. D., Barnes, S. M., & Chard, K. M. (2014). Comparing effectiveness of CPT to CPT-C among U.S. veterans in an interdisciplinary residential PTSD/TBI treatment program. *Journal of Traumatic Stress, 27*(4), 438–445.

Walter, K. H., Glassman, L. H., Michael Hunt, W., Otis, N. P., & Thomsen, C. J. (2018a). Evaluation of an integrated treatment for active duty service members with comorbid posttraumatic stress disorder and major depressive disorder: Study protocol for a randomized controlled trial. *Contemporary Clinical Trials, 64*, 152–160.

Walter, K. H., Levine, J. A., Highfill-McRoy, R. M., Navarro, M., & Thomsen, C. J. (2018b). Prevalence of posttraumatic stress disorder and psychological comorbidities among U.S. active duty service members, 2006-2013. *Journal of Traumatic Stress, 31*(6), 837–844.

Walter, K. H., Hunt, W. M., Otis, N. P., Kline, A. C., Miggantz, E. L., Thomsen, C. J., & Glassman, L. H. (2023). Comparison of behavioral activation-enhanced cognitive processing therapy and cognitive processing therapy among U.S. service members: A randomized clinical trial. *Psychiatry Research, 326*, 1–10.

Yamokoski, C., Flores, H., Facemire, V., Maieritsch, K., Perez, S., & Fedynich, A. (2023). Feasibility of an intensive outpatient treatment program for posttraumatic stress disorder within the veterans health care administration. *Psychological Services, 20*(3), 506–515.

Chapter 3
Delivering CPT in the Context of Emotion Dysregulation

John Nanney

Introduction

Emotion regulation is the ability to manage the internal experience and external expression of affect (Gratz & Roemer, 2004; Gross, 1998). Difficulties with Emotion Regulations (DERs) are common among those with post-traumatic stress disorder (PTSD) and are associated with the severity of PTSD symptoms (Seligowski et al., 2015). Emotion regulation includes several overlapping facets including the ability to identify emotions, to accept/tolerate emotional experiences without self-judgment, to engage in goal-driven behavior despite emotional arousal, and to inhibit impulsive, potentially harmful, emotion-driven behaviors (Gratz & Roemer, 2004). This latter facet, often labeled as *negative urgency*, reflects the tendency to act rashly when under distress (Cyders & Smith, 2008). Maladaptive impulsive reactions to distress often manifest as high-risk "crises" that cause significant functional impairment, sometimes to the point that the individual becomes a safety risk to themselves or others.

Negative urgency is the emotion regulation facet most specifically tied to PTSD (Contractor et al., 2018). It is associated with all PTSD symptom clusters (Roley et al., 2017), and is a proximal mechanism linking PTSD to numerous dangerous behaviors including suicidality (Wiblin et al., 2021), interpersonal aggression (Dutra & Sadeh, 2018; Nomamiukor et al., 2022), and substance misuse (Hahn et al., 2015; Mirhashem et al., 2017; Tripp et al., 2015). Unsurprisingly, dangerous emotion-driven behaviors (e.g., substance use, suicidality, and aggression) are often present within the same individual. Alcohol misuse significantly contributes to suicide attempts (Borges et al., 2017) and impulsive aggression (Elbogen et al., 2014; Miles et al., 2016); emotion-driven aggression is associated with self-directed

J. Nanney (✉)
Intelligent Clinical Design, LLC, St. Louis, MO, USA

J. S. Wachen, T. E. Galovski (eds.), *Cognitive Processing Therapy for Complex Cases*, CBT: Science Into Practice,
https://doi.org/10.1007/978-3-031-87356-0_3

aggression particularly among those with PTSD (Fanning et al., 2016); and both PTSD and substance misuse each independently increase the odds of an individual engaging in self-directed or other-directed violence, separately or concurrently (Fanning et al., 2016).

Dangerous emotion-driven behaviors not only co-occur within individuals, but may dynamically emerge within a single crisis, with one crisis behavior potentiating another (Bryan & Rudd, 2018). Such episodes of dangerous emotion-driven behaviors are consistent with contemporary theories of suicide like the *fluid vulnerability theory* (Rudd, 2006). This theory posits that individuals possess differing degrees of chronic risk for suicide, but suicidal behavior typically emerges only when an acute life stressor activates intense emotions and a chain of impulsive, emotion-driven acts, labeled as the *suicide mode*, which may end in a serious suicide attempt. Indeed, case examples of typical suicide modes in contemporary treatment manuals for suicide prevention (e.g., Brief Cognitive Behavioral Therapy for Suicide Prevention [BCBT-SP]; Bryan & Rudd, 2018) include chains of impulsive reactions to acute emotional stressors as predicates for suicidal behavior. For example, someone with PTSD may be triggered by trauma cues, drink excessive alcohol to numb their intense distress, get into a fight, and then become suicidal as they reproach themselves over these responses. Likewise, case examples from interventions for concurrent PTSD and substance use disorders (e.g., Concurrent Treatment of PTSD and SUD Prolonged Exposure [COPE]; Back et al., 2014]) highlight PTSD-related impulsive substance use predicating impulsive violence and suicide, and interventions for PTSD and intimate partner violence (e.g., Strength at Home; Taft et al., 2016) note substance use and suicidality as risk factors for impulsive aggression. What in the suicide literature is referred to as a *suicide mode* may thus be understood as a subclass of a more general *emotional crisis mode* that may or may not include suicidality, but often does include some dangerous emotion-driven behaviors.

Treatment of PTSD and Co-Occurring Dangerous Emotion-Driven Behaviors

Some clinicians and scholars have argued that PTSD treatment among those with significant emotion dysregulation or emotional crisis behaviors (e.g., suicide, substance misuse, self- or other-directed aggression) should begin with a stabilization phase to increase self-regulation before beginning trauma-focused therapy (Cloitre et al., 2002; LoSavio et al., 2022). Such clients are thought to be incapable of tolerating the emotions evoked in trauma-focused therapies without engaging in dangerous emotion-driven acts, potentially interfering with successful trauma treatment or even placing the individual and the community at greater risk (LoSavio et al., 2019).

For clients with PTSD and emotion regulation difficulties, however, there is no evidence that preparatory treatment yields better outcomes than immediately initiating trauma-focused interventions (Dedert et al., 2021). Moreover, PTSD treatment strategies that include an initial stabilization phase necessarily extend overall treatment length, contributing to high rates of drop-out, even before trauma-focused elements begin (Dedert et al., 2021). Delaying or withholding direct trauma processing may also implicitly suggest that trauma-focused therapy is dangerous or that clients are too fragile to engage explicitly trauma-related content. Such cognitions are only likely to strengthen the trauma-related schemas which underpin PTSD (Resick et al., 2017).

Fortunately, Cognitive Processing Therapy for PTSD (CPT; Resick et al., 2024) is a broad-spectrum intervention that addresses not only traumatogenic cognitions, but each component of emotion regulation as well (Martin et al., 2020; Resick et al., 2024). CPT helps clients clarify and name their emotions and to tolerate the natural emotions that stem from trauma and distressing events. CPT also helps clients recognize that some emotions stem from distorted interpretations of events but that reframing these interpretations can lead to more effective emotions and actions (Resick et al., 2017). CPT thus teaches clients how to respond to strong emotions thoughtfully, rather than responding as if the emotional tendency were a mandate to act. Accordingly, research indicates emotion regulation difficulties do not increase treatment drop-out or compromise efficacy, and such difficulties significantly improve over the course of CPT (Shnaider et al., 2022).

CPT has also demonstrated safety and efficacy among clients with specific emotional crisis behaviors that often accompany PTSD. There is evidence that CPT reduces suicidal ideation, beginning with the first session (Bryan et al., 2016; Gradus et al., 2013; Holliday et al., 2018; Post et al., 2021) CPT is also shown to be safe and effective in reducing PTSD among those with hazardous drinking (Held et al., 2021) and may reduce problematic drinking itself (Dondanville et al., 2019). Hazardous drinking does not appear to be associated with higher treatment drop-out or need for lengthier intervention (Dondanville et al., 2019; LoSavio et al., 2023; Straud et al., 2021). Borderline Personality Disorder (BPD), the diagnosis most emblematic of dangerous emotion dysregulation, is not found to negatively influence CPT outcomes (Clarke et al., 2008; Holder et al., 2017). Although some patients may exhibit exacerbation of symptoms in the initial stages of CPT, these initial exacerbations typically do not lead to adverse events or poorer end-state functioning (Larsen et al., 2022). Intervening to address emotional crisis behaviors through the lens of CPT, rather than abandoning the trauma-focus, appears to allow the emotion-regulating processes of CPT to take hold, yielding safe and positive outcomes (Burback et al., 2023; Tripp et al., 2021).

CPT in the Context of Dangerous Emotion-Driven Behaviors

Since CPT provides broad and effective coverage of emotion regulation issues while directly addressing underlying trauma, the most efficient and effective treatment plan for those with co-occurring dangerous emotion-driven behaviors likely should remain parsimonious, with minimal deviation into non-CPT content. Fidelity to the CPT model is associated with stronger outcomes (Farmer et al., 2017; Holder et al., 2018). Stopping CPT for several weeks or spending substantial time in CPT sessions teaching non-trauma-focused skills may dilute or delay the essential processing of trauma-related cognitions that underlie PTSD and any associated dangerous behaviors. Therefore, when using CPT with clients who engage in dangerous emotion-driven acts, a foundational strategy is to emphasize throughout treatment how cognitive processing skills can be used to regulate strong emotions in the specific contexts most associated with the clients' crisis behaviors.

The main threat to successful completion of CPT for clients with heightened emotion dysregulation is the emergence of a potentially treatment-disrupting crisis *before* clients have mastered the emotion regulation skills inherent to CPT. To mitigate this risk, Crisis Response Planning (CRP; Bryan & Rudd, 2018) can be integrated into CPT to provide individualized plans to reduce the likelihood or severity of dangerous emotion-driven behaviors during treatment (Rozek & Bryan, 2020). CRP provides an idiographic "game plan" for clients to safely navigate their emotional crises while they learn essential CPT skills. Bryan and colleagues initially described a case example illustrating the integration of CRP with CPT (2024) and recently reported findings from a randomized trial indicating that CRP prior to CPT quickly reduced preexisting suicidal ideation and protected against the onset of suicidal thoughts (Bryan et al., 2024). Following this lead, the present chapter describes a more generalized approach for managing dangerous emotion-driven behaviors within CPT while also suggesting CPT-consistent interventions for clients with specific emotion regulation needs.

Cognitive Processing Therapy for PTSD with Dangerous Emotion-Driven Behaviors

Assessment

Thorough and precise assessment is the foundation of good intervention. Extensively assessing the specific contexts and functional mechanisms that generate the client's most disruptive symptoms allows the clinician to develop an idiographic treatment plan to mitigate the client's specific pattern of dangerous emotion-driven behaviors. This case conceptualization approach allows for targeted interventions that minimize interference with the standard CPT process such that treatment is not extended, over-complicated, or diluted by unnecessary diversions. The assessment phase of

CPT for clients with dangerous emotion-driven behavior (CPT-DEB) should likely be more detailed and extensive than is typical. The Life Events Checklist-Interview Format (Weathers et al., 2013a) and a thorough psychosocial history can provide a solid understanding of how social ecologies and specific Criterion A traumas influence client functioning, past and present. Administration of the Clinician-Administered PTSD Scale for *DSM-5* (CAPS-5; Weathers et al., 2018), in addition the PTSD Checklist for *DSM-5* (PCL-5; Weathers et al., 2013b), is also recommended to gain more thorough knowledge of current trauma symptoms. In addition to the standard CAPS questions, clinicians can ask clients to describe in detail the most salient and severe manifestation of each reported symptom, both within the last month and over the course of the client's lifetime, as well as how the client typically copes with the symptom and any outcomes that commonly ensue. Such information allows clinicians to sketch hypotheses about potentially dangerous emotion-driven behaviors that might occur during therapy, their relationship to traumatic stress symptoms, and the contexts in which they are most likely to emerge. Client responses may also illustrate their current repertoire coping behaviors and knowledge of potential coping skills.

The Difficulties with Emotion Regulation Scale (DERS; Gratz & Roemer, 2004) is also recommended when assessing clients with trauma-related concerns. The DERS measures several ER facets. Subscales of most immediate interest may be Limited Access to Emotion Regulation Strategies and Difficulties Controlling Impulsive Behaviors When Distressed. Endorsement of items on these subscales point generally toward the importance of addressing emotional crisis behavior and coping skills in CPT. More importantly, specific item endorsements provide a starting point for qualitative follow-up questions to fully assess the nature and severity of high-risk behavior. Specific deficits in one or more other facets on the DERS are also noteworthy as they may suggest adding additional emphasis or skill development when they are addressed in CPT. Lack of Emotional Awareness and Lack of Emotional Clarity suggest clients may need greater psychoeducation and resources for identifying and naming specific emotions. The Lack of Emotional Acceptance subscale even includes several items that are analogous to potential stuck points regarding the meaning of trauma-related emotions (e.g., "When I am upset, I feel like I am weak.") Higher scores on this facet suggest that natural trauma-related emotions may evoke self-judgment, and therapists should remain attuned to potential stuck points related to emotions/emotional expression. Item endorsement around Lack of Coping Skills should prompt discussion of what coping skills the client *has* found helpful, currently and in the past, as these likely may be important elements of the initial Crisis Response Plans.

To supplement the DERS, the Negative Urgency subscale of the UPPS-P Impulsivity Scale (Cyders et al., 2007) provides supplemental assessment of dysfunctional emotion-driven behaviors. As with other measures, clinicians should probe for the most salient/extreme examples of behaviors the client may be referencing in their item endorsement. For example, if the patient endorses "When I'm upset, I become out of control," clinicians should directly inquire about what contexts typically predicate the client becoming "out of control" as well as the behaviors and outcomes that this denotes.

Suicide risk should always be explicitly assessed and documented using a well-defined method. Although there are no well-validated algorithms for assigning level of suicide risk (Bryan & Rudd, 2018), several structured interviews and rating scales regarding suicidality are available including the Columbia Suicide Severity Rating Scale (C-SSRS; Posner et al., 2011), the Suicide Status Form-4 (Jobes, 2023), and the Suicide Risk Assessment Documentation Template from BCBT-SP (Bryan & Rudd, 2018). Each of these approaches generally addresses the nature and severity of any suicidal ideation or behavior and they can be supplemented with data from the psychosocial history, the DERS, and the UPPS-P when assessing suicide risk. When considering the constellation of information relevant to suicide risk the following principles should be considered:

- Suicide risk may be differentiated into acute and chronic timeframes. Acute risk of suicide refers to risk of suicide occurring within the next few hours to days and is most germane to determining if a client can remain safe outside of a restricted environment (i.e., a hospital). Chronic risk refers to risk of suicide over longer-periods of time (i.e., months to years). Acute and chronic risk levels may differ. A client with a history of suicide attempts, borderline personality disorder, and polysubstance abuse likely is at high chronic risk of suicide. But if they are currently sober, stable, and in therapy, their acute risk of suicide may be low.
- History of prior attempts informs both acute and chronic risk. Clients with multiple prior suicide attempts should be treated as higher risk than those with a single or no prior attempts (Bryan & Rudd, 2006).
- Objective indicators of recent resolved planning of a suicide attempt (i.e., considering specific methods of suicide, practicing or rehearsing an attempt) are more strongly associated with acute suicide risk than indicators of suicidal desire (i.e., articulating a desire to die, having few reasons to live, having passive thoughts of suicide; Bryan & Rudd, 2006; Joiner Jr. et al., 1999).
- Access to firearms significantly increases risk of lethal suicide (Anestis, 2023).
- Clients without a history of suicidal ideation or attempts are not free of suicide risk. Factors such as agitation, impulsivity, and suicide-related beliefs like guilt and shame are as strongly related to suicide risk as suicidal ideation and history of attempts (Bryan et al., 2014).

Acute suicide risk should be specifically assessed at baseline and all subsequent sessions. High acute risk of suicide implies the need for immediate hospitalization which takes precedence over any other outpatient psychological interventions, including CPT. High acute suicide risk may take multiple forms, but is generally characterized by more specific resolved planning, subjective or objective evidence of intent to die by suicide, access to lethal means, and unwillingness to participate in risk-reducing intervention. Research suggests clients with elevated levels of both acute and chronic risk (e.g., history of suicide attempts and current suicidal ideation) are just as able to complete and benefit from CPT as clients with no prior attempts or ideation (Roberge et al., 2021). Thus, it appears that most clients, even with elevated levels of suicide risk, can safely participate in and benefit from CPT, especially if suicidality is closely monitored and addressed during treatment.

For clients who do report dangerous emotion-driven behaviors, the next step is development of a Crisis Response Plan (CRP; Bryan & Rudd, 2018). CRPs focus on the contexts that generate a client's most dangerous emotion-driven behaviors (Rozek & Bryan, 2020). These should always include suicidality (Bryan & Rudd, 2018), but may also include binge-drinking, self-injurious behavior, or serious forms of aggression like intimate partner violence (IPV), aggressive driving, or impulsive community violence. A CRP provides clients with a highly specific plan for situations most likely to cause serious harm to themselves or others (Miles et al., 2015). Each CRP is collaboratively developed with the client. The CRP is optimally a simple checklist that the client can always keep with them. Essential elements of the CRP are as follows:

1. Personal warning signs that an emotional crisis is imminent.
2. Specific actions that clients can do themselves to provide distraction or otherwise cope effectively with the situation.
3. Reasons for coping with the situation effectively/avoiding dangerous behaviors.
4. Supportive friends or family who can provide help if needed.
5. Professional sources of support including the therapist, crisis hotlines, or emergency services.

Optimally, a single CRP will cover each of the situations/crisis behaviors that the client has described in the assessment. At times, distinct CRPs may be needed to cover different situations that may evoke dangerous crisis behaviors (e.g., trauma reminders versus triggers for substance use). The goal, however, is to simplify and specify the client's response to relevant crises. Thus, the clinician and client should develop the minimum number of CRPs needed to provide concrete response options across all contexts likely to generate dangerous behaviors. Once each CRP is developed, the clinician should review each step of the CRP(s) and ask the client to rate on a scale of 0–10 their likelihood of using the plan. If the client responds with anything lower than a 7, ask if there is anything that might be changed to make the plan more usable and adjust accordingly. CRPs should be given to clients as wallet-size paper copies and can easily be photographed and uploaded to smartphones.

The presence of a firearm in the home, particularly a loaded and unsecured firearm, dramatically increases the risk of lethal suicide (Anestis, 2023), homicide (Studdert et al., 2022), and intimate partner violence (Zeoli & Webster, 2010). Clients with PTSD, particularly veterans, are also significantly more likely to have positive views of firearms (Wamser-Nanney et al., 2021) and to keep unsecured firearms in the home (Semenza et al., 2023). Assessment for PTSD should thus routinely include questions about access to firearms. With clients who endorse gun access, clinicians should further inquire about typical methods of storage. For clients with PTSD, especially those with dangerous emotion-driven behaviors, reducing ready access to firearms may be an essential supplement to the CRP. Clinicians approaching the topic of firearms may benefit from taking an approach akin to Motivational Interviewing (Miller & Rollnick, 2012):

1. Engage the client by asking them general, nonthreatening questions about firearms in general (e.g., "What types of guns do you own/collect?"; "Do you enjoy hunting?").
2. Focus the conversation on gun safety by guiding the client to discuss their views about gun safety or the safety procedures they employ as a responsible gun-owner.
3. Evoke from the client personal reasons for potentially limiting their access to guns at this specific time. Example questions may include, "What are your thoughts about locking up or securing firearms for someone who is in an emotional crisis?" or "Can you tell me about some times it was probably good that you did not have a gun available?" Based upon the client's response, the clinician should listen for and encourage elaboration of "change talk" where the client is acknowledging the potential utility of limiting gun access in a crisis.
4. If the client has acknowledged that it may be beneficial to restrict their access given their current risk, create a plan for what they might do to ensure their safety during treatment.

Therapists should be respectful of the client's right to maintain their firearms. Clinicians should emphasize that safety is their primary goal and that any changes to current gun access would be temporary, lasting only until the client has achieved greater symptom reduction and emotional stability. Clinicians may need to clarify that forcible removal of guns from client possession is an option only in rare circumstances in which the client has made direct credible threats to harm themselves or others (Emergency Risk Protective Orders; ERPO) and only in jurisdictions where ERPOs are available (Frattaroli & Sharfstein, 2021). Clinicians should, therefore, be aware of any ERPO laws in their locality (Shultz et al., 2020). Storing the firearm unloaded, locked, and in a restricted location (i.e., a safe) separate from any ammunition is a preferred storage outcome. Clinicians may thus want to have gun locks on-hand for clients. For clients at higher risk, combinations or keys to the gun safe or lock would optimally be given to a family member or friend.

Intervention

Clients with severe emotion-driven behaviors may benefit from a more concentrated therapy course as it reduces opportunities for external events to predicate crisis behaviors before the mechanisms of CPT take hold. Considering available resources, such clients may benefit from massed CPT (e.g., Galovski et al., 2022; Held et al., 2020, see Chap. 14 of this book for an overview) or meeting more frequently than the typical one-session-per week paradigm. Intensive scheduling of CPT yields positive outcomes and minimal adverse events even in clients with complex presentations (Galovski et al., 2020; Sciarrino et al., 2020). Sessions may also require additional time each week to discuss the client's response to any emotional crises and to review/update the Crisis Response Plan(s). Scheduling longer sessions (e.g., 60–75 min) may be useful to ensure that trauma-focused elements are still delivered at an adequate pace.

Clients typically should be given the opportunity to choose between CPT with or without the written account, but therapists should recall that symptom improvement may be more immediate and dropout less frequent in standard CPT than when including the written account (Resick et al., 2008). If the need for improvement seems particularly urgent, clinicians may thus encourage use of CPT without the trauma narrative. Alternatively, clients who experience significant dissociation, particularly if it is part of their typical crisis behaviors, may benefit from including the written account (Resick et al., 2012).

Session 1 should begin by reviewing any emotional crises and how the CRP was or was not helpful in those contexts. The client and therapist should problem solve any identified difficulties or limitations and problem solve/revise accordingly. Faithful completion of CPT-1 psychoeducation remains essential as it lays the conceptual foundation for the remainder of CPT, including elements most likely to reduce the chances of unsafe behavior. Session 1 content should likely be administered in the standard CPT-1 psychoeducation sequence, though certain additional points may be helpful to add. When discussing the cognitive model of trauma, consider noting that clients often interpret their emotional reactions to the trauma based on their previous beliefs regarding emotions and emotional expression. For example, clients who learned that strong emotional experiences or expression were "not okay" may judge themselves for their natural trauma-related emotions, leading to emotion-related stuck points and avoidance. Also, clients who experienced invalidation of their trauma responses may come to believe that they must express their emotions more strongly and more dramatically to get needed assistance. For such clients, therapists may consider modifying the instructions of the Impact Statement slightly, asking clients to discuss how the trauma affected beliefs about emotions and emotional expression. Clinicians should also discuss with clients any concerns they have about emotional distress stemming from the Impact Statement assignment and how they plan to cope with that emotion, perhaps referencing the CRP.

Session 1 may also be briefly expanded upon traditional CPT-1 under certain, limited circumstances. If initial assessment or problem solving of the CRP demonstrate notable deficits in coping skills, the therapist may consider a brief skill instruction following assignment of the impact statement. Skill instruction should be limited to the client's individual needs as illustrated in assessment measures or narrative description of symptoms, crisis events, or CRPs. Of note, relaxation and mindfulness training is commonly included in the BCBT-SP approach to suicidal crisis management (Bryan & Rudd, 2018), and CPT psychoeducation provides logical predicates for teaching each of these skills. CPT-1 reviews physiological responses to trauma including the common fight or flight reaction and describes how this reaction may become paired with trauma-related cues. Relaxation skills are specifically effective in reducing such physiological arousal and may benefit clients for whom physiological arousal is a common component of emotional crisis. Likewise, for clients whose emotional crises typically include rumination, discussion of the cognitive theory of trauma provides a basis for briefly introducing mindfulness skills at the end of session as a method for gaining distance these thoughts. The PTSD Coach App (Tiet et al., 2019) provides short and accessible relaxation and mindfulness exercises that clients may find particularly convenient. Alternatively, scripts for brief training in relaxation and mindfulness for crisis prevention are found in BCBT-SP (Bryan & Rudd, 2018).

Subsequent sessions should generally begin with review and problem solving of any client challenges in using the CRP in emotional crises, but CRP review should provide a segue to review of CPT practice assignments. Rarely is an emotion-driven behavior entirely unrelated to trauma, and clinicians should inquire about how CPT practice assignments provide an added perspective on the relevant emotional crisis and should readily add CPT worksheets to the CRP as appropriate. Likewise, when introducing new worksheets, always include examples consistent with the client's typical crisis situations. If a client engages in dangerous emotion-driven behaviors between sessions, always thoroughly review the client's thinking in the crisis using the worksheet appropriate to the treatment stage. Clients can be allowed two "crisis" sessions where they can choose to focus directly on emergent issues rather than CPT (Galovski et al., 2012). Crisis sessions may be good opportunities to teach/review coping skills like relaxation or mindfulness. Whenever possible, however, crises should also be approached using the cognitive therapy concepts and techniques appropriate to the treatment phase. Notably, when crisis behaviors are functionally related to PTSD, as is commonly the case, the content of emotional crisis worksheets and trauma-related stuck point worksheets should begin to converge. Optimally, cognitive processing progressively becomes a central focus of any CRP.

Case Example

Kyle is a 41-year-old Army Veteran who served as an infantryman during Operation Iraqi Freedom (OIF). Kyle reported childhood exposure to verbal and physical abuse. He noted being diagnosed with Attention-Deficit/Hyperactivity Disorder (ADHD) in middle-school and described problems with his temper as a teenager and young adult.

Kyle's unit frequently received hostile fire. As his index trauma, Kyle identified a situation in which an Improvised Explosive Device (IED) detonated adjacent to an armored combat vehicle containing a close friend, Jason. Kyle was riding in another vehicle immediately to the rear. Kyle recalled that he often rode with his friend but did not on this occasion. Kyle participated in rescue operations immediately after the explosion, and he saw Jason's deceased body. Kyle said he felt "sick" and immediately thought that he "should have been there" or "should have been the one to die." Kyle was diagnosed with PTSD after returning stateside and endorsed experiencing substantial symptom-related impairment ever since.

During the CAPS-5, Kyle reported frequent intrusive memories and dreams as well as intense physiological and emotional reactions to loud noises, particularly those that sound like gunfire or explosions. Such cues often lead him to feel heart pounding, muscle tension, stomach discomfort, and a mix of anxiety and anger. Kyle avoids situations in which he might experience potentially triggering sounds. He does not like driving on unfamiliar roads. Recently, a neighbor began remodeling their home, and associated noises, including an occasional jackhammer, have been highly distressing to Kyle. Specifically, Kyle endorsed intense hyperarousal symptoms including anger/irritability and verbal conflicts with his wife. Kyle also reported strong feelings of guilt and shame since the trauma and beliefs that he is now a "failure" and "deserves to die." Kyle's baseline PCL-5 was 63.

Kyle acknowledged that he copes with his emotional distress through intermittent alcohol use. Kyle's wife has become very concerned about his safety given that Kyle keeps several a loaded firearm in the home "for protection." Kyle's wife reported that she has found the gun in differing locations lately despite no obvious reason for Kyle to move them. On the Difficulties with Emotion Regulation Scales (DERS), Kyle acknowledged having few healthy coping strategies when experiencing strong emotions, tending to rely on impulsive substance use or interpersonal conflicts/arguments to discharge his tension. He did note recently downloading a relaxation app on his phone. On the Negative Urgency subscale of the UPPS-P, Kyle endorsed several items indicating problems controlling himself when upset. When probed for details, Kyle mentioned his tendency to engage in conflicts, but also noted suicidal ideation in response to distress.

Kyle acknowledged on the C-SSRS thinking of death and specific thoughts of suicide in the last month. He also acknowledged having a suicide plan, but he denied any intent. Kyle also indicated that in the last month he once picked up and handled his gun when thinking of suicide, but he again denied intent and or any further actions toward ending his life. Given his recent suicidal ideation, planning, and preparatory behavior, Kyle's acute risk of suicide was relatively high, but because he consistently denied any intent, Kyle was rated as being at intermediate acute risk of suicide and judged to be suitable for outpatient care. Kyle's PTSD, substance use, and impulsivity increase his chronic risk for suicide, but he has never attempted suicide previously, and he stated that he has only rarely experienced suicidal ideation before the prior six months. Kyle was thus rated as having intermediate chronic suicide risk. Given that Kyle did not require hospitalization and his dangerous emotional crises appeared directly related to PTSD, he was judged to be a strong candidate for CPT. Since Kyle reported engaging in several potentially dangerous emotion-driven behaviors, the therapist worked with Kyle to develop a CRP:

Therapist: *Kyle, I appreciate you sharing this information with me. I'm wondering how concerned you are about your safety given what we've discussed.*

Kyle: *Honestly, it's upsetting to think about all this, what might happen if I really get out of control. I don't want to die and don't want to keep hurting my family.*

Therapist: *I can tell that you want help and are quite concerned about protecting yourself and your family. How about we work together to come up with a plan for exactly what you can do when you find yourself in a situation when you are feeling or might begin to feel some of those intense emotions we talked about?*

Kyle: *That sounds great. I often feel like I just don't know what to do when I'm so upset.*

The therapist then asked Kyle to describe the most recent situation in which emotions made him feel "out of control." Kyle said he recently was driving home from work and saw a truck on fire on the side of the road. Kyle stated he was already "keyed up" because he was driving, and when he saw the truck, he immediately began having intrusive memories as well as the "unbelievable sickness" he experienced during his index trauma. Agitated, Kyle stopped at a bar on his way home and had "a couple" drinks. When he returned home and could not find his firearm, he yelled at his wife, accusing her of hiding it from him. His wife denied moving the gun, which Kyle later found underneath clothes in his dresser drawer. Kyle said he could not believe he forgot where he put his gun, thinking "anything can happen, and I have to be ready." Kyle said he felt "pathetic" and thought about killing himself to "save everyone," and he acknowledged handling the gun on that occasion. Kyle said he stopped himself at that moment and began crying. The next day, Kyle agreed to his wife's request that he seek therapy, though he did not tell her about the suicidal ideation or handling the gun.

Kyle identified the following warning signs that he may need to use his CRP:

1. Hearing the jackhammer/stressful driving scenarios
2. Heart pounding or racing/muscles getting tight
3. Feeling the urge to drink
4. Sharp increases in anxiety or anger

Next, the therapist helped Kyle identify specific things he could do when he notices any of these signs:

1. Get out of the house or the car as soon as is possible/safe
2. Open and use the relaxation app
3. Listen to a favorite podcast
4. Look at a picture of his family
5. Call his wife
6. Call the therapist

Kyle rated his likelihood of using this plan in an appropriate scenario as a 9 out of 10.

The therapist then talked to Kyle about how he might make his environment safer by limiting the ease of access to his gun:

Therapist: *Kyle, I can understand you wanting to have access to a gun and I'm not here to keep you from doing that. My only concern is that having the gun so easily accessible in the times of crisis makes it more likely that you might do something unsafe in the moment. Tell me, how do you think the situation you told me about earlier would have been different, if you did not already have the gun in your hand?*

Kyle: *I'm not sure, but I guess I might not have thought about shooting myself and I definitely wouldn't have looked at it and thought about that possibility like I did.*

Therapist: *So having that gun right there made you more likely to think about and maybe even start to do something that might be very dangerous.*

Kyle: *Yeah, I am glad I didn't do something that night. I'm just really concerned about having my gun taken away. It does make me feel safer.*

Therapist: *I understand. Would you be willing to talk about ways that you might be able to keep the gun in the home, but just less "around you" and accessible as it is now?*

Kyle: *Yeah, I guess.*

Therapist: *Thanks Kyle, I appreciate it, and we would only agree to something that still preserves your sense of safety.*

Kyle and therapist then agreed that Kyle, along with his wife, would unload and place a gun lock on the firearm and then store it separate from ammunition in a small hard lockable safe. Kyle agreed to allow his wife to keep possession of the keys to the safe for now, but only until he "gets a little better." After discussing treatment options, Kyle and the therapist agreed to a course of CPT. They agreed to meet twice weekly for 60-min sessions.

CPT 1 began with a review of an emotional crisis Kyle experienced in the prior week. Kyle explained that the hammering on his neighbor's house was "unrelenting" that day, such that he became very "wound up." Kyle was about to finally confront the neighbor about the noise, but when he grabbed his phone to record the situation, Kyle remembered having his CRP in his photos. Kyle decided to get his headphones and head out the door to get away from the house and the neighbor. Kyle said he opened the relaxation app, but in the moment, the relaxation recording was "too soft" and only agitated him further. Kyle did, however, put on his favorite current events podcast and began jogging, both of which were quite helpful. After about 30 min, Kyle was able to calm down safely and return home. In reviewing the CRP, Kyle and the therapist took out the relaxation app and replaced it with "Go for a jog." Kyle said he found jogging while listening to something upbeat or though-provoking to be quite helpful and said he was confident (9/10) he would use that strategy again.

The therapist proceeded to the standard psychoeducation content of CPT 1, utilizing the emotional crises already reported by Kyle as examples:

Therapist: *It sounds like you work pretty hard to avoid thinking about or feeling things like you did at the time of "the explosion," but do you think the emotions just go away when you push them down like that?*

Kyle: *I guess not. They always show back up when I just can't control the situation like with the noise from the neighbors. I try to hold it in but eventually I blow-up.*

Therapist: *Yes, you lose control, but when you finally let out the emotions by yelling at someone about the noise, does that do anything to help you deal with the feelings about the explosion?*

Kyle: *No, I guess not. I'm not really thinking about the explosion anymore. I'm just irritated at whoever or what is bothering me.*

Therapist: *Exactly, so in some way, the anger/aggression about the noises helps you to avoid really grappling with the trauma?*

Kyle: *I don't know. Maybe ...*

And then later…

Therapist: *Do you think there are times that certain thoughts strengthen or manufacture some of the emotions that get you "out of control"? Like, what were you thinking when you were getting "wound up" about the noises from the [neighbor's] house?*

Kyle: *"I can't stand that guy."* [chuckling].

Therapist: *How did you feel when you said that to yourself?*

Kyle: *Just made me angrier.*

Therapist: *Any other thoughts come to mind?*

Kyle: Ummm… *"I can't control anything."*

Therapist: *Ahh… what happened when you said that to yourself?*

Kyle: *That's when I "lost it."*

Therapist: *I can see how that might happen. I wonder if "I can't control anything" might be one of those stuck points we talked about. And that brings me to my first between session activity I have for you …".*

The therapist assigned the Impact Statement as usual, and Kyle completed it before the next session. During the subsequent course of therapy, Kyle was able to use his Crisis Response Plan during two other instances in which he got "out of control," on one occasion even needing to call his wife while on a jog, asking her to come get him because he was still having thoughts about being a "failure" and "deserving to die." Kyle's wife was able to reassure him that he was not a failure, helping him to see the various ways he was being a good father. This crisis occurred before Session 6. Kyle did not complete any worksheets regarding this event, but after reviewing the crisis and Kyle's response, the therapist said the following:

Therapist: *I noted that the things you said to yourself during the crisis like "I failed" and "I deserve to die" are similar to some of the Stuck Points we've been talking about.*

Kyle: *Yeah, I guess they are a lot like "I should have been able to save Jason" and "I should have been the one to die" in the explosion.*

Therapist: *Maybe we should complete an Exploring Questions worksheet about these thoughts?*

Kyle: *Okay.*

Therapist: *So, tell me, what is the evidence for the thought "I should have been able to save Jason"?*

Using the Exploring Questions worksheet (previously called the Challenging Questions Worksheet), Kyle described thinking that Jason was always a "better" soldier than he was, stating that he "knows" if the positions were reversed, Jason either would have found a way to save him or would have been able to move on without developing PTSD. Together, Kyle and the therapist were able to utilize questions to identify that it is highly unlikely than anyone could have saved a soldier who was in Jason's position during the explosion. Further, they concluded that there is no way to know how trauma will influence anyone else, and that Kyle's development of PTSD was a function of a mixture of largely unknown and uncontrollable factors—not an indication of his value or worth. Finally, the therapist asked the following set of questions regarding the Stuck Point, "It should have been me."

Therapist: *Think about all the other guys you know who didn't make it back, besides Jason. Can you think of any of them who should have died?*

Kyle: *Well, no.*

Therapist: *Can you think of any others who shouldn't have died, besides Jason? Any others who were good soldiers but died anyway?*

Kyle: *Sure, some of our best guys didn't make it. Not just Jason.*

Therapist: *So, in a war zone, does that violence and destruction care about or know how to tell the difference between who it should take and who it should spare?*

Kyle: *I guess not. I guess it's sort of random. It takes who it takes. You can't control it.*

Therapist: *Exactly. Now Kyle, thinking about all the guys who died, how many deserved to die?*

Kyle: *None of them, really.*

Therapist: *And do you think any of them in their past maybe did some things like the things you've done recently. Do you think any of them ever "lost control" and did something they regretted later?*

Kyle: *I'm sure. There were some wild dudes over there.*

Therapist: *So, if they didn't deserve to die, why do you deserve to die?*

Kyle: *I don't know.*

Therapist: *Do you wonder if maybe "It should have been me" or "I deserve to die" might be more of a habit than a fact for you? How much do you really think about it before you tell yourself now that you deserve to die?*

Kyle: *None really. The words just sort of say themselves. Like after the explosion, it just sort of came to me like that and I couldn't let it go.*

Therapist: *So, sort of like a habit? I wonder if every time the thought crosses your mind, maybe you should just immediately respond to yourself, "Habit!"*

Kyle: *I like that idea, Doc.*

Kyle continued to benefit from Socratic Questioning regarding his stuck points, including those echoed in the typical thoughts that drove his dangerous emotion-driven behaviors. Kyle's reported fewer such thoughts, fewer intense emotions, and no further out of control behaviors. When Kyle completed his final impact statement, he said, "Jason died because he was in a war. Some people die in a war, no matter who they are or what they did. Some people in war get PTSD, like me, and some of those people end up being out of control sometimes and hurt people they care about. All kinds of people, no matter who they are or what they did. It sucks but in war, and sometimes in life, horrible stuff comes at you: no matter good or bad or anywhere in between." Kyle's PCL-5 score at termination was 17.

Future Directions

The adaptation of CPT described in this chapter, CBT-DEB, has not been empirically validated as such, although the core components all have demonstrated efficacy individually. Future research should thus evaluate if this approach provides improved outcomes compared to traditional CPT or a sequence of CRP followed by CPT. CBT-DEB could also be compared to other extant models that address dangerous crisis behaviors and trauma within a combined or sequential package (e.g., Dialectical Behavior Therapy with Prolonged Exposure Therapy [DBT-PE]; Harned, 2022). Finally, the core elements of CBT-DEB may be further developed, perhaps by adding a module session regarding the effects of trauma on emotional experience and expression. Although this topic should be covered throughout the CBT-DEB package, an additional module regarding emotions may be a useful addition.

Summary

Emotion regulation difficulties, common among those with PTSD, sometimes lead to dangerous behaviors. The perceived risk of evoking this danger has limited the extensive use of evidence-based interventions for PTSD, including Cognitive Processing Therapy (CPT), particularly when clients are perceived to have elevated risk of emotion dysregulation. Empirical research, however, indicates that CPT is a robust and effective intervention for emotion regulation difficulties that accompany PTSD and can safely and effectively be administered even among those with more hazardous emotion-driven behaviors. Careful and precise assessment, along with the use of Crisis Response Planning (CRP) can help to mitigate the risk of dangerous emotion-driven behavior interfering with positive CPT outcomes. Careful attention to beliefs about emotion and limited, individualized instruction in emotion-regulation skills may further improve CPT outcomes among those with more serious emotion regulation difficulties.

Competing Interests
The author has no conflicts of interest to declare that are relevant to the content of this chapter.

References

Anestis, M. D. (2023). Firearm access and suicide rates: An unambiguously robust association. *Archives of Suicide Research, 1-5*, 701. https://doi.org/10.1080/13811118.2023.2192753

Back, S. E., Killeen, T. K., Cotton, B. D., & Carroll, K. M. (2014). *Concurrent treatment of PTSD and substance use disorders using prolonged exposure (COPE): Therapist guide*. Treatments That Work.

Borges, G., Bagge, C., Cherpitel, C., Conner, K., Orozco, R., & Rossow, I. (2017). A meta- analysis of acute use of alcohol and the risk of suicide attempt. *Psychological Medicine, 47*(5), 949–957. https://doi.org/10.1017/S0033291716002841

Burback, L., Dhaliwal, R., Reeson, M., Erick, T., Hartle, K., Chow, E., et al. (2023). Trauma focused psychotherapy in patients with suicidal ideation: A scoping review. *Current Research in Behavioral Sciences, 100102*, 100102. https://doi.org/10.1016/j.crbeha.2023.100102

Bryan, C. J., Bryan, A. O., Khazem, L. R., Aase, D. M., Moreno, J. L., Ammendola, E., Bauder, C. R., Hiser, J., Daruwala, S. E., & Baker, J. C. (2024). Crisis response planning rapidly reduces suicidal ideation among U.S. military veterans receiving massed cognitive processing therapy for PTSD. *Journal of Anxiety Disorders, 102*, 102824. https://doi.org/10.1016/j.janxdis.2023.102824

Bryan, C. J., Clemans, T. A., Hernandez, A. M., Mintz, J., Peterson, A. L., Yarvis, J. S., et al. (2016). Evaluating potential iatrogenic suicide risk in trauma-focused group cognitive behavioral therapy for the treatment of PTSD in active-duty military personnel. *Depression and Anxiety, 33*, 549–557. https://doi.org/10.1002/da.22456

Bryan, C. J., & Rudd, M. D. (2006). Advances in the assessment of suicide risk. *Journal of Clinical Psychology, 62*(2), 185–200. https://doi.org/10.1002/jclp.20222

Bryan, C. J., & Rudd, M. D. (2018). *Brief cognitive-behavioral therapy for suicide prevention*. Guilford Publications.

Bryan, C. J., David Rudd, M., Wertenberger, E., Etienne, N., Ray-Sannerud, B. N., Morrow, C. E., Peterson, A. L., & Young-McCaughon, S. (2014). Improving the detection and prediction of suicidal behavior among military personnel by measuring suicidal beliefs: An evaluation of the suicide cognitions scale. *Journal of Affective Disorders, 159*, 15–22. https://doi.org/10.1016/j.jad.2014.02.021

Contractor, A. A., Caldas, S., Weiss, N. H., & Armour, C. (2018). Examination of the heterogeneity in PTSD and impulsivity facets: A latent profile analysis. *Personality and Individual Differences, 125*, 1–9. https://doi.org/10.1016/j.paid.2017.12.022

Clarke, S. B., Rizvi, S. L., & Resick, P. A. (2008). Borderline personality characteristics and treatment outcome in cognitive-behavioral treatments for PTSD in female rape victims. *Behavior Therapy, 39*(1), 72–78. https://doi.org/10.1016/j.beth.2007.05.002

Cloitre, M., Koenen, K. C., Cohen, L. R., & Han, H. (2002). Skills training in affective and interpersonal regulation followed by exposure: A phase-based treatment for PTSD related to childhood abuse. *Journal of Consulting and Clinical Psychology, 70*(5), 1067–1074. https://doi.org/10.1037/0022-006X.70.5.1067

Cyders, M. A., Smith, G. T., Spillane, N. S., Fischer, S., Annus, A. M., & Peterson, C. (2007). Integration of impulsivity and positive mood to predict risky behavior: Development and validation of a measure of positive urgency. *Psychological Assessment, 19*(1), 107–118. https://doi.org/10.1037/1040-3590.19.1.107

Cyders, M. A., & Smith, G. T. (2008). Emotion-based dispositions to rash action: Positive and negative urgency. *Psychological Bulletin, 134*(6), 807–828. https://doi.org/10.1037/a0013341

Dedert, E. A., LoSavio, S. T., Wells, S. Y., Steel, A. L., Reinhardt, K., Deming, C. A., Ruffin, R. A., Berlin, K. L., Kimbrel, N. A., Wilson, S. M., Boeding, S. E., & Clancy, C. P. (2021). Clinical effectiveness study of a treatment to prepare for trauma-focused evidence-based psychotherapies at a veterans affairs specialty posttraumatic stress disorder clinic. *Psychological Services, 18*(4), 651–662. https://doi.org/10.1037/ser0000425

Dondanville, K. A., Wachen, J. S., Hale, W. J., Mintz, J., Roache, J. D., Carson, C., et al. (2019). Examination of treatment effects on hazardous drinking among service members with posttraumatic stress disorder. *Journal of Traumatic Stress, 32*(2), 310–316. https://doi.org/10.1002/jts.22393

Dutra, S. J., & Sadeh, N. (2018). Psychological flexibility mitigates effects of PTSD symptoms and negative urgency on aggressive behavior in trauma-exposed veterans. *Personality Disorders, 9*, 315–323. https://doi.org/10.1037/per0000251

Elbogen, E. B., Johnson, S. C., Wagner, H. R., Sullivan, C., Taft, C. T., & Beckham, J. C. (2014). Violent behaviour and post-traumatic stress disorder in US Iraq and Afghanistan veterans. *The British Journal of Psychiatry, 204*(5), 368–375. https://doi.org/10.1192/bjp.bp.113.134627

Fanning, J. R., Lee, R., & Coccaro, E. F. (2016). Comorbid intermittent explosive disorder and posttraumatic stress disorder: Clinical correlates and relationship to suicidal behavior. *Comprehensive Psychiatry, 70*, 125–133. https://doi.org/10.1016/j.comppsych.2016.05.018

Farmer, C. C., Mitchell, K. S., Parker-Guilbert, K., & Galovski, T. E. (2017). Fidelity to the cognitive processing therapy protocol: Evaluation of critical elements. *Behavior Therapy, 48*, 195–206. https://doi.org/10.1016/j.beth.2016.02.009

Frattaroli, S., & Sharfstein, J. M. (2021). Extreme risk protection orders—A tool for clinicians to prevent gun violence. *JAMA Health Forum, 2*(4), e210948. https://doi.org/10.1001/jamahealthforum.2021.0948

Galovski, T. E., Blain, L. M., Mott, J. M., Elwood, L., & Houle, T. (2012). Manualized therapy for PTSD: Flexing the structure of cognitive processing therapy. *Journal of Consulting and Clinical Psychology, 80*(6), 968–981. https://doi.org/10.1037/a0030600

Galovski, T. E., Nixon, R. D., & Kaysen, D. (2020). *Flexible applications of cognitive processing therapy: Evidence-based treatment methods*. Academic Press.

Galovski, T. E., Werner, K. B., Weaver, T. L., Morris, K. L., Dondanville, K. A., Nanney, J., Wamser-Nanney, R., McGlinchey, G., Fortier, C. B., & Iverson, K. M. (2022). Massed cognitive processing therapy for posttraumatic stress disorder in women survivors of intimate partner violence. *Psychological Trauma: Theory, Research, Practice and Policy, 14*(5), 769–779. https://doi.org/10.1037/tra0001100

Gradus, J. L., Suvak, M. K., Wisco, B. E., Marx, B. P., & Resick, P. A. (2013). Treatment of posttraumatic stress disorder reduces suicidal ideation. *Depression and Anxiety, 30*, 1046–1053. https://doi.org/10.1002/da.22117

Gratz, K. L., & Roemer, L. (2004). Multidimensional assessment of emotion regulation and dysregulation: Development, factor structure, and initial validation of the difficulties in emotion regulation scale. *Journal of Psychopathology and Behavioral Assessment, 26*, 41–54. https://doi.org/10.1023/B:JOBA.0000007455.08539.94

Gross, J. J. (1998). The emerging field of emotion regulation: An integrative review. *Review of General Psychology, 2*(3), 271–299. https://doi.org/10.1037/1089-2680.2.3.271

Hahn, A. M., Tirabassi, C. K., Simons, R. M., & Simons, J. S. (2015). Military sexual trauma, combat exposure, and negative urgency as independent predictors of PTSD and subsequent alcohol problems among OEF/OIF veterans. *Psychological Services, 12*, 378–383. https://psycnet.apa.org/doi/10.1037/ser0000060

Harned, M. S. (2022). *Treating trauma in dialectical behavior therapy: The DBT prolonged exposure protocol (DBT PE)*. Guilford Publications.

Held, P., Klassen, B. J., Boley, R. A., Wiltsey Stirman, S., Smith, D. L., Brennan, M. B., Van Horn, R., Pollack, M. H., Karnik, N. S., & Zalta, A. K. (2020). Feasibility of a 3-week intensive treatment program for service members and veterans with PTSD. *Psychological trauma: theory, research, practice and policy, 12*(4), 422–430. https://doi.org/10.1037/tra0000485

Held, P., Steigerwald, V. L., Smith, D. L., Kaysen, D., Van Horn, R., & Karnik, N. S. (2021). Impact of hazardous alcohol use on intensive PTSD treatment outcomes among veterans. *European Journal of Psychotraumatology, 12*, 1888541. https://doi.org/10.1080/20008198.2021.1888541

Holder, N., Holliday, R., Pai, A., & Surís, A. (2017). Role of borderline personality disorder in the treatment of military sexual trauma-related posttraumatic stress disorder with cognitive processing therapy. *Behavioral Medicine, 43*, 184–190. https://doi.org/10.1080/08964289.2016.1276430

Holder, N., Holliday, R., Williams, R., Mullen, K., & Surís, A. (2018). A preliminary examination of the role of psychotherapist fidelity on outcomes of cognitive processing therapy during an RCT for military sexual trauma-related PTSD. *Cognitive Behaviour Therapy, 47*, 76–89. https://doi.org/10.1080/16506073.2017.1357750

Holliday, R., Holder, N., Monteith, L. L., & Surís, A. (2018). Decreases in suicide cognitions after cognitive processing therapy among veterans with posttraumatic stress disorder due to military sexual trauma: A preliminary examination. *The Journal of Nervous and Mental Disease, 206*(7), 575–578. https://doi.org/10.1097/NMD.0000000000000840

Jobes, D. A. (2023). *Managing suicidal risk: A collaborative approach*. The Guilford Press.

Joiner, T. E., Jr., Walker, R. L., Rudd, M. D., & Jobes, D. A. (1999). Scientizing and routinizing the assessment of suicidality in outpatient practice. *Professional Psychology: Research and Practice, 30*(5), 447–453. https://doi.org/10.1037/0735-7028.30.5.447

Larsen, S. E., Mackintosh, M.-A., La Bash, H., Evans, W. R., Suvak, M. K., Shields, N., Lane, J. E. M., Sijercic, I., Monson, C. M., & Wiltsey Stirman, S. (2022). Temporary PTSD symptom increases among individuals receiving CPT in a hybrid effectiveness-implementation trial: Potential predictors and association with overall symptom change trajectory. *Psychological Trauma: Theory, Research, Practice, and Policy, 14*(5), 853–861. https://doi.org/10.1037/tra0000545

LoSavio, S. T., Dillon, K. H., Murphy, R. A., & Resick, P. A. (2019). Therapist stuck points during training in cognitive processing therapy: Changes over time and associations with training outcomes. *Professional Psychology: Research and Practice, 50*, 255–263. https://psycnet.apa.org/doi/10.1037/pro0000224

LoSavio, S. T., Holder, N., Wells, S. Y., & Resick, P. A. (2022). Clinician concerns about cognitive processing therapy: A review of the evidence. *Cognitive and Behavioral Practice., 31*, 152. https://doi.org/10.1016/j.cbpra.2022.08.005

LoSavio, S. T., Straud, C. L., Dondanville, K. A., Fridling, N. R., Schuster Wachen, J., Young-McCaughan, S., Mintz, J., Yarvis, J. S., Peterson, A. L., & Resick, P. A. (2023). Treatment responder status and time to response as a function of hazardous drinking among active duty military receiving variable-length cognitive processing therapy for posttraumatic stress disorder. *Psychological Trauma: Theory, Research, Practice, & Policy, 15*, 386–393. https://doi.org/10.1037/tra0001268

Martin, C., Stayton, L., & Chard, K. M. (2020). Emotion in cognitive processing therapy for PTSD. In *Emotion in posttraumatic stress disorder* (pp. 491–511). Academic Press.

Miles, S. R., Menefee, D. S., Wanner, J., Teten Tharp, A., & Kent, T. A. (2016). The relationship between emotion dysregulation and impulsive aggression in veterans with posttraumatic stress disorder symptoms. *Journal of Interpersonal Violence, 31*(10), 1795–1816. https://doi.org/10.1177/0886260515570746

Miles, S. R., Thompson, K. E., Stanley, M. A., & Kent, T. A. (2015). Cognitive behavioral treatments for posttraumatic stress disorder: A review of the evidence base focusing on patients over the age of 65. *American Journal of Geriatric Psychiatry, 24*(3), 192–205. https://doi.org/10.1016/j.jagp.2015.11.001

Miller, W. R., & Rollnick, S. (2012). *Motivational interviewing: Helping people change*. Guilford Press.

Mirhashem, R., Allen, H. C., Adams, Z. W., van Stolk-Cooke, K., Legrand, A., & Price, M. (2017). The intervening role of urgency on the association between childhood maltreatment, PTSD, and substance-related problems. *Addictive Behaviors, 69*, 98–103. https://doi.org/10.1016/j.addbeh.2017.02.012

Nomamiukor, F. O., Suresky, R. E., May, C. L., & Wisco, B. E. (2022). Understanding internalizing and externalizing symptoms in trauma exposed community members. *Psychological Trauma: Theory, Research, Practice, and Policy*. Advance online publication. https://doi.org/10.1037/tra0001388

Posner, K., Brown, G. K., Stanley, B., et al. (2011). The Columbia-suicide severity rating scale: Initial validity and internal consistency findings from three multisite studies with adolescents and adults. *American Journal of Psychiatry., 168*(12), 1266–1277. https://doi.org/10.1176/appi.ajp.2011.10111704

Post, L. M., Held, P., Smith, D. L., Black, K., Van Horn, R., Pollack, M. H., et al. (2021). Impact of intensive treatment programs for posttraumatic stress disorder on suicidal ideation in veterans and service members. *Psychological Services, 18*, 671–678. https://psycnet.apa.org/doi/10.1037/ser0000518

Resick, P. A., Galovski, T. E., Uhlmansiek, M. O., Scher, C. D., Clum, G. A., & Young-Xu, Y. (2008). A randomized clinical trial to dismantle components of cognitive processing therapy for posttraumatic stress disorder in female victims of interpersonal violence. *Journal of Consulting and Clinical Psychology, 76*(2), 243–258. https://doi.org/10.1037/0022-006X.76.2.243

Resick, P. A., LoSavio, S. T., Monson, C. M., Kaysen, D. L., Wachen, J. S., Galovski, T. E., Wiltsey Stirman, S., Nixon, R. D. V., & Chard, K. M. (2024). State of the science of cognitive processing therapy. *Behavior Therapy, 55*(6), 1205–1221. https://doi.org/10.1016/j.beth.2024.04.003

Resick, P. A., Wachen, J. S., Dondanville, K. A., Pruiksma, K. E., Yarvis, J. S., Peterson, A. L., Mintz, J., the STRONG STAR Consortium, Borah, E. V, Brundige, A., Hembree, E. A., Litz, B. T., Roache, J. D., & Young-McCaughan, S. (2017). Effect of group vs individual cognitive processing therapy in active-duty military seeking treatment for posttraumatic stress disorder: A randomized clinical trial. *JAMA Psychiatry, 74*(1), 28–36. https://doi.org/10.1001/jamapsychiatry.2016.2729

Resick, P. A., Suvak, M. K., Johnides, B. D., Mitchell, K. S., & Iverson, K. M. (2012). The impact of dissociation on PTSD treatment with cognitive processing therapy. *Depression and Anxiety, 29*(8), 718–730. https://doi.org/10.1002/da.21938

Roberge, E. M., Harris, J. A., Weinstein, H. R., & Rozek, D. C. (2021). Treating veterans at risk for suicide: An examination of the safety, tolerability, and outcomes of cognitive processing therapy. *Journal of Traumatic Stress, 34*(6), 1228–1237. https://doi.org/10.1002/jts.22662

Roley, M. E., Contractor, A. A., Weiss, N. H., Armour, C., & Elhai, J. D. (2017). Impulsivity facets' predictive relations with DSM–5 PTSD symptom clusters. *Psychological Trauma: Theory, Research, Practice, and Policy, 9*(1), 76–79. https://doi/10.1037/tra0000146.

Rozek, D. C., & Bryan, C. J. (2020). Integrating crisis response planning for suicide prevention into trauma-focused treatments: A military case example. *Journal of Clinical Psychology, 76*, 852–864. https://doi.org/10.1002/jclp.22920

Rudd, M. D. (2006). Fluid vulnerability theory: A cognitive approach to understanding the process of acute and chronic suicide risk. In T. E. Ellis (Ed.), *Cognition and suicide: Theory, research, and therapy* (pp. 355–368). American Psychological Association. https://doi.org/10.1037/11377-016

Sciarrino, N. A., Warnecke, A. J., & Teng, E. J. (2020). A systematic review of intensive empirically supported treatments for posttraumatic stress disorder. *Journal of Traumatic Stress, 33*(4), 443–454. https://doi.org/10.1002/jts.22556

Shultz, B. N., Lye, C. T., D'Onofrio, G., Gluck, A. R., Miller, J., Kraschel, K. L., & Ranney, M. L. (2020). Understanding the role of law in reducing firearm injury through clinical interventions. *Journal of Law, Medicine & Ethics, 48*(S4), 146–154. https://doi.org/10.1177/1073110520979416

Semenza, D. C., Magee, L. A., Anestis, M. D., & Buggs, S. A. L. (2023). Identity, experience, and threat: Assessing key correlates of firearm ownership and related behaviors in a representative sample of five US states. *Preventive Medicine Reports, 34*, 102269. https://doi.org/10.1016/j.pmedr.2023.102269

Shnaider, P., Boyd, J. E., Cameron, D. H., & McCabe, R. E. (2022). The relationship between emotion regulation difficulties and PTSD outcomes during group cognitive processing therapy for PTSD. *Psychological Services, 19*(4), 751–759. https://doi.org/10.1037/ser0000546

Seligowski, A. V., Lee, D. J., Bardeen, J. R., & Orcutt, H. K. (2015). Emotion regulation and posttraumatic stress symptoms: A meta-analysis. *Cognitive Behavior Therapy, 44*, 87–102. https://doi.org/10.1080/16506073.2014.980753

Straud, C. L., Dondanville, K. A., Hale, W. J., Wachen, J. S., Mintz, J., Litz, B. T., et al. (2021). The impact of hazardous drinking among active duty military with posttraumatic stress disorder: Does cognitive processing therapy format matter? *Journal of Traumatic Stress, 34*, 210–220. https://doi.org/10.1002/jts.22609

Studdert, D. M., Zhang, Y., Holsinger, E. E., Prince, L., Holsinger, A. F., Rodden, J. A., et al. (2022). Homicide deaths among adult cohabitants of handgun owners in California, 2004 to 2016: A cohort study. *Annals of Internal Medicine, 175*(6), 804–811. https://doi.org/10.7326/M21-3762

Taft, C. T., Creech, S. K., Gallagher, M. W., Macdonald, A., Murphy, C. M., & Monson, C. M. (2016). Strength at home couples program to prevent military partner violence: A randomized controlled trial. *Journal of Consulting and Clinical Psychology, 84*(11), 935–945. https://doi.org/10.1037/ccp0000129

Tiet, Q. Q., Duong, H., Davis, L., French, R., Smith, C. L., Leyva, Y. E., & Rosen, C. (2019). PTSD coach mobile application with brief telephone support: A pilot study. *Psychological Services, 16*(2), 227–232. https://doi.org/10.1037/ser0000245

Tripp, J. C., McDevitt-Murphy, M. E., Avery, M. L., & Bracken, K. L. (2015). PTSD symptoms, emotion dysregulation, and alcohol-related consequences among college students with a trauma history. *Journal of Dual Diagnosis, 11*, 107–117. https://doi.org/10.1080/15504263.2015.1025013

Tripp, J. C., Haller, M., Trim, R. S., Straus, E., Bryan, C. J., Davis, B. C., Lyons, R., Hamblen, J. L., & Norman, S. B. (2021). Does exposure exacerbate symptoms in veterans with PTSD and alcohol use disorder? *Psychological Trauma: Theory, Research, Practice and Policy, 13*(8), 920–928. https://doi.org/10.1037/tra0000634

Wamser-Nanney, R., Nanney, J. T., & Constans, J. I. (2021). Trauma exposure, posttraumatic stress symptoms, and attitudes toward guns. *Psychology of Violence, 11*, 376–384. https://psycnet.apa.org/doi/10.1037/vio0000356

Weathers, F. W., Blake, D. D., Schnurr, P. P., Kaloupek, D. G., Marx, B. P., & Keane, T. M. (2013a). *The life events checklist for DSM-5 (LEC-5)—Interview.* [measurement instrument]. Scale available from the National Center for PTSD at www.ptsd.va.gov

Weathers, F.W., Litz, B.T., Keane, T.M., Palmieri, P.A., Marx, B.P., & Schnurr, P.P. (2013b). *The PTSD checklist for DSM-5 (PCL-5).* Scale available from the National Center for PTSD at www.ptsd.va.gov.

Weathers, F. W., Bovin, M. J., Lee, D. J., Sloan, D. M., Schnurr, P. P., Kaloupek, D. G., Keane, T. M., & Marx, B. P. (2018). *The Clinician-Administered PTSD Scale for DSM-5* (CAPS-5): Scale available from the National Center for PTSD at www.ptsd.va.gov.

Wiblin, J., Holder, N., Holliday, R., Jeon-Slaughter, H., LePage, J., & Surís, A. (2021). A factor analysis of the suicide cognitions scale in veterans with military sexual trauma-related posttraumatic stress disorder. *Journal of Trauma & Dissociation, 22*, 319–331. https://doi.org/10.1080/15299732.2020.1869643

Zeoli, A. M., & Webster, D. W. (2010). Effects of domestic violence policies, alcohol taxes and police staffing levels on intimate partner homicide in large US cities. *Injury Prevention, 16*(2), 90–95. https://doi.org/10.1136/ip.2009.024620

Chapter 4
Delivering CPT in the Context of Serious Mental Illness

Stephanie A. Sacks

Trauma Exposure, Post-Traumatic Stress Disorder, and Serious Mental Illness

Individuals with serious mental illnesses (SMI), defined as schizophrenia-spectrum and bipolar-spectrum disorders, are extremely vulnerable to trauma exposure and to the development of post-traumatic stress disorder (PTSD; Breslau et al., 2004; Grubaugh et al., 2011; Kessler et al., 2005). Research has found that rates of trauma exposure in individuals with SMI ranges from 49% to 100% (Grubaugh et al., 2011), with sexual and physical assault rates across the lifespan being exceedingly high (Davidson et al., 2009; Gearon et al., 2003; Goodman et al., 1999; Lysaker & Larocco, 2008). Individuals with SMI also have higher rates of repeated traumatization and violent victimization, compared to the general population (Brekke et al., 2001; Hiday et al., 1999).

The lifetime prevalence estimate of PTSD amongst civilians with schizophrenia-spectrum disorders is between 55% and 57% (Dallel et al., 2018; Seow et al., 2016) and 10.8% in civilians with co-occurring bipolar disorders (Nabavi et al., 2015). Among veterans utilizing services at the Veterans Health Administration, recent data found that of those that met criteria for an SMI, 34.9% also had a co-occurring schizophrenia-spectrum or bipolar disorder (Serious Mental Illness Treatment, Research, and Evaluation Center, 2020).

S. A. Sacks (✉)
Cognitive Behavioral Therapy Center of the Palm Beaches, Boca Raton, USA

Nova Southeastern University, Fort Lauderdale, USA

University of Southern California, Los Angeles, CA, USA
e-mail: drsacks@cbtpalmbeach.com

J. S. Wachen, T. E. Galovski (eds.), *Cognitive Processing Therapy for Complex Cases*, CBT: Science Into Practice,
https://doi.org/10.1007/978-3-031-87356-0_4

The comorbidity of PTSD and SMI is associated with many deleterious outcomes. In individuals with SMI, co-occurring PTSD is associated with higher risk of substance use disorders, more severe psychotic illness, poorer cognitive functioning, higher rates of homelessness, more frequent hospitalizations, increased suicidal thoughts and behaviors and greater health care utilization (Calhoun et al., 2006; Grubaugh et al., 2011; Insel, 2008).

Current Evidence for Cognitive Processing Therapy for PTSD with SMI

There is a growing evidence base supporting the efficacy of cognitive behavioral treatments for posttraumatic stress disorder (PTSD) with individuals who have coexisting serious mental illness (SMI) (Grubaugh et al., 2021). Early evidence suggests that unmodified gold-standard evidence-based interventions (e.g., cognitive processing therapy (CPT), prolonged exposure therapy, eye movement desensitization and reprocessing) are well tolerated and effective in treating posttraumatic stress disorder (PTSD) in this patient group (de Bont, van den Berg, et al., 2013a, b; Feingold et al., 2018; Frueh et al., 2009; Grubaugh et al., 2017; Nishith et al., 2024; Sacks et al., 2025; Van den Berg et al., 2015, 2018; van den Berg & van der Gaag, 2012).

To date, there are only a few studies showing the efficacy of cognitive processing therapy (CPT) for those with SMI. One study included veterans who met criteria for PTSD and a schizophrenia-spectrum disorder who were being treated with CPT by clinicians recently trained by the Veterans Health Administration Cognitive Processing Therapy Training Program (Sacks et al., 2025). Veterans with PTSD and schizophrenia-spectrum disorders who received CPT experienced a statistically significant decrease in PTSD symptoms and depression symptoms. When compared to those with PTSD and no psychosis, the study found no significant differences between groups, meaning that those with PTSD and psychosis experienced as much improvement following CPT as veterans with no schizophrenia-spectrum disorders (Sacks et al., 2025). A second study (Feingold et al., 2018) evaluated the effectiveness of CPT with civilians with SMI who were involved in the criminal justice system and, after being evaluated for trauma-related symptoms, were referred to the trauma-informed treatment portion of a jail diversion program. In this study, participants who began CPT experienced significant decreases in PTSD and depression symptoms. CPT completers, operationalized as SMI individuals who completed all 12 sessions of CPT or were early completers due to scores below clinical cutoffs for probable PTSD, experienced an average pre- to post-treatment score change of over 20 points on the PTSD Checklist, more than double the ten-point change used to indicate clinical significance (Monson et al., 2008), as well as significant decrease in depressive symptoms (Feingold et al., 2018). A third study reported results from an open pilot trial of CPT conducted at a community behavioral health center with patients with PTSD and SMI (Nishith et al., 2024). There were significant improvements in PTSD, depression, and functioning from pre- to post-treatment, lending further support to the benefits of CPT for individuals with SMI.

Although early evidence shows substantial promise for the treatment of PTSD in those with SMI using CPT, clinicians are often reluctant to treat PTSD with individuals with SMI (Frueh et al., 2006; Gairns et al., 2013; Salyers et al., 2004) due to clinician fears that treating PTSD would exacerbate psychiatric SMI symptoms, concerns that those with SMI would not have the cognitive capacity, interest or motivation to address PTSD in therapy, and inadequate training in the use of evidence-based PTSD treatments with those with SMI (Frueh et al., 2006). These findings all underscore the need for clinician access to accurate and up-to-date guidance, education, and clinical resources and strategies in order to feel competent and empowered in their use of CPT to treat PTSD in clients with co-occurring SMI. This chapter provides clinicians with clinical tools, guidance and an empirical rebuttal to the perceived barriers to the provision of CPT for PTSD in those with SMI.

Recent research has shown that clients with SMI are often very interested and motivated in having their PTSD symptoms treated and that they have the cognitive capacity to undergo CPT as prescribed (Feingold et al., 2018; Sacks et al., 2025). There is very little evidence of SMI symptom exacerbation when undergoing an evidence-based PTSD treatment (van den Berg et al., 2016); instead, there is evidence that treating PTSD effectively can lead to secondary improvement in SMI symptoms such as paranoia (van den Berg et al., 2018).

Clinical Guidance for Using CPT with Clients with SMI

There are several important considerations and nuances that clinicians should be aware of for the effective implementation of CPT with those with SMI. First, we will discuss pertinent pre-treatment assessment and treatment-planning issues. Next, this chapter will provide specific guidance and recommendations regarding how to most effectively implement CPT with patients with SMI throughout the course of CPT.

Assessment and Treatment Planning

It is important that clinicians imbue clinical interactions with positive regard, empowerment and acknowledgement of the client's agency and choice. This is particularly important when working with clients with SMI due to the elevated challenges with engagement and attrition in this population (Dixon et al., 2016). Challenges with treatment engagement and attrition are due to a multitude of factors, including elevated rates of unstable housing and homelessness (Leickly & Townley, 2021; Pratt, 2012), difficulties with access to consistent and reliable transportation (Olmos-Ochoa et al., 2019), persistent psychosocial crises (Olmos-Ochoa et al., 2019), elevated rates of criminal justice involvement (Hawthorne et al., 2012), and high rates of exposure to additional traumas (Grubaugh et al., 2011). In addition, this population has a high prevalence of physical health concerns (de Hert et al., 2011), substance use disorders (Buckley, 2006), and medication nonadherence (Buckley, 2006), all of which can interfere with trauma processing due to its impact on destabilization of psychotic and manic symptoms. Clients with SMI also may suffer from clinical symptoms such as paranoia, which can impact rapport and the building of a trusting therapeutic relationship (Green & Phillips, 2004; Hooker et al., 2011) and they may experience challenges with receiving timely and appropriate access to mental health care (Lawrence & Kisely, 2010).

Prior to initiating a clinical assessment of symptoms with clients with SMI, it is important to clearly discuss clients' expectations of the assessment process, procedures, methods, and treatment options in order to provide an avenue for clients to ask questions about clinical interactions. It can be especially helpful, because of numerous cognitive symptoms prevalent in clients with SMI (Bo et al., 2017; Burdick et al., 2011; Rajji et al., 2013), to provide clients with information about the assessment and client treatment options in both, verbal and written form, as well as to have clients, in their own words, describe their understanding about the assessment process, their choices and all available treatment options. Beginning the conversation of assessment with a clear rationale can put clients with SMI at ease that the information gathered, though it may feel intrusive or uncomfortable, will ultimately serve their care (i.e., appropriate treatment planning and treatment matching), thereby reducing confusion and/or paranoia regarding the assessment process. Due to the nature of the information being gathered, providers should also discuss confidentiality, as well as limits of confidentiality, including when reporting would be appropriate, in order to empower clients with information and choice and to lay the groundwork for this, should reporting be necessary. This is particularly important with clients with SMI, given the high prevalence of childhood physical abuse and sexual abuse compared to the general population (Arseneault et al., 2011; Bendall et al., 2008; Powers et al., 2016). In fact, studies have found a strong association between exposure to childhood trauma, particularly childhood sexual abuse, and future hallucinatory experiences (Daalman et al., 2012; Hammersley et al., 2003; Misiak et al., 2016; Sheffield et al., 2013).

A crucial step prior to initiating CPT with clients with PTSD and SMI is to engage clients in a thorough and systematic evaluation of all mental health symptoms, including, but not limited to, all SMI symptoms and trauma-related symptoms. In addition, clinicians should determine a clear clinical history, including age of onset of all symptoms, course of symptoms, hospitalizations, medications prescribed and their effects, history of mental health treatment and treatment effects, factors that facilitate stabilization, factors that tend to destabilize the client, living arrangements, social supports, and current stressors.

Assessment of schizophrenia-spectrum symptoms can be achieved by using the Structured Clinical Interview for DSM Disorders—Psychotic Module (SCID; First et al., 2016) along with either the Positive And Negative Syndrome Scale (PANSS;

Kay et al., 1987) or the Scale for the Assessment of Positive Symptoms and Scale for the Assessment of Negative Symptoms (SAPS/SANS; Andresen, 1984, 1985). For clinicians who are not familiar with these scales, training is widely available (Opler et al., 2017). For the assessment of bipolar disorder symptoms, clinicians can begin with a screener, such as the Mood Disorders Questionnaire (MDQ; Hirschfeld et al., 2000); however, clinicians are advised that the MDQ is a screener that can yield false positives when taken at face value; thus, in order to accurately assess the diagnostic picture, it is best to use the SCID (First et al., 2016) to ensure that symptoms are congruent with *DSM-5* criteria, that they resulted in negative consequences for the client, and that they were not due to substance use.

Routine screening measures for trauma exposure (Trauma History Questionnaire or Life Events Checklist), and for PTSD (PTSD Checklist-5), and the gold-standard assessment measure for PTSD, the Clinician Administered PTSD Scale-5 (CAPS-5), are reliable and valid and have been found to have strong psychometric properties when utilized with individuals with SMI (Mueser et al., 2001; Lu et al., 2022; Gray et al., 2004).

Neurocognitive Symptoms

Because clients with SMI often struggle with symptoms that may manifest during the clinical assessment, such as cognitive disorganization, tangentiality, or pressured speech, it can be useful to help clients titrate their responses by providing a verbal cue such as "In a sentence or two, can you please tell me about X?" In addition, clinicians can introduce the idea that they may need to interrupt the client if the conversation derails in order to be most efficient and effective during the assessment. Clinicians should keep in mind that when affect is intensified or when speaking about emotion-laden material, cognitive disorganization symptoms can exacerbate (Anticevic & Corlett, 2012).

Negative Symptoms

Clinicians should keep in mind that some clients with SMI, possibly because of their SMI symptoms such as blunted affect, or as a result of psychotropic medication side effects, may display affect that is muted or incongruent with their description of their emotions during or after a trauma. Clinicians should rely on the client's verbal report of distress, not simply their affect, to assist in their case conceptualization, as research has found that flat or blunted affect in individuals with schizophrenia-spectrum disorders does not reflect a diminished subjective internal experience of that emotion (Kring et al., 1993; Sweet et al., 1998).

Delusions

A common question regarding assessment of trauma exposure in those with SMI is how to differentiate between a delusion of traumatic content and a bona fide Criterion A traumatic event. Delusions are fixed, false beliefs held with high regard and high conviction, despite contrary evidence (Paolini et al., 2016). They are a common feature of schizophrenia-spectrum disorders and can cause substantial distress and impairment (Upthegrove, 2018). Research has found that reports of traumatic events in those with SMI are generally accurate and reliable (Goodman et al., 1999); therefore, clinicians should lead with an assumption that traumatic events endorsed actually occurred as reported. There are times, however, when clients with SMI may report a delusion that includes traumatic content, thus clinicians are advised on how differentiate this phenomenon. An example that illustrates the report of a traumatic delusion is below:

Gerry is a 52yo White, lesbian, cisgender woman admitted to an inpatient psychiatric unit due to acute exacerbation of psychotic symptoms. Upon admission, she reports that, at her friend's house three months prior, a herd of horses entered her home and sexually assaulted her while her friends, who were present, did nothing to help her. Gerry was distressed when recounting this experience, particularly because it appeared that no one took her concerns seriously or believed that this had actually occurred. She requested to have a one-on-one nurse during the nighttime to ensure that such an event would not happen again as now she was worried that this herd of horses was following her. Gerry was angered when the treatment team denied this request.

If a clinician suspects that a report of a trauma from a client with SMI may actually be a delusion, there are three factors to help differentiate how to conceptualize this distressing experience—the consistency of the report, how unusual/bizarre the report, and what specifically is causing the client most distress regarding the report. First, clinicians are encouraged to ask numerous Socratic questions to clarify the details of what the client says occurred and then can compare reports of the distressing experience from the client over time. While it is not uncommon that some peripheral details about bona fide Criterion A trauma memories will vary to some extent over time, the central details remain consistent (Bagri, 2017; Bryant, 2015; Payne et al., 2004; Paz-Alonso & Goodman, 2008; Shors & Millon, 2016). In contrast, delusions can vary much more widely in their reports, and can include changes in some of the most meaningful and central features, including what happened, who perpetrated (if relevant), and whether it occurred at all. The more variable the reports over time in these significant central features, the greater possibility this could point to a delusion, though a careful assessment is needed. Other times, delusions may be more realistic or plausible, therefore making it very difficult to identify it as such during the assessment phase, thereby leading to an inaccurate conclusion that a delusion is a Criterion A trauma. In these instances, clinicians may notice that a

delusion might shift over time while the client attempts to answer unanswerable questions, typically during the examination of real evidence in CPT, thereby making the event described as a trauma less plausible over time.
Second, delusions tend to be quite unusual and bizarre (Cermolacce et al., 2010), whereas trauma memories are not. Specifically, delusions typically include highly unusual and implausible circumstances, setting, details, or people involved. Third, clients who report traumatic delusions may be more or equally distressed by the possibility that anyone may question whether or not the experience happened, compared to the distress about the reported experience itself. Conversely, distress about a Criterion A trauma in the context of PTSD is explicitly linked to the traumatic event, rather than how others in general may perceive the report of the event. It is important to note that there may also be other circumstances in which clients may become concerned or preoccupied with not being believed and/or supported upon disclosure of traumatic events experienced. For example, in cases of institutional betrayal (e.g., military settings, academic institutions) or in circumstances when sexual assault reporting was not believed or was deemed "unfounded" (e.g., by law enforcement), clients who experience Criterion A traumas may also experience substantial distress due to not being believed and/or when actions are not taken to punish a perpetrator. In these situations, these feelings tend to be circumscribed to the institutions that were not validating or supportive specifically, not anyone who may not believe that the trauma occurred generally (Monteith et al., 2022; Murphy-Oikonen et al., 2022).

Hallucinations and Perceptual Aberrations

Some clients with schizophrenia-spectrum disorders may report unusual perceptual experiences that are trauma-related. In order to accurately diagnose and conceptualize this symptomatology, clinicians should consider whether perceptual aberrations are trauma-related intrusions or psychotic-spectrum hallucinations. In the case of the former, clients may indicate hearing voices or sounds (e.g., hearing a perpetrator's voice during the assault), seeing images or visions (e.g., eyes of a deceased friend) or gustatory, olfactory, or tactile perceptual experiences that mimicked the circumstances of the traumatic event(s) experienced. In the case of the latter, schizophrenia-spectrum hallucinations are perceptual experiences that are unrelated to traumatic event(s) experienced. Another useful approach for distinguishing whether an unusual perceptual experience is a PTSD intrusion or a schizophrenia-spectrum hallucination is to clarify the timeline of when the symptom emerged. If the symptom emerged prior to the trauma(s) experienced, then it cannot be a PTSD intrusion.

Mania

Due to the brief nature of true manic episodes, it is unlikely that clients with SMI will present to CPT during an active manic phase. However, if manic symptoms emerge during the course of CPT, clinicians and patients can collaboratively make the decision to utilize a flexible adaptation of CPT based on case formulation and the client's acute treatment needs. This approach allows clinicians and patients to make a strategic departure from the CPT protocol, while ideally incorporating elements of the CPT framework (e.g., non-avoidance, accessing natural emotions, identification and evaluation of stuck points), in order to address specific concerns such as an assessment of mania, psychoeducation about the manic episode and client stabilization (Vieta & Sanchez-Moreno, 2008) for an identified number of sessions. Another essential component of this approach is a clear plan for how and when to return to the CPT protocol. These treatment decisions should also include coordination with psychiatry or other prescribing providers in order to support use of stabilizing pharmacotherapy, as well as utilization of measures to prevent risks for the clients.

Considerations for Treatment Planning

After it is established that a client meets criteria for PTSD and an SMI, clinicians can begin discussing CPT as a gold-standard treatment option. Clinicians should keep in mind that clients with SMI characteristically struggle with neurocognitive symptoms that affect processing speed, attention and verbal memory (Green et al., 2004; Zanelli et al., 2022). As such, clients with SMI greatly benefit from written and verbal information regarding CPT so that they can absorb the content via multiple avenues and can be better-informed about what the treatment entails. Clinicians can utilize patient handouts and pamphlets from reliable sources, such as the National Center for PTSD (www.ptsd.va.gov). In addition, clinicians may use verbal comprehension checks to ensure that clients are understanding the CPT content and process, and that clients can describe the treatment, treatment roles and expectations in their own words. It is not unusual for individuals with SMIs to have received involuntary treatment for mental health symptoms at some point in their lives; for example, due to the need for stabilization of acute symptom exacerbation (Maina et al., 2021). Given this, clinicians should empower clients with SMI who are considering CPT to know that their involvement with CPT is a voluntary and collaborative process.

Once clients choose to undergo CPT, there are several psychosocial, logistical, and clinical considerations that clinicians should address in order to set clients with SMI up for success. First, a common psychosocial stressor for clients with SMI is unstable housing or lack of privacy in housing. It can be helpful to discuss the logistics surrounding space and privacy given the importance of practice assignment completion and the necessity for clients to connect to and sit with natural emotions during CPT practices. There are often opportunities for problem-solving these space-related challenges; there may be a local library with private spaces, clinic rooms to reserve for practice assignment completion, or the use of parked cars or other spaces where clients can have privacy. Clinicians should note that, while research shows that practice assignment completion in CPT can facilitate PTSD symptom change (Stirman et al., 2018; Wachen, 2024), it is also true that therapist skill in incorporating homework effectively into the CPT protocol is very important (Woolley et al., 2023). Therefore, given that many clients with SMI face numerous psychosocial challenges, including unstable housing, that may complicate their ability to complete daily practice assignments, clinicians should focus their efforts on providing a clear rationale for practice and beginning practice assignments with clients in session when homework is introduced in order to increase clarity and understanding of what each assignment entails. Clinicians are encouraged to assign every CPT practice assignment to clients and to encourage completion, while practicing practicality regarding whether daily worksheets are possible for every client, regardless of their psychosocial circumstances.

Second, given that many clients with SMI will be taking psychotropic medications and/or using case management services, CPT therapists should discuss the value of having communication with the client's treatment team in order to ensure that all providers are on the same page and supportive of the work of CPT. This is particularly important given that many providers are unaware of the emerging literature on the effectiveness of EBTs for PTSD, such as CPT, for clients with SMIs, and therefore often hold antagonistic views towards the treatment of PTSD in those with SMI (Frueh et al., 2006; Gairns et al., 2013; Salyers et al., 2004). In these cases, once CPT therapists have secured authorization forms from clients consenting to communication with treatment team members, CPT therapists are in the position of educators and champions of CPT. Clinicians are encouraged to call and/or meet with each treatment team member working with the client to provide information about CPT and its appropriateness for the client—the benefits to PTSD symptoms, the benefits to secondary symptoms, and the cost of not providing an EBT for PTSD. This clear communication and championing of CPT will increase the chances that the client is receiving consistent and hopeful messages regarding the appropriateness, utility, or effectiveness of CPT for their PTSD symptoms.

Third, it is not uncommon for clients with SMI to struggle with medication noncompliance (Semahegn et al., 2020). CPT clinicians are encouraged to discuss with clients the importance of aiming for full medication compliance during CPT in order to maintain momentum in treatment and, thus, to facilitate greater and more efficient recovery from PTSD. A discussion of factors that predict or precede medication noncompliance, ways to collaboratively identify medication noncompliance, factors that have promoted medication compliance, as well as the use of motivational enhancement techniques, can be useful to encourage maintaining medication consistency during CPT.

Fourth, because clients with SMI will struggle with non-PTSD symptoms, clinicians are encouraged to identify if there are symptoms that would be useful to track concurrent to PTSD and depression symptoms during CPT. For example, if a client struggles with daily auditory hallucinations as part of a schizophrenia-spectrum disorder, and if those symptoms impact client engagement with CPT or perpetuate avoidance for any reason, clinicians can use well-validated measures like the Mental Health Research Institute Unusual Perceptions Schedule (MUPS; Carter et al., 1995), Auditory Vocal Hallucination Rating Scale (AVHRS; Steenhuis et al., 2019), Psychotic Symptom Rating Scales (PSYRATS; Haddock et al., 1999), and Beliefs About Voices Questionnaire-Revised (Chandwick et al., 2000) to assess psychotic symptoms. To assess mania or hypomania, clinicians can use the Young Mania Rating Scale (YMRS; Young et al., 2000), which is an interview-based assessment measure, or the Altman Self-Report Mania Scale (Altman et al., 1997).

Fifth, since SMI symptoms are occurring in a parallel manner with PTSD symptoms during CPT, and a significant change in SMI symptoms can be a barrier to sticking with the CPT protocol, it is recommended that, prior to CPT, clinicians and clients with SMI spend time identifying early warning signs of SMI symptom exacerbation and encouraging the utilization of a relapse prevention plan and/or skills for effectively managing those symptoms. Early identification allows for early, brief interventions that can temper SMI emerging symptoms, and thus allow the continuation of CPT. Often this can be achieved by utilizing a "stressor" session during the CPT protocol (Galovski et al., 2012). There is no evidence that gold-standard PTSD treatments lead to an exacerbation of SMI symptoms (van den Berg et al., 2016); however, factors like medication noncompliance, sleep disturbance, stress, and substance use have been found to predict symptom relapse (Alvarez-Jimenez et al., 2012; Semahegn et al., 2020). There are multiple methods for the early identification of emerging SMI symptoms such as psychosis or mania, including Wellness Recovery Action Plan (WRAP) or the GOALS Program (Johnson & Fulford, 2009; Norton & Flynn, 2020).

Therapists should be prepared for the possibility that identifying early warning signs of SMI symptoms can impact the therapeutic relationship. Consider a client with bipolar II disorder who, after being in a major depressive episode (MDE) for many weeks, begins to emerge out of the MDE and is feeling much better. Soon, the client describes staying up until 4 am each night to work on numerous creative projects and getting only 3 hours of sleep before going to work. Since decreased need for sleep is an early warning sign for hypomania for this client, their CPT therapist identifies this. The client may have a negative reaction to the therapist's attempt to thwart their "great mood" after weeks of profound depression. This example underscores the importance of a priori discussions about the importance and rationale for the identification of early warning signs. This example also illustrates numerous opportunities to use the CPT framework to address this concern swiftly, before returning to the CPT protocol. For example, the therapist can use Socratic questions to discuss the emerging symptoms ("Is decreased need for sleep something that we should attend to for any reason?") and the impact of this discussion on the clinical relationship ("How are you feeling and thinking about me given that I've brought up the possibility that you may be experiencing an early warning sign of hypomania?"). In addition, the clinician can use other CPT skills, such as ABC worksheets to clarify the client's thoughts and feelings, and cognitive restructuring worksheets including the Examining Questions Worksheet (previously called Challenging

Questions Worksheet) and the Alternative Thoughts Worksheet (previously called Challenging Beliefs Worksheet) to address any potential symptom-based and/or relational stuck points. Similar scenarios may also emerge with clients with a schizophrenia-spectrum disorders who may not be believed about a delusion or their hallucinatory experiences.

The working alliance is a powerful predictor of psychotherapy outcomes, including for evidence-based PTSD treatments (Ellis et al., 2017; Howard et al., 2022; McLaughlin et al., 2014; Sijercic et al., 2021). Given that struggles with safety, trust, power/control, esteem, and intimacy can manifest in current relationships, including with the therapist (Ellis et al., 2017; Held et al., 2022; McLaughlin et al., 2014; Norcross & Wampold, 2018; Sijercic et al., 2021), clinicians are strongly encouraged to inquire often about how clients are experiencing them, their ability to understand them, and their experience with CPT (Basset & Sacks, 2022).

CPT-Specific Clinical Guidance

Once therapists have initiated CPT, there are several important clinical recommendations when working with clients with SMI, including (1) broadening the lens for detecting assimilated stuck points; (2) tips/guidelines for engaging in Socratic dialogue; (3) strategies for navigating client neurocognitive impairment, which is a core feature of those with SMI; 4) methods for addressing stuck points in patients with bipolar disorder that foster balanced, fact-based thinking; and (5) addressing trauma themes.

Detecting Assimilation

With regard to assimilated stuck points, it is important that clinicians understand that (1) assimilated stuck points may include more unusual and/or creative meaning-making in individuals with SMI, particularly those with schizophrenia-spectrum disorders, compared to clients without an SMI, and (2) that trauma-related perceptual aberrations can be a breeding ground for assimilated stuck points. These issues are discussed in turn.

Some clients with SMI, especially those with schizophrenia-spectrum disorders, may make meaning of why the trauma happened or may judge how the trauma unfolded in ways that may appear to be a delusion because of its unusual or bizarre language and/or content. However, when working with clients with SMI, it is essential that clinicians inquire about any and all beliefs that clients may have formed in attempt to make sense of the trauma(s) they have experienced. This includes beliefs regarding unacceptability of the trauma having occurred at all, undoing beliefs about the trauma, hindsight bias, judgments regarding how the trauma occurred, and negative attributions about their and/or others' internal or external reactions as the trauma unfolded, among others. Here are examples of these types of assimilated stuck points: "The trauma happened because an evil genius shifted the earth at the moment of the trauma," "The trauma happened because he had telepathic powers and could tell that I thought he was attractive," "The trauma happened because she was born inside of a swamp," or "If I had transformed myself into another lifeform, the trauma would not have happened." Though these example stuck points are related to specific Criterion A traumas, they do illustrate slightly different, more unusual/bizarre, less reality-based examples of attempts to reconcile pre-trauma beliefs and the trauma experience. Clinicians are encouraged to approach finding assimilated stuck points with clients with SMI with openness, curiosity and a non-judgmental attitude, and are best served to inquire about any and all unusual meaning-making clients have done regarding their trauma(s). These types of assimilated stuck points should be added to the stuck point log, prioritized in CPT, and addressed exactly as other assimilated stuck points are handled in CPT.

Below is a clinical example to illustrate this practice:

Therapist: *"You've been doing an excellent job identifying important stuck points and writing them on your Stuck Point Log. One stuck point that you've mentioned that feels particularly stuck is the idea that the trauma happened because an evil genius shifted the earth and caused your injuries. Can you help me understand makes you think that?"*

Client: *"I just think that the earth shifted in the moment right before I was shot and that movement caused me to get hurt."*

Therapist: *"When you say the earth shifted, what do you mean?"*

Client: *"I mean that the earth spun at a different rate than it normally would."*

Therapist: *"What do we know about what typically causes the Earth to spin?"*

Client: *"I'm not really sure."*

Therapist: *"Since we don't know what typically causes the Earth to spin, perhaps we can do some research on that to better understand what causes the Earth to spin under typical circumstances? That might help us understand your situation better."*

Client: *"Ok."*

Therapist: *"Have you ever heard of the Earth changing the speed that it spins?"*

Client: *"Not before this, no."*

Therapist: *"What were the nature of your injuries?"*

Client: *"I had a gunshot wound in my shoulder. I had to get surgery on it and had to get the bullet removed."*

Therapist: *"How are gunshot wounds typically caused?"*

Client: *"By being shot by a gun."*

Therapist: *"What do we know about what causes a gun to be discharged?"*

Client: *"Well, someone has to pull the trigger."*

Therapist: *"At the time of your trauma, was there someone holding a gun?"*

Client: *"Yes, there was a man standing behind a bush outside of my house."*

Therapist: *"Right before you were shot, what happened?"*

Client: *"The man came out from behind the bush, pointed his gun towards me and said that if I didn't give him my wallet, that he would shoot me."*

Therapist: *"Then what happened?"*

Client: *"I struggled to get my wallet out of my pocket and he started yelling at me to hurry and threatened that he would shoot me."* [Client begins crying]

Therapist: *"What happened next?"*

Client: *"He yelled at me that I was stalling and he told me that I left him no choice but to shoot me."*

Therapist: *"What took place next?"*

Client: *"I was shot."*

Therapist: *"I understand. So, prior to you being shot, you were standing outside of your house and a man emerged from behind a bush and told you that if you didn't give him your wallet, that he would shoot you. You struggled to get your wallet out and then he said he had no choice but to shoot you, and then you remember being shot? Am I getting that right?"*

Client: *"Yeah, that's right. It was terrible."*

Therapist: *"I hear you. Based on what you're sharing with me, could it be possible that the reason that you incurred your injuries was because this man who told you he would shoot you, shot you?"*

Client: *"I guess it's possible."*

Trauma-related perceptual aberrations are fertile soil for assimilated stuck points. Clinicians should be prepared to ask questions about the *content* and the *meaning* of these perceptual experiences so as to not miss essential assimilated stuck points. Assimilated stuck points may be in the *content* of trauma-related perceptual aberrations. For example, if a client indicates that they hear the voice of a perpetrator saying "this is your fault," clinicians might inquire about what the client makes of this experience, to which the client might respond with "the rape was my fault." Below is an example clinical interaction to illustrate this:

Therapist: *"In your impact statement, you wrote about a voice that you hear that sounds like the perpetrator's voice, and how that haunts you. Is there anything that you've heard the voice say that you think is relevant to why you've been stuck or to how you've made sense of the trauma?"*

Client: *"Yes, I hate hearing that voice, it always scares me and makes me feel guilty."*

Therapist: *"What about it makes you feel guilty?"*

Client: *"He always tells me that the rape was my fault."*

Therapist: *"And what do you make of that?"*

Client: *"It makes me think that the rape was my fault, if he was saying it was."*

Therapist: *"Do you think this might be an important stuck point for us to add to your log?"*

Client: *"Oh yeah, I think the rape was my fault all of the time because his voice tells me so."*

Therapist: *"Let's take a minute and have you add that stuck point to your log. How do you think we would phrase it?"*

Client: *"I would write 'the rape was my fault.'"*

Therapist: *"Excellent job finding that important stuck point."*

Assimilated stuck points may also be found in the appraisal of trauma-related perceptual aberrations. For example, if a client sees the vision of a friend who died in front of them (index trauma), the way that they make sense of this perceptual experience may be an assimilated stuck point. For example, a client may make meaning of seeing their deceased friend by telling themselves "he should still be alive," which is an assimilated stuck point.

Socratic Dialogue

As CPT clinicians know, Socratic dialogue is the cornerstone of CPT. When working with clients with co-occurring SMI, clinicians should pay special care to how they set the stage for Socratic dialogue and how they handle SMI-specific roadblocks. Setting the stage for Socratic dialogue is imperative when working with clients with SMI, rather than simply launching into questions. The reason for this is that many clients, particularly those with a schizophrenia-spectrum disorder, often struggle with paranoia and self-defeating thoughts regarding their ability to do things correctly. Thus, it can be quite useful to provide education about and rationale for Socratic dialogue. Specifically, clinicians can be transparent about the fact that fostering curiosity is one of the variables most associated with psychological health. Specifically in CPT, we use a lot of questions to help us be curious about stuck points in order to sort out what is absolutely a fact and what might not be. Clinicians can also communicate to clients that they will be asking many different questions and that the client is encouraged to try to answer the questions as best as possible, with knowledge that they may not have answers to every question. Clinicians can also discuss the role of avoidance in limiting curiosity about stuck points and how asking questions in CPT allows us to move past avoidance to a place of more clarity about the relevant facts surrounding the trauma.

As mentioned previously, another powerful tool when working with clients with SMI, and one that inherently strengthens the clinical relationship, is inquiring how the client experiences the therapist and how the client is thinking and feeling about the clinical relationship. This can be an extremely useful question to utilize after engaging in Socratic dialogue about a stuck point. For example, a therapist might ask "How has me asking you these questions about this stuck point shaped how you think and feel about our working relationship?" or "What was your experience of me and of our working relationship as I was asking you questions about your stuck point?"

Neurocognitive Symptoms

It is well documented that individuals with schizophrenia-spectrum disorders and bipolar disorders struggle with a host of neurocognitive impairments (Green et al., 2004; Zanelli et al., 2022), including deficits in attention, verbal learning and memory, executive functions and several other domains. While some of these impairments will likely show up during CPT, there are numerous compensatory strategies that clinicians can introduce to clients in order to ensure clients maximally benefit from CPT. It is not uncommon that clients with SMI derail due to cognitive disorganization, racing thoughts or flight of ideas, while engaging in Socratic dialogue about stuck points, particularly assimilated stuck points. It can be useful to have the client write down the assimilated stuck point on an ABC worksheet in column B and then circle or highlight it to draw attention and anchor the conversation to the stuck point being addressed. When a client derails, therapists can use this visual cue as a reminder to re-ground the conversation in the specific stuck point. In addition, clinicians should set up the expectation that they may need to interrupt clients if the conversation derails. Therapists can also encourage clients to self-identify derailing by holding up a finger when it occurs or by verbally noting "I just went to another stuck point," or "I just started talking about something else."

As described above in the context of assessment, comprehension checks can also be used during treatment as an effective way to assist clients with SMI with strengthening their understanding of CPT concepts and integrating information gleaned during Socratic dialogue. Clinicians may say "Please tell me, in your own words, what you are understanding from what I explained," or "Tell me in a sentence or two, what you are gathering from what you're hearing." This allows clinicians to enhance their case conceptualization and to fill in information that was missed. Using this skill after lengthy Socratic dialogue about a stuck point can also aid in the cognitive processing. In order to help a client integrate and consolidate information that was elucidated via questioning, CPT therapists might ask "Tell me what you are taking with you from this conversation about this stuck point?", "What is information that was clarified and/or new to you from this discussion about the stuck point?" or "How has what we discussed today via questioning impacted how you're thinking about the original stuck point?"

Clinicians should ensure that they begin CPT homework with clients in session and that clients have a solid understanding of what they are being asked to do between sessions. Clinicians may also encourage the use of alerts and alarms to remind clients to complete therapy-related practice assignments, and may consider scheduling brief calls between sessions to facilitate client engagement in CPT practice assignments, especially when clients are first learning a more sophisticated cognitive skill or worksheet.

Stuck Points and Bipolar Disorder

Clients with bipolar disorder tend to have extreme, conflicting beliefs, particularly about themselves, success and social approval (Mansell et al., 2007), which waiver in valence depending on their mood states (e.g., depression vs hypomania/mania). This tendency to swing from cognitive distortions at one extreme to another may present itself in CPT, particularly in stuck points related to control ("I have no control" and "I have control over everything") and esteem ("I am worthless," "I can accomplish things no one else can"). Clinicians should note that since the window of mania and hypomania is very brief (4–7 days), it is more likely that clients with bipolar disorders will present to CPT while in a depressed episode or while experiencing dysthymia, rather than a hypomanic or manic episode given the brevity of these episodes (4–7 days). However, as noted previously, if clients do present in an acute manic phase, the session should focus on accurate assessment, psychoeducation, pharmacology consultation/discussion and client stabilization.

Trauma Themes

Once CPT begins to focus on trauma themes (safety, trust, power/control, esteem, intimacy), clinicians should be aware of two SMI-specific challenges that they might face. First, flexibility in some of the themes in CPT may be attenuated because these beliefs may also be impacted by SMI symptoms (e.g., safety and trust). Second, some behavioral practice assignments in the later stages of CPT (e.g., giving and receiving compliments, doing one nice thing for oneself each day) may be particularly challenging for clients with SMI due to SMI symptoms like anhedonia and social skills deficits.

With regard to the first challenge, some clients with SMI may experience delusions which are fixed, false beliefs held with high regard. One very common type of delusion is persecutory delusions or paranoia. These beliefs include fears that others are out to get them and that others are intending serious harm. These beliefs differ from PTSD-related safety and trust stuck points in (1) the extent with which they are held with conviction and the lack of insight into the possibility that safety concerns could be excessive, (2) they often include more specific threats, instead of global hypervigilance fears (e.g., "My neighbor is bugging my house and trying to steal my thoughts"), and (3) these threats often include unusual, bizarre or implausible situations.

In these circumstances, paranoid beliefs may be premorbid to PTSD and/or are exacerbated by PTSD such that fears about safety and danger may be more engrained and stuck than for someone with PTSD but no paranoia. It is also possible that when inquiring about safety or trust stuck points in CPT, clients may begin describing a persecutory or paranoid delusion. If this occurs in CPT, clinicians should aim to bring the focus back to a circumscribed trauma-related stuck point (e.g., "people are dangerous"), rather than address a paranoid delusion in CPT, in order to remain as effective as possible in treating PTSD. Below is an example transcript of how a clinician may handle such a situation.

Therapist: *"Let's discuss what safety beliefs you found when reading the safety theme handouts for practice last week. How have you been thinking about self- and other- safety since the trauma occurred? How do you think the trauma has shaped how you think about safety?"*

Client: *"Well, I know that I don't feel very safe now anywhere. I think that the world is dangerous and that people are out to harm me, especially in large crowds because my trauma happened in a large crowd. Another thought that I have is that my boss is dangerous and is trying to put thoughts into my mind that are not my own, and that he can also read my mind."*

Therapist: *"I see. Tell me more about your thoughts about large crowds. What are you telling yourself will happen in a large crowd?"*

Client: *"Oh, I think that if I am in a crowd, I will be assaulted."*

Therapist: *"And what might that sound like?"*

Client: *"I think that's a stuck point. If I am in a crowd, I will be assaulted."*

Therapist: *"Exactly, great work. Let's have you write that in your stuck point log."*

[Client writes down stuck point.]

Therapist: *"You also mentioned something about the world and dangerousness. What are you telling yourself there? Could there be another stuck point in there about safety?"*

Client: *"Yeah, the world is dangerous. Should I write that one down too?"*

Therapist: *"Absolutely! You are getting really good at finding these stuck points. Excellent work."*

In this example, the clinician did not engage the paranoid delusion and also did not agree with it being true. Rather, the clinician conceptualized that this belief was related to SMI symptoms, made the clinical decision in real-time to step aside of that belief and then focused the session on PTSD-specific safety stuck points. Even using this approach, it is still possible that some clients with paranoid delusions may struggle to effectively evaluate certain stuck points about safety, such as "people will hurt me" because the paranoid thoughts may be used as "evidence" for these beliefs. In those instances, clinicians can repeat to clients that evidence can only include hard facts that are agreed upon universally and then can then refocus on finding additional evidence against the stuck point. Just like with non-SMI clients with PTSD, some clients with SMI may struggle to differentiate between "hard facts" and opinions or other beliefs/stuck points. In these instances, it can be useful to utilize educational information or resources that are well-vetted to clarify what facts exist for a given stuck point. Clinicians can also encourage the utilization of behavioral experiments to gather data regarding stuck points. For example, if a client is evaluating the stuck point "no one ever wants to help me," the clinician may Socratically encourage the client to experiment with asking for different types of help from many different people (i.e., help taking out the trash, help carrying books, help with loading a grocery bag onto the bus/metro, help with holding a door open) and then have the client take notes of what occurs in each instance. Clinicians are advised to explore and/or encourage these experiments Socratically, as part of the Alternative Thoughts (Challenging Beliefs) Worksheet work, rather than formally assigning these practices as separate homework. For example, if the client is evaluating the stuck point "no one ever wants to help me" the clinician may say "You've mentioned the stuck point that 'no one ever wants to help me,' and you've shared that this stuck point often keeps you from asking others for help or support due to your expectation that you will not receive it. Given that we are hoping to gather some evidence for and against this Stuck Point, do you have any ideas about how we can test this idea out in the world? What could you take on as a challenge to identify some new data regarding this Stuck Point? What do you think could be ways that you could gather some real-time information about whether this Stuck Point is true or not?"

During the latter sessions of CPT, clients are encouraged to engage in several behavioral practice assignments (e.g., giving and receiving compliments, doing one nice thing for oneself each day). An activity like giving compliments may be challenging for clients with SMI-related social skills deficits as they may lack the skills to know how to initiate or participate in such an interaction. Clinicians are advised to inquire Socratically about how clients are considering engaging in these practices. For example, a therapist might say "How might you go about giving a compliment this week? What could be an example of how you might do this?" If the client expresses being unsure how to do this or if they give an example of an inappropriate compliment (e.g., complimenting a co-worker's physique), then clinicians can engage in a brief role play to model an appropriate compliment. The therapist can first model the skill and then encourage the client to practice the skill via a brief role play. This is an example of a very brief and appropriate adjustment to the CPT framework that is guided by case conceptualization and congruent with the objectives of the assignment (to obtain new data) and the objectives of CPT (cognitive flexibility).

Another SMI symptom that may present a challenge during CPT is anhedonia. In order to support clients with SMI to take steps to engage in behavioral practice assignments, such as doing one nice activity for themselves each day, clinicians can help clients break tasks down into smaller portions, encourage the use of alarms and other compensatory memory/organizational strategies and discuss the importance of "putting the cart before the horse," or doing the activity while uncomfortable, instead of waiting until the client feels like doing the activity. In addition, clinicians should consider the socioeconomic background of clients and help generate cost-effective ideas for pleasurable activities, so that clients have numerous compelling options of activities to practice that are within their budgets. This is particularly important with clients with SMI, as individuals with SMI suffer from housing instability and homelessness at disproportionate rates (Gutwinski et al., 2021) and may not have disposable income.

Medication-Related Considerations

Patients with SMI are often prescribed psychotropic medication, and, for many of these clients, medication is essential for the stabilization and management of SMI symptoms (Carolan et al., 2019). It can be helpful for clinicians to educate themselves on the common medications prescribed for SMI symptoms; for example, mood stabilizers, like Lithium and Lamictal, for Bipolar Disorders and antipsychotic medications, such as Quetiapine or Haloperidol, for schizophrenia-spectrums symptoms. As clinicians become more educated about exactly how these medications work for core SMI symptoms and their common side effect profiles, clinicians are better equipped to work collaboratively with their SMI clients for if, or when, medication-related challenges surface during the course of CPT. For example, lethargy and sleepiness is a common side effect for clients taking antipsychotic medication. This knowledge may shape conversations and decisions made surrounding the timing of therapy appointments in order to capitalize on the client's most alert times of the day. It is also common for many clients with SMI to be prescribed antidepressant medications and, due to the high rates of co-occurring substance use disorders, they may be prescribed medications such as Naltrexone for Alcohol Use Disorders or Methadone maintenance treatment for Heroin Use Disorder. As discussed earlier in this chapter, gathering information about medications prescribed and history with medication compliance and noncompliance is an essential first step in the pre-treatment assessment process. Once this information is gathered, clinicians can proactively obtain education about medications utilized by their clients, communicate with the client's prescribing provider (after obtaining informed consent for communication) and discuss side effects and contingency for medication noncompliance with clients openly. These conversations with clients allow for the anticipation of and the active and collaborative decision-making surrounding the possible use of "stressor" sessions (Galovski et al., 2012) that may focus on acute effects of medication noncompliance or the emergence of treatment-interfering side effects in order to facilitate patient engagement with CPT.

Summary and Future Directions

In sum, PTSD is highly prevalent in individuals with SMI, and these clients are often eager to and extremely capable of engaging in CPT for PTSD. While there are some barriers to the provision of CPT with clients with SMI, this chapter, along with other published resources, can empower therapists to take on this work and to provide much needed PTSD treatment to this underserved and very deserving population. There is emerging research indicating that individuals with SMI can have PTSD effectively treated with CPT and that CPT for these clients can be as effective as for those without an SMI. However, this area of research is in its infancy. Clinicians, researchers, and administrators who work with clients with PTSD and SMI are in excellent positions to progress this body of research and are encouraged to do so.

As described in this chapter, clinicians will position their SMI clients best by attending to several important pre-treatment assessment and treatment planning steps before initiating CPT. Clinicians are encouraged to freely utilize the numerous tips, guidelines, and recommendations contained within this chapter to make CPT as effective as possible with clients with SMI throughout the course of CPT- while finding and prioritizing pertinent assimilated stuck points, during their use of Socratic dialogue, -and when navigating trauma themes and theme-congruent behavioral practice assignments.

Competing Interests Stephanie Sacks receives income for the training of professionals in Cognitive Processing Therapy (CPT) for PTSD.

References

Altman, E. G., Hedeker, D., Peterson, J. L., & Davis, J. M. (1997). The Altman self-rating mania scale. *Society of biological psychiatry, 42*, 948–955. https://doi.org/10.1016/S0006-3223(96)00548-3

Alvarez-Jimenez, M., Priede, A., Hetric, S. E., Bendall, S., Killackey, E., Parker, A. G., McGorry, P. D., & Gleeson, J. F. (2012). Risk factors for relapse following treatment for first episode psychosis: A systematic review and meta-analysis of longitudinal studies. *Schizophrenia Research, 139*(1–3), 116–128. https://doi.org/10.1016/j.schres.2012.05.007

Andresen, N. C. (1984). *The scale for the assessment of positive symptoms*. University of Iowa Press.

Andresen, N. C. (1985). *The scale for the assessment of positive symptoms*. University of Iowa Press.

Anticevic, A., & Corlett, P. R. (2012). Cognitive-emotion dysinteraction in schizophrenia. *Frontiers in Psychology, 3*, 392. https://doi.org/10.3389/fpsyg.2012.00392

Arseneault, L., Cannon, M., Fisher, H. L., Polanczyk, G., Moffitt, T. E., & Caspi, A. (2011). Childhood trauma and children's emerging psychotic symptoms: A genetically sensitive longitudinal cohort study. *The American Journal of Psychiatry, 168*(1), 65–72. https://doi.org/10.1176/appi.ajp.2010.10040567

Bagri, G. (2017). Remembering emotional central and peripheral information: How different memory tasks and individual differences influence eyewitness testimony. *American Journal of Forensic Psychology, 35*(2), 21–42.

Basset, G., & Sacks, S. A. (2022, November). Strengthening the working alliance in cognitive processing therapy for PTSD: Improving relational responsiveness to help reduce drop-out and enhance client outcomes. In *Pre-meeting institute workshop. 38th annual conference for the International Society for Traumatic Stress Studies*.

Bendall, S., Jackson, H. J., Hulbert, C. A., & McGorry, P. D. (2008). Childhood trauma and psychotic disorders: A systematic, critical review of the evidence. *Schizophrenia Bulletin, 34*(3), 568–579. https://doi.org/10.1093/schbul/sbm121

Bo, Q., Mao, Z., Li, X., Wang, Z., Wang, C., & Ma, X. (2017). Use of the MATRICS consensus cognitive battery (MCCB) to evaluate cognitive deficits in bipolar disorder: A systematic review and meta-analysis. *PLoS One, 12*(4), e0176212. https://doi.org/10/1371/journal.pone.0176212

Brekke, J. S., Prindle, C., Bae, S. W., & Long, J. D. (2001). Risks for individuals with schizophrenia who are living in the community. Psychiatric services (), 52(10), 1358–1366. doi:https://doi.org/10.1176/appi.ps.52.10.1358.

Breslau, N., Peterson, E. L., Poisson, L. M., Schultz, L. R., & Lucia, V. C. (2004). Estimating post-traumatic stress disorder in the community: Lifetime perspective and the impact of typical traumatic events. *Psychological Medicine, 34*(5), 889–898. https://doi.org/10.1017/s0033291703001612

Bryant, R. A. (2015). The complex fabric of trauma and autobiographical memory. In L. A. Watson & D. Bernsten (Eds.), *Clinical perspectives on autobiographical memory* (pp. 17–40). Cambridge University Press. https://doi.org/10.1017/CBO9781139626767.003

Buckley, P. F. (2006). Prevalence and consequences of the dual diagnosis of substance abuse and severe mental illness. *Journal of Clinical Psychiatry, 67*(Suppl 7), 5–9. https://doi.org/10.4088/jcp.0706e01

Burdick, K. E., Goldberg, T. E., Cornblatt, B. A., Keefe, R. S., Gopin, C. B., Derosse, P., Braga, R. J., & Malhotra, A. K. (2011). The MATRICS consensus cognitive battery in patients with bipolar I disorder. *Neuropsychopharmacology: official publication of the American College of neuropsychopharmacology, 36*(8), 1587–1592. https://doi.org/10.1038/npp.2011.36

Calhoun, P. S., Bosworth, H. B., Stechuchak, K. A., Strauss, J. L., & Butterfield, M. I. (2006). The impact of posttraumatic stress disorder on quality of life and health service utilization among veterans who have schizophrenia. *Journal of Traumatic Stress, 19*, 393–397. https://doi.org/10.1002/jts.20114

Carolan, A., Keating, D., Strawbridge, J., & Ryan, C. (2019). Optimising prescribing for patients with severe mental illness: The need for criteria. *Evidence Based Mental Health, 22*(4), 139–141. https://doi.org/10.1136/ebmental-2019-300099

Carter, D. M., Mackinnon, A., Howard, S., Zeegers, T., & Copolov, D. (1995). The development and reliability of the mental Health Research Institute unusual perceptions schedule (MUPS): An instrument to record auditory hallucinatory experience. *Schizophrenia Research, 16*(2), 157–165. https://doi.org/10.1016/0920-9964(94(00069-k

Cermolacce, M., Sass, L., & Parnas, J. (2010). What is bizarre in bizarre delusions? A critical review. *Schizophrenia Bulletin, 36*(4), 667–679. https://doi.org/10.1093/schbul/sbq001

Chandwick, P., Lees, S., & Birchwood, M. (2000). The revised beliefs about voices questionnaire (BAVQ-R). *The British Journal of Psychiatry: the Journal of Mental Science, 177*, 229–232. https://doi.org/10.1192/bjp.177.3.229

Daalman, K., Diederen, K. M., Derks, E. M., van Luttenveld, R., Kahn, R. S., & Sommer, I. E. (2012). Childhood trauma and auditory verbal hallucinations. *Psychological Medicine, 42*(12), 2475–2484. https://doi.org/10.1017/S0033291712000761

Dallel, S., Cancel, A., & Fakra, E. (2018). Prevalence of posttraumatic stress disorder in schizophrenia spectrum disorders: A systematic review. *Neuropsychiatry Journal, 8*(3). https://doi.org/10.4172/Neuropsychiatry.1000430

Davidson, G., Shannon, C., Mulholland, C., & Campbell, J. (2009). A longitudinal study of the effects of childhood trauma on symptoms and functioning of people with severe mental health problems. *Journal of Trauma & Dissociation: the Official Journal of the International Society for the Study of Dissociation (ISSD), 10*(1), 57–68. https://doi.org/10.1080/15299730802485169

de Bont, P. A., van den Berg, D. P., van der Vleugel, B. B., de Roos, C., Mulder, C. L., Becker, E. S., de Jongh, A., van der Gaag, M., & van Minnen, A. (2013a). A multi-site single blind clinical study to compare the effects of prolonged exposure, eye movement desensitization and reprocessing and waiting list on patients with a current diagnosis of psychosis and co morbid post traumatic stress disorder: Study protocol for the randomized controlled trial treating trauma in psychosis. *Trials, 23*(14), 151. https://doi.org/10.1186/1745-6215-14-151

de Bont, P. A., Van Minnen, A., & de Jongh, A. (2013b). Treating PTSD in patients with psychosis: A within-group controlled feasibility study examining the efficacy and safety of evidence-based PE and EMDR protocols. *Behavior Therapy, 44*(4), 717–730. https://doi.org/10.1016/j.beth.2013.07.002

de Hert, M., Corell, C. U., Bobes, J., Cetkovich-Bakmas, M., Cohen, D., Asai, I., Detraux, J., Guatam, S., Moller, H.-J., Ndetei, D. M., Newcomer, J. W., Uwakwe, R., & Leucht, S. (2011). Physical illness in patients with severe mental disorders. I. Prevalence, impact of medications and disparities in health care. *World Psychiatry, 10*(1), 52–77. https://doi.org/10.1002/j.2051-5545.2011.tb00014.x

Dixon, L. B., Holoshitz, Y., & Nossel, I. (2016). Treatment engagement of individuals experiencing mental illness: Review and update. *World Psychiatry: Official journal of the World Psychiatric Association (WPA), 15*(1), 13–20. https://doi.org/10.1002/wps.20306

Ellis, A. E., Simiola, V., Brown, L., Courtois, C., & Cook, J. M. (2017). The role of evidence-based therapy relationships on treatment outcomes for adults with trauma: A systemic review. *Journal of Trauma and Dissociation, 19*(2), 185–213. https://doi.org/10.1080/15299732.2017.1329771

Feingold, Z. R., Fox, A., & Galovski, T. E. (2018). Effectiveness of evidence-based psychotherapy for posttraumatic distress within a jail diversion program. *Psychological Services, 15*(4), 409–418. https://doi.org/10.1037/ser0000194

First, M. B., Williams, J. B. W., Karg, R. S., & Spitzer, R. L. (2016). *Structured clinical interview for DSM-5 disorders, clinician version (SCID-5-CV)*. American Psychiatric Association.

Frueh, B., Cusack, K. J., Grubaugh, A. L., Sauvageot, J. A., & Wells, C. (2006). Clinicians' perspectives on cognitive-behavioral treatment for PTSD among persons with severe mental illness. *Psychiatric Services, 57*(7), 1027–1031. https://doi.org/10.1176/ps.2006.57.7.1027

Frueh, B., Grubaugh, A. L., Cusack, K. J., Kimble, M. O., Elhai, J. D., & Knapp, R. G. (2009). Exposure-based cognitive-behavioral treatment of PTSD in adults with schizophrenia or schizoaffective disorder: A pilot study. *Journal of Anxiety Disorders, 23*(5), 665–675. https://doi.org/10.1016/j.janxdis.2009.02.005

Gairns, S., Alvarez-Jimenez, M., Hulbert, C., McGorry, P., & Bendall, S. (2013). Perceptions of clinicians treating young people with first-episode psychosis for post-traumatic stress disorder. *Early Intervention in Psychiatry., 9*, 12. https://doi.org/10.1111/eip.12065

Galovski, T. E., Blain, L. M., Mott, J. M., Elwood, L., & Houle, T. (2012). Manualized therapy for PTSD: Flexing the structure of cognitive processing therapy. *Journal of Consulting and Clinical Psychology, 80*, 968–981. https://doi.org/10.1037/a0030600

Gearon, J. S., Kaltman, S. I., Brown, C., & Bellack, A. S. (2003). Traumatic life events and PTSD among women with substance use disorders and schizophrenia. Psychiatric services (), 54(4), 523–528. doi:https://doi.org/10.1176/appi.ps.54.4.523.

Goodman, L. A., Thompson, K. M., Weinfurt, K., Corl, S., Acker, P., Mueser, K. T., & Rosenberg, S. D. (1999). Reliability of reports of violent victimization and posttraumatic stress disorder among men and women with serious mental illness. *Journal of Traumatic Stress, 12*(4), 587–599. https://doi.org/10.1023/A:1024708916143

Gray, M., Litz, B., Hsu, J., & Lombardo, T. (2004). Psychometric properties of the life events checklist. (PDF) *Assessment, 11*, 330-341. https://doi.org/10.1177/1073191104269954 PILOTS ID:6825.

Green, M. F., Kern, R. S., & Heaton, R. K. (2004). Longitudinal studies of cognition and functional outcome in schizophrenia: Implications for MATRICS. *Schizophrenia Research, 72*(1), 41–51. https://doi.org/10.1016/j.schres.2004.09.009

Green, M. J., & Phillips, M. L. (2004). Social threat perception and the evolution of paranoia. *Neuroscience and Biobehavioral Reviews, 28*(3), 333–342. https://doi.org/10.1016/j.neubiorev.2004.03.006

Grubaugh, A. L., Zinzow, H. M., Paul, L., Egede, L. E., & Frueh, B. C. (2011). Trauma exposure and posttraumatic stress disorder in adults with severe mental illness: A critical review. *Clinical Psychology Review, 31*, 883–899. https://doi.org/10.1016/j.cpr.2011.04.003

Grubaugh, A. L., Veronee, K., Ellis, C., Brown, W., & Knapp, R. G. (2017). Feasibility and efficacy of prolonged exposure for PTSD among individuals with a psychotic spectrum disorder. *Frontiers in Psychology, 8*, 977. https://doi.org/10.3389/fpsyg.2017.00977

Grubaugh, A. L., Brown, W. J., Wojtalik, J. A., Myers, U. S., & Eack, S. M. (2021). Meta-analysis of the Treatment of posttraumatic stress disorder in adults with comorbid severe mental illness. *The Journal of Clinical Psychiatry, 82*(3), 20r13584. https://doi.org/10.4088/JCP.20r13584

Gutwinski, S., Schreiter, S., Deutscher, K., & Fazel, S. (2021). The prevalence of mental disorders among homeless people in high-income countries: An updated systematic review and meta-regression analysis. *PLoS Medicine, 18*(8), e1003750. https://doi.org/10.1371/journal.pmed.1003750

Haddock, G., McCarron, J., Tarrier, N., & Faragher, E. B. (1999). Scales to measure dimensions of hallucinations and delusions: The psychotic symptom rating scales (PSYRATS). *Psychological Medicine, 29*(4), 879–889. https://doi.org/10.1017/s0033291799008661

Hammersley, P., Dias, A., Todd, G., Bowen-Jones, K., Reilly, B., & Bentall, R. P. (2003). Childhood trauma and hallucinations in bipolar affective disorder: Preliminary investigation. *The British Journal of Psychiatry: the Journal of Mental Science, 182*, 543–547. https://doi.org/10.1192/bjp.182.6.543

Hawthorne, W. B., Folson, D. P., Sommerfeld, D. H., Lanouette, N. M., Lewis, M., Aarons, G. A., Conklin, R. M., Solozano, E., Lindamer, L. A., & Jeste, D. V. (2012). Incarceration among adults who are in the public health system: Rates, risk factors, and short-term outcomes. *Psychiatric Services, 63*(1), 26–32. https://doi.org/10.1176/appi.ps.201000505

Held, P., Meade, E. A., Kovacevic, M., Smith, D. L., Pridgen, S., Coleman, J. A., & Klassen, B. J. (2022). Building strong therapeutic relationships quickly: The effect of the perceived working alliance on veterans' intensive PTSD treatment outcomes. *Psychotherapy (Chicago, Ill.), 59*(3), 470–480. https://doi.org/10.1037/pst0000447

Hiday, V. A., Swartz, M. S., Swanson, J. W., Borum, R., & Wagner, H. R. (1999). Criminal victimization of persons with severe mental illness. Psychiatric services (), 50(1), 62–68. doi:https://doi.org/10.1176/ps.50.1.62.

Hirschfeld, R. M. A., Williams, J. B. W., Spitzer, R. L., Calabrese, J. R., Flynn, L., Keck, P. E., Lewis, L., McElroy, S. L., Post, R. M., Rapport, D. J., Russell, J. M., Sachs, G. S., & Zajecka. (2000). Development and validation of a screening instrument for bipolar spectrum disorder: The mood disorders questionnaire. *American Journal of Psychiatry, 157*(11), 1873–1875. https://doi.org/10.1176/appi.ajp.157.11.1873

Hooker, C. I., Tully, L. M., Verosky, S. C., Fisher, M., Holland, C., & Vinogradov, S. (2011). Can I trust you? Negative affective priming influences social judgments in schizophrenia. *Journal of Abnormal Psychology, 120*(1), 98–107. https://doi.org/10.1037/a0020630

Howard, R., Berry, K., & Haddock, G. (2022). Therapeutic alliance in psychological therapy for posttraumatic stress disorder: A systematic review and meta-analysis. *Clinical Psychology and Psychotherapy, 29*, 373–399. https://doi.org/10.1002/cpp.2642

Insel, T. R. (2008). Assessing the economic costs of serious mental illness. *The American Journal of Psychiatry, 165*(6), 663–665. https://doi.org/10.1176/appi.ajp.2008.08030366

Kay, S. R., Fiszbein, A., & Opler, L. A. (1987). The positive and negative syndrome scale (PANSS) for schizophrenia. *Schizophrenia Bulletin, 13*(2), 261–276. https://doi.org/10.1093/schbul/13.2.261

Kessler, R. C., Berglund, P., Demler, O., Jin, R., Merikangas, K. R., & Walters, E. E. (2005). Lifetime prevalence and age-of-onset distributions of DSM-IV disorders in the national comorbidity survey replication. *Archives of General Psychiatry, 62*, 593–602. https://doi.org/10.1001/archpsyc.62.6.593

Johnson, S. L., & Fulford, D. (2009). Preventing mania: A preliminary examination of the GOALS program. *Behavior Therapy, 40*(2), 103–113. https://doi.org/10.1016/j.beth.2008.03.002

Kring, A. M., Kerr, S. L., Smith, D. A., & Neale, J. M. (1993). Flat affect in schizophrenia does not reflect diminished subjective experience of emotion. *Journal of Abnormal Psychology, 102*(4), 507–517. https://doi.org/10.1037/0021-843x.102.4.507

Leickly, E., & Townley, G. (2021). Exploring factors related to supportive housing tenure and stability for people with serious mental illness. *Journal of Community Psychology, 49*(6), 1787–1805.

Lawrence, D., & Kisely, S. (2010). Inequalities in healthcare provision for people with severe mental illness. *Journal of Psychopharmacology (Oxford, England), 24*(4 Suppl), 61–68. https://doi.org/10.1177/1359786810382058

Lu, W., Yanos, P. T., Waynor, W., Jia, Y., Siriram, A., Leong, A., Gill, K., & Mueser, K. T. (2022). Psychometric properties of post-traumatic stress disorder (PTSD) checklist for DSM-5 in persons with serious mental illness. *European Journal of Psychotraumatology, 13*(1), 2038924. https://doi.org/10.1080/20008198.2022.2038924

Lysaker, P. H., & Larocco, V. A. (2008). The prevalence and correlates of trauma-related symptoms in schizophrenia spectrum disorder. *Comprehensive Psychiatry, 49*(4), 330–334. https://doi.org/10.1016/j.comppsych.2007.12.003

Mansell, W., Morrison, A., Reid, G., Lowens, I., & Tai, S. (2007). The interpretation of, responses to, changes in internal states: An integrative cognitive model of mood swings and bipolar disorders. *Behavioural and Cognitive Psychotherapy, 35*(5), 515–539. https://doi.org/10.1017/S1352465807003827

Maina, G., Rosso, G., Carezana, C., Mehanović, E., Risso, F., Villari, V., Gariglio, L., & Cardano, M. (2021). Factors associated with involuntary admissions: A register-based cross-sectional multicenter study. *Annals of General Psychiatry, 20*(1), 3. https://doi.org/10.1186/s12991-020-00323-1

McLaughlin, A. A., Keller, S. M., Feeny, N. C., Youngstrom, E. A., & Zoellner, L. A. (2014). Patterns of therapeutic alliance: Rupture-repair episodes in prolonged exposure for posttraumatic stress disorder. *Journal of Consulting and Clinical Psychology, 82*(1), 112–121. https://doi.org/10.1037/a0034696

Norcross, J. C., & Wampold, B. E. (2018). A new therapy for each patient: Evidence-based relationships and responsiveness. *Journal of Clinical Psychology, 74*, 1889–1906. https://doi.org/10.1002/jclp.22678

Misiak, B., Moustafa, A. A., Kiejna, A., & Frydecka, D. (2016). Childhood traumatic events and types of auditory verbal hallucinations in first-episode schizophrenia patients. *Comprehensive Psychiatry, 66*, 17–22.

Monson, C. M., Gradus, J. L., Young-Xu, Y., Shnurr, P. P., Price, J. L., & Schumm, J. A. (2008). Change in posttraumatic stress disorder symptoms: Do clinicians and patients agree? *Psychological Assessment, 20*, 131–138. https://doi.org/10.1037/1040-3590.20.2.131

Monteith, L. L., Holder, N., Iglesias, C. D., & Holliday, R. (2022). Institutional betrayal and closeness among women veteran survivors of military sexual trauma: Associations with self-directed violence and mental health symptoms. *Journal of trauma & dissociation: the official journal of the International Society for the Study of Dissociation (ISSD)*, 1–19. Advance online publication. doi:https://doi.org/10.1080/15299732.2022.2120152.

Mueser, K. T., Salyers, M. P., Rosenberg, S. D., Ford, J. D., Fox, L., & Carty, P. (2001). Psychometric evaluation of trauma and posttraumatic stress disorder assessments in persons with severe mental illness. *Psychological Assessment, 13*(1), 110–117. https://doi.org/10.1037/1040-3590.13.1.110

Murphy-Oikonen, J., McQueen, Miller, A., Chambers, L., & Hiebert, A. (2022). Unfounded sexual assault: Women's experiences of not being believed by the police. *Journal of Interpersonal Violence, 37*(11–12), NP8916. https://doi.org/10.1177/0886260520978190

Nabavi, B., Mitchell, A. J., & Nutt, D. (2015). A lifetime prevalence of comorbidity between bipolar affective disorder and anxiety disorders: A meta-analysis of 52 interview-based studies of psychiatric population. *eBioMedicine, 2*(10), 1405–1419. https://doi.org/10.1016/j.ebiom.2015.09.006

Nishith, P., Morse, G., & Dell, N. A. (2024). Effectiveness of cognitive processing therapy for PTSD in serious mental illness. *Journal of Behavioral and Cognitive Therapy, 34*(1), 100486.

Norton, M. J., & Flynn, C. (2020). The evidence base for wellness recovery action planning (WRAP): A protocol for a systematic literature review and meta-analysis. *International Journal of Environmental Research and Public Health, 18*(24), 13365. https://doi.org/10.3390/ijerph182413365

Olmos-Ochoa, T. T., Niv, N., Hellemann, G., Cohen, A. N., Oberman, R., Goldberg, R., & Young, A. S. (2019). Barriers to participation in web-based and in-person weight management interventions for serious mental illness. *Psychiatric Rehabilitation Journal, 42*(3), 220–228. https://doi.org/10.1037/prj0000363

Opler, M. G. A., Yavorsky, C., & Daniel, D. G. (2017). Positive and negative syndrome scale (PANSS) training: Challenges, solutions, and future directions. *Innovations in clinical neuroscience, 14*(11–12), 77–81.

Paolini, E., Moretti, P., & Compton, M. T. (2016). Delusions in first-episode psychosis: Principal component analysis of twelve types of delusions and demographic and clinical correlates of resulting domains. *Psychiatry Research, 243*, 5–13. https://doi.org/10.1016/j.psychres.2016.06.002

Payne, J. D., Nadel, L., Britton, W. B., & Jacobs, J. (2004). The biopsychology of trauma and memory. In D. Reisberg & P. Hertel (Eds.), *Memory and emotion, series in affective science*. Oxford Academic. Accessed 26 Aug 2023 from. https://doi.org/10.1093/acprof:oso/9780195158564.003.0003

Paz-Alonso, P. M., & Goodman, G. S. (2008). Trauma and memory: Effects of post-event misinformation, retrieval order, and retention interval. *Memory (Hove, England), 16*(1), 58–75. https://doi.org/10.1080/09658210701363146

Powers, A., Fani, N., Cross, D., Ressler, K. J., & Bradley, B. (2016). Childhood trauma, PTSD, and psychosis: Findings from a highly traumatized, minority sample. *Child Abuse & Neglect, 58*, 111–118. https://doi.org/10.1016/j.chiabu.2016.06.015

Pratt, L. A. (2012). Characteristics of adults with serious mental illness in the United States household population in 2007. *Psychiatric Services, 63*(10), 1042–1046. https://doi.org/10.1176/appi.ps.201100442

Rajji, T. K., Voineskos, A. N., Butters, M. A., Miranda, D., Arenovich, T., Menon, M., Ismail, Z., Kern, R. S., & Mulsant, B. H. (2013). Cognitive performance of individuals with schizophrenia across seven decades: A study using the MATRICS consensus cognitive battery. *The American Journal of Geriatric Psychiatry: Official Journal of the American Association for Geriatric Psychiatry, 21*(2), 108–118. https://doi.org/10.1016/j.jagp.2012.10.011

Sacks, S. A., Chard, K. M, & Healy, E. T. (2025). Cognitive processing therapy for veterans with posttraumatic stress disorder and co-occurring schizophrenia-spectrum disorders: Data from the veterans affairs CPT training program. Manuscript in preparation.

Salyers, M. P., Evans, L. J., Bond, G. R., & Meyer, P. S. (2004). Barriers to assessment and treatment of posttraumatic stress disorder and other trauma-related problems in people with severe mental illness: Clinician perspectives. *Community Mental Health Journal, 40*, 17–31. https://doi.org/10.1023/A:1024794232175

Semahegn, A., Torpey, K., Manu, A., Assefa, N., Tesfaye, G., & Ankomah, A. (2020). Psychotropic medication non-adherence and its associated factors among patients with major psychiatric disorders: A systematic review and meta-analysis. *Systematic Reviews, 9*(1), 17. https://doi.org/10.1186/s13643-020-1274-3

Serious Mental Illness Treatment, Research, and Evaluation Center (SMITREC). (2020). *Care for veterans with psychosis in the veterans health administration, FY20, 22nd Annual National Psychosis Registry Report*.

Seow, L. S. E., Ong, C., Mahesh, M. V., Sagayadevan, V., Shafie, S., Chong, S. A., & Subramaniam, M. (2016). A systematic review on comorbid post-traumatic stress disorder in schizophrenia. *Schizophrenia Research, 176*(2–3), 441–451. https://doi.org/10.1016/j.schres.2016.05.004

Sheffield, J. M., Williams, L. E., Blackford, J. U., & Heckers, S. (2013). Childhood sexual abuse increases risk of auditory hallucinations in psychotic disorders. *Comprehensive Psychiatry, 54*(7), 1098–1104. https://doi.org/10.1016/j.comppsych.2013.05.01

Shors, T. J., & Millon, E. M. (2016). Sexual trauma and the female brain. *Frontiers in Neuroendocrinology, 41*, 87–98. https://doi.org/10.1016/j.yfrne.2016.04.001

Sijercic, I., Liebman, R. E., Stirman, S. W., & Monson, C. M. (2021). The effect of therapeutic alliance on dropout in cognitive processing therapy for posttraumatic stress disorder. *Journal of Traumatic Stress, 34*(4), 819–828. https://doi.org/10.1002/jts.22676

Steenhuis, L. A., Pijnenborg, G. H. M., Visser, E., van de Willige, G., van Beilen, M., Nauta, M., Aleman, A., & Bartels-Velthuis, A. A. (2019). The development, validity, and reliability of the auditory vocal hallucination rating scale questionnaire (AVHRS-Q). *Social Psychiatry and Psychiatric Epidemiology, 54*(8), 927–935. https://doi.org/10.1007/s00127-019-01692-z

Stirman, S. W., Gutner, C. A., Suvak, M. K., Adler, A., Calloway, A., & Resick, P. (2018). Homework completion, patient characteristics, and symptom change in cognitive processing therapy for PTSD. *Behavior Therapy, 49*(5), 741–755. https://doi.org/10.1016/j.beth.2017.12.001

Sweet, L. H., Primeau, M., Fichtner, C. G., & Lutz, G. (1998). Dissociation of affect recognition and mood state from blunting in patients with schizophrenia. *Psychiatry Research, 81*(3), 301–308. https://doi.org/10.1016/s0165-1781(98)00121-8

Upthegrove, R. (2018). Delusional beliefs in the clinical context. In L. Bortolotti (Ed.), *Delusions in context* (pp. 1–34). Springer International Publishing.

van den Berg, D. P., & van der Gaag, M. (2012). Treating trauma in psychosis with EMDR: A pilot study. *Journal of behavior therapy and experimental psychiatry., 43*(1), 664–671. https://doi.org/10.1016/j.jbtep.2011.09.011
van den Berg, D. P., De Bont, P. A., Van Der Vleugel, B. M., de Roos, C., De Jongh, A., Van Minnen, A., & Van der Gaag, M. (2015). Prolonged exposure vs eye movement desensitization and reprocessing vs wait list for posttraumatic stress disorder in patients with a psychotic disorder: A randomized clinical trial. *JAMA Psychiatry, 72*(3), 259–267. https://doi.org/10.1001/jamapsychiatry.2014.2637
van den Berg, D. P. G., de Bont, P. A. J. M., van der Vleugel, B. M., de Roos, C., de Jongh, A., van Minnen, A., & van der Gaag, M. (2016). Trauma-focused treatment in PTSD patients with psychosis: Symptom exacerbation, adverse events, and revictimization. *Schizophrenia Bulletin, 42*(3), 693–702. https://doi.org/10.1093/schbul/sbv172
Van den Berg, D., de Bont, P. A. J. M., van der Vleugel, B. M., de Roos, C., de Jongh, A., van Minnen, A., & van der Gaag, M. (2018). Long-term outcomes of trauma-focused treatment in psychosis. *The British Journal of Psychiatry: the Journal of Mental Science, 212*(3), 180–182. https://doi.org/10.1192/bjp.2017.30
Vieta, E., & Sanchez-Moreno, J. (2008). Acute and long-term treatment of mania. *Dialogues in Clinical Neuroscience, 10*(2), 165–179. https://doi.org/10.31887/DCNS.2008.10.2/evieta
Wachen, J. S. (2024). The use of practice assignments in cognitive processing therapy to promote cognitive and emotional change: A case study. *Journal of Clinical Psychology, 80*(5), 1161–1176. https://doi.org/10.1002/jclp.23632
Woolley, M. G., Smith, B. N., Micol, R. L., Farmer, C. C., & Galovski, T. E. (2023). Evaluating the relative contribution of patient effort and therapist skill in integrating homework into treatment for posttraumatic stress disorder. *Psychological trauma: theory, research, practice and policy*., Advance online publication, *16*, S742. https://doi.org/10.1037/tra0001459
Young, R. C., Biggs, J. T., Ziegler, V. E., & Meyer, D. A. (2000). Young Mania Rating Scale. In *Handbook of psychiatric measures* (pp. 540–542). American Psychiatric Association.
Zanelli, J., Reichenberg, A., Sandin, S., Morgan, C., Dazzan, P., Pilecka, I., Marques, T. R., Morgan, K., Young, A. H., & Mollon, J. (2022). Dynamic and static cognitive deficits in schizophrenia and bipolar disorder after the First episode. *Schizophrenia Bulletin, 48*(3), 590–598. https://doi.org/10.1093/schbul/sbab150

Chapter 5
Delivering CPT in the Context of Substance Use Disorders

Shannon M. Kehle-Forbes, Brittany C. Davis, Amy Williams, and Nicole Christ

Post-traumatic stress disorder (PTSD) and substance use disorder (SUD) comorbidity is widespread. Among those with SUD, over 35% have PTSD and 90% have trauma exposure (Grant et al., 2016). Between 15% and 42% of individuals with SUD have PTSD, and 28–52% of those with PTSD have a SUD (Barrett et al., 2014; Blanco et al., 2013; Drapkin et al., 2011; Heltemes et al., 2014; Gielen et al., 2012; Pietrzak et al., 2011; Simpson et al., 2019). Compared to those without SUD, those with PTSD and SUD have more severe PTSD symptoms and are more likely to have comorbid mental health diagnoses, perpetrate violence, have poor vocational and psychosocial functioning, report health complaints, and think about and attempt suicide. U.S. veterans with PTSD and alcohol use disorder (AUD) are three times more likely to attempt suicide than veterans with PTSD without AUD (Norman et al., 2018). Clients with comorbid PTSD and SUD have worse treatment outcomes than those with either condition in isolation. Attrition rates from PTSD treatment are higher among those with untreated comorbid SUD, and the presence of untreated

S. M. Kehle-Forbes (✉)
Women's Health Sciences Division, National Center for PTSD, Department of Veterans Affairs, Boston, MA, USA

Center for Care Delivery & Outcomes Research, Minneapolis VA Healthcare System, Minneapolis, MN, USA
e-mail: Shannon.Kehle-Forbes@va.gov

B. C. Davis
James A. Haley Veteran's Hospital, Tampa, FL, USA

A. Williams
The Headstrong Project, NY, New York, USA

N. Christ
Center for Care Delivery & Outcomes Research, Minneapolis VA Healthcare System, Minneapolis, MN, USA

J. S. Wachen, T. E. Galovski (eds.), *Cognitive Processing Therapy for Complex Cases*, CBT: Science Into Practice,
https://doi.org/10.1007/978-3-031-87356-0_5

PTSD decreases the likelihood of clients meeting their SUD treatment goals (Berke et al., 2019; Ouimette et al., 2003). Conversely, PTSD symptom reduction leads to reduced substance use and cravings (Coffey et al., 2006; Hien et al., 2018). The increased severity and worse prognosis for clients with co-occurring SUD and PTSD, combined with the potential benefits of reducing PTSD symptoms on SUD-related outcomes highlight the importance of successfully addressing both conditions.

Historically, there has been apprehension to engage clients with SUD in PTSD treatment until the individual had established several months of sobriety. This largely stems from a clinician belief that trauma-focused treatment will exacerbate PTSD symptoms (van Minnen et al., 2012) combined with the notion that cravings can be exacerbated due to increased PTSD severity (Simpson et al., 2012). However, examinations have revealed that these concerns may not be well supported. While comorbid SUD may increase the complexity of a presentation, PTSD treatment has remained effective across SUD severities, treatment types, and format of treatment delivery (Kline et al., 2023). Recent meta-analyses have found that treatment for SUD, either with or without a non-trauma-focused therapy for PTSD (e.g., coping skills), results in meaningful reductions in both PTSD and SUD symptoms (Roberts et al., 2022; Simpson et al., 2017). However, the delivery of trauma-focused therapies, such as cognitive processing therapy (CPT), alongside SUD treatment yields larger improvements in both PTSD and SUD outcomes. Importantly, none of the included studies found that trauma-focused therapy resulted in worse substance use, relapse, or symptom severity than SUD treatment only or non-trauma-focused therapies concurrent to SUD treatment. These emerging data led to recommendations in the Department of Veterans Affairs/Department of Defense Clinical Practice Guidelines for PTSD that guideline-consistent treatments for PTSD should be delivered alongside evidence-based SUD care (VA/DoD Clinical Practice Guideline Work Group, 2023).

While much of the research that has been conducted regarding trauma-focused therapy with clients with comorbid SUD has examined exposure-based treatments, there is increasing evidence regarding the use of CPT in this client population. Below, we provide a brief overview of the evidence supporting its use, then discuss its clinical application in clients with comorbid SUD.

Evidence Regarding Use of CPT with Co-occurring SUD

An early study of CPT in veterans with SUD involved a chart review of medical records to examine differences among outpatients with PTSD, PTSD and current AUD, and PTSD and past AUD who initiated CPT (Kaysen et al., 2014). The study found no difference in the number of sessions attended by AUD diagnostic status or in the number of participants completing at least 12 CPT sessions (i.e., those considered to be "treatment completers") among the three groups. Further, results from this study found no interaction between AUD diagnosis and treatment outcome;

PTSD and depression symptoms improved over the course of treatment regardless of the presence or absence of AUD diagnosis and there was no difference in treatment discontinuation between the groups. Of note, those with diagnoses of past AUD presented with more severe PTSD symptoms than those with PTSD alone. Despite this, there were no differences in post-treatment symptom severity between these groups, suggesting that individuals with initially higher symptom severity can both tolerate and benefit from CPT. Finally, the post-treatment severity scores for PTSD and depression were comparable to those reported in CPT trials, suggesting that substance use did not decrease the effectiveness of CPT.

A second study that conducted a retrospective review of records found similarly promising results. Baig et al. (2021) compared the effect of group CPT to Seeking Safety, a non-trauma-focused treatment frequently used with dually diagnosed individuals, in U.S. veterans with PTSD and co-occurring alcohol use disorder. Clients who completed CPT experienced greater reductions in PTSD symptom severity than those who completed Seeking Safety. These findings mirror the conclusions of the meta-analyses discussed above in that while both CPT and Seeking Safety significantly reduced PTSD symptom severity, the greatest effects are found in those whom complete CPT.

Several recent randomized clinical trials (RCTs) have further shed light on the delivery of CPT among clients with co-occurring SUD. In one study (Simpson et al., 2021), individual CPT resulted in reasonably comparable outcomes to a first-line treatment for addiction recovery, Relapse Prevention (RP). Specifically, both CPT and RP demonstrated substantial pre- to post-treatment reductions in PTSD severity and number of days drinking. Compared to an assessment only control group, CPT demonstrated statistically significant PTSD symptom reduction whereas RP did not. Interestingly, neither CPT nor RP outperformed the assessment only group in reducing number of drinking days, though they both demonstrated significantly reduced heavy drinking days compared to the control group. Finally, although there was a slightly greater reduction in PTSD severity in CPT and a slightly greater reduction in days drinking in RP, there was no significant difference in either metric between the two groups. However, individuals in RP demonstrated a 45% greater reduction in heavy drinking days compared to CPT participants.

ElBarazi et al. (2022) evaluated the comparable tolerability and effectiveness of sertraline to CPT in individuals dually diagnosed with PTSD and SUD. Sertraline is a recommended treatment for PTSD (VA/DoD Clinical Practice Guideline Work Group, 2023) that also has a positive impact on substance use outcomes (e.g., Brady et al., 2005; Huang et al., 2020). Both the CPT and the sertraline groups produced greater reductions in PTSD, substance use, and depression symptoms than the control group. However, in comparing CPT to sertraline, CPT demonstrated significantly greater reductions in PTSD severity at post-treatment, to a large effect. Finally, participants in the CPT group demonstrated greater reductions in SUD risk factors and greater increases in SUD protective factors compared to either the sertraline or control group. Given that sertraline alone did demonstrate significant effects compared to the control group, it is possible that combined CPT + sertraline may have even greater effects on individuals with comorbid PTSD and SUD, though this has yet to be examined. Notably, as much of the literature centers around veteran samples, primarily with alcohol use disorder, this study demonstrates the effectiveness of CPT in a non-U.S., non-veteran community sample with a diverse sampling of substance use disorder types and severities.

Finally, in a secondary analysis of data from a randomized clinical trial, Straud et al. (2021) attempted to answer the question of whether CPT treatment format (i.e., group vs. individual) impacted PTSD treatment outcomes in a sample of active-duty service members with PTSD and with or without hazardous drinking. Consistent with prior research, results demonstrated there was no difference in treatment discontinuation or number of sessions attended by group (hazardous vs. nonhazardous drinking or group vs. individual format). All groups evidenced significant improvement in pre- to post-treatment PTSD severity and hazardous drinking with medium-to-large effects, regardless of treatment format or drinking status. These findings suggest that individual and group CPT appear to produce comparable reductions in PTSD severity in for those with co-occurring hazardous drinking. Importantly, no individuals experienced increased drinking behavior from pre- to post-treatment. Nevertheless, despite these positive treatment outcomes, approximately one-third of hazardous drinkers retained "hazardous drinking" status following CPT, though the small proportion of hazardous drinkers in this sample (16.8%) limits the interpretations of this finding. Though the study was underpowered to examine treatment format differences in retention of hazardous drinking status, one advantage to individual therapy may be that it offers more flexible options for clinicians to tailor the content of treatment to meet an individual's specific presenting problems or substance-related stuck points. Relatedly, another secondary analysis of data from a CPT trial with active duty servicemembers found that those with hazardous drinking were as likely to achieve good end-state functioning and no more likely to drop out of variable-length individual CPT than those without hazardous drinking (LoSavio et al., 2023). Interestingly, and partially consistent with findings by Straud et al. (2021), there was evidence that those with hazardous drinking experienced greater PTSD symptom reductions than those without (LoSavio et al., 2023).

In sum, CPT has demonstrated effectiveness for individuals with co-occurring PTSD and SUD across the randomized and non-randomized trials conducted to-date. Although medication and substance use-focused interventions (e.g., Relapse Prevention, Seeking Safety) produce improvements in PTSD severity, CPT consistently demonstrated equal or greater reductions. While additional research is needed to confirm these initial findings, these studies strongly suggest CPT is both a tolerable and effective treatment for individuals with comorbid PTSD and SUD. In the studies reviewed above, CPT was delivered without modifications to account for the dual diagnosis. However, by nature of the treatment, CPT may present an opportunity to tailor the elements of treatment to meet the unique presentation and needs of these individuals. Below we discuss the clinical application of CPT for clients with co-occurring SUD, including minor modifications we often employ to account for the comorbidity.

Clinical Application of CPT for Clients with Comorbid SUD

As previously discussed within this chapter, there are many reasons that support the importance of PTSD treatment for clients with a PTSD/SUD comorbidity. Historically, a sequential approach to treatment was normative—requiring some length of abstinence (~90 days) prior to being offered PTSD treatment (Ouimette & Brown, 2003; Tripp et al., 2020). Unfortunately, this approach often led to prolonged distress and potential risk of not receiving PTSD treatment. To date, clinician fears continue to hinder providing trauma-focused care to their clients with PTSD/SUD. Clinicians report being less likely to engage in or offer CPT alongside active SUD (Thomas et al., 2023). Many may elect to engage in sequential model of care and it is often unclear whether clients are being involved in this decision making. These fears may occur in the most skilled providers; those who are proficient in trauma-focused treatment but may have little to no experience working with those struggling with alcohol and other substance use disorders. Although beliefs may be rooted in the concern of the client, this perpetuates a therapeutic approach that is not supported by research, fragilizes the client, and removes client choice from the treatment plan. Providers who have difficulty managing this comorbidity may ask themselves questions such as:

- *What if my clients can't handle doing trauma work?*
- *Will doing trauma work increase their use?*
- *Will this work worsen their symptoms?*

Over the last 20 years, research has continued to challenge the notion that SUD comorbidity is a barrier to trauma-focused care (VA/DoD Clinical Practice Guideline Work Group, 2023). CPT is a widely implemented intervention for the treatment of PTSD, and as reviewed above, clients with a PTSD/SUD comorbidity have been shown to have tolerance for the intervention and reduction of trauma symptoms (Kaysen et al., 2014; Peck et al., 2018; Simpson et al., 2022), as well as reduction of heavy alcohol use (Haller et al., 2016). The following section is designed to empower clinicians to implement CPT with minimal modifications while still addressing both PTSD and problematic substance use. Housed in cognitive-behavioral theory, the concepts presented and the practice assignments implemented within the therapy protocol easily lend themselves to include substance use recovery. A case example is embedded within this section to provide additional guidance. With this information, clinicians should feel more confident in treating complex clients with PTSD/SUD comorbidity.

Case Example: Background

Sarah, a 35-year-old Caucasian cisgender female, presented for treatment following an incident in which she drove under the influence of alcohol and crashed her vehicle. While not physically injured, Sarah was charged with a DUI and the loss of her vehicle resulted in unemployment. She had been struggling with the aftermath of a physically and emotionally abusive relationship to which she attributed her alcohol use. Sarah was diagnosed with PTSD and AUD, and agreed to begin therapy with the goals of reducing her PTSD symptoms as well as the frequency and amount of alcohol use. The therapist and Sarah agreed to a course of CPT to focus on the intimate partner violence (IPV) in her previous relationship. Sarah disclosed childhood abuse which was also addressed in addition to IPV. CPT was delivered on a weekly basis with 50-min sessions for about four months via 12 CPT sessions and one emergency/crisis session.

Setting the Stage: Considerations Prior to Starting CPT

Prior to starting the CPT protocol, clinicians should discuss the client's treatment goals related to both PTSD symptom reduction and substance use. Information should be gathered regarding current and past patterns of both frequency and amount of use, providing markers for assessment during the CPT protocol. Abstinence from substances is not required for CPT treatment, and the clinician should not assume that as a treatment goal. The client's substance use goal should be driven by them, by asking specifically how they would like to reduce their use (e.g., abstain, harm reduction, moderation). Goals should be frequently revisited over the course of treatment, as it is common for goals to change or require modifications. Table 5.1 presents sample language for use at different stages of CPT, including the initial discussion regarding substance use.

This preliminary work is also an opportunity to review the expectations of treatment with regard to substance use. Clients are encouraged to fully engage in the CPT protocol and increase self-efficacy around their ability to tolerate distress without substance use. Therefore, clients are asked to refrain from use prior to, during, and immediately after both therapy sessions and practice assignments. Clients should be informed that, as a part of their standard check-in each week, the clinician will assess their substance use and cravings. Queries should be directive and open-ended (e.g., "How much have you used since our last appointment?"), staying away from leading statements such as "You didn't use over the past week, right?" or "You're doing so great in treatment. You haven't been having cravings, have you?"

Clinicians should also establish a clear policy of what will happen if a client comes to session when high, intoxicated, or in active detox or recovery from a substance (e.g., hungover). The guiding principle remains whether the client can engage with the therapeutic material of trauma-focused treatment. Depending on the degree of impairment, the therapist may problem-solve about their use, remind them of

Table 5.1 Sample language for addressing SUD in the context of CPT

Prior to Session 1: SUD Assessment & Setting Expectations
• Tell me, how much are you drinking each day throughout the week? Are you using any other substances? Have you in the past? • There are a lot of different ways people reduce their use, some people choose to completely cut out alcohol where others learn to moderate their use. What are your goals for your substance use? • In addition to checking in each week regarding your out of session assigned worksheets, I'll be checking in with you each week about your substance use. • In cognitive therapy, it's important for you to be clear-headed about how you're thinking and feeling. Sometimes people who are struggling with substance use come to therapy when using or drinking, which clouds one's ability to get the benefits of treatment. If this happens during our sessions, I will make sure you are safe, and we will reschedule for a later time.
Early Treatment: Discussing SUD-Related Avoidance
• When people with PTSD experience memories or symptoms that intrude on them in an unwanted or unexpected way, it is common to want to escape or avoid them. There are many ways to avoid including drinking or using drugs. This usually works in the short-term but because it doesn't work in the long-term, people often drink or use more often to try and keep PTSD in check. In fact, people with PTSD and substance use are more likely to relapse than those with substance use alone. In the long-term, avoidance keeps you from recovering.
Mid-Treatment: Discussing Increased Use
• It seems like there has been a slight increase in your use. Let's take a moment to identify some of your thoughts associated with your use this past week, revisit your current substance use goals, and also target some ways that you may be able to practice strategies to move towards your goal this week. • It sounds like the weekend was difficult for you in terms of staying on track with your goal of not smoking after the fight with your partner. Could we do a CBW on what was going through your mind after the argument? Maybe that is tied to the slip?
End Stage: Evaluating Progress & SUD Treatment Needs
• Let's take some time to process your overall gains. Overall, your PTSD symptoms have continued to drop and I can see what your mood has improved. However, since about mid-treatment you have not reported a reduction in your alcohol use. Have you hit your reduction goal? If not, we can explore what your next steps in treatment may look like.
Addressing Use Prior to CPT Sessions
• "I understand that this is very difficult, and that you have been using a substance to cope with distress for a long time. This process is something new, and it will eventually get easier. For us to work on your trauma we cannot have you use any substances before, during, or directly after our sessions or practice assignments. It seemed like today something got in the way of that. Can you tell me what occurred? Do you think that you will be able to attend our next session without using?" • "You reported drinking a lot last night. It seems like you aren't able to concentrate on our session today. I really want to provide you the best care, but that also requires you being able to engage in the material. Instead of the session today—why don't you tell me the reasons for drinking last night?"

treatment rationale around abstaining, and encourage them to continue their practice of cognitive skills prior to the next session. Depending on the severity of the client's substance use, additional parameters may also be set as an expectation (e.g., breathalyzer prior to session) (McCarthy & Petrakis, 2011). Example language for setting these parameters is provided in Table 5.1.

Case Example: Pre-treatment

Prior to initiating CPT, the therapist and Sarah discussed her pattern of drinking which tended to be restricted to the evenings and on weekends. She agreed that she would be able to attend therapy sessions while sober as well as to complete assignments while not drinking. Her goals related to AUD were to decrease the number of days during the week that she drank and, if she drank, to limit it to one glass of wine. She agreed to track her urges to drink, the days that she drank, and the most she drank on any given day.

CPT: Initial Stage

The purpose of CPT is to decrease trauma symptoms and resolve PTSD. While the clinician and client are tracking substance use in terms of frequency, amount, and cravings, the focus of the initial stage of CPT should be on psychoeducation and identifying stuck points related to the index trauma. Within the CPT manual, substance use is conceptualized as an avoidance behavior, utilized as a maladaptive way that clients may distance themselves from their trauma memory which keeps them stuck in PTSD. This is discussed with the client in Session 1 (see Table 5.1 for example language). For clients with SUD, the clinician may spend additional time on this conceptualization and reinforce pre-treatment rationale for abstaining during practice assignments and before and immediately after sessions.

For many clients, trauma-related cognitions will be related to problematic substance use and relapse. Although it is not necessary to specifically ask clients to attend to these beliefs in the impact statement, the clinician is encouraged to listen for relevant stuck points in Session 2 when creating the Stuck Point Log. This is especially true if the trauma involved alcohol or another substance. Clinicians may also identify maladaptive thinking surrounding the function of their substance use and how it relates to their trauma symptoms. For any SUD-related cognitions, it may be helpful to add them to the Stuck Point Log to address in treatment after assimilated cognitions are addressed.

Examples of SUD-related cognitions that may be added to Stuck Point Log include:

- Drinking is the only way I can get to sleep.
- Smoking pot is the only way I can get along with my spouse.
- I should just be able to drink like a normal person.
- I was raped because I was drinking.... It was my fault.
- I can't tolerate talking about my trauma without drinking.
- I can't be intimate with my spouse unless I'm drunk.
- Being high is the only time I feel in control.

Case Example: Initial Stage

In the initial Impact Statement and Stuck Point Log, Sarah identified assimilated stuck points related to shame and self-loathing. She also asserted that her drinking helped her escape these thoughts. Her Stuck Point Log, although primarily focused on trauma-related cognitions, included beliefs also related to her recent DUI and alcohol use. For example, "I am weak", "I screw everything up", and "I can't tolerate being around men without drinking."

Therapist: *Thank you for reading your Impact Statement. I noticed that you focused on the abuse from your partner, but also included some thoughts related to the events from present day. Let's take some time to identify stuck points...let's start with the abuse from your partner.*

Sarah: *This is really hard...The thought that stands out to me and causes so much distress is that the abuse was my fault. My friends and the police have made statements that I didn't cause this. But I really FEEL like the abuse was my fault. I also think that there is something wrong with me, and I will be abused again because I can't do anything right.*

Therapist: *Those are very powerful statements to catch. Let's go ahead and put each separate statement on your log. I also notice you included some thoughts about your current alcohol use. What are some of those thoughts that stand out to you?*

Sarah: *It really comes down to me believing I can't handle life without drinking. It's the only way I can be around men. It is the only way I can do what I need to do each day with thoughts about the abuse constantly in my head. It's the only sway I can sleep. I can't function without it.*

Therapist: *Let's also add each of those thoughts to your Stuck Point Log. I think we will see over time that there will be a lot of overlapping thoughts between your use and the abuse and your PTSD symptoms. That is why catching all of your stuck point thoughts may be meaningful to treatment. As thoughts come up that seem like they could be stuck points related to your traumas, how you view yourself, others, and the world, as well as your thoughts surrounding your misuse of alcohol—try to catch them and place them on your Stuck Point Log. However, to really target your trauma symptoms, we will first focus on the thoughts deeply tied to the abuse, such as those thoughts about self-blame. As treatment progresses, we will start to expand to include challenging other thoughts on your log.*

CPT: Middle Stage

The middle stage of CPT includes processing the trauma and learning to challenge stuck points, prioritizing assimilated cognitions over over-accommodated cognitions. Although we encourage the client to track their substance use throughout the week and continue to assess at each session, as is typical in CPT, the focus in early sessions is on assimilated stuck points. Once assimilated stuck points have been addressed and trauma symptoms have started to decrease, the clinician may start to challenge substance use and over-accommodated stuck points. However, if substance use is interfering with treatment conduct or progress, the therapist may on occasion directly address substance-related stuck points earlier in treatment with the goal of resolving the exacerbation so that CPT can continue.

Within Session 4, guilt- and shame-based assimilated cognitions are challenged by assisting the client in understanding the difference between intention, responsibility, and the unforeseeable. Following this discussion, clients may identify and include additional substance-related stuck points on their log, as guilt and shame cognitions are also common with those struggling with substance use disorders. These cognitions may be related to their self-perception of relapse, letting others down, or engaging in behaviors that have gone against their moral compass.

As assimilated stuck points begin to resolve, clinicians should begin to weave in SUD-related cognitions by assigning specific Challenging Beliefs Worksheets (CBWs; note the label for CBWs has recently been changed to Alternative Thoughts Worksheets) for activating events related to cravings, use, or lapses. The clinician may also start to have more active discussions on the relationship between substance use and trauma-related symptoms, reviewing the negative impact of use, and identifying coping strategies to promote decreased substance use (see Table 5.1 for example language).

Case Example: Middle Stage

At each session, Sarah reported on the number of days she experienced cravings, the intensity of the urges, how many days she drank, and the amount she drank. Her use slightly decreased with attention and tracking. However, as Sarah's PTSD symptoms ameliorated utilizing CPT, the therapist noted that there was not a correlating reduction in her alcohol use. Although she had reduced her drinking but was still binge drinking once or twice per week. Sarah agreed to complete CBWs on her thoughts related to cravings and her use. Sarah and the therapist had identified a trigger of being emotionally distressed. However, Sarah's distress had largely been alleviated. Her belief that "I drink because it's the only way I can handle my PTSD symptoms" became a cognition to be challenged based on her behavior.

Therapist: *We are about halfway through the treatment. I'd like for us to take a few moments to check in regarding your progress and treatment goals. You have been working really hard, challenging beliefs around guilt and self-blame. I have noticed that you have shifted your language about the abuse being your fault and are now understanding that you were not in control of your partner's actions.*

Sarah: *Yes, I agree. I am noticing I am starting to look at the events from our relationship differently. It's difficult because a lot of the time I still FEEL guilty, but I'm able to take a step back and look at the whole picture. The worksheets are really helping with that part.*

Therapist: *That's excellent, we will make sure that we continue to focus on that as we progress. Shifting gears, I would like to make an observation and provide some feedback, is that something you would be comfortable with?*

Sarah**:** *Yes, of course. I'm really trying to make the most of this.*

Therapist: *When we started, you identified that your use of alcohol was closely tied with feeling distressed.*

Sarah: *Yes, I agree. I did not think I could handle thinking about my trauma or being around people without drinking.*

Therapist: *Lately, your distress has significantly decreased. However, you are continuing to report high cravings to drink and have only had a slight decrease in your use.*

Sarah: *Hmm... I haven't really thought about that very much. But, I guess you are right about that... if I look back at my tracking week to week there hasn't been a lot of changes with my drinking.*

Therapist: *Would you be open to challenging the thought "I drink because I can't handle my PTSD symptoms without alcohol" this week. This might give you some additional insight into your use and help us strategize how to continue to reduce your drinking.*

Sarah: *Sure, I can do that.*

CPT: Ending Stage of Treatment

Within Sessions 8–12, the focus is shifted away from assimilated cognitions to over-accommodated cognitions. For each of the schema-based topics (safety, trust, power and control, esteem, and intimacy), the CPT therapist can target SUD-related stuck points specific to that area (e.g., Power/Control = The only way I can control my emotions around men is by drinking). Session 10 lends a natural place to introduce relapse prevention and preparation for discharge. When assigning engagement in a daily pleasurable activity, focus on examples that replace use-based activities or avoid use-based triggers (e.g., people, places, situations). The clinician is encouraged to be nuanced in this discussion, so that the client can understand the difference between avoidance of trauma reminders/cognitions versus being in situations that place them at risk for relapse.

At the end of treatment, the overall discussion focuses on both the progress made as well as suggested next steps in relation to both PTSD and substance use. Based upon the needs of the client, an additional session may be added post-CPT dedicated to the development of a relapse prevention plan and to strategize next steps to maintain treatment gains. For many, as PTSD symptoms improve, so do their problematic use patterns; however, this is not the case for all. Additional insights into the client's pattern of use may suggest it is more habitual in nature or may not be closely linked to trauma-symptoms. In these circumstances, the next recommended steps in treatment may be substance-focused interventions (see Table 5.1 for example language).

Case Example: Ending Stage

Sarah completed CPT and her PTSD remitted. Her course of treatment included 12 CPT sessions and one emergency session (described in more detail below) that occurred after CPT Session 4 following an episode of binge drinking. Apart from the emergency session, the early sessions focused on assimilated stuck points with only brief monitoring of SUD symptoms during homework review. Around Session 7 as Sarah's PTSD symptoms began to improve, the therapist began to integrate SUD-specific stuck points alongside other over-accommodated beliefs. In the last sessions of CPT, she and the therapist were able to cover the relevant CPT protocol items and spend additional time on identifying triggers for Sarah's use. Without the layer of PTSD symptoms, Sarah continued to drink out of habit and boredom. Following completion of CPT, Sarah and her therapist enacted several behavioral interventions to address her boredom (e.g., working out) as well as make changes in her environment and routine (e.g., heading straight to the gym after work, stocking the refrigerator with nonalcoholic beverages). These additional, cognitive-behavioral interventions assisted Sarah in reaching her goal of reduced frequency and amount of drinking. Therapy was terminated based on mutual agreement.

Therapist: *You've made some remarkable progress over the course of treatment. I noticed that your thoughts about yourself in your Impact Statement have drastically shifted from our first session. Tell me, what are some of the things that you noticed have shifted?*

Sarah: *Not just my thoughts, but I'm feeling so differently about myself. For such a long time I blamed myself for the abuse from my partner. I justified what he was doing to me because I thought I had done something wrong. I think that's because I thought the abuse I suffered as a child was also my fault. I know this was not my fault. I deserve better, I want to be better.*

Therapist: *That is amazing. Congratulations... your hard work has really paid off. I know for a long time you reported that you were drinking to cover up your feelings. You have also made notable changes in your drinking. What are your thoughts on your moderation of alcohol? Where are you at in relation to your goals?*

Sarah: *Well....I do think that I have significantly reduced my drinking...and I'm surprised to learn some things about myself and alcohol.*

Therapist: *What do you mean?*

Sarah: *Well...I was surprised that I had cravings to drink even when I was feeling good. I would not say that I have hit my goal yet. I realize this is not as easy as I thought, but I've been trying to use the strategies we discussed. I have been practicing occupying my time with healthy activities, going to the gym and cooking. I have not been buying alcohol, so there is not any in my home. At work events I have been ordering mocktails to feel like I'm having a drink with my colleagues. I know you mentioned that I could be referred to a psychiatrist for medications to assist with my cravings, but that is not something I want to do...at least not yet. I'm hoping the more I practice the easier it will be.*

Therapist: *It seems like you are being honest with yourself and confronting what is hard. That is what I hope continues. You seem to understand your resources if you need additional assistance, which includes reaching back out to me as needed.*

Additional Clinical Considerations

Use of Emergency or Crisis Sessions

CPT, like other manualized trauma-focused treatments, is individualistic and remains client-centered. When treating PTSD/SUD, clinicians may need to exercise flexibility to match the needs of their client; as they may present with increased psychosocial stressors, interpersonal conflicts (e.g., legal, marital, occupational), and potential exposure to additional trauma (e.g., drug overdose, deaths). CPT is already designed to be variable in length to match the needs of the client in practicing their skills to resolve trauma-related symptoms. However, if clinically warranted, the use of an "emergency or crisis session" may be considered as an option to address present stressors that may arise over the course of the treatment episode.

An emergency or crisis session is an off-protocol session that may still use the concepts learned in CPT but is focused on the present stressor rather than the trauma. These sessions should not be the initial "go to" response of the clinician as many crises presented over the course of treatment would not warrant an entire session deviation. Additionally, crises may be easier to discuss in treatment rather than their trauma, and the discussion of a stressor may be a form of avoidance. This is a tricky balance, as clinicians are encouraged to utilize clinical skills as to when an off-protocol session may be warranted, and when it may be better to challenge avoidance. Variability in length of care and the use of one or two emergency or crisis session(s) have not been shown to result in poorer treatment outcomes (Galovski et al., 2012).

It should be noted that a common pitfall of clinicians is assuming that a lapse or a relapse warrants an emergency or stressor session. Where lapses and relapses may be emotionally provocative, and potentially scary for both the client and clinician, in most cases a lapse/relapse can be worked into the CPT session material and would not require a deviation of care.

Case Example: Crisis Session

Between Session 4 and Session 5, Sarah and her therapist decided to utilize an emergency session after Sarah became intoxicated during an evening event for work at a local restaurant work event, leading to a meeting with her boss about her use. Sarah's re-experiencing symptoms were triggered by interactions with several male coworkers, which led to her consuming much more alcohol than planned. She left early after several conversations with coworkers and clients that she is unable to remember. The following day, her boss called a meeting to express concerns about her drinking and discuss potential consequences of overuse at work events should it happen again. Her shame-based thoughts (e.g., "I'm an idiot", "I keep screwing up") were mixed with fear and hopelessness for the future (e.g., "I embarrassed myself and ruined my career," "I am never going to be successful because of my mental health problems"). In addition to addressing the connection between her thoughts and feelings, the therapist helped problem-solve around the current situation as well as how to handle social requests with her alcohol use goals.

Clients Under the Influence in Session

When working with clients with SUD, the client may arrive to session under the influence of a substance or demonstrating signs of recent use that would impact their session (e.g., hungover, withdrawal symptoms). As stated within the pre-treatment planning session, a brief safety check and explanation as to why a session would not be beneficial at this time would be reviewed. If this becomes a pattern or the clinician is concerned about a steady increase in use, higher levels of care (e.g., intensive outpatient, residential, detox) or concurrent interventions (e.g., medication assisted therapies for substance use disorders) may be included in the treatment planning.

Treatment Across a Continuum of Care

Substance use treatment occurs across a continuum of care. In an ideal world, the client will be able to manage their substance use while appropriately engaging in CPT. However, it is not uncommon to have to adjust treatment plans to appropriately accommodate the needs of the client. Over the course of treatment, it may be mutually determined to increase the level of care to accommodate their substance use needs (e.g., detox, residential, intensive outpatient). If this occurs, the continuation of CPT would be determined largely based upon the restrictions of the clinician. For example, the case presented within this chapter focused on the delivery of CPT on a weekly basis as an outpatient. However, CPT has been delivered in residential settings with success while concurrently engaging in SUD programming (Peck et al., 2018).

Lastly, to promote efficacy and confidence working with this population, clinicians are encouraged to rely on the assistance of their resources. The terminology "it takes a village" is commonly utilized in SUD treatment communities. For a PTSD provider, this may be consultation with peers or formal consultation groups, and familiarizing themselves with community resources (e.g., mutual help groups; Alcoholics Anonymous; SMART Recovery). Based upon the clinician's work setting, they may also collaborate with psychiatry services to encourage discussions around medication assisted therapy (MAT) for alcohol and opioid disorders. It sometimes does truly take a village to provide effective care, while also preventing burnout. PTSD/SUD work can be difficult at times, however, providing care to clients that may have never been offered treatment can be an immensely validating experience.

Future Directions in Applying CPT in the Context of SUD

As described above, the application of CPT among clients with comorbid SUD has largely examined CPT with few modifications. Integrated treatments for PTSD and SUD, that include elements of both an evidence-based PTSD and SUD treatment within the sample protocol, have been widely tested and found effective. However, these protocols have almost exclusively integrated prolonged exposure therapy (e.g., concurrent treatment of PTSD and substance use disorders using prolonged exposures [COPE]; Back et al., 2014), rather than CPT. To date, there have been only preliminary case studies of integrated CPT treatments. In an initial case study (McCarthy & Petrakis, 2011), the CPT protocol was enhanced to integrate standard practices from the addiction field, including specific monitoring and targeting of alcohol-related behavior through treatment. Modifications also included additional psychoeducation on the function of alcohol use as avoidance and enhancing client understanding of the connection between PTSD and alcohol use. This modified CPT protocol resulted in clinically meaningful gains on both PTSD and alcohol use outcomes. More recently, Vujanovic et al. (2019) developed and pilot tested an integrated protocol that combined CPT and relapse prevention for SUD. They similarly found that the integrated treatment held promise for successfully reducing symptoms of PTSD and SUD. An RCT of an integrated CPT/relapse prevention protocol compared to relapse prevention alone in the treatment of co-occurring PTSD and SUD was recently funded; findings will provide more definitive data about the effectiveness of integrated approaches.

The role of group CPT in the treatment of comorbid PTSD and SUD warrants further study. The CPT protocol can be delivered in either individual or group format, both of which have demonstrated significant reductions in PTSD and depressive symptoms (Jeffreys et al., 2014; Lamp et al., 2019; Resick et al., 2017). However, in head-to-head comparisons, individual CPT results in greater reductions in PTSD and depressive symptoms than group CPT (Jeffreys et al., 2014; Lamp et al., 2019; Resick et al., 2017). As highlighted above, initial data suggest that individual and group CPT may result in similar benefits for those with comorbid SUD. These findings warrant further study given that group therapy may be a better fit and increase the implementability of CPT within SUD treatment settings, where group programming is common.

Finally, while the data reviewed above demonstrate that treatment discontinuation rates from CPT are similar for those with and without SUD, meta-analyses show that discontinuation is higher from integrated treatments that include a trauma-focus than those that don't specifically engage with trauma memories. Therefore, strategies for better engaging clients in CPT are warranted. Applying contingency management strategies to session attendance has been shown to increase engagement in PE among those with comorbid SUD (Schacht et al., 2017); a similar approach may be effective for CPT, although it may not be feasible in a variety of settings. Qualitative research has found that concerns about the negative impact of during-treatment symptom worsening differentiates those who do and do not complete trauma-focused therapy; as such, explicitly eliciting and challenging such beliefs within the context of CPT may be useful (Kehle-Forbes et al., 2022). Further, qualitative research suggests if the client is engaged in other treatment programs concurrent to CPT, involving the full care team to support the goal of completion may be an effective engagement strategy. Finally, massed CPT has been shown to reduce treatment discontinuation rates while retaining the treatment's potency (Galovski et al., 2022). Although it has not yet been studied in those with comorbid PTSD and SUD, massed PE has yielded promising results in this population (Watkins et al., 2023) and similar effects would be hypothesized for massed CPT. These and other engagement strategies should be the focus of future research with the goal of further improvement of CPT outcomes for this important client population.

Summary

In contrast to longstanding clinical lore, a growing body of data has shown that trauma-focused therapy is effective and tolerable to clients with comorbid SUD. Therapists can feel confident in providing CPT with few modifications to those with substance use. Setting shared expectations and boundaries regarding substance use, providing psychoeducation about the link between PTSD and substance use, integrating identification and challenging of stuck points related to substance use, and evaluating the need for additional SUD-related treatment during the termination process are minor modifications to the protocol that acknowledge and address the presence of SUD while maintaining CPT's trauma focus. Additional research is needed to guide clinicians in how to best integrate CPT and SUD treatments, the role of group CPT in treating those with comorbid SUD, and better engaging clients in CPT.

Competing Interests Shannon Kehle-Forbes, Ph.D. has received research grants on topics related to this chapter from the U.S. Department of Defense, U.S. Department of Veterans Affairs, and the Patient Centered Outcomes Research Institute. Brittany Davis, Ph.D. has received research grants on topics related to this chapter from the U.S. Department of Defense and Department of Veterans Affairs. Amy Williams, Ph.D. Dr. Williams receives honoraria for training and consulting in

CPT from the Patient Centered Outcomes Research Institute, Department of Veterans Affairs, and Texas Health and Human Services.

References

Back, S. E., Killeen, T. K., Cotton, B. D., & Carroll, K. M. (2014). *Concurrent treatment of PTSD and substance use disorders using prolonged exposure (COPE): Therapist guide*. Treatments That Work.

Baig, M. R., Ouyang, S., Mata-Galán, E., Dawes, M. A., & Roache, J. D. (2021). A comparison of cognitive processing therapy and seeking safety for the treatment of posttraumatic stress disorder in veterans. *Psychiatric Quarterly, 92*, 735–750. https://doi.org/10.1007/s11126-020-09850-2

Barrett, E. L., Teesson, M., & Mills, K. L. (2014). Associations between substance use, post-traumatic stress disorder and the perpetration of violence: A longitudinal investigation. *Addictive Behaviors, 39*(6), 1075–1080. https://doi.org/10.1016/j.addbeh.2014.03.003

Berke, D. S., Kline, N. K., Wachen, J. S., McLean, C. P., Yarvis, J. S., Mintz, J., Young-McCaughan, S., Peterson, A. L., Foa, E., Resick, P. A., Litz, B. T., & STRONG STAR Consortium. (2019). Predictors of attendance and dropout in three randomized controlled trials of PTSD treatment for active duty service members. *Behaviour Research and Therapy, 118*, 7–17. https://doi.org/10.1016/j.brat.2019.03.003

Blanco, C., Xu, Y., Brady, K., Pérez-Fuentes, G., Okuda, M., & Wang, S. (2013). Comorbidity of posttraumatic stress disorder with alcohol dependence among US adults: Results from National Epidemiological Survey on alcohol and related conditions. *Drug and Alcohol Dependence, 132*(3), 630–638. https://doi.org/10.1016/j.drugalcdep.2013.04.016

Brady, K. T., Sonne, S., Anton, R. F., Randall, C. L., Back, S. E., & Simpson, K. (2005). Sertraline in the treatment of co-occurring alcohol dependence and posttraumatic stress disorder. *Alcoholism: Clinical and Experimental Research, 29*(3), 395–401. https://doi.org/10.1097/01.ALC.0000156129.98265.57

Coffey, S. F., Stasiewicz, P. R., Hughes, P. M., & Brimo, M. L. (2006). Trauma-focused imaginal exposure for individuals with comorbid posttraumatic stress disorder and alcohol dependence: Revealing mechanisms of alcohol craving in a cue reactivity paradigm. *Psychology of Addictive Behaviors, 20*(4), 425. https://doi.org/10.1037/0893-164X.20.4.425

ElBarazi, A., Badary, O. A., Elmazar, M. M., & Elrassas, H. (2022). Cognitive processing therapy versus medication for the treatment of comorbid substance use disorder and post-traumatic stress disorder in Egyptian patients (randomized clinical trial). *Journal of evidence-based. Psychothérapies, 22*(2), 63. https://doi.org/10.24193/jebp.2022.2.13

Drapkin, M. L., Yusko, D., Yasinski, C., Oslin, D., Hembree, E. A., & Foa, E. B. (2011). Baseline functioning among individuals with posttraumatic stress disorder and alcohol dependence. *Journal of Substance Abuse Treatment, 41*(2), 186–192. https://doi.org/10.1016/2Fj.jsat.2011.02.012

Galovski, T. E., Blain, L. M., Mott, J. M., Elwood, L., & Houle, T. (2012). Manualized therapy for PTSD: Flexing the structure of cognitive processing therapy. *Journal of Consulting and Clinical Psychology, 80*(6), 968–981. https://doi.org/10.1037/a0030600

Galovski, T. E., Werner, K. B., Weaver, T. L., Morris, K. L., Dondanville, K. A., Nanney, J., McGlinchey, G., Fortier, C. B., & Iverson, K. M. (2022). Massed cognitive processing therapy for posttraumatic stress disorder in women survivors of intimate partner violence. *Psychological trauma: theory, research, practice, and policy, 14*(5), 769. https://doi.org/10.1037/tra0001100

Gielen, N., Havermans, R., Tekelenburg, M., & Jansen, A. (2012). Prevalence of post-traumatic stress disorder among patients with substance use disorder: It is higher than clinicians think it is. *European Journal of Psychotraumatology, 3*(1), 17734. https://doi.org/10.3402/ejpt.v3i0.17734

Grant, B. F., Saha, T. D., Ruan, W. J., Goldstein, R. B., Chou, S. P., Jung, J., Zhang, H., Smith, S. M., Pickering, R. P., Huang, B., & Hasin, D. S. (2016). Epidemiology of DSM-5 drug use disorder: Results from the National Epidemiologic Survey on alcohol and related conditions–III. *JAMA Psychiatry, 73*(1), 39–47. https://doi.org/10.1001/jamapsychiatry.2015.2132

Haller, M., Norman, S. B., Cummins, K., Trim, R. S., Xu, X., Cui, R., Allard, C. B., Brown, S. A., & Tate, S. R. (2016). Integrated cognitive behavioral therapy versus cognitive processing therapy for adults with depression, substance use disorder, and trauma. *Journal of Substance Use Treatment, 62*, 38–48. https://doi.org/10.1016/j.jsat.2015.11.005

Heltemes, K. J., Clouser, M. C., MacGregor, A. J., Norman, S. B., & Galarneau, M. R. (2014). Co-occurring mental health and alcohol misuse: Dual disorder symptoms in combat injured veterans. *Addictive Behaviors, 39*(2), 392–398. https://doi.org/10.1016/j.addbeh.2013.06.001

Hien, D. A., Smith, K. Z., Owens, M., López-Castro, T., Ruglass, L. M., & Papini, S. (2018). Lagged effects of substance use on PTSD severity in a randomized controlled trial with modified prolonged exposure and relapse prevention. *Journal of Consulting and Clinical Psychology, 86*(10), 810. https://doi.org/10.1037/ccp0000345

Huang, Z. D., Zhao, Y. F., Li, S., Gu, H. Y., Lin, L. L., Yang, Z. Y., Niu, Y. M., Zhang, C., & Luo, J. (2020). Comparative efficacy and acceptability of pharmaceutical management for adults with post-traumatic stress disorder: A systematic review and meta-analysis. *Frontiers in Pharmacology, 11*, 559. https://doi.org/10.3389/fphar.2020.00559

Jeffreys, M. D., Reinfeld, C., Nair, P. V., Garcia, H. A., Mata-Galan, E., & Rentz, T. O. (2014). Evaluating treatment of posttraumatic stress disorder with cognitive processing therapy and prolonged exposure therapy in a VHA specialty clinic. *Journal of Anxiety Disorders, 28*(1), 108–114. https://doi.org/10.1016/j.janxdis.2013.04.010

Kaysen, D., Schumm, J., Pedersen, E. R., Seim, R. W., Bedard-Gilligan, M., & Chard, K. (2014). Cognitive processing therapy for veterans with comorbid PTSD and alcohol use disorders. *Addictive Behaviors, 39*(2), 420–427. https://doi.org/10.1016/j.addbeh.2013.08.016

Kehle-Forbes, S. M., Ackland, P. E., Spoont, M. R., Meis, L. A., Orazem, R. J., Lyon, A., Valenstein-Mah, H. R., Schnurr, P. P., Zickmund, S. L., Foa, E. B., Chard, K. M., Alpert, E., & Polusny, M. A. (2022). Divergent experiences of US veterans who did and did not complete trauma-focused therapies for PTSD: A national qualitative study of treatment dropout. *Behaviour Research and Therapy, 154*, 104123. https://doi.org/10.1016/j.brat.2022.104123

Kline, A. C., Panza, K. E., Lyons, R., Kehle-Forbes, S. M., Hien, D. A., & Norman, S. B. (2023). Trauma-focused treatment for comorbid post-traumatic stress and substance use disorder. *Nature Reviews Psychology, 2*(1), 24–39. https://doi.org/10.1038/s44159-022-00129-w

Lamp, K. E., Avallone, K. M., Maieritsch, K. P., Buchholz, K. R., & Rauch, S. A. (2019). Individual and group cognitive processing therapy: Effectiveness across two veterans affairs posttraumatic stress disorder treatment clinics. *Psychological Trauma: Theory, Research, Practice, and Policy, 11*(2), 197. https://doi.org/10.1037/tra0000370

LoSavio, S. T., Straud, C. L., Dondanville, K. A., Fridling, N. R., Wachen, J. S., McMahon, C. J., Mintz, J., Young-McCaughan, S., Yarvis, J. S., Peterson, A. L., & Resick, P. A. (2023). Treatment responder status and time to response as a function of hazardous drinking among active-duty military receiving variable-length cognitive processing therapy for posttraumatic stress disorder. *Psychological Trauma: Theory, Research, Practice, and Policy, 15*(3), 386–393. https://doi.org/10.1037/tra0001268

McCarthy, E., & Petrakis, I. (2011). Case report on the use of cognitive processing therapy—Cognitive, enhanced to address heavy alcohol use. *Journal of Traumatic Stress, 24*(4), 474–478. https://doi.org/10.1002/jts.20660

Norman, S. B., Haller, M., Hamblen, J. L., Southwick, S. M., & Pietrzak, R. H. (2018). The burden of co-occurring alcohol use disorder and PTSD in US military veterans: Comorbidities, functioning, and suicidality. *Psychology of Addictive Behaviors, 32*(2), 224. https://doi.org/10.1037/adb0000348

Ouimette, P. E., & Brown, P. J. (2003). Trauma and substance abuse: Causes, consequences, and treatment of comorbid disorders. *American Psychological Association.* https://doi.org/10.1037/10460-000
Ouimette, P., Moos, R. H., & Finney, J. W. (2003). PTSD treatment and 5-year remission among patients with substance use and posttraumatic stress disorders. *Journal of Consulting and Clinical Psychology, 71*(2), 410. https://doi.org/10.1037/0022-006X.71.2.410
Peck, K. R., Coffey, S. F., McGuire, A. P., Voluse, A. C., & Connolly, K. M. (2018). A cognitive processing therapy-based treatment program for veterans diagnosed with co-occurring post-traumatic stress disorder and substance use disorder: The relationship between trauma-related cognitions and outcomes of a 6-week treatment program. *Journal of Anxiety Disorders, 59*, 34–41. https://doi.org/10.1016/j.janxdis.2018.09.001
Pietrzak, R. H., Goldstein, R. B., Southwick, S. M., & Grant, B. F. (2011). Prevalence and Axis I comorbidity of full and partial posttraumatic stress disorder in the United States: Results from wave 2 of the National Epidemiologic Survey on alcohol and related conditions. *Journal of Anxiety Disorders, 25*(3), 456–465. https://doi.org/10.1016/2Fj.janxdis.2010.11.010
Resick, P. A., Wachen, J. S., Dondanville, K. A., Pruiksma, K. E., Yarvis, J. S., Peterson, A. L., Mintz, J., & Strong Star Consortium. (2017). Effect of group vs individual cognitive processing therapy in active-duty military seeking treatment for posttraumatic stress disorder: A randomized clinical trial. *JAMA Psychiatry, 74*(1), 28–36. https://doi.org/10.1001/jamapsychiatry.2016.2729
Roberts, N. P., Lotzin, A., & Schäfer, I. (2022). A systematic review and meta-analysis of psychological interventions for comorbid post-traumatic stress disorder and substance use disorder. *European Journal of Psychotraumatology, 13*(1), 2041831.
Schacht, R. L., Brooner, R. K., King, V. L., Kidorf, M. S., & Peirce, J. M. (2017). Incentivizing attendance to prolonged exposure for PTSD with opioid use disorder patients: A randomized controlled trial. *Journal of Consulting and Clinical Psychology, 85*(7), 689. https://doi.org/10.1037/ccp0000208
Simpson, T. L., Stappenbeck, C. A., Varra, A. A., Moore, S. A., & Kaysen, D. (2012). Symptoms of posttraumatic stress predict craving among alcohol treatment seekers: Results of a daily monitoring study. *Psychology of Addictive Behaviors, 26*(4), 724. https://doi.org/10.1037/a0027169
Simpson, T. L., Lehavot, K., & Petrakis, I. L. (2017). No wrong doors: Findings from a critical review of behavioral randomized clinical trials for individuals with co-occurring alcohol/drug problems and posttraumatic stress disorder. *Alcoholism: Clinical and Experimental Research, 41*(4), 681–702. https://doi.org/10.1111/acer.13325
Simpson, T. L., Rise, P., Browne, K. C., Lehavot, K., & Kaysen, D. (2019). Clinical presentations, social functioning, and treatment receipt among individuals with comorbid life-time PTSD and alcohol use disorders versus drug use disorders: Findings from NESARC-III. *Addiction, 114*(6), 983–993. https://doi.org/10.1111/add.14565
Simpson, T. L., Goldberg, S. B., Louden, D. K., Blakey, S. M., Hawn, S. E., Lott, A., Browne, K. C., Lehavot, K., & Kaysen, D. (2021). Efficacy and acceptability of interventions for co-occurring PTSD and SUD: A meta-analysis. *Journal of Anxiety Disorders, 84*, 102490. https://doi.org/10.1016/j.janxdis.2021.102490
Simpson, T. L., Kaysen, D. L., Fleming, C. B., Rhew, I. C., & Jaffe., A.E., Desai, S., Hien, D.A., Berliner, L., Donovan, D., & Resick, P.A. (2022). Cognitive processing therapy or relapse prevention for comorbid posttraumatic stress disorder and alcohol use disorder: A randomized clinical trial. *PLoS One, 17*(11), e0276111. https://doi.org/10.1371/journal.pone.0276111
Straud, C. L., Dondanville, K. A., Hale, W. J., Wachen, J. S., Mintz, J., Litz, B. T., Roache, J. D., Yarvis, J. S., Young-McCaughan, S., Peterson, A. L., Resick, P. A., & STRONG STAR Consortium. (2021). The impact of hazardous drinking among active duty military with posttraumatic stress disorder: Does cognitive processing therapy format matter? *Journal of Traumatic Stress, 34*(1), 210–220. https://doi.org/10.1002/jts.22609
Thomas, F. C., Loskot, T., Mutschler, C., Burdo, J., Lagdaman, J., Sijercic, I., Lane, J. E. M., Liebman, R. E., Finley, E. P., Monson, C. M., & Wiltsey-Stirman, S. (2023). Initiating cognitive

processing therapy (CPT) in community settings: A qualitative investigation of therapist decision-making. *Administration and Policy in Mental Health and Mental Health Services Research, 50*(1), 137–150. https://doi.org/10.1007/s10488-022-01229-8

Tripp, J. C., Worley, M. J., Straus, E., Angkaw, A. C., Trim, R. S., & Norman, S. B. (2020). Bidirectional relationship of posttraumatic stress disorder (PTSD) symptom severity and alcohol use over the course of integrated treatment. *Psychology of Addictive Behaviors, 34*(4), 506–511. https://doi.org/10.1037/adb0000564

van Minnen, A., Harned, M. S., Zoellner, L., & Mills, K. (2012). Examining potential contraindications for prolonged exposure therapy for PTSD. *European Journal of Psychotraumatology, 3*(1), 18805. https://doi.org/10.3402/ejpt.v3i0.18805

VA/DoD Clinical Practice Guideline. (2023). *Management of Posttraumatic Stress Disorder and Acute Stress Disorder Work Group.* U.S. Government Printing Office.

Vujanovic, A. A., Smith, L. J., Tipton, K. P., & Schmitz, J. M. (2019). A novel, integrated cognitive-behavioral therapy for co-occurring posttraumatic stress and substance use disorders: A case study. *Cognitive and Behavioral Practice, 26*(2), 307–322. https://doi.org/10.1016/2Fj.cbpra.2018.03.003

Watkins, L. E., Patton, S. C., Drexler, K., Rauch, S. A., & Rothbaum, B. O. (2023). Clinical effectiveness of an intensive outpatient program for integrated treatment of comorbid substance abuse and mental health disorders. *Cognitive and Behavioral Practice, 30*(3), 354–366. https://doi.org/10.1016/j.cbpra.2022.05.005

Chapter 6
Delivering CPT in the Context of Traumatic Brain Injury and Physical Health Conditions

Amy Jak and Kristine Dell

Scope of the Problem

Events that result in physical trauma, including traumatic brain injury (TBI), often result in psychological trauma, so it is perhaps unsurprising that post-traumatic stress disorder (PTSD) is one of the most commonly occurring mental health conditions following TBI (Dilley & Avent, 2011). PTSD and history of mild traumatic brain injury (mTBI; also known as concussion) are highly comorbid conditions in military and Veteran populations, and they also commonly co-occur in civilian trauma, including following car accidents, assault, and interpersonal violence (IPV) (Van Praag et al., 2019). PTSD co-occurs in approximately 20% of those with history of concussion, a rate that is higher than seen in individuals with other non-TBI injuries (e.g., orthopedic injuries) (Albrecht et al., 2020). While the general expectation after concussion is full recovery, mental health factors, such as PTSD and depression, as well as sleep problems and chronic pain, all are known to contribute to persistent and increased symptom reporting well beyond the period of expected neurological recovery. The intersection of physical and psychological trauma presents some unique treatment considerations for clinicians delivering cognitive processing therapy (CPT). This chapter will provide empirical background on this common comorbidity, including other physical health comorbidities such as sleep and pain that may further complicate the PTSD/mTBI picture, unique treatment considerations to consider when working with this population, and future considerations.

A. Jak (✉) · K. Dell
VA San Diego Healthcare System and University of California San Diego Department of Psychiatry, San Diego, CA, USA
e-mail: ajak@ucsd.edu

J. S. Wachen, T. E. Galovski (eds.), *Cognitive Processing Therapy for Complex Cases*, CBT: Science Into Practice,
https://doi.org/10.1007/978-3-031-87356-0_6

Research Overview

TBI

A traumatic brain injury is an event in which an external force to the head results in a change in consciousness (loss (LOC) or alteration (AOC) of consciousness), potentially post-traumatic amnesia (PTA; a period of time in which one is conscious and alert but not yet effectively storing new memories), and immediate neurological symptoms like confusion, nausea, and/or headache (VA/DoD, 2021). Severity of TBI (mild, moderate, or severe) is determined by these injury details (duration of LOC/AOC, length of PTA, presence or absence of brain imaging findings, and Glasgow Coma Rating Scale score (if available) (VA/DoD, 2021). Approximately 80–85% of the 1.4 million TBIs diagnosed annually in the USA are classified as mild (CDC, 2006; Congressional Research Service, 2007; DVBIC, 2017), implying briefer LOC, shorter periods of PTA, and more rapid recovery trajectory, typically returning fully to baseline functioning. This chapter will focus predominantly on mTBI (used interchangeably with concussion) given it is the predominant type of TBI and most likely to present comorbidly with PTSD.

Symptoms such as headache, sensitivities to light/sound, dizziness/nausea, fatigue, attentional lapses, slowed psychomotor processing speed, and irritability are common acute symptoms following concussion (McCrea, 2008), though the vast majority of those symptoms resolve in 7–10 days or an outer limit of normal recovery of 90 days (Iverson, Gardner, et al., 2017a). Nonetheless, 15–30% of individuals do not recover along this timeline (Belanger et al., 2009) and 40–72% of those with mTBI history reported persistent symptoms over a year later (Belanger et al., 2009). While etiology of these enduring symptoms may seem obviously tied to the concussive event, the evidence supporting this association is much more nebulous; acute symptoms following concussion are largely neurologic, but persistent symptoms beyond the expected recovery window are strongly related to non-neurologic etiologies. PTSD figures prominently into protracted recoveries following concussion in this comorbid population (McCrea, 2008) (see Fig. 6.1).

PTSD and concussion are often interconnected, particularly in treatment seeking Veterans and service members, with reciprocal influences of physical and psychological trauma on persistence of symptoms in the post-acute phase following concussion (Stein et al., 2015; Gardner et al., 2023; Howlett et al., 2022). Among Veterans seeking treatment for protracted recovery following concussion, up to 73% carry a diagnosis of PTSD (Taylor et al., 2012). History of concussion also increases risk of PTSD in civilian populations (Bryant et al., 2010), with particularly prominent rates in survivors of interpersonal violence (IPV) (Galovski, Werner, et al., 2021b; Iverson, Dardis, & Pogoda, 2017b; Lagarde et al., 2014) because the context in which an injury occurs notably impacts risk for PTSD following concussion. Those whose injuries are caused by assault or violence are at greater risk to develop

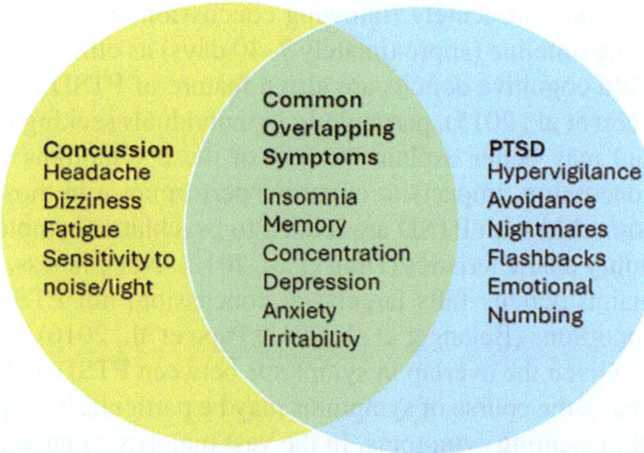

Fig. 6.1 Common distinct and overlapping symptoms between TBI and PTSD

PTSD (Stein et al., 2019). Concussions sustained in civilian (non-sport) and military settings show higher rates of mental health conditions than in sport-related settings; athletes are at comparatively lower risk to develop mental health conditions following sport-related concussion as compared to the broader civilian population (Howlett et al., 2022) but certainly sport-related concussion still increases risk for mental health concerns. Though psychiatric comorbidities can and do co-occur with moderate to severe TBI, mTBI/concussion is more strongly linked with psychiatric comorbidities than moderate to severe TBI (Kim et al., 2023).

Symptoms that may have initially been caused by a concussion are most likely maintained in the post-acute period by non-TBI factors (Lange et al., 2013). These persistent symptoms are commonly experienced by uninjured individuals and/or are nonspecific and overlap with any number of preexisting and/or comorbid conditions (Lange et al., 2013; McLean et al., 2009; Iverson & Lange, 2003; Wang et al., 2006) but tend to nonetheless be attributed to concussion. Comorbidity between concussion and PTSD is particularly relevant to acute concussion symptoms that persist beyond the expected recovery window. In fact, presence of mental health comorbidities better predicts persistent "postconcussive" symptoms than does history of concussion itself (Meares et al., 2008; Schneiderman et al., 2008; Porter et al., 2018). The role of social-psychological factors also cannot be underestimated in persistence of symptoms following concussion; expectations, misattribution, and an idealized view of preinjury functioning all can notably influence recovery trajectories (McCrea, 2008). Thoughtful interpretation of self-reported symptoms is therefore important. In summary, the initial concussive event may have resulted in *expected* postconcussive symptoms, but prolonged *persistence* of these symptoms is likely independent of, or only indirectly related to, the concussion.

Cognitive complaints are one of the most common concerns in those seeking treatment following concussion. While objective mild neuropsychological deficits may present acutely following concussion, cognitive symptoms resolve along the same timeline (approximately 7–10 days) as other symptoms following concussion. Mild cognitive deficits are also a feature of PTSD however (Aupperle et al., 2012; Scott et al., 2015), particularly in individuals seeking treatment (O'Neil et al., 2017) and may better explain the root of these symptoms in protracted recoveries after concussion. Impacts to cognitive performance in those with history of concussion comorbid with PTSD are related to psychiatric symptom severity, but not to mTBI injury characteristics (Drag et al., 2012). Nonetheless, attribution of cognitive complaints/deficits falls largely on concussion, not PTSD or other behavioral health conditions (Belanger et al., 2013; Pape et al., 2016).

Given the overlap in symptoms between PTSD and concussion in the post-acute phase, the course of symptoms may be particularly helpful in disentangling etiology of presenting symptoms. In the vast majority of cases, the recovery following concussion is linear (symptoms present acutely and prominently and lessen progressively over time) but in PTSD, symptoms may be delayed in their onset and worsen over time. Therefore, PTSD is much more likely to be the underlying etiology of symptom courses described as worsening over time or that vary over time (e.g., present, remit, re-present) than is history of concussion (Vasterling et al., 2018).

Taken together, the empirical literature supports a picture that is the largely the opposite of many of commonly held beliefs by both patients and providers regarding concussion when it co-occurs with mental health conditions. One of the most consequential misunderstandings regarding the comorbidity of mTBI and PTSD is that in these cases, ***PTSD is likely the driver of persistent symptoms, not mTBI***. PTSD has potentially longer lasting cognitive symptoms than mTBI, and treatment of PTSD makes great strides in reducing not only PTSD symptoms but also "postconcussive" symptoms, including cognitive functioning. Despite this evidence regarding the likely primary role of mental health conditions in persistence of symptoms following mTBI, mental health treatment is often relegated to secondary or tertiary consideration (Jak, 2017).

A diathesis-stress model helps characterize this process whereby acute symptoms are directly related to the neurological consequences of concussion but subsequently become reinforced by a negative feedback loop (Hou et al., 2012; McCrea, 2008). That is, a concussive event occurs causing acute neurobehavioral symptoms. Without realistic expectation management at the time of the acute event, the distressing neurobehavioral symptoms can lead to increased stress, subsequently feeding avoidance and exacerbating mood symptoms, which in turn may further increase neurobehavioral symptoms. In the context of the compelling research literature and informed by a diathesis-stress framework, CPT holds great promise for this population.

CPT in TBI

Structured Psychotherapy for PTSD Is Feasible and Effective in Those with a Concussion History

The oft-intertwined nature of concussion and PTSD begs the question of why trauma-focused therapies have *not* been more widely applied for those with this comorbidity. In the post-acute phase after concussion, emphasis has historically been (mis)placed on "TBI treatment", often to the detriment of the contribution of PTSD to the symptom and functional presentation in those with persistent symptoms following concussion. But treating PTSD in this population is paramount. Despite evidence to the contrary, concern lingers that the memory and attention symptoms and emotional control problems associated with concussion and/or PTSD may complicate or possibly impede recovery from either problem (Bogdanova & Verfaellie, 2012; Sayer et al., 2009; Verfaellie et al., 2013). CPT is actually a good choice for use in those with comorbid PTSD and TBI because of its structure, directive nature, concrete goals, and psychoeducation. Still, hesitancy remains regarding use of CPT for patients with comorbid history of concussion; anecdotal and research evidence suggest that this hesitancy is rooted in concern that CPT is too cognitively complex for those with potentially mild cognitive deficits (Cook et al., 2014) and/or poor follow-through on homework (Sripada et al., 2013).

There is no empirical evidence that concussion, in and of itself, should prohibit participation in empirically supported treatments for PTSD. CBT approaches to PTSD are effective across the TBI severity spectrum (Vasterling et al., 2018). Research supports that those with a history of concussion benefit notably from evidence-based PTSD treatment. The benefits and feasibility of CBT (Bryant et al., 2003; Potter et al., 2016; Tiersky et al., 2005), and more specifically CPT, in this population have strong empirical support (Boyd et al., 2016; Davis et al., 2013). As an example, in a residential TBI/PTSD program, CPT was effective in reducing PTSD and depressive symptoms and level of TBI severity did not impact PTSD treatment outcomes (Chard et al., 2011; Walter et al., 2014a). A recent review of 12 studies that applied CPT to comorbid PTSD and history of mTBI in military populations showed significant reduction in PTSD symptoms across all studies and no significant differences in attendance or completion rates (Mikolić et al., 2019). Furthermore, time since concussive injury, presence of loss of consciousness LOC or PTA, and number and mechanism of concussions are not associated with number of treatment sessions attended, do not significantly impact treatment adherence, and do not moderate treatment response in terms of change in PTSD (or depressive) symptoms (Crocker et al., 2019; Davis et al., 2013; Jak et al., 2019; Ragsdale & Voss Horrell, 2016; Shorer et al., 2020; Wolf et al., 2018). Individual psychotherapy, however, may be more efficacious than group therapy for those with both PTSD and history of TBI (Wachen et al., 2022).

It is not surprising then, that the Department of Veterans Affairs and Department of Defense *Clinical Practice Guidelines (CPGs) for mTBI Treatment* highlight the importance of treating all mental health comorbidities in those with protracted recoveries from concussion (VA/DoD, 2021). Similarly, VA/DoD CPGs for PTSD state: "The evidence shows good tolerance and efficacy for trauma focused-focused PTSD treatments in patients with other common impairing comorbid conditions including…TBI…" (VA/DoD, 2023). Trauma-focused therapy is NOT contraindicated in those with history of mTBI and in fact, is likely an active ingredient in reducing ostensibly postconcussive symptoms in adults (Jak et al., 2019; Wolf et al., 2018) and children (Shorer et al., 2020).

Structured Psychotherapy for PTSD Is Effective in Reducing Neurobehavioral Symptoms

Perhaps the more compelling question is whether empirically supported treatments for PTSD also reduce neurobehavioral symptoms in this population, and the answer to this question is yes. CPT has been shown to lead clinically significant reductions in PTSD, neurobehavioral, and cognitive symptoms (Boyd et al., 2016; Jak et al., 2019; Walter et al., 2012). Early clinical trial data examining efficacy of CPT in a comorbid PTSD and TBI population in a residential treatment setting provided initial insight into CPT in those with TBI (Walter et al., 2014b) and subsequent trials in this population have shown reduction of neurobehavioral symptoms following CPT (Jak et al., 2019) and prolonged exposure (Wolf et al., 2018). These trials highlight treatment of PTSD as a key mechanism for improving mood and neurobehavioral symptoms, including neurocognitive functioning, in those with PTSD and history of persistent postconcussive symptoms.

Barriers to Engagement in Psychotherapy for PTSD and Persistent Postconcussive Symptoms

There are likely multifaceted reasons why individuals with persistent symptoms in the post-acute phase after concussion are not more systematically directed to engage in mental health interventions. Despite psychoeducational efforts to combat it, heavy stigma is still prominent for mental health diagnoses and treatment, stigma that contributes to treatment avoidance (Mittal et al., 2013). It may be more palatable to seek treatment for a medical condition, such as TBI. A potential consequence of continually linking current symptoms to concussion/brain damage is inadvertently implying permanence of symptoms, leaving little room for belief in change or improvement. Expectation management (i.e., psychoeducation and communication of realistic but positive expectations of recovery) in these cases is essential; the concussive event as a catalyst in a negative cycle and the capability to disrupt that cycle are key features in this process of expectation management.

Iatrogenic effects may be related to strong media focus on negative outcomes tied solely and directly to concussion that are inconsistent with the vast majority of scientific literature on concussion outcomes and could unintentionally be doing harm. Certainly, concussive injuries should never be taken lightly, but scientific data suggest good outcomes in most cases.

Interestingly, one of the strongest predictors of good recovery following concussion is expectation of positive outcomes. Individuals holding maladaptive beliefs about long-term negative consequences of concussive symptoms are significantly more likely to have protracted and poor outcomes (Whittaker et al., 2007); psychoeducation regarding expected symptoms and trajectory of recovery provided at the time of injury significantly improves likelihood of full recoveries as compared to those who do not receive this expectation management (Mittenberg et al., 2001). It stands to reason then, that failure to receive appropriate expectation management or presence of poorly informed negative expectations of recovery contribute to higher risk for persistent symptoms. Treatment recommendations may serve to mitigate some negative expectations of concussion recovery, such as the updated concussion consensus recommendations for a graded or progressive return to activity, as tolerated, as opposed to complete avoidance of any activity for extended periods of time (McCrory et al., 2017). The VA/DOD *Clinical Practice Guidelines (CPGs) for mTBI Treatment* also recommend a symptom-focused approach "with an emphasis on education and avoiding symptom misattribution" (VA/DoD, 2021).

Holistic Intervention Approaches

Because the majority of persistent symptoms in those with history of concussion overlap with mental health conditions and mental health usually explains a greater proportion of variance than does history of mTBI, transdiagnostic treatments that target conditions together and holistically are recommended. And though history of TBI should not preclude engagement in trauma-focused therapy, memory, attention, and/or executive difficulties associated with either PTSD or TBI can present unique challenges to treatment attendance, engagement, or ability to complete homework in between sessions. Thus augmentation or modifications of standard empirically supported trauma-focused therapies may be needed to optimize treatment in the context of co-occurring conditions (Vasterling et al., 2018). Combined therapies may better meet treatment guidelines for cohesively targeting comorbidities, more holistically address patient concerns, and streamline care, thereby reducing barriers to receiving treatment. Research into these combined therapies is still in its infancy, however, to date, enhanced or modified trauma-focused therapies have met with good success.

One modified treatment includes principles of cognitive rehabilitation taken from Cognitive Symptom Management and Rehabilitation Training (CogSMART) and Compensatory Cognitive Training (CCT). These are evidence-based compensatory cognitive training interventions that have been shown to improve functional cognition in persons with a wide range of presenting concerns, including history of traumatic brain injury and neuropsychiatric disorders (Mendella et al., 2015; Twamley et al., 2012; Vidarsdottir et al., 2019, 2020). Specifically, CogSMART has been shown in clinical trials to improve cognition, functional capacity, postconcussive symptom severity, and quality of life in both civilians and Veterans with persistent symptoms following TBI (Fure et al., 2021; Howe et al., 2020; Storzbach et al., 2017; Twamley et al., 2014, 2015). Integrating compensatory cognitive strategies into an evidence-based treatment for PTSD targets a common comorbidity and takes advantage of the fact that systematically treating one category of symptoms may also reduce symptom burden arising from other conditions (Boyd et al., 2016; LaFrance et al., 2014; Walter et al., 2012). SMART-CPT (Jak et al., 2019) integrates compensatory cognitive training components of CogSMART into CPT to form a hybrid intervention that optimizes treatment of comorbid PTSD and history of concussion. In a clinical trial comparing standard CPT to SMART-CPT, *both* interventions resulted in clinically significant reductions in PTSD and neurobehavioral symptoms, and those in the SMART-CPT group experienced additional benefits to their objective attention, memory, and executive functioning, significantly above and beyond that of the CPT group (Jak et al., 2019).

Executive dysfunction may be particularly important to attend to in comorbid presentations as it may contribute to the development and maintenance of PTSD via failure to implement adaptive coping mechanisms (Vasterling et al., 2018). Particularly as it applies to CPT, individuals with executive functioning deficits may have difficulty implementing strategies, such as cognitive restructuring (Vasterling et al., 2018). Poorer baseline executive functioning contributes to premature dropout from therapy (Crocker et al., 2018) and is associated with reduced treatment gains from trauma-focused therapy (Crocker et al., 2018, 2023). However, SMART-CPT, given its additional focus on compensatory cognitive strategies including in the domain of executive functioning, was successful in achieving similar PTSD symptom improvement regardless of baseline cognitive flexibility (Crocker et al., 2018). Modifying trauma-focused therapy to accommodate executive dysfunction may bolster treatment effectiveness in adults (Crocker et al., 2018, 2023) as well as children (Shorer et al., 2020).

Though formal satisfaction data are not available for SMART-CPT, implementation research with CogSMART/CCT, a component of SMART-CPT, shows high satisfaction with the cognitive intervention by both providers and patients; 99% of surveyed providers and 95% of patients would recommend CogSMART/CCT to others (Lindamer et al., 2022). Providers found the treatment to be beneficial to patients and afforded the flexibility to combine with other treatments. CogSMART/CCT in real world settings is frequently adapted to accommodate the characteristics of individual patients. The perceived mechanisms of change in the intervention (i.e., psychoeducation, skill development, practice, problem solving, and generalization) can be kept consistent across patients, while the implementation details (i.e., specific strategies, length and number of sessions) are easily modifiable and personalized (Lindamer et al., 2022). Providers commented that "[CogSMART/CCT is] super useful in building patient confidence, practical and easy to combine with other approaches" and "Helpful as both a stand-alone intervention or blend in with other approaches...." (Lindamer et al., 2022). Anecdotal comments regarding SMART-CPT from patients are quite positive, with one individual calling it "life changing".

Additional Comorbidities: Pain and Sleep

Pain is highly prevalent among those who have sustained a concussion, as high 40–70% (Abel et al., 2016; Cifu et al., 2013; Nampiaparampil, 2008). The co-occurrence of PTSD, history of concussion, and pain is so common in Veterans and service members that it has been dubbed the Polytrauma Clinical Triad (Lew et al., 2009). Since this pattern of comorbidities was initially studied and the moniker coined, additional studies have continued to reveal how commonly (up to 80% of the time) this triad presents in military/Veteran (Cifu et al., 2013; Laughter et al., 2022; Walker et al., 2018) as well as civilian (Peixoto et al., 2018) populations. Similar to the relationship between number of mTBIs and PTSD, multiple concussive events also lead to higher rates of pain (75%) than single concussive events (57%) (Lindquist et al., 2017). The triad can lead to higher pain ratings and greater need for care (Song et al., 2020). Some pharmacologic interventions for pain can contribute to cognitive complaints and increased risk for abuse or overdose (Song et al., 2020) and do not address to intertwined nature of the triadic presentation. Transdiagnostic treatments that target the components of the triad more holistically are likely to achieve better outcomes though at present, most available treatments follow a sequential or parallel model of treatment (McGeary et al., 2022) with integrated treatments targeting two but not all three components of the triad (e.g., Boersma et al., 2019; Jak et al., 2019; Gilliam et al., 2020).

Attending to comorbidities also has the potential to attenuate development of persistent symptoms following concussion; there is evidence that pain is a strong predictor of continued symptom burden in this population (Meares et al., 2008; Schwab et al., 2017). As with all symptoms potentially attributed to concussion, postconcussive-like symptoms are not unique sequelae solely of concussion, and the presence of chronic pain should be considered when interpreting patients' physical, cognitive, and psychological complaints (Iverson & McCracken, 1997; Smith-Seemiller et al., 2003). Pain should not preclude use of CPT and in fact it may have benefits to pain even when it is not an explicit component of treatment. This may be due to shared etiologic framework (Kovacevic et al., 2024), such as shared vulnerabilities and neurobiological mechanisms (e.g., common circuits underlie both emotional and physiological distress/threat) and/or mutual maintenance via factors like avoidance behaviors, anxiety sensitivity, and/or dysfunctional cognitions (Murphy et al., 2022). For those with both PTSD and chronic pain engaged in CPT, there is evidence that pain intensity abates as PTSD symptom severity improves. (Held et al., 2024). Applying the lens of a mutual maintenance framework, the cognitive restructuring in CPT to challenge trauma-focused beliefs may generalize to challenge maladaptive cognitions about pain as well. There is, however, variability in the degree to which CPT may collaterally result in improvements in pain; post-traumatic headache pain following TBI, in particular, may not improve following CPT and require more targeted behavioral pain interventions (McGeary et al., 2022).

Broadly, poor sleep is pervasive in those with PTSD, history of TBI, or both (McCarthy et al., 2019; Rojczyk et al., 2023) all of which also further co-occurs with pain (Balba et al., 2018; Hoot et al., 2018; Khokhar et al., 2021). Upwards of 70% of those with PTSD endorse poor sleep (Maher et al., 2006). Like pain, sleep is another comorbidity particularly associated with increased symptom severity and slower recovery in those with both PTSD and persistent symptoms following concussion (Gilbert et al., 2015). When history of concussion is also present, PTSD symptom severity still seems to be a larger contributor than sleep disturbances to persistence of symptoms (Lu et al., 2019).

Sleep disturbances in PTSD often respond poorly to treatment-as-usual for trauma (Colvonen et al., 2019; Spoormaker & Montgomery, 2008). Close to half of patients still report impaired sleep following CBT-oriented PTSD treatment (Zayfert & DeViva, 2004). Consistent with sleep difficulties comorbid in many mental health conditions, trauma-focused treatments such as CPT may attenuate (Galovski et al., 2016; Gutner et al., 2013) but not fully resolve insomnia (Pruiksma et al., 2016; Sullan et al., 2021). It is equivocal as to whether poor sleep does (Pruiksma et al., 2023; Sullan et al., 2021) or does not (Galovski et al., 2016) impact CPT treatment gains. Cognitive Behavioral Therapy for Insomnia (CBT-I) is effective in TBI, but combined therapies using trauma-focused interventions and CBT-I in those who also have a history of concussion could have enhanced benefits; it would allow for simultaneous and streamlined targeting of both symptoms of PTSD and insomnia, and particularly elements of insomnia that may interfere with PTSD treatment (Almklov et al., 2022). See Chap. 7 for more information on delivering CPT in the context of sleep disturbance.

Case Example: SMART-CPT

To provide a more in-depth look at one integrated treatment for PTSD and history of concussion, a detailed example of SMART-CPT is presented below. Table 6.1 summarizes the main topics covered in each weekly session of SMART-CPT. The CPT content follows exactly the familiar CPT protocol and the CogSMART content is incorporated with this standard CPT. While some modifications have been made to the visual presentation of worksheets (e.g., reorganized layout, employed color-coding) to assist anyone with cognitive challenges to more quickly orient and process the task demands, the content has not been modified. Following Table 6.1 is a description of how CogSMART content is included in CPT sessions, along with helpful tips garnered from real-world delivery of SMART-CPT. The CogSMART manual that more fully details the compensatory strategies and content is available at no cost at cogsmart.com and the full SMART-CPT manual is available upon request from the author.

Table 6.1 SMART-CPT session content

Session		
	CPT content	CogSMART content
1	Introduction to treatment and psychoeducation about PTSD	TBI psychoeducation, choosing a calendar
2	Impact of trauma, identifying trauma-related cognitive distortions ("stuck-points"), psychoeducation about emotions	Identify a "home" for important items, calendar use
3	Identifying thoughts and feelings, initial stuck point challenging	Taking breaks, sleep and fatigue strategies
4	Continuation of Session 3 topics	Prospective memory techniques, routines, linking tasks, automatic places
5	Specific work on challenging stuck points	Calendar—weekly planning session, prioritizing to-do lists
6	Identification of patterns of problematic thinking	Attention strategies—active effort, breaks, self-talk
7	Continued work on challenging stuck points, introduction of generating alternative thoughts	External (e.g., calendars, note taking, alarms) and internal (e.g., categorizing, visual imagery) memory strategies
8	Challenging safety stuck points, generating alternative thoughts	Overlearning, name learning, and retrieval strategies; organization strategies
9	Challenging trust stuck points, generating alternative thoughts	Goal setting and planning
10	Challenging power/control stuck points, generating alternative thoughts	Cognitive flexibility and problem solving, brainstorming
11	Challenging esteem stuck points, generating alternative thoughts	Review and use of cognitive strategies
12	Challenging intimacy stuck points, generating alternative thoughts, termination	Additional resources

Session 1

Psychoeducation regarding natural recovery from mTBI should complement the information reviewed regarding PTSD (e.g., its development, conceptualization as a disorder of recovery, automatic thoughts, and avoidance). More specifically, reviewing the subset of postconcussive symptoms overlapping with PTSD symptoms (memory challenges, mood changes, concentration and sleep difficulties) dovetails with assisting in identifying ways to change existing (or persistent) habits in favor of more helpful ways to cope. Patients have noted this starts treatment with optimism that there are skills they can build throughout the course of therapy that target multiple areas of concern, and that generally, there was an expectation of recovery, even from longstanding symptoms. For some, however, the psychoeducation that concussion symptoms typically resolve within three months generated global negative beliefs that "I should be better by now" or "It is my fault that I still experience symptoms." These comments can be countered with language that acknowledges that they may not have recovered along the expected timeline, but that symptom improvement or resolution is still possible with the new skills they will learn. These beliefs can also be identified as stuck points to be addressed in the context of CPT skills. Similar to PTSD's conceptualization as a disorder of recovery, acknowledging that repetitive or more severe head injury histories can complicate the recovery trajectory may prove helpful.

The cognitive compensatory strategy introduced at Session 1 focuses on choosing a calendar (e.g., electronic, paper, etc.). Any calendar type that works for the patient is acceptable, but there should only be one calendar source. That is, one should not use an electronic calendar *and* a wall calendar; multiple sources of information lead to increased cognitive demands and higher likelihood of error. If there is any resistance to need to use a calendar ("I've never had to use one before" or other reference to not wanting to appear as using a memory "crutch"), framing calendar use as a tool that the vast majority of busy and highly successful individuals use, regardless of mental health or brain injury status, can be helpful. Patients report that therapist prompts (e.g., to bring the calendar with them to session, penciling in future therapy and calendar review sessions, as well as time to complete homework) assisted in routinizing use of the skill throughout and beyond the course of treatment. Secondly, it scaffolded use of other compensatory skills presented in later sessions such as other external and internal memory strategies, examining sleep hygiene, and completing self-care activities. Additionally, referencing calendar entries emerged as a helpful tool in challenging stuck points throughout future sessions, notably those related to power/control as well as esteem. Comments such as "I have no control over what is decided or what happens to me" can be challenged with "If we take a look at your calendar, who decides when to review it, what to record, and if you participate in or complete all these entries?" "I never do anything correctly" presents an opportunity to comment with something like: "If we take a look at your calendar, look at all the things you choose to do and predominantly do well (work/school, what you eat, physical and social activities, etc.). Would you say this serves as some evidence that you have accomplished different things?"

Session 2

The trauma-focused work for the second session is primarily focused on formulating why one has not recovered naturally from the event and initiating the process of identifying stuck points. Patients reported that several questioning methods endemic to stand-alone CPT were helpful in identifying the spectrum on which avoidance behaviors might occur, such as direct, self-generated choices of avoiding people, places, or activities that serve as reminders of the traumatic events (which are easier to identify), to more indirect ways that it manifests (e.g., inconsistent attendance or completion of homework assignments, overscheduling activities that reduce time to attend sessions or complete homework, etc.). Making a home for important items refers to coming up with a singular and consistent place for keeping everyday items (commonly keys, phone, wallet/purse, and glasses). Establishing the habit of always putting these items on a table by the door, a basket in the entryway, a tray on a dresser, or other similar concept that meets the individuals home setting and needs, is essential in reducing the cognitive demands of searching for these items. Other items as needed can go in this "home" as needed, such as documents for a specific appointment. In conjunction with the calendar use introduced in the initial session, the addition of making a "home" for important items served as a tangible way to address behavioral patterns that might emerge from the intersection of an organizational skills deficit with avoidance. Patients reported placing wallets, keys, their session binder, and other important items in a consistent "home" reduced opportunities for automatic responses of "I couldn't locate my binder so I wasn't able to do the homework/attend our session" or, "I couldn't drive to/attend the social event because I couldn't find my keys". Once the organizational skills difficulties began to improve, so too does their recognition of trauma-related stuck points and avoidance behaviors.

Session 3

The layout of the A-B-C worksheets introduced at the prior session provides a straightforward framework for individuals to begin identifying relationships between events, thoughts, and feelings. At times, however, common stumbling blocks emerge during the first few times patients complete the worksheets. More specifically, some may struggle with the wording of "Belief/Stuck Point" for Column B, it might be helpful to ask them to state the automatic thought (or "the thought or statement that pops in your head immediately") following the event in Column A. Additionally, if entries within Column B are in the form of a question (e.g., "Why do these things keep happening to me?"), it is helpful to ask "What would you say is the answer to that question? That answer is what we will place in Column B as the 'Belief/Stuck Point'". The layout of the worksheet has been streamlined and color-coded to further assist individuals who may struggle to track the components of the task.

Revisiting calendar use may also aid in the introduction of the compensatory strategies for this session pertaining to fatigue management. At times, the discussion of incorporating "active breaks" or initializing sleep hygiene practices are met with the response that insufficient time exists to implement the suggested methods. After examining those statements within the A-B-C worksheet framework while reviewing the calendar, patients frequently arrive at an agreement that while there might not be time to address all of the suggestions, there is usually time to trial at least one. Secondly, reviewing their calendar provided information to plan for nights where prioritizing sleep hygiene was more important, compared to other evenings.

Sessions 4 and 5

Strategies to enhance prospective memory are the cognitive focus of these sessions. Prospective memory refers to remembering to do something in the future, which is one of the most common functional complaints among individuals engaging in SMART-CPT. The calendar use and home for everyday items covered in prior sessions contribute to prospective memory, though this session will further build on those initial strategies. Specifically, a focus is now on habits and systems to ensure checking one's calendar 2–3 times per day. Linking this, or any new habit one wishes to develop, to things already done regularly (like meals, walking the dog, or brushing teeth) will increase the likelihood of firmly establishing this new behavior and subsequently having it become automatic, thereby reducing memory load. Even the consistent structure of every SMART-CPT session (review, CPT material, active break, cognitive strategies, home exercises) is an in vivo example of repeating routines as a cognitive strategy to reduce mental load. Putting therapy sessions and homework assignments into one's calendar and using calendar planning sessions to keep on top of these therapy tasks are a helpful way to integrate the CPT components with the SMART components of these sessions. Additionally, putting tasks that need done (e.g., homework pages) somewhere that has to be touched (e.g., on a breakfast chair that the patient sits in everyday or in front of the door they always exit from) helps task completion if the worksheet can't be missed. Therapists should check in about what did or did not work well regarding these exercises and the home exercises; not doing the homework is an opportunity to approach with curiosity what worked and what didn't for the patient and engage in a continual process of fine tuning the strategies for their individual situation. It's also an opportunity to explore any avoidance behaviors that may be intertwined with cognitive lapses when it comes to homework, session attendance, or things undone in the patient's home life. That is, explore whether there are elements of avoidance or forgetting (or both).

Session 6

This session focuses on attention and mental energy. The active breaks that are embedded into every session of SMART-CPT are modeling in vivo the importance of taking breaks regularly and optimally before one hits a metaphorical wall. Because threats to focus, attention, and mental energy can be internal or external, there is a table that many patients find helpful as a quick reference about strategies to try depending on the source of the distraction.

Sessions 7 and 8

Calendar use, calendar checking, and to-do lists are an ongoing strategy that permeate almost every session of SMART-CPT, but some additional memory strategies are addressed in Sessions 7 and 8. While many of the best memory strategies are *external* aids (e.g., calendars, alarms, recordings, making lists/taking written notes), there are additional *internal* strategies (e.g., visualization, self-talk) that are presented in these sessions. Often patients rely most heavily on external strategies in their everyday lives but have endorsed value in the internal strategies when an important thought or to-do item comes to them while driving, showering, or working out and using the external strategies isn't possible. The vast majority of the memory strategies throughout SMART-CPT are *prospective* memory strategies, however, Session 8 does address *retrieval* strategies (pulling something out of your memory bank). Many of the retrieval strategies are built on the foundation of habits and systems already covered in earlier sessions.

Sessions 9 and 10

Session 9 returns to goal setting and calendar use/planning sessions, now fine-tuning calendar use to incorporate the component parts of one's goals into their calendar. As some (many) patients are likely to still have goals that they are struggling with, Session 10 introduces a problem-solving method guiding the individual to define the problem, brainstorm possible solutions, and to evaluate the feasibility, cost, and likelihood of success for each suggestion. Patients have reported that despite the difference in worksheet layout, the general process shared similarities with the A-B-C and Challenging Beliefs worksheets completed throughout the previous nine sessions. Therapists can capitalize on this generalizable skill to assist anyone who may be struggling temporarily with the problem-solving method. After selecting a possible solution to a problem that they wish to trial, individuals are encouraged to schedule the solution-focused activity(ies) into their calendar; they often do so without prompting at this stage of treatment, resultant from consistent habit building for calendar use throughout treatment.

Additional Suggestions

Language matters when working with this comorbid presentation. To reduce risk of attribution error, use neutral terms that convey meaning but do not overpathologize; as an example, use "concussion" rather than "mTBI", or "protracted recovery" instead of "postconcussion syndrome" (McLean et al., 2009). When covering information on building in cognitive breaks in Session 3, individuals who also present with pain may need further breaks built in to properly manage both cognitive efficiency and pain.

Future Directions

Massed treatment for CPT has been shown to be as effective in reducing trauma symptoms as standard treatment delivery timelines and possibly results in improved treatment retention rates (Galovski et al., 2022; Held et al., 2022, 2023; Sciarrino et al., 2020). To date, alternate schedules of delivery of CPT in those with comorbid physical health conditions or with holistic treatments to simultaneously targeting co-occurring conditions have not yet been widely studied and would be a worthwhile focus of future investigations. Other elements that may reduce attrition and/or encourage engagement in treatment in those with PTSD and history of concussion would also help optimize interventions for this population. Because much of the work in this comorbid group has been conducted in Veterans and service members (overwhelmingly male cohorts) more work needs to be done to target females. CPT results in effective reduction of trauma symptoms in those with PTSD stemming from IPV and appears to be equally effective regardless of presence or absence of mTBI history (single or multiple mTBIs) (Galovski, Smith, et al., 2021a). But despite the high likelihood of co-occurring PTSD and history of concussion in this vulnerable IPV population, broad systematic study of integrated or holistic treatments for IPV survivors who have experienced head injury is limited. Women with history of IPV, concussion, and current PTSD may exhibit more severe pretreatment PTSD symptoms and subsequently more attenuated symptom change when compared to IPV survivors without history of mTBI and may also be at particular risk of not completing a full course of CPT (Galovski et al., 2022). Therefore, additional research into optimal treatments for this vulnerable group are needed. Finally, the representation of racially and ethnically diverse communities in research examining hybrid, holistic, or transdiagnostic treatments for PTSD when co-occurring with concussion or other physical health conditions is also limited; future studies need to attend to inclusion of minoritized communities so that we are confident that any treatment advances will serve the full population of those presenting for care.

Summary

The intersection of physical and psychological trauma presents unique treatment considerations for clinicians delivering CPT. The evidence is compelling that PTSD and history of concussion frequently co-occur, that PTSD can be a dominant factor in persistence of what are labelled "postconcussive" symptoms, and that empirically supported trauma-focused therapies are indicated and equally efficacious for those with or without history of concussion. Acute symptoms following concussion are largely neurologic and the general expectation after concussion is full recovery, but persistent symptoms beyond the expected recovery window are strongly related to non-neurologic or non-TBI etiologies; PTSD as well as insomnia and chronic pain figure prominently into protracted recoveries and increased symptom reporting beyond the period of expected neurological recovery. Given the overlap in symptoms between PTSD and concussion in the post-acute phase, the course of symptoms may be particularly helpful in disentangling etiology of presenting symptoms. In the vast majority of cases, the recovery following concussion is linear, but PTSD is much more likely to be the underlying etiology of symptom courses described as worsening over time or that vary over time than is history of concussion. One of the most important take-home messages about treatment-seeking individuals with PTSD and protracted recovery following concussion is that PTSD is likely the driver of persistent symptoms, not concussion. PTSD has potentially longer lasting cognitive symptoms than concussion, and treatment of PTSD makes great strides in reducing not only PTSD symptoms but also "postconcussive" symptoms, including cognitive complaints. Any hesitation about the appropriateness of CPT for those with a history of concussion is unfounded; CPT is *not* contraindicated in those with history of concussion and in fact, is likely an active ingredient in reducing both trauma and neurobehavioral symptoms. Despite this evidence regarding the likely primary role of mental health conditions in persistence of symptoms following concussion, mental health treatment is often relegated to secondary or tertiary consideration. Systematic intervention for co-occurring conditions targeting the overall constellations of presenting symptoms are the optimal treatments. Siloed conceptualizations where treatment of comorbid mental health conditions and concussion treatment are distinct entities should give way to transdiagnostic thinking. Hybrid treatments, though still nascent in an empirical sense, show good efficacy to target trauma and neurobehavioral symptoms effectively and efficiently.

Competing Interests The authors have no conflicts of interest to declare that are relevant to the content of this chapter.

References

Abel, E. A., Brandt, C. A., Czlapinski, R., & Goulet, J. L. (2016). Pain research using veterans health administration electronic and administrative data sources. *Journal of Rehabilitation Research and Development, 53*(1), 1–12. https://doi.org/10.1682/jrrd.2014.10.0246

Albrecht, J. S., Abariga, S. A., Rao, V., & Wickwire, E. M. (2020). Incidence of new neuropsychiatric disorder diagnoses following traumatic brain injury. *Journal of Head Trauma Rehabilitation, 35*(4), E352–e360. https://doi.org/10.1097/htr.0000000000000551

Almklov, E. A., Rivera, G. L., & Orff, H. (2022). Chapter 13–CBT-I in patients with a history of traumatic brain injury. In S. Nowakowski, S. N. Garland, M. A. Grandner, & L. J. Cuddihy (Eds.), *Adapting cognitive behavioral therapy for insomnia* (pp. 265–290). Academic Press. https://doi.org/10.1016/B978-0-12-822872-2.00009-8

Aupperle, R. L., Melrose, A. J., Stein, M. B., & Paulus, M. P. (2012). Executive function and PTSD: Disengaging from trauma. *Neuropharmacology, 62*, 686–694. https://doi.org/10.1016/j.neuropharm.2011.02.008

Balba, N. M., Elliott, J. E., Weymann, K. B., Opel, R. A., Duke, J. W., Oken, B. S., Morasco, B. J., Heinricher, M. M., & Lim, M. M. (2018). Increased sleep disturbances and pain in veterans with comorbid traumatic brain injury and posttraumatic stress disorder. *Journal of Clinical Sleep Medicine, 14*(11), 1865–1878. https://doi.org/10.5664/jcsm.7482

Belanger, H. G., Barwick, F. H., Kip, K. E., Kretzmer, T., & Vanderploeg, R. D. (2013). Postconcussive symptom complaints and potentially malleable positive predictors. *The Clinical Neuropsychologist, 27*, 1–13. https://doi.org/10.1080/13854046.2013.774438

Belanger, H. G., Kretzmer, T., Vanderploeg, R. D., & French, L. M. (2009). Symptom complaints following combat-related traumatic brain injury: Relationship to traumatic brain injury severity and posttraumatic stress disorder. *Journal of the International Neuropsychological Society, 16*, 194–199. https://doi.org/10.1017/S1355617709990841

Boersma, K., Södermark, M., Hesser, H., Flink, I. K., Gerdle, B., & Linton, S. J. (2019). Efficacy of a transdiagnostic emotion-focused exposure treatment for chronic pain patients with comorbid anxiety and depression: A randomized controlled trial. *Pain, 160*(8), 1708–1718. https://doi.org/10.1097/j.pain.0000000000001575

Bogdanova, Y., & Verfaellie, M. (2012). Cognitive sequelae of blast-induced traumatic brain injury: Recovery and rehabilitation. *Neuropsychology Review, 22*(1), 4–20. https://doi.org/10.1007/s11065-012-9192-3

Boyd, B., Rodgers, C. S., Aupperle, R. L., & Jak, A. J. (2016). Case report on the effects of cognitive processing therapy on psychological, neuropsychological, and speech symptoms in comorbid PTSD and TBI. *Cognitive and Behavioral Practice, 23*(2), 173–183. https://doi.org/10.1016/j.cbpra.2015.10.001

Bryant, R. A., Moulds, M., Guthrie, R., & Nixon, R. D. (2003). Treating acute stress disorder following mild traumatic brain injury. *American Journal of Psychiatry, 160*(3), 585–587.

Bryant, R. A., O'Donnell, M. L., Creamer, M., McFarlane, A. C., Clark, C. R., & Silove, D. (2010). The psychiatric sequelae of traumatic injury. *American Journal of Psychiatry, 167*(3), 312–320. https://doi.org/10.1176/appi.ajp.2009.09050617

CDC. (2006). *Facts about traumatic brain injury* (TBI fact sheets, Issue.

Chard, K. M., Schumm, J. A., McIlvain, S. M., Bailey, G. W., & Parkinson, R. B. (2011). Exploring the efficacy of a residential treatment program incorporating cognitive processing therapy-cognitive for veterans with PTSD and traumatic brain injury. *Journal of Traumatic Stress, 24*(3), 347–351. https://doi.org/10.1002/jts.20644

Cifu, D. X., Taylor, B. C., Carne, W. F., Bidelspach, D., Sayer, N. A., Scholten, J., & Campbell, E. H. (2013). Traumatic brain injury, posttraumatic stress disorder, and pain diagnoses in OIF/OEF/OND veterans. *Journal of Rehabilitation Research and Development, 50*(9), 1169–1176. https://doi.org/10.1682/jrrd.2013.01.0006

Colvonen, P. J., Ellison, J., Haller, M., & Norman, S. B. (2019). Examining insomnia and PTSD over time in veterans in residential treatment for substance use disorders and PTSD. *Behavioral Sleep Medicine, 17*, 524–535.

Congressional Research Service. (2007). *United States military casualty statistics: Operation Iraqi freedom and operation enduring freedom,* (CRS Report for Congress., Issue.

Cook, J. M., Dinnen, S., Simiola, V., Thompson, R., & Schnurr, P. P. (2014). VA residential provider perceptions of dissuading factors to the use of two evidence-based PTSD treatments. *Professional Psychology: Research and Practice, 45*, 136–142. https://doi.org/10.1037/a0036183

Crocker, L. D., Jurick, S. M., Thomas, K. R., Keller, A. V., Sanderson-Cimino, M., Boyd, B., Rodgers, C., Twamley, E. W., & Jak, A. J. (2018). Worse baseline executive functioning is associated with dropout and poorer response to trauma-focused treatment for veterans with PTSD and comorbid traumatic brain injury. *Behavior Research and Therapy, 108*, 68–77. https://doi.org/10.1016/j.brat.2018.07.004

Crocker, L. D., Jurick, S. M., Thomas, K. R., Keller, A. V., Sanderson-Cimino, M., Hoffman, S. N., Boyd, B., Rodgers, C., Norman, S. B., Lang, A. J., Twamley, E. W., & Jak, A. J. (2019). Mild traumatic brain injury characteristics do not negatively influence cognitive processing therapy attendance or outcomes. *Journal of Psychiatric Research, 116*, 7–13. https://doi.org/10.1016/j.jpsychires.2019.05.022

Crocker, L. D., Sullan, M. J., Jurick, S. M., Thomas, K. R., Davey, D. K., Hoffman, S. N., Twamley, E. W., & Jak, A. J. (2023). Baseline executive functioning moderates treatment-related changes in quality of life in veterans with posttraumatic stress disorder and comorbid traumatic brain injury. *Journal of Traumatic Stress, 36*(1), 94–105. https://doi.org/10.1002/jts.22883

Davis, J. J., Walter, K. H., Chard, K. M., Parkinson, R. B., & Houston, W. S. (2013). Treatment adherence in cognitive processing therapy for combat-related PTSD with history of mild TBI. *Rehabilitation Psychology, 58*(1), 36–42. https://doi.org/10.1037/a0031525

Dilley, M., & Avent, C. (2011). Long-term neuropsychiatric disorders after traumatic brain injury. In T. Uehara (Ed.), *Psychiatric disorders: Worldwide advances*. BoD–Books on Demand. https://www.intechopen.com/chapters/20981

Drag, L. L., Spencer, R. J., Walker, S. J., Pangilinan, P. H., & Bieliauskas, L. A. (2012). The contributions of self-reported injury characteristics and psychiatric symptoms to cognitive functioning in OEF/OIF veterans with mild traumatic brain injury. *Journal of the International Neuropsychological Society, 18*, 576–584.

DVBIC. (2017). *DoD Worldwide Numbers for TBI*. http://dvbic.dcoe.mil/dod-worldwide-numbers-tbi

Fure, S. C. R., Howe, E. I., Andelic, N., Brunborg, C., Sveen, U., Røe, C., Rike, P. O., Olsen, A., Spjelkavik, Ø., Ugelstad, H., Lu, J., Ponsford, J., Twamley, E. W., Hellstrøm, T., & Løvstad, M. (2021). Cognitive and vocational rehabilitation after mild-to-moderate traumatic brain injury: A randomised controlled trial. *Annals of Physical Rehabilitation Medicine, 64*(5), 101538. https://doi.org/10.1016/j.rehab.2021.101538

Galovski, T. E., Harik, J. M., Blain, L. M., Elwood, L., Gloth, C., & Fletcher, T. D. (2016). Augmenting cognitive processing therapy to improve sleep impairment in PTSD: A randomized controlled trial. *Journal of Consulting and Clinical Psychology, 84*(2), 167–177. https://doi.org/10.1037/ccp0000059

Galovski, T. E., Smith, B. N., Micol, R. L., & Resick, P. A. (2021a). Interpersonal violence and head injury: The effects on treatment for PTSD. *Psychological Trauma: Theory, Research, Practice, and Policy, 13*(3), 376–384. https://doi.org/10.1037/tra0000976

Galovski, T. E., Werner, K. B., Iverson, K. M., Kaplan, S., Fortier, C. B., Fonda, J. R., Currao, A., Salat, D., & McGlinchey, R. E. (2021b). A multi-method approach to a comprehensive examination of the psychiatric and neurological consequences of intimate partner violence in women. *Frontiers in Psychiatry–Psychopathology, 12*. https://doi.org/10.3389/fpsyt.2021.569335

Galovski, T. E., Werner, K. B., Weaver, T. L., Morris, K. L., Dondanville, K. A., Nanney, J., Wamser-Nanney, R., McGlinchey, G., Fortier, C. B., & Iverson, K. M. (2022). Massed cognitive processing therapy for posttraumatic stress disorder in women survivors of intimate partner violence. *Psychological Trauma: Theory, Research, Practice, and Policy, 14*(5), 769–779. https://doi.org/10.1037/tra0001100

Gardner, R. C., Barnes, D. E., Li, Y., Boscardin, J., Peltz, C., & Yaffe, K. (2023). Medical and psychiatric risk factors for dementia in veterans with and without traumatic brain injury (TBI): A Nationwide cohort study. *Journal of Prevention of Alzheimers Disease, 10*(2), 244–250. https://doi.org/10.14283/jpad.2023.16

Gilbert, K. S., Kark, S. M., Gehrman, P., & Bogdanova, Y. (2015). Sleep disturbances, TBI and PTSD: Implications for treatment and recovery. *Clinical Psychology Review, 40*, 195–212. https://doi.org/10.1016/j.cpr.2015.05.008

Gilliam, W. P., Schumann, M. E., Craner, J. R., Cunningham, J. L., Morrison, E. J., Seibel, S., Sawchuk, C., & Sperry, J. A. (2020). Examining the effectiveness of pain rehabilitation on chronic pain and post-traumatic symptoms. *Journal of Behavioral Medicine, 43*(6), 956–967. https://doi.org/10.1007/s10865-020-00160-3

Gutner, C. A., Casement, M. D., Stavitsky Gilbert, K., & Resick, P. A. (2013). Change in sleep symptoms across cognitive processing therapy and prolonged exposure: A longitudinal perspective. *Behavior Research and Therapy, 51*(12), 817–822. https://doi.org/10.1016/j.brat.2013.09.008

Held, P., Kovacevic, M., Petrey, K., Meade, E. A., Pridgen, S., Montes, M., Werner, B., Miller, M. L., Smith, D. L., Kaysen, D., & Karnik, N. S. (2022). Treating posttraumatic stress disorder at home in a single week using 1-week virtual massed cognitive processing therapy. *Journal of Traumatic Stress, 35*(4), 1215–1225. https://doi.org/10.1002/jts.22831

Held, P., Mundle, R. S., Pridgen, S., Smith, D. L., Coleman, J. A., Klassen, B. J., & Burns, J. W. (2024). Reductions in PTSD severity precede reductions in pain intensity among veterans receiving intensive treatment. *Psychological Trauma: Theory, Research, Practice, and Policy.* https://doi.org/10.1037/tra0001761

Held, P., Smith, D. L., Pridgen, S., Coleman, J. A., & Klassen, B. J. (2023). More is not always better: 2 weeks of intensive cognitive processing therapy-based treatment are noninferior to 3 weeks. *Psychological Trauma, 15*(1), 100–109. https://doi.org/10.1037/tra0001257

Hoot, M. R., Levin, H., Smith, A. N., Goldberg, G., Wilde, E. A., Walker, W. C., Eapen, B. C., Nolen, T., & Pugh, N. L. (2018). Pain and chronic mild traumatic brain injury in the US military population: A chronic effects of Neurotrauma consortium study. *Brain Injury, 32*(10), 1169–1177. https://doi.org/10.1080/02699052.2018.1482427

Hou, R., Moss-Morris, R., Peveler, R., Mogg, K., Bradley, B. P., & Belli, A. (2012). When a minor head injury resutls in enduring symptoms: A prospective investigation of risk factors for postconcussional syndrome after mild traumatic brain injury. *Journal of Neurology, Neurosurgery, and Psychiatry, 83*, 217–223.

Howe, E. I., Fure, S. C. R., Løvstad, M., Enehaug, H., Sagstad, K., Hellstrøm, T., Brunborg, C., Røe, C., Nordenmark, T. H., Søberg, H. L., Twamley, E., Lu, J., & Andelic, N. (2020). Effectiveness of combining compensatory cognitive training and vocational intervention vs. treatment as usual on return to work following mild-to-moderate traumatic brain injury: Interim analysis at 3 and 6 month follow-up. *Frontiers Neurology, 11*, 561400. https://doi.org/10.3389/fneur.2020.561400

Howlett, J. R., Nelson, L. D., & Stein, M. B. (2022). Mental health consequences of traumatic brain injury. *Biological Psychiatry, 91*(5), 413–420. https://doi.org/10.1016/j.biopsych.2021.09.024

Iverson, G. L., Gardner, A. J., Terry, D. P., Ponsford, J. L., Sills, A. K., Broshek, D. K., & Solomon, G. S. (2017a). Predictors of clinical recovery from concussion: A systematic review [10.1136/bjsports-2017-097729]. *British Journal of Sports Medicine, 51*(12), 941. http://bjsm.bmj.com/content/51/12/941.abstract

Iverson, G. L., & Lange, R. T. (2003). Examination of "postconcussion-like" symptoms in a healthy sample. *Applied Neuropsychology, 10*(3), 137–144. https://doi.org/10.1207/s15324826an1003_02

Iverson, G. L., & McCracken, L. M. (1997). Postconcussive' symptoms in persons with chronic pain. *Brain Injury, 11*(11), 783–790. https://doi.org/10.1080/026990597122990

Iverson, K. M., Dardis, C. M., & Pogoda, T. K. (2017b). Traumatic brain injury and PTSD symptoms as a consequence of intimate partner violence. *Comprehensive Psychiatry, 74*, 80–87. https://doi.org/10.1016/j.comppsych.2017.01.007

Jak, A. J. (2017). The primary role of mental health treatment in resolution of persistent postconcussive symptoms. *Current Treatment Options in Psychiatry, 4*(3), 231–240. https://doi.org/10.1007/s40501-017-0119-8

Jak, A. J., Jurick, S., Crocker, L. D., Sanderson-Cimino, M., Aupperle, R., Rodgers, C. S., Thomas, K. R., Boyd, B., Norman, S. B., Lang, A. J., Keller, A. V., Schiehser, D. M., & Twamley, E. W. (2019). SMART-CPT for veterans with comorbid post-traumatic stress disorder and history of traumatic brain injury: A randomised controlled trial. *Journal of Neurology, Neurosurgery, and Psychiatry, 90*, 331–341. https://doi.org/10.1136/jnnp-2018-319315

Khokhar, B. R., Lindberg, M. A., & Walker, W. C. (2021). Post-mTBI pain interference in a U.S. military population: A chronic effects of Neurotrauma consortium study. *Military Medicine, 186*(3–4), e293–e299. https://doi.org/10.1093/milmed/usaa249

Kim, S. Y., Soumoff, A. A., Raiciulescu, S., Kemezis, P. A., Spinks, E. A., Brody, D. L., Capaldi, V. F., Ursano, R. J., Benedek, D. M., & Choi, K. H. (2023). Association of Traumatic Brain Injury Severity and Self-Reported Neuropsychiatric Symptoms in wounded military service members. *Neurotrauma Reports, 4*(1), 14–24. https://doi.org/10.1089/neur.2022.0063

Kovacevic, M., Montes, M., Tirone, V., Pridgen, S., Smith, D. L., Burns, J. W., & Held, P. (2024). Treating a common comorbidity: Pain outcomes following a 3-week cognitive processing therapy–based intensive treatment for posttraumatic stress disorder address. *Journal of Traumatic Stress, 37*(1), 47–56. https://doi.org/10.1002/jts.22979

LaFrance, W. C., Baird, G. L., Barry, J. J., Blum, A. S., Frank Webb, A., Keitner, G. I., Machan, J. T., Miller, I., & Szaflarski, J. P. (2014). Multicenter pilot treatment trial for psychogenic nonepileptic seizures: A randomized clinical trial. *JAMA Psychiatry, 71*(9), 997–1005. https://doi.org/10.1001/jamapsychiatry.2014.817

Lagarde, E., Salmi, L., Holm, L. W., Contrand, B., Masson, F., Ribéreau-Gayon, R., Laborey, M., & Cassidy, J. D. (2014). Association of Symptoms Following Mild Traumatic Brain Injury with Posttraumatic Stress Disorder vs Postconcussion syndrome. *JAMA Psychiatry, 71*(9), 1032–1040. https://doi.org/10.1001/jamapsychiatry.2014.666

Lange, R. T., Brickell, T. A., Ivins, B., Vanderploeg, R. D., & French, L. M. (2013). Variable, not always persistent, postconcussion symptoms after mild TBI in U.S. military service members: A five-year cross-sectional outcome study. *Journal of Neurotrauma, 30*(11), 958–969. https://doi.org/10.1089/neu.2012.2743

Laughter, S., Khan, M., Banaag, A., Madsen, C., & Koehlmoos, T. P. (2022). Prevalence of Polytrauma clinical triad among active duty service members. *Military Medicine, 187*(7–8), e856–e861. https://doi.org/10.1093/milmed/usab199

Lew, H. L., Otis, J. D., Tun, C., Kerns, R. D., Clark, M. E., & Cifu, D. X. (2009). Prevalence of chronic pain, posttraumatic stress disorder, and persistent postconcussive symptoms in OIF/OEF veterans: Polytrauma clinical triad. *Journal of Rehabilitation Research and Development, 46*(6), 697–702.

Lindamer, L., Almklov, E., Pittman, J. O. E., Shi, S., Maye, J., Jak, A., Twamley, E. W., & Rabin, B. (2022). Multi-method study of the implementation of cognitive symptom management and rehabilitation training (CogSMART) in real-world settings. *BMC Health Services Research, 22*(1), 1542. https://doi.org/10.1186/s12913-022-08941-z

Lindquist, L. K., Love, H. C., & Elbogen, E. B. (2017). Traumatic brain injury in Iraq and Afghanistan veterans: New results from a national random sample study. *The Journal of Neuropsychiatry and Clinical Neurosciences, 29*(3), 254–259.

Lu, L. H., Reid, M. W., Cooper, D. B., & Kennedy, J. E. (2019). Sleep problems contribute to post-concussive symptoms in service members with a history of mild traumatic brain injury without posttraumatic stress disorder or major depressive disorder. *NeuroRehabilitation, 44*(4), 511–521. https://doi.org/10.3233/nre-192702

Maher, M. J., Rego, S. A., & Asnis, G. M. (2006). Sleep disturbances in patients with post-traumatic stress disorder: Epidemiology, impact and approaches to management. *CNS Drugs, 20*(7), 567–590. https://doi.org/10.2165/00023210-200620070-00003

McCarthy, E., DeViva, J. C., Norman, S. B., Southwick, S. M., & Pietrzak, R. H. (2019). Self-assessed sleep quality partially mediates the relationship between PTSD symptoms and functioning and quality of life in U.S. veterans: Results from the National Health and resilience in veterans study. *Psychological Trauma: Theory, Research, Practice and Policy, 11*, 869–876.

McCrea, M. (2008). *Mild traumatic brain injury and Postconcussion syndrome*. Oxford University Press.

McCrory, P., Meeuwisse, W., Dvorak, J., Aubry, M., Bailes, J., Broglio, S., Cantu, R. C., Cassidy, D., Echemendia, R. J., Castellani, R. J., Davis, G. A., Ellenbogen, R., Emery, C., Engebretsen, L., Feddermann-Demont, N., Giza, C. C., Guskiewicz, K. M., Herring, S., Iverson, G. L., et al.

(2017). Consensus statement on concussion in sport-the 5th international conference on concussion in sport held in Berlin, October 2016. *British Journal of Sports Medicine, 51*, 838. https://doi.org/10.1136/bjsports-2017-097699

McGeary, D. D., Resick, P. A., Penzien, D. B., McGeary, C. A., Houle, T. T., Eapen, B. C., Jaramillo, C. A., Nabity, P. S., Reed, D. E., Moring, J. C., Bira, L. M., Hansen, H. R., Young-McCaughan, S., Cobos, B. A., Mintz, J., Keane, T. M., & Peterson, A. L. (2022). Cognitive behavioral therapy for veterans with comorbid posttraumatic headache and posttraumatic stress disorder symptoms: A randomized clinical trial. *JAMA Neurology, 79*(8), 746–757. https://doi.org/10.1001/jamaneurol.2022.1567

McLean, S. A., Kirsch, N. L., Tan-Schriner, C. U., Sen, A., Frederiksen, S., Harris, R. E., Maixner, W., & Maio, R. F. (2009). Health status, not head injury, predicts concussion symptoms after minor injury. *American Journal of Emergency Medicine, 27*(2), 182–190. https://doi.org/10.1016/j.ajem.2008.01.054

Meares, S., Shores, E. A., Taylor, A. J., Batchelor, J., Bryant, R. A., Baguley, I. J., Chapman, J., Gurka, J., Dawson, K., Capon, L., & Marosszeky, J. E. (2008). Mild traumatic brain injury does not predict acute postconcussion syndrome. *Journal of Neurology, Neurosurgery, and Psychiatry, 79*(3), 300–306. https://doi.org/10.1136/jnnp.2007.126565

Mendella, P. D., Burton, C. Z., Tasca, G. A., Roy, P., St. Louis, L., & Twamley, E. W. (2015). Compensatory cognitive training for people with first-episode schizophrenia: Results from a pilot randomized controlled trial. *Schizophrenia Research, 162*, 108–111.

Mikolić, A., Polinder, S., Retel Helmrich, I. R. A., Haagsma, J. A., & Cnossen, M. C. (2019). Treatment for posttraumatic stress disorder in patients with a history of traumatic brain injury: A systematic review. *Clinical Psychology Review, 73*, 101776. https://doi.org/10.1016/j.cpr.2019.101776

Mittal, D., Drummond, K. L., Blevins, D., Curran, G., Corrigan, P., & Sullivan, G. (2013). Stigma associated with PTSD: Perceptions of treatment seeking combat veterans. *Psychiatric Rehabilitation Journal, 36*(2), 86–92. https://doi.org/10.1037/h0094976

Mittenberg, W., Canyock, E. M., Condit, D., & Patton, C. (2001). Treatment of post-concussion syndrome following mild head injury. *Journal of Clinical and Experimental Neuropsychology, 23*(6), 829–836. https://doi.org/10.1076/jcen.23.6.829.1022

Murphy, J. L., Driscoll, M. A., Odom, A. S., & Hadlandsmyth, K. (2022). Post traumatic stress Disorder & Chronic Pain *PTSD. Research Quarterly, 33*(2).

Nampiaparampil, D. E. (2008). Prevalence of chronic pain after traumatic brain injury: A systematic review. *Journal of the American Medical Association, 300*, 711–719.

O'Neil, M. E., Laman-Maharg, B., Schnurr, P. P., Carlson, K. F., Twamley, E. W., Peterson, C., Storzbach, D., Helfand, M., & Sayer, N. A. (2017). Objective cognitive impairment and subjective cognitive problems in veterans initiating psychotherapy for posttraumatic stress disorder: An exploratory study. *Applied Neuropsychology. Adult, 1-8*, 247. https://doi.org/10.1080/23279095.2017.1395334

Pape, T. L., Herrold, A. A., Smith, B., Babcock-Parziale, J., Harp, J., Shandera-Ochsner, A., Jenkins, S., Evans, C. T., Schleenbaker, R., & High, W. M. (2016). Algorithm for symptom attribution and classification following possible mild traumatic brain injury. *The Journal of Head Trauma Rehabilitation, 31*(6), E10–e22. https://doi.org/10.1097/htr.0000000000000220

Peixoto, C., Hyland, L., Buchanan, D. M., Langille, E., & Nahas, R. (2018). The polytrauma clinical triad in patients with chronic pain after motor vehicle collision. *Journal of Pain Research, 11*, 1927–1936. https://doi.org/10.2147/jpr.S165077

Porter, K. E., Stein, M. B., Martis, B., Avallone, K. M., McSweeney, L. B., Smith, E. R., Simon, N. M., Gargan, S., Liberzon, I., Hoge, C. W., & Rauch, S. A. M. (2018). Postconcussive symptoms (PCS) following combat-related traumatic brain injury (TBI) in veterans with posttraumatic stress disorder (PTSD): Influence of TBI, PTSD, and depression on symptoms measured by the neurobehavioral symptom inventory (NSI). *Journal of Psychiatric Research, 102*, 8–13. https://doi.org/10.1016/j.jpsychires.2018.03.004

Potter, S. D., Brown, R. G., & Fleminger, S. (2016). Randomised, waiting list controlled trial of cognitive-behavioural therapy for persistent postconcussional symptoms after predominantly mild-moderate traumatic brain injury. *Journal of Neurology, Neurosurgery, and Psychiatry, 87*(10), 1075–1083. https://doi.org/10.1136/jnnp-2015-312838

Pruiksma, K. E., Taylor, D. J., Wachen, J. S., Mintz, J., Young-McCaughan, S., Peterson, A. L., Yarvis, J. S., Borah, E. V., Dondanville, K. A., Litz, B. T., Hembree, E. A., & Resick, P. A. (2016). Residual sleep disturbances following PTSD treatment in active duty military personnel. *Psychological Trauma, 8*(6), 697–701. https://doi.org/10.1037/tra0000150

Pruiksma, K. E., Taylor, D. J., Wachen, J. S., Straud, C. L., Hale, W. J., Mintz, J., Young-McCaughan, S., Peterson, A. L., Yarvis, J. S., Borah, E. V., Dondanville, K. A., Litz, B. T., & Resick, P. A. (2023). Self-reported sleep problems in active-duty US Army personnel receiving posttraumatic stress disorder treatment in group or individual formats: Secondary analysis of a randomized clinical trial. *Journal of Clinical Sleep Medicine, 19*(8), 1389–1398. https://doi.org/10.5664/jcsm.10584

Ragsdale, K. A., & Voss Horrell, S. C. (2016). Effectiveness of prolonged exposure and cognitive processing therapy for U.S. veterans with a history of traumatic brain injury. *Journal of Trauma Stress, 29*(5), 474–477. https://doi.org/10.1002/jts.22130

Rojczyk, P., Seitz-Holland, J., Kaufmann, E., Sydnor, V. J., Kim, C. L., Umminger, L. F., Wiegand, T. L. T., Guenette, J. P., Zhang, F., Rathi, Y., Bouix, S., Pasternak, O., Fortier, C. B., Salat, D., Hinds, S. R., Heinen, F., O'Donnell, L. J., Milberg, W. P., McGlinchey, R. E., et al. (2023). Sleep quality disturbances are associated with white matter alterations in veterans with posttraumatic stress disorder and mild traumatic brain injury. *Journal of Clinical Medicine, 12*(5). https://doi.org/10.3390/jcm12052079

Sayer, N. A., Rettman, N. A., Carlson, K. F., Bernardy, N., Sigford, B. J., Hamblen, J. L., & Friedman, M. J. (2009). Veterans with history of mild traumatic brain injury and posttraumatic stress disorder: Challenges from provider perspective. *Journal of Rehabilitation Research and Development, 46*(6), 703–716.

Schneiderman, A. I., Braver, E. R., & Kang, H. K. (2008). Understanding sequelae of injury mechanisms and mild traumatic brain injury incurred during the conflicts in Iraq and Afghanistan: Persistent postconcussive symptoms and posttraumatic stress disorder. *American Journal of Epidemiology, 167*(12), 1446–1452. https://doi.org/10.1093/aje/kwn068

Schwab, K., Terrio, H. P., Brenner, L. A., Pazdan, R. M., McMillan, H. P., MacDonald, M., Hinds, S. R., & Scher, A. I. (2017). Epidemiology and prognosis of mild traumatic brain injury in returning soldiers: A cohort study. *Neurology, 88*(16), 1571–1579. https://doi.org/10.1212/wnl.0000000000003839

Sciarrino, N. A., Warnecke, A. J., & Teng, E. J. (2020). A systematic review of intensive empirically supported treatments for posttraumatic stress disorder. *Journal of Traumatic Stress, 33*(4), 443–454. https://doi.org/10.1002/jts.22556

Scott, J. C., Georg, G. E., Wrocklage, K. M., Crnich, C., Jordan, J., Southwick, S. M., Krystal, J. H., & Schweinsburg, B. C. (2015). A quantitative meta-analysis of neurocognitive functioning in posttraumatic stress disorder. *Psychological Bulletin, 141*(1), 105–140. https://doi.org/10.1037/a0038039

Shorer, M., Segev, S., Rassovsky, Y., Fennig, S., Apter, A., & Peleg, T. P. (2020). Efficacy of psychological intervention for children with concurrent posttraumatic stress disorder and mild traumatic brain injury. *Journal of Traumatic Stress, 33*(3), 330–337. https://doi.org/10.1002/jts.22512

Smith-Seemiller, L., Fow, N. R., Kant, R., & Franzen, M. D. (2003). Presence of post-concussion syndrome symptoms in patients with chronic pain vs mild traumatic brain injury. *Brain Injury, 17*(3), 199–206. https://doi.org/10.1080/0269905021000030823

Song, K., Wang, C. P., McGeary, D. D., Jaramillo, C. A., Eapen, B. C., Amuan, M., McGeary, C. A., Potter, J. S., & Pugh, M. J. (2020). Five-year pain intensity and treatment trajectories of Post-9/11 veterans with mild traumatic brain injury. *The Journal of Pain, 21*(9–10), 1005–1017. https://doi.org/10.1016/j.jpain.2019.12.009

Spoormaker, V. I., & Montgomery, P. (2008). Disturbed sleep in post-traumatic stress disorder: Secondary symptom or Core feature? *Sleep Medicine Review, 12*, 169–184.

Sripada, R. K., Rauch, S. A., Tuerk, P. W., Smith, E., Defever, A. M., Mayer, R. A., Messina, M., & Venners, M. (2013). Mild traumatic brain injury and treatment response in prolonged exposure for PTSD. *Journal of Traumatic Stress, 26*(3), 369–375. https://doi.org/10.1002/jts.21813

Stein, M. B., Jain, S., Giacino, J. T., Levin, H., Dikmen, S., Nelson, L. D., Vassar, M. J., Okonkwo, D. O., Diaz-Arrastia, R., Robertson, C. S., Mukherjee, P., McCrea, M., Mac Donald, C. L., Yue, J. K., Yuh, E., Sun, X., Campbell-Sills, L., Temkin, N., Manley, G. T., & Investigators, a. t. T.-T. (2019). Risk of posttraumatic stress disorder and major depression in civilian patients after mild traumatic brain injury: A TRACK-TBI study. *JAMA Psychiatry, 76*(3), 249–258. https://doi.org/10.1001/jamapsychiatry.2018.4288

Stein, M. B., Kessler, R. C., Heeringa, S. G., Jain, S., Campbell-Sills, L., Colpe, L. J., Fullerton, C. S., Nock, M. K., Sampson, N. A., Schoenbaum, M., Sun, X., Thomas, M. L., & Ursano, R. J. (2015). Prospective longitudinal evaluation of the effect of deployment-acquired traumatic brain injury on posttraumatic stress and related disorders: Results from the Army study to assess risk and resilience in Servicemembers (Army STARRS). *American Journal of Psychiatry, 172*(11), 1101–1111. https://doi.org/10.1176/appi.ajp.2015.14121572

Storzbach, D., Twamley, E. W., Roost, M. S., Golshan, S., Williams, R. M., O'Neil, M., Jak, A. J., Turner, A. P., Kowalski, H. M., Pagulayan, K. F., & Huckans, M. (2017). Compensatory cognitive training for operation enduring freedom/operation Iraqi freedom/operation new Dawn veterans with mild traumatic brain injury. *Journal of Head Trauma Rehabilitation, 32*(1), 16–24. https://doi.org/10.1097/htr.0000000000000228

Sullan, M. J., Crocker, L. D., Thomas, K. R., Orff, H. J., Davey, D. K., Jurick, S. M., Twamley, E. W., Norman, S. B., Schiehser, D. M., Aupperle, R., & Jak, A. J. (2021). Baseline sleep quality moderates symptom improvement in veterans with comorbid PTSD and TBI receiving trauma-focused treatment. *Behaviour Research and Therapy, 143*, 103892. https://doi.org/10.1016/j.brat.2021.103892

Taylor, B. C., Hagel, E. M., Carlson, K. F., Cifu, D. X., Cutting, A., Bidelspach, D. E., & Sayer, N. A. (2012). Prevalence and costs of co-occurring traumatic brain injury with and without psychiatric disturbance and pain among Afghanistan and Iraq war veteran VA users. *Medical Care, 50*, 342–356.

Tiersky, L. A., Anselmi, V., Johnston, M. V., Kurtyka, J., Roosen, E., Schwartz, T., & DeLuca, J. (2005). A trial of Neuropsychologic rehabilitation in mild-Spectrum traumatic brain injury. *Archives of Physical Medicine and Rehabilitation, 86*(8), 1565–1574. http://www.sciencedirect.com/science/article/B6WB6-4GT5YXG-H/2/18f68f595e15725463b0fb3e0258080f

Twamley, E. W., Jak, A. J., Delis, D. C., Bondi, M. W., & Lohr, J. B. (2014). Cognitive symptom management and rehabilitation therapy (CogSMART) for veterans with traumatic brain injury: Pilot randomized controlled trial. *Journal of Rehabilitation Research and Development, 51*, 59–70.

Twamley, E. W., Thomas, K. R., Gregory, A. M., Jak, A. J., Bondi, M. W., Delis, D. C., & Lohr, J. B. (2015). CogSMART compensatory cognitive training for traumatic brain injury: Effects over 1 year. *Journal of Head Trauma Rehabilitation, 30*(6), 391–401. https://doi.org/10.1097/htr.0000000000000076

Twamley, E. W., Vella, L., Burton, C. Z., Heaton, R. K., & Jeste, D. V. (2012). Compensatory cognitive training for psychosis: Effects in a randomized controlled trial. *Journal of Clinical Psychiatry, 73*, 1212–1219.

VA/DoD. (2021). *VA/DoD clinical practice guideline. (2021). Management and Rehabilitation of Post-Acute Mild Traumatic Brain Injury (mTBI) Washington, DC: U.S. Government Printing Office*. U.S. Government Printing Office.

VA/DoD. (2023). *VA/DoD clinical practice Guideline for management of posttraumatic stress disorder and acute stress disorde*. U.S. Government Printing Office.

Van Praag, D. L. G., Cnossen, M. C., Polinder, S., Wilson, L., & Maas, A. I. R. (2019). Post-traumatic stress disorder after civilian traumatic brain injury: A systematic review and meta-analysis of prevalence rates. *Journal of Neurotrauma, 36*(23), 3220–3232. https://doi.org/10.1089/neu.2018.5759

Vasterling, J. J., Jacob, S. N., & Rasmusson, A. (2018). Traumatic brain injury and posttraumatic stress disorder: Conceptual, diagnostic, and therapeutic considerations in the context of co-occurrence. *Journal of Neuropsychiatry and Clinical Neurosciences, 30*, 90–100. https://doi.org/10.1176/appi.neuropsych.17090180

Verfaellie, M., Lafleche, G., Spiro, A., Tun, C., & Bousquet, K. (2013). Chronic postconcussion symptoms and functional outcomes in OEF/OIF veterans with self-report of blast exposure. *Journal of the International Neuropsychological Society, 19*(1), 1–10. https://doi.org/10.1017/S1355617712000902

Vidarsdottir, O. G., Roberts, D. L., Twamley, E. W., Gudmundsdottir, B., Sigurdsson, E., & Magnusdottir, B. B. (2019). Integrative cognitive remediation for early psychosis: Results from a randomized controlled trial. *Psychiatry Research, 273*, 690–698.

Vidarsdottir, O. G., Twamley, E. W., Roberts, D. L., Sigurdsson, E., Gudmundsdottir, B., & Magnusdottir, B. B. (2020). Integrative cognitive remediation for early psychosis: A 12-month follow-up. *Psychiatry Research, 288, 112964.*

Wachen, J. S., Mintz, J., LoSavio, S. T., Kennedy, J. E., Hale, W. J., Straud, C. L., et al. (2022). The impact of prior head injury on outcomes following group and individual cognitive processing therapy among military personnel. *Journal of Traumatic Stress, 35*(6), 1684–1695.

Walker, W. C., Hirsch, S., Carne, W., Nolen, T., Cifu, D. X., Wilde, E. A., Levin, H. S., Brearly, T. W., Eapen, B. C., & Williams, R. (2018). Chronic effects of Neurotrauma consortium (CENC) multicentre study interim analysis: Differences between participants with positive versus negative mild TBI histories. *Brain Injury, 32*(9), 1079–1089. https://doi.org/10.1080/02699052.2018.1479041

Walter, K. H., Dickstein, B. D., Barnes, S. M., & Chard, K. M. (2014a). Comparing effectiveness of CPT to CPT-C among U.S. veterans in an interdisciplinar residential PTSD/TBI treatment program. *Journal of Traumatic Stress, 27*, 438–445.

Walter, K. H., Dickstein, B. D., Barnes, S. M., & Chard, K. M. (2014b). Comparing effectiveness of CPT to CPT-C among U.S. veterans in an interdisciplinary residential PTSD/TBI treatment program. *Journal of Traumatic Stress, 27*(4), 438–445. https://doi.org/10.1002/jts.21934

Walter, K. H., Kiefer, S. L., & Chard, K. M. (2012). Relationship between posttraumatic stress disorder and postconcussive symptom improvement after completion of a posttraumatic stress disorder/traumatic brain injury residential treatment program. *Rehabilitation Psychology, 57*(1), 13–17. https://doi.org/10.1037/a0026254

Wang, Y., Chan, R. C., & Deng, Y. (2006). Examination of postconcussion-like symptoms in healthy university students: Relationships to subjective and objective neuropsychological function performance. *Archives of Clinical Neuropsychology, 21*(4), 339–347. https://doi.org/10.1016/j.acn.2006.03.006

Whittaker, R., Kemp, S., & House, A. (2007). Illness perceptions and outcome in mild head injury: A longitudinal study. *Journal of Neurology, Neurosurgery, and Psychiatry, 78*(6), 644–646. https://doi.org/10.1136/jnnp.2006.101105

Wolf, G. K., Mauntel, G. J., Kretzmer, T., Crawford, E., Thors, C., Strom, T. Q., & Vanderploeg, R. D. (2018). Comorbid posttraumatic stress disorder and traumatic brain injury: Generalization of prolonged-exposure PTSD treatment outcomes to Postconcussive symptoms, cognition, and self-efficacy in veterans and active duty service members. *Journal of Head Trauma Rehabiliation, 33*(2), E53–e63. https://doi.org/10.1097/htr.0000000000000344

Zayfert, C., & DeViva, J. C. (2004). Residual insomnia following cognitive behavioral therapy for PTSD. *Journal of Traumatic Stress, 17*(1), 69–73. https://doi.org/10.1023/B:JOTS.0000014679.31799.e7

Chapter 7
Delivering CPT in the Context of Sleep Disturbance

Kimberly B. Werner

Delivering CPT in the Context of Sleep Disturbance

Scope of the Problem

The co-occurrence of post-traumatic stress disorder (PTSD) and sleep impairment represents a significant clinical challenge when engaging patients in therapy. Sleep disturbance is a common and often debilitating symptom of a variety of mental health conditions with as many as 90% of individuals with PTSD reporting difficulty sleeping (Milanak et al., 2019). High rates of insomnia (35–61%; Colvonen et al., 2018) and trauma-related nightmares (50–96%; Leskin et al., 2002; Neylan et al., 1998) are consistently reported within the PTSD population. Clinicians and researchers have noted that sleep impairment is a hallmark feature of PTSD (Spoormaker & Montgomery, 2008), while others have argued that sleep impairment is only one of many PTSD symptoms to be considered. Regardless of whether sleep disturbances are considered a secondary symptom or core feature, patients may report significant interference that can deleteriously impact treatment engagement and PTSD remittance during a course of cognitive processing therapy (CPT). As such, the impact of sleep impairment and the utility of incorporating sleep-focused treatments as complementary treatments along with trauma-focused therapies have begun to be investigated to target sleep in PTSD (Weber & Wetter, 2022).

Insomnia, characterized by difficulties initiating or maintaining sleep, alongside distress or functional impairment during waking hours, is a prevalent concern among individuals with PTSD. Nightmares which often reenact traumatic events and impede restorative sleep, can further exacerbate the sleep-related challenges

K. B. Werner (✉)
College of Nursing, University of Missouri-St. Louis, St. Louis, MO, USA
e-mail: wernerk@umsl.edu

J. S. Wachen, T. E. Galovski (eds.), *Cognitive Processing Therapy for Complex Cases*, CBT: Science Into Practice,
https://doi.org/10.1007/978-3-031-87356-0_7

faced by individuals with PTSD. Beyond insomnia and nightmares, individuals with PTSD encounter an array of additional sleep disturbances encompassing not only sleep initiation, maintenance, and quality but also sleep-related disorders such as sleep apnea, sleep state misperception, and restless leg syndrome, collectively contributing to the multifaceted nature of sleep impairment within this population. The co-occurrence of these disturbances complicates the clinical landscape, necessitating a nuanced understanding for effective intervention strategies to target not only PTSD, but also these comorbid and debilitating disorders.

Theoretical frameworks attempt to explain how difficulties with sleep and nightmares not only constitute core symptomatology of PTSD, but also persist following successful CPT and PTSD remission. The biopsychosocial model integrates biological, psychological, and social factors to understand the etiology and maintenance of sleep disturbances in PTSD. According to this framework, sleep disturbances arise from a complex interplay of neurobiological dysregulation, psychological vulnerability (e.g., maladaptive cognitions, emotional dysregulation), and environmental stressors (e.g., trauma-related triggers, social support deficits) (Germain et al., 2008). Trauma-focused therapies like CPT address these factors by targeting the underlying neurobiological mechanisms of PTSD, challenging maladaptive cognitions, and enhancing coping skills. However, residual manifestations of sleep disturbances may persist due to the lingering effects of trauma-related arousal and environmental stressors on sleep physiology and functioning.

The Nightmare Cognitive Arousal Processing (Night-CAP) model posits that existing sleep disturbances underly and predict the development of PTSD (Youngren et al., 2020). This model focuses on the role of nightmares in the perpetuation of sleep disturbance in PTSD, while the cognitive-behavioral model emphasizes the role of maladaptive beliefs and behaviors in perpetuating sleep disturbances in PTSD. According to this framework, individuals with PTSD may develop dysfunctional beliefs about sleep (e.g., "I will never feel safe enough to sleep") and engage in behaviors that maintain sleep disturbances (e.g., excessive time awake in bed, avoidance of sleep-related cues). Nightmares and other sleep disturbances are viewed as learned responses to trauma-related stimuli, reinforced by negative cognitions and behaviors. Cognitive-behavioral therapies, such as CPT and cognitive behavioral therapy for insomnia (CBT-I), aim to modify these maladaptive beliefs and behaviors, thereby reducing the frequency and severity of sleep disturbances. However, as described below, residual levels of sleep disturbances may persist due to unresolved trauma-related cognitions and behaviors even after successful treatment.

The bidirectional nature of the relationship between insomnia and PTSD is a complex entanglement of symptoms and etiology between these two disorders (Richards et al., 2020). Within this reciprocal relationship, traumatic experiences can disrupt sleep patterns, while sleep disturbances, in turn, can exacerbate symptoms of PTSD perpetuating a cycle of mutual reinforcement. Preexisting sleep issues before trauma exposure have been identified as potential risk factors for developing PTSD (Bryant et al., 2010; Wang et al., 2020), while insomnia symptoms immediately following a traumatic event may serve as predictive markers for

PTSD onset (Koren et al., 2002; Wright et al., 2011). Research even suggests that sleep-related factors, such as sleep duration and difficulties falling or staying asleep, can predict the severity of PTSD symptoms on subsequent days (Biggs et al., 2020). Sleep disturbances, notably insomnia, not only exacerbate the severity of PTSD symptoms but also negatively impact quality of life, daily functioning (Brownlow et al., 2016), and may increase the risk of substance misuse (Nishith et al., 2001; Miller et al., 2017). The bidirectional relationship between sleep disturbance and trauma provides important context for addressing sleep-related difficulties in PTSD treatment in order to optimize therapeutic outcomes.

Neurobiological mechanisms underpinning the relationship between sleep and PTSD underscore the interplay between these phenomena and can provide potential approaches for intervention (Richards et al., 2020). Dysregulation of the hypothalamic-pituitary-adrenal (HPA) axis, alterations in neurotransmitter systems (e.g., serotonin, noradrenaline), and disruptions in the sleep-wake cycle have all been implicated in both PTSD and sleep disturbances. For instance, hyperarousal, a symptom of PTSD, is associated with heightened sympathetic activity and dysregulated stress response systems, which can behaviorally present as sleep-onset insomnia and frequent awakenings during the night. Individuals with PTSD often exhibit alterations in sleep architecture when objectively assessed with polysomnography, including decreased rapid eye movement (REM) sleep latency, increased REM density, and disturbances in slow-wave sleep (Kobayashi et al., 2007). These sleep abnormalities not only contribute to the symptomatic profile of PTSD but also have implications for cognitive functioning, emotional processing, and overall psychosocial well-being.

Experiences of sleep disturbance, while part of the PTSD symptom criteria, can complicate PTSD expression, significantly impacting overall well-being and recovery. The pervasive impact of sleep impairment on health and well-being extends beyond mere symptomatology into various domains of functioning and quality of life. Sleep disturbances have been implicated in a range of adverse health outcomes, including cardiovascular disease, dysregulated stress response systems, and increased risk of comorbid psychiatric conditions (Harvey, 2008). Sleep impairment has been associated with deleterious effects on cognitive functioning, emotional regulation, and psychosocial well-being, impairing individuals' ability to cope with traumatic memories and navigate daily challenges (Germain et al., 2008). Harvey (2008) conducted a longitudinal study investigating the impact of sleep disturbances on physiological arousal and stress response systems. Their findings revealed a significant association between sleep impairment and heightened sympathetic activity, as evidenced by increased heart rate variability and cortisol levels. These physiological alterations not only exacerbate symptoms of PTSD, but also contribute to the development of comorbid medical conditions, such as cardiovascular disease and metabolic disorders. Studies have consistently documented the deleterious effects of sleep disturbances on social relationships, occupational functioning, and overall quality of life (Pigeon et al., 2013). Individuals grappling with PTSD and sleep impairment often report difficulties maintaining employment, fulfilling familial roles, and engaging in recreational activities, potentially exacerbating feelings of isolation and distress.

Furthermore, Germain et al. (2008) explored the cognitive and emotional consequences of sleep impairment in individuals with PTSD. Their research, as well as their report on others' research, demonstrated that sleep disturbances disrupt neural circuits associated with cognitive processing and emotional regulation, impairing individuals' ability to effectively cope with traumatic memories and regulate negative affect. Consequently, sleep impairment perpetuates a cycle of maladaptive coping strategies, exacerbating symptoms of PTSD and compromising overall psychosocial well-being. This can also manifest as inability to engage with treatment when targeting cognitive distortions and stuck points within the context of CPT.

Sleep disturbance can not only have a significant impact on a person's quality of life, including their ability to function at work, school, and in relationships, but also impede the ability to engage in treatment for PTSD. The disruptive effects of sleep disturbances on emotional regulation, memory consolidation, and daily functioning underscore the need to address this comorbidity when evaluating clients' needs and symptomatology as well as designing a treatment plan. The impact of sleep on PTSD can be profound and multifaceted, with disturbances in sleep architecture, neurobiological dysregulation, and bidirectional relationships exacerbating the complexity of the disorder. By elucidating these mechanisms, we can gain deeper insights into the interplay between PTSD and sleep disturbances, paving the way for more effective intervention strategies that address the comprehensive needs of individuals grappling with these comorbidities.

Research Overview

While CPT has been shown to be effective in reducing symptoms of PTSD, including sleep disturbance symptomatology, recent research has indicated that CPT alone may not be effective in reducing subjective or objective measured sleep impairment (Haynes et al., 2020). Historically, research has indicated even with successful CPT treatment reducing PTSD symptoms, overall sleep impairment remained above clinical cutoffs (Galovski et al., 2016). In a study comparing CPT and prolonged exposure (PE) treatment for PTSD in 108 female rape survivors who completed treatment (Galovski et al., 2009), significant improvements in sleep quality as well as subscales of sleep quantity, efficiency, and onset, as measured by the Pittsburgh Sleep Quality Index, were reported in both treatment groups. Despite these reductions in sleep dysfunction and PTSD symptomatology, neither treatment group met the level of remission from sleep disturbance, once again reinforcing the refractory nature of sleep impairment in this population. More recent evaluation of data from the same study, expanding to the intent to treat sample ($N = 171$) and using a long-term follow-up approach (mean 6 years posttreatment), indicated the treatment gains were maintained through the long-term follow-up assessment but affirmed that CPT nor PE improved sleep to "normal sleep levels" (Gutner et al., 2013).

Research in veteran and active-duty service member samples also reported similar improvements in sleep associated with reductions in PTSD severity following CPT; however, most also indicated sleep-related treatment gains were small and did not return to "normal sleep levels". Pruiksma et al. (2016) investigated nightmares and disturbed sleep in a sample of active-duty service members and found that both experiences of nightmares (62%) and insomnia (92%) were prevalent at baseline. These difficulties persisted posttreatment for both CPT and group present-centered therapy patients, with insomnia reported in over half (59%) and nightmares in 13% of the participants who no longer met the criteria for PTSD following treatment. Additional research in veterans exposed to military sexual trauma with PTSD (Holder et al., 2019), veterans receiving outpatient CPT (Haynes et al., 2020), and active-duty service members with PTSD (Pruiksma et al., 2016) indicate high rates of insomnia and sleep disturbance at baseline with marginal improvements in insomnia over the course of treatment. Consistent with other research, sleep scores remained in clinical ranges posttreatment, despite significant and clinically meaningful improvements in PTSD severity and diagnosis.

While CPT has proven to be successful in treating PTSD and may indirectly improve insomnia and other sleep dysfunction, CPT has not been shown to lower sleep disturbances to a level deemed clinically normal. Researchers suggest that these PTSD treatments may target certain factors contributing to sleep disturbances, such as feeling unsafe, unwanted trauma memories, hypervigilance, and cognitive distortions. However, other behavioral elements, including irregular sleep patterns, prolonged wakefulness in bed, ineffective stimulus control, and maladaptive beliefs about sleep, are not explicitly targeted by these treatments. Consequently, these underlying symptoms that may remain unaddressed could explain the persistence of insomnia in certain cases. Taken together, these findings stress the importance of augmenting PTSD interventions with sleep-focused treatments.

Guided by the augmentation approach, Galovski et al. (2016) examined the efficacy of 3 weeks of sleep-directed hypnosis prior to CPT for PTSD in a sample of 108 female interpersonal assault survivors. Data indicated that 3 weeks of sleep-directed hypnosis improved insomnia symptoms and global sleep quality, particularly in sleep latency. However, treatment conditions did not differ across total sleep time or experience of nightmares and, although reductions in PTSD symptoms were reported during the hypnosis component, the sleep-directed treatment before CPT did not augment gains in PTSD treatment over the long-term. While sleep impairment was severe at baseline and statistically significant improvements were displayed posttreatment, average sleep scores were still close to clinical cutoffs at both posttreatment and follow-up assessments. These findings hold for objectively measured (actigraphy) sleep outcomes as well (Arditte Hall et al., 2021). That said, the relative ease and short time frame of hypnosis treatment as an adjunct could be beneficial to implement prior to CPT for clients with significant sleep disturbance who might experience difficulty in CPT engagement. Pigeon et al. (2022) implemented CBT-I prior to starting CPT in 110 civilian participants exposed to interpersonal violence who had PTSD and insomnia. After treatment, participants who received CBT-I plus CPT experienced decreases in PTSD and insomnia symptoms as compared to those who were in the attention control group. However, mean scores for sleep disturbance remained above clinical cutoffs at posttreatment. Findings from a recent pilot study (Taylor et al., 2023) indicated larger symptom improvements for PTSD and insomnia when combining cognitive behavioral therapy for insomnia and nightmares (CBT-I&N) and CPT, regardless of if CBT-I&N preceded or followed traditional CPT treatment.

When focusing specifically on sleep-focused treatment in individuals with trauma exposure and PTSD, some efficacy has been found for three treatments—CBT-I; imagery rehearsal therapy (IRT); and exposure, relaxation, and rescripting therapy (ERRT)—to reduce sleep disturbance (e.g., insomnia and nightmares) in PTSD populations (see meta-analysis Ho et al., 2016; review Casement & Swanson, 2012). While not in combination with CPT, these treatments have been shown to significantly improve nightmares, insomnia, sleep quality, and sleep efficiency in individuals with PTSD (see review Isaac et al., 2022). Overall results from multiple randomized control trials indicated that CBT-I alone or in combination with IRT or EERT were beneficial for treating sleep impairment in PTSD (Ho et al., 2016; Isaac et al., 2022). While study samples, treatment provided, and measures implemented differed across these RCTs, improvements in insomnia severity and nightmare frequency were reported. Further, PTSD symptoms were also reduced following successful sleep-focused treatments with moderate to large effect sizes (Casement & Swanson, 2012; Ho et al., 2016; Isaac et al., 2022). Overall findings across four RCTs indicated that six to eight sessions of CBT-I significantly improved insomnia severity at follow-up and long-term 6-month follow-up assessment (Germain et al., 2012; Talbot et al., 2014; Taylor et al., 2017; Walters et al., 2020). This is consistent with previous reviews (Taylor & Pruiksma, 2014) and research (Ulmer et al., 2011; Margolies et al., 2013) on sleep treatments within PTSD populations.

These studies add to the literature by highlighting the importance of integrating behavioral sleep medicine into the comprehensive treatment approach for PTSD, although additional research is needed to fully understand the relationship between insomnia, nightmares, and PTSD symptomatology. While some findings have been promising, and CBT-I, IRT, ERRT, and sleep directed hypnosis have been shown to reduce insomnia in PTSD populations, overall reductions in sleep impairment have not reached the level of remission and "normal sleep". Due to the limited research and marginal strength of existing findings on adjunct treatments for PTSD, insomnia, and nightmares, there is a need for studies to provide additional evidence and replicate findings to establish the most effective treatment.

The majority of existing research has aimed to address sleep disturbances prior to treating PTSD (Miller et al., 2020). Addressing sleep issues first may ameliorate sleep deprivation, thereby improving patients' ability to cognitively engage and regulate emotions during treatment, which could facilitate better processing of traumatic experiences. Implementing sleep-focused treatments first also may reduce stigma around the therapy process, leading to reduced anticipation and anxiety as well as a smoother transition and greater confidence in subsequent PTSD treatments (Baddeley & Gros, 2013). This approach could also enhance the patient-provider relationship before delving into trauma-related material as part of PTSD therapy, potentially strengthening the therapeutic alliance. That said, a rationale also exists for addressing PTSD prior to addressing sleep disturbances. Prioritizing PTSD treatment may alleviate hyperarousal symptoms that could be leading to sleep disruption and, therefore enhance the PTSD treatment process by addressing lingering issues related to sleep specifically. Trauma-related cognitive distortions could be addressed in CPT which could indirectly improve sleep impairment. From a practicality of treatment delivery, trauma-focused clinicians may feel more comfortable delivering CPT and may feel insufficiently informed about the full clinical picture to tackle sleep disturbances first.

Clinical Applications

Addressing sleep disturbance within CPT and integrating sleep-focused interventions within CPT can contribute to comprehensive trauma recovery. While CBT-I and other sleep-focused treatments are predominantly focused on improving nocturnal symptoms, these treatments have also been shown to positively impact daytime functioning and well-being (Ho et al., 2016). Addressing sleep disturbance and nightmares can help reduce hyperarousal, enhance cognitive processing, and improve overall treatment engagement and outcomes (Colvonen et al., 2018). Both the American Psychological Association (APA) and, 2017 Department of Veterans Affairs Department of Defense (VA/DoD;, 2018) clinical practice guidelines recommend CBT-I as a first-line treatment for insomnia within a PTSD population. However, in the 2023 revision of the VA/DoD clinical practice guidelines (2023), the (a) recommendation of independent assessment of co-occurring sleep disturbances and (b) recommendation of CBT-I for insomnia in patients with PTSD were removed after review. The guidelines indicated insufficient evidence to support these recommendations.

Relevant to nightmares, in a position paper in 2018, the American Academy of Sleep Medicine (Morgenthaler et al., 2018) recommended IRT as a treatment for PTSD-related nightmares. The paper further noted that cognitive behavioral therapy, CBT-I, eye movement desensitization and reprocessing, and ERRT may be used for the treatment of PTSD-associated nightmares. However, the VA/DoD note in their 2023 clinical practice guidelines (VA/DoD, 2023) that there is insufficient evidence to provide a recommendation for or against any treatment of PTSD-related nightmares, including IRT. The APA does not currently have guidelines related to the primary treatment of nightmares in PTSD (APA, 2017).

While clinical treatment guidelines have generally not been established or agreed upon to treat sleep disturbance within a PTSD population, this section explores practical strategies for delivering CPT in the context of sleep disturbance. Existing research does suggest that incorporating sleep-focused interventions into trauma-focused treatments, such as CPT, can lead to significant improvements in sleep quality, PTSD symptoms, and overall functioning. As described above, studies examining the efficacy of combining sleep-focused techniques with CPT have reported significant results that may have clinical impact on patients who are experience sleep disturbance along with PTSD. This evidence, as well as data outside of CPT augmentation trials, have indicated that CBT-I and IRT may be effective techniques to reduce insomnia symptomatology prior to CPT. That said, prior to considering any treatment, thorough assessment and evaluation of sleep disturbance should be completed.

The first step is to identify the trauma-related sleep impairment through assessment. A number of self-report sleep assessments have shown strong validity and reliability in traumatized samples. The Pittsburgh Sleep Quality Index (Buysse et al., 1989) as well as the Insomnia Severity Index (Bastien et al., 2001) are commonly used to evaluate symptoms of insomnia and sleep quality. For ongoing tracking of the client's sleep disturbance, daily sleep diaries can be used to evaluate any change in sleep domains, experiences of nightmares, and daytime dysfunction associated with nocturnal disruption. The therapist could conduct a functional analysis of the client's sleep disturbance to identify the factors that were maintaining the problem specific to PTSD. If sleep assessment identifies significant sleep disturbance that would prevent the client from engaging with the therapist and moving through CPT, adjunct, manualized therapies such as CBT-I and IRT should be considered prior to beginning with CPT. If sleep disturbance reaches clinical levels, clients may benefit from referral to a sleep impairment protocol utilizing objective measurement of sleep and sleep architecture such as polysomnography. If sleep impairment seems to be a predominant factor, and may serve as a barrier to CPT engagement, treatment of insomnia prior to CPT initiation may be considered. Clinicians should consider the severity of the sleep impairment, and, when indicated, potentially consider referral to a sleep specialist. If sleep impairment is less severe and potentially manageable, integration of sleep-focused treatment prior to or within CPT sessions may be appropriate. If this approach is utilized, sleep disturbance should be monitored through the therapeutic process using weekly assessment or daily sleep diary monitoring.

When clinical focus on the impact of sleep impairment, as well as factors that may be underlying the trauma-related sleep impairment are warranted, the literature does provide us some strategies that could serve to integrate approaches from CBT-I, IRT, and other augmentation sleep-focused treatments that could be integrated or augment CPT. Addressing co-occurring sleep impairments in PTSD through integration and augmentation with CPT involves a multifaceted approach that combines core CPT skills with evidence-based techniques tailored to sleep issues. That said, clinicians should be trained in sleep-focused treatments to ensure fidelity and best practices. If the clinician is not trained in appropriate treatments, referral to a specialist should be considered.

Sleep hygiene education and monitoring is an approach that is aligned with CBT-I methodology (Perlis et al., 2005) and could be incorporated as part of CPT augmentation. The integration of evidence-based sleep-focused interventions, such as sleep hygiene education, cognitive restructuring of sleep-related thoughts, and relaxation techniques, can enhance the effectiveness of CPT and improve treatment outcomes. These strategies include teaching patients about the importance of keeping a consistent sleep schedule, creating a relaxing and dedicated sleep environment, limiting consumption of caffeine and use of electronic devices before bed, and engaging in relaxing activities before sleep. These practices can improve sleep quality and reinforce the progress made in CPT sessions. Another strategy is to encourage patients to self-monitor using daily sleep diaries to track time into bed and out of bed, the number of awakenings and total time awake, sleep quality, and any intrusive thoughts that occur prior to falling asleep or awaking during the night.

Clinicians can incorporate core CPT skills to identify and challenge negative beliefs related to the traumatic event that contribute to sleep difficulties. For instance, if a patient believes they are responsible for the trauma and this belief triggers nightmares, work on reevaluating this belief by gathering evidence to counter it. This process can reduce the emotional intensity tied to traumatic memories and subsequently lessen their impact on sleep. That said, as noted in the CPT manual (Resick et al., 2016), patients could fixate on sleep disturbance as an avoidance strategy to engage in other trauma-related material during sessions. Therefore, authors recommend that sleep-related items should be a focus of additional worksheets outside of normal session to allow for the primary focus directly on trauma-related material and sleep as an important but secondary target.

Further application of cognitive restructuring techniques to address sleep-related thoughts that perpetuate insomnia or nightmares could also be implemented. For example, if a patient anticipates nightmares before sleep, assist them in identifying these anxious thoughts and challenge them with evidence-based reasoning. This can alleviate sleep-related anxiety and create a more conducive mindset for sleep. As discussed in the identification and modification of trauma-related beliefs CPT approach, it is important to distinguish between primary and secondary concerns related to the trauma experience and focus on trauma-related stuck points and beliefs during session.

Finally, aligned with the findings from Galovski et al. (2016), hypnosis and deep relaxation techniques improved sleep prior to initiation of CPT. Augmenting CPT with relaxation techniques such as deep relaxation breathing, or mindfulness meditation may help with the reduction of insomnia symptoms. These techniques help manage arousal and anxiety levels, making it easier for patients to relax prior to treatment as well as before bedtime.

By integrating these evidence-based techniques into the core framework of CPT, therapists can offer a comprehensive approach to addressing the co-occurring sleep impairments in PTSD. Customizing treatment to the individual's needs and combining established therapeutic modalities enhances the overall effectiveness of therapy and contributes to the patient's recovery journey. If sleep disturbance remains following a successful course of CPT, where PTSD remits, the client may benefit from a course of CBT-I (Perlis et al., 2005) or IRT (Krakow & Zadra, 2010), both of which have shown efficacy for treating insomnia in individuals with PTSD (Thünker & Pietrowsky, 2012). That said, both modalities require training in their respective structured approaches to ensure fidelity to the treatment. As such, clinicians should receive adequate training in these treatment modalities or consider referring clients to trained professionals.

Case Example

The following case example illustrates how clinicians could incorporate sleep-focused approaches into CPT delivery for individuals who endorse significant sleep disturbance in the context of PTSD.

Patient Background Sarah is a 32-year-old woman who recently experienced a traumatic event in which she was involved in a car accident that resulted in the death of a close friend. She has been diagnosed with PTSD and is also struggling with sleep disturbances. She frequently has nightmares related to the accident and has difficulty falling asleep and staying asleep.

Assessment The therapist assessed the client's sleep disturbance using the ISI and deemed that, while the client is experiencing symptoms of insomnia, the symptoms are manageable within the context of the CPT delivery. To track sleep symptoms, in addition to the CPT worksheets, the clinician will ask the client to complete a sleep diary including a reporting of overall restfulness of sleep, sleep onset latency, total sleep time, sleep quality, any wakefulness after sleep onset, and if any nightmares occurred.

Treatment Plan Throughout the course of CPT, the therapist and patient develop a treatment plan that includes CPT, relaxation techniques, and lifestyle changes. The therapist begins by working with the client to identify her negative and distorted thoughts about sleep. Throughout CPT and aligned with CPT processes, the therapist assists the client in challenging these thoughts and developing more realistic and helpful beliefs. The therapist teaches and encourages the client to use relaxation techniques, such as deep breathing and progressive muscle relaxation, to help her relax before bed. Finally, the therapist can work with the client to make lifestyle changes, such as establishing a regular sleep schedule and avoiding caffeine and alcohol before bed.

Session 1: Assessment, Psychoeducation, and Introduction to CPT

Therapist (incorporating a brief sleep assessment into CPT Session 1): *Sarah, I'd also like to understand more about your sleep and how it's been impacted since the accident. Can you tell me about your sleep patterns and any specific difficulties you've been facing?*

Sarah: *Well, ever since the accident, I've been having trouble falling asleep. I keep having nightmares about the accident, and it's like I'm reliving it all over again. Even when I do fall asleep, I wake up several times during the night, sweating and feeling anxious.*

Therapist: *It sounds like your sleep is really being affected by the trauma you experienced. These types of sleep difficulties are common with PTSD. Through CPT,* *we'll work on understanding and challenging the thoughts and beliefs that are maintaining your distressing symptoms, including sleep. In addition to engaging with the trauma memory and identifying and examining stuck points, we can discuss different strategies to improve your daily habits around relaxation and sleep by focusing on some strategies to improve your environment and make it more conducive to relaxation and sleep.*

Session 2: Identifying Stuck Points Affecting Sleep

Therapist (after patient reads impact statement and as the stuck point log is being developed): *Let's also highlight some of the stuck points that might be related to your difficulties with sleep. For example, when you have nightmares, it sounds like certain beliefs are getting triggered. These beliefs might be related to your safety, the world, or yourself. Are there any sleep-related stuck points that you can identify?*

Sarah: *That makes sense. So, you're saying that my nightmares might be linked to my thoughts about the accident? I think a stuck point might be "I'm in danger when I am asleep."*

Therapist: *Exactly. By identifying and examining these thoughts, we can help reduce the emotional distress and the impact they have on your sleep. There also may be certain stuck points that you are experiencing that impact your ability to relax and get restful sleep. In addition to processing the trauma, we'll also work on improving your sleep hygiene and developing relaxation techniques that can help you manage your anxiety and fall asleep more easily.*

Session 3: Identifying and Challenging Stuck Points and Negative Beliefs

Therapist (during the process of examining assimilated stuck points): *Sarah, let's also identify some of the thoughts that come up when you have nightmares or when you're struggling to sleep.*

Sarah: *Well, one thought that comes up a lot when I am trying to get to sleep or after I wake up from a nightmare is that I could have done something to prevent the accident. Like, I keep thinking I should have driven slower or taken a different route. I start to feel panicky and just toss and turn or even have to leave bed because my anxiety is high.*

Therapist: *I agree—that sounds like a stuck point to me. Let's examine this thought. Is it possible that you're placing unrealistic expectations on yourself? Could there have been other factors beyond your control that contributed to the accident?* [Therapist and Sarah gently challenge the stuck point and therapist suggests some deep breathing techniques and recommends a progressive muscle relaxation app for Sarah to begin to use prior to bedtime to help her relax and reduce her anxiety.]

Session 4: Modifying Negative Beliefs and Sleep Techniques

Therapist: *Sarah, we've been working on challenging and modifying your stuck points related to the accident. How have you been applying these techniques?*

Sarah: *I've been trying to remind myself that accidents can happen to anyone and that it's not solely my fault. And for sleep, I've been practicing the deep breathing and progressive muscle relaxation before bed. It's been helping me calm down and fall asleep faster.*

Therapist: *That's great to hear, Sarah. Challenging those negative beliefs takes time, but with practice, it can really make a difference. And the relaxation techniques you're using are evidence-based ways to manage anxiety, which can improve your sleep.*

Sessions 5–11

Over the course of the remainder of the protocol, CPT progresses as per the protocol. Beyond the assimilated, sleep-related stuck points, the therapist and Sarah identify several over-accommodated stuck points as well (e.g., "I'll never get adequate sleep again", "It is not safe to fall asleep—bad things happen when you are not fully on guard," and "I don't deserve to feel rested and well while my friend died in the accident"). These stuck points were preventing Sarah from relaxing and were contributing to anxiety that prevented sleep. The therapist also augmented the CPT protocol by continuing to check in on sleep hygiene items (Sarah was taking a lot of naps during the day and had a habit of drinking coffee in the late afternoon to help boost her energy). Sarah continued practicing her relaxation techniques, made minor tweaks in her list of sleep hygiene items, and used CPT techniques to challenge her sleep-related stuck points.

Session 12: Review and Future Steps

Therapist: *Sarah, as we wrap up, I'm proud of the progress you've made in challenging your stuck points and improving your PTSD including your sleep difficulties! Keep practicing the techniques we've discussed and remember that this is a gradual process. If nightmares or sleep troubles persist, we can continue to address them in our sessions or we can certainly offer you a referral for additional work on any remaining insomnia.*

Sarah: *Thank you, Dr. Smith. I do feel like things are getting better, and I'm hopeful that my sleep will continue to improve.*

Therapist: *You're welcome, Sarah. Remember, our goal is to help you regain a sense of safety, control, and restful sleep. Keep up the good work, and we'll continue working together to overcome the impact of the trauma.*

Outcome: After 12 weeks of treatment, the client reported significant improvement in her sleep. She reported that she was sleeping through the night more often and that she was having far fewer nightmares. She also reported that she was feeling more rested and alert during the day.

This case example integrates CPT to address Sarah's co-occurring sleep disorder and PTSD. As covered in this chapter, it is clear that trauma-related beliefs can contribute to sleep disturbances, including insomnia and nightmares, in individuals with PTSD. CPT focuses on challenging and modifying these negative beliefs, which can in turn alleviate symptoms like nightmares and improve sleep quality. The integration of relaxation techniques and sleep hygiene practices enhances the effectiveness of treatment, aligning with research that supports the use of these strategies to manage sleep difficulties in PTSD patients.

Future Directions

Research in the treatment of sleep impairment in PTSD is an important area of study, given the significant impact that sleep disturbances can have on individuals with PTSD as well as the refractory nature of sleep impairment following CPT. Future research is needed to rigorously investigate the efficacy of targeted interventions specifically designed to address sleep disturbances in individuals with PTSD. These studies should include detailed and longitudinal assessment and tracking of sleep and PTSD symptoms throughout the study implementation. Further research into the neurological and cognitive underpinnings of the relationship between PTSD and insomnia could assist in the disentanglement of these two disorders as well as provide novel treatment targets and approaches to address each. Identification of biomarkers could also help predict treatment response or inform personalized treatment approaches. Future research specifically targeting treatment approach is also warranted for sleep disturbance in PTSD. Examining the feasibility and acceptability of treatments and exploring the use of technology-based interventions, such as mobile apps or wearable devices, for monitoring and treating sleep impairment in PTSD could provide real-time feedback and support for individuals with PTSD, potentially increasing engagement with treatment and improving outcomes.

Summary

Sleep disturbances, particularly insomnia and nightmares, are significant impairments in PTSD and, oftentimes, remain above clinical cutoffs following successful treatment for PTSD. Research has provided evidence for a bidirectional relationship between PTSD and sleep disturbance and overlapping neurological and cognitive underpinnings that facilitate the perpetuation of symptoms. Data suggest efficacy of sleep-focused treatments, such as CBT-I, IRT, ERRT, and sleep-directed hypnosis treatment to supplement CPT and address sleep disturbance in PTSD clients. Further research is warranted to rigorously examine the effectiveness of these interventions, as well as to explore additional modalities tailored specifically to the complex interplay of PTSD and sleep disturbance. Understanding the underlying mechanisms through which PTSD and sleep disturbance interact is crucial for developing targeted and effective therapeutic approaches. Finally, investigating the long-term outcomes and mechanisms to which treatments are efficacious is essential for optimizing treatment strategies and improving the overall well-being of individuals suffering from PTSD-related sleep disturbances.

Competing Interests The authors have no conflicts of interest to declare that are relevant to the content of this chapter.

References

American Psychological Association. (2017). *Clinical practice guidelines for the treatment of posttraumatic stress disorder (PTSD) in Adults*; https://www.apa.org/ptsd-guideline/ptsd.pdf

Arditte Hall, K. A., Werner, K. B., Griffin, M. G., & Galovski, T. E. (2021). The effects of cognitive processing therapy+ hypnosis on objective sleep quality in women with posttraumatic stress disorder. *Psychological Trauma: Theory, Research, Practice, and Policy, 13*(6), 652.

Baddeley, J. L., & Gros, D. F. (2013). Cognitive behavioral therapy for insomnia as a preparatory treatment for exposure therapy for posttraumatic stress disorder. *American Journal of Psychotherapy, 67*(2), 203–214.

Bastien, C. H., Vallières, A., & Morin, C. M. (2001). Validation of the insomnia severity index as an outcome measure for insomnia research. *Sleep Medicine, 2*(4), 297–307.

Biggs, Q. M., Ursano, R. J., Wang, J., Wynn, G. H., Carr, R. B., & Fullerton, C. S. (2020). Post traumatic stress symptom variation associated with sleep characteristics. *BMC Psychiatry, 20*, 1–10.

Brownlow, J. A., McLean, C. P., Gehrman, P. R., Harb, G. C., Ross, R. J., & Foa, E. B. (2016). Influence of sleep disturbance on global functioning after posttraumatic stress disorder treatment. *Journal of Traumatic Stress, 29*(6), 515–521.

Bryant, R. A., Creamer, M., O'Donnell, M., Silove, D., & McFarlane, A. C. (2010). Sleep disturbance immediately prior to trauma predicts subsequent psychiatric disorder. *Sleep, 33*(1), 69–74.

Buysse, D. J., Reynolds, C. F., III, Monk, T. H., Berman, S. R., & Kupfer, D. J. (1989). The Pittsburgh sleep quality index: A new instrument for psychiatric practice and research. *Psychiatry Research, 28*(2), 193–213.

Casement, M. D., & Swanson, L. M. (2012). A meta-analysis of imagery rehearsal for post-trauma nightmares: Effects on nightmare frequency, sleep quality, and posttraumatic stress. *Clinical Psychology Review, 32*(6), 566–574. https://doi.org/10.1016/j.cpr.2012.06.002

Colvonen, P. J., Straus, L. D., Stepnowsky, C., McCarthy, M. J., Goldstein, L. A., & Norman, S. B. (2018). Recent advancements in treating sleep disorders in co-occurring PTSD. *Current Psychiatry Reports, 20*, 1–13.

Department of Veteran Affairs, Department of Defense. (2023). *VA/DoD Clinical practice guidelines for the management of posttraumatic stress disorder and acute stress reactions*; https://www.healthquality.va.gov/guidelines/MH/ptsd/VA-DoD-CPG-PTSD-Full-CPGAug242023.pdf

Galovski, T. E., Harik, J. M., Blain, L. M., Elwood, L., Gloth, C., & Fletcher, T. D. (2016). Augmenting cognitive processing therapy to improve sleep impairment in PTSD: A randomized controlled trial. *Journal of Consulting and Clinical Psychology, 84*(2), 167.

Galovski, T. E., Monson, C., Bruce, S. E., & Resick, P. A. (2009). Does cognitive–behavioral therapy for PTSD improve perceived health and sleep impairment? *Journal of Traumatic Stress: Official Publication of The International Society for Traumatic Stress Studies, 22*(3), 197–204.

Germain, A., Buysse, D. J., & Nofzinger, E. (2008). Sleep-specific mechanisms underlying posttraumatic stress disorder: Integrative review and neurobiological hypotheses. *Sleep Medicine Reviews, 12*(3), 185–195.

Germain, A., Richardson, R., Moul, D. E., Mammen, O., Haas, G., Forman, S. D., Rode, N., Begley, A., & Nofzinger, E. A. (2012). Placebo-controlled comparison of prazosin and cognitive-behavioral treatments for sleep disturbances in US military veterans. *Journal of Psychosomatic Research, 72*(2), 89–96. https://doi.org/10.1016/j.jpsychores.2011.11.010

Isaac, F., Toukhsati, S. R., DiBenedetto, M., & Kennedy, G. A. (2022). Cognitive behavioral therapy-based treatments for insomnia and nightmares in adults with trauma symptoms: A systematic review. In *Current psychology* (pp. 1–11). https://doi.org/10.1007/s12144-022-03512-1

Gutner, C. A., Casement, M. D., Gilbert, K. S., & Resick, P. A. (2013). Change in sleep symptoms across cognitive processing therapy and prolonged exposure: A longitudinal perspective. *Behaviour Research and Therapy, 51*(12), 817–822.

Harvey, A. G. (2008). Insomnia, psychiatric disorders, and the transdiagnostic perspective. *Current Directions in Psychological Science, 17*(5), 299–303.

Haynes, P. L., Skobic, I., Epstein, D. R., Emert, S., Parthasarathy, S., Perkins, S., & Wilcox, J. (2020). Cognitive processing therapy for posttraumatic stress disorder is associated with negligible change in subjective and objective sleep. *Behavioral Sleep Medicine, 18*(6), 809–819.

Ho, F. Y. Y., Chan, C. S., & Tang, K. N. S. (2016). Cognitive-behavioral therapy for sleep disturbances in treating posttraumatic stress disorder symptoms: A meta-analysis of randomized controlled trials. *Clinical Psychology Review, 43*, 90–102.

Holder, N., Holliday, R., Wiblin, J., & Surís, A. (2019). A preliminary examination of the effect of cognitive processing therapy on sleep disturbance among veterans with military sexual trauma-related posttraumatic stress disorder. *Traumatology, 25*(4), 316.

Kobayashi, I., Boarts, J. M., & Delahanty, D. L. (2007). Polysomnographically measured sleep abnormalities in PTSD: A meta-analytic review. *Psychophysiology, 44*(4), 660–669.

Koren, D., Arnon, I., Lavie, P., & Klein, E. (2002). Sleep complaints as early predictors of posttraumatic stress disorder: A 1-year prospective study of injured survivors of motor vehicle accidents. *American Journal of Psychiatry, 159*(5), 855–857.

Krakow, B., & Zadra, A. (2010). Imagery rehearsal therapy: Principles and practice. *Sleep Medicine Clinics, 5*(2), 289–298.

Leskin, G. A., Woodward, S. H., Young, H. E., & Sheikh, J. I. (2002). Effects of comorbid diagnoses on sleep disturbance in PTSD. *Journal of Psychiatric Research, 36*(6), 449–452.

Margolies, S. O., Rybarczyk, B., Vrana, S. R., Leszczyszyn, D. J., & Lynch, J. (2013). Efficacy of a cognitive-behavioral treatment for insomnia and nightmares in Afghanistan and Iraq veterans with PTSD. *Journal of Clinical Psychology, 69*(10), 1026–1042.

Milanak, M. E., Zuromski, K. L., Cero, I., Wilkerson, A. K., Resnick, H. S., & Kilpatrick, D. G. (2019). Traumatic event exposure, posttraumatic stress disorder, and sleep disturbances in a national sample of US adults. *Journal of Traumatic Stress, 32*(1), 14–22.

Miller, K. E., Brownlow, J. A., & Gehrman, P. R. (2020). Sleep in PTSD: Treatment approaches and outcomes. *Current Opinion in Psychology, 34*, 12–17.

Miller, K. E., Brownlow, J. A., Woodward, S., & Gehrman, P. R. (2017). Sleep and dreaming in posttraumatic stress disorder. *Current Psychiatry Reports, 19*, 1–10.

Morgenthaler, T. I., Auerbach, S., Casey, K. R., Kristo, D., Maganti, R., Ramar, K., et al. (2018). Position paper for the treatment of nightmare disorder in adults: An American Academy of sleep medicine position paper. *Journal of Clinical Sleep Medicine, 14*(6), 1041–1055.

Neylan, T. C., Marmar, C. R., Metzler, T. J., Weiss, D. S., Zatzick, D. F., Delucchi, K. L., et al. (1998). Sleep disturbances in the Vietnam generation: Findings from a nationally representative sample of male Vietnam veterans. *American Journal of Psychiatry, 155*(7), 929–933.

Nishith, P., Resick, P. A., & Mueser, K. T. (2001). Sleep difficulties and alcohol use motives in female rape victims with posttraumatic stress disorder. *Journal of Traumatic Stress, 14*, 469–479.

Perlis, M. L., Jungquist, C., Smith, M. T., & Posner, D. (2005). *Cognitive behavioral treatment of insomnia: A session-by-session guide*. Springer.

Pigeon, W. R., Campbell, C. E., Possemato, K., & Ouimette, P. (2013). Longitudinal relationships of insomnia, nightmares, and PTSD severity in recent combat veterans. *Journal of Psychosomatic Research, 75*(6), 546–550.

Pigeon, W. R., Crean, H. F., Cerulli, C., Gallegos, A. M., Bishop, T. M., & Heffner, K. L. (2022). A randomized clinical trial of cognitive-behavioral therapy for insomnia to augment PTSD treatment in survivors of interpersonal violence. *Psychotherapy and Psychosomatics, 91*(1), 50.

Pruiksma, K. E., Taylor, D. J., Wachen, J. S., Mintz, J., Young-McCaughan, S., Peterson, A. L., et al. (2016). Residual sleep disturbances following PTSD treatment in active duty military personnel. *Psychological Trauma: Theory, Research, Practice, and Policy, 8*(6), 697.

Resick, P. A., Monson, C. M., & Chard, K. M. (2016). Cognitive processing therapy for PTSD: A comprehensive manual. .

Richards, A., Kanady, J. C., & Neylan, T. C. (2020). Sleep disturbance in PTSD and other anxiety-related disorders: An updated review of clinical features, physiological characteristics, and psychological and neurobiological mechanisms. *Neuropsychopharmacology, 45*(1), 55–73.

Spoormaker, V. I., & Montgomery, P. (2008). Disturbed sleep in post-traumatic stress disorder: Secondary symptom or core feature? *Sleep Medicine Reviews, 12*(3), 169–184.

Talbot, L. S., Maguen, S., Metzler, T. J., Schmitz, M., McCaslin, S. E., Richards, A., Perlis, M. L., Posner, D. A., Weiss, B., Ruoff, L., Varbel, J., & Neylan, T. C. (2014). Cognitive behavioral therapy for insomnia in posttraumatic stress disorder: A randomized controlled trial. *Sleep, 37*(2), 327–341. https://doi.org/10.5665/sleep.3408

Taylor, D. J., & Pruiksma, K. E. (2014). Cognitive and behavioural therapy for insomnia (CBT-I) in psychiatric populations: A systematic review. *International Review of Psychiatry, 26*(2), 205–213. https://doi.org/10.3109/09540261.2014.902808

Taylor, D. J., Peterson, A. L., Pruiksma, K. E., Young-McCaughan, S., Nicholson, K., Mintz, J., & STRONG STAR Consortium. (2017). Internet and in-person cognitive behavioral therapy for insomnia in military personnel: A randomized clinical trial. *Sleep, 40*(6), 1–12. https://doi.org/10.1093/sleep/zsx075

Taylor, D. J., Pruiksma, K. E., Mintz, J., Slavish, D. C., Wardle-Pinkston, S., Dietch, J. R., Dondanville, K. A., Young-McCaughan, S., Nicholson, K. L., Litz, B. T., Keane, T. M., Peterson, A. L., Resick, P. A., & Consortium to Alleviate PTSD. (2023). Treatment of comorbid sleep disorders and posttraumatic stress disorder in U.S. active duty military personnel: A pilot randomized clinical trial. *Journal of Traumatic Stress, 36*(4), 712–726. https://doi.org/10.1002/jts.22939

Thünker, J., & Pietrowsky, R. (2012). Effectiveness of a manualized imagery rehearsal therapy for patients suffering from nightmare disorders with and without a comorbidity of depression or PTSD. *Behaviour Research and Therapy, 50*(9), 558–564.

Ulmer, C. S., Edinger, J. D., & Calhoun, P. S. (2011). A multi-component cognitive-behavioral intervention for sleep disturbance in veterans with PTSD: A pilot study. *Journal of Clinical Sleep Medicine, 7*(1), 57–68.

VA/DOD Clinical Practice Guideline for the Management of Posttraumatic Stress Disorder and Acute Stress Disorder: Clinician summary. (2018). *Focus (American Psychiatric Publishing), 16*(4), 430–448. https://doi.org/10.1176/appi.focus.16408

Walters, E. M., Jenkins, M. M., Nappi, C. M., Clark, J., Lies, J., Norman, S. B., & Drummond, S. P. A. (2020). The impact of prolonged exposure on sleep and enhancing treatment outcomes with evidence-based sleep interventions: A pilot study. *Psychological trauma: theory, research, practice and policy, 12*(2), 175–185. https://doi.org/10.1037/tra0000478

Wang, C., Ramakrishnan, S., Laxminarayan, S., Dovzhenok, A., Cashmere, J. D., Germain, A., & Reifman, J. (2020). An attempt to identify reproducible high-density EEG markers of PTSD during sleep. *Sleep, 43*(1), zsz207.

Weber, F. C., & Wetter, T. C. (2022). The many faces of sleep disorders in post-traumatic stress disorder: An update on clinical features and treatment. *Neuropsychobiology, 81*(2), 85–97.

Wright, K. M., Britt, T. W., Bliese, P. D., Adler, A. B., Picchioni, D., & Moore, D. (2011). Insomnia as predictor versus outcome of PTSD and depression among Iraq combat veterans. *Journal of Clinical Psychology, 67*(12), 1240–1258.

Youngren, W. A., Hamilton, N. A., & Preacher, K. J. (2020). Assessing triggers of posttrauma nightmares. *Journal of Traumatic Stress, 33*(4), 511–520. https://doi.org/10.1002/jts.22532

Part III
Cognitive Processing Therapy with Specific Populations

Chapter 8
Treating Survivors of Sexual Assault with CPT

Rachel A. Wamser and Julia Richardson

Sexual assault is the trauma ecology that prompted the initial development of cognitive processing therapy (CPT) and thus, in many ways, is the quintessential or model CPT trauma type. Since its inception, CPT has amassed considerable efficacy in mitigating trauma symptoms following an array of trauma types and presentations (Chard, 2005; Galovski et al., 2012; Resick et al., 2021). However, the initial application of this intervention stemmed from the experiences of female sexual assault survivors (Resick & Schnicke, 1992). Many of these pioneering participants of the early trials conducted at the University of Missouri—St. Louis, Center for Trauma Recovery (e.g., Resick & Schnicke, 1993; Resick et al., 2002; Galovski et al., 2009, 2012, 2013) had experienced the type of sexual assault with the highest likelihood of resulting in PTSD, rape (Kessler et al., 2017). Moreover, for a considerable portion of the survivors who participated in the early treatment trials, sexual assault was one of many traumatic events they had endured across their lifespan, and many were recruited from an impoverished community. Thus, although no sexual assault CPT case is necessarily "clean" or "easy," the research participants' clinical presentations were quite complex.

The initial CPT studies were also conducted during a time when the full range of traumatic stress, both the full range of traumatic experiences as well as trauma symptoms, were not always diagnostically recognized (Resick & Schnicke, 1992, 1993; Resick et al., 2002). At that time, the *Diagnostic Statistical Manual (DSM-III* and *DSM-IV*) required specification of an "index event" and the PTSD diagnosis did not fully take into account several of the key symptoms of PTSD, particularly ones that may be aided by CPT such as trauma-related cognitions and feelings (APA,

R. A. Wamser (✉) · J. Richardson
Department of Psychological Sciences, University of Missouri—St. Louis, St. Louis, MO, USA
e-mail: WamserR@umsl.edu

J. S. Wachen, T. E. Galovski (eds.), *Cognitive Processing Therapy for Complex Cases*, CBT: Science Into Practice,
https://doi.org/10.1007/978-3-031-87356-0_8

2013). However, these symptoms, which are now part of *DSM-5,* were embedded in the initial conceptualization of CPT. Thus, CPT is a trauma treatment that was designed to mitigate the extensive array of trauma-related challenges following a trauma ecology with layers of complexity, including victim blaming, rape myths, substance involvement, and possible interpersonal betrayal and social contract injustices.

With this important historical context in mind, this chapter will focus on implementing CPT with individuals who have experienced a sexual assault. The chapter will review the current evidence base for this form of trauma and CPT, as well as discuss relevant clinical strategies, including addressing rape myths using CPT with special populations. The chapter will also include a detailed case example that will demonstrate the use of CPT with an index trauma of sexual assault. We then conclude this chapter by offering some avenues for future work to continue to bolster the CPT literature and, hopefully, aid the recovery process for sexual assault survivors.

Sexual Assault and CPT Research

Sexual assault research is foundational to CPT. As noted above, the initial research to develop and support the use of CPT was conducted with female sexual assault survivors in both group and individual formats (Resick & Schnicke, 1992, 1993; Resick et al., 2002), but this literature base has expanded across various trauma types, including military sexual trauma (for a meta-analytic review see Asmundson et al., 2019). Treatment gains from CPT appear to hold over time, with long-term follow-up of female rape victims suggesting that CPT elicits lasting changes in PTSD symptoms over a 5- to 10-year period (Resick et al., 2012). CPT is one of only four interventions for PTSD that is considered to have strong research support by both the APA (2017) and the US Department of Veterans Affairs and Department of Defense (2023). In addition to PTSD symptoms, sexual dysfunction may occur following sexual trauma, and CPT is associated with reductions in sexual difficulties among women (Wells et al., 2019).

CPT has demonstrated efficacy in treating PTSD among sexual assault survivors in numerous randomized controlled trials (RCTs). Resick et al.'s (2002) first RCT compared CPT+ Account (CPT + A) to prolonged exposure (PE) and a waitlist control group and found that CPT + A and PE performed equally well with respect to PTSD and depression symptoms. However, evidence indicated that those in the CPT + A condition had greater reductions in guilt (Resick et al., 2002), hopelessness (Gallagher & Resick, 2012), suicidal ideation (Gradus et al., 2013), and health concerns (Galovski et al., 2009). In an RCT dismantling components of CPT + A with female sexual assault survivors, those in the cognitive therapy-only (CPT) condition showed greater symptom reduction compared to those in the written account (WA) condition (Resick et al., 2008). Further, the findings of this study indicated no advantage of CPT + A over CPT. Indeed, those in the CPT condition improved faster than those in the CPT + A and WA groups (Resick et al., 2008).

In an RCT contrasting CPT to PE among women who had been raped, younger women fared better in CPT and older women had better outcomes in PE. Findings regarding gender differences among CPT clients have been mixed. CPT was found to be less effective for men with a sexual assault history than women (Mullen et al., 2014; Surís et al., 2013), although the sample sizes for males were small in both of these studies. Similarly, in a larger study of military sexual trauma (MST) victims in an intensive treatment, males demonstrated lower treatment gains compared to females (Voelkel et al., 2015). In contrast, Galovski et al. (2013) reported similar rates of change of PTSD symptom improvement among civilian male and female victims of interpersonal assault. However, women demonstrated greater improvement in PTSD symptoms at three months post-treatment. Gender differences in CPT outcomes among survivors of sexual assault may be explained in part by gender socialization. Male rape myths perpetuate the idea that men cannot be raped, making it more difficult for men to come to terms with their victimization, in turn hindering recovery (Davies, 2002).

Several forms of individual CPT have demonstrated efficacy with sexual assault survivors, including CPT, CPT with a written account (CPT + A), variable-length CPT (Galovski et al., 2012; Resick et al., 2021), and CPT for survivors of childhood sexual abuse (CSA) (CPT-SA; Chard, 2005). In choosing a format for CPT, it is important to consider the client's preferences. Some clients may prefer to have the opportunity to share in detail by writing a narrative about their assault, while others may prefer to engage in their trauma memory through Socratic questions. CPT + A may also be advantageous for sexual assault survivors who experience moderate-to-high levels of dissociation (Resick et al., 2008). CPT-SA, a 16-session protocol geared toward those who experienced CSA, may be preferred by therapists and clients who want to spend additional time focused on other areas (e.g., development, assertiveness, communication, and social support) that may be impacted by developmental trauma (Chard, 2005). Group-based CPT has also been shown to be effective for adolescent survivors of commercial sexual exploitation in a pilot study in Cambodia, including significant reductions in PTSD and depression (Clemans et al., 2021). This pilot study is notable in that it was used with adolescents, delivered CPT in a group format, and was conducted in a non-Western culture. Another CPT RCT with Congolese rape survivors found that CPT was associated with larger PTSD reductions than supportive therapy (Bass et al., 2013). Taken together, these studies show the robust nature of the intervention across a variety of cultures and healthcare settings.

Clinical Considerations for CPT with Sexual Assault Survivors

One of the first tasks of CPT is identifying an index trauma for which the client will write their impact statements and account (if applicable). Sexual assault survivors often present with a history of multiple sexual traumas, including multiple rapes or a history of childhood sexual abuse (Resick et al., 2002). In the case of multiple assaults, the index event should be the trauma with the most linked PTSD symptoms (i.e., most intrusion and avoidance symptoms).

Further, several factors related to the circumstances of the assault(s) may warrant special consideration for treatment. First, sexual assaults may occur at the victim's home, which may increase the client's risk to experience more frequent trauma reminders, feelings of distress, and a lack of safety. Second, the client's relationship to the perpetrator may impact trauma processing. Specifically, if the perpetrator was initially trusted by the victim, as in marital rape, CSA, and MST, the patient may be more likely to blame themselves for trusting the perpetrator. The goal of restructuring this type of cognition should be to aid the client in appropriately applying blame and responsibility. Third, the client's developmental level at the time of the trauma may impact their presentation and treatment. For instance, CSA survivors may have failed to develop adequate emotion regulation skills (Messman-Moore & Bhuptani, 2017), and relevant stuck points may be targeted within CPT. Individuals who were assaulted in adolescence may have more difficulty in relationships or have issues in identity development, and these challenges can be targeted within the CPT modules.

Endorsement of rape myths are a key treatment consideration for sexual assault survivors receiving CPT. The client's belief in these myths, perhaps confirmed by the reactions of others in the person's life, may be important factors in the development and maintenance of stuck points. Examples of rape myths include "if the victim didn't physically fight back, they can't really say it was rape," or "if the victim was drunk, they are at least partially responsible for their rape." Rape myths also interact with a Just World Belief (JWB) framework and result in, and reinforce, self-blaming assimilated stuck points. These myths and their endorsement may also interact with gender issues and negatively affect both male and female adult sexual assault victims (McMahon & Farmer, 2011; Payne et al., 1999). Thus, these victims may question their own experience as being a sexual assault, may not be believed by others, and do not necessarily reflect subscription to the JWB.

Although rape myths can serve to invalidate, trivialize, and blame both male and female victims for their sexual assault, men have the added burden of a set of rape myths that suggest their experience of sexual assault is not even possible (Groth & Burgess, 1980). Male rape myths can include beliefs such as (1) men cannot be raped; (2) if a victim has a physical response (e.g., erection or ejaculation) then he must have wanted it; (3) it is not possible for women to sexually assault men; (4) male sexual assault or abuse perpetrated by a man causes homosexuality; (5) "real" men are able to prevent or defend themselves against sexual assault; and (6) sexual assault is not as severe for a man as it is for a woman (Turchik & Edwards, 2012;

Struckman-Johnson & Struckman-Johnson, 1992). CPT providers should keep these rape myths in mind during treatment to ensure that if these beliefs are endorsed by their patient, they are addressed within the course of treatment.

The identification of stuck points is essential to the cognitive restructuring mechanism of CPT and typically begins in Sessions 2–3. In CPT with sexual assault survivors, the therapist should be attuned to assimilated stuck points about the assault characterized by hindsight bias (e.g., "I should have known better than to go to that party"), and erroneous self-blame (e.g., "It is my fault it happened"). The therapist should also help the client identify over-accommodated stuck points such as "I cannot trust my own judgment," "If I let anyone get close to me, they will hurt me," and "I am unlovable." Similarly to all trauma survivors suffering from PTSD, rape survivors tend to endorse high levels of self-blame, viewing themselves, rather than the perpetrators, as the cause of the assault (Resick et al., 2016). Stuck points related to self-blame (assimilated stuck points) should be prioritized in CPT with sexual assault survivors, leveraging the use of Socratic dialogue.

There are additional post-trauma beliefs and emotional presentations that may warrant unique considerations in CPT with sexual assault survivors. Survivors may feel intense shame associated with beliefs that they are permanently damaged or that something bad about them led them to be assaulted. Schema-level shame may need to be initially addressed earlier in treatment, rather than introducing it in the Trust, Esteem, and Intimacy modules (Resick et al., 2016). Schema-level shame also may require additional worksheets and more extensive Socratic dialogue due to the deeper nature of these beliefs. Relatedly, for some cases, variable-length CPT may be leveraged for those who may benefit from additional sessions to more fully mitigate shame and related cognitions.

Specific Sexual Assault Populations

Military Sexual Trauma (MST) MST refers to sexual assault or harassment that occurs during military service. MST is common, with over 40% of women and 4% of men disclosing MST, and risk factors include combat exposure and being a Marine (Barth et al., 2016). There are indications that rates have increased, which may be a function of improved recognition and reporting efforts. The DoD has encouraged reporting; however, it is recognized that MST is often unreported (Galovski et al., 2022a). CPT has been used effectively within the VA healthcare system and within other veteran care facilities to treat MST as well as among civilians (Holliday et al., 2018; Surís et al., 2013). One CPT RCT noted the importance of targeting self-blame for the MST, distress regarding having to work with the perpetrator, and worry for concerns for the consequences if reported (Holliday et al., 2018). In one RCT evaluating the effects of CPT in a sample of veterans with MST-related PTSD, CPT was associated with improvements in self-reported and clinician-assessed PTSD symptoms (Surís et al., 2013).

MST survivors have unique challenges in reporting experiences, including difficulty accessing individuals to disclose to, lack of knowledge regarding how to report, a complicated reporting and investigation system, as well as interference experiences (Dardis et al., 2018). Fears of retaliation, judgment, concerns for personal safety, and negative repercussions may also be experienced by these survivors (Dardis et al., 2018). Reporting barriers also include a perceived need to protect unit cohesion, lack of confidentiality and consequences, and an absence of resources (Burns et al., 2014). Anonymous data from female veterans indicated that 90% reported at least one form of MST, and reported that women were told that sexual violence were socially acceptable in the military and to expect these experiences (Wolff & Mills, 2016). These beliefs may worsen trauma symptoms, engender feelings of mistrust and betrayal, and therefore may be key themes in treatment. MST is also associated with higher rates of institutional betrayal, which is related to higher symptoms (Andresen et al., 2019).

Sexual Minorities LGBTQ+ sexual assault survivors also may warrant special considerations in CPT. For example, sexual minorities may in some circumstances experience sexual assault as a hate crime against their sexuality. Sexual assault within this context can add another layer of victimization for these individuals that can lead to internalized homophobia and identity struggles (Davies, 2002). For all clients, including men and sexual minorities, the broader social constructions of gender and sexuality may significantly impact their meaning-making process of their sexual victimization experiences. See Chap. 10 for further information on treating individuals with marginalized and intersectional identities using CPT.

Substance-Involved Sexual Assault Victims Sexual assaults often occur within the context of substances, which can complicate treatment. Substances can negatively impact one's memories for the events, making trauma processing more difficult as well as provide perceived evidence that it was the victim's fault. These types of assaults are more likely to have been perpetrated by an acquaintance (Lorenz & Ullman, 2016), and include lower threat perceptions and less fear (Clum et al., 2002). These aspects may contribute to survivors of substance-involved SA being less likely to acknowledge the experience as "rape." Critically, these survivors are less likely to report the assault to authorities and seek health care (Wolitzky-Taylor et al., 2011). Survivors of sexual assault with substances involved may be further isolated and vulnerable, as victim substance use is associated with more negative social reactions to disclosure (see Lorenz & Ullman, 2016). Indeed, when substances are involved, these survivors disclose more negative cognitions, such as self-blame (Littleton et al., 2009; Peter-Hagene & Ullman, 2016). These factors may contribute to a unique pattern for recovery for this subgroup, where there are fewer initial PTSD symptoms, but a slower recovery (Gong et al., 2019).

In a dismantling study of CPT among women who had been sexually assaulted, those whose assault was substance-involved had more severe residual PTSD at 6-month follow-up, although groups had similar levels of PTSD at posttreatment (Jaffe et al., 2021). When treatment condition was examined, those with a substance-involved sexual assault had the largest effect in symptom reduction for the CPT condition, compared to CPT + A as well as the written account-only group. This seems to provide empirical support that, as indicated in the CPT manual, a written account may not always be indicated for clients without a clear trauma memory. For a substance-involved SA, the memory of the SA may be unclear; however, there may be other memories or moments that are traumatic such as memories leading up to the assault, brief moments of lucidity, regaining consciousness or alertness, seeing the aftermath of the assault, and realizing that an assault occurred. Even in the absence of a clear trauma memory, victims may suffer from intense distress at reminders related to the assault, such as where it occurred and other situational cues. Some clients may benefit from writing an account, piecing these memory fragments together to help try and form a more cohesive and coherent narrative, thereby potentially allowing them to integrate the experience cognitively and affectively. A few case studies have observed that some substance-involved sexual assault survivors have struggled with rumination in attempting to engage with the memory of the event (Gauntlett-Gilbert et al., 2004; Padmanabhanunni & Edwards, 2013), thus, clinicians should be mindful of ensuring that there is not an unhealthy press to have a complete trauma account.

Case Example

"Amy" was a 29-year-old Korean-American female who presented to a trauma specialty clinic specifically for trauma-focused services. She was a former Marine with a history of sexual assault, intimate partner violence (IPV), as well as MST. She also suffered from emotional abuse as a child. Amy was an aspiring business owner who had previously received services from her local VA clinic for trauma-related difficulties, including PTSD symptoms and insomnia, but did not find it effective and also spoke negatively of going to treatment at the VA due to institutional barriers related to her traumatic event. She spoke at length that while in the waiting room, others assumed it was her boyfriend, and later fiancé, who was the veteran, not her. This occurred a few times. Amy also disclosed that she had felt unsupported by her fellow service members during her tour after disclosing the sexual assault and IPV.

Assessment Amy was eager to participate in CPT during the assessment process. She had good insight and motivation to reduce her PTSD symptoms, to mitigate her moderate insomnia, and to improve her impaired social and family relationships. She was concerned that, without help, she would "drive her fiancé away," and she was often tearful about this fear. Amy's avoidance of trauma-related content was initially low, but she was experiencing high levels of trauma-related cognitions and hyperarousal symptoms. Amy also had low and flat mood, and anhedonia as well as a strong fear of driving. This made treatment complicated as she drove to the clinic from a neighboring state. At intake, she had stopped driving without her fiancé, except for occasionally a 5-min drive to McDonalds. He drove her to the initial few sessions. She had also cut herself off from all social functions, despite classifying herself as an extrovert.

Amy presented to treatment with high levels of PTSD (PCL-5 score at intake = 48) and notable insomnia, both sleep onset and maintenance issues. As noted, Amy was engaged to a fellow veteran, and described the relationship as supportive. She had one sister, and they were estranged and not speaking at the time of treatment. This was very distressing to Amy as she missed her two nieces. Amy had a complicated and tense relationship with her parents, and they were not perceived as being supportive of her and did not entirely believe her trauma history. As a child, Amy experienced significant corporal punishment and felt very emotionally neglected and abused. At intake, she discussed cultural issues and beliefs regarding parenting, and felt that her mother was on the "extreme end" of the other families she grew up with who also shared the same cultural background. Amy described being expected to have tolerated the assaults and to not need treatment for her symptoms. She also shared that her parents blamed her for entering into the relationship.

As Amy had experienced multiple traumatic events, the therapist and Amy collaboratively discussed her full trauma history to determine a focal point for CPT. She felt strongly that the sexual assaults were the driver of her PTSD and should be her index trauma. These assaults were perpetrated by her prior boyfriend (a civilian) when she was stationed in New Orleans a few years prior. This was Amy's most distressing trauma as the perpetrator used her own gun against her and the trauma occurred in her home in her bedroom closet. She was very upset that as a Marine, she was not able to protect herself physically, which was also complicated by her petite stature. Amy found the IPV, which was mostly psychological in nature and involved controlling behaviors, to be less distressing to her in terms of her intrusive ideation and sleep challenges. Of note, the emotional abuse seemed consistent with the childhood emotional abuse perpetrated by her mother, thus the psychological IPV seemed to be easily assimilated for her. The focus on the sexual assault also made sense as it included the use of a gun, which has very high mortality salience and lethality. CPT focused on this index trauma, and the CPT modules regarding esteem, trust, and intimacy were conceptualized to be very helpful in assisting Amy to overcome the psychological IPV and childhood emotional abuse.

CPT with Amy Amy had previously had some exposure to PTSD psychoeducation and had completed a few sessions of EMDR. The therapist nevertheless delivered CPT Session 1 as usual, checking to see if the content was repetitive or not to Amy. To Amy, it felt "new," perhaps due to the different setting, time in her life, or way the information was presented. This also suggests the importance of repeated exposure to trauma and PTSD education. Indeed, despite being a veteran who had a fair amount of prior treatment at the VA, she felt that the PTSD psychoeducation content made her feel "less crazy," particularly the discussions of difficulties sleeping, challenges trusting others, and increased arousal. Cognitive theory was helpful and novel, especially the just-world myth that was consistent with messages from her parents and family that parental approval and obedience are very important. For Amy, she also agreed with the notion that "bad things always happen to her" and that the assault was in line with her prior self-schemas, but that the trauma did contribute to large shifts in her beliefs regarding her power, trust, and intimacy. Amy spontaneously took a few notes on her phone during the content regarding over-accommodation, assimilation, and stuck points. Amy did a nice job giving a brief description of the assault with moderate level of details and affect, and CPT was chosen, not CPT + A.

Amy returned to Session 2 with her impact statement which was a bit brief and lacked details. She was tearful, embarrassed, and highly avoidant and distressed. She discussed her three earnest attempts to write the statement. Amy explained that she felt anxious and distressed, and didn't believe she could do it. She revealed that she jotted something down quickly in the waiting room. The therapist praised these repeated efforts and reiterated the concept of anticipatory anxiety. Amy then read her impact statement, cradling herself in the warm, fuzzy floor-length sweater she had worn despite the summer heat. She did not become very distressed or tearful during her reading, and the therapist warmly praised the work she was able to do. The therapist then asked Amy questions, guiding her to elaborate on why she believes the assault occurred and how it impacted her sense of safety, trust, power and control, esteem, and intimacy. They then spent the session expanding the statement, adding in additional details. Amy's distress level was moderate but well-tolerated. The therapist and Amy agreed that she would complete it again, in addition to the Session 2 assignments. She was motivated to have another opportunity to overcome her avoidance.

Amy understood the concept of stuck points fairly well, and she recognized that her beliefs tended to be rather negative and distressing. Yet, she felt that they were all accurate and very "true" to her. A few times Amy laughed at herself that she is guilty of these types of thoughts "about everything." The therapist introduced the Stuck Point log, and asked Amy to identify stuck points from her impact statement and write them on the log. Amy was quickly able to identify her over-accommodated beliefs (e.g., "Men cannot be trusted," "If I get close to anyone, they will hurt me"), but had a harder time pinpointing her self-blame beliefs as stuck points. After the therapist helped her recognize these beliefs, she maintained how strongly she believed them. Amy flatly, and firmly, stated that the sexual assault and IPV were her fault, as was the emotional abuse—with percentages being "90% true." The therapist allowed Amy some space with these reactions, and moved through the CPT content at a slower pace. When Amy disclosed her self-blame and assimilated stuck points in the first session, the therapist refrained from challenging them directly, which was difficult but prudent. As treatment continued, Amy revealed why she felt it was her fault, and the therapist believed that it would have been premature to shut down that conversation too early by challenging these stuck points right away.

Amy proudly came to Session 3 with a much more detailed and richer impact statement. Her impact statement clearly indicated that she felt as though she was responsible for the sexual assault, and included statements such as "he should not have been able to get my gun," and that she should have "known better" and ended the relationship earlier. Her impact statement also mentioned her difficulties in feeling safe and trusting men, including her fiancé, as well as challenges feeling close and connected to her friends and family.

Amy became tearful when the therapist discussed the JWB, and it brought up the emotional abuse from her mother and the reactions she received when she disclosed the IPV and sexual assaults to her family, friends, and colleagues—particularly her fellow service members. She slowly and tearfully discussed that she consistently received overt negative and blaming reactions to the abuse she suffered, across contexts, including rape and IPV myths. The large theme in these reactions was that she "must have done something" to contribute to the IPV and that she likely deserved it. She was also questioned, explicitly, for how a civilian obtained her weapon and used it against her. Importantly, he had broken into her home, and had hidden in her closet. He had previously moved into her rental home, and after the IPV began, she broke up with him and he moved out. The therapist and Amy spent time discussing several critical details regarding how she could not have prevented the rape—including that he had hidden in her bedroom closet and was holding her gun, thus she was raped at gun point, making it very dangerous and challenging for her to fight back, irrespective of her level of fitness and military background. They also noted her small stature. The therapist gently wondered if perhaps it was safer to "freeze" in this context. Amy nodded, slowly, and agreed that most rape victims should prioritize staying alive and safe. She was not sure if that applied to her, but agreed to consider these details over the course of the week.

Amy also came to Session 3 with seven completed A-B-C worksheets, three of which were relatively complete and three were directly trauma-related, including the one tasked to be focused on the index trauma. The trauma-focused sheets were less developed and she again was embarrassed that she found that her avoidance symptoms made it challenging for her to fully immerse herself in this process. Amy had sat in the waiting room, holding a large mug of tea with her sweater cardigan, and filled in a few more details prior to session. She benefited from reviewing the worksheets in session, as she disclosed that she was "over-thinking" a bit about what to include. The therapist normalized this process and Amy and the therapist reviewed the ABC worksheets, which included some work challenges, and some distress regarding moving. Amy did a good job identifying and challenging her beliefs and feelings, as well as coming up with more helpful beliefs. The non-trauma-related worksheets were centered on feeling hurt or slighted by others and having large affective responses of anger and then withdrawing from her relationships without discussing her feelings. Amy recognized this theme, and mentioned that in her family of origin and the collectivistic culture she was raised in, hurt and angry feelings were not shown or expressed. She elaborated that these negative feelings "build up," however, and then she often feels overcome by them and completely avoids the person, or "rages" at them. Using Socratic dialogue, the therapist guided Amy to identify a stuck point from this theme ("Expressing emotion means I am weak").

Therapist: *Can you tell me a little bit about where that belief comes from?*

Amy: *Sure, that is what my parents taught me. We don't show emotions in my family.*

Therapist: *I see, can you say more about that? We've briefly touched on how your cultural background and childhood experiences have contributed to that belief; I'd like to hear more so I can understand better.*

Amy then described issues relating to coming from a collectivist culture and "saving face," and how both of her parents did not "allow" emotional expressions. After listening to this, the therapist shifted the discussion back to the stuck point.

Therapist: *I understand the cultural value of focusing on the "greater good" and putting others before oneself, that is in many respects a really positive thing. I wonder though if there are times when not showing emotion may actually be less helpful for you? And for your family?*

Amy: *Oh yes, I hold it in and blow up!* [Smiling] *They don't like that.*

Therapist: *I understand, and that is common. You are in good company with a lot of trauma survivors. But it sounds like holding in all feelings, sort of pretending that they don't exist isn't working for you?*

Amy: *No, it's not. I am actually really sensitive.*

Therapist: *So, perhaps, I am just thinking out loud here, but I wonder if there are other ways to approach emotions, feelings we all have, that is both in line with your culture but also honors yourself too? And may even help your relationships?*

Amy: *Maybe some of them, like I feel more comfortable showing feelings to like my fiancé, basically people not in my family.*

Therapist: *They won't see you as "weak" if you have feelings then?*

Amy: *No.... actually my fiancé would probably feel better if I could show my feelings before they explode.*

Amy and the therapist then worked toward developing some more adaptive and nuanced thoughts regarding expressing feelings to others, differentiating between different people in her life. This exercise went well and was also leveraged later in treatment when discussing trust.

Over the course of a few early sessions, the therapist observed that Amy's level of insight into her trauma-related beliefs was less developed at first, and she benefited a great deal from the stuck point examples in the handouts. She circled those that she felt applied to her, which were most of them, including those related to self-blame and believing that she deserved the abuse and assault, not fighting back, feeling the need to push people away and not let anyone close to her, and feeling that she must be on guard all of the time. The only ones that Amy did not readily identify with tended to be those related to negative perceptions regarding authority figures and the government. Her affect during this discussion was minimal, almost numb and flat, despite the veracity with which she believed these stuck points and the pervasiveness of them. Indeed, she presented as though she was almost resigned to believing these self-blame and negative beliefs, and that they would likely not change.

By Session 4, Amy had started to drive herself to session. Her driving phobia was not a direct target of CPT, but was something she identified as being trauma-related. Interestingly, CPT afforded her the language and understanding of exposure therapy, and she took it upon herself to create the equivalent of an exposure hierarchy. Amy had a moderate degree of compliance with the ABC sheets, with some sheets more complete than others. Over the course of CPT, she greatly improved her level of detail on the homework assignments and the amount of time she spent on them. Amy completed the Challenging Questions worksheets (now called Exploring Questions in the recently published CPT manual) very well for her assimilated stuck points. The therapist praised her a great deal for this work. Sessions 4 and 5 were devoted to Amy and the therapist carefully unpacking and challenging these assimilated stuck points, first regarding her beliefs regarding the perpetrator gaining access to her home and gun, and then her belief that the assault was her fault and that she is to blame, especially as he is a civilian and she is a Marine. It was very useful to leverage a large dry-erase board easel in session to have the visual space to include details of the assault and the context, including how the perpetrator had lived with her, thus he knew how to access her home and where she kept her gun.

Therapist: *You did a great job identifying your stuck points about trusting men and getting close to others. I wonder if we can identify any stuck points about the assault itself. You said to me when we discussed your impact statement that you believe he should not have been able to get your gun, is that still correct?*

Amy: *Well, it's true. He shouldn't have been able to get my gun. I am a Marine! I can't believe he could use my own gun against me. It was my fault that it wasn't locked away.*

Therapist: *I understand you feel like because you are a Marine and have special training, it is really upsetting that you were not able to protect yourself. Can we unpack this a bit?*

Amy: *Sure.*

Therapist: *Okay, bear with me as I try to better understand this belief. How tall are you?*

Amy: *I am short—five one.*

Therapist: *And how tall is the perpetrator?*

Amy: *He's tall, six feet.*

Therapist: *So, he has your gun when you entered the bedroom, and he is a great deal taller than you, making it also harder for you from a physical standpoint, right?*

Amy: *Yes, he already had it.*

Therapist: *So, please correct me as I am not a Marine. But given that he had the gun already and it was dark I assume? And you were not expecting him to be hiding in your closet, let alone with your gun, right?* [Amy nods]. *I am wondering how your special training could have helped you in that moment?*

Amy nods and appears to be taking this in. The therapist pauses and waits. Amy begins to cry softly.

Therapist: *It's tough. Thanks for letting me push you a bit on this.*

Amy nods: *It is tough. I just feel, I just wish—*

Therapist (slowly nodding): *Yes… you wish it was different.* [pauses]. *But wishing it were different and being responsible seem different to me. You wish you could have overpowered him. I understand that.*

Amy: *I do. That's it. I am angry about it, it was humiliating.*

Therapist: *That makes sense, I would be angry too. You should be angry. But do you hear what I mean about the difference between regret and responsibility?*

Amy: *Yes… It just still feels like it is my fault.*

Therapist: *I hear that. That makes sense to me too, and a lot of victims feel that way at the beginning of treatment. It may take time for your heart to catch up to your brain. [Pause]. Let's keep going with this, if that's okay?* [Amy nods]. *Let's pretend for a second that you had locked the gun away that day. What would have happened then?*

Amy: *He wouldn't have been able to threaten me with a weapon.*

Therapist: *Could he still have attacked you? When he entered your home to attack you, he could not have known that the gun wasn't locked up, right?*

Amy: *That's true, or I could have moved it.*

Therapist: *Exactly! And when you came home from work, did you have any indication he would be hiding in the dark bedroom with your gun?*

Amy: *No. It was a complete shock.*

Therapist: *Yes, of course it was. Amy, how could you have known he was there then?*

Amy [softly becoming tearful]: *I couldn't.*

Therapist: *No, you couldn't.* [long pause]. *You are doing great. Really great. Can I ask you then, how could it have been your fault?*

Amy: *I guess it wasn't.*

Therapist: *No, it wasn't. That's what I believe. I hear a few of those stuck points we talked about—that it is your fault, that you should have known he was hiding in the closet, that being a Marine should have protected you, and that he shouldn't have gotten your gun. All of these suggest that you are to blame for the rape. Now that we have unpacked this a bit, can we write some of the key details down on the dry erase board? I wonder if seeing it can help you release some of this blame.*

The therapist and Amy then drew a large web, with her assimilated stuck points and smaller circles with evidence to counteract these thoughts. This visual depiction was most helpful to help Amy decrease her belief in her assimilated stuck points. The therapist and Amy both took a picture of this work, to help her remember the fuller context of the assault in a more accurate way.

As part of ongoing sessions, the therapist often returned to asking Amy Question 3 on the Challenging Questions worksheet, regarding in what ways her beliefs were not including all of the information. The patterns of Problematic Thinking Worksheet (now called Thinking Patterns Worksheet) that is part of Session 5 was very useful for the therapist as a concrete, and removed, way to help Amy move toward more balanced thinking. After the therapist introduced the Patterns of Problematic Thinking worksheet, Amy was quickly able to identify that she was prone to oversimplifying and ignoring important parts of the situation. Like many CPT clients, Amy seemed to benefit from a "less-is-more" removed approach and stance toward her stuck points. The therapist observed that Amy seemed to make significant progress if the therapist relied on reflective comments and wondering aloud, compared to more direct challenging questions. Often by "planting a seed" in one session, Amy would return to the next session reporting that she had shifted her beliefs in a positive, more compassionate manner. Amy found the Levels of Responsibility handout and sample Challenging Questions Worksheets to be very helpful. She benefited a great deal from seeing the completed worksheets and, often over the course of a week, would seem to be able to generalize those examples to herself. Assessment measures indicated that her PTSD symptoms were still above clinical cutoff, but had dropped by about 10% by Session 5.

At Session 6, Amy's score on the PCL-5 was below clinical cutoff, and her sleep had improved. She also reported improvements in her assimilated stuck points, and now believed that the assault was not her fault approximately 90% of the time. She continued to believe that she had some degree of responsibility (10%–20%), as well as some lingering desires to have prevented it or "known better." Nevertheless, these cognitions were decreasing in severity and frequency. Amy benefited from being reminded that it may take time for her thinking to "catch up," akin to a new habit. When the therapist discussed the CPT themes that would be addressed in upcoming sessions, Amy readily expressed her desire to complete them and noted how they all apply to her, "as [I] am messed up" she lamented. She was crying and laughing as she said this. When the topic of safety was introduced, Amy began discussing her childhood and discussing how she felt physically safe, but not emotionally safe with her mother, who was described as very strict and relying on emotional abuse and physical punishment to ensure compliance. She emphasized how she never felt loved by her mother or that she was "good enough." Amy and the therapist then integrated her childhood experiences with her more recent traumatic events, which served to confirm her lack of safety—both emotional and physical safety. She acknowledged that she feels less physically safe in the world now, but also did note that she now believes she doesn't need to be quite so "on guard" all of the time. Amy's improvements in driving really appeared to help her, and reinforced her progress. Amy and the therapist discussed the Session 8 worksheets, and she readily recognized her own thoughts in these examples. She often had good humor about these as well.

Amy did very well with the Safety, Trust, and Power/Control themes of CPT during Sessions 8, 9, and 10. She had some family stressors that she also brought up in treatment, but started to apply the cognitive skills from CPT to help her manage her emotions. Amy was very motivated to address her beliefs related to trust, as she was fearful of losing her fiancé after a fight. She was also concerned that he would think that she was "crazy" if she did not let him into her "world" or displayed significant bouts of affect. Amy disclosed that she really wanted to become a mother one day, and wanted to be able to be trusting and connected with other people. Amy felt as though she trusted herself, but her other-focused trust was very impaired. She recognized that she was not sure if she had ever trusted anyone, including her father. She did not trust her mother and was not speaking with her sister. The therapist and Amy spent session time focused on degrees of trust, which helped Amy realize that she trusted her fiancé, and some old friends. She even set goals to contact a few of them, and did so over the course of the next few weeks. The Trust Star worksheet was very beneficial for Amy, and was used in the following session as well to monitor treatment progress. The therapist and Amy spent time discussing the various people in her life, her level of trust for each of them, and how these individuals have demonstrated trust to her (or not).

At Session 10, Amy had made good progress on her feelings of other-focused trust; however, the therapist and Amy agreed that this was going to be an ongoing issue for her given that she had, understandably, struggled to fully trust anyone before. What was notable about Amy, though, was her motivation to change this relational pattern, once she and the therapist discussed how not trusting others is inconsistent with her life goals and values, particularly regarding getting married to her fiancé and her hope to become a mother. Following introducing the Power/Control theme, Amy seemed to visibly soften toward herself and some of her friends and family, with the exception of her mother and estranged sister. She even went to a few social gatherings, and made progress on her business—including renting a workspace. Amy recognized how hard she was working to make things appear "perfect," including her appearance, home, and workplace. She made the connection that she tries hard to control things as she is fearful and over-compensates due to her low self-esteem.

At Session 10, Amy's assimilated stuck points were mostly resolved, and she began to give herself "permission" to let go of her perceived responsibility for the assaults, IPV, and emotional abuse. Amy's childhood adversities with her mother were not the focus of treatment, and were not Criterion A events, but identifying that those early experiences had shaped her views of herself as being "bad" and "damaged," that others could not be trusted, and her familial and cultural beliefs in the JWB, self-sacrificing, and "saving face" had an incredible impact on loosening the "grips" of the other stuck points. She appeared to visibly relax in session and began to identify what beliefs she wished to retain from her family and culture, and those she did not want to "pass on," to her potential daughters (Amy was very keen on having girl offspring). The therapist used this visualization to help Amy's motivation. Amy's esteem was low at the beginning of treatment, but had improved prior to this module. She nevertheless was excited by the behavioral assignment of self-care and discussed how much she enjoys hot baths.

Session 11 included reviewing the Esteem module and homework, and her self-care activities had gone well. Now, her PCL-5 score was a 17 and she was sleeping fairly well and driving again. Amy and the therapist discussed some of the childhood experiences and issues with her sister, which were the focus of her practice assignments. She had encountered her sister at a recent family gathering, and her sister pretended as though she was invisible, which was very hurtful. This stressor provided a nice opportunity to practice CPT skills with Amy, helping her to be her own therapist, and discussing termination. Amy and the therapist focused on helping her to identify what she could (and could not) control with regards to her sister, and what she wants for herself and her family relationships. She resolved to no longer avoid family functions because of her sister, and had a small degree of hope that if she continued to be around her sister, they would repair their relationship. Amy lamented that she may never know or understand why her sister stopped speaking to her, but she missed her other uncles and her nieces. Amy's stressors also tied nicely into the Intimacy module, and she readily expressed a desire to be more connected to others and have a richer life. She cried in session when discussing her stuck points related to being alone, and her fears that she will always feel alone. Amy agreed to challenge her intimacy-related stuck points using the Challenging Beliefs worksheet (now called Alternate Thoughts Worksheet) over the next week. When the therapist raised the issue of termination, Amy felt optimistic that she could continue to use the CPT skills on her own.

Amy was eager to rewrite her impact statement. When she shared her new impact statement in Session 12, Amy recognized the significant progress she had made regarding her assimilated stuck points. Her new impact statement was quite different, and she was surprised at the content included in her original one when the therapist read it to her. Amy no longer believed any of her traumatic events or adverse experiences reflected on her, and she felt she had a good life ahead of her. Amy was able to appropriately apply blame to the perpetrator of her assault, rather than to herself. She felt as though she could trust her fiancé, and was excited about her new store. Amy seemed much more comfortable with herself, and even had stopped wearing so much make-up to session. Amy and the therapist discussed additional goals for her, and this process seemed energizing to her, including her home renovations, getting married, and reconnecting with friends and family. She felt comfortable knowing when she may need to seek treatment if symptoms arose again.

Future Directions

The empirical evidence to support the use of CPT for sexual assault survivors is clear, and has been for decades (e.g., Resick et al., 2002, 2008). This line of research has provided ample evidence for the use of CPT among survivors of sexual assault in different settings and in special populations. It is important now to build on this literature to better serve these survivors. Like other trauma treatments, attrition is common. This is partially a function of PTSD—avoidance symptoms encourage avoiding trauma treatment. CPT attempts to counteract this with an explicit discussion of avoidance and how tempting avoiding trauma-related material and treatment can be, but how it ultimately forestalls recovery. Perhaps some clients need additional interventions to aid them in overcoming these understandable urges to prematurely dropout of therapy. It may also be fruitful to improve attrition specifically among special populations, such as men, MST survivors, and diverse groups. Another potential area for further consideration is empirical studies regarding when to leverage the WA component for sexual assault survivors. Further, circumstances of sexual assaults and survivors' experiences are idiosyncratic, and it may be useful to continue to grow our understanding of other special sub-groups of sexual assault survivors and how to best treat them within the context of CPT, such as those who experienced revictimization, or suffered an assault by a family member or clergy.

There are several directions for the future of research on CPT for sexual assault survivors. Namely, varied formats of CPT have been studied more recently. Specifically, intensive, or massed, CPT, administered over the course of several days to 3 weeks, has demonstrated promising results with veterans and female survivors of IPV and other co-occurring traumas (Galovski et al., 2022b; Held et al., 2023). While massed CPT has not been studied specifically among survivors of sexual assault, some of the participants in these trials had undergone sexual assault. See Chap. 14 to learn more about this promising direction for future research with potential to expand accessibility of the treatment. Similarly, telehealth-based CPT has demonstrated equivalence to in-person CPT in several trials (e.g., Maieritsch et al., 2015), which have included sexual assault survivors. See Chap. 16 for more information on this format of CPT. Implementation research is another critical future direction for research on CPT for sexual assault survivors. More work is needed to understand barriers and facilitators of its adoption, adherence to the protocol, and real-world effectiveness among this population. Finally, the role of CPT in prevention and early intervention for sexual assault survivors is understudied. CPT, either in totality or the techniques of CPT could be leveraged as a preventative or early intervention approach for those who recently experienced sexual trauma.

Competing Interests The authors have no conflicts of interest to declare that are relevant to the content of this chapter and did not receive any grant support that pertains to this work.

References

American Psychiatric Association. (2013). *Diagnostic and statistical manual of mental disorders: DSM-5* (5th ed.). American Psychiatric Association.

American Psychological Association (APA). (2017). *Clinical practice guideline for the treatment of posttraumatic stress disorder (PTSD) in adults*. Retrieved from: https://www.apa.org/ptsd-guideline

Andresen, F. J., Monteith, L. L., Kugler, J., Cruz, R. A., & Blais, R. K. (2019). Institutional betrayal following military sexual trauma is associated with more severe depression and specific posttraumatic stress disorder symptom clusters. *Journal of Clinical Psychology, 75*(7), 1305–1319. https://doi.org/10.1002/jclp.22773

Asmundson, G. J. G., Thorisdottir, A. S., Roden-Foreman, J. W., Baird, S. O., Witcraft, S. M., Stein, A. T., Smits, J. A. J., & Powers, M. B. (2019). A meta-analytic review of cognitive processing therapy for adults with posttraumatic stress disorder. *Cognitive Behaviour Therapy, 48*(1), 1–14. https://doi.org/10.1080/16506073.2018.1522371

Barth, S. K., Kimerling, R. E., Pavao, J., McCutcheon, S. J., Batten, S. V., Dursa, E., Peterson, M. R., & Schneiderman, A. I. (2016). Military sexual trauma among recent veterans: Correlates of sexual assault and sexual harassment. *American Journal of Preventive Medicine, 50*(1), 77–86. https://doi.org/10.1016/j.amepre.2015.06.012

Bass, J. K., Annan, J., McIvor Murray, S., Kaysen, D., Griffiths, S., Cetinoglu, T., Wachter, K., Murray, L. K., & Bolton, P. A. (2013). Controlled trial of psychotherapy for Congolese survivors of sexual violence. *The New England Journal of Medicine, 368*(23), 2182–2191. https://doi.org/10.1056/NEJMoa1211853

Burns, B., Grindlay, K., Holt, K., Manski, R., & Grossman, D. (2014). Military sexual trauma among US servicewomen during deployment: A qualitative study. *American Journal of Public Health, 104*(2), 345–349. https://doi.org/10.2105/AJPH.2013.301576

Chard, K. M. (2005). An evaluation of cognitive processing therapy for the treatment of posttraumatic stress disorder related to childhood sexual abuse. *Journal of Consulting and Clinical Psychology, 73*(5), 965–971. https://doi.org/10.1037/0022-006X.73.5.965

Clemans, T. A., White, K. L., Fuessel-Herrmann, D., Bryan, C. J., & Resick, P. A. (2021). Acceptability, feasibility, and preliminary effectiveness of group cognitive processing therapy with female adolescent survivors of commercial sexual exploitation in Cambodia. *Journal of Child & Adolescent Trauma, 14*(4), 571–583. https://doi.org/10.1007/s40653-021-00405-6

Clum, G. A., Nishith, P., & Calhoun, K. S. (2002). A preliminary investigation of alcohol use during trauma and peritraumatic reactions in female sexual assault victims. *Journal of Traumatic Stress, 15*(4), 321–328. https://doi.org/10.1023/A:1016255929315

Dardis, C. M., Reinhardt, K. M., Foynes, M. M., Medoff, N. E., & Street, A. E. (2018). "Who are you going to tell? Who's going to believe you?": Women's experiences disclosing military sexual trauma. *Psychology of Women Quarterly, 42*(4), 414–429. https://doi.org/10.1177/0361684318796783

Davies, M. (2002). Male sexual assault victims: A selective review of the literature and implications for support services. *Aggression and Violent Behavior, 7*(3), 203–214. https://doi.org/10.1016/S1359-1789(00)00043-4

Departments of Veterans Affairs and Defense (VA/DoD). (2023). *VA/DoD clinical practice guideline for the management of posttraumatic stress disorder and acute stress disorder*. Author. Retrieved from: https://www.healthquality.va.gov/guidelines/MH/ptsd/

Gallagher, M. W., & Resick, P. A. (2012). Mechanisms of change in cognitive processing therapy and prolonged exposure therapy for PTSD: Preliminary evidence for the differential effects of hopelessness and habituation. *Cognitive Therapy and Research, 36*(6), 750–755. https://doi.org/10.1007/s10608-011-9423-6

Galovski, T. E., Blain, L. M., Chappuis, C., & Fletcher, T. (2013). Sex differences in recovery from PTSD in male and female interpersonal assault survivors. *Behaviour Research and Therapy, 51*(6), 247–255. https://doi.org/10.1016/j.brat.2013.02.002

Galovski, T. E., Blain, L. M., Mott, J. M., Elwood, L., & Houle, T. (2012). Manualized therapy for PTSD: Flexing the structure of cognitive processing therapy. *Journal of Consulting and Clinical Psychology, 80*(6), 968–981. https://doi.org/10.1037/a0030600

Galovski, T. E., Monson, C., Bruce, S. E., & Resick, P. A. (2009). Does cognitive–behavioral therapy for PTSD improve perceived health and sleep impairment? *Journal of Traumatic Stress, 22*(3), 197–204. https://doi.org/10.1002/jts.20418

Galovski, T. E., Street, A. E., Creech, S., Levahot, K., Kelly, U., & Yano, E. M. (2022a). State of the knowledge of VA military sexual trauma research. *Journal of General Internal Medicine, 37*(3), 825–832. https://doi.org/10.1007/s11606-022-07580-8

Galovski, T. E., Werner, K. B., Weaver, T. L., Morris, K. L., Dondanville, K. A., Nanney, J., Wamser-Nanney, R., McGlinchey, G., Fortier, C. B., & Iverson, K. M. (2022b). Massed cognitive processing therapy for posttraumatic stress disorder in women survivors of intimate partner violence. *Psychological Trauma: Theory, Research, Practice, and Policy, 14*(5), 769–779. https://doi.org/10.1037/tra0001100

Gauntlett-Gilbert, J., Keegan, A., & Petrak, J. (2004). Drug-faciliated sexual assault: Cognitive approaches to treating the trauma. *Behavioural and Cognitive Psychotherapy, 32*(2), 215–223. https://doi.org/10.1017/S1352465804001481

Gong, A. T., Kamboj, S. K., & Curran, H. V. (2019). Post-traumatic stress disorder in victims of sexual assault with pre-assault substance consumption: A systematic review. *Frontiers in Psychiatry, 10*. https://doi.org/10.3389/fpsyt.2019.00092

Gradus, J. L., Suvak, M. K., Wisco, B. E., Marx, B. P., & Resick, P. A. (2013). Treatment of posttraumatic stress disorder reduces suicidal ideation. *Depression and Anxiety, 30*(10), 1046–1053. https://doi.org/10.1002/da.22117

Groth, A. N., & Burgess, A. W. (1980). Male rape: Offenders and victims. *The American Journal of Psychiatry, 137*(7), 806–810. https://doi.org/10.1176/ajp.137.7.806

Held, P., Smith, D. L., Pridgen, S., Coleman, J. A., & Klassen, B. J. (2023). More is not always better: 2 weeks of intensive cognitive processing therapy-based treatment are noninferior to 3 weeks. *Psychological Trauma: Theory, Research, Practice, and Policy, 15*(1), 100–109. https://doi.org/10.1037/tra0001257

Holliday, R., Holder, N., & Surís, A. (2018). Reductions in self-blame cognitions predict PTSD improvements with cognitive processing therapy for military sexual trauma-related PTSD. *Psychiatry Research, 263*, 181–184. https://doi.org/10.1016/j.psychres.2018.03.007

Jaffe, A. E., Kaysen, D., Smith, B. N., Galovski, T., & Resick, P. A. (2021). Cognitive processing therapy for substance-involved sexual assault: Does an account help or hinder recovery? *Journal of Traumatic Stress, 34*(4), 864–871. https://doi.org/10.1002/jts.22674

Kessler, R. C., Aguilar-Gaxiola, S., Alonso, J., Benjet, C., Bromet, E. J., et al. (2017). Trauma and PTSD in the WHO world mental health surveys. *European Journal of Psychotraumatology, 8*(sup5), 1353383. https://doi.org/10.1080/20008198.2017.1353383

Littleton, H., Grills, A., & Axsom, D. (2009). Impaired and incapacitated rape victims: Assault characteristics and post-assault experiences. *Violence and Victims, 24*, 439–457. https://doi.org/10.1891/0886-6708.24.4.439

Lorenz, K., & Ullman, S. E. (2016). Alcohol and sexual assault victimization: Research findings and future directions. *Aggression and Violent Behavior, 31*, 82–94. https://doi.org/10.1016/j.avb.2016.08.001

Maieritsch, K., Smith, T., Hessinger, J., Ahearn, E., Eickhoff, J., & Zhao, Q. (2015). Randomized controlled equivalence trial comparing videoconference and in person delivery of cognitive processing therapy for PTSD. *Journal of Telemedicine and Telecare, 22*, 238. https://doi.org/10.1177/1357633X15596109

McMahon, S., & Farmer, G. L. (2011). An updated measure for assessing subtle rape myths. *Social Work Research, 35*(2), 71–81. https://doi.org/10.1093/swr/35.2.71

Messman-Moore, T. L., & Bhuptani, P. H. (2017). A review of the long-term impact of child maltreatment on posttraumatic stress disorder and its comorbidities: An emotion dysregulation perspective. *Clinical Psychology: Science and Practice, 24*(2), 154–169. https://doi.org/10.1111/cpsp.12193

Mullen, K., Holliday, R., Morris, E., Raja, A., & Surís, A. (2014). Cognitive processing therapy for male veterans with military sexual trauma-related posttraumatic stress disorder. *Journal of Anxiety Disorders, 28*(8), 761–764. https://doi.org/10.1016/j.janxdis.2014.09.004

Padmanabhanunni, A., & Edwards, D. (2013). Treating the psychological sequelae of proactive drug-facilitated sexual assault: Knowledge building through systematic case based research. *Behavioural and Cognitive Psychotherapy, 41*(3), 371–375. https://doi.org/10.1017/S1352465812000896

Payne, D. L., Lonsway, K. A., & Fitzgerald, L. F. (1999). Rape myth acceptance: Exploration of its structure and its measurement using the Illinois rape myth acceptance scale. *Journal of Research in Personality, 33*(1), 27–68. https://doi.org/10.1006/jrpe.1998.2238

Peter-Hagene, L. C., & Ullman, S. E. (2016). Longitudinal effects of sexual assault victims' drinking and self-blame on posttraumatic stress disorder. *Journal of Interpersonal Violence, 0886260516636394*. https://doi.org/10.1177/0886260516636394

Resick, P. A., Galovski, T. E., Uhlmansiek, M. O., Scher, C. D., Clum, G. A., & Young-Xu, Y. (2008). A randomized clinical trial to dismantle components of cognitive processing therapy for posttraumatic stress disorder in female victims of interpersonal violence. *Journal of Consulting and Clinical Psychology, 76*(2), 243–258. https://doi.org/10.1037/0022-006X.76.2.243

Resick, P. A., Monson, C. M., & Chard, K. M. (2016). Cognitive processing therapy for PTSD: A comprehensive manual. .

Resick, P. A., Nishith, P., Weaver, T. L., Astin, M. C., & Feuer, C. A. (2002). A comparison of cognitive-processing therapy with prolonged exposure and a waiting condition for the treatment of chronic posttraumatic stress disorder in female rape victims. *Journal of Consulting and Clinical Psychology, 70*(4), 867–879. https://doi.org/10.1037/0022-006x.70.4.867

Resick, P. A., & Schnicke, M. K. (1992). Cognitive processing therapy for sexual assault victims. *Journal of Consulting and Clinical Psychology, 60*(5), 748–756. https://doi.org/10.1037/0022-006X.60.5.748

Resick, P. A., & Schnicke, M. K. (1993). *Cognitive processing therapy for rape victims: A treatment manual.* (pp. xi, 178). Sage Publications, Inc.

Resick, P. A., Wachen, J. S., Dondanville, K. A., LoSavio, S. T., Young-McCaughan, S., Yarvis, J. S., Pruiksma, K. E., Blankenship, A., Jacoby, V., Peterson, A. L., Mintz, J., & STRONG STAR Consortium. (2021). Variable-length cognitive processing therapy for posttraumatic stress disorder in active duty military: Outcomes and predictors. *Behaviour Research and Therapy, 141*, 103846. https://doi.org/10.1016/j.brat.2021.103846

Resick, P. A., Williams, L. F., Suvak, M. K., Monson, C. M., & Gradus, J. L. (2012). Long-term outcomes of cognitive–behavioral treatments for posttraumatic stress disorder among female rape survivors. *Journal of Consulting and Clinical Psychology, 80*(2), 201–210. https://doi.org/10.1037/a0026602

Struckman-Johnson, C., & Struckman-Johnson, D. (1992). Acceptance of male rape myths among college men and women. *Sex Roles: A Journal of Research, 27*(3–4), 85–100. https://doi.org/10.1007/BF00290011

Surís, A., Link-Malcolm, J., Chard, K., Ahn, C., & North, C. (2013). A randomized clinical trial of cognitive processing therapy for veterans with PTSD related to military sexual trauma. *Journal of Traumatic Stress, 26*(1), 28–37. https://doi.org/10.1002/jts.21765

Turchik, J. A., & Edwards, K. M. (2012). Myths about male rape: A literature review. *Psychology of Men & Masculinity, 13*(2), 211–226. https://doi.org/10.1037/a0023207

Voelkel, E., Pukay-Martin, N. D., Walter, K. H., & Chard, K. M. (2015). Effectiveness of cognitive processing therapy for male and female U.S. veterans with and without military sexual trauma. *Journal of Traumatic Stress, 28*(3), 174–182. https://doi.org/10.1002/jts.22006

Wells, S. Y., Glassman, L. H., Talkovsky, A. M., Chatfield, M. A., Sohn, M. J., Morland, L. A., & Mackintosh, M. A. (2019). Examining changes in sexual functioning after cognitive processing therapy in a sample of women trauma survivors. *Women's Health Issues, 29*(1), 72–79.

Wolff, K. B., & Mills, P. D. (2016). Reporting military sexual trauma: A mixed-methods study of women veterans' experiences who served from world war II to the war in Afghanistan. *Military Medicine, 181*(8), 840–848. https://doi.org/10.7205/MILMED-D-15-00404

Wolitzky-Taylor, K. B., Resnick, H. S., McCauley, J. L., Amstadter, A. B., Kilpatrick, D. G., & Ruggiero, K. J. (2011). Is reporting of rape on the rise? A comparison of women with reported versus unreported rape experiences in the national women's study-replication. *Journal of Interpersonal Violence, 26*(4), 807–832. https://doi.org/10.1177/0886260510365869

Chapter 9
Treating Military Personnel and Veterans with Cognitive Processing Therapy

Kristen H. Walter, Stephanie Y. Wells, Hannah E. Walker, and Rosalba M. Gomez

Across the world, individuals serve in armed forces for national defense. Yet, the various contexts of military service can notably differ. In some countries, service is mandatory, while in others it is a volunteer force. Service may be while on active duty or through component forces, such as the Guard or Reserves. Military experiences may also markedly differ whether service occurs in the home country, abroad, or whether at war or peacetime. For providers working with military populations, a general understanding of the military structure and environment for which their patients serve will help provide valuable context and clinical information regarding trauma exposure. Knowledge and recognition of these military factors can facilitate trauma-focused treatment, including trauma processing and Socratic dialogue that are central to the successful delivery of cognitive processing therapy (CPT).

Military service can provide numerous opportunities, such as skill acquisition, education, training, stable employment, career advancement, travel, access to healthcare, and a sense of purpose through service. Furthermore, these opportunities are available to those who may have more limited access otherwise due to geographic location, financial resources, or other social determinants of health. Along

K. H. Walter (✉)
Psychological Health & Readiness, Naval Health Research Center, San Diego, CA, USA

School of Public Health, San Diego State University, San Diego, CA, USA
e-mail: kristen.h.walter.civ@health.mil

S. Y. Wells
Durham Center of Innovation to Accelerate Discovery and Practice Transformation (ADAPT), Durham VA Health Care System, Durham, NC, USA

VA Mid-Atlantic Mental Illness Research, Education, and Clinical Center, Durham, North, USA

H. E. Walker · R. M. Gomez
Durham VA Medical Center, Durham, NC, USA

J. S. Wachen, T. E. Galovski (eds.), *Cognitive Processing Therapy for Complex Cases*, CBT: Science Into Practice,
https://doi.org/10.1007/978-3-031-87356-0_9

with potential benefits, there is an increased risk of trauma exposure through military service, including life-threatening experiences to the service member themselves, their comrades, combatants, and civilians. The training may inherently involve physical and psychological risks. Beyond the risks associated with national defense, service members may also experience traumas that civilians face, including vehicular or other accidents, as well as interpersonal traumas (e.g., physical and sexual assault, domestic violence).

There are nuanced aspects of military context that can complicate recovery from trauma exposure. For example, interpersonal violence could occur within a hierarchical, chain of command structure in which the victim reports to their perpetrator and has routine contact with them. The dangerous contexts of military operations may also result in comorbid injuries at the time of trauma exposure (e.g., traumatic brain injury [TBI]) that can impact posttraumatic stress disorder (PTSD) development and symptomatology. Service members may also take actions consistent with the warrior ethos, such as placing the mission first or never leaving a fallen comrade. However, some actions taken during service may violate service members' morals. This chapter is intended to bring awareness to the distinct facets of military service that may affect the experience and aftermath of trauma exposure, and how these factors can be addressed through CPT to facilitate recovery from PTSD.

Efficacy and Effectiveness of CPT in Military Populations

CPT was originally developed and tested on civilian sexual assault survivors and was shown to be effective in treating PTSD among female interpersonal violence survivors (Resick et al., 2002). Following September 11, 2001, and the ensuing Iraq and Afghanistan conflicts, there was recognition that effective PTSD treatments for military personnel were needed for those returning from deployment (Hoge et al., 2006). To address this need, CPT was first empirically tested on a veteran sample (Monson et al., 2006). This initial randomized controlled trial (RCT) conducted with veterans found a large improvement in PTSD symptom severity among those who completed CPT compared to those in the waitlist group, as well as reduced depression, anxiety, and guilt (Monson et al., 2006). Several RCTs and clinic evaluation studies have now been conducted to examine CPT's effectiveness in military populations.

Overall, studies have found that CPT significantly reduces PTSD symptoms in these populations with improvements of medium or large magnitude (e.g., Forbes et al., 2012; Held et al., 2022, 2023; Resick et al., 2017). CPT also typically results in greater improvements in PTSD compared to non-trauma focused treatments (Resick et al., 2015) and similar outcomes to other evidence-based PTSD treatment, such as prolonged exposure (Schnurr et al., 2022). CPT also mitigates related concerns, such as depression (Resick et al., 2017; Schnurr et al., 2022; Walter et al., 2023), suicidality (Resick et al., 2017) and guilt (Monson et al., 2006), and improves social functioning (Monson et al., 2006; Schnurr et al., 2022).

The use of CPT with military populations in a variety of formats, settings, and across trauma types is also effective. CPT can be delivered effectively in individual, group, or combined individual and group formats. When individual and group formats were compared in an active duty sample, both resulted in significant PTSD symptom reductions; however, the individual format showed greater effectiveness than the group format (Resick et al., 2017). Individual and group formats can be delivered through telehealth with similar benefits when compared to in-person CPT (Maieritsch et al., 2016; Peterson et al., 2022). Furthermore, these formats can be provided in outpatient, intensive outpatient (Held et al., 2022, 2023; Zalta et al., 2018), and residential settings (Walter et al., 2014), with the latter settings showing lower dropout rates than for outpatient CPT (Held et al., 2022; Walter et al., 2014; Zalta et al., 2018). CPT also has demonstrated effectiveness across types of military traumas experienced, such as combat (e.g., Resick et al., 2015; Resick et al., 2017) and military sexual trauma (MST; Surís et al., 2013a, 2013b).

While there is clear evidence that CPT can meaningfully improve PTSD and comorbid concerns in military populations, it is not without limitations. For example, although approximately 37–49% of military personnel no longer met criteria for PTSD following CPT (Resick et al., 2017; Schnurr et al., 2022), a substantial number continue to meet diagnostic criteria after treatment. However, retaining a PTSD diagnosis following CPT does not preclude service members and veterans from experiencing meaningful symptom improvements. Also, dropout rates from CPT among military personnel can be problematic and range from 15%–46% (Litz et al., 2021; Peterson et al., 2022; Resick et al., 2017; Schnurr et al., 2022). In addition to common factors that can affect dropout, such as avoidance, there are military-specific factors that may influence the rates of premature termination. These include changes in duty location, deployment or training exercises, and concerns about stigma and confidentiality (Hoge et al., 2014). Collectively, the research shows that CPT can effectively and meaningfully reduce trauma-related symptoms among military populations in various formats and settings. Identifying ways to enhance CPT treatment response and reduce dropout are important avenues for both clinical research and practice.

Treatment Response for Military Versus Civilian Populations

Although CPT can effectively reduce PTSD secondary to both combat (Resick et al., 2015; Resick et al., 2017) and military sexual trauma (MST) exposure (Surís et al., 2013a, 2013b), effect sizes in clinical trials with military samples typically are smaller than those with civilians (Steenkamp et al., 2020). There are various potential explanations for differing clinical outcomes. Although not specific to military populations, PTSD often co-occurs with both mental (e.g., depression, panic, anger and aggression, substance use, suicidal ideation) and physical health conditions (e.g., chronic pain, TBI; Blakey et al., 2018; Gonzalez et al., 2016; Loignon et al., 2020; Norman et al., 2018) that could negatively impact response to CPT. The types of traumatic events that service members experience may differ from those of civilians and present additional clinical considerations. For example, combat trauma may involve exposure to chronic, inescapable, life-threatening events, the potential for multiple traumatic losses and combat-related morally injurious experiences, and exposure to the aftermath of battle (e.g., seeing dead bodies or injured people; Steenkamp et al., 2020). Many military personnel have also lost comrades to suicide, with approximately 64% of a clinical sample of service members reporting such exposure (Schmied et al., 2023). Specific aspects of military culture such as hypermasculinity and situational awareness may be reinforced in military settings and lead to more treatment resistance of certain PTSD symptoms like anger, aggression, or hypervigilance. The presence of comorbidities, complexities of military traumas (e.g., complicated grief, morally injurious events), maintenance of symptoms that may be perceived as advantageous in military settings, and reinforcement of stuck points consistent with the warrior ethos (e.g., I will never quit; The mission always comes first) may impact response to CPT in this population. It is imperative for clinicians to be cognizant of military-specific factors that could affect treatment response. Thus, we will review MST, TBI, and morally injurious events that are common among this population and provide clinical considerations for working with each factor.

Military Sexual Trauma

MST refers to sexual assault or sexual harassment that occurs during military service (VA, 2021), including if a service member is on or off base, or on or off duty. Perpetrators of MST can be anyone, including civilians or service members, superiors or subordinates in the chain of command, intimate partners, friends, acquaintances, or strangers, and can be of any gender. A recent meta-analysis found that 15.7% of service members and veterans experience MST during their service (38.4% of women and 3.9% of men), and rates vary by definition of MST (Wilson, 2018). Although women are more likely to experience sexual trauma than men, the number of men and women affected by MST is comparable due to the greater proportion of men serving in the United States (US) military (Murdoch et al., 2007). Risk factors for MST include being younger age, female, growing up in a difficult home environment, lack of college degree, enlisted status, and prior trauma history (Allard et al., 2011; Surís & Lind, 2008). Marginalized groups, including people of color and sexual and gender minorities, are also at an elevated risk for MST, possibly due to having more limited societal standing and greater hesitancy to disclose (Bell et al., 2018).

Veterans with MST have a higher risk for developing PTSD compared to veterans with other sexual trauma (e.g., child sexual abuse, civilian sexual assault; Surís et al., 2004) or combat trauma (Kang et al., 2005). Among those who endorse MST, 51.1% of women and 52.5% of men screen positive met criteria for PTSD (Kimerling et al., 2010). However, the rates of both MST and MST-related PTSD are likely conservative estimates given that both are underreported, particularly for men. MST also increases the risk for revictimization after military service, which may result in greater risk for developing PTSD and the severity of PTSD symptoms (Surís et al., 2013a, 2013b).

There are several aspects of military culture that clinicians should be aware of when treating service members and veterans who experienced MST. One critical complexity of MST is that military personnel depend on their comrades for safety and other basic needs. Thus, MST perpetrated by a fellow service member or superior may be perceived as a significant violation or betrayal of those basic needs. Many military personnel who experience MST have a working relationship with their perpetrator, and depending on their duties, may rely on their perpetrator for protection in dangerous or life-threatening situations (Surís & Lind, 2008). MST may therefore lead to a breach in these important bonds and one's sense of trust in others, resulting in feelings of powerlessness (Andresen et al., 2019; Surís & Lind, 2008). If the perpetrator is of superior rank, they may also have influence over the survivor's career, making it difficult to report without concern for occupational consequences or further victimization. Military units also prioritize cohesiveness, particularly within the context of deployments or combat, which may lead to more hesitancy to disclose MST if there is a fear of retaliation (Dardis et al., 2018). Given that MST may occur in proximity to where individuals live and work, service members might continue to live and work near their perpetrator long after their MST experience, increasing their risk for chronic stress and revictimization. Taken together, MST can have a significant impact on both work and social settings, along with the potential challenges faced if the assault is reported (Holland et al., 2016).

Clinical Considerations for Working with Military Populations with MST

Given the complexity of MST, there are special considerations for providing CPT to military personnel. Like civilians, many MST survivors have a prior trauma history (e.g., child trauma, other sexual or intimate partner violence), and may require follow-ups or additional treatment sessions due to the recurrence rate of PTSD. Many survivors experience negative cognitions related to self-blame, possibly due to MST occurring while one was intoxicated or to not reporting the trauma. As stated above, MST often occurs within a complex dynamic between a service member and a superior or a comrade. Therefore, there are strong deterrents to reporting MST due to the real consequences that reporting may have on one's daily functioning. Survivors may also have cognitions about being unlovable or being unable to maintain healthy relationships.

Fortunately, CPT is well-equipped to address these beliefs, through Socratic questioning about the difference between responsibility and blame, as well as themes of self-esteem and intimacy. CPT specifically addresses five themes that are often impacted by trauma (i.e., safety, trust, power and control, esteem, intimacy; Resick et al., 2024). With regard to MST, these themes can be a natural transition to begin Socratic dialogue about power hierarchies and coercion from other military personnel and superior officers, self-blame related to lack of reporting, lack of control related to fear of losing one's job, safety concerns, difficulties trusting other military personnel or those demographically similar to one's perpetrator, feelings of weakness or being inferior to military peers, and difficulties with emotional and sexual intimacy.

Clinical Vignette: Woman MST Survivor

Below is an example Impact Statement and Stuck Point Log for a 60-year-old single, Black, female Army veteran with a history of child neglect, community violence exposure, and MST. She joined the military after high school with the hope of a better life. After several months of pervasive sexual harassment by a superior officer, she was raped by him. After her service contract, she did not re-enlist. Although the trauma occurred many years earlier, she continues to blame herself for the rape and how it impacted her career. She also reports low self-esteem, difficulty with trust, and a fear of men and the world overall.

> I would have never been raped if I reported the harassment when it first began. I was weak. I was scared that if I reported him, I would lose my job because he was buddies with my captain. They would not have helped me. But now it doesn't matter, because I didn't report it, and I am broken as a result. I am not sure if this happened because of my weakness, or if I am just a bad person, and that is why bad things have happened to me over and over again in my life. The world is such a scary place, and I always feel unsafe. Even though the rape happened years ago, I am still so scared of men, even people I work with now in a completely new setting. I hate looking at myself in the mirror because I hate what I see. I see an ugly, weak person. I am damaged because of the rape. I can't maintain friendships, and I haven't had a romantic relationship in ages because I am too scared to let people get close to me and I cannot trust people. In relationships, I rarely feel comfortable having sex with my partners, and eventually, they just leave me. Everyone leaves me. My family and friends think I am crazy. I hate myself for allowing the rape to happen, but sometimes it feels as though I deserved it because I was too scared to file the report.

After the patient reads their Impact Statement aloud, the therapist and patient create the Stuck Point Log together and add Stuck Points based on the Impact Statement and subsequent discussion. Based on this Impact Statement, some Stuck Points may include:

Assimilated	Overaccommodated
"If I reported the harassment, the rape would never have occurred."	*"Everyone will leave me."*
"It's my fault the rape happened because I was weak."	*"I am weak."* *"I am ugly."*
"I was raped because I am a bad person."	*"I am damaged."*

Assimilated	Overaccommodated
"I should have reported the harassment sooner."	*"I am unsafe."*
"I deserved to be raped because I was too scared to file the harassment report."	*"I cannot trust people."*
"I allowed the rape to happen."	*"I am a bad person".*
"If I reported the rape, the military would not have helped me." *"It is the military's fault I was raped"*	*"All men are dangerous."* *"No one in the military can be trusted"*

Although more women experience MST, men are also at risk, oftentimes in the context of hazing. Aspects of military culture (e.g., strength and masculinity) are highly threatened by sexual victimization (Turchik & Edwards, 2012), which may lead to cognitive dissonance, shame, self-blame, and identity dysphoria in men with MST (Allard et al., 2011). The value of strength and hypermasculinity is ever-present in military culture and may send a message that experiencing sexual trauma and feeling emotions is tied to weakness, femininity, or their sexual identity. Men may therefore be more apt to deny a history of MST and not engage in treatment. This may also encourage individuals to avoid trauma memories and emotions, which may make CPT quite challenging for military personnel, particularly those who are male identifying. Further, while both men and women commonly experience sexual dysfunction after MST (Allard et al., 2011), males with MST endorse greater sexual dysfunction than women, and may cite their MST as destroying their romantic relationships (O'Brien et al., 2008). Exploring stuck points related to self-blame, betrayal, weakness, sexual identity, and intimacy may be particularly important to assess and address during CPT with male MST survivors.

Clinical Vignette: Male Survivor of MST

This is an example of Socratic dialogue between a therapist and a male identifying client. The client is a 34-year-old, single, biracial, male veteran. He enlisted in the Marine Corps after high school and served on three combat deployments to the Middle East during his military service. During his early training, this veteran was sexually assaulted by four other Marines in the barracks after an evening of heavy alcohol consumption. The veteran continues to have self-blame related to his intoxication, ongoing distrust of his comrades, and both ongoing identity dysphoria and sexual dysfunction.

Therapist: *One stuck point that seems particularly strong for you is, "If I was physically aroused during the assault, I must have wanted it."*

Veteran: *Yes, the fact that my body wanted it is how I know that I must have wanted it on some level. I did not fight back hard enough in the moment, so I must have wanted it.*

Therapist: *Okay, let's talk about that a bit. Can you tell me a bit more about what things you think you might have been able to do at the time the assault happened?*

Veteran: *One of them was covering my mouth, so I was not able to yell, Although I did try to break free to call for help. I tried to fight them off, but they held me down. If I had not been drinking, I would have been able to fight harder.*

Therapist: *So, it sounds like you tried to fight them off, you tried to yell, and still the assault continued. What might that have communicated to them if you were doing those things?*

Veteran: *I mean, I guess it showed I didn't want it, especially because they had to hold me down. They kept telling me to be quiet and stop moving around.*

Therapist: *Hmmm, okay, so it sounds like they were aware based on your body language, movements, and yelling, that you did not want this to happen.*

Veteran: *I don't know if they did know that because one of them told me, "I can tell how much you want this" because I became physically aroused when they were touching me.*

Therapist: *I see, so one of the men who assaulted you said you wanted it because you had a physical reaction to being touched.*

Veteran: *Yes, so even though I was trying to get free of their grip and call for help, my body still wanted it. I just can't get the thought out of my head that I must have liked it.*

Therapist: *What were you thinking or feeling at the time?*

Veteran: *I was scared, I was thinking I needed to get away.*

Therapist: *What about the physical aspect of being touched? Is it possible that your body can become physically aroused by being touched in certain ways?*

Veteran: *Yes, I guess so. It had just never happened before with a man.*

Therapist: *Is it possible that our biological systems of arousal do not discriminate between the touch of a man* versus *a woman?*

Veteran: *I supposed it is possible, yes.*

Therapist: *So, in this situation, I hear you saying that you tried to yell, and you tried to fight them off. Given those circumstances, it sounds like you did not want the assault to happen despite the physical arousal that occurred. What else you could have done in the situation beyond what you tried?*

Veteran: *I cannot think of anything else I could have done. I think that maybe they did know I did not want it to happen because they had to hold me down the entire time. If the arousal was just a biological response, then I guess they used that to justify their actions.*

Therapist: *Absolutely. Putting this all together, is there any part of the situation that makes you think that you wanted this to happen or that you communicated to them that you wanted it?*

Veteran: *No, they took advantage of me when I had been drinking, and they made me think it was my fault when I never asked for this. How am I supposed to trust my fellow Marines to have my back and protect me after something like this?*

Therapist: *That sounds like another important stuck point for you. In particular, it sounds like the assault has made it difficult for you to know who is trustworthy given such a strong betrayal by these Marines.*

Veteran: *Exactly. As Marines, we are brothers. We are trained to have each other's back no matter what, not to turn on each other. Now I cannot trust any of them.*

Therapist: *You have been on three combat deployments during your military service. Are there any Marines from those deployments that you trusted to have your back in dangerous situations?*

Veteran: *Yes, there were several guys on my squad who I could trust with my life. Even Marines that I have known since bootcamp…I know they would have my back.*

Therapist: *Okay, so it sounds like there are some Marines who are trustworthy. As we move forward in CPT, we are going to spend some time thinking about trust on a continuum, as opposed to in a constricted or "black and white" way. It is hard to feel like you can trust anyone after such a devastating betrayal, and still, it sounds like there are some Marines out there that you have trusted with your life when the situation has demanded it. I wonder if those Marines you trusted then are still people you trust now, even if the degree of trust has changed?*

Veteran: *Yes, that is true. Even though it is hard with all that has happened to me, I still trust them with my life.*

The impact of MST is far-reaching, and it can impact many areas of functioning (Galovski et al., 2022). Clinicians should be cognizant of the unique facets of MST compared to civilian sexual trauma. In addition to the shame, isolation, sense of betrayal, and possible chronicity associated with all sexual trauma exposure, the complexity of MST extends further. Specifically, there may be an inability to escape the trauma environment or perpetrator, a fear for retaliation and loss of occupational success, a fear that the one may be punished rather than the perpetrator, and a fear for one's safety and protection if they are in an active war zone. Clinicians can offer education to all veterans that CPT is an effective treatment for MST-related PTSD, as many may be unaware.

Traumatic Brain Injury and Cognitive Impairment

TBIs, defined as an injury to the head caused by an external force, are common among both civilian and military populations. From 2000 to 2022, there were a reported 468,424 TBIs in the Department of Defense (DoD) worldwide (Traumatic Brain Injury Center of Excellence [TBICoE];, 2022). Most of these injuries were sustained in non-deployed settings following motor vehicular accidents, falls, sports and recreational activities, and military training. TBIs were also considered a "signature injury" of US military combat operations in Iraq and Afghanistan (Okie, 2005). Despite the increased attention to the assessment, diagnosis, and treatment of TBI, much remains unknown, and the existing literature suffers from methodological limitations that preclude definitive conclusions (Phipps et al., 2020). TBIs are classified as mild, moderate, or severe based on alteration/loss of consciousness (LOC) and posttraumatic amnesia (PTA) criteria. Mild TBIs (mTBI), or "concussions," account for the majority of TBIs in both the civilian and military populations. In the US DoD, 82.3% of TBIs were classified as mild, 11.1% were moderate, and 2.02% were severe or penetrating (TBICoE;, 2022). Although mTBIs are the most common, moderate to severe TBIs can be easier to diagnose given that objective data are often documented during medical care. Because mTBI is the most common injury, and TBIs of greater severity can show significant heterogeneity in resulting impairment, this section will primarily focus on treatment of PTSD for military populations with a history of mTBI.

Neurobehavioral symptoms that may result following TBI include an array of cognitive, affective, and physical changes such as sensitivity to light, headaches, changes in taste/smell, nausea, forgetfulness, poor concentration, low frustration tolerance, sleep problems, fatigue, and anxiety/tension. Although some research shows that recovery is expected within weeks to months following mTBI (Iverson, 2005; Porter & Johnson, 2020), other research indicates that a sizeable portion of service members and veterans report persistent symptoms (McDonald et al., 2021). It is important to know that although symptoms can result from an mTBI, they are not specific to the injury and are often reported by healthy individuals without a history of mTBI (Iverson & Lange, 2003). Also, a systematic review of the literature found that there were minimal, if any, significant differences in mental health symptoms among military populations with and without a history of mTBI (O'Neil et al., 2013). Further complicating the symptom presentation is the significant overlap between a history of mTBI and psychological disorders, such as PTSD and depression. Among veterans who were diagnosed with a history of mTBI, 67% had a PTSD diagnosis in their medical record, 34% had a depression diagnosis, and 29% had both. The comorbidity between mTBI history and PTSD may be tied to shared, event-specific factors and symptom overlap (Vasterling et al., 2012).

From a clinical perspective, these findings collectively demonstrate the lack of specificity of neurobehavioral symptoms, and that they alone may not result from a history of mTBI, given their overlap with symptoms of other conditions. Because of this, it can be difficult to determine the precise etiology of neurobehavioral symptoms, and it may be most advantageous for clinicians to focus on addressing the presenting concerns and reducing barriers. This approach may improve symptoms and functioning while reducing the potential for the inadvertent development of symptoms in response to diagnosis or treatment (Yang et al., 2018). Further, this recommendation aligns with the US Department of Veterans Affairs (VA) and DoD Clinical Practice Guideline for the Management of Concussion-mild Traumatic Brain Injury (2016), which suggests assessing for both psychiatric symptoms and comorbid disorders during a thorough history and examination for patients with symptoms attributed to mTBI. These practice guidelines also recommend treating comorbid conditions per their specific VA/DoD clinical practice guidelines (VA/DoD, 2021), such as with CPT for PTSD (VA/DoD, 2023).

Treatment Outcomes for Military Populations with PTSD and TBI History

Providers may be hesitant to use CPT with service members and veterans with a history of mTBI due to assumptions that cognitive limitations may exist or concerns that they may reduce treatment effectiveness (Bogdanova & Verfaellie, 2012). Additionally, neurobehavioral symptoms attributed to mTBI may be perceived to negatively impact trauma-focused treatment and that treatment should primarily focus on these cognitive, affective, and physical symptoms (Crocker et al., 2018). Although it is critical to acknowledge that the research for treating PTSD in the context of an mTBI history in military populations is evolving and critical questions remain unanswered, it is also important to note that results from a review of the extant literature supports the use of CPT for military personnel with a history of mTBI (Mikolić et al., 2019).

In the outpatient literature, several studies have evaluated CPT engagement and treatment effectiveness for service members with PTSD and mild-to-moderate TBI. One study did not show a difference in the number of CPT sessions attended for those with PTSD (9.6) and those with both PTSD and mTBI (7.9), or on the rate of CPT treatment completion, which was greater than 61% for veterans in both groups (Davis et al., 2013). However, subsequent research examining data across three clinical trials of trauma-focused treatments (including CPT) among active duty service members showed that history of TBI predicted lower session attendance and greater dropout (Berke et al., 2019). Research has also investigated whether injury characteristics of mTBI (i.e., presence of LOC or PTA, time since injury, number of mTBIs, and mechanisms of injury) are related to CPT session attendance. Findings indicated that none of the injury characteristics were associated with number of CPT sessions attended (Crocker et al., 2019). While initial results present mixed findings, these suggest that military populations with PTSD and a history of mTBI can engage in CPT for PTSD and receive a sufficient treatment dose (i.e., 8 sessions; Maguen et al., 2020) and a history of mTBI should not prevent individuals from receiving CPT, irrespective of injury characteristics (Crocker et al., 2019).

In addition to engagement and attendance, studies have explored treatment outcomes following CPT in military populations with PTSD and a history of mTBI. Preliminary clinic data showed that PTSD and depression outcomes did not significantly differ after CPT between veterans with PTSD with and without a history of TBI (Ragsdale & Voss Horrell, 2016). Similar to findings regarding attendance, Crocker et al. (2019) found that the five injury characteristics did not impact treatment response across two treatment conditions, CPT and an integrated treatment combining CPT and compensatory cognitive training (SMART-CPT; discussed in more detail later in this section). However, LOC differentially predicted outcomes when considering the treatments separately. Specifically, veterans who denied experiencing LOC experienced greater improvements in PTSD and depression symptom severity in CPT compared to SMART-CPT.

The modality and setting of CPT delivery has also been examined among service members with PTSD and a history of TBI. Individual CPT has been found to be more effective than group CPT for service members with PTSD and a history of TBI with neurobehavioral symptoms, while group and individual modalities were equally effective for those without TBI and neurobehavioral symptoms (Wachen et al., 2022). This suggests that the cognitive effects of TBI may be more pronounced in a group treatment format. CPT was shown to be effective for individuals with a TBI history when delivered in specialized, residential treatment programs within the VA where veterans receive CPT in a combined individual and group format, along with other programming, such as psychosocial groups, occupational therapy, and speech therapy (Chard et al., 2011). Following treatment, there were significant reductions in PTSD and depression symptoms (Chard et al., 2011), neurobehavioral symptoms (Walter et al., 2012), and suicidal ideation (Pease et al., 2023), as well as improvements in occupational performance and satisfaction with that performance (Speicher et al., 2014). In comparing the effectiveness of CPT delivered with or without the trauma account in a residential setting for veterans with PTSD and a history of TBI, program results showed comparable outcomes between the treatments for PTSD but greater decreases in depression for veterans who received CPT with the trauma account (Walter et al., 2014). While initial outcome data imply that history of TBI should not preclude military populations with PTSD from being offered or engaging in CPT, it appears that modality (individual over group), format (standard vs. adapted versions; discussed more below) may yield greater therapeutic gains, and CPT can be effectively delivered in outpatient and residential settings.

Research has also begun to focus on whether PTSD and TBI with cognitive impairment are predictive of CPT treatment response. Executive functioning (EF) refers to cognitive skills that are critical in daily life, such as planning, organization, and regulating thoughts and behaviors. EF is also essential in CPT for evaluating evidence for and against beliefs, inhibiting maladaptive beliefs, and identifying alternative thoughts. In CPT, veterans with poorer pretreatment EF showed higher rates of treatment dropout and a reduced PTSD symptom response following treatment compared to those with better pretreatment EF (Crocker et al., 2018). Importantly, findings showed that veterans with worse pretreatment cognitive flexibility benefitted less from standard CPT, though significant PTSD symptom improvement was observed in a version of CPT enhanced with compensatory cognitive training. EF appears to be an important cognitive skill in predicting both treatment attendance and outcome in CPT, and assessment of EF can help determine the appropriateness of CPT compared to adapted versions.

Clinical Considerations for Working with Military Populations with a History of TBI

A central clinical consideration for working with military populations with PTSD and a history of mTBI is similar to treating those without a history of TBI—focusing on the current symptom presentation—which may or may not consist of cognitive limitations. CPT relies on cognitive skills, including critical thinking, working memory, and concentration, to name a few. At the start of treatment, it is common for patients to be confused by treatment concepts or the practice assignments, but this confusion typically diminished over the course of treatment. Because of this, it is recommended that CPT be delivered as intended to start and then modifications be made if the patient continues to demonstrate comprehension difficulties or the inability to complete practice assignments with basic understanding. It should be noted that for some patients, significant cognitive limitations may be observable at initial intake that could warrant adaptions to the protocol at treatment outset.

One adaptation for cognitive limitations, regardless of TBI history, is modified CPT worksheets. These worksheets were developed for individuals with cognitive limitations that affect their ability to complete the worksheets in the standard format, and are included in the CPT manual. It is recommended that the standard ABC sheet be used as intended in treatment as they are generally effective for those with TBI histories. However, if a patient expresses difficulty understanding the Alternative Thoughts Worksheet (previously called the Challenging Questions Worksheet), a modified version of this worksheet can be used. The modified worksheets allow the CPT protocol content to be delivered, while still facilitating comprehension among those with PTSD and cognitive limitation.

There are also adaptations to the treatment protocol for military personnel with PTSD and a history of mild-to-moderate TBI. Jak et al. (2019) integrated CPT with compensatory cognitive training, which provides instruction on internal, external, and environmental strategies to improve and manage cognitive skill deficits. In the hybrid treatment, compensatory cognitive training from the Cognitive Symptom Management and Rehabilitation Therapy (CogSMART) was integrated into CPT and referred to as SMART-CPT. Like CPT, SMART-CPT was developed as a 12-session protocol, but sessions are 75 min in duration (compared to 60 for CPT) to accommodate the compensatory cognitive training content. SMART-CPT retains the content and structure of CPT (without the trauma account) and adds the following components from CogSMART: PTSD and TBI comorbidity psychoeducation; compensatory strategies for memory, attention, and EF and how they apply to CPT; simplified language; written summaries and mini-reviews throughout treatment for repetition and review; short breaks during session; and modified worksheets that divide assignments into smaller section to facilitate completion. When SMART-CPT was compared to CPT, both treatments resulted in clinically significant improvements in PTSD symptom severity, neurobehavioral symptoms, and quality of life (Jak et al., 2019). SMART-CPT produced additional benefits in neurocognitive domains of verbal learning/memory, attention/working memory, and novel problem solving. See Chap. 6 for further details about SMART-CPT and additional considerations for delivering CPT in the context of TBI.

Although providers may hesitate to use evidence-based PTSD treatments with military personnel with a TBI history, the existing literature supports the use of CPT for those with histories of mild-to-moderate TBI (Mikolić et al., 2019). CPT can be delivered effectively to military populations with PTSD and histories of mild-to-moderate TBI in various formats, including with or without the trauma account, using standard or modified worksheets, or CPT alone or integrated with cognitive compensatory strategies (SMART-CPT). When resources allow, CPT appears the most effective when delivered to military personnel with PTSD individually rather than in a group setting (Resick et al., 2017), including among those with a TBI history (Wachen et al., 2022), and can be delivered with other disciplines in more intensive treatment settings to reduce PTSD and neurobehavioral symptoms. These CPT options are available and effective for military populations with PTSD and a history of mild-to-moderate TBI and can be selected based on factors, such as the existence and degree of cognitive limitations and patient preference.

Moral Injury

There has been increased attention in recent years to the importance of treating PTSD related to morally injurious events. However, there is not a consistently accepted definition of moral injury, and the definition has evolved over time with input from scholars and clinicians. Dr. Jonathan Shay originally wrote about the concept of moral injury in his Shay, 1994 book titled, *Achilles in Vietnam: Combat Trauma and the Undoing of Character*, where he compared Vietnam soldiers' experiences to that of Homer in the *Iliad.* Litz et al. (2009) later published a seminal paper that defined morally injurious events as, "perpetrating, failing to prevent, or bearing witness to acts that transgress deeply held moral beliefs and expectations may be deleterious in the long-term, emotionally, psychologically, behaviorally, spiritually, and socially" (p. 1). Although the definition of moral injury may vary, the overarching principle is that someone has violated or has experienced a betrayal of moral beliefs and/or expectations that contributes to psychological pain, including but not limited to PTSD.

Given the increased attention on treating moral injury and PTSD related to morally injurious events, several recent studies examined the impact of CPT for PTSD related to morally injurious events or among those who have experienced these events. In one study, a history of moral injury or morally injurious index trauma did not adversely impact reductions in PTSD and depression symptoms among military personnel engaged in CPT through a 3-week intensive treatment (Held et al., 2021). These results suggested that following an intensive outpatient program for PTSD, service members and veterans with PTSD and moral injury can significantly improve symptoms following CPT. Furthermore, a recent study examining data from five clinical trials of CPT in military and veteran samples found that both those with and without morally injurious index traumas experienced significant reductions in PTSD and depression, and that reductions among those with morally injurious trauma were non-inferior to those without a morally injurious trauma (LoSavio et al., 2023).

RCTs have also evaluated CPT among active duty and veteran populations that commonly experience morally injurious events. Litz et al. (2021) conducted an RCT comparing CPT to Adaptive Disclosure (AD), a treatment intended to address moral injury, PTSD related to combat, and traumatic loss. AD and CPT resulted in similar PTSD and depressive symptom reductions, with approximately 25% of service members in both treatment groups showing improvement in or recovery from PTSD symptoms. Treatment completers had greater improvement or recovery rates following CPT and AD (45% and 41%, respectively). Of note, improvement and recovery rates in this study were calculated using at least a 22-point reduction in CAPS-IV scores from pretreatment. This is greater than the reliable change index found for the CAPS-5 in other Veteran samples (e.g., 12–13 points, Marx et al., 2022). Additionally, dropout rates did not significantly differ between CPT and AD (40% and 37%, respectively). Given a large proportion of service members in the intent-to-treat sample did not improve or recover, it is important to continue to better understand how to maximize CPT in populations where morally injurious events are common. Notably, improvement and recovery rates were greater in the completer sample, which highlights the importance of continued efforts to increase completion rates in CPT. Overall, the literature suggests that individuals who have experienced a morally injurious event or have PTSD related to moral injury can benefit from CPT and have significant symptom reduction. Clinicians should therefore feel comfortable offering CPT to military personnel presenting with moral injury-related concerns.

Clinical Considerations When Working with Military Populations with Moral Injury

Morally injurious events occur in both military and civilian populations. Although civilians can experience morally injurious events (e.g., first responder who cannot save someone's life), there are aspects of military culture, training, and duties that may contribute to unique facets of moral injury in military populations. Most notably, military service often requires military personnel to engage in behaviors or bear witness to acts that are not typically expected of civilians. For example, some service members may be given orders to wound or kill combatants, be repeatedly exposed to injured or dead bodies, or have to move or dispose of dead bodies. The military also has "rules of engagement" that outline the circumstances and means in which service members can use force. Thus, there are times when service members are forced to make split-second decisions regarding threat and need to decide whether to engage with force. The inherent ambiguity in these situations can lead to the loss of life of civilians who may have been mistaken for combatants, which can result in moral injury. Similarly, service members may need to make quick decisions about whose life to try to save, such as the life of a child in the warzone or the life of a comrade.

These potentially morally injurious events can weigh heavily on individuals and become a burden to carry long after the event itself. When service members return stateside or reintegrate back into civilian life, they may experience feelings of guilt or shame related to their actions, which were previously adaptive for survival, but are no longer effective in civilian life. Given that many of these morally injurious events occur within the context of combat or an active warzone, there is not often an opportunity to fully process or grieve these experiences due to the need to survive and perform duties. Therefore, encouraging the expression of natural emotions related to moral injury is important during CPT.

Military personnel also may experience moral injury related to betrayal by authority figures, the government, or the military institution. The military is known for its camaraderie and "brotherhood" among members, and therefore, betrayals by one another or the overall institution can have a devastating impact on well-being. Training is focused on looking out for oneself and one's fellow service members, so situations where someone is left behind or sexually assaulted can be perceived as violations of these values. These betrayals can also lead to an overall sense of disillusionment with the military. Similarly, one may experience moral injury if they question the larger purpose of conflicts and feel that the outcomes were not what they intended when they made the decision to serve. This often leads to military personnel questioning the purpose of their service or feeling misled by the military.

Clinical Vignette: Morally Injurious Event

This is an example of Socratic dialogue between a therapist and a veteran who has PTSD related to a morally injurious event. The veteran is a 42-year-old, single, White, male who enlisted in the Army and was deployed to Iraq in 2003. On his first deployment, he fatally shot a young child after being given orders by a superior officer to shoot anyone who appeared to be a threat or was holding a weapon. He presented to treatment with guilt and shame, and beliefs that he should not have followed orders in this instance. He believed that the child would still be alive if he had not shot them, and that he is a horrible person for killing a child.

Therapist: *It seems like the stuck point "I should not have followed orders because then the child would be alive" is what you are really feeling stuck on and making you feel the most guilt.*

Veteran: *Yes, I can't get it out of my head, and it makes me feel like a horrible person that I killed a child. I shouldn't have listened to the orders I was given.*

Therapist: *It sounds like this has really been weighing on you. Tell me more about what was happening at the time that makes you think you should not have followed orders.*

Veteran: *We were on a reconnaissance mission in a local village. I was there, along with my commanding officer and several other soldiers nearby. It was hard to tell at the time who was a threat and who was a civilian. There was a child nearby who ran out of a house, and he was carrying something bulky under his shirt. It looked like it could be a weapon, and I had been told to shoot if someone was a threat. I hesitated for a moment, but then I shot him. Now I don't think I should have listened to those orders. If I had not shot the child, he'd still be alive.*

Therapist: *It sounds like there was some uncertainty during the situation that made it hard to know if the child was a threat or not, and you had to make the best decision you could at the time. What were you thinking and feeling before you shot the child?*

Veteran: *It all happened so fast it is hard to remember. I recall feeling panicked, and I froze for a few seconds. I remember not knowing if it was the right call because I couldn't tell for sure if he had a weapon under his shirt. I didn't want to shoot the child, but I didn't have a choice.*

Therapist: *How come you didn't think you had a choice?*

Veteran: *I had been given orders and I had to follow the chain of command. If I didn't follow orders, I could have been court martialed, which would have really hurt my career. I was just starting out in the military and didn't want to ruin my career and my reputation. I also was afraid to make a mistake if the child was a threat and get myself or anyone else killed.*

Therapist: *It makes sense that you were doing what you had been trained to do and wanted to protect your career. It sounds like even though you didn't want to shoot the child, you were trying to protect yourself and others. What do you think would have happened to the child though if you had not followed orders and didn't shoot in that moment?*

Veteran: *I think someone else would have shot him given the orders.*

Therapist: *Hm, so it sounds like the child may have died even if you hadn't shot because he appeared to be a threat and you were all given those same orders. It sounds like you were in a challenging position where there wasn't a good choice.*

Veteran: *Yeah, I just wish this child didn't die. I didn't sign up to go to war to kill children. So, I just think that I am a horrible person for doing this.*

Therapist: *It makes a lot of sense that you wish the child hadn't died and is a painful reality of war. I know you said you think you are a horrible, what makes someone a horrible person?*

Veteran: *I think someone who doesn't care about other people, disregards their feelings, tries to harm others on purpose, and doesn't feel remorse.*

Therapist: *If you were a horrible person who didn't care about other people and didn't feel remorse, do you think you'd be in therapy for this right now?*

Veteran: *I guess I hadn't thought about it like that before. I mean, I guess not.*

Therapist: *It sounds like underneath the guilt and shame you have been feeling, there is a lot of grief and sadness about what you had to do as a part of your job.*

Veteran: (tearful) *Yeah, I just wasn't prepared for this at my age at the time. I was just a kid. I didn't realize what I'd have to do over there or how it would continue to affect me.*

Acts that transgress against a person's moral code can occur during military service and impact psychological health and functioning in profound and complex ways. Clinical knowledge regarding the best approaches to treating the effects of moral injury is evolving, but research to date supports the use of CPT in treating PTSD related to morally injurious events and among those who have experienced such events. Fortunately, CPT is well poised to address moral injury through the identification and examination of moral injury-related stuck points and the encouragement of the expression of natural emotions. Understanding the contexts in which morally injurious events often occur in military settings, including competing demands and immediate nature of decisions, is essential for clinicians working with military populations. This contextual information facilitates Socratic questioning and cognitive restructuring in CPT, which can address the psychological effects of morally injurious events experienced by service members and veterans.

Summary

CPT has been shown to be effective for treating PTSD in military populations. Military service provides opportunities for professional and personal development but may also present trauma exposures that are both similar to and unique from those of civilians. Awareness of the contextual factors of military service can provide essential information for evaluating beliefs in the delivery of CPT. Clinical concerns related to MST, TBI, and moral injury are common in treating service members and veterans with PTSD using CPT. For many military personnel, CPT in the standard format may be the appropriate treatment option, but for others, modified worksheets or adapted versions of the CPT protocol could offer enhanced clinical benefit. Clinical trials have started to identify which service members and veterans may respond best to these CPT treatments options, but additional work is needed to improve treatment response for those with military-related PTSD. Military culture and environmental factors add a great deal of nuance to trauma presentations, which clinicians should be cognizant of when working with military populations.

Acknowledgments The authors greatly appreciate Tony An, Aileen Chang, and Julia Hollingsworth for assisting with literature searches for this chapter, Sarah Jurick for reviewing content, and Michelle Stoia for her editorial assistance.

Disclaimer: Kristen H. Walter, Stephanie Y. Wells, and Hannah E. Walker are employees of the US Government. This work and works cited in this chapter were part of their official duties. The views expressed in this article are those of the authors and do not necessarily reflect the official policy or position of the Department of the Navy, Department of Defense, Department of Veterans Affairs, nor the US Government.

Competing Interests
The authors have no conflicts of interest to declare that are relevant to the content of this chapter.

References

Allard, C. B., Nunnink, S., Gregory, A. M., Klest, B., & Platt, M. (2011). Military sexual trauma research: A proposed agenda. *Journal of Trauma & Dissociation: The Official Journal of the International Society for the Study of Dissociation (ISSD), 12*(3), 324–345. https://doi.org/10.1080/15299732.2011.542609

Andresen, F. J., Monteith, L. L., Kugler, J., Cruz, R. A., & Blais, R. K. (2019). Institutional betrayal following military sexual trauma is associated with more severe depression and specific post-traumatic stress disorder symptom clusters. *Journal of Clinical Psychology, 75*(7), 1305–1319. https://doi.org/10.1002/jclp.22773

Bell, M. E., Dardis, C. M., Vento, S. A., & Street, A. E. (2018). Victims of sexual harassment and sexual assault in the military: Understanding risks and promoting recovery. *Military Psychology, 30*(3), 219–228. https://doi.org/10.1080/15299732.2011.542609

Berke, D. S., Kline, N. K., Wachen, J. S., McLean, C. P., Yarvis, J. S., Young-McCaughan, S., Peterson, A. L., Foa, E., Resick, P. A., Litz, B. T., & STRONG STAR Consortium. (2019). Predictors of attendance and dropout in three randomized controlled trials of PTSD treatment for active duty service members. *Behaviour Research and Therapy, 118*, 7–17. https://doi.org/10.1016/j.brat.2019.03.003

Blakey, S. M., Wagner, H. R., Naylor, J., Brancu, M., Lane, I., Sallee, M., Kimbrel, N. A., & Elbogen, E. B. (2018). Chronic pain, TBI, and PTSD in military veterans: A link to suicidal ideation and violent impulses? *The Journal of Pain, 19*(7), 797–806. https://doi.org/10.1016/j.brat.2019.03.003

Bogdanova, Y., & Verfaellie, M. (2012). Cognitive sequelae of blast-induced traumatic brain injury: Recovery and rehabilitation. *Neuropsychology Review, 22*(1), 4–20. https://doi.org/10.1007/s11065-012-9192-3

Chard, K. M., Schumm, J. A., McIlvain, S. M., Bailey, G. W., & Parkinson, R. B. (2011). Exploring the efficacy of a residential treatment program incorporating cognitive processing therapy-cognitive for veterans with PTSD and traumatic brain injury. *Journal of Traumatic Stress, 24*(3), 347–351. https://doi.org/10.1002/jts.20644

Crocker, L. D., Jurick, S. M., Thomas, K. R., Keller, A. V., Sanderson-Cimino, M., Boyd, B., Rodgers, C., Twamley, E. W., & Jak, A. J. (2018). Worse baseline executive functioning is associated with dropout and poorer response to trauma-focused treatment for veterans with PTSD and comorbid traumatic brain injury. *Behaviour Research and Therapy, 108*, 68–77. https://doi.org/10.1016/j.brat.2018.07.004

Crocker, L. D., Jurick, S. M., Thomas, K. R., Keller, A. V., Sanderson-Cimino, M., Hoffman, S. N., Boyd, B., Rodgers, C., Norman, S. B., Lang, A. J., Twamley, E. W., & Jak, A. J. (2019). Mild traumatic brain injury characteristics do not negatively influence cognitive processing therapy attendance or outcomes. *Journal of Psychiatric Research, 116*, 7–13. https://doi.org/10.1016/j.jpsychires.2019.05.022

Dardis, C. M., Reinhardt, K. M., Foynes, M. M., Medoff, N. E., & Street, A. E. (2018). "Who are you going to tell? Who's going to believe you?": Women's experiences disclosing military sexual trauma. *Psychology of Women Quarterly, 42*, 414–429. https://doi.org/10.1177/0361684318796783

Davis, J. J., Walter, K. H., Chard, K. M., Parkinson, R. B., & Houston, W. S. (2013). Treatment adherence in cognitive processing therapy for combat-related PTSD with history of mild TBI. *Rehabilitation Psychology, 58*(1), 36–42. https://doi.org/10.1037/a0031525

Forbes, D., Lloyd, D., Nixon, R. D., Elliott, P., Varker, T., Perry, D., Bryant, R. A., & Creamer, M. (2012). A multisite randomized controlled effectiveness trial of cognitive processing therapy for military-related posttraumatic stress disorder. *Journal of Anxiety Disorders, 26*(3), 442–452. https://doi.org/10.1016/j.janxdis.2012.01

Galovski, T. E., Street, A. E., Creech, S., Levahot, K., Kelly, U., & Yano, E. M. (2022). State of the knowledge of VA military sexual trauma research. *Journal of General Internal Medicine, 37*(3), 825–832. https://doi.org/10.1007/s11606-022-07580-8

Gonzalez, O. I., Novaco, R. W., Reger, M. A., & Gahm, G. A. (2016). Anger intensification with combat-related PTSD and depression comorbidity. *Psychological Trauma: Theory, Research, Practice, and Policy, 8*, 9–16. https://doi.org/10.1037/tra0000042

Held, P., Kovacevic, M., Petrey, K., Meade, E. A., Pridgen, S., Montes, M., et al. (2022). Treating posttraumatic stress disorder at home in a single week using 1-week virtual massed cognitive processing therapy. *Journal of Traumatic Stress, 35*(4), 1215–1225. https://doi.org/10.1002/jts.22831

Held, P., Smith, D. L., Pridgen, S., Coleman, J. A., & Klassen, B. J. (2023). More is not always better: 2 weeks of intensive cognitive processing therapy-based treatment are noninferior to 3 weeks. *Psychological Trauma: Theory, Research, Practice, and Policy, 15*(1), 100–109. https://doi.org/10.1037/tra0001257

Held, P., Klassen, B. J., Steigerwald, V. L., Smith, D. L., Bravo, K., Rozek, D. C., Van Horn, R., & Zalta, A. (2021). Do morally injurious experiences and index events negatively impact intensive PTSD treatment outcomes among combat veterans? *European Journal of Psychotraumatology, 12*(1), 1877026. https://doi.org/10.1080/20008198.2021.1877026

Hoge, C. W., Auchterlonie, J. L., & Milliken, C. S. (2006). Mental health problems, use of mental health services, and attrition from military service after returning from deployment to Iraq or Afghanistan. *JAMA, 295*(9), 1023–1032. https://doi.org/10.1001/jama.295.9.1023

Hoge, C. W., Grossman, S. H., Auchterlonie, J. L., Riviere, L. A., Milliken, C. S., & Wilk, J. E. (2014). PTSD treatment for soldiers after combat deployment: Low utilization of mental health care and reasons for dropout. Psychiatric services (), 65(8), 997–1004. doi:https://doi.org/10.1176/appi.ps.201300307

Holland, K. J., Rabelo, V. C., & Cortina, L. M. (2016). Collateral damage: Military sexual trauma and help-seeking barriers. *Psychology of Violence, 6*(2), 253–261. https://doi.org/10.1037/a0039467

Iverson, G. L. (2005). Outcome from mild traumatic brain injury. *Current Opinion in Psychiatry, 18*(3), 301–317. https://doi.org/10.1097/01.yco.0000165601.29047.ae

Iverson, G. L., & Lange, R. T. (2003). Examination of "postconcussion-like" symptoms in a healthy sample. *Applied Neuropsychology, 10*(3), 137–144. https://doi.org/10.1207/S15324826AN1003_02

Jak, A. J., Jurick, S., Crocker, L. D., Sanderson-Cimino, M., Aupperle, R., Rodgers, C. S., Thomas, K. R., Boyd, B., Norman, S. B., Lang, A. J., Keller, A. V., Schiehser, D. M., & Twamley, E. W. (2019). SMART-CPT for veterans with comorbid post-traumatic stress disorder and history of traumatic brain injury: A randomised controlled trial. *Journal of Neurology, Neurosurgery, and Psychiatry, 90*(3), 333–341. https://doi.org/10.1136/jnnp-2018-319315

Kang, H., Dalager, N., Mahan, C., & Ishii, E. (2005). The role of sexual assault on the risk of PTSD among gulf war veterans. *Annals of Epidemiology, 15*(3), 191–195. https://doi.org/10.1016/j.annepidem.2004.05.009

Kimerling, R., Street, A. E., Pavao, J., Smith, M. W., Cronkite, R. C., Holmes, T. H., & Frayne, S. M. (2010). Military-related sexual trauma among veterans' health administration patients returning from Afghanistan and Iraq. *American Journal of Public Health, 100*(8), 1409–1412. https://doi.org/10.2105/AJPH.2009.171793

Litz, B. T., Rusowicz-Orazem, L., Doros, G., Grunthal, B., Gray, M., Nash, W., & Lang, A. J. (2021). Adaptive disclosure, a combat-specific PTSD treatment, versus cognitive-processing therapy, in deployed marines and sailors: A randomized controlled non-inferiority trial. *Psychiatry Research, 297*, 113761. https://doi.org/10.1016/j.psychres.2021.113761

Litz, B. T., Stein, N., Delaney, E., Lebowitz, L., Nash, W. P., Silva, C., & Maguen, S. (2009). Moral injury and moral repair in war veterans: A preliminary model and intervention strategy. *Clinical Psychology Review, 29*(8), 695–706. https://doi.org/10.1016/j.cpr.2009.07.003

Loignon, A., Ouellet, M.-C., & Belleville, G. (2020). A systematic review and meta-analysis on PTSD following TBI among military/veteran and civilian populations. *The Journal of Head Trauma Rehabilitation, 35*(1), E21. https://doi.org/10.1097/HTR.0000000000000514

LoSavio, S. T., Hale, W., Straud, C. L., Wachen, J. S., Mintz, J., Young-McCaughan, S., Vacek, S. N., Yarvis, J. S., Sloan, D. M., McGeary, D. D., Taylor, D. J., Keane, T. M., Peterson, A. L., & Resick, P. A. (2023). Impact of morally injurious traumatic event exposure on cognitive processing therapy outcomes among veterans and service members. *Journal of Military, Veteran and Family Health, 9*(2), 40–51. https://doi.org/10.3138/jmvfh-2022-0048

Maieritsch, K. P., Smith, T. L., Hessinger, J. D., Ahearn, E. P., Eickhoff, J. C., & Zhao, Q. (2016). Randomized controlled equivalence trial comparing videoconference and in person delivery of cognitive processing therapy for PTSD. *Journal of Telemedicine and Telecare, 22*(4), 238–243. https://doi.org/10.1177/1357633X15596109

Maguen, S., Holder, N., Madden, E., Li, Y., Seal, K. H., Neylan, T. C., Lujan, C., Patterson, O. V., DuVall, S. L., & Shiner, B. (2020). Evidence-based psychotherapy trends among posttraumatic stress disorder patients in a national healthcare system, 2001–2014. *Depression and Anxiety, 37*(4), 356–364. https://doi.org/10.1002/da.22983

Marx, B. P., Lee, D. J., Norman, S. B., Bovin, M. J., Sloan, D. M., Weathers, F. W., Keane, T. M., & Schnurr, P. P. (2022). Reliable and clinically significant change in the clinician-administered PTSD scale for DSM-5 and PTSD checklist for DSM-5 among male veterans. *Psychological Assessment, 34*(2), 197–203. https://doi.org/10.1037/pas0001098

McDonald, S. D., Walker, W. C., Cusack, S. E., Yoash-Gantz, R. E., Pickett, T. C., Cifu, D. X., Mid-Atlantic Mirecc Workgroup, V, & Tupler, L. A. (2021). Health symptoms after war zone deployment-related mild traumatic brain injury: Contributions of mental disorders and lifetime brain injuries. *Brain Injury, 35*(11), 1338–1348. https://doi.org/10.1080/02699052.2021.1959058

Mikolić, A., Polinder, S., Retel Helmrich, I. R. A., Haagsma, J. A., & Cnossen, M. C. (2019). Treatment for posttraumatic stress disorder in patients with a history of traumatic brain injury: A systematic review. *Clinical Psychology Review, 73*, 101776. https://doi.org/10.1016/j.cpr.2019.101776

Monson, C. M., Schnurr, P. P., Resick, P. A., Friedman, M. J., Young-Xu, Y., & Stevens, S. P. (2006). Cognitive processing therapy for veterans with military-related posttraumatic stress disorder. *Journal of Consulting and Clinical Psychology, 74*(5), 898. https://doi.org/10.1037/0022-006X.74.5.898

Murdoch, M., Pryor, J. B., Polusny, M. A., & Gackstetter, G. D. (2007). Functioning and psychiatric symptoms among military men and women exposed to sexual stressors. *Military Medicine, 172*, 718–725. https://doi.org/10.7205/MILMED.172.7.718

Norman, S. B., Haller, M., Hamblen, J. L., Southwick, S. M., & Pietrzak, R. H. (2018). The burden of co-occurring alcohol use disorder and PTSD in U.S. military veterans: Comorbidities, functioning, and suicidality. *Psychology of Addictive Behaviors, 32*, 224–229. https://doi.org/10.1037/adb0000348

O'Brien, C., Gaher, R. M., Pope, C., & Smiley, P. (2008). Difficulty identifying feelings predicts the persistence of trauma symptoms in a sample of veterans who experienced military sexual trauma. *The Journal of Nervous and Mental Disease, 196*(3), 252–255. https://doi.org/10.1097/NMD.0b013e318166397d

O'Neil, M. E., Carlson, K., Storzbach, D., Brenner, L., Freeman, M., Quiñones, A., Motu'apuaka, M., Ensley, M., & Kansagara, D. (2013). Complications of mild traumatic brain injury in veterans and military personnel: A systematic review. *Department of Veterans Affairs (US).*

Okie, S. (2005). Traumatic brain injury in the war zone. *The New England Journal of Medicine, 352*(20), 2043–2047. https://doi.org/10.1056/NEJMp058102

Pease, J. L., Martin, C. E., Rowe, C., & Chard, K. M. (2023). Impact of residential PTSD treatment on suicide risk in veterans. *Suicide & Life-Threatening Behavior, 53*(2), 250–261. https://doi.org/10.1111/sltb.12939

Peterson, A. L., Mintz, J., Moring, J. C., Straud, C. L., Young-McCaughan, S., McGeary, C. A., Litz, B. T., Velligan, D. I., Macdonald, A., Mata-Galan, E., Holliday, S. L., Dillon, K. H., Roache, J. D., Bira, L. M., Nabity, P. S., Medellin, E. M., Hale, W. J., & Resick, P. A. (2022). In-office, in-home, and telehealth cognitive processing therapy for posttraumatic stress disorder in veterans: A randomized clinical trial. *BMC Psychiatry, 22*(1), 41. https://doi.org/10.1186/s12888-022-03699-4

Phipps, H., Mondello, S., Wilson, A., Dittmer, T., Rohde, N. N., Schroeder, P. J., Nichols, J., McGirt, C., Hoffman, J., Tanksley, K., Chohan, M., Heiderman, A., Abou Abbass, H., Kobeissy, F., & Hinds, S. (2020). Characteristics and impact of U.S. military blast-related mild traumatic brain injury: A systematic review. *Frontiers in Neurology, 11*, 559318. https://doi.org/10.3389/fneur.2020.559318

Porter, S. J., & Johnson, D. E. (2020). Clinical use of the automated neuropsychological assessment metrics TBI-mil expanded battery in evaluating concussion recovery: A retrospective study. *Military Medicine, 185*(9–10), e1722–e1727. https://doi.org/10.1093/milmed/usaa075

Ragsdale, K. A., & Voss Horrell, S. C. (2016). Effectiveness of prolonged exposure and cognitive processing therapy for U.S. veterans with a history of traumatic brain injury. *Journal of Traumatic Stress, 29*(5), 474–477. https://doi.org/10.1002/jts.22130

Resick, P. A., Monson, C. M., & Chard, K. M. (2024). *Cognitive processing therapy for PTSD: A comprehensive therapist manual* (2nd ed.). The Guilford Press.

Resick, P. A., Nishith, P., Weaver, T. L., Astin, M. C., & Feuer, C. A. (2002). A comparison of cognitive-processing therapy with prolonged exposure and a waiting condition for the treatment of chronic posttraumatic stress disorder in female rape victims. *Journal of Consulting and Clinical Psychology, 70*(4), 867–879. https://doi.org/10.1037/0022-006x.70.4.867

Resick, P. A., Wachen, J. S., Dondanville, K. A., Pruiksma, K. E., Yarvis, J. S., Peterson, A. L., Mintz, J., the STRONG STAR Consortium, Borah, E. V, Brundige, A., Hembree, E. A., Litz, B. T., Roache, J. D., & Young-McCaughan, S. (2017). Effect of group vs individual cognitive processing therapy in active-duty military seeking treatment for posttraumatic stress disorder: A randomized clinical trial. *JAMA Psychiatry, 74*(1), 28–36. https://doi.org/10.1001/jamapsychiatry.2016.2729

Resick, P. A., Wachen, J. S., Mintz, J., Young-McCaughan, S., Roache, J. D., Borah, A. M., Borah, E. V., Dondanville, K. A., Hembree, E. A., Litz, B. T., & Peterson, A. L. (2015). A randomized clinical trial of group cognitive processing therapy compared with group present-centered therapy for PTSD among active duty military personnel. *Journal of Consulting and Clinical Psychology, 83*(6), 1058. https://doi.org/10.1037/ccp0000016

Shay, J. (1994). *Achilles in Vietnam: Combat trauma and the undoing of character*. Simon and Schuster.

Schmied, E. A., Jun, H., Glassman, L., Pippard, N., & Walter, K. H. (2023). Investigating the effects of suicide exposure among active duty service members. *Journal of Traumatic Stress, 36*(2), 310–324. https://doi.org/10.1002/jts.22909

Schnurr, P. P., Chard, K. M., Ruzek, J. I., Chow, B. K., Resick, P. A., Foa, E. B., Marx, B. P., Friedman, M. J., Bovin, M. J., Caudle, K. L., Castillo, D., Curry, K. T., Hollifield, M., Huang, G. D., Chee, C. L., Astin, M. C., Dickstein, B., Renner, K., Clancy, C. P., et al. (2022). Comparison of prolonged exposure vs cognitive processing therapy for treatment of posttraumatic stress disorder among US veterans: A randomized clinical trial. *JAMA Network Open, 5*(1), e2136921–e2136921. https://doi.org/10.1001/jamanetworkopen.2021.36921

Speicher, S. M., Walter, K. H., & Chard, K. M. (2014). Interdisciplinary residential treatment of posttraumatic stress disorder and traumatic brain injury: Effects on symptom severity and occupational performance and satisfaction. *The American Journal of Occupational Therapy: Official Publication of the American Occupational Therapy Association, 68*(4), 412–421. https://doi.org/10.5014/ajot.2014.011304

Steenkamp, M. M., Litz, B. T., & Marmar, C. R. (2020). First-line psychotherapies for military-related PTSD. *JAMA, 323*(7), 656–657. https://doi.org/10.1001/jama.2019.20825

Surís, A., Holliday, R., Weitlauf, J. C., North, C. S., & the Veteran Safety Initiative Writing Collaborative. (2013a). Military sexual trauma in the context of veterans' life experiences. *Federal Practitioner., 30*(suppl 3), 16s–20s.

Surís, A., Lind, L., Kashner, T. M., Borman, P. D., & Petty, F. (2004). Sexual assault in women veterans: An examination of PTSD risk, health care utilization, and cost of care. *Psychosomatic Medicine, 66*(5), 749–756. https://doi.org/10.1097/01.psy.0000138117.58559.7b

Surís, A., & Lind, L. (2008). Military sexual trauma: A review of prevalence and associated health consequences in veterans. *Trauma, Violence & Abuse, 9*(4), 250–269. https://doi.org/10.1177/1524838008324419

Surís, A., Link-Malcolm, J., Chard, K., Ahn, C., & North, C. (2013b). A randomized clinical trial of cognitive processing therapy for veterans with PTSD related to military sexual trauma. *Journal of Traumatic Stress, 26*(1), 28–37. https://doi.org/10.1002/jts.21765

VA/DoD. (2016). *Clinical practice guideline for the management of concussion-mild traumatic brain injury*. https://www.va.gov/covidtraining/docs/mTBICPGFullCPG50821816.pdf

VA/DoD. (2021). *Clinical practice guideline for the management and rehabilitation of post-acute mild traumatic brain injury*. https://www.healthquality.va.gov/guidelines/Rehab/mtbi/VADoDmTBICPGFinal508.pdf

VA/DoD Clinical Practice Guideline. (2023). *Management of posttraumatic stress disorder and acute stress disorder work group*. U.S. Government Printing Office. https://www.healthquality.va.gov/guidelines/MH/ptsd/VADoDPTSDCPGFinal012418.pdf

Traumatic Brain Injury Center of Excellence (2022). *DoD TBI Worldwide Numbers*. https://health.mil/Military-Health-Topics/Centers-of-Excellence/Traumatic-Brain-Injury-Center-of-Excellence/DOD-TBI-Worldwide-Numbers

Turchik, J. A., & Edwards, K. M. (2012). Myths about male rape: A literature review. *Psychology of Men & Masculinity, 13*, 211–226. https://doi.org/10.1037/a0023207

U.S. Department of Veterans Affairs. (2021, May). *Military sexual trauma*. https://mentalhealth.va.gov/mentalhealth/docs/mst_general_factsheet.pdf

Vasterling, J. J., Bryant, R. A., & Keane, T. M. (2012). Understanding the interface of traumatic stress and mild traumatic brain injury: Background and conceptual framework. In J. J. Vasterling, R. A. Bryant, & T. M. Keane (Eds.), *PTSD and mild traumatic brain injury* (pp. 3–11). The Guilford Press.

Wachen, J. S., Mintz, J., LoSavio, S. T., Kennedy, J. E., Hale, W. J., Straud, C. L., Dondanville, K. A., Moring, J., Blankenship, A. E., Vandiver, R., Young-McCaughan, S., Yarvis, J. S., Peterson, A. L., Resick, P. A., & STRONG STAR Consortium. (2022). The impact of prior head injury on outcomes following group and individual cognitive processing therapy among military personnel. *Journal of Traumatic Stress, 35*(6), 1684–1695. https://doi.org/10.1002/jts.22870

Walter, K. H., Hunt, W. M., Otis, N. P., Kline, A. C., Miggantz, E. L., Thomsen, C. J., & Glassman, L. H. (2023). Comparison of behavioral activation-enhanced cognitive processing therapy and cognitive processing therapy among U.S. service members: A randomized clinical trial. *Psychiatry Research, 326*, 115330. https://doi.org/10.1016/j.psychres.2023.115330

Walter, K. H., Kiefer, S. L., & Chard, K. M. (2012). Relationship between posttraumatic stress disorder and postconcussive symptom improvement after completion of a posttraumatic stress disorder/traumatic brain injury residential treatment program. *Rehabilitation Psychology, 57*(1), 13–17. https://doi.org/10.1037/a0026254

Walter, K. H., Varkovitzky, R. L., Owens, G. P., Lewis, J., & Chard, K. M. (2014). Cognitive processing therapy for veterans with posttraumatic stress disorder: A cross-sectional and longitudinal comparison between outpatient and residential PTSD treatment. *Journal of Consulting and Clinical Psychology, 82*, 551–561. https://doi.org/10.1037/a0037075

Wilson, L. C. (2018). The prevalence of military sexual trauma: A meta-analysis. *Trauma, Violence, & Abuse, 19*(5), 584–597. https://doi.org/10.1177/1524838016683459

Yang, C. C., Chiu, H. C., Xiao, S. H., Tsai, Y. H., Lee, Y. C., Ku, Y. T., Lin, R. S., Lin, W. C., & Huang, S. J. (2018). Iatrogenic effect? Cautions when utilizing an early health education for post-concussion symptoms. *Archives of Clinical Neuropsychology, 33*(2), 131–142. https://doi.org/10.1093/arclin/acx060

Zalta, A. K., Held, P., Smith, D. L., Klassen, B. J., Lofgreen, A. M., Normand, P. S., et al. (2018). Evaluating patterns and predictors of symptom change during a three-week intensive outpatient treatment for veterans with PTSD. *BMC Psychiatry, 18*(1), 242. https://doi.org/10.1186/s12888-018-1816-6

Chapter 10
Treating Individuals with Marginalized Identities Using Cognitive Processing Therapy

Elizabeth N. Collazo, Christine Serpe, Sebastian Bliss, Julie Klunk-Gillis, Cara Herbitter, and Nicholas A. Livingston

Scope of the Problem

Marginalized individuals, or those who are not white, cisgender (individuals for whom their gender aligns with their sex assigned at birth), and heterosexual, are routinely subjected to oppression-based stress experiences due to society's under-valuing and stigmatization of certain "minority" or marginalized identities (Meyer, 1995, 2003). People of color (POC) as well as sexual and gender minorities (SGM) are routinely impacted by oppression-based stress experiences grounded in racism and anti-SGM oppression. These experiences tend to be cumulative and compounded among individuals with intersectional identities, or oppression-based stress experiences rooted in various forms of oppression when an individual holds multiple marginalized identities (Crenshaw, 1989; Robinson & Ross, 2013). Therefore, it is not surprising that these experiences have been linked to negative mental health outcomes, such as symptoms of posttraumatic stress disorder (PTSD;

E. N. Collazo (✉) · N. A. Livingston
U.S. Department of Veteran Affairs, VA Boston Healthcare System, Boston, MA, USA

Department of Psychiatry, Boston University Chobanian & Avedisian School of Medicine, Boston, MA, USA

National Center for PTSD, Behavioral Science Division, Boston, MA, USA
e-mail: Elizabeth.Savarese@va.gov

C. Serpe · J. Klunk-Gillis · C. Herbitter
U.S. Department of Veteran Affairs, VA Boston Healthcare System, Boston, MA, USA

Department of Psychiatry, Boston University Chobanian & Avedisian School of Medicine, Boston, MA, USA

S. Bliss
U.S. Department of Veteran Affairs, VA Boston Healthcare System, Boston, MA, USA

J. S. Wachen, T. E. Galovski (eds.), *Cognitive Processing Therapy for Complex Cases*, CBT: Science Into Practice,
https://doi.org/10.1007/978-3-031-87356-0_10

Williams et al., 2018). Despite the increasing evidence of the link between oppression-based stress experiences and PTSD, the effectiveness of cognitive processing therapy (CPT; Resick et al., 2024) for marginalized individuals remains understudied (Galovski et al., 2020). Furthermore, current literature is limited on guidance on how to address trauma related to intersectionality and oppression-based stress from a CPT framework. This chapter provides context and illustration of ways clinicians can adapt CPT when working with people with marginalized identities.

We will use a scholar-practitioner-advocate model (Mallinckrodt et al., 2014) to provide a framework for this important clinical work. The scientist-practitioner-advocate model is an alternative model and extension of the scholar-practitioner-advocate framework that better addresses this gap in training, practice, and scientific inquiry by drawing from feminist and multicultural principles. The model remains committed to rigorous scientific and clinical training while focusing on social justice in all aspects of training, practice, and research. This framework allows for the examination of power, privilege, oppression, and intersectionality as they influence clinical work and research. As such, this chapter will be grounded in the scientist–practitioner–advocate model as we consider the many identity and contextual factors that influence our treatment of marginalized individuals utilizing CPT.

While some elements of the scientist–practitioner–advocate model may be novel to many practitioners, one aspect—sharing power and knowledge—is something that is inherent to well-delivered cognitive behavioral treatment, particularly CPT. In CPT, the clinician is a guide who engages in shared decision-making with the patient and allows the patient to challenge potentially maladaptive thoughts through the use of Socratic questioning. A central component of the scientist–practitioner–advocate model is the specific focus on sharing power; in clinical work, the clinician and client are curious co-learners, rather than an expert and a non-expert. We will demonstrate how this may play out in treatment with a clinical example later in this chapter. Therefore, this model would indicate that CPT, a gold-standard evidence-based treatment for PTSD, be implemented in clinical practice while also focusing on how stressors affecting individuals with intersectional identities may impact and/or be the focus of treatment for marginalized folks, then adapting interventions accordingly.

Criterion A and Insidious Trauma Among Marginalized People

Feminist scholars have argued in favor of a more expansive definition of trauma in order to validate and capture the impacts of the insidious nature of oppression, while allowing the subject to demarcate the nature of their experience(s) (Root, 1992; Brown, 2004). Currently, the *Diagnostic and Statistical Manual of Mental Disorders* (DSM-5) guides clinicians in assessing for the presence of PTSD by first identifying the traumatic event, also known as a Criterion A trauma, according to event type and means of experiencing/learning about the event (APA, 2013). To be considered a Criterion A trauma, the event must involve exposure to actual or threatened death, serious injury, and/or sexual violence (APA, 2013). Next, the means through which the individual experienced the event are assessed in terms of proximity; experienced directly (e.g., it happened to me), witnessed (e.g., I saw it happen to someone else), learned it happened to a loved one (e.g., it happened to my sibling in another state), or repeated exposure to adverse details through work (e.g., first responders, combat drone operators; APA, 2013). Although this current definition allows for multiple types of traumatic events (e.g., childhood sexual abuse, murder of a family member), it does not account for the traumatic impact of oppression-based stress experiences, thereby potentially excluding individuals who would benefit from evidence-based treatments for PTSD. As such, it is important to understand how insidious trauma is linked to PTSD symptoms and how this can be incorporated into CPT.

Defined by feminist psychologist Maria P. P. Root (1992), insidious trauma is expansive enough to capture the deleterious effects of chronic social oppression imposed upon marginalized individuals throughout their lives (e.g., POC, SGM). While defining trauma within psychology and psychiatry continues to be debated, some argue in favor of less subjective and sociopolitical definitions of harm (see Holmes et al., 2016; APA, 2013), discounting the experiences of the oppressed. As elucidated in Miller's (2009) critique of psychiatry's attempts to divest and decontextualize racial trauma from mainstream definitions, we as a field not only ignore the impact of oppression, but also lack funding and resources for something not built into our mainstream models of assessment and practice. However, literature continues to validate the influence of insidious trauma on PTSD symptoms and suggests that these symptoms can in fact emerge as a result of systemic discrimination, microaggressions, and social inequalities based on one's belonging to a social identity group (e.g., Barr et al., 2022; Szymanski & Balsam, 2011). Furthermore, support for incorporating insidious trauma into the treatment of marginalized individuals presenting with PTSD symptoms can be found in the history of the PTSD diagnosis as well as ethical guidelines. Specifically, Criterion A has been expanded in several iterations of the DSM-5 to account for our ongoing understanding of the impact of trauma, which research supports as including insidious trauma (Holmes et al., 2016). Furthermore, psychologists' ethical duty to practice with beneficence and in a manner consistent with social justice highlights the importance of incorporating insidious trauma into the treatment of marginalized individuals presenting with PTSD symptoms in order to grant access to beneficial evidence-based treatments to all individuals (Holmes et al., 2016).

Marginalized individuals are unable to divest from a culture of oppression, and these individuals may present with Criterion A trauma and/or insidious trauma resulting in significant levels of distress. Therefore, treating trauma-related distress requires close attention to the influence of all factors in the manifestation of symptoms in order to promote recovery. CPT may be a useful treatment in this regard as it allows for the restructuring of the negative alterations in cognition and mood caused by Criterion A trauma or oppression-based stress experiences (e.g., "I was raped because I am bisexual"). Additionally, emerging literature suggests that insidious trauma may also uniquely influence and exacerbate non-identity specific trauma cognitions (e.g., "I should have been more careful"; Dworkin et al., 2018). For instance, SGM people may come to internalize trauma-related beliefs about self-blame as a result of chronic societal messages related to SGM identity as a "choice" or that it is an invalid identity. Ultimately, sociocultural invalidation and oppression can create new or exacerbate existing trauma-related cognitions, such as self-blame and trauma causality. Challenging these distortions may be difficult without a clinical conceptualization that captures the influence of oppression on one's identity and sense of self.

Regardless of the presence of a Criterion A or non-criterion A trauma, it is important to make CPT accessible for all individuals presenting with PTSD symptoms who have encoded an event as traumatic in order to treat these symptoms. Identification of the trauma that impacts PTSD symptoms most often, on average, is an important part of CPT (Resick et al., 2008). As indicated in the CPT manual, not addressing these experiences can result in continued PTSD symptoms (e.g., cognitive distortions; Resick et al., 2008). In other words, CPT cannot be beneficial for marginalized individuals if intersectionality is disregarded in treatment (Valentine et al., 2023; Williams et al., 2021).

Research Support and Treatment Gaps

CPT has been shown to be effective for a wide range of people and flexible across diverse contexts, and is also amenable to adaptation (Bass et al., 2013; Galovski et al., 2020; Valentine et al., 2017). This latter feature is a relative strength of CPT, as marginalized people may not benefit equally from evidence-based treatments compared to their non-marginalized or majority counterparts (Beard et al., 2017; Rimes et al., 2019). For example, POC and SGM individuals have reported pervasive experiences of discrimination in healthcare (Livingston et al., 2019; Mays et al., 2017; Washington & Randall, 2023; White & Fontenot, 2019), even opting to avoid healthcare (Clark et al., 2022), terminate treatment early (Mays et al., 2017; McClendon et al., 2020), or conceal their SGM identities from healthcare providers (Durso & Meyer, 2013); such experiences present barriers to seeking or remaining in treatment, benefiting from it, and have been associated with poor health outcomes (Durso & Meyer, 2013; Mays et al., 2017; Ruben et al., 2019). Some marginalized individuals have expressed a preference for providers who are knowledgeable about their experiences and seek to actively affirm them (e.g., Berke et al., 2016). However, affirmative care alone is inadequate to address the unique needs and experiences of marginalized individuals.

Marginalized people report health care needs that are commensurate with the unique challenges they face, such as ongoing threats to their safety, discrimination, and internalized negative beliefs about themselves in relation to their marginalized identities, which exacerbate distress and may complicate PTSD treatment and recovery. Beyond increased risk for exposure to traumatic events, POC and SGM individuals experience ongoing external stressors, such as discrimination and microaggressions (Grant et al., 2011; Nadal et al., 2016, 2019; Moody & Lewis, 2019). Marginalized individuals may experience insidious trauma and oppression-based stress as equally or even more high impact relative to Criterion A trauma, underscoring the significance of these stressors and their impacts in therapy (Cardona et al., 2021; Livingston et al., 2019; Williams et al., 2022).

Treatments that are responsive to the insidious trauma and oppression-based stress affecting marginalized people are essential and have already begun demonstrating promise. For instance, transdiagnostic cognitive behavioral interventions that target depression, anxiety, and health risk behaviors have been tailored to and shown to be effective for SGM people (Pachankis et al., 2015, 2020). While interventions like these are not trauma-focused or PTSD-centered, PTSD treatments are well-suited for adaptations that can better meet the mental health needs of clients (Livingston et al., 2020), particularly given the overlapping impacts of trauma and oppression-based stress on marginalized people (Livingston et al., 2020; Salomaa et al., 2023; Arnett et al., 2019; Reisner et al., 2016; Szymanski & Balsam, 2011). Protocols and adaptations that address this overlap have begun to emerge, such as the Healing from Racial Trauma protocol (Williams et al., 2022) and culturally adaptive Prolonged Exposure for African Americans (Williams et al., 2014), but treatment outcomes have not yet been assessed. Regardless, it is clear that treatment adaptation is warranted when a marginalized group faces unique risk factors (Lau, 2006), such as the added burden of trauma and oppression-based stress.

Clinical Applications

In this section, we will discuss practical strategies for the application of CPT with marginalized clients. Although previous studies have reported on the use of modifications/adaptations to CPT, outcomes related to these modifications are understudied (Marques et al., 2019). However, one recent study highlighted that fidelity-consistent modifications to CPT were effective in reducing symptomology in a community sample, and may even improve treatment outcomes (Marques et al., 2019). This study highlighted that fidelity-consistent modifications included tailoring interventions to the client as well as cultural adaptations that ultimately did not change the core principle of CPT (Marques et al., 2019). As such, the strategies we will present are intended to serve as principle-driven guideposts for clinical consideration and discussion with clients as part of a dynamic, culturally attuned approach to providing CPT without changing the core principles of this treatment. Throughout the treatment process, a dynamic sizing approach is recommended, which is the practice of flexibly generalizing culturally-relevant insights into care while also thoughtfully tuning care for the individual (Sue, 2006). Dynamic sizing challenges clinicians to conduct an ongoing assessment of whether culture-specific information about a group applies to the individual client who is part of that group.

Setting the Stage: CPT in the Context of Oppression-Based Stress

Several models address the impact of racism on mental health, from an early biopsychosocial stress framework (Clark et al., 1999) to a race-based traumatic stress model that described how racism can lead to traumatic stress reactions (Carter, 2007). Drawing upon the race-based stress literature (Clark et al., 1999), Minority Stress Theory (2003) described the influence of chronic and minority stressors and indignities (e.g., a lack of gender affirming restrooms; race-based microaggressions) on proximal distress (e.g., shame about their identity), and focused on group-specific experiences in explanation of health disparities. Initially focused on sexual minorities, Minority Stress Theory was later extended to apply to gender minorities (Hendricks & Testa, 2012). Meyer (2003) called for the expansion of the minority stress framework to include the underlying psychological mechanisms that linked stress and mental health inequity, and Hatzenbuehler (2009) proposed a psychological mediation framework to locate the cognitive and affective processes impacted by minority stress. In this framework, Hatzenbuehler emphasized the roles of both general and minority-specific psychological processes impacting mental health. "General" psychological processes that help explain the connection between trauma and minority stressors on marginalized people include coping and emotion regulation (e.g., rumination, coping-motivated substance use), social and interpersonal processes (e.g., social isolation), and cognitive mechanisms (e.g., learned hopelessness, negative views of the self). In contrast, compounding "group-specific" processes are those that are activated in response to minority stressors, such as expectations of rejection, shame (in relation to their marginalized identity[ies]), and identity concealment or code switching. As drivers of poorer mental health among marginalized people, these mechanisms are, and should be, primary targets of intervention in their own right, or in tandem with other post-trauma stress reactions in PTSD treatment.

When considering these models, it is also important to remember the concept of intersectionality, which explains how systems of oppression simultaneously impact individuals with multiple marginalized identities (Crenshaw, 1989; Robinson & Ross, 2013). This means, for example, that a queer woman of color may face stressful experiences due to oppressive systems that perpetuate racism, homonegativity, and sexism. An abundance of research has focused on single marginalized identities as there is currently no agreed upon standardized methodology to capture intersectional experiences (Robinson & Ross, 2013). However, research that has explored intersectionality thus far highlight poorer psychological health outcomes amongst those with multiple marginalized identities compared to those with one or fewer marginalized identities (Calabrese et al., 2015; Jeong et al., 2016). As such, clinicians must always consider this concept in conjunction with Minority Stress Theory as well as in our treatment of marginalized individuals.

As previously described, emerging treatment frameworks that address stress among marginalized individuals target the underlying processes that contribute to the relationship between proximal and distal stressors. Consistent with Hatzenbuehler (2009), CPT may be well suited to address the link between oppression-based stress and trauma-related symptoms by attending to the cognitive and affective processes that impede recovery. CPT aims to challenge and modify maladaptive beliefs associated with traumatic experiences that contribute to emotional distress and interfere with recovery. Through psychoeducation, structured exercises, and Socratic Questions, clients are encouraged to systematically analyze their beliefs, weigh real evidence for and against inaccurate beliefs, and gradually develop a more balanced and accurate view of why their trauma occurred as well as more balanced current beliefs about the world, self, and others, thereby improving PTSD symptomatology and resulting in enhanced functioning and overall well-being. A preliminary and critical element in CPT involves the writing of an impact statement to explore and understand a client's beliefs about the underlying cause of a traumatic event. Clients are asked to reflect on "why" they believe the trauma event(s) occurred, and to also explore how the trauma(s) affected their lives according to five themes: safety, trust, power/control, intimacy, and esteem. The written impact statement is then used in the collaborative identification and recording of assimilated (e.g., "If I had locked the door, I wouldn't have been stabbed") and over-accommodated (e.g., "Everyone will hurt me eventually") beliefs, also known as "stuck points" (Resick et al., 2024).

Understanding and Avoiding Pitfalls: PTSD Treatment Through a Cultural Lens

Prior to beginning CPT, clinicians first assess trauma, PTSD symptoms, and interrelated impacts; then, once CPT is initiated, clinicians provide psychoeducation to the client during the first session. As discussed previously in this chapter, the DSM-5 conceptualization of PTSD and other trauma-related disorders may not provide a comprehensive account of the ways in which trauma is experienced by marginalized individuals. Considering this and that CPT requires clients to identify an index trauma, it is important to assess for the traumatic event(s) that causes the most distress and PTSD symptoms. As such, clinicians would benefit from ensuring they are assessing for both Criterion A trauma and other insidious trauma and oppression-based stressors as part of patient-centered care. We also recommend emphasizing the index trauma as an "anchor point" as opposed to the "worst event" as the latter can be incredibly invalidating to marginalized individuals, especially if they experience equivalent distress in relation to multiple traumas. It is also important, regardless of the index trauma, to acknowledge that many traumatic events are connected and disentangling which events caused which thoughts is very difficult; therefore, the clinician should explain that additional events will be incorporated into CPT. The CPT manual already explains that this is a routine part of CPT after session 5; however, we recommend allowing for flexibility if these events arise sooner than session 5. For example, the impact statement can be a powerful tool that allows marginalized clients to explore the impact their cumulative traumas have had on their thoughts and beliefs. We also encourage clinicians to specifically discuss the flexibility of the format of this statement (e.g., use of bullet points, poetry).

Similar to multicultural considerations for conceptualizing Criterion A trauma and its impacts, we also encourage clinicians to recognize how the additional diagnostic criteria for PTSD can identify and pathologize several behaviors which, for marginalized clients, may serve non-pathological functions firmly grounded in their personal and intergenerational histories, as well as their everyday realities. For example, without doing so, a clinician could inadvertently conceptualize avoidance of others as an avoidance behavior (consistent with criterion C) and overlook that this behavior might be necessary to some extent among marginalized people who live in hostile settings. We will discuss several criteria that may commonly present in treatment, though we encourage clinicians to be mindful of ways in which other criteria, particularly concerning safety and "exaggerated" beliefs about systems and agents of oppression, may have a basis in reality for the client and should be treated accordingly in the course of CPT. Overall, instead of challenging these thoughts or behaviors, we encourage clinicians to engage in discussion related to decreasing distress, returning to baseline following a threat, increasing feelings of safety and empowerment, and expanding on adaptive coping, which we will discuss further later in this chapter. It is also important to keep in mind that each individual will present with unique cultural beliefs, preferences, and values. These should be honored throughout this process regardless of how other clients you have treated in similar communities responded (e.g., one woman of color chooses to engage in activism and another does not; both are potentially adaptive and values-congruent options).

Avoidance vs. Necessary Safety-Seeking Behaviors

When assessing safety-related avoidance behaviors and associated beliefs, it is important to understand whether avoidance of certain contexts, locations, or institutions is based on unrealistic expectations or whether this avoidance is appropriate. For example, if a transgender woman has been avoiding using women's bathrooms in public after experiencing repeated harassment and threats upon doing so, avoidance of women's bathrooms should not be pathologized as trauma-related avoidance. Instead, a clinician would validate this avoidance as realistic and, if the client wishes, discuss ways that they can still engage in necessary activities in a manner that is aligned with their values. In this instance, a transgender woman might prefer to identify locations that offer single-stall restrooms or gender-neutral restrooms; however, this client may not find those options suitable for a variety of reasons and instead opt to utilize the restroom in safe-spaces that can be identified throughout communities she frequents. Ultimately, it is important to consider the client's preferences and which strategies are right for them.

Hypervigilance vs. Vigilance

Similar to safety-related avoidance, clinicians should assess whether a client's hypervigilance is based on low-probability fears (e.g., a terrorist attack at the grocery store) or on realistic concerns and experiences of being intensely surveilled by others in a range of contexts. Although considerations of what is or is not realistic is an intervention highlighted throughout the CPT manual, this is especially important when working with Black men and other POC who have individually and/or collectively been disproportionate targets of police attention and violence (e.g., a client having a fear of or pronounced reaction to being pulled over in their car for speeding). This can also be true of SGM, who may discuss being surveilled for a variety of reasons, such as being scrutinized in bathrooms based on gender expression or when holding hands with a same-gender partner.

The Risk of Over-Pathologizing

Clinicians must also exercise caution around assuming that a client with one or more marginalized identities is experiencing life-interfering problems related to these identities. As with failing to assess and address cultural manifestations of trauma, the clinician can also invalidate a client by over-pathologizing their presentation and overlooking individual and community resilience factors. Thus, in both symptom assessment and treatment with marginalized clients, it is of crucial importance to discuss how we are not pathologizing marginalized identities, but acknowledging the distress that can be caused by trauma and oppression more broadly. As such, we will acknowledge the impact of oppressive systems on the individual and how these systems can cause distress as well as adaptations that allow the individual to navigate these oppressive systems in a safe manner. Emphasis should be placed, therefore, on addressing distress in a values-aligned manner, not attempting to pathologize every thought and/or behavior.

Introducing CPT Through a Multicultural and Feminist Framework

Although the first session of CPT focuses on providing psychoeducation to the client while providing sufficient opportunity for them to ask questions, another important consideration for introducing CPT is the discussion of power and control as well as addressing intersectionality and the cultural context in which we live. For instance, traumatic events are commonly associated with feelings of powerlessness and being out of control. This may be especially true for marginalized individuals who are routinely regarded as second-class citizens and face oppression from privileged individuals as well as systems that continue to reinforce the oppression of marginalized individuals. As such, it is important to present (and enact) CPT in such a manner that emphasizes the power and control of the client throughout treatment and acknowledges the client's expertise in their own lived experiences. Furthermore, it is important to address up-front how intersectionality and cultural contexts will be incorporated into treatment as many marginalized individuals may avoid engaging openly, or at all, if these topics are not initiated and prioritized by the clinician.

It may additionally be important to engage in discussion about the client's previous experiences and/or thoughts about therapy in order to further elucidate this intersectional and feminist framework. This is strongly advised in situations where it is known or suspected that the client has had negative experiences in mental health treatment in the past, or with clinicians or within clinics. Being attentive to these considerations can also help initiate discussion regarding past experiences or other cultural barriers to treatment. Although discussion of avoidance is a routine part of the first session of CPT, it is incredibly important to acknowledge how cultural factors and systems of oppression may also increase avoidance (e.g., fear of and/or previous experiences with a white clinician invalidating a POC's experiences, front desk staff misgendering a client, cultural beliefs about therapy, etc). A marginalized client may choose not to share this information early in the therapy process; however, routine attention to and prioritization of intersectionality and cultural factors is not only necessary to engage in multicultural treatment, but also will likely aid the client and clinician's therapeutic relationship. Of course, as is key in dynamic sizing (Sue, 2006) which urges a fluid and adaptive application of culture-specific knowledge to an individual client, if a particular cultural factor, experience, or hypothesis does not apply to a client, it does not apply and does not have to continue to be discussed. However, assessment is an important part of treatment and clinicians routinely explore factors that may not yet have been spoken about in treatment (e.g., a client only identifies anger in worksheets and a clinician explores other emotions that may also be affecting the client). Ultimately, it is best to explore and increase discussion about cultural factors and experiences than to not address these at all.

Stuck Points

In CPT, stuck points represent cognitive distortions that either arose or were solidified as a result of traumatic experience(s) and result in "manufactured" or secondary emotions (e.g., inappropriate guilt/shame in response to beliefs about the trauma, not the event itself) that reinforce unhelpful coping strategies (e.g., avoidance, thought suppression, rumination) and distress (LoSavio et al., 2017). Avoidance is both a symptom and ineffective coping strategy fundamental to diagnosing and treating PTSD (APA, 2013), and similarly, repeated oppression-based stress experiences may result in coping styles designed to avoid future rejection or stigmatization, promoting hopelessness and negative self-schemas (Hatzenbuehler, 2009). Therefore, capturing insidious trauma within a PTSD treatment framework could prove fruitful for overall recovery as there is likely overlap between the internalization of trauma-related and discrimination-related beliefs.

The *Healing from Racism Trauma Protocol* (Williams et al., 2022) and the *Transcending Protocol* (Ouellette et al., 2023) offer a unified cognitive-behavioral approach to address the effects of oppression-based stress on mental health among POC and transgender and gender diverse (TGD) people, respectively. These protocols include elements consistent with CPT, such as an impact statement and use of stuck points (Ouellette et al., 2023) as well as back and forth dialogue between clinician and client that helps the client challenge undue cognitions caused by their trauma(s), and make meaning of them (Williams et al., 2022). This form of back-and-forth dialogue, or Socratic questioning, in *Healing from Racial Trauma* and the impact statement in *Transcending* asks clients to reflect on their experiences of trauma and oppression-based stress, which is then used for the identification of identity-related stuck points (e.g., "I'm not Mexican enough"; "I will never be a 'real' man/woman"). Clinicians using CPT with marginalized clients would benefit from becoming familiar with the *Healing from Racial Trauma* and *Transcending* protocols, as these may assist with making modifications to the current treatment protocol in CPT that lend to discussions about identity-related stressors and processes (e.g., avoidant coping styles). From a cognitive perspective, helping clients to address beliefs about discriminatory events, and to appropriately contextualize them within a framework of oppression may assist with offsetting proximal stressors (e.g., internalized stigma; Ouellette et al., 2023; Williams et al., 2022), and overall trauma recovery.

Internalized Stigma

Internalized stigma reflects both a process and outcome of an individual internalizing negative self-views due to repeated exposure to oppressive systems in society that regard marginalized individuals or identities as negative, wrong, or otherwise inferior (Ouellette et al., 2023; Williams et al., 2022). Internalization of these prejudicial beliefs can drive manufactured emotions that can be by themselves a target of intervention as well as complimentary targets of treatment focused on other traumatic impacts within the CPT framework. For example, a transgender woman who was raped may endorse a variety of trauma-related beliefs (e.g., "it is my fault"), identity-related beliefs (e.g., "transgender identity isn't natural"), and a combination of the two (e.g., "If I didn't transition, the rape wouldn't have happened"). Clinicians who only attend to beliefs that appear directly related to the trauma, and not to those that may exacerbate traumatic symptoms, may overlook critical nuances that relate to trauma recovery as well as opportunities to have a concurrent positive impact on the client's recovery, such as resilience and self-acceptance.

In manualized CPT, stuck points are challenged throughout the course of therapy using Socratic dialogue and strategies that assist clients in more critically examining beliefs thereby arriving at new and more helpful conclusions that promote recovery (Resick et al., 2024). Using a more expansive and principle-driven approach to the CPT protocol, it is possible to understand and jointly address the influence of insidious trauma as it relates to trauma-related cognitions (i.e., stuck points), as well as help the client challenge internalized stigma by questioning how these thoughts developed and highlighting the context of various oppressive systems (e.g., racism; Williams et al., 2022). This allows clients to separate society's oppressive beliefs from that of their own, which can increase opportunities to practice adaptive beliefs about one's identity and/or group (Williams et al., 2022).

Socratic Questioning

According to Farmer et al. (2017), reliable change is most likely to occur from clinicians who are skillful in Socratic dialogue and prioritize challenging assimilated stuck points prior to over-accommodated ones. Socratic dialogue is central to cognitive restructuring and relies on questions that clarify, challenge, and explore stuck points in order to assist clients with developing a new understanding (Beck et al., 1979; Resick et al., 2017). Navigating Socratic questioning around identity-related stuck points can be particularly tricky if clinicians are unfamiliar with a client's particular background and experiences or the sociocultural climate. For example, a client who received a dishonorable discharge under the United States military's Don't Ask Don't Tell policy, banning sexual minority individuals from serving openly in the military, may believe "being gay is criminal." A clinician without adequate knowledge about military culture or queer history in the Department of Defense may work to challenge this stuck point from their sociocultural lens and not that of the client, or perhaps underestimate the impacts of this policy on the mental health of SGM service members and Veterans (Livingston et al., 2019). Cultural humility may help bridge this gap and remain therapeutically consistent with CPT as it relies on curiosity, gentle open-ended questioning, and warmth, to better understand a client's lived experience (Mosher et al., 2017).

Therefore, regardless of prior knowledge of the client's experiences, the clinician should remain curious throughout CPT and seek to understand the origin of various thoughts. In this example, a clinician may ask the client to question: the origin of these thoughts, the current laws/policies, the origin of those law/policies (similar to internalized stigma), and any discrepancies between this law and personal, cultural, interpersonal, and/or religious beliefs, as applicable. It is important to note that the new understanding we hope clients arrive at through Socratic questioning is one that is aligned with their own values and experiences as opposed to the clinician's values and experiences. In other words, we caution clinicians away from guiding clients to the "right" answer or a particular point they are trying to make when engaging in this intervention. In order to understand where intervention is needed, clinicians should collaborate with the client to identify adaptive thoughts and maladaptive thoughts, a routine part of CPT, while also considering potential bias clinicians may place on this process. This determination requires understanding the individual client, their history, and the sociopolitical context, then engaging in Socratic questioning that may help clients challenge maladaptive thoughts.

Reality-Based Beliefs

Understanding the origins of various thoughts assists clinicians in distinguishing potentially maladaptive thoughts from adaptive thoughts. Specifically, marginalized clients may identify beliefs over the course of CPT that appear on the surface to be stuck points but are actually based in the reality of that client's lived experience and sociocultural contexts. It is important, therefore, to understand that not all thoughts that cause distress are maladaptive or stuck points. Some of the thoughts that may be highlighted while conducting CPT with marginalized individuals may be related to: lack of trust in authority figures or larger systems (e.g., police, government, employer's institution), safety concerns related to the world being a dangerous place, fears related to identity disclosure (e.g., anticipatory distress), and fears related to harm and/or negative consequences as a result of speaking up about oppression. Given the current sociopolitical climate, many of these thoughts are firmly grounded in reality, especially during times of increased sociopolitical tension targeted toward marginalized individuals. A client's particular identities (e.g., intersectionality), geographic location (e.g., state, town), and other sociodemographic considerations (e.g., employer, setting) are additional factors to consider when contextualizing these thoughts. Rather than assuming that beliefs such as these are inherently irrational and subjecting them to the challenging processes of CPT, we recommend inquiring more into the origins of these beliefs and the context(s) in which these beliefs are formed. If the beliefs are indeed based in reality, to challenge these beliefs would be inappropriate and potentially damaging to the therapeutic relationship. If a client engages in ruminative thinking around a realistic belief, it may still be appropriate to inquire about whether this ruminative process is helpful, eliciting the emotional consequences of this rumination as needed.

We recommend caution in labeling realistic and adaptive beliefs formed out of experiences of marginalization as "stuck points," as this term is specifically used for beliefs that are inaccurate. Identifying inaccurate beliefs should be a collaborative process, as detailed in the CPT manual. Extra caution may be warranted for beliefs in this regard, as labeling a realistic belief about oppression as a "stuck point" would suggest that, if the client only stopped perseverating on their oppression, they would no longer be oppressed, which is invalidating and inaccurate. However, this does not mean that such beliefs cannot and should not be addressed. Indeed, the identification, validation, and culturally humble, client-centered discussion of these beliefs may be immensely therapeutic. We recommend first validating concerns that accurately reflect a client's context and then discussing finding balance in order to promote psychological flexibility, a process that may buffer against oppression-based stress (Bhambhani et al., 2020; Matos et al., 2017). Of course, this balance must also include discussion of each client's values. For example, in cases where an SGM client may fear disclosing their identities, but value being open about their identities, balance may be found by evaluating the environment for safety symbols (e.g., trans-affirming signage, presence of other SGM individuals). Other situations may be more complex, such as evaluating the safety of authority figures, and require additional research both on the part of the clinician and the client (e.g., understanding state laws or guidelines that protect POC individuals in police interactions, knowing the institutional policies related to discrimination and retaliation in the workplace). Ultimately, the point of these discussions is not to place the burden of problem-solving on the client, a burden that should be explored with the client, but to offer a potential method for balancing values and realistic concerns. Primarily, we want to promote client empowerment and recovery in a manner that is best suited for the client's context and values.

Additional Adaptations to CPT Processes and Techniques

Assessing the Context of Treatment

To aid in determining whether symptoms are pathological or potentially adaptive, it is helpful to assess the physical contexts in which the client is living and engaging in outside of session. For example, if a Latinx client lives in a neighborhood where he is regularly exposed to the sounds of gunshots or police presence patrols, or if a Muslim immigrant client lives in a community with strong white nationalist values, this information could inform the clinician's understanding of the function of hypervigilance or other safety behaviors as these clients engage in their daily lives.

Number of Sessions

Given the multifaceted nature of insidious trauma as well as the rapport and trust building process that must occur between a therapist and client, we recommend being as flexible as possible with the number of sessions, which has become a standard practice with CPT (Galovski et al., 2012), Of note, many marginalized individuals have experienced systemic (e.g., oppression) and cultural barriers to treatment and have rightful concerns about trusting therapists, especially those from non-marginalized backgrounds. Further, the effects of insidious trauma are far-reaching and might impact clients in ways that do not conform to a limited number of sessions (e.g., 12 sessions). As such, additional sessions may be required to build trust, to address various and other insidious trauma experiences, and/or to meet a client's needs (e.g., a patient with a head injury may require more time to understand material). Helping clients recover from these experiences may also require additional emotional regulation, coping, interpersonal, and empowerment-based skill-building interventions as well, which can complement and enhance the efficacy of CPT for marginalized people who experience ongoing oppression-based stressors. Although this may not always be necessary and these processes can be incorporated into CPT, we believe providing this flexibility in length of treatment, as needed, is aligned with a multicultural and feminist adaption of CPT.

Empowerment/Power and Control

Although there is a Power and Control module in CPT, we recommend that empowerment be one of the ultimate goals of CPT for marginalized individuals that is highlighted throughout treatment. Specifically, empowering clients to manage distress in a manner that not only promotes recovery from PTSD symptoms, but also allows marginalized individuals to feel empowered enough to enact their values and experience daily life with minimal distress. Throughout any discussion in CPT, we must balance reality with managing distress. One of our roles as clinicians is to help clients develop tools to find this balance in their daily lives, especially when trauma may skew and/or intensify distress.

In the Power and Control module, specifically, one of the tools highlighted to assist clients in empowerment through healthy behaviors is being assertive. Although we agree that this should be promoted, the context of each individual is also necessary to take into consideration, especially when considering negative stereotypes that tend to be applied to women of color in particular when being assertive. A common theme that may arise in this section is dissonance between silence or speaking up. We recommend spending extra time cultivating tools to help a client navigate this process. Tools might include evaluating the safety of the environment, practicing speaking up in a manner that is consistent with a client's values, and practicing what to do in situations where assertiveness is responded to poorly, which may involve checking institutional policies that protect marginalized individuals in these situations.

What Would You Say to a Friend?

A useful tool in Socratic question commonly used by clinicians to challenge stuck points is asking a client what they would tell a friend with similar thoughts. Although we agree that this tool can be effective, we recommend using caution when asking this question to marginalized individuals. For example, an individual with internalized stigma may hold negative beliefs not just about themselves, but also the communities they belong to (e.g., their racial group). In instances like these, this question is unlikely to be effective if the client considers a friend with similar identities. Similarly, if an individual is currently isolated, especially if due to living in a setting that devalues their identity, we caution away from this question. Further, for thoughts that are very specific to a personal journey (e.g., I should stay away from my family because they don't accept my gender identity), we caution away from asking this question as it may be taken as invalidation (e.g., "This is specific to my family members" or "I would tell someone in the same situation to do the same thing"). In instances where the helpfulness of this intervention is questionable, clinicians may consider rewording the question to a more general format. For instance, "Sometimes it is helpful to imagine an important person in your life and/or someone you admire in a similar situation and consider what you might tell them if they had a similar thought." This allows more room for flexibility around the intervention, both highlighting that the client may be treating themselves more harshly than they would others and allowing the client an opportunity to say they do not think this intervention is helpful by not phrasing this as a question.

Validation vs. Problem Solving

As described previously, clients with marginalized identities may hold beliefs that appear to be stuck points but actually reflect the reality of their lived experiences. In these cases, validating reality is not only called for on a rational basis, it will likely also help maintain and potentially strengthen the therapeutic working relationship. In addition to validation, it can also be tempting for the clinician to move quickly toward problem-solving, perhaps out of discomfort with sitting with the client's reality or out of a desire to help the client change their circumstances. Although there may be certain situations where problem-solving is appropriate and welcomed by the client, as described with the transgender client in *Avoidance* vs. *Appropriate Safety-Seeking Behaviors*, we caution against jumping directly to this intervention. An indiscriminate application of problem-solving strategies may reinforce the damaging message that systems and ideologies of oppression are problems that the client can and should solve individually, or that convey to the client that the clinician has a removed or overly simplified view of the client's concerns and their solutions. Therefore, we recommend validation as a primary strategy for these reality-based beliefs, along with other empowerment and regulation strategies described in this chapter. If there are potential problems within the client's control to solve, we advise broaching these in a collaborative and client-centered way (e.g., "Would it be helpful for us to brainstorm some ways for you to feel safer when you have to go to campus?"), and only after taking time to validate the client's worldview.

Use of Affirming Language

Attention to language and adoption of the client's language can be a subtle but powerful tool in working with marginalized clients, within respectful limitations. Some words may be specific to CPT or discussion of trauma, while others may be related to culture or identity. For instance, a client may prefer to use the term "stressful event" instead of "trauma" and the clinician should respect this. We also recommend having open discussions about words that may potentially sound evaluative and/or place labels on a patient's symptoms, even if those words are routinely utilized by clinicians in the context of CPT. For example, using words like "maladaptive, unhelpful, or ineffective" to describe certain beliefs or behaviors may seem invalidating to marginalized patients, especially if those beliefs are understandable given the patient's lived experiences and, thus, potentially adaptive, helpful, or effective in certain circumstances. As such, it is important to discuss what words feel best for the patient and/or simply describe the thought/behavior without prescribing a label to it, instead focusing on the function of the thought or behavior itself and when it functions to allow the patient to engage in values-aligned activities or achieve their goal versus when it does not. Additionally, while attempting to identify internalized stigma and stuck points related to identity, a clinician may look to the language the client uses to identify themselves or their community; at times, the clinician may find words that could be considered pejorative in mainstream culture. However, an open-minded inquiry may be indicated to determine whether the client's terms point to internalized stigma or instead to an adaptive reclamation of weaponized language (e.g., "queer") or to another subcultural use of the word that the clinician may be unfamiliar with. Within respectful limitations, clinicians should match the language the client prefers to use, especially if requested by the client (e.g., use Latine instead of Latinx, do not use the word queer if requested not to use it).

Similarly, clinicians who work with PTSD may find the highlighting of client strengths and resiliency to be invaluable in encouraging them through the difficult work of trauma-focused treatment. However, in some cases, "resiliency" may be another name for necessary adaptations to chronically stressful environments, interpersonal invalidations, and systemic oppression. Thus, the clinician's attempts to highlight a client's "resiliency" without this consideration may be interpreted by the client as neglecting how systemic oppression forced them to be resilient. This may also be interpreted as the clinician attempting to find a "silver lining" or send the message that "what doesn't kill you make you stronger," both of which can be incredibly invalidating for marginalized individuals. Although we believe highlighting a client's strengths is a necessary and important component of treatment, it is important to call attention to and directly name this process by which marginalized individuals must adapt to oppressive systems and are then complimented by being called "resilient." Clinicians should inquire if the client prefers different language to be used, while also explaining the importance of incorporating one's own strengths into CPT.

Managing Assumptions and Getting Things Right

There are two overarching principles that guide both the aforementioned clinical recommendations as well as other potential cultural and contextual considerations that may impact CPT work with marginalized clients. The first involves the clinician observing their assumptions about the client, the client's identities, and the client's contexts of daily living. This may include reflecting about failures to appreciate the extent to which the client experiences oppression as well as an overestimation of the burden of oppression for the client. In either of these cases, the clinician is encouraged to engage in self-reflective practice to first identify their assumptions about these domains of client experience and then engage in open, curious discussion with the client to align their assumptions or hypotheses with the client's reality.

The second principle is that culturally responsive CPT is less about perfect application of the prescribed techniques, or "getting it right," and more about maintaining an attitude of open-mindedness, flexibility, and thoughtfulness when considering how trauma and trauma responses may intersect with culture, context, and experiences of marginalization. A clinician could make the same statement to two different clients and one would find this validating, while the other may find it invalidating. However, concerns about perfectionism and fears of therapeutic ruptures can lead to an avoidance of naming and addressing crucial cultural and contextual factors that not only shape the client's trauma experience but also may shape the therapeutic relationship. Thus, the clinician is encouraged to engage in these conversations with an orientation toward ongoing growth rather than toward the achievement of perfect competency. When mistakes are made, clinicians should name the mistake, offer an apology, and seek to continue to improve as they would with other potentially rapport-rupturing mistakes.

Case Example

In this case example, we present a patient–therapist dialogue to help conceptualize the culturally responsive adaptations described throughout this chapter. This case example demonstrates a therapist and client collaborating on an ABC Worksheet, one of the first interventions utilized in CPT designed to help the client identify potentially triggering situations (i.e., Activating event), stuck points (i.e., Beliefs), and how these thoughts impact their emotions and behaviors (i.e., Consequences), in order to challenge their thinking in new ways, restructure trauma-related cognitions, and make new meaning. Of note, this case example will present a discussion regarding over-accommodated stuck points. Although assimilated stuck points are typically prioritized prior to addressing over-accommodated stuck points, it may be helpful to discuss over-accommodated stuck points at the same time or even first with marginalized clients depending on the context in which these arise. For example, if the client does not yet feel comfortable enough to address the assimilated stuck points, but shows interest in learning the cognitive skill, it may be helpful for the clinician to start where the client feels comfortable while building trust through this exercise (e.g., identifying how oppressive systems interact with the stuck points identified). In this example, the client is a queer cisgender woman of color and a veteran of the United States Army. The therapist is a white, heterosexual, cisgender woman who has never served in the military.

Therapist: *You mentioned that you have a lot of thoughts about trust and safety. Tell me more.*

Client: *Yeah. It's pretty simple. I can't trust people and there aren't safe places for me.*

Therapist: *Ok. I'm curious about both of those statements.*

Veteran: *People hurt each other. I always get hurt when I trust someone. I can't trust people. And I am not safe. Especially when people see me or know more about me.*

Therapist: *How so?*

Client: *I am a queer Black woman. The military wasn't safe for me—the comments about how I look, who I dated, the shitty jobs I got, the way people looked at me. And then I got out and had nowhere to go—the military dropped me on my ass. I couldn't even find comfort or solidarity in queer spaces because people are either racist or judge you for being a veteran.*

Therapist: *I understand why you would not feel safe in those spaces or around people in those spaces, especially when it sounds like they are actively being oppressive towards you.*

Client: *Yeah. Just being me in the world puts me at risk.*

Therapist: *That is a hard reality to sit with. It is true in so many ways. And at the same time, it sounds like you were looking for spaces and people that are safe. I imagine that is something you still value or would seek out if it were available.*

Client: *In a world of rainbows and sunshine where that could actually happen, sure. But that's not reality. And I'm not really sure that you could ever understand that.*

Therapist: *You're right that the world is not rainbows and sunshine. And as a White, heterosexual person, it is important to acknowledge the privilege I have. I'm never going to fully understand what it's like to walk in your shoes. I can say, though, that a very important part of the clinical work I do involves acknowledging the world we live in and the oppressive systems that continue to harm marginalized individuals, especially POC and SGM. I always want the work we do to highlight that world because that impacts not just your daily experiences, but even the PTSD symptoms we are working on here. My hope is that through collaboration, I can bring my understanding of the skills or tools that might be helpful to you in the context of the world we live in, while you bring your understanding of your needs, values, and history. And together, we find a path forward that works for you. How do you feel about that?*

Client: *Hmm. A lot of people say a lot of things and then do another.*

Therapist: *That's true. I also know trust is difficult as we've been talking about. But I will work hard to not just tell you I value these discussions but show you how through our clinical work.*

Client: *We'll see.*

Therapist: *That's fair. I want to remind you that, through these worksheets, we're not trying to deny reality or change your thoughts from one extreme, like I can't trust anyone, to the other extreme, I can trust everyone. The point of this work is to add flexibility to your thoughts so that we can find a balance between reality and engaging in values-aligned activities that will decrease your distress. With that in mind, would you be willing to work on an ABC sheet together?*

Client: *That makes me feel a little better. I guess I'll give it a try.*

Therapist: *I appreciate that. So, let's pick one stuck point to start with. You mentioned, "No one can be trusted" and "Nowhere is safe." Where would you like to start?*

Client: *I can't trust anyone. That one.*

Therapist: *Ok. Let's think of a recent situation where this stuck point showed up.*

Client: *Um. Here in the waiting room actually. I was sitting with a bunch of men, no one who looked like me, while waiting for this appointment. I was thinking even though we are all veterans, I can't trust them. I can't trust anyone.*

Therapist: *So, let's put this on a sheet. A—situation: Sitting in the waiting room with a bunch of men. B—thought: I can't trust anyone. C—emotion—how did you feel?*

Client: *Angry. Anxious.*

Therapist: *So, having the thought I can't trust anyone led to feeling angry and anxious. Were there things happening in the waiting room that led to this thought, or just a general feeling?*

Client: *Both. There's a general feeling of being unsafe is mostly White spaces and it is hard for me to talk about trust without thinking about safety. They are linked. Then on top of that, people tend to stare at me. Whether it's because I'm Black or because of my gender expression or both, I don't know—but I see the looks and I just think, "Wow. You really can't trust anyone in any location, even the ones made for me."*

Therapist: *Yes, I think safety and trust go hand in hand so that makes sense, especially in spaces that are meant to be safe. In that moment, did you have both trust and safety thoughts or just trust-related stuck points?*

Client: *I was mostly thinking about trust but was on guard because without trust I don't feel safe.*

Therapist: *Okay, so then we would add that feeling of being on guard to the C column. Now, the questions on the bottom of the worksheet are meant to help us start to find balance in these thoughts. The first one is, "Are my thought is Column B realistic?" I want to preface that one by saying that there are absolutely components of this experience that are grounded in reality, like we discussed earlier. But just thinking about the thought "I can't trust anyone." Is that thought by itself realistic is every single situation you're in?*

Client: *I guess not. I trust my partner. And my sister.*

Therapist: *Ok. So a couple people you can trust.*

Client: *Yes.*

Therapist: *What about in here? What are your thoughts about trust in therapy?*

Client: *Well, I trust you to a degree, but I'm not sure yet. And I don't always trust the people I sit with in the lobby.*

Therapist: *Absolutely fair. Thinking about trust with different people or trust at different degrees or levels is actually one step ahead. With that in mind, why would you not trust, for example, me in the same way you trust your sister or your partner?*

Client: *Well, I can tell you about my trauma and my experiences in the military so far, but I haven't known you for long and I don't know you like I know them. I don't have other information that would help me.*

Therapist: *Exactly. So, talking this through, we've established that "I can't trust anyone" might not be 100% accurate because there are a couple of people you trust and at varying degrees. So, what about that next part on the sheet? What can you tell yourself on such occasions in the future?*

Client: *I guess I can trust some people some of the time.*

Therapist: *Does that feel any different when you tell yourself that?*

Client: *A little.*

Therapist: *Ok, so we'll continue to chip away at these stuck points together through CPT. You can see the link between what you're thinking and feeling already. And we'll continue to ground these thoughts in reality, which includes experiences of discrimination and bias. Sometimes not trusting is justified and necessary, and maybe there are some places where it might be helpful to shift thinking, like trying to make a new friend. That's a skill we'll practice throughout treatment.*

Summary

In this chapter, we highlighted how CPT may be applied using a multicultural and feminist framework when working with marginalized individuals, and in a way that balances the core tenets of CPT while privileging the presenting concerns (e.g., oppression-based stress, ongoing trauma) and preferences of clients from marginalized backgrounds. A large part of this work includes collaborating with clients to identify cultural contexts that impact each part of treatment, from initiation and potential treatment barriers to engaging in interventions. Several important considerations include directly naming and addressing cultural contexts, balancing reality (e.g., ongoing threats to safety, trust, esteem) with managing distress, incorporating client's preferences and values into thought and behavior modification, and highlighting the client's empowerment in and beyond treatment. Multiculturally adapted CPT ultimately seeks to understand each client in a multifaceted manner, which acknowledges personal histories, values, and sociodemographic contexts in order to provide effective interventions that address core issues in the contexts in which clients live.

**Disclaimer: The views expressed in this chapter are those of the authors and do not necessarily reflect the position or policy of the US Department of Veterans Affairs or the US government.

Conflict of Interest Statement The authors have no conflicts of interest to declare that are relevant to the content of this chapter.

References

American Psychiatric Association. (2013). *Diagnostic and statistical manual of mental disorders* (5th ed.). https://doi.org/10.1176/appi.books.9780890425596

Arnett, J. E., Frantell, K. A., Miles, J. R., & Fry, K. M. (2019). Anti-bisexual discrimination as insidious trauma and impacts on mental and physical health. *Psychology of Sexual Orientation and Gender Diversity, 6*(4), 475–485. https://doi.org/10.1037/sgd0000344

Barr, S. M., Snyder, K. E., Adelson, J. L., & Budge, S. L. (2022). Posttraumatic stress in the trans community: The roles of anti-transgender bias, non-affirmation, and internalized transphobia. *Psychology of Sexual Orientation and Gender Diversity, 9*(4), 410–421.

Bass, J. K., Annan, J., McIvor Murray, S., Kaysen, D., Griffiths, S., Cetinoglu, T., Wachter, K., Murray, L. K., & Bolton, P. A. (2013). Controlled trial of psychotherapy for Congolese survivors of sexual violence. *New England Journal of Medicine, 368*(23), 2182–2191. https://doi.org/10.1056/nejmoa1211853

Beard, C., Kirakosian, N., Silverman, A. L., Winer, J. P., Wadsworth, L. P., & Björgvinsson, T. (2017). Comparing treatment response between LGBQ and heterosexual individuals attending a CBT- and DBT-skills-based partial hospital. *Journal of Consulting and Clinical Psychology, 85*(12), 1171–1181. https://doi.org/10.1037/ccp0000251

Beck, A. T., Rush, A. J., Shaw, B. F., & Emery, G. (1979). *Cognitive therapy of depression: A treatment manual*. Guilford Press.

Berke, D. S., Maples-Keller, J. L., & Richards, P. (2016). LGBTQ perceptions of psychotherapy: A consensual qualitative analysis. *Professional Psychology: Research and Practice, 47*(6), 373–382. https://doi.org/10.1037/pro0000099

Bhambhani, Y., Flynn, M. K., Kellum, K. K., & Wilson, K. G. (2020). The role of psychological flexibility as a mediator between experienced sexual racism and psychological distress among men of color who have sex with men. *Archives of Sexual Behavior, 49*(2), 711–720. https://doi.org/10.1007/s10508-018-1269-5

Brown, L. S. (2004). Feminist paradigms of trauma treatment. *Psychotherapy: Theory, Research, Practice, Training, 41*(4), 464–471. https://doi.org/10.1037/0033-3204.41.4.464

Calabrese, S. K., Meyer, I. H., Overstreet, N. M., Haile, R., & Hansen, N. B. (2015). Exploring discrimination and mental health disparities faced by black sexual minority women using a minority stress framework. *Psychology of Women Quarterly, 39*(3), 287–304. https://doi.org/10.1177/0361684314560730

Cardona, N. D., Madigan, R. J., & Sauer-Zavala, S. (2021). How minority stress becomes traumatic invalidation: An emotion-focused conceptualization of minority stress in sexual and gender minority people. *Clinical Psychology: Science and Practice, 29*(2), 185–195. https://doi.org/10.1037/cps0000054

Carter, R. T. (2007). Racism and psychological and emotional injury: Recognizing and assessing race-based traumatic stress. *The Counseling Psychologist, 35*(1), 13–105. https://doi.org/10.1177/0011000006292033

Clark, K. D., Luong, S., Lunn, M. R., Flowers, E., Bahalkeh, E., & Lubensky, M. E. (2022). Healthcare mistreatment, state-level policy protections, and healthcare avoidance among

gender minority people. *Sexuality Research and Social Policy, 19*(4), 1717–1730. https://doi.org/10.1007/s13178-022-00748-1
Clark, R., Anderson, N. B., Clark, V. R., & Williams, D. R. (1999). Racism as a stressor for African Americans. A biopsychosocial model. *The American Psychologist, 54*(10), 805–816. https://doi.org/10.1037/0003-066x.54.10.805
Crenshaw, K. W. (1989). Demarginalizing the intersection of race and sex: A black feminist critique of antidiscrimination doctrine, feminist theory and antiracist politics. *University of Chicago Legal Forum, 1989*, 139–167.
Durso, L. E., & Meyer, I. H. (2013). Patterns and predictors of disclosure of sexual orientation to healthcare providers among lesbians, gay men, and bisexuals. *Sexuality Research and Social Policy, 10*(1), 35–42. https://doi.org/10.1007/s13178-012-0105-2
Dworkin, E. R., Gilmore, A. K., Bedard-Gilligan, M., Lehavot, K., Guttmannova, K., & Kaysen, D. (2018). Predicting PTSD severity from experiences of trauma and heterosexism in lesbian and bisexual women: A longitudinal study of cognitive mediators. *Journal of Counseling Psychology, 65*(3), 324–333. https://doi.org/10.1037/cou0000287
Farmer, C. C., Mitchell, K. S., Parker-Guilbert, K., & Galovski, T. E. (2017). Fidelity to the cognitive processing therapy protocol: Evaluation of critical elements. *Behavior Therapy, 48*(2), 195–206. https://doi.org/10.1016/j.beth.2016.02.009
Galovski, T. E., Blain, L. M., Mott, J. M., Elwood, L., & Houle, T. (2012). Manualized therapy for PTSD: Flexing the structure of cognitive processing therapy. *Journal of Consulting and Clinical Psychology, 80*(6), 968–981.
Galovski, T. E., Nixon, R. D., & Kaysen, D. (2020). *Flexible applications of cognitive processing therapy: Evidence-based treatment methods*. Academic Press.
Grant, J. M., Mottet, L., Tanis, J., Harrison, J., Herman, J. L., & Keisling, M. (2011). Injustice at every turn: A report of the national transgender discrimination survey. *Washington National Center for Transgender Equality and National Gay and Lesbian Task Force., 11*, 450. https://doi.org/10.1016/S0016-7878(90)80026-2
Hatzenbuehler, M. L. (2009). How does sexual minority stigma "get under the skin"? A psychological mediation framework. *Psychological Bulletin, 135*(5), 707–730. https://doi.org/10.1037/a0016441
Hendricks, M. L., & Testa, R. J. (2012). A conceptual framework for clinical work with transgender and gender nonconforming clients: An adaptation of the minority stress model. *Professional Psychology: Research and Practice, 43*(5), 460–467. https://doi.org/10.1037/a0029597
Holmes, S. C., Facemire, V. C., & DaFonseca, A. M. (2016). Expanding criterion a for posttraumatic stress disorder: Considering the deleterious impact of oppression. *Traumatology, 22*(4), 314–321. https://doi.org/10.1037/trm0000104
Jeong, Y. M., Veldhuis, C. B., Aranda, F., & Hughes, T. L. (2016). Racial/ethnic differences in unmet needs for mental health and substance use treatment in a community-based sample of sexual minority women. *Journal of Clinical Nursing, 25*(23–24), 3557–3569. https://doi.org/10.1111/jocn.13477
Lau, A. S. (2006). Making the case for selective and directed cultural adaptations of evidence-based treatments: Examples from parent training. *Clinical Psychology: Science and Practice, 13*(4), 295–310. https://doi.org/10.1111/j.1468-2850.2006.00042.x
Livingston, N. A., Berke, D. S., Ruben, M. A., Matza, A. R., & Shipherd, J. C. (2019). Experiences of trauma, discrimination, microaggressions, and minority stress among trauma-exposed LGBT veterans: Unexpected findings and unresolved service gaps. *Psychological Trauma: Theory, Research, Practice, and Policy, 11*(7), 695–703. https://doi.org/10.1037/tra0000464
Livingston, N. A., Berke, D., Scholl, J., Ruben, M., & Shipherd, J. C. (2020). Addressing diversity in PTSD treatment: Clinical considerations and guidance for the treatment of PTSD in LGBTQ populations. *Current Treatment Options in Psychiatry, 7*(2), 53–69. https://doi.org/10.1007/s40501-020-00204-0

LoSavio, S. T., Dillon, K. H., & Resick, P. A. (2017). Cognitive factors in the development, maintenance, and treatment of post-traumatic stress disorder. *Current Opinion in Psychology, 14*, 18–22. https://doi.org/10.1016/j.copsyc.2016.09.006

Mallinckrodt, B., Miles, J. R., & Levy, J. J. (2014). The scientist-practitioner-advocate model: Addressing contemporary training needs for social justice advocacy. *Training and Education in Professional Psychology, 8*(4), 303–311.

Marques, L., Valentine, S. E., Kaysen, D., Mackintosh, M. A., Dixon De Silva, L. E., Ahles, E. M., Youn, S. J., Shtasel, D. L., Simon, N. M., & Wiltsey-Stirman, S. (2019). Provider fidelity and modifications to cognitive processing therapy in a diverse community health clinic: Associations with clinical change. *Journal of Consulting and Clinical Psychology, 87*(4), 357–369. https://doi.org/10.1037/ccp0000384

Matos, M., Carvalho, S. A., Cunha, M., Galhardo, A., & Sepodes, C. (2017). Psychological flexibility and self-compassion in gay and heterosexual men: How they relate to childhood memories, shame, and depressive symptoms. *Journal of LGBT Issues in Counseling, 11*(2), 88–105. https://doi.org/10.1080/15538605.2017.1310007

Mays, V. M., Jones, A. L., Delany-Brumsey, A., Coles, C., & Cochran, S. D. (2017). Perceived discrimination in health care and mental health/substance abuse treatment among blacks, Latinos, and whites. *Medical Care, 55*(2), 173–181.

McClendon, J., Dean, K. E., & Galovski, T. (2020). Addressing diversity in PTSD treatment: Disparities in treatment tngagement and outcome among patients of color. *Current Treatment Options in Psychiatry, 7*(3), 275–290. https://doi.org/10.1007/s40501-020-00212-0

Meyer, I. H. (1995). Minority stress and mental health in gay men. *Journal of Health and Social Behavior, 36*(1), 38–56. https://doi.org/10.2307/2137286

Meyer, I. H. (2003). Prejudice, social stress, and mental health in lesbian, gay, and bisexual populations: Conceptual issues and research evidence. *Psychology of Sexual Orientation and Gender Diversity, 1*(S), 3–26. https://doi.org/10.1037/2329-0382.1.S.3

Miller, G. H. (2009). Commentary: The trauma of insidious racism. *Journal of the American Academy of Psychiatry and the Law, 37*(1), 41–44.

Moody, A. T., & Lewis, J. A. (2019). Gendered racial microaggressions and traumatic stress symptoms among black women. *Psychology of Women Quarterly, 43*(2), 201–214.

Mosher, D. K., Hook, J. N., Captari, L. E., Davis, D. E., DeBlaere, C., & Owen, J. (2017). Cultural humility: A therapeutic framework for engaging diverse clients. *Practice Innovations, 2*(4), 221–233. https://doi.org/10.1037/pri0000055

Nadal, K. L., Erazo, T., & King, R. (2019). Challenging definitions of psychological trauma: Connecting racial microaggressions and traumatic stress. *Journal for Social Action in Counseling & Psychology, 11*(2), 2–16.

Nadal, K. L., Whitman, C. N., Davis, L. S., Erazo, T., & Davidoff, K. C. (2016). Microaggressions toward lesbian, gay, bisexual, transgender, queer, and genderqueer people: A review of the literature. *Journal of Sex Research, 53*(4–5), 488–508. https://doi.org/10.1080/00224499.2016.1142495

Ouellette, M. J., Mutschler, C., Roth, S. L., Mccabe, R. E., Tissera, T., Patel, H., Boyd, J. E., Nicholson, A. A., Lopes, J., Jeffs, L., Schneider, M. A., Mckinnon, M. C., Ouellette, M. J., Mutschler, C., Roth, S. L., Mccabe, R. E., Tissera, T., Patel, H., Boyd, J. E., et al. (2023). The transcending protocol: A cognitive-behavioral approach for addressing the psychosocial impact of minority stress in transgender and gender diverse individuals. *Journal of LGBTQ Issues in Counseling, 17*(1), 57–76. https://doi.org/10.1080/26924951.2022.2096168

Pachankis, J. E., Hatzenbuehler, M. L., Rendina, H. J., Safren, S. A., & Parsons, J. T. (2015). LGB-affirmative cognitive-behavioral therapy for young adult gay and bisexual men: A randomized controlled trial of a transdiagnostic minority stress approach. *Journal of Consulting and Clinical Psychology, 83*(5), 875–889. https://doi.org/10.1037/ccp0000037

Pachankis, J. E., McConocha, E. M., Clark, K. A., Wang, K., Behari, K., Fetzner, B. K., Brisbin, C. D., Scheer, J. R., & Lehavot, K. (2020). A transdiagnostic minority stress intervention for gender diverse sexual minority women's depression, anxiety, and unhealthy alcohol use: A randomized controlled trial. *Journal of Consulting and Clinical Psychology, 88*(7), 613–630. https://doi.org/10.1037/ccp0000508

Reisner, S. L., Hughto, J. M. W., Gamarel, K. E., Keuroghlian, A. S., Mizock, L., & Pachankis, J. E. (2016). Discriminatory experiences associated with posttraumatic stress disorder symptoms among transgender adults. *Journal of Counseling Psychology, 63*(5), 509–519. https://doi.org/10.1037/cou0000143

Resick, P. A., Monson, C. M., & Chard, K. M. (2024). *Cognitive processing therapy for PTSD: A comprehensive manual*. The Guilford Press. https://psycnet.apa.org/record/2016-49603-000

Resick, P. A., Monson, C. M., & Chard, K. M. (2008). *Cognitive processing therapy: Veteran/military version*. Department of Veterans' Affairs.

Resick, P. A., Wachen, J. S., Dondanville, K. A., Pruiksma, K. E., Yarvis, J. S., Peterson, A. L., Mintz, J., the STRONG STAR Consortium, Borah, E. V., Brundige, A., Hembree, E. A., Litz, B. T., Roache, J. D., & Young-McCaughan, S. (2017). Effect of group vs individual cognitive processing therapy in active-duty military seeking treatment for posttraumatic stress disorder: A randomized clinical trial. *JAMA Psychiatry, 74*(1), 28–36. https://doi.org/10.1001/jamapsychiatry.2016.2729

Rimes, K. A., Ion, D., Wingrove, J., & Carter, B. (2019). Sexual orientation differences in psychological treatment outcomes for depression and anxiety: National cohort study. *Journal of Consulting and Clinical Psychology, 87*(7), 577–589. https://doi.org/10.1037/ccp0000416

Robinson, M., & Ross, L. E. (2013). Gender and sexual minorities: Intersecting inequalities and health. *Ethnicity and Inequalities in Health and Social Care, 6*(4), 91–96.

Root, M. P. P. (1992). Reconstructing the impact of trauma on personality. In L. S. Brown & M. Ballou (Eds.), *Personality and psychopathology: Feminist reappraisals* (pp. 229–265). The Guilford Press.

Ruben, M. A., Livingston, N. A., Berke, D. S., Matza, A. R., & Shipherd, J. C. (2019). Lesbian, gay, bisexual, and transgender veterans' experiences of discrimination in health care and their relation to health outcomes: A pilot study examining the moderating role of provider communication. *Health Equity, 3*(1), 480–488. https://doi.org/10.1089/heq.2019.0069

Salomaa, A. C., Livingston, N. A., Bryant, W. T., Herbitter, C., Harper, K., Sloan, C. A., Hinds, Z., Gyuro, L., Valentine, S. E., & Shipherd, J. C. (2023). A bottom-up approach to developing a unified trauma-minority stress model for transgender and gender diverse people. *Psychological Trauma: Theory, Research, Practice and Policy, 15*(4), 618–627. https://doi.org/10.1037/tra0001373

Sue, S. (2006). Cultural competency: From philosophy to research and practice. *Journal of Community Psychology, 34*(2), 237–245.

Szymanski, D. M., & Balsam, K. F. (2011). Insidious trauma: Examining the relationship between heterosexism and lesbians' PTSD symptoms. *Traumatology, 17*(2), 4–13. https://doi.org/10.1177/1534765609358464

Valentine, S. E., Borba, C. P. C., Dixon, L., Vaewsorn, A. S., Guajardo, J. G., Resick, P. A., Wiltsey Stirman, S., & Marques, L. (2017). Cognitive processing therapy for spanish-speaking latinos: A formative study of a model-driven cultural adaptation of the manual to enhance implementation in a usual care setting. *Journal of Clinical Psychology, 73*(3), 239–256. https://doi.org/10.1002/jclp.22337

Valentine, S. E., Smith, A. M., Miller, K., Hadden, L., & Shipherd, J. C. (2023). Considerations and complexities of accurate PTSD assessment among transgender and gender diverse adults. *Psychological Assessment, 35*(5), 383–395.

Washington, A., & Randall, J. (2023). "We're not taken seriously": Describing the experiences of perceived discrimination in medical settings for black women. *Journal of Racial and Ethnic Health Disparities, 10*(2), 883–891.

Williams, M. T., Holmes, S., Zare, M., Haeny, A., & Faber, S. (2022). An evidence-based approach for treating stress and trauma due to racism. *Cognitive and Behavioral Practice, 30*(4), 565–588.

Williams, M. T., Malcoun, E., Sawyer, B. A., Davis, D. M., Bahojb Nouri, L., & Bruce, S. L. (2014). Cultural adaptations of prolonged exposure therapy for treatment and prevention of posttraumatic stress disorder in African Americans. *Behavioral Sciences, 4*(2), 102–124.

Williams, W. C., Morelli, S. A., Ong, D. C., & Zaki, J. (2018). Interpersonal emotion regulation: Implications for affiliation, perceived support, relationships, and Well-being. *Journal of Personality and Social Psychology, 115*(2), 224–254. https://doi.org/10.1037/pspi0000132

Williams, M. T., Osman, M., Gran-Ruaz, S., & Lopez, J. (2021). Intersection of racism and PTSD: Assessment and treatment of racial stress and trauma. *Current Treatment Options in Psychiatry, 8*(4), 167–185.

White, B. P., & Fontenot, H. B. (2019). Transgender and non-conforming persons' mental healthcare experiences: An integrative review. *Archives of Psychiatric Nursing, 33*(2), 203–210. https://doi.org/10.1016/j.apnu.2019.01.005

Chapter 11
Delivering Cognitive Processing Therapy in the Context of Suicide Risk, Violence Risk, and Intense Psychosocial Stressors

Nicholas Holder and Ryan Holliday

Cognitive processing therapy (CPT) is currently advised as a first-line treatment for those diagnosed with posttraumatic stress disorder (PTSD; Departments of Veterans Affairs and Defense, 2023; Haagen et al., 2015; Hamblen et al., 2019), with many organizations supporting national trainings on CPT delivery (Dondanville et al., 2022; Rosen et al., 2016). Unfortunately, PTSD rarely occurs without clinical complexity. In addition to comorbid mental and physical health diagnoses, the psychosocial and interpersonal circumstances that individuals diagnosed with PTSD face are strong contributors to this complexity. While PTSD symptoms are the primary target of CPT, clinicians are regularly required to help patients navigate PTSD treatment in the context of suicide risk, risk of continued exposure to violence, and intense psychosocial stressors. A substantial proportion of individuals diagnosed with PTSD die by suicide each year (Holliday et al., 2020). In addition, re-traumatization is common among those with PTSD (Kessler et al., 2017), and re-traumatization elevates risk for more severe symptom presentations (Brewin et al., 2000; Kessler et al., 2017) and further re-traumatization (Iverson et al., 2022; Jaffe et al., 2019). Psychosocial stressors further contribute to complexity. An estimated

N. Holder (✉)
San Francisco Veterans Affairs Health Care System, San Francisco, CA, USA

University of California, San Francisco School of Medicine, San Francisco, CA, USA

Center for Data to Discovery and Delivery Innovation (3DI COIN), San Francisco, CA, USA
e-mail: Nicholas.Holder@va.gov

R. Holliday
Rocky Mountain Mental Illness Research, Education, and Clinical Center for Suicide Prevention, Aurora, CO, USA

University of Colorado Anschutz Medical Campus, Aurora, CO, USA

VA Pacific Islands Health Care System, Honolulu, USA

J. S. Wachen, T. E. Galovski (eds.), *Cognitive Processing Therapy for Complex Cases*, CBT: Science Into Practice,
https://doi.org/10.1007/978-3-031-87356-0_11

27.4% of individuals experiencing homelessness also meet diagnostic criteria for PTSD (Ayano et al., 2020). There are similar associations between PTSD and criminal–legal involvement (Taylor et al., 2020), with incarcerated individuals experiencing twice the rate of PTSD relative to community peers (Baranyi et al., 2018). Importantly, there is a reciprocal relationship between these psychosocial stressors and PTSD, with stressors worsening PTSD and PTSD contributing to poorer psychosocial functioning (e.g., unemployment; irritable behavior contributing to criminogenic behavior such as physical assault).

In most cases, clinical complexity is not a reason to deny a patient access to CPT. Rather, this serves as an opportunity to flexibly deliver the CPT treatment protocol in order to optimally meet the patient's needs. Delivering CPT in these contexts requires careful assessment, thoughtful case conceptualization, and an adaptable approach to care. With the correct enhancements and supports in place, CPT can assist patients in navigating challenging environments by both directly treating PTSD as well as providing generalizable skills.

Research Overview

Suicide Risk

When considering "high risk" patients with PTSD, patients reporting suicidal thoughts or behavior are often among the first populations that come to mind. Clinicians often voice hesitancy with providing CPT to individuals who report ongoing, recent, or historical suicidal thoughts or behaviors (Cook et al., 2014; LoSavio et al., 2024). Clinicians may be concerned about whether CPT can help attenuate suicide risk or, conversely, if CPT may exacerbate suicide risk. Encouragingly, considerable research has identified CPT as not only a safe intervention for many with elevated suicide risk, but also an intervention that can help to *reduce* suicide risk (Rozek et al., 2022). See Chap. 3 for an in-depth review of assessing and managing emotional dysregulation and resultant emotion-driven crisis behaviors, including suicidal behaviors.

Generally, clinical practice guidelines encourage treating comorbid mental health conditions, including PTSD and other common comorbidities (e.g., depression), to reduce suicide risk (Departments of Veterans Affairs and Defense, 2024). In a national Department of Veterans Affairs (VA) study, the risk of death by suicide was substantially reduced by treating PTSD symptoms to remission (Forehand et al., 2022). In addition to the *indirect* reduction in suicide risk due to the attenuation of PTSD symptoms, CPT also appears to *directly* reduce suicide risk. In a recent systematic review, Rozek et al. (2022) concluded that many of those who received CPT reported reductions in suicidal ideation as well as suicide-related beliefs (Holliday et al., 2018a) and perceived burdensomeness (Blain et al., 2021). Further, of the treatments identified in this systematic review, CPT had the greatest number of included studies (i.e., 11) investigating suicide-related outcomes (Rozek et al., 2022).

In addition to demonstrated benefit of CPT in attenuating risk for suicide, CPT also has *not* been shown to lead to exacerbation of suicide risk. Among participants reporting suicidal ideation at baseline, Bryan et al. (2016) found that new onset suicidal ideation was rare in a trial comparing group CPT to non-trauma-focused group treatment. Further, worsening of existing suicidal ideation was also rare in this trial, with no statistically significant differences in rates of worsening of suicidal ideation between the treatments (Bryan et al., 2016). Randomized clinical trials have also shown that suicide attempts during and after CPT are uncommon, even in clinically complex (e.g., comorbid borderline personality disorder) presentations of PTSD (e.g., Bohus et al., 2020; Schnurr et al., 2022). These results appear to generalize from clinical trials to routine clinical practice. In a study of routine clinical practice in a VA medical center, only 1.0% of the sample engaged in suicidal behavior after initiating CPT (Roberge et al., 2021). Taken together, these data suggest that worsening of suicide risk observed during CPT may be more consistent with the variable nature of suicide risk rather than an iatrogenic effect of CPT.

When considering delivery of CPT in the context of elevated suicide risk, it is important to consider limitations in the current PTSD research literature. Research studies have typically used vague terminology that is not consistent with stratification tools to describe suicide risk (Bakalar et al., 2017; Holliday et al., 2019b). Vague terminology makes it difficult to determine suicide risk among trial participants (and particularly the threshold of suicide risk of excluded participants). The inability to extrapolate suicide risk from trials impacts our current knowledge of what severity of risk (e.g., those with recent suicide attempts vs. those with suicidal ideation many months prior) is best suited for CPT. Nonetheless, providers should have confidence that CPT has the potential to attenuate suicide risk, both directly through improvements in suicide-related outcomes and indirectly through improvements in PTSD symptoms. The iatrogenic risk of CPT appears to be minor, but research in this area is limited.

Risk of Violence Exposure

Survivors of trauma are at elevated risk of future trauma exposure (Kessler et al., 2017), and patients often present to treatment in the context of ongoing violence. For example, in studies designed to support adaptation of CPT for Latine communities, the impact of community violence was highlighted by patients (Marques et al., 2016) and cited as challenge by clinicians (Valentine et al., 2017). This is particularly true for socioeconomically disadvantaged patients, particularly those without the ability to escape such circumstances (e.g., unemployed or experiencing housing instability). We will discuss navigating CPT in the context of psychosocial stressors, such as homelessness, later in the chapter. Research in delivering CPT to those at risk of ongoing violence is limited. In fact, early clinical trials specifically excluded participants who were in an ongoing physically abusive relationship (e.g., Galovski et al., 2012; Resick et al., 2002; Surís et al., 2013). Key concerns with regard to risk of violence exposure include whether CPT can be effective for patients at risk of violence exposure and whether participating in CPT is appropriate for those at risk of ongoing violence exposure.

Trauma-focused psychotherapy, including CPT, has more recently been investigated in patients at risk of violence exposure. Peterson et al. (2020) conducted a non-randomized trial of trauma-focused psychotherapy, including CPT, in deployed military personnel. Results suggested preliminary effectiveness of delivering trauma-focused treatments in this setting, although benefits were less robust and not-statistically significant for CPT. Further, two recent systematic reviews have described the literature regarding delivery of trauma-focused treatment in the context of ongoing threat of violence exposure (Ennis et al., 2021; Yim et al., 2024). Overall, both reviews report that psychological interventions can be delivered in these settings and that patients living in settings with risk of ongoing violence experience reductions in PTSD symptoms following treatment. Both reviews also highlight high heterogeneity between studies and variable quality in methods as points of caution in interpretation.

Two studies report on the influence of violence exposure on CPT engagement and outcomes specifically. In a secondary analysis of data from a CPT randomized clinical trial Iverson et al. (2011b) found that patients who were in a relationship with past year intimate partner violence (IPV) were less likely to begin CPT compared to those without a history of IPV or IPV that occurred more than a year prior. However, after beginning treatment, patients with past year intimate partner violence completed CPT at similar rates to other participants. Additionally, higher frequency of IPV was associated with *greater* benefit from CPT from pre- to post-treatment, and similar benefit from pre-treatment to 6-month follow-up. Kaysen et al. (2020) reported similar findings from a study of CPT in the Democratic Republic of the Congo. Patients from areas with high and low conflict and risk of violence experienced similar benefit from CPT and similar rates of treatment completion. In addition to improvements in PTSD symptoms, effective treatment of PTSD with CPT may result in a *reduced* risk of future exposure to violence (Iverson et al., 2011a). Although more research in this area is needed, initial results suggest CPT can be safely and effectively delivered to those at ongoing risk of violence exposure.

Homelessness and Housing Instability

Homelessness and housing instability are associated with increased risk of trauma exposure (Tsai et al., 2020). Given this, it is unsurprising that individuals experiencing homelessness have high rates of PTSD diagnosis (Ayano et al., 2020). Homelessness can create a substantial barrier to accessing and engaging in mental health care, and mental health symptoms can create a substantial barrier to establishing stable housing. This tension often creates a challenge for clinicians in trying to determine how to approach prioritizing and sequencing care. As with other areas of risk, clinicians should consider whether individuals experiencing homelessness can effectively participate in CPT and whether CPT can effectively treat PTSD symptoms for these patients.

A recent scoping review highlights the scarcity of clinical trials studying the delivery of trauma-focused psychotherapy to individuals experiencing homelessness (Bennett et al., 2022). While some trials do explicitly exclude participants experiencing homelessness (e.g., Bohus et al., 2020), most trials neither explicitly identify homelessness as an exclusion criteria nor report on whether any included participants were experiencing homelessness (e.g., Galovski et al., 2012; Resick et al., 2002; Surís et al., 2013). While at first glance this may seem to suggest that CPT is not being provided to individuals experiencing homelessness, several clinical effectiveness and program evaluation studies show that this is not the case. Feingold et al. (2018) studied the effectiveness of various evidence-based psychotherapies, including CPT, as part of a jail diversion program. In their sample, 30% of participants were experiencing homelessness or housing instability. Housing was not significantly associated with treatment completion, suggesting that individuals experiencing homelessness and housing instability are capable of engaging in evidence-based psychotherapy despite this substantial psychosocial stressor. In a study of a residential PTSD treatment program for veterans (which included CPT), Holliday et al. (2021b) found that PTSD symptoms improved for veterans experiencing homelessness from pre-treatment to discharge, but recurred at follow-up. One notable characteristic of the research on homelessness and CPT is that studies have delivered CPT with additional services/interventions (Feingold et al., 2018; Holliday et al., 2021b; Yamokoski et al., 2023), such as providing housing during treatment and case management to facilitate post-discharge planning.

Criminal–Legal Involvement

Criminal–legal involvement is associated with high rates of PTSD (Baranyi et al., 2018; Taylor et al., 2020). Similar to other intense psychosocial stressors, many individuals who are involved in the criminal–legal system are disproportionately likely to have experienced trauma (Fovet et al., 2021; Saxon et al., 2001). Notably, such experiences can occur within the context of criminal–legal involvement (e.g., assault during incarceration). Despite this, studies of the effectiveness of CPT are lacking for individuals engaged with the criminal–legal system. As with other high-risk individuals, protections for vulnerable prison populations make research in these settings challenging.

Two studies to date have explored evidence-based psychotherapy programs that included CPT for criminal–legal involved individuals—both are studies that also included individuals experiencing homelessness or housing instability (Feingold et al., 2018; Holliday et al., 2021b). In their study of individuals in a jail diversion program where 53% of patients received CPT, Feingold et al. (2018) found significant improvement in PTSD and depression symptoms from pre- to post-treatment.

Holliday et al. (2021b) found that criminal–legal involved residential PTSD treatment participants, including those entering programing following jail or prison, experienced significant PTSD symptom reduction from pre- to post-treatment that persisted through four-month follow-up. Together, these studies include data from only 112 criminal–legal involved participants, highlighting the strong need for additional research in this area, with one such study in progress (Zielinski et al., 2022).

Case Example: Aaron

Identifying Information and Chief Complaint

Aaron is a 29-year-old, Black, gay, single, male, Army veteran. He is unemployed and he is currently residing in temporary housing at a local extended stay hotel provided by a local Veteran Service Organization (VSO; an umbrella term for organizations that serve veterans through a wide range of psychosocial services). In addition to concerns regarding housing and employment, Aaron reports primary mental health concerns of trauma-related nightmares, always being down on himself, and difficulty trusting others.

History of Presenting Illness

Aaron reports being diagnosed with "depression, anxiety, and PTSD" by mental health providers in the past. Aaron has participated in psychotherapy and has been prescribed psychotropic medications (e.g., selective serotonin reuptake inhibitors, atypical antipsychotic medications, prazosin, trazodone) on and off since childhood. When asked about his treatment experiences, he described skill-based (rather than trauma-focused) psychotherapy (e.g., grounding, mindful breathing, suicide safety planning).

Aaron has a history of chronic suicidal ideation and three suicide attempts. The Columbia Suicide Severity Rating Scale (CSSRS; Posner et al., 2011) was used to assess current and historical suicidal ideation and behavior. Currently, Aaron endorsed suicidal ideation (i.e., "It would be easier if I weren't around"). While he reports considering a method for suicide (i.e., firearm), he denies a specific plan for suicide (e.g., does not own a firearm) and suicidal intent at this time. Aaron reports a history of three suicide attempts: (1) at age 13, he took a handful of medication with the intention to overdose; (2) at age 22 (during military service) he sat in his room with a loaded firearm; and (3) at age 26 (post-military service) he purchased a firearm, but received a phone call from a friend who encouraged him to go to the hospital before he got home. Aaron denies suicidal behavior since the most recent attempt.

Aaron reports an extensive trauma history—he witnessed domestic violence perpetrated by his father against his mother as a child, was sexually assaulted at age 14, joined the Army and experienced military sexual assault, witnessed aftermath of violence (e.g., serious injuries/death) in his military occupation, and experienced IPV in several romantic relationships post-military service (including a recent relationship). Based on clinical interview and the PCL-5, Aaron reported symptoms consistent with a diagnosis of PTSD anchored to military sexual assault. Aaron also meets criteria for comorbid major depressive disorder; however, his anxiety is trauma-related rather than characteristic of a generalized anxiety disorder or specific phobia. Aaron denies substance use aside from alcohol (i.e., drinking one to two drinks three days per week), which has reduced since living in the extended stay hotel. He reports having control over his drinking, and he denies a history of legal or social consequences from drinking.

Aaron recently moved across the United States to pursue a romantic relationship with a partner he met online. Aaron has no other friends or family in the area and planned to live with his romantic partner while he found work and housing. However, the romantic partner was physically and sexually abusive, and Aaron left the relationship within a few weeks. Given his plan to live with this partner, Aaron was subsequently homeless prior to contacting his local VSO.

Case Considerations

When working with patients who are experiencing substantial psychosocial stressors or other issues of risk, thorough assessment and case conceptualization are critical to help decide how best to move forward. In Aaron's case, initial focus should be upon factors most pressing, specifically determinations of suicide risk and risk for continued exposure to violence. In addition, it is paramount to understand his current psychosocial circumstances and his case management needs (i.e., housing instability, unemployment). From there, a determination about the appropriateness for CPT can be made.

Clinical Application

Modifications to CPT and Important Considerations in Context of Suicide Risk

As noted above, clinicians may cite "suicidality" generally as a barrier to providing CPT (Cook et al., 2014; LoSavio et al., 2024). Research suggests that CPT is indicated for many patients who have a history of suicidal thoughts or behaviors, and CPT can, in fact, help to reduce suicide risk (Rozek et al., 2022). Clinicians are therefore entrusted with navigating this tension—a task which requires careful assessment of suicide risk, incorporation of assessment data into case conceptualization, integration of suicide risk management strategies into CPT, and a flexible (yet high-fidelity) approach to CPT delivery.

Assessment and Suicide Risk Stratification

High quality suicide risk assessment is the foundation to effective clinical care for all patients, including those with PTSD who are experiencing concurrent suicidal ideation or have engaged in recent suicidal behavior. It is recommended that risk assessment include both a structured, validated tool for assessing suicide risk (e.g., CSSRS; Posner et al., 2011) as well as a clinical interview (Holliday et al., 2018b). This information can then be synthesized to inform a risk stratification based on both temporality and severity (Wortzel et al., 2014). In terms of temporality, clinicians should consider "acute" and "chronic" risk. Acute risk refers to the patient's risk of suicide in the near term—in the upcoming hours or days. Chronic risk refers to the patient's risk of suicide over the long-term—throughout their life. Each of these periods of risk is also stratified by severity of risk—low, intermediate, or high. Throughout the course of treatment, clinicians should consider acute and chronic risk, especially factors which may fluctuate or exacerbate risk (e.g., patient report of a risk factor such an impending eviction).

Appropriateness of CPT Based on Suicide Risk Stratification

In the absence of other complicating factors, patients who are deemed to be at low acute risk for suicide are likely appropriate for CPT (Holliday et al., 2021a). These patients may experience suicidal ideation, but do not have intent or a plan (Wortzel et al., 2014). Sometimes patients in this risk classification have consideration of a method, but this consideration is vague, based on a potential future contingency, and does not include preparatory behaviors (e.g., "I've thought about shooting myself if my wife left me, but I don't own a gun"). For these patients, effective treatment of PTSD, which may be driving suicidal thoughts, is a preferred method for mitigating suicide risk.

The treatment recommendation for patients at intermediate acute risk for suicide is less clear (Holliday et al., 2021a). Patients at intermediate acute risk experience suicidal ideation and have a suicide plan (Wortzel et al., 2014). The characteristic that distinguishes intermediate from high acute risk may only be lack of suicidal intent. Patients in this risk classification have demonstrated ability to be able to maintain safety autonomously (e.g., engaged in treatment and uses a Safety Plan during periods of elevated distress). The decision about whether CPT is indicated for these patients is anchored in confidence in patient's ability to independently maintain safety and the degree to which PTSD symptoms are conceptualized to be driving suicide risk. CPT is unlikely to be appropriate for a patient at intermediate acute risk of suicide with a recent suicide attempt (i.e., past month) and those who have not demonstrated the ability to independently maintain safety in the presence of distress.

Patients determined to be at high acute risk for suicide are not immediately appropriate for CPT (Holliday et al., 2021a). These patients have suicidal ideation, plan, and intent, and lack the ability to independently maintain safety (Wortzel et al., 2014). These circumstances typically warrant a higher level of care, such as hospitalization. Nonetheless, it is important to note that hospitalization, while indicated for some individuals, should always be considered as a last resort, and may be contraindicated at times (Paris, 2004). For patients at high acute risk of suicide, treatment should focus primarily on stabilizing and providing foundational skills for treatment (e.g., skills-based approaches such as dialectical behavior therapy [DBT] or brief cognitive behavioral therapy for suicide prevention [BCBT-SP]) that ultimately facilitate transition to a trauma-focused treatment.

When selecting a skills-focused intervention, clinicians should also consider the larger trajectory of care. For example, interventions with conceptual overlap with CPT (e.g., BCBT-SP) may facilitate transition more easily than interventions that encourage differing approaches to therapy and managing negative automatic thoughts (e.g., accepting rather than reframing cognitions; Holder et al., in press). Importantly, research indicates that treatments focused only on coping skills are not substantially effective in addressing PTSD symptoms in the absence of trauma-focused elements (Harned et al., 2018). Given the importance of ultimately engaging in a trauma-focused treatment, patients who are deemed inappropriate for CPT at one assessment point should be continually re-evaluated as coping skills are developed (Holder et al., in press). As part of shared-decision making, patients should be educated about the short-term purpose of skills-based interventions and the long-term goal to address PTSD symptoms through a trauma-focused psychotherapy is indicated (Holder et al., in press). To further increase the likelihood that trauma-focused psychotherapy will occur upon stabilization, therapists should consider setting a specific, scheduled timeline for re-evaluation (e.g., after every four sessions).

Modifying CPT on the Basis of Suicide Risk

One important modification for individuals at elevated suicide risk is incorporation of suicide risk management approaches into CPT. Safety planning or similar interventions (e.g., Crisis Response Planning) are indicated for patients at intermediate to high acute risk and those at intermediate to high chronic risk prior to initiating CPT. Safety planning is a structured, collaborative process by which patients identify warning signs for suicide, sequential strategies for maintaining safety (i.e., internal coping, external coping, reaching out for help, contacting professional/emergency services). In addition, safety planning incorporates lethal means safety (i.e., making environment safer)—a critical component of suicide prevention. Providers may choose to check-in with patients regarding use of the safety plan and spend time updating the safety plan as needed during the CPT out of session practice review (Holliday et al., 2019a). As the provider progresses through CPT, patients may have a better understanding of concepts introduced in the safety plan. For example, after covering A-B-C worksheets, patients may better be able to identify situations and thoughts that contribute to suicidal ideation. This provides an opportunity to update the safety plan, enhancing cohesion between interventions. Similarly, new skills (e.g., Challenging Beliefs Worksheets, now called Alternative Thoughts Worksheets in the revised CPT manual) can be incorporated as additional tools in the safety plan as they are introduced in CPT.

Regular administration of a structured suicide assessment tool as part of measurement-based care is indicated for patients with suicide risk concerns. While screening measures such as the CSSRS have robust empirical support, should providers be hesitant to include this approach in their clinical care, reviewing the suicide items for self-report measures of depression symptom severity (e.g., Patient Health Questionnaire—9 item version [PHQ-9]) may be one method of integrating risk assessment into routine practice. Nonetheless, providers should be aware that reviewing suicide items on briefer measures, such as the PHQ-9, may create more false-negatives than suicide-specific measures (e.g., CSSRS; Viguera et al., 2015). Additionally, the suicide items on depression screening tools can be ambiguous, conflating thoughts of death with suicidal ideation. Endorsement of these vague items often requires clarification and further assessment of suicidal intent, means, and plan. Finally, depression screening items do not assess for recent suicide attempts, a leading risk factor for future suicidal behavior.

Even for those with low acute suicide risk, this routine suicide risk assessment can be used as a tool to address and monitor potential patient concerns that trauma-focused treatment will exacerbate suicide risk. Similarly, this may also capture dynamic fluctuations in risk due to factors outside of CPT. While initial suicide risk assessment may be more time-intensive, these recommended weekly assessments can be brief and focused on identifying any changes from the previous week (Holliday et al., 2021a).

PTSD-related beliefs also often drive suicide risk. Stuck points that contribute both to PTSD symptom severity and drive suicide risk provide excellent opportunities for CPT intervention. For example, a law enforcement officer experiencing survivor's guilt following the death of a fellow officer may hold the beliefs that "I don't deserve to be alive." and "I should have died with them." Engaging in Socratic dialogue (and assigning worksheets) on these stuck points may be prioritized over other trauma-related beliefs in order to best address suicide risk.

Case Example: Aaron

Aaron's suicide risk is classified using data collected from the CSSRS and clinical interview. First, in conceptualizing his chronic suicide risk, he has several notable risk factors. Relevant to suicidal behavior, he has a history of two prior suicide attempts and has been hospitalized once to prevent a suicide attempt. He endorsed chronic suicidal ideation, meets diagnostic criteria for major depressive disorder and PTSD, has a substantial trauma history, and has limited social support and a turbulent living situation. These characteristics are consistent with *high chronic risk for suicide*. Next, in conceptualizing acute suicide risk, Aaron endorsed current suicidal ideation with consideration of method, substantial current psychosocial stressors (housing instability, unemployment, recent break-up, and recent exposure to IPV) and is endorsing substantial distress due to symptoms of PTSD and depression. He denies a definite suicide plan and intent and has displayed an ability to independently maintain his own safety. He also has awareness of coping skills and demonstrated ability to utilize such skills during periods of distress. Further, despite experiencing recent IPV, he was able to autonomously exit this relationship and access transitional housing and psychotherapy services. He is future-oriented, reports his desire to "get a job and make it," and is committed to engaging in mental health treatment. Based on this assessment, Aaron is at *intermediate acute risk of suicide*.

Patients at intermediate acute suicide risk are appropriate for outpatient treatment, and treatment of associated mental health conditions is often beneficial in reducing this suicide risk. While some modifications to a trauma-focused treatment would be appropriate for a patient at intermediate acute suicide risk (i.e., pre-treatment safety planning session; regular, formal suicide risk assessment; safety plan updates as appropriate based on risk assessment), this level of risk is not a contraindication for trauma-focused psychotherapy. Further, Aaron has completed several rounds of skills-focused psychotherapy without remission of his PTSD symptoms. He has shown the capacity to use these skills as a foundation from which to increase his safety when navigating trauma-focused elements.

As part of the decision-making process for Aaron, the therapist's goal is to help him understand his PTSD diagnosis, learn about PTSD treatment options, make connections between PTSD treatment and his personal treatment goals, and help him to understand how treatment will be flexibly and personally applied to his unique presenting circumstances. Intermediate acute risk for suicide is an important part of these presenting circumstances, and it is not uncommon for patients to share concerns about CPT worsening mental health symptoms, including suicidal ideation. As part of the shared-decision making process, it will be important to talk with Aaron about how to address suicide risk within the context of CPT:

Clinician: *We have several psychotherapy treatments that we typically recommend for treating PTSD, and we have good rates of success with these treatments.*

Aaron: *I'll be honest—I just don't see how. It isn't like we can go back in time and make it not happen. I have been in therapy since I was a kid, what is another year going to do?*

Clinician: *You're right—we can't go back in time and make it not happen. I also hear you about the therapy you have been through since you were a kid—while it has been helpful, it also hasn't really helped your PTSD symptoms. The treatments you have participated in before are very different than what I would recommend for PTSD treatment for you today.*

Aaron: *Different how?*

Clinician: *The treatments that are most effective at treating PTSD are what are called "trauma-focused psychotherapies." These treatments focus on processing the traumas that you have had to live through. Depending on the treatment we choose there may be a different way that we do this processing, but in any of these treatments, the key to addressing the PTSD symptoms is to directly target the traumas you have survived.*

Aaron: *I don't know about all that. You are right—it is different. I have spent my whole life trying to not think about what happened to me. I'm not sure I'm ready to do all that.*

Clinician: *We do have other options that I will mention. We can talk to our psychiatry colleagues and discuss medication options. For some people, medications are helpful in managing PTSD symptoms. There are also non-trauma-focused psychotherapies that we can offer for PTSD. There is a wider range of these non-trauma-focused psychotherapies, but generally they focus on current struggles rather than trauma. We would develop strategies and skills to help you to manage these current day problems. There are two reasons that I bring up these options second. One, these overall are less effective in treating PTSD symptoms. Two, these are much more similar to the types of treatment that you have done in the past that haven't been as helpful. That said, I want to make sure you know all about all of these options so we can make the decision together that works best for you right now.*

Aaron: *I know I have to do something different, because what I have been doing hasn't been working. Do you really think I can handle all that? What if I just get stuck in my head like I always do and end up in a spiral and kill myself?*

Clinician: *However we decide to go forward, I completely agree that suicidal thinking is something we need to pay attention to. As we get started, I think it would be helpful to spend a week or two talking about suicide and some of the skills they taught you in the inpatient program—like a safety plan. After that, I would want us to have conversations each week about where you are at with regard to suicidal thoughts. That way, we can keep an eye out for changes and we are on the same page about what we will do if suicidal thinking does get worse.*

Aaron: *That makes sense to me. Tell me more about these therapies you are suggesting.*

As discussed with Aaron as part of the shared decision-making process, one important aspect of care will be to routinely assess suicide risk throughout the CPT treatment course. The therapist's plan is to administer the CSSRS screening tool at the beginning of each treatment session (alongside other measures of PTSD and depression symptom severity). As with other measurement-based care approaches, providing Aaron with feedback on changes in his suicide risk over time and describing adjustments to the treatment plan corresponding to these changes will facilitate buy-in for completing the measures.

Modifications to CPT and Important Considerations in the Context of Violence Exposure

Similar to suicide risk addressed above, risk of violence exposure creates a challenging tension for clinicians to navigate for patients diagnosed with PTSD. Research on providing CPT to patients at risk of ongoing violence exposure is limited; however, preliminary findings support that CPT is effective and appropriate for those who may be at risk of experiencing ongoing violence. As with suicide risk, delivery of CPT to these patients requires careful assessment of violence risk, incorporation of assessment data into case conceptualization, integration of risk management strategies into CPT, and a flexible, yet high-fidelity, approach to CPT delivery.

Assessment and Appropriateness of CPT in the Context of Risk of Violence Exposure

Risk of ongoing violence exposure can occur due to a patient's neighborhood or current living situation, occupational setting, or social setting (i.e., IPV or domestic violence). When assessing for risk for violence exposure (especially IPV or domestic violence), it is essential that screening occurs individually in a private setting, without others (including intimate partners) present (Doyle et al., 2022). During these processes, patients should be notified of any limits to confidentiality or mandatory reporting requirements prior to screening. While screening tools for violence exposure exist for measuring IPV or domestic violence (e.g., the extended Hurt, Insult, Threaten, Scream tool [E-HITS]; Iverson et al., 2015), standardized measures for other types of violence exposure are not as commonly implemented across healthcare systems (Cowlishaw et al., 2022). Further, tools for stratifying violence risk (e.g., Danger Assessment; Messing et al., 2017) are also less commonly implemented than suicide risk stratification tools, and these tools are typically specifically designed for IPV and domestic violence (Cowlishaw et al., 2022).

In making determinations of the appropriateness of CPT, similar considerations should be made to those of suicide risk—what is the current assessment of safety and how relevant are PTSD symptoms to the conceptualization of current distress? Importantly, patients may never leave the situation that is increasing risk of violence exposure—be that a decision to remain in a relationship, the necessity of living in a particular neighborhood, or the dangers associated with a particular occupation. Clinicians should carefully consider the broad life circumstances of patients in relationships where there is ongoing risk of exposure to violence. For example, patients may depend on abusive partners for financial support or housing, and volatility in the relationship may call into question child custody. Moreover, perpetrators of violence may react to changes in beliefs or improvements in symptoms by attempting to reassert control or increasing threats of violence. Open and transparent dialogue regarding the risks and benefits of continued treatment through shared decision-making is particularly important for these patients to reinforce autonomy and self-efficacy in treatment (Doyle et al., 2022; Sorrentino et al., 2021). This transparency is especially true for patients of minoritized populations (e.g., LGBTQ+, BIPOC) who may experience systemic threats to safety. Further, even in such instances, providers can consider providing resources and potentially referrals (e.g., sexual health screening following sexual assault by partner or relative), should the patient consider accessing these resources in the future.

Modifying CPT on the Basis of Risk of Violence Exposure

After the decision has been made to move forward to CPT, maintaining safety remains a priority of care for those at risk of violence exposure. Considerations for maintaining safety are particularly important and may be more broad for those whose risk of violence exposure comes through IPV (Doyle et al., 2022). In order to maintain safety, clinicians should first complete a safety plan with regard to the risk of IPV. This safety plan may include resources such as emergency shelter numbers as well as actions to take in the face during a violent incident. More information can be found online as well as in the MyPlan Safety app (Glass et al., 2022). Next, clinicians should proactively discuss communication, documentation, and therapy material transmission practices with patients. Discussing with patients how they can refer to treatment (e.g., a "wellness class") can help maintain appropriate privacy. The therapist and patient should consider how to maintain document security and establish a safe setting to complete practice assignments. One potential option is the use of the "CPT Coach" mobile application, which provides a centralized source of materials and is password-secured (Rodriguez-Paras et al., 2017). Another option is to dedicate a space for patients to work on and leave assignments after session. Massed treatment approaches, where CPT is delivered with greater frequency over a shorter period of time, may also provide an opportunity to deliver treatment in a narrow window of safety (Galovski et al., 2022).

When working with patients at increased risk of violence exposure, clinicians should carefully consider stuck points in terms of what is factual vs. what is "stuck." This is particularly true for stuck points related to safety and power/control. Danger may be more likely than possible for some patients. Similarly, power and control may be limited for patients remaining in a violent relationship. When engaging in Socratic dialogue around nuanced stuck points regarding safety and power/control, clinicians should communicate in a way that validates the realities and dangers experienced by patients. The goal of CPT is to identify realistic, balanced beliefs—even though these beliefs at times are not "positive." Consistent with this, studies of delivery of CPT in communities with high risk of violence exposure have hypothesized that increasing realistic beliefs (even when realistic beliefs indicate danger) may reduce PTSD symptoms (Kaysen et al., 2020). Clinically, it is common for patients in abusive relationships to feel empowered when reducing assimilated stuck points related to self-blame (e.g., "I should have known better than to say anything when he was drinking") and modifying all-or-none beliefs about their own autonomy (e.g., "Nothing I do ever makes things better").

Case Example: Aaron

In addition to suicide risk, a safety related concern is Aaron's risk for violence exposure, considering his recent departure from an abusive romantic relationship. However, Aaron has also taken action to remove himself from the abusive relationship. The provider can consider brief screening to assess for exposures between sessions. While there are risks of violence exposure, particularly given his prior reliance on his romantic partner for shelter and financial support, Aaron is at a stage where treatment of his mental health symptoms will be a strong support to maintaining his safety, making CPT a strong treatment option. Reinforcing patient autonomy and reducing clinician/patient power disparities through shared decision-making is also important when working with patients holding marginalized identities and trauma survivors (particularly IPV and military sexual assault survivors).

When describing treatment options with Aaron, it is important to anchor treatment principles to his stated treatment goals. For CPT in particular, it would be important to make connections between stuck points and his desired behavior change in romantic relationships. For instance, his challenges with other-trust (alternating from being overly trusting and untrusting) have impacted relationship selection and challenges with self-trust have impacted his employment, financial situation, and housing. A strong introduction to CPT would help connect the importance of these beliefs in Aaron's recovery, connect the origins of these beliefs to his trauma history, and describe how CPT treatment principles will address these beliefs. More specifically, these stuck points could be targeted during the trust modules with discussion on beliefs surrounding the recent relationship experience.

Modifications to CPT and Important Considerations in the Context of Intense Psychosocial Stressors

Assessing the Appropriateness of CPT in the Context of Intense Psychosocial Stressors

Individuals experiencing intense psychosocial stressors are often simultaneously exposed to trauma. As stated by Dinnen et al. (2014) in their commentary on homeless veterans, "failing to recognize the association between trauma and [intense psychosocial stressors] may lead to further victimization, exacerbate mental health symptomatology, and hinder a provider's ability to effectively intervene on behalf of [patients]." Addressing PTSD is central to assisting patients in navigating situations such as housing instability or criminal–legal involvement. For instance, PTSD, and associated comorbidity (e.g., depression, substance use), may drive factors that exacerbate housing instability or criminogenic behavior (e.g., avoidance resulting in unemployment and insufficient financial resources).

Resources for providing basic needs should also be in place prior to undertaking CPT. Research on providing CPT to individuals experiencing housing instability have been described in residential treatment settings or as part of other programs that provide shelter (Holliday et al., 2021a; Yamokoski et al., 2023) as well as in outpatient settings (Feingold et al., 2018). Consistent with meeting basic needs, a multidisciplinary approach (with referrals to both physical healthcare services and social support services) is typically indicated for those experiencing intense psychosocial stressors (Holliday et al., 2022). Care coordination is critical in multidisciplinary treatment settings as is setting appropriate boundaries and expectations of each team member (Holliday et al., 2022). For patients who begin CPT, this multidisciplinary approach can be an asset to the clinician intending to focus on treating PTSD symptoms. The mental health clinician should be aware of social service and physical health needs and treatment plans, but should defer questions about these needs to the specialized multidisciplinary team member. Frequent team check-ins can provide both clinician and patient confidence in a cohesive treatment plan.

For providers functioning outside of healthcare systems, this multidisciplinary approach may be less accessible. Especially in these cases, clinicians should consider the resource needs and capabilities of their patient. Some patients experiencing housing instability may have the capability of engaging with CPT without additional supports, for example, a patient who is couch surfing with friends or family. However, a patient who is experiencing unsheltered homelessness (e.g., street dwelling) is less likely to have this capability. As with other concerns of risk, clinicians should aim for transparency in the risks and benefits of treatment as well as transparency in their own expertise and capabilities. Referrals to outside agencies that can support housing needs should be strongly considered. When referrals are placed, providers should aim to complete a release of information as early as possible to open lines of multidisciplinary communication.

For patients referred to a treatment court due to mental health-related criminal–legal involvement, it is important for clinicians to consider the individual's level of treatment motivation (and stage of behavior change; Slattery et al., 2013). Nonetheless, CPT and other trauma-focused treatments can help to address relationships between PTSD and criminal–legal involvement (Taylor et al., 2020). As with other patient populations, reinforcing patient autonomy in the treatment process in CPT and anchoring to patient goals (rather than systemic goals) can help boost engagement in CPT for criminal–legal-involved patients. As with patients who are at risk of violence exposure through IPV, there are privacy-related concerns for individuals who are engaging in CPT while incarcerated. Settings may vary in terms of what resources incarcerated individuals have access to in order to maintain appropriate privacy while engaging with CPT. Clinicians working in these settings should work with administrators to identify appropriate options and then proactively problem-solve with patients the options that are most realistic for them.

Modifying CPT for Intense Psychosocial Stressors

A key consideration in the delivery of CPT to individuals experiencing intense psychosocial stressors is the use of an "emergency" session. When patients arrive in the context of an acute stressor, it is oftentimes possible to address this throughout the course of a typical CPT therapy session. While CPT (especially initially) focuses on trauma-related beliefs, the skills and worksheets imparted through CPT are generalizable across life circumstances. Using an ongoing stressor as an example in a worksheet can help patients to make personal connections in the therapy material and learn the scope of the skill. This also helps when psychosocial stressors are functioning as avoidance mechanisms (e.g., crisis of the week). Even when the situation cannot be incorporated into the session content, clinicians can reserve ten to 15 minutes *at the end of session* for problem-solving, solution-generating, and case management.

On some occasions, the seriousness of the stressor may warrant a departure from CPT. Such a session can provide reinforcement of coping skills and review of available resources (e.g., emergency shelters to leave an abusive relationship) that may be beneficial to the patient. When using an emergency session, it is important to allow patients to make the ultimate decision whether to depart from CPT and to make clear such a departure delays addressing and processing traumatic experiences. In these instances, the clinician should clearly note the intention to immediately return to CPT at the next session (Galovski et al., 2020). See Chap. 15 for guidance on diverging from CPT to navigate challenges to optimal therapy outcomes during a course of CPT. Brief departures from CPT to conduct emergency sessions have not been shown to negatively impact outcomes (Galovski et al., 2012).

Consistent with previous sections, proactively problem-solving for out of session practice is important for those facing intense psychosocial stressors (e.g., where to complete practice, where to store therapy materials). Patients who are living in (or have lived through) these intense psychosocial stressors may also present with more entrenched beliefs, particularly with over-accommodated stuck points. Clinicians should identify when to use CPT skills to restructure beliefs versus when beliefs are accurate reflections of challenging life circumstances (Williams et al., 2022). Validating and acknowledging objective reality (including challenges to having basic needs met) is critically important, as is attending to the potentially less accurate perceptions of what these circumstances mean about the patient and/or their future. Striking a balance between validating reality, exploring context, and gently challenging inaccurate perceptions is likely to help build therapeutic rapport while also modelling strong CPT skills.

Case Example: Aaron

Aaron is experiencing several serious psychosocial stressors—housing instability, unemployment, lack of social support, and economic instability. His emergent needs are being met by the local VSO—with temporary shelter as well as access to food and transportation. However, these resources are time-limited. Effective coordination with social work and case management services will be critical for Aaron's long-term recovery. As part of the assessment, therapists should consider the impact of these psychosocial stressors on both the appropriateness and ability to engage with trauma-focused psychotherapy, such as CPT. Aaron currently has access to transitional housing where he can complete between-session work, secure locations to store therapy materials, and access to Internet. However, this may change over the treatment course, and continued assessment and discussion of alternative options with Aaron is warranted.

Aaron's psychosocial stressors are significant and have the strong potential to impact treatment; however, Aaron also has case management support and both the time and willingness to remain engaged with mental health treatment. Delivering trauma-focused psychotherapy to Aaron may require enhanced flexibility in how assignments are delivered or stored, careful coordination with the social work team, and potential incorporation of stressor sessions to assist with the management of psychosocial stressors.

When presenting for the second CPT treatment session, Aaron describes distress from difficulties acquiring and maintaining housing which serves as a challenge to maintaining CPT progress. There are several considerations to weigh—(1) is this an emergency that requires departure from CPT? (2) is this a significant stressor such that therapist should discuss the pros and cons of using an "emergency session" with Aaron and let him decide the course of action? (3) is this avoidance of trauma and therapist should dissuade use of session time to address in order to remain trauma-focused?

Despite elevations in distress, the therapist determines that Aaron's suicide risk is commensurate with his baseline—intermediate acute risk, high chronic risk. In addition, he has strategically placed his safety plan in several locations—photo on his phone, in his wallet, and in his nightstand drawer. With further assessment, the therapist determines Aaron is not at immediate risk of losing housing. He has appropriately connected with his case manager about the concern, and there is a plan in place to move forward with housing. There is not additional problem-solving that could be addressed through an emergency session. Instead, the thoughts and emotions that the patient describes in relation to the stressor can be addressed through CPT tools and are excellent non-trauma-focused A-B-C worksheets for practice after CPT session 2.

Clinician: *Talking through the process with your case manager was the way to go—they know a lot more about getting the housing figured out than I will. That said, the way we think about what is going on with housing and the feelings that come along with it—that is some of the stuff we want to work on in here. So here is what I'm weighing here—getting your housing sorted out is important and very stressful, AND I think CPT can give you some tools to help with emotions that come up around the uncertainty of housing. Like we talked about last week, I also know that avoidance thing is something PTSD draws us into all the time* *that keeps us from moving forward in new ways. The more we stay stuck in avoidance, the harder it is to break out.*

Aaron: *Yeah—I mean, I'm avoiding talking about all this, I'm not going to lie about that. I kind of did part of that impact statement, but I don't think I did it right because it was hard.*

Clinician: *What do you think about this plan—I want to make sure that we have a chance to talk about that impact statement. You put in work on that, and I want us to have the chance to talk about that work. We can make time for us to talk about the housing situation too. I think it will make a great example for us to use when talking about this new CPT tool.*

Aaron: *Anything that you think will help with this housing stress is fine.*

Aaron reads through his impact statement. The therapist praises his effort and uses Socratic dialogue to elicit more information and identify additional stuck points. The therapist and patient discuss the concept of stuck points in more depth and collaboratively identify stuck points in his impact statement. Together, they are able to identify two relevant stuck points (1) I will never get housing and (2) There is nothing I can do to help my housing situation. After discussing the identifying emotions handout, the therapist gives Aaron an introduction to A-B-C sheets and later uses the opportunity to link A-B-C worksheets to Aaron's ongoing stressor.

Clinician: *Now let's apply this to your housing situation. In the "A" column we are looking to identify the situation that brought up the thoughts and emotions. How would you write the situation down on the worksheet?*

Aaron: *Well, my case manager called me and said that my housing was rejected.*

Clinician: *Perfect—that is a great example of a situation. After this situation, you were thinking and feeling a certain way. What we want to do in this sheet is notice the connections between situations, thoughts, and emotions. Which do you think is easier for you to notice, how you were thinking about or feeling about the situation?*

Aaron: *Feeling for sure—I felt pissed and down and like I will never get housing.*

Clinician: *I'm hearing that you identified both feelings AND thoughts in there. Let's figure out how to put these into the sheet. For emotions, we can always use that Identifying Emotions Handout to help us separate the emotions from the thoughts. In what you mentioned, which ones are on the handout?*

Aaron: *Well, pissed is angry and down is sad. I guess that leaves never getting housing.*

Clinician: *Exactly—I would write in pissed and down in "C." What you are left with is "I'm never going to get housing" and that is one of those stuck points we wrote down earlier. We will put that down in "B." Let's check our work. If a friend told you that their case manager said their housing was rejected, could you imagine them saying "I will never get housing?"*

Aaron: *Yeah—I can.*

Clinician: *How would you expect them to feel every time that they told themselves that?*

Aaron: *Pretty down and pretty pissed.*

Clinician: *That gives us confidence that we have filled it out right. We can see the connection between the situation, the thought, and the emotion. We can also see how every time we think that thought, our emotions get stronger and stronger. Now—let's talk the bottom of the form. If your friend told you that thought, would you say it is realistic.*

Aaron: *There aren't guarantees in life—so yeah—it is realistic.*

Clinician: *Alright—is your friend telling himself that helpful? Meaning, is it helping him to get housing or feel better?*

Aaron: *Well no, it isn't helping.*

Clinician: *That's where this next piece comes into play—is there something that your friend could say that is both realistic AND helpful?*

Aaron: *Well, the case manager is trying a bunch of things to help get housing.*

Clinician: *Great example, based on what we talked about before that is absolutely a fact. How might you imagine it would feel different telling yourself "I'll never get housing"* vs. *"the case manager is trying a bunch of things to help get housing."*

Aaron: *A little different—anxious that it might not work.*

Clinician: *What about those pissed off and down feelings?*

Aaron: *Nah—not that so much, which is better in some ways.*

Clinician: *I think we have a great example here—changing the way we think about the situation changes the way we are feeling. Doesn't make everything magically better, but it does give us more manageable emotions based on thoughts that are realistic and helpful. What questions do you have for me about this A-B-C Worksheet?*

When presenting for the sixth CPT treatment session, Aaron again comes with challenges with his housing. Again, the therapist considers making the decision to depart from CPT, collaboratively deciding whether or not to depart from CPT with an "emergency session," or encouraging continuing CPT.

Clinician: *Hi Aaron, good to see you. Let's set our agenda for today. We want to start with our check-in about suicide. Next, I want to talk through the Thinking Patterns worksheets we introduced last week. Last, we will introduce the final worksheet in CPT. What do you think of that plan—anything to add?*

Aaron: *Honestly, I can't do it today. I just can't.*

Clinician: *What is going on?*

Aaron: *The hotel funds ran out—I have to go to a shelter or live on the street. I didn't do any worksheets this week either. I talked with the case manager yesterday, and she has an apartment lined up, but I can't move in until next week. I don't know what to do. I don't feel safe.*

Clinician: *That makes sense why today would be a challenging day to do CPT. I mentioned what we would do with a CPT session today. We could also use this week as an emergency session. We could discuss some problem solving to help you make some short-term housing decisions, talk about ways to maintain your emotional and physical safety, and plan to return to CPT next week after you* *have moved into your apartment. I want to leave it up to you, do you think today should be a CPT session or an emergency session?*

Aaron: *Thanks, I think that today has to be an emergency session.*

As part of the emergency session, it will be important to continue suicide risk assessment and appropriately respond to changes in acute suicide risk. It would be helpful to discuss with Aaron logistics around the physical security of his therapy materials as part of his housing change. Rather than using physical worksheets or printouts of his safety plan, keeping photographs on his phone, digital versions in his phone, or abbreviated versions in his wallet would be most appropriate at this time. As part of problem solving, the therapist can consider consultation with the case manager to ensure that Aaron has an accurate understanding of his current housing options; however, it is important to maintain the role as a mental health provider. As appropriate throughout the emergency session, making connections to CPT materials or concepts will be helpful to maintain a cohesive therapeutic frame. In addition, it will be important to reinforce the temporary deviation from the CPT protocol. If Aaron's housing situation increases in stability as expected, the therapist should plan to quickly return to the CPT protocol. If Aaron's housing situation deteriorates in stability, the therapist will need to think about the most appropriate treatment to most directly impact housing stability.

Summary

Initial research suggests that CPT is safe and effective to deliver to many in the context of suicide risk, risk of exposure to violence, housing instability, and criminal–legal involvement. However, these are understudied areas. Clinical complexity is often the norm, rather than the exception, when treating PTSD with CPT. Nonetheless, CPT can often be delivered effectively despite these factors. An overarching theme of delivering CPT in the context of risk and intense psychosocial stressors is the need for strong assessment, clear case conceptualization, and a flexible approach to CPT delivery. Further, it is important to set up the patient for success by proactively anticipating, discussing, and troubleshooting barriers to care (see Chap. 15 for explicit guidance). Identifying a multidisciplinary team, including case management supports, can help therapists stay focused on the trauma work while ensuring that patients' social needs are being actively addressed. While there may be changes to the scaffolding of CPT, it is notable that the core approaches to CPT are largely unchanged for patients in the context of risk and intense psychosocial stressors. Clinicians should still follow the four key elements of CPT: encouraging expression of natural emotion, using Socratic dialogue, prioritizing assimilated vs. over-accommodated stuck points, and encouraging between-session practice.

Acknowledgments The authors would like to sincerely thank Dr. Amy M. Williams for her mentorship. We appreciate her assistance in conceptualizing and revising this chapter. Further, Dr.

Williams has been instrumental in her support and dissemination of trauma-focused evidence-based treatment, including the training of both authors.

Competing Interests The authors have no conflicts of interest to declare that are relevant to the content of this chapter.

References

Ayano, G., Solomon, M., Tsegay, L., Yohannes, K., & Abraha, M. (2020). A systematic review and meta-analysis of the prevalence of post-traumatic stress disorder among homeless people. *Psychiatric Quarterly, 91*(4), 949–963.

Bakalar, J. L., Carlin, E. A., Blevins, C. L., & Ghahramanlou-Holloway, M. (2017). Generalizability of evidence-based PTSD psychotherapies to suicidal individuals: A review of the Veterans Administration and Department of Defense Clinical Practice Guidelines. *Military Psychology, 28*(5), 331–343.

Baranyi, G., Cassidy, M., Fazel, S., Priebe, S., & Mundt, A. P. (2018). Prevalence of posttraumatic stress disorder in prisoners. *Epidemiologic Reviews, 40*(1), 134–145.

Bennett, A., Crosse, K., Ku, M., Edgar, N. E., Hodgson, A., & Hatcher, S. (2022). Interventions to treat post-traumatic stress disorder (PTSD) in vulnerably housed populations and trauma-informed care: A scoping review. *BMJ Open, 12*(3), e051079.

Blain, R., Pukay-Martin, N., Martin, C., Dutton-Cox, C., & Chard, K. (2021). Residential cognitive processing therapy decreases suicidality by reducing perceived burdensomeness in veterans with posttraumatic stress disorder. *Journal of Traumatic Stress, 34*(6), 1199–1208.

Bohus, M., Kleindienst, N., Hahn, C., Muller-Engelmann, M., Ludascher, P., Steil, R., et al. (2020). Dialectical behavior therapy for posttraumatic stress disorder (DBT-PTSD) compared with cognitive processing therapy (CPT) in complex presentations of PTSD in women survivors of childhood abuse: A randomized clinical trial. *JAMA Psychiatry, 77*(12), 1235–1245.

Brewin, C., Andrews, B., & Valentine, J. (2000). Meta-analysis of risk factors for posttraumatic stress disorder in trauma-exposed adults. *Journal of Consulting and Clinical Psychology, 68*(5), 748–766.

Bryan, C. J., Clemans, T. A., Hernandez, A. M., Mintz, J., Peterson, A. L., Yarvis, J. S., et al. (2016). Evaluating potential iatrogenic suicide risk in trauma-focused group cognitive behavioral therapy for the treatment of PTSD in active duty military personnel. *Depression and Anxiety, 33*(6), 549–557.

Cook, J. M., Dinnen, S., Simiola, V., Thompson, R., & Schnurr, P. P. (2014). VA residential provider perceptions of dissuading factors to the use of two evidence-based PTSD treatments. *Professional Psychology: Research and Prractice, 45*(2), 136–142.

Cowlishaw, S., Sbisa, A., Freijah, I., Kartal, D., Mulligan, A., Notarianni, M., et al. (2022). Health service interventions for intimate partner violence among military personnel and veterans: A framework and scoping review. *International Journal of Environmental Research and Public Health, 19*(6), 3551.

Departments of Veterans Affairs and Defense. (2023). *VA-DoD clinical practice guideline for the management of posttraumatic stress disorder and acute stress disorder*. Author.

Departments of Veterans Affairs and Defense. (2024). *VA-DOD clinical practice guideline for the assessment and management of patients at risk for suicide*. Author.

Dinnen, S., Kane, V., & Cook, J. M. (2014). Trauma-informed care: A paradigm shift needed for services with homeless veterans. *Professional Case Management, 19*(4), 161–170.

Dondanville, K. A., Fina, B. A., Straud, C. L., Tyler, H., Jacoby, V., Blount, T. H., et al. (2022). Evaluating a community-based training program for evidence-based treatments for PTSD using the RE-AIM framework. *Psychological Services, 19*(4), 740–750.

Doyle, K. W., Knetig, J. A., & Iverson, K. M. (2022). Practical implications of research on intimate partner violence experiences for the mental health clinician. *Current Treatment Options in Psychiatry, 9*(3), 280–300.

Ennis, N., Sijercic, I., & Monson, C. M. (2021). Trauma-focused cognitive-behavioral therapies for posttraumatic stress disorder under ongoing threat: A systematic review. *Clinical Psychology Review, 88*, 102049.

Feingold, Z. R., Fox, A. B., & Galovski, T. E. (2018). Effectiveness of evidence-based psychotherapy for posttraumatic distress within a jail diversion program. *Psychological Services, 15*(4), 409–418.

Forehand, J. A., Dufort, V., Gradus, J. L., Maguen, S., Watts, B. V., Jiang, T., et al. (2022). Association between post-traumatic stress disorder severity and death by suicide in US military veterans: Retrospective cohort study. *British Journal of Psychiatry, 221*(5), 676–682.

Fovet, T., Wathelet, M., Amad, A., Horn, M., Belet, B., Benradia, I., et al. (2021). Trauma exposure and PTSD among men entering jail: A comparative study with the general population. *Journal of Psychiatric Research, 145*, 205–212.

Galovski, T. E., Blain, L. M., Mott, J. M., Elwood, L., & Houle, T. (2012). Manualized therapy for PTSD: Flexing the structure of cognitive processing therapy. *Journal of Consulting and Clinical Psychology, 80*(6), 968–981.

Galovski, T. E., Nixon, R. D. V., & Kaysen, D. (2020). *Flexible applications of cognitive processing therapy: Evidence-based treatment methods*. Academic Press.

Galovski, T. E., Werner, K. B., Weaver, T. L., Morris, K. L., Dondanville, K. A., Nanney, J., et al. (2022). Massed cognitive processing therapy for posttraumatic stress disorder in women survivors of intimate partner violence. *Psychological Trauma: Theory, Research, Practice, Policy, 14*(5), 769–779.

Glass, N., Clough, A., Messing, J. T., Bloom, T., Brown, M. L., Eden, K. B., Campbell, J. C., Gielen, A., Laughon, K., Grace, K. T., Turner, R. M., Alvarez, C., Case, J., Barnes-Hoyt, J., Alhusen, J., Hanson, G. C., & Perrin, N. A. (2022). Longitudinal impact of the my plan app on health and safety among college women experiencing partner violence. *Journal of Interpersonal Violence, 37*(13–14), 11436–11459.

Haagen, J. F., Smid, G. E., Knipscheer, J. W., & Kleber, R. J. (2015). The efficacy of recommended treatments for veterans with PTSD: A metaregression analysis. *Clinical Psychology Review, 40*, 184–194.

Hamblen, J. L., Norman, S. B., Sonis, J. H., Phelps, A. J., Bisson, J. I., Nunes, V. D., et al. (2019). A guide to guidelines for the treatment of posttraumatic stress disorder in adults: An update. *Psychotherapy, 56*(3), 359–373.

Harned, M. S., Gallop, R. J., & Valenstein-Mah, H. R. (2018). What changes when? The course of improvement during a stage-based treatment for suicidal and self-injuring women with borderline personality disorder and PTSD. *Psychotherapy Research, 28*(5), 761–775.

Holder, N., Ranney, R. M., Delgado, A. K., Purcell, N., Iwamasa, G. Y., Batten, A., Neylan, T. C., Shiner, B., & Maguen, S. (in press). Transitioning into trauma-focused evidence-based psychotherapy for posttraumatic stress disorder from other treatments: A qualitative investigation. *Cognitive Behaviour Therapy*. Available Online Ahead of Print. https://doi.org/10.1080/16506073.2024.2408386

Holliday, R., Holder, N., Monteith, L. L., & Suris, A. (2018a). Decreases in suicide cognitions after cognitive processing therapy among veterans with posttraumatic stress disorder due to military sexual trauma: A preliminary examination. *Journal of Nervous and Mental Disease, 206*(7), 575–578.

Holliday, R., Monteith, L., & Wortzel, H. (2018b). Understanding, assessing, and conceptualizing suicide risk among veterans with posttraumatic stress. *Federal Practicioner, 35*(4), 24–27.

Holliday, R., Rozek, D. C., Smith, N. B., McGarity, S., Jankovsky, M., & Monteith, L. L. (2019a). Safety planning to prevent suicidal self-directed violence among veterans with posttraumatic stress disorder: Clinical considerations. *Professional Psychology: Research and Practice, 50*(4), 215–227.

Holliday, R., Holder, N., Olson-Madden, J. H., & Monteith, L. L. (2019b). Treating posttraumatic stress disorder in the presence of acute suicide risk in veterans and active duty service members: A call for research. *Journal of Nervous and Mental Disease, 207*(7), 611–614.

Holliday, R., Borges, L. M., Stearns-Yoder, K. A., Hoffberg, A. S., Brenner, L. A., & Monteith, L. L. (2020). Posttraumatic stress disorder, suicidal ideation, and suicidal self-directed violence among U.S. military personnel and veterans: A systematic review of the literature from 2010 to 2018. *Frontiers in Psycholology, 11*, 1998.

Holliday, R., Holder, N., Williams, A. M., & Monteith, L. L. (2021a). Treating PTSD in the context of concurrent suicide risk: Current evidence and navigating complicating factors. *Current Treatment Options in Psychiatry, 8*(4), 213–228.

Holliday, R., Gross, G. M., Desai, A., Smith, N. B., & Harpaz-Rotem, I. (2021b). A preliminary investigation of VA PTSD residential treatment for veterans admitted from unstable housing or incarceration. *Journal of Social Distress and Homelessness, 31*(2), 238–243.

Holliday, R., Desai, A., Stimmel, M., Liu, S., Monteith, L. L., & Stewart, K. E. (2022). Meeting the health and social service needs of veterans who interact with the criminal justice system and experience homelessness: A holistic conceptualization and recommendations for tailoring care. *Current Treatment Options in Psychiatry, 9*(3), 174–185.

Iverson, K. M., Gradus, J. L., Resick, P. A., Suvak, M. K., Smith, K. F., & Monson, C. M. (2011a). Cognitive-behavioral therapy for PTSD and depression symptoms reduces risk for future intimate partner violence among interpersonal trauma survivors. *Journal of Consulting and Clinical Psychology, 79*(2), 193–202.

Iverson, K. M., Resick, P. A., Suvak, M. K., Walling, S., & Taft, C. T. (2011b). Intimate partner violence exposure predicts PTSD treatment engagement and outcome in cognitive processing therapy. *Behavior Therapy, 42*(2), 236–248.

Iverson, K. M., King, M. W., Gerber, M. R., Resick, P. A., Kimerling, R., Street, A. E., & Vogt, D. (2015). Accuracy of an intimate partner violence screening tool for female VHA patients: A replication and extension. *Journal of Traumatic Stress, 28*(1), 79–82.

Iverson, K., Rossi, F., Nillni, Y., Fox, A., & Galovski, T. (2022). PTSD and depression symptoms increase women's risk for experiencing future intimate partner violence. *International Journal of Environmental Research and Public Health, 19*(19), 12217.

Jaffe, A. E., DiLillo, D., Gratz, K. L., & Messman-Moore, T. L. (2019). Risk for revictimization following interpersonal and noninterpersonal trauma: Clarifying the role of posttraumatic stress symptoms and trauma-related cognitions. *Journal of Traumatic Stress, 32*(1), 42–55.

Kaysen, D., Stappenbeck, C. A., Carroll, H., Fukunaga, R., Robinette, K., Dworkin, E. R., et al. (2020). Impact of setting insecurity on cognitive processing therapy implementation and outcomes in eastern Democratic Republic of the Congo. *European Journal of Psychotraumatology, 11*(1), 1735162.

Kessler, R. C., Aguilar-Gaxiola, S., Alonso, J., Benjet, C., Bromet, E. J., Cardoso, G., et al. (2017). Trauma and PTSD in the WHO world mental health surveys. *European Journal of Psychotraumatology, 8*(5), 1353383.

LoSavio, S. T., Holder, N., Wells, S. Y., & Resick, P. A. (2024). Clinician concerns about cognitive processing therapy: A review of the evidence. *Cognitive and Behavioral Practice, 31*(2), 152–175.

Marques, L., Eustis, E. H., Dixon, L., Valentine, S. E., Borba, C. P. C., Simon, N., et al. (2016). Delivering cognitive processing therapy in a community health setting: The influence of Latino culture and community violence on posttraumatic cognitions. *Psychological Trauma: Theory, Research, Practice, Policy, 8*(1), 98–106.

Messing, J. T., Campbell, J. C., & Snider, C. (2017). Validation and adaptation of the danger assessment-5: A brief intimate partner violence risk assessment. *Journal of Advanced Nursing, 73*(12), 3220–3230.

Paris, J. (2004). Is hospitalization useful for suicidal patients with borderline personality disorder? *Journal of Personality Disorders, 18*(3), 240–247.

Peterson, A. L., Foa, E. B., Resick, P. A., Hoyt, T. V., Straud, C. L., Moore, B. A., et al. (2020). A nonrandomized trial of prolonged exposure and cognitive processing therapy for combat-related posttraumatic stress disorder in a deployed setting. *Behavior Therapy, 51*(6), 882–894.

Posner, K., Brown, G. K., Stanley, B., Brent, D. A., Yershova, K. V., Oquendo, M. A., et al. (2011). The Columbia-suicide severity rating scale: Initial validity and internal consistency findings from three multisite studies with adolescents and adults. *American Journal of Psychiatry, 168*(12), 1266–1277.

Resick, P. A., Nishith, P., Weaver, T. L., Astin, M. C., & Feuer, C. A. (2002). A comparison of cognitive-processing therapy with prolonged exposure and a waiting condition for the treatment of chronic posttraumatic stress disorder in female rape victims. *Journal of Consulting and Clinical Psychology, 70*(4), 867–879.

Roberge, E. M., Harris, J. A., Weinstein, H. R., & Rozek, D. C. (2021). Treating veterans at risk for suicide: An examination of the safety, tolerability, and outcomes of cognitive processing therapy. *Journal of Traumatic Stress, 34*(6), 1228–1237.

Rodriguez-Paras, C., Tippey, K., Brown, E., Sasangohar, F., Creech, S., Kum, H. C., et al. (2017). Posttraumatic stress disorder and mobile health: App investigation and scoping literature review. *JMIR mHealth and uHealth, 5*(10), e156.

Rosen, C. S., Matthieu, M. M., Wiltsey Stirman, S., Cook, J. M., Landes, S., Bernardy, N. C., et al. (2016). A review of studies on the system-wide implementation of evidence-based psychotherapies for posttraumatic stress disorder in the veterans health administration. *Admistration and Policy in Ment Health and Mental Health Services Research, 43*(6), 957–977.

Rozek, D. C., Baker, S. N., Rugo, K. F., Steigerwald, V. L., Sippel, L. M., Holliday, R., et al. (2022). Addressing co-occurring suicidal thoughts and behaviors and posttraumatic stress disorder in evidence-based psychotherapies for adults: A systematic review. *Journal of Traumatic Stress, 35*(2), 729–745.

Saxon, A. J., Davis, T. M., Sloan, K. L., McKnight, K. M., McFall, M. E., & Kivlahan, D. R. (2001). Trauma, symptoms of posttraumatic stress disorder, and associated problems among incarcerated veterans. *Psychiatric Services, 52*(7), 959–964.

Schnurr, P. P., Chard, K. M., Ruzek, J. I., Chow, B. K., Resick, P. A., Foa, E. B., et al. (2022). Comparison of prolonged exposure vs cognitive processing therapy for treatment of posttraumatic stress disorder among US veterans: A randomized clinical trial. *JAMA Network Open, 5*(1), e2136921.

Slattery, M., Dugger, M. T., Lamb, T. A., & Williams, L. (2013). Catch, treat, and release: Veteran treatment courts address the challenges of returning home. *Substance Use and Misuse, 48*(10), 922–932.

Sorrentino, A. E., Iverson, K. M., Tuepker, A., True, G., Cusack, M., Newell, S., & Dichter, M. E. (2021). Mental health care in the context of intimate partner violence: Survivor perspectives. *Psychological Services, 18*(4), 512–522.

Surís, A., Link-Malcolm, J., Chard, K., Ahn, C., & North, C. (2013). A randomized clinical trial of cognitive processing therapy for veterans with PTSD related to military sexual trauma. *Journal of Traumatic Stress, 26*(1), 28–37.

Taylor, E. N., Timko, C., Nash, A., Owens, M. D., Harris, A. H. S., & Finlay, A. K. (2020). Posttraumatic stress disorder and justice involvement among military veterans: A systematic review and meta-analysis. *Journal of Traumatic Stress, 33*(5), 804–812.

Tsai, J., Schick, V., Hernandez, B., & Pietrzak, R. H. (2020). Is homelessness a traumatic event? Results from the 2019–2020 national health and resilience in veterans study. *Depression and Anxiety, 37*(11), 1137–1145.

Valentine, S. E., Borba, C. P., Dixon, L., Vaewsorn, A. S., Guajardo, J. G., Resick, P. A., et al. (2017). Cognitive processing therapy for Spanish-speaking Latinos: A formative study of a model-driven cultural adaptation of the manual to enhance implementation in a usual care setting. *Journal of Clinical Psychology, 73*(3), 239–256.

Viguera, A. C., Milano, N., Laurel, R., Thompson, N. R., Griffith, S. D., Baldessarini, R. J., & Katzan, I. L. (2015). Comparison of electronic screening for suicidal risk with the patient

health questionnaire item 9 and the Columbia suicide severity rating scale in an outpatient psychiatric clinic. *Psychosomatics, 56*(5), 460–469.
Williams, A. M., Baier, A. L., Woolley, M. G., & Galovski, T. E. (2022). Integrating social determinants of health within cognitive therapy. *Current Treatment Options in Psychiatry, 9*(3), 215–228.
Wortzel, H. S., Homaifar, B., Matarazzo, B., & Brenner, L. A. (2014). Therapeutic risk management of the suicidal patient: Stratifying risk in terms of severity and temporality. *Journal of Psychiatric Practice, 20*(1), 63–67.
Yamokoski, C., Flores, H., Facemire, V., Maieritsch, K., Perez, S., & Fedynich, A. (2023). Feasibility of an intensive outpatient treatment program for posttraumatic stress disorder within the veterans health care administration. *Psychological Services, 20*(3), 506–515.
Yim, S., Lorenz, H., & Salkovskis, P. (2024). The effectiveness and feasibility of psychological interventions for populations under ongoing threat: A systematic review. *Trauma, Violence, & Abuse, 25*(1), 577–592.
Zielinski, M. J., Smith, M. K. S., Kaysen, D., Selig, J. P., Zaller, N. D., Curran, G., & Kirchner, J. E. (2022). A participant-randomized pilot hybrid II trial of group cognitive processing therapy for incarcerated persons with posttraumatic stress and substance use disorder symptoms: Study protocol and rationale. *Health Justice, 10*(1), 30.

Chapter 12
Cultural Adaptation of Cognitive Processing Therapy: Fidelity Consistent Treatment Adaptations for the Global Majority

Debra L. Kaysen and Luzimar Vega

"Mental health and wellbeing are fundamental to quality of life, enabling people to experience life as meaningful and to be creative and active citizens" (World Health Organization, 2005, pg. 17). In 2005, Member States of the World Health Organization (WHO) European Region convened with the intent of developing action plans to address the growing burden and impact of mental and behavioral disorders. Despite bringing this issue to the front of the global stage, mental illness and behavioral disorders remain responsible for 32% of the world's years lived with disability (Kilbourne et al., 2018) and 7.4% of the global burden of disease (Becker & Kleinman, 2013). The sobering reality is that mental and behavioral disorders remain the number one cause of disability globally (Wainberg et al., 2017).

Trauma exposure is an associated risk factor for various mental and behavioral disorders, thus contributing to the global burden of disease (Atwoli et al., 2015; Hoppen et al., 2021; Koenen et al., 2017). Globally, the potential exposure to trauma varies widely between countries, but most individuals are likely to experience at least one potentially traumatic event throughout their lifetime (Benjet et al., 2016; Hoppen et al., 2021; Magruder et al., 2017). While various potentially traumatic events (e.g., motor vehicle accident; natural disaster; physical/sexual assault; the murder/suicide of a loved one) can lead to psychological distress, exposure to ongoing conflict and the aftermath of these events increases the risk for psychological dysfunction, including posttraumatic stress disorder (PTSD; Atwoli et al., 2015). In 43 countries with a history of war between 1989 and 2019, almost all of which were

D. L. Kaysen (✉)
Department of Psychiatry & Behavioral Sciences, Stanford University, Palo Alto, CA, USA
e-mail: dkaysen@stanford.edu

L. Vega
James A. Haley Veterans' Hospital, Department of Veteran Affairs, Tampa, FL, USA
e-mail: Luzimar.Vega@va.gov

J. S. Wachen, T. E. Galovski (eds.), *Cognitive Processing Therapy for Complex Cases*, CBT: Science Into Practice,
https://doi.org/10.1007/978-3-031-87356-0_12

classified as low/middle income countries (LMIC), rates of PTSD were estimated at 26.51%, with approximately 316 million adult war survivors endorsing symptoms of PTSD and/or depression (Hoppen et al., 2021). Upwards of 75% of individuals in LMIC's with a psychological or behavioral health problem do not have access to care (Becker & Kleinman, 2013). Further, despite accounting for 80% of the global population, individuals in LMIC's account for less than 20% of those utilizing resources (Magruder et al., 2017). This disparity is not unique to LMIC's, as in some high-income countries only one third of those in need of mental health care have access to it, with lower income and diverse communities in high-income countries experiencing the majority of the disparity in provision of that care (Kilbourne et al., 2018). The chasm that is the global mental health treatment gap is further perpetuated by limited resources, poor mental health infrastructure, lack of providers with adequate training, lack of culturally competent providers, stigma associated with mental health, stigma associated with being a mental health provider, poorly adapted treatment materials, and ongoing conflicts (Becker & Kleinman, 2013; Kazlauskas, 2017; McClendon et al., 2020; Wainberg et al., 2017).

As covered throughout this book, cognitive processing therapy (CPT) was developed to treat sexual assault survivors struggling with symptoms of PTSD. Over time, CPT has been updated, developed, and validated as a modality effective in addressing symptoms of PTSD resulting from a variety of traumas (Resick et al., 2017). At the time of this chapter, CPT has been adapted and modified for a variety of settings (e.g., Egypt, Democratic Republic of Congo, Northern Iraq, Southern Iraq, China, Japan, Germany, Israel) and populations (e.g., Native Americans, Bosnian refugees, Karen refugees, Syrian refugees, Congolese refugees, Latino). CPT has been translated into various languages, including French, Spanish, German, Arabic, Kurdi, Chinese, Japanese, and Ukrainian. Lastly, CPT has been adapted for those with limited cognitive or literacy skills. Adaptations across CPT vary and have utilized the input of experts within the target communities in order to review and modify the materials accordingly (Kaysen et al., 2013; Pearson et al., 2019; Valentine et al., 2017). Such modifications can include changes in language, the content of the modules, or how the materials are utilized. The goal of this chapter is to help bridge the gap between theory and practice so that providers are able to identify and implement appropriate adaptations for CPT with diverse populations.

Culture is multifaceted and includes aspects of one's identity such as ethnicity, race, gender identity, country of origin, religion, sexual orientation, language, able-bodiedness, socioeconomic status, and age, along with many other characteristics, in combination, and makes up who we are (Alizadeh & Chavan, 2016; Zolfaghari et al., 2016). Culture is not static, but instead changes over time with new experiences and learning. In understanding mental health, cultural norms, mores, stories, societal structures, and language all impact the understanding of mental health to include mental health education, assessment, diagnosis, and intervention (Qureshi et al., 2021). It includes cultural understandings of the origin of symptoms, as well as beliefs about recovery. Moreover, culture in psychotherapy occurs as part of a dyadic, or in the case of group, multifaceted, relational, and reciprocal set of relationships (Kousteni, 2022).

Although the medical model of psychopathology treats mental health disorders as fixed and independent of culture, there remain open questions regarding the cross-cultural applicability of diagnostic lexicons and resulting treatments which have historically been developed in high-income countries when applied to individuals from markedly different cultures and settings (Gopalkrishnan, 2018; Nadkarni et al., 2024; Subudhi, 2014). Without considering the implications of both culture and context, diagnoses and treatments may be less acceptable and less effective for the populations that need them. This argues for the need for thoughtful, culturally competent, and fidelity-congruent adaptations for CPT to ensure its relevancy and effectiveness across populations.

Cultural adaptation can be thought of as the systematic modification of a treatment, in this case CPT, to match the culture, language, and context of a client in a way that makes the treatment a better match for their values and beliefs (Ennis et al., 2020; Heim & Kohrt, 2019). In adaptation, there is a continuum from implementing treatments as they were developed, adaptation to increase the cultural fit, and developing new treatments for each new cultural group (Hwang, 2009). In addition, there is a tension in knowing when to focus on the individual in the room versus generalizing within a cultural group, given the risks of stereotyping or being overly reductionist.

A large systematic review of the literature on adaptation of treatments highlighted differing aspects of adaptation, including the target of adaptation (i.e., what is modified), the degree of adaptation, and the process of adaptation (Hall et al., 2016). Targets of adaptation include modification of the content, including adding, deleting, or modifying components of the intervention, altering aspects of intervention delivery via changing the type of provider (e.g., lay providers, healthcare workers) or treatment modality (e.g., telehealth, mobile health, changing worksheets), and considering the context of intervention delivery such as altering the setting within which an intervention is delivered (e.g., church, primary care). There is also an emphasis on not altering core components, or key aspects of fidelity, as these types of modifications are seen as risky and may reduce the efficacy of interventions (Miller et al., 2020; Wiltsey Stirman et al., 2017). This, of course, presumes that we are able to accurately identify what the core components are of any given intervention.

Degree of adaptation refers to the level of adaptation ranging from surface to deep adaptations (Resnicow et al., 2000). Surface-level structural adaptations are those that address the fit of the intervention for the population through making changes to observable characteristics. Examples of surface-level modifications include using culturally appropriate messages, language, and materials to improve appeal, acceptability, and face validity of the intervention. Deep structural changes are those that address factors that may be unique to a specific group and include historical, cultural, environmental, and social factors such as norms, beliefs about causality of symptoms or theoretical models of recovery, core values, and world views.

Stakeholder involvement in the process of adaptation has also been varied across studies and can include intervention developers or experts, practitioners, community leaders or implementers, individuals from the community, and/or people with lived experience (Ennis et al., 2020; Naeem et al., 2023; Orengo-Aguayo et al., 2020; Valentine et al., 2017). The way in which these stakeholders might be involved also can vary. This can include involving stakeholders through key informant interviews, focus groups, community based participatory research, and standing stakeholder committees.

Research Support

There have now been several studies where CPT has been adapted in low and middle income countries. This includes research conducted in the Democratic Republic of Congo (DRC), Northern Iraq, Southern Iraq, Egypt, and Tanzania (Bass et al., 2013; Bolton et al., 2014; ElBarazi, et al., 2022; Greene et al., 2021; Weiss et al., 2015). Adaptations, when they are described in the research literature, tend to consist of modifications to content, delivery, and modality (Ennis et al., 2020). Modifications across these studies have overall been relatively modest and have included reducing the jargon in the manual, describing concepts behaviorally, delivery by non-mental health professionals via task sharing, and including more content on basic mental health and psychotherapy techniques.

Generally, CPT adapted for communities in LMIC's has demonstrated efficacy across outcomes. CPT has demonstrated large and consistent reductions in PTSD symptoms in DRC, Iraq, Egypt, and Tanzania (Bass et al., 2013; Bolton et al., 2014; ElBarazi, et al., 2022; Greene et al., 2021; Weiss et al., 2015). CPT also has demonstrated reductions in other comorbid conditions, including depression, anxiety, substance use, percent of days abstinent, and traumatic grief (Bass et al., 2013, Elbarazi et al., 2022; Greene et al., 2021; Weiss et al., 2015). Secondary outcomes such as perceived stigma, emotional support seeking, dissociation, social functioning, and substance use risk factors have also improved (Hall et al., 2014; Murray et al., 2018). In DRC and Northern Iraq, CPT was associated with improved daily functioning, although this was not found for CPT delivered in Southern Iraq (Bass et al., 2013; Bolton et al., 2014; Weiss et al., 2015). Moreover, in a 6-year follow-up of group CPT delivered to sexual assault survivors in the DRC, CPT was found to have long-term effects, with approximately half of the women maintaining treatment gains (Bass et al., 2022). In general, this study found low rates of relapse, with relapse rates for PTSD, depression, and anxiety of around 20%. This is largely comparable to relapse rates found in studies conducted in the United States. Overall, this body of research supports the use of CPT, with some adaptation, across a wide range of diverse populations and contexts.

Specific Cultural Adaptations for CPT

For work in many LMIC's, adaptations needed to be made for the treatment context (Bernal & Adames, 2017; Chen et al., 2017). This includes adaptations for working with clients with lower levels of literacy. In some settings, such as in Northern Iraq, literacy varied based on gender and whether individuals were in rural or urban locations (Bolton et al., 2014). In other settings, such as the DRC, treatment was being provided in almost exclusively low literacy contexts (Bass et al., 2013). These adaptations included using pictures as cues for core CPT skills, working daily practice of skills into people's everyday routines (such as following prayer), or simplifying the CPT skills so they could be memorized (Kaysen et al., 2013). Other changes may be less about culture and more about working in low resource contexts, with a limited mental health workforce (Bolton, 2019). This may be leveraging community health workers or nurses, or utilizing NGO staff or paraprofessionals. This can also involve modifications in where CPT may be delivered, such as in refugee camps, in people's homes, in libraries, or in community health clinics. Treatment delivery location may at times reflect access to space and expediency but also can reflect cultural values. For example, for Bosnian refugees in the United States, treatment was often delivered in people's homes, as coming to the clinic was seen as a barrier due to agoraphobia and concerns about stigma (Schulz, Huber, & Resick, 2006). In Iraq, sessions were, at times, held in libraries when there were concerns about patient privacy in being seen coming to the clinic.

Other changes made to CPT reflect changes needed to increase cultural fit. For example, given a lack of a talk therapy tradition in the DRC, CPT added in a session of psychoeducation on what talk therapy is and on group therapy (Bass et al., 2013). In Iraq, based on feedback from the clinicians, the Patterns of Problematic Thinking worksheet (now called Thinking Patterns Worksheet) was dropped from CPT due to being seen as too abstract (Kaysen et al., 2013). There may be modifications needed to capture how trauma influences people's stuck points. For example, the CPT module on esteem did not resonate with the Kurdish community in Northern Iraq (Kaysen et al., 2013). After discussing the symptoms associated with the Esteem module, the topic was changed to Respect which included respect for self and others, including one's tribe and community. In Iraq as well, to address concerns about therapists and clients of opposite gender being alone together for clients from more conservative religious backgrounds, clients were allowed to have a family member of their choosing present for sessions. This increased cultural fit as well as safety for clients and therapists. In working with a rural community of Native Americans, content on historical trauma and stuck points was added, as were culturally specific stories, examples, and metaphors (Pearson et al., 2019).

Consideration should be given to what examples or metaphors are used throughout the course of therapy. For example, when describing cognitive theory to a patient, the example of distinguishing between types of furniture may be used to explain this concept. However, that example may not resonate as readily with patients of different backgrounds. Instead, the use of examples and metaphors that are congruent with individual patient's lived experiences improves the applicability and adaptability of the protocol across populations. A therapist could use differentiating between type of animals or types of vehicles, depending on the setting and experiences of the client. Other metaphors commonly used in CPT are metaphors illustrating the importance of between-session practice. Clinicians may use learning a sport, schoolwork, or a musical instrument as metaphors for the importance of sustained practice in building up a skill. However, this example will be more meaningful if it fits skills that individuals in that context are using. For rural women in the Democratic Republic of Congo, for example, we used the example of learning to cook or sew, which was something that many of the women learned and which was something that got better with practice. Learning a sport or homework from school would not have been meaningful metaphors for the Congolese women.

In sum, adaptations may include changing where treatment is delivered, aspects of the content of CPT, and use of metaphors and examples that best fit the current setting. However, key aspects of CPT such as the use of Socratic dialogue, the focus on assimilated beliefs prior to over-accommodated beliefs, and the core components of teaching cognitive flexibility, reducing avoidance, and creating space for emotional processing remain intact.

Engaging in culturally sensitive treatment doesn't begin at session 1 of CPT, but instead begins prior to the first encounter. Considering how mental health and symptom presentation manifest and are interpreted by those of other cultures is a core piece of this process. Although the DSM-5 provides a helpful framework clinically and empirically for CPT, the diagnostic labels may not be meaningful for our clients and may not fit their way of understanding their symptoms. Developing sensitivity thus requires providers to understand the nuance of mental health for such individuals and how to bridge the gap for treatment purposes while still building a treatment rationale. Let's look at a case example in order to illustrate this point:

Case Example

Mr. Sanchez is a 65-year-old Puerto Rican male who transitioned to live with his daughter in a local city after hurricane Maria destroyed his home in 2017. Mr. Sanchez has a history of cardiovascular problems and lost his left leg below the knee several years prior secondary to chronic limb ischemia. Following an appointment with his cardiologist, a referral to mental health was placed. After completing the initial evaluation, he was diagnosed with PTSD and scheduled for follow-up to discuss the diagnosis and treatment options.

Therapist: *Thank you again for making it in today Mr. Sanchez.*
Mr. Sanchez*: Of course.*
Therapist: *I wanted to take time today to go over the results of the evaluation and talk about some potential treatment options. Does that sound ok?*
Mr. Sanchez: *Sure. No problem.*

Therapist: *We talked about a lot of things that have happened in your life and the different symptoms you are experiencing now. Based on everything we talked about, it appears that you are struggling with symptoms of posttraumatic stress disorder, or PTSD. What are your thoughts about that?*

Mr. Sanchez: *PTSD? What is that?*

Therapist: *PTSD is a mental illness that can happen after we experience a trauma.*

Mr. Sanchez: *Mental illness? Trauma? I don't have those. I came here because of my heart, not because of some trauma or mental thing.*

Therapist: *Yes, your cardiologist sent you here because of some things you two discussed. From what you and I also talked about, you described having a lot of different symptoms after hurricane Maria.*

Mr. Sanchez: *Yes, but that's because of my health problems.*

Therapist: *You do have health problems but you also have PTSD. I know that can sound scary, but the good news is that we have treatments that work to address the symptoms so that they aren't impacting you.*

Mr. Sanchez: *No, that doesn't sound right. I don't know about this PTSD.*

Therapist: *It can be really scary for some people hearing that they have a diagnosis. What worries you about the diagnosis of PTSD?*

Mr. Sanchez*: I am not scared or worried. I just don't have PTSD. I have a heart condition. Why is no one taking that seriously?*

As you can see, the client in this example is not open to the diagnosis or the potential treatment options, which were only worsened given the provider's approach to the discussion with the client. Let's see what happens when things slow down and space is given to consider the patient's perspective.

Therapist: *Thank you again for making it in today Mr. Sanchez.*

Mr. Sanchez: *Of course.*

Therapist: *I wanted to take time today to go over the results of the evaluation and talk about some potential treatment options. Does that sound ok?*

Mr. Sanchez*: Sure. But I still don't see why I'm here.*

Therapist: *Thank you. I know that you and I went over a lot of information in the first two sessions together about your history and what's been going on.*

Mr. Sanchez: *Yeah, it was a lot.*

Therapist: *It was, and I really appreciate you taking the time to go over it all with me as I think there are things that can help. In going over everything that's happened, it really sounded to me like you experienced a lot of changes after hurricane Maria.*

Mr. Sanchez*: I really did.*

Therapist: *Do you remember what things you noticed about those changes?*

Mr. Sanchez*: Yes. Well, prior to Maria I had some health issues but I feel like those were better. I was taking my medications and following what my doctor was saying. After Maria they all got worse.*

Therapist*: What were the things that got worse?*

Mr. Sanchez: *Well, I noticed I had to take more of my heart medications as I felt like I was going to have a heart attack almost every day. That really worried me. My* *sleep also has not been good and I have bad dreams. I feel a lot of tension all the time and my daughter keeps saying that I am always irritable and tense in the home. I don't want to be that way but I can't help it. We also got into a fight a few days ago because she wants to take me to visit Puerto Rico and I just can't. I got really upset and she doesn't seem to understand how it will affect me. I feel like it will give me a heart attack.*

Therapist: *You've really described how worried you've been about your health and how it got worse after Maria. It has made things difficult at home with your daughter and her family. You have been focused on getting better and are frustrated that you aren't seeing any progress.*

Mr. Sanchez: *Exactly. I have been listening to my doctor and trying things but I am not getting better. It's why my doctor said I should come to see you. But I don't think I need a psychologist.*

Therapist: *You have been working really hard and he wanted to make sure you got all the support you need. In thinking about all of these negative changes, I am curious if you've noticed how these heart experiences, tension, and irritability change when you think about what happened during the hurricane?*

Mr. Sanchez*: I don't know…I mean I haven't really thought about that. [pauses] When I stop and think, my heart gets worse when I think about the hurricane. Just the thought of going back to Puerto Rico made me feel like I did during the hurricane. I don't want to feel that again.*

Therapist: *Many people describe feeling like that after an event like Maria; after what many of us call a trauma. They may have their bodies react like the event is happening again.*

Mr. Sanchez: *Other people have that happen?*

Therapist: *Yes, after a trauma sometimes people's bodies, or alarm system, acts like the trauma is happening again. That can feel like your heart racing, or like your muscles are tense, or like it is hard to breathe, or like your blood pressure is going up as if they are going to have a heart attack. Even though it feels that way, their doctor is telling them that's not a heart event. Oftentimes, what's really happening is our body reacting to the trauma memory. It is really happening in your body but it is because your brain is telling your body you are in danger. So while it isn't the result of a heart condition, it can definitely impact us physically. What do you make of that?*

Mr. Sanchez: *So it's something else besides my heart?*

Therapist: *Yes. Are you interested in learning a little more about this?*

Mr. Sanchez: *Yes. Now I am curious.*

Therapist: *There are other problems someone may have after a trauma. They might have unwanted thoughts or feelings about the event come up, nightmares, problems with sleep or feeling irritable. It can really impact people's lives and families. How do those fit for you?*

Mr. Sanchez: *That fits with a lot of my experiences. I just figured it was my heart.*

Therapist: *When people have that collection of reactions it can be something we call posttraumatic stress disorder, or PTSD.*

Mr. Sanchez: *Oh, so this PTSD…this is what I have seen on the TV. Doesn't that mean that I am crazy? Am I going to be this way forever?*

Therapist: *Not at all. PTSD means that we weren't able to recover after a trauma. That doesn't mean we never will. We have several treatments that are effective in reducing, or even eliminating the symptoms. Would you like to hear more about them?*

Mr. Sanchez: *Ok, I am open to that.*

As you can see with the second example, there were a few key differences across the interactions. First, the provider took the time to have the patient outline the difficulties they have been experiencing and how these have in turn impacted their life. Psychoeducation was then used to assist the patient in understanding how the noted difficulties were reflective of PTSD and not cardiovascular in origin. Having the patient engage in the discussion, not forcing any labels at the outset, using the patient's language, and by being patient, he was able to not only be open to the diagnosis of PTSD, but was also open to learning more about the treatments available.

Socratic Method

While there are several techniques and foundational skills inherent to CPT, none is as critical as the utilization of the Socratic Method. Named after the Greek philosopher Socrates, this therapeutic technique assists patients in confronting dysfunctional beliefs, or stuck points as they are called in CPT, with their own knowledge and lived experiences to bring about meaningful change (Waltman et al., 2021). From a philosophical perspective, the Socratic Method comprises two key components: the dialogue (or elenchus) and the dialect. The key feature of the dialogue is to create tension and confusion, forcing the individual to identify and acknowledge the cognitive errors or fallacies behind their beliefs. This then prepares them to explore other possibilities and give way to change, also known as the dialect (Overholser, 2019).

Theoretically, the structure and process of the Socratic Method lends itself well to working with individuals from diverse backgrounds. However, there are several factors that result in this seemingly straightforward approach being difficult for providers to use effectively with diverse patients. First, many providers initially learning the technique tend to confound the Socratic Method with leading questions to create change. They may try to convince the person or try to "get them off the hook." It is true that the utilization of questions in therapy is a key skill in creating new understanding, learning, and change. However, how this is achieved with the Socratic Method is much more complex than by simply asking leading questions in therapy, which can unintentionally result in the therapist acting as the expert in the patient's life (Kazantzis & Stuckey, 2018).

When the therapist acts as the expert of the patient in front of them, it results in the provider bringing in their own lived experiences, their own assumptions, and their own interpretations into the therapeutic space, often resulting in patients of different backgrounds, cultures, and lived experiences feeling marginalized in therapy (Okamoto et al., 2019). True Socratic dialogue instead places the patient in the role of the expert and allows the patient's lived experiences, assumptions, and interpretations to be explored in order to achieve change. At its core, the Socratic Method is about suspending our own assumptions and collaboratively exploring the patient's thoughts inquisitively. Taking time to clarify the belief systems, explore all of the assumptions around these systems, and exploring all of the evidence in favor and in conflict with these systems are all key components to this method. However, effective use of the Socratic Method does require patient-specific adjustments in order to remain effective. When adapted thoughtfully, the Socratic Method gives space for the patient as an individual in therapy, allows for trauma processing to occur, and naturally builds the therapeutic alliance (Overholser, 2019; Waltman et al., 2021).

In order to successfully utilize the Socratic Method with patients, several factors should be taken into account. Consideration should be given to the patient's culture, language, and life experiences. For example, are there language barriers or factors related to dialect that should be considered? Are there words or phrases in CPT that don't have direct translations? Are there cultural components vital in this patient's life and experience of trauma that are being inadequately explored? Are we utilizing the "templated" metaphors or examples, or are we taking the time to adjust our use of them in order for them to more effectively resonate with the patient? Are we exploring the patient as a whole when it comes to their stuck points and belief systems or are we unintentionally missing key factors in their presentation?

While work continues to be done to modify and adapt the CPT protocol cross-culturally, it is on each individual provider to ensure that they go beyond the group-based adaptations and ensure that individually based adaptations congruent to the model are also taking place. This creates a therapeutic space that is truly collaborative and aligned with the patient's needs, leading to not only improved engagement but improved treatment outcomes. Arguably, when the Socratic Method is conducted as intended, it is a culturally attuned way of providing care as it centers the clients' lived experiences and knowledge.

Once buy-in is obtained for treatment, it is critical that providers continue to provide care from a culturally sensitive perspective. As noted earlier, the Socratic Method is not only a key component to CPT, but in providing culturally competent care. Let's take a moment to look at an example to see how things can go in therapy when this method is, and is not, incorporated properly.

Case Example

Ms. Farih is a 40-year-old female Muslim from Iraq. She and her family were provided asylum in the United States in 2008. She recently sought to engage in mental health services secondary to trauma symptoms that stem not only from her exposure to war, but from a sexual assault that occurred in her late 20's. After completing an evaluation in which she was diagnosed with PTSD, her treatment options were reviewed and CPT was collaboratively identified as her treatment of choice. She came into session four with the following ABC worksheet completed on the stuck point "I am forever marked" [because of her trauma].

Therapist: *I see you did a great job really working on the practice this week. Really lovely job noticing the thoughts and feelings relationships. Was there any particular ABC worksheet you found you struggled with?*

Farih*:* *Well several were hard, but I really had a hard time on this one.*

Therapist: *Okay, what did you write on the worksheet?*

Farih: *Well, in column A I wrote "I was raped." For my thought in column B I had "I am forever marked," and in column C I wrote "shame, disgust, and anger." I am not sure if my thought is a stuck point though, because I really believe that the sexual assault marked me forever.*

Therapist*:* *That sounds like a good one for us to focus on. What do you think?*

Farih: *That one causes me a lot of pain. So, yes, that would be helpful.*

Therapist: *OK. Nice job noticing the thought. And the emotion makes sense too—shame. What makes you think that the sexual assault marked you forever? How did you get to that idea?*

Farih: *That is what my family has told me. It is what my faith tells me.*

Therapist: *Forever is a long time. Do you know what is going to happen in the future?*

Farih: *I don't but I know that this is a shame that will never leave me.*

Therapist: *Never is a strong word. Are there other ways to think about this?*

Farih: *Not that I can think of.*

Therapist: *Does everyone in your family think this? Do any people disagree?*

Farih: *Yes, women who have been assaulted are seen as being damaged forever.*

Therapist: *Are there people in the world who don't see rape as being the woman's fault?*

Farih: *I don't think you understand. It doesn't matter what those people think.*

This therapist is doing a good job of checking in on the practice exercises and is emphasizing that the client has identified a clear stuck point that is linked to an emotion that makes sense, given the belief. However, the therapist's responses are not building rapport or moving the client forward. There are a few places where the therapist is both not staying with the CPT protocol and also not considering the client's cultural framework. The first error is that the therapist is focusing on an over-accommodated stuck point. Given that this is early in CPT, rather than focusing on the over-accommodated stuck point of "The sexual assault marked me forever," it would be better, and more consistent with CPT, to go back to the index trauma and the assimilated stuck point. The therapist is also forgetting some of the principles of Socratic dialogue. They are assuming they know the answer and are trying to convince their client rather than helping the client find the answer that fits for them. This can lead to the client feeling invalidated. It can lead as well to failing to consider deeply held cultural beliefs and helping the client find culturally congruent ways of getting themselves unstuck. Let's have a redo!

Therapist: *I see you did a great job really working on the homework this week. Really lovely job noticing the thoughts and feelings relationships. Was there any particular ABC worksheet you found you struggled with?*

Farih: *Well several were hard, but I really had a hard time on this one. I am not sure if it's a stuck point because I really believe that the sexual assault marked me forever.*

Therapist: *Let's see what's going on with that stuck point. What do you think?*

Farih*:* *That one causes me a lot of distress. So, yes, that would be helpful.*

Therapist: *OK. Nice job noticing the thought. And the emotion makes sense too—shame. I can see why this one causes you a lot of distress. That seems like a really hard thing to say to yourself. But this belief is the kind that we work on a little later in CPT. It may be helpful instead to figure out how you got to that idea and how it relates to the rape itself right now. How did you make sense of why the rape happened?*

Farih: *Women who are raped are a shame on their family.*

Therapist: *What was it that happened during the rape that you feel most ashamed of? Maybe it would be most helpful to look at that part together.*

Farih*:* *I keep telling myself that he picked me because he thought I was too forward.*

Therapist: *Now that sounds like a stuck point to me. What do you mean by too forward? How were you too forward?*

Farih*:* *My family is more conservative. I am more liberal. I let myself be alone in a room with him. He may have seen that as me being interested in him.*

Therapist*:* *That may be another stuck point—the rape happened because I was alone in a room with him. Tell me a little more about that.*

Farih: *He was an old family friend. I had grown up with him. He came to the house when my parents weren't home and asked to come in to wait for them. I thought it would be fine. But then, after he came in, he grabbed me and raped me. It never would have happened if I hadn't let him in.*

Therapist*:* *So we have a few stuck points. 'The rape happened because I was too forward.' 'The rape happened because alone in a room with him.' And 'it never would have happened if I hadn't let him in.' It makes total sense why you are feeling so distressed. Let's take a moment and write these down on your stuck point log. Now when you think about these three beliefs, which one is most tied to your emotions about the rape?*

Farih: *The last one. It never would have happened if I hadn't let him in. I just feel so ashamed of what I did when I think about that.*

Therapist: *Then let's focus on that one for now. We will come back to the other ones later. I'm curious, what did you know at the time when you let him in?*

Farih: *He had never done anything like this before. Our families have been friends for a long time. I thought of him like a brother.*

Therapist: *What were the norms in your house about a situation like this? What had you been taught?*

Farih: *I was taught not to be alone with men outside our family. But I was also taught to be hospitable. To not turn someone away.*

Therapist: *You had grown up with him. So how did you know that this time it would be different?*

Farih: *I guess I didn't.*

Therapist: *Did you have a reason to turn him away?*

Farih: *I'm not sure. Not really. Not at that time.*

Therapist: *What might have happened if you had turned him away?*

Farih: *He might have been offended. I guess he might have pushed his way in anyway. Honestly, at the time, I didn't think much of it.* [pauses to think].

Therapist: *So you didn't know this would happen. Is there something else you could tell yourself?*

Farih: *I couldn't have known he would rape me. He violated my trust and the trust of my family.*

So how is this example different? First, the therapist goes back to the index trauma to figure out where the belief is coming from that Ms. Farih has a "mark" on her. The therapist identifies assimilation stuck points and collaboratively they pick one to focus on, based on her emotions. The therapist also is very careful to ask questions about the context of the event itself and about the expectations and rules at the time. Remember—good Socratic dialogue isn't about what the therapist knows, it is about what the client discovers! It is not only important that the therapist remains curious and not jump to conclusions through the discovery process but also go through the exploration without inadvertently buying into a stuck point.

In sum, we hope this chapter illustrates general guidelines on how best to apply CPT when culturally adapting the treatment. The key to culturally adapting CPT across cultural contexts is to ensure that the essential elements of CPT remain in place. This includes good use of Socratic dialogue throughout the treatment, emphasis on processing natural emotions while allowing for cognitive change to shift manufactured emotions, and targeting assimilation before over-accommodation. Socratic dialogue itself, through the emphasis on client autonomy, inherent wisdom, and creating their own meaning or alternative thought, lends itself quite well to a culturally humble approach. Factors that may change are aspects of CPT such as language, specific metaphors, cultural understanding of trauma reactions, layout or format of worksheets, or labels for specific modules. The context of delivery is an aspect of cross-cultural adaptation that is often not directly addressed but is equally as important as other factors. This includes aspects such as who is providing the intervention, where and how they are delivering CPT, and the frequency and length of sessions. To do this work, we have to hold the dialectic of having a good reason for making changes, based on the client's needs, and not assuming that treatment can't or won't work just because of cultural differences while also holding the possibility of changing aspects of CPT to increase client fit and to better meet their needs.

Competing Interests Debra Kaysen's research is supported, in part, by the Patient Centered Outcomes Research Institute (PTSD-2019C1-15,636, 15065sc) and the National Institute on Minority Health and Health Disparities (R01-MD011574, R01-MD018201). Dr. Kaysen receives honoraria from Lyssn and is on the Scientific Advisory board for Nema Health. She has previously received honoraria from Psychwire, the Navy Seal Foundation, and Jazz Pharmaceuticals. Dr. Kaysen receives honoraria periodically for conducting workshops on Cognitive Processing Therapy. She receives royalties from Elsevier for a book on delivery of CPT. The content is solely the responsibility of the authors and does not necessarily represent the official views of the National Institutes of Health, the Patient Centered Outcomes Research Institute, the Veterans Administration, or any other funding agency.

References

Alizadeh, S., & Chavan, M. (2016). Cultural competence dimensions and outcomes: A systematic review of the literature. *Health & Social Care in the Community, 24*(6), e117–e130.

Atwoli, L., Stein, D. J., Koenen, K. C., & McLaughlin, K. A. (2015). Epidemiology of posttraumatic stress disorder: Prevalence, correlates and consequences. *Current Opinion in Psychiatry, 28*(4), 307–311. https://doi.org/10.1097/YCO.0000000000000167

Bass, J. K., Annan, J., McIvor Murray, S., Kaysen, D., Griffiths, S., Cetinoglu, T., Wachter, K., Murray, L. K., & Bolton, P. A. (2013). Controlled trial of psychotherapy for Congolese survivors of sexual violence. *New England Journal of Medicine, 368*(23), 2182–2191.

Bass, J. K., Murray, S. M., Lakin, D. P., Kaysen, D., Annan, J., Matabaro, A., & Bolton, P. A. (2022). Maintenance of intervention effects: Long-term outcomes for participants in a group talk-therapy trial in the Democratic Republic of Congo. *Global Mental Health, 9*, 347–354.

Becker, A. E., & Kleinman, A. (2013). Mental health and the global agenda. *New England Journal of Medicine, 369*(1), 66–73. https://doi.org/10.1056/NEJMra1110827

Benjet, C., Bromet, E., Karam, E. G., Kessler, R. C., Mclaughlin, K. A., Ruscio, A. M., Shahly, V., Stein, D. J., Petukhova, M., Hill, E., Alonso, J., Atwoli, L., Bunting, B., Bruffaerts, R., Caldas-De-Almeida, J. M., De Girolamo, G., Florescu, S., Gureje, O., Huang, Y., Lepine, J. P., Kawakami, N., Kovess Masfety, V., Medina-Mora, M. E., Navarro-Mateu, F., Piazza, M., Posada-Villa, J., Scott, K. M., Shalev, A., Slade, T., Ten Have, M., Torres, Y., Viana, M. C., Zarkov, Z., & Koenen, K. C. (2016). The epidemiology of traumatic event exposure worldwide: Results from the World Mental Health Survey Consortium. *Psychological Medicine, 46*, 327–343.

Bernal, G., & Adames, C. (2017). Cultural adaptations: Conceptual, ethical, contextual, and methodological issues for working with ethnocultural and majority-world populations. *Prevention Science, 18*(6), 681–688.

Bolton, P. (2019). Global mental health and psychotherapy: Importance of task-shifting and a systematic approach to adaptation. In *Global mental health and psychotherapy* (pp. 11–24). Academic Press.

Bolton, P., Bass, J. K., Zangana, G. A. S., Kamal, T., Murray, S. M., Kaysen, D., Lejuez, C. W., Lindgren, K., Pagoto, S., Murray, L. K., & Van Wyk, S. S. (2014). A randomized controlled trial of mental health interventions for survivors of systematic violence in Kurdistan, Northern Iraq. *BMC Psychiatry, 14*, 1–15.

Chen, J. A., Olin, C. C., Stirman, S. W., & Kaysen, D. (2017). The role of context in the implementation of trauma-focused treatments: Effectiveness research and implementation in higher and lower income settings. *Current Opinion in Psychology, 14*, 61–66.

ElBarazi, A. S., Tikamdas, R., Ahmed, S., & Ramadan, S. (2022). Cognitive processing therapy for the treatment of PTSD, depression and anxiety in Syrian refugees in Egypt. *Intervention Journal Of Mental Health And Psychosocial Support In Conflict Affected Areas, 20*(2), 179–187.

Ennis, N., Shorer, S., Shoval-Zuckerman, Y., Freedman, S., Monson, C. M., & Dekel, R. (2020). Treating posttraumatic stress disorder across cultures: A systematic review of cultural adaptations of trauma-focused cognitive behavioral therapies. *Journal of Clinical Psychology, 76*(4), 587–611.

Greene, M. C., Likindikoki, S., Rees, S., Bonz, A., Kaysen, D., Misinzo, L., Njau, T., Kiluwa, S., Turner, R., Ventevogel, P., & Mbwambo, J. K. (2021). Evaluation of an integrated intervention to reduce psychological distress and intimate partner violence in refugees: Results from the Nguvu cluster randomized feasibility trial. *PLoS One, 16*(6), e0252982.

Gopalkrishnan, N. (2018). Cultural diversity and mental health: Considerations for policy and practice. *Frontiers in Public Health, 6*, 179.

Hall, B. J., Bolton, P. A., Annan, J., Kaysen, D., Robinette, K., Cetinoglu, T., Wachter, K., & Bass, J. K. (2014). The effect of cognitive therapy on structural social capital: Results from a randomized controlled trial among sexual violence survivors in The Democratic Republic of the Congo. *American Journal of Public Health, 104*(9), 1680–1686.

Hall, G. C. N., Ibaraki, A. Y., Huang, E. R., Marti, C. N., & Stice, E. (2016). A meta-analysis of cultural adaptations of psychological interventions. *Behavior Therapy, 47*(6), 993–1014. https://doi.org/10.1016/j.beth.2016.09.005

Heim, E., & Kohrt, B. A. (2019). Cultural adaptation of scalable psychological interventions. *Clinical Psychology in Europe, 1*(4), 1–22.

Hoppen, T. H., Priebe, S., Vetter, I., & Morina, N. (2021). Global burden of post-traumatic stress disorder and major depression in countries affected by war between 1989 and 2019: A systematic review and meta-analysis. *BMJ Global Health, 6*(7), 1–13. https://doi.org/10.1136/bmjgh-2021-006303

Hwang, W.-C. (2009). The formative method for adapting psychotherapy (FMAP): A community-based developmental approach to culturally adapting therapy. *Professional Psychology: Research and Practice, 40*(4), 369–377. https://doi.org/10.1037/a0016240

Kazlauskas, E. (2017). Challenges for providing health care in traumatized populations: Barriers for PTSD treatments and the need for new developments. *Global Health Action, 10*(1), 1322399. https://doi.org/10.1080/16549716.2017.1322399

Kazantzis, N., & Stuckey, M. E. (2018). Inception of a discovery: Re-defining the use of Socratic dialogue in cognitive behavioral therapy. *International Journal of Cognitive Therapy, 11*, 117–123.

Kaysen, D., Lindgren, K., Zangana, G. A. S., Murray, L., Bass, J., & Bolton, P. (2013). Adaptation of cognitive processing therapy for treatment of torture victims: Experience in Kurdistan, Iraq. *Psychological Trauma: Theory, Research, Practice, and Policy, 5*(2), 184.

Kilbourne, A. M., Beck, K., Spaeth-Rublee, B., Ramanuj, P., O'Brien, R. W., Tomoyasu, N., & Pincus, H. A. (2018). Measuring and improving the quality of mental health care: A global perspective. *World Psychiatry, 17*(1), 30–38. https://doi.org/10.1002/wps.20482

Koenen, K. C., Ratanatharathorn, A., Ng, L., McLaughlin, K. A., Bromet, E. J., Stein, D. J., Karam, E. G., Ruscio, A. M., Benjet, C., Scott, K., & Atwoli, L. (2017). Posttraumatic stress disorder in the world mental health surveys. *Psychological Medicine, 47*(13), 2260–2274. https://doi.org/10.1017/S0033291717000708

Kousteni, I. D. (2022). Toward an extended view of evidence-based psychotherapy: Diversity and societal factors. *Journal of Humanistic Psychology, 62*(1), 31–43. https://doi.org/10.1177/0022167818762651

Magruder, K. M., McLaughlin, K. A., & Elmore Borbon, D. L. (2017). Trauma is a public health issue. *European Journal of Psychotraumatology, 8*(1). https://doi.org/10.1080/20008198.2017.1375338

McClendon, J., Dean, K. E., & Galovski, T. (2020). Addressing diversity in PTSD treatment: Disparities in treatment engagement and outcome among patients of color. *Current Treatment Options in Psychiatry, 7*(3), 275–290. https://doi.org/10.1007/s40501-020-00212-0

Miller, C. J., Wiltsey-Stirman, S., & Baumann, A. A. (2020). Iterative decision-making for evaluation of adaptations (IDEA): A decision tree for balancing adaptation, fidelity, and intervention impact. *Journal of Community Psychology, 48*(4), 1163–1177.

Murray, S. M., Augustinavicius, J., Kaysen, D., Rao, D., Murray, L. K., Wachter, K., Annan, J., Falb, K., Bolton, P., & Bass, J. K. (2018). The impact of cognitive processing therapy on stigma among survivors of sexual violence in eastern Democratic Republic of Congo: Results from a cluster randomized controlled trial. *Conflict and Health, 12*, 1–9.

Nadkarni, A., Hanlon, C., & Patel, V. (2024). Mental health care models in low-and middle-income countries. In *Tasman's psychiatry* (pp. 3347–3393). Springer International Publishing.

Naeem, F., Sajid, S., Naz, S., & Phiri, P. (2023). Culturally adapted CBT–the evolution of psychotherapy adaptation frameworks and evidence. *The Cognitive Behaviour Therapist, 16*, e10.

Orengo-Aguayo, R., Stewart, R. W., Villalobos, B. T., Hernandez Rodriguez, J., Dueweke, A. R., de Arellano, M. A., & Young, J. (2020). Listen, don't tell: Partnership and adaptation to implement trauma-focused cognitive behavioral therapy in low-resourced settings. *American Psychologist, 75*(8), 1158.

Overholser, J. C. (2019). *The socratic method of psychotherapy*. Columbia University Press.

Okamoto, A., Dattilio, F. M., Dobson, K. S., & Kazantzis, N. (2019). The therapeutic relationship in cognitive–behavioral therapy: Essential features and common challenges. *Practice Innovations, 4*(2), 112.

Pearson, C. R., Kaysen, D., Huh, D., & Bedard-Gilligan, M. (2019). Randomized control trial of culturally adapted cognitive processing therapy for PTSD substance misuse and HIV sexual risk behavior for native American women. *AIDS and Behavior, 23*, 695–706.

Qureshi, O., Endale, T., Ryan, G., Miguel-Esponda, G., Iyer, S. N., Eaton, J., De Silva, M., & Murphy, J. (2021). Barriers and drivers to service delivery in global mental health projects. *International Journal of Mental Health Systems, 15*(1). https://doi.org/10.1186/s13033-020-00427-x

Resick, P. A., Monson, C. M., & Chard, K. M. (2017). *Cognitive processing therapy for PTSD: A comprehensive manual*. The Guilford Press.

Resnicow, K., Soler, R., Braithwaite, R. L., Ahluwalia, J. S., & Butler, J. (2000). Cultural sensitivity in substance use prevention. *Journal of Community Psychology, 28*, 271–290. https://doi.org/10.1002/(SICI)1520-6629(200005)28:3<271::AID-JCOP4>3.0.CO;2

Schulz, P. M., Huber, L. C., & Resick, P. A. (2006). Practical adaptations of cognitive processing therapy with Bosnian refugees: Implications for adapting practice to a multicultural clientele. *Cognitive and Behavioral Practice, 13*(4), 310–321.

Subudhi, C. (2014). Culture and mental illness. In A. Francis, P. La Rosa, L. Sankaran, & S. P. Rajeev (Eds.), *Social work practice in mental health: Cross-cultural perspectives* (Vol. 141, pp. 132–140). Allied Publishers.

Valentine, S. E., Borba, C. P., Dixon, L., Vaewsorn, A. S., Guajardo, J. G., Resick, P. A., Wiltsey Stirman, S., & Marques, L. (2017). Cognitive processing therapy for Spanish-speaking Latinos: A formative study of a model-driven cultural adaptation of the manual to enhance implementation in a usual care setting. *Journal of Clinical Psychology, 73*(3), 239–256. https://doi.org/10.1002/jclp.22337

Wainberg, M. L., Scorza, P., Shultz, J. M., Helpman, L., Mootz, J. J., Johnson, K. A., Neria, Y., Bradford, J.-M. E., Oquendo, M. A., & Arbuckle, M. R. (2017). Challenges and opportunities in global mental health: A research-to-practice perspective. *Current Psychiatry Reports, 19*(5). https://doi.org/10.1007/s11920-017-0780-z

Waltman, S. H., Codd, R. T., III, McFarr, L. M., & Moore, B. A. (2021). *Socratic questioning for therapists and counselors: Learn how to think and intervene like a cognitive behavior therapist*. Routledge/Taylor & Francis Group.

Wiltsey Stirman, S., Gamarra, J. M., Bartlett, B. A., Calloway, A., & Gutner, C. A. (2017). Empirical examinations of modifications and adaptations to evidence-based psychotherapies: Methodologies, impact, and future directions. *Clinical Psychology: Science and Practice, 24*(4), 396.

Weiss, W. M., Murray, L. K., Zangana, G. A. S., Mahmooth, Z., Kaysen, D., Dorsey, S., Lindgren, K., Gross, A., Murray, S. M., Bass, J. K., & Bolton, P. (2015). Community-based mental health treatments for survivors of torture and militant attacks in southern Iraq: A randomized control trial. *BMC Psychiatry, 15*, 1–16.

World Health Organization. (2005). *Mental health: Facing the challenges, building solutions: Report from the WHO European ministerial conference*. WHO Regional Office for Europe.

Zolfaghari, B., Möllering, G., Clark, T., & Dietz, G. (2016). How do we adopt multiple cultural identities? A multidimensional operationalization of the sources of culture. *European Management Journal, 34*(2), 102–113.

Part IV
Alternative Formats of CPT Delivery

Chapter 13
Group Cognitive Processing Therapy

Caroline R. Scheid, Colleen Martin, and Kathleen M. Chard

Scope of the Problem

Cognitive Processing Therapy (CPT) is an evidenced-based and manualized treatment designed to address symptoms of posttraumatic stress disorder (PTSD). CPT is a 12-session protocol (typically delivered in 7–15 sessions based on treatment response) that facilitates natural recovery from PTSD by having clients challenge unhelpful cognitions about traumatic event(s), as well as about themselves, others, and the world. Numerous clinical guidelines identify CPT as a first line evidence-based treatment for PTSD, including the VA/DoD Clinical Practice Guideline for the Management of Posttraumatic Stress Disorder and Acute Stress Disorder (VA/DoD, 2023). The American Psychological Association (APA) also "strongly recommends" implementing CPT for adults with PTSD in its Clinical Practice Guidelines for the Treatment of PTSD (APA, 2017). The treatment was originally developed to address PTSD symptoms for individuals who had experienced sexual assault (Resick and Schnicke, 1993), but since its initial creation, CPT has been expanded to address a variety of trauma types and implementation modalities. For example, CPT has been successfully delivered with veterans (e.g., Holder et al., 2020; Monson et al., 2006; Schnurr et al., 2022) and active-duty military personnel (e.g., Resick

C. R. Scheid (✉) · C. Martin
Cincinnati VA Medical Center, Trauma Recovery Center, Cincinnati, OH, USA
e-mail: Caroline.Scheid@va.gov; Colleen.Martin4@va.gov

K. M. Chard
Cincinnati VA Medical Center, Cincinnati, OH, USA

Department of Psychiatry and Behavioral Neuroscience, University of Cincinnati School of Medicine, Cincinnati, OH, USA
e-mail: Kathleen.Chard@va.gov

J. S. Wachen, T. E. Galovski (eds.), *Cognitive Processing Therapy for Complex Cases*, CBT: Science Into Practice,
https://doi.org/10.1007/978-3-031-87356-0_13

et al., 2015, 2017), along with different delivery methods that include individual, group-only, or combined group and individual formats (Chard, 2005; Resick et al., 2017).

Group CPT provides numerous boons, both for patients and clinicians, as an efficient form of treatment delivery. For patients, both group-only formats or combined individual and group treatments allow trauma-impacted individuals to identify shared experiences, emotions, or thought patterns, among other commonalities with group participants. Group sessions further enable therapeutic opportunities for socialization and symptom normalization. From a cost or practical perspective, potential benefits of group-only programming are the opportunities for resource-saving and widespread implementation. Specifically, one or two clinicians are able to provide CPT for multiple individuals at one time, which reduces clinician burden and allows for numerous clients to receive treatment simultaneously.

Group CPT can be conducted in two formats, with corresponding pros and cons. First, group-only CPT may maximize the number of clients who receive services, especially if available providers trained in CPT are limited (e.g., in corrections facilities; Zielinski et al., 2023). A disadvantage of group-only treatment is that patients do not receive as much individual attention from the therapist to more deeply process their trauma or get personalized assistance with worksheets if they are having difficulties understanding the material. A second option, combined group and individual CPT, in contrast, may be optimal for programs aiming to address PTSD symptoms comprehensively and from multiple angles, such as in residential treatment facilities or intensive outpatient treatment programs. This format may be appropriate for individuals who need a higher level of care for the treatment of PTSD symptoms (e.g., Walter et al., 2014). Overall, given the various benefits and potential challenges of group CPT, it is important to consider the research, clinical applications and considerations, and future directions for this treatment modality to optimize its administration and benefit for participants.

Research Overview

Group-Only CPT

Research on group-only CPT has demonstrated its effectiveness for trauma-exposed populations. CPT conducted in a group format has resulted in significant decreases in PTSD symptoms and associated psychiatric sequelae (e.g., depression symptoms; Alvarez et al., 2011; Jeffreys et al., 2014; Resick et al., 2017;). However, findings showed that individual CPT conferred greater benefits for PTSD symptoms, although participants in group CPT still experienced significant reductions in PTSD symptoms in active-duty service member and veteran samples (Jeffreys et al., 2014; Lamp et al., 2019; Resick et al., 2017). Studies on group-only CPT are predominately observational research. For example, Jeffreys et al. (2014) utilized chart review to identify that individual CPT benefited veterans more than group-only or combined group and individual CPT, although all demonstrated reductions in PTSD symptoms over treatment. In a retrospective, observational veteran sample, Spiller et al. (2022) also found that individual treatment (i.e., Prolonged Exposure or CPT) outperformed group-only CPT in reduction of PTSD symptoms at the completion of treatment. However, no significant differences in outcomes existed between group CPT and individual CPT and PE at a 4-month follow-up, so findings supported sustained benefit over time for group-only CPT (Spiller et al., 2022).

One randomized clinical trial of active-duty service members compared individual CPT with group-only CPT and found twice the effect size for individual CPT over group-only CPT (Resick et al., 2017). In this RCT, individual CPT and group-only CPT reduced depression symptoms and suicidality equally well (Resick et al., 2017). Notably, more recent analyses of the same sample from this study found that group and individual CPT performed equally in reducing PTSD symptoms, except for military personnel who had a history of head injury and were experiencing current post-concussive symptoms (e.g., headaches, memory problems, irritability, sleep problems; Wachen et al., 2022). This suggests that the persistent cognitive effects of head injury (i.e., inattention, concentration difficulties) may hamper treatment improvement in a group format. Taken together, group-only CPT has shown strong research support in relation to reductions in psychopathology, even when compared to individual treatment, but this may vary by presenting concerns (e.g., head injury) of the population.

Prior research has highlighted the utility of group-only CPT over other group treatments for individuals with PTSD. Group CPT has been shown to outperform present-centered therapy delivered in a group format in a randomized clinical trial of active-duty service members (Resick et al., 2015). Another study corroborated the superiority of group CPT for reducing PTSD symptoms compared to treatment as usual for male veterans in a residential program (Alvarez et al., 2011). Therefore, research has supported CPT as a leading option for group programming to address PTSD symptoms.

Combined Group and Individual CPT

Variations in group CPT delivery have also been examined in veteran samples in order to maximize treatment accessibility and decreases in symptomatology. For example, Chard (2005) tested a combined individual and group format of CPT delivery, which demonstrated significantly more improvement in PTSD symptoms as compared to wait-list, with gains remaining at 1-year follow-up for adult survivors of child sexual abuse. This approach may be particularly useful for residential programming or intensive outpatient treatment programs, such that individuals attend a variety of individual and group sessions throughout their treatment. Although this combined administration format is less frequently studied—likely due to its resource- and time-intensive approach—individuals who have received this type of CPT have also been shown to benefit (Jeffreys et al., 2014). Research has found that veterans in individual-only outpatient treatment experienced greater reductions in PTSD symptoms, compared to veterans receiving combined group and individual CPT in residential treatment (Walter et al., 2014). However, these results may be confounded by differences in demographic characteristics, programming (e.g., outpatient versus residential), or severity of symptoms at pre-treatment, rather than the treatment modality, per se (Walter et al., 2014). Rather, the level of treatment may be a more important factor for individuals seeking and selecting PTSD treatment, instead of the modality in particular. Nonetheless, further research is warranted in this area.

Additional Considerations from the Literature

Emotional Regulation Difficulties

CPT delivered in a group format has been studied in samples with psychiatric complexities to further understand its effectiveness to treat PTSD symptoms in various populations. There is conflicting evidence regarding the efficacy of PTSD treatments for individuals presenting with greater difficulties with emotion regulation. Some studies have favored a phase-based approach for those high in emotion dysregulation, which involves teaching coping skills prior to engaging in trauma-focused treatment (e.g., Cloitre et al., 2010); however, in a recent study examining group CPT with individuals high in emotion regulation difficulties, pre-treatment emotion regulation difficulties did not significantly influence changes in PTSD symptoms across treatment and at post-treatment (Schnaider et al., 2022). In addition to significant improvement in PTSD symptoms, emotion regulation also significantly improved from pre- to post-treatment for these individuals engaged in group-only CPT (Schnaider et al., 2022). In fact, it appears that group-only CPT is effective in addressing both types of symptoms without a phase-based approach to PTSD treatment. See Chap. 3 for further information about delivering CPT in the context of emotional dysregulation.

Substance Use Disorders

Substance use disorders (SUD) are a common co-occurrence with PTSD diagnoses (Pietrzak et al., 2011), and several studies have tested the ability of group CPT to decrease PTSD symptoms in this population. In active-duty military members with PTSD and comorbid hazardous drinking, group-only CPT has been effective in significantly reducing PTSD symptoms (Straud et al., 2021; Dondanville et al., 2019). Similar results were found in a sample of veterans in residential PTSD treatment, such that veterans diagnosed with PTSD with and without comorbid SUD did not have significantly different outcomes in PTSD symptoms after treatment (McDowell & Rodriguez, 2013). Given that individuals diagnosed with PTSD and comorbid

SUD experienced similar reductions in PTSD symptoms as compared to those without comorbid SUD in group-only CPT, having a SUD does not preclude someone from benefitting from CPT in a group format. See Chap. 5 for additional information on delivering CPT in the context of SUD.

Telehealth

A recent topic of interest as it relates to research in group CPT is the delivery of this treatment via telehealth interventions. In veterans, who received group CPT via telehealth services as compared to those treated in-person, no significant differences were found in clinician-assessed PTSD symptoms in both a pilot study (Morland et al., 2011) and in a randomized non-inferiority trial at post-treatment and 6-month follow-up (Morland et al., 2014). See Chap. 16 for a detailed description of implementing CPT via telehealth.

Altogether, the previous findings highlight the ability of group CPT to effectively treat PTSD symptoms even when the clinical presentation includes comorbidities or logistical barriers that may lead some providers to hesitate about implementing trauma-focused treatment. By demonstrating group-only CPT's effectiveness in samples with virtual administration, in-person format, and psychological comorbidities, research supports the use of CPT for a wide variety of individuals with PTSD.

Clinical Application

There are many factors to consider when planning implementation of group CPT. The current section aims to address examples of key points to address when delivering CPT in a group format, along with common challenges that may arise. First, the desire to discuss traumatic details should be addressed early on in group programming. Second, group facilitators should incorporate discussion of common Stuck Points in groups to promote skill-building and support. Third, this section provides options for addressing group conflict and adherence to CPT assignments. Last, information on implementation options, including CPT+A, combined group and individual treatment, and massed treatment delivery is provided.

Trauma Disclosure

For trauma-focused groups, it is important to clearly establish expectations regarding disclosure or processing of trauma details at the outset of groups. Disclosure of explicit trauma details in group may cause dysregulation in the individual disclosing and may be triggering or distressing for other participants. Therefore, it is imperative that group members are aware of and abide by group guidelines to withhold trauma disclosure or processing in group therapy, and the CPT manual explicitly recommends implementing a rule against trauma disclosures in group (Resick et al., 2024). To establish this expectation, group facilitators are recommended to lead an initial discussion during the first group therapy session about "rules" for the group. This discussion also provides potential downstream benefits to foster a sense of choice and ownership over treatment expectations for participants. During the discussion of group rules, facilitators should encourage collaboration among members and clearly document the chosen rules or guidelines (e.g., write on whiteboard or posterboard). If not proposed by group members, facilitators may then add the rule to withhold disclosure of specific trauma details or processing during group sessions due to the aforementioned reasons. Ideally, this rule should be reinforced throughout treatment, possibly by posting the group rules in a visible and consistent location on display for sessions (e.g., door of the group room) and adding this expectation to participants' treatment contracts at the outset of therapy. As needed, facilitators may also verbally remind participants on an individual or group basis regarding the group expectations about trauma disclosure. In fact, group leaders should revisit and review group rules at any time that would be clinically appropriate and relevant during treatment.

Despite clear groundwork to deter trauma disclosure or processing in group, participants may begin to share potentially distressing information at times during group treatment. On such occasions, facilitators may gently and directly intercede or guide individuals toward reflecting more on their thoughts or reactions to specific events, rather than trauma details explicitly. As always, the focus of the facilitator should be to validate the experience of participants, rather than specifically encouraging detailed trauma accounts among group members. It is important to note that this redirection is different than colluding with avoidance because the aim is to foster a safe and supportive environment for all group members, rather than leaving individuals with the impression they cannot safely share trauma memories with other people. Leaders may review the rationale behind the group rule to reinforce the expectation and reasoning behind this guideline. At the same time, leaders may want to help clients identify Stuck Points related to the trauma information that the client is wanting to share and begin working on them collaboratively with the rest of the group in session. In programs offering both group and individual treatment, leaders are recommended to refer participants to individual therapists to address clinical needs around trauma disclosure and processing. Individual therapists should also reinforce this message by encouraging clinically relevant trauma disclosure and processing within individual sessions, if needed. For group-only CPT, facilitators may offer the opportunity to discuss more details with the group leaders outside of group, if clinically indicated and practically feasible. This team-based perspective promotes space for individuals to be heard and practice approaching the trauma, while maintaining appropriate boundaries for group sessions.

Common Stuck Points

Negative alterations in cognitions are central in PTSD symptoms (e.g., Brown et al., 2019; Dekel et al., 2013), and CPT refers to these cognitions as "Stuck Points." One major benefit of group CPT is the opportunity for participants to recognize and relate to other group members' thoughts and feelings, including common Stuck Points. When groups are learning new CPT skills or reviewing previous assignments, facilitators utilize shared Stuck Points to illustrate skills during group sessions. For example, group leaders guide members through discussion and completion of CPT worksheets on smart/whiteboards or large posterboards. With this approach, group members can collectively challenge distressing thoughts while simultaneously accruing cognitive skills. In doing so, they may learn from other members while asking questions to foster greater understanding for all participants. Further, this process enables normalization of emotions associated with negative cognitions, while promoting more adaptive thinking. Specifically, group members can witness other individuals who also hold similar trauma-impacted beliefs while seeing that other participants with PTSD are able to challenge these unhelpful thoughts and bolster more adaptive cognitions.

In CPT, it is recommended to begin examining assimilated Stuck Points prior to overaccommodated Stuck Points. Assimilated Stuck Points occur when traumatic experiences are assimilated into prior beliefs (i.e., "I should have prevented the trauma"; Resick et al., 2024). Common assimilated Stuck Points to discuss in group sessions may include—but are not limited to—"The trauma is my fault." Group leaders are encouraged to start conversations about identifying Stuck Points for skill practice and discussion by asking group members to volunteer example Stuck Points in group from their own Stuck Point Logs, especially as they possibly relate to why they believe the trauma happened (e.g., "I should have known the trauma would happen").

Collaboratively, group leaders and members then select Stuck Points for the focus of group sessions. Facilitators help guide selection of stuck points that are broad enough to apply to many individuals with PTSD (e.g., "The trauma was my fault"), rather than examples unique to one individual and their trauma. Choosing broadly relevant Stuck Points maximizes potential benefits for all participants. This general focus may present challenges for individuals who are not able to explore unique Stuck Points (e.g., "The trauma happened because I invited my friend over"). Nonetheless, group members are encouraged to challenge individualized Stuck Points during their own practice between sessions, and group discussion of Stuck Points is focused on building understanding of cognitive skills. Additionally, group members may also apply discussions of assimilated Stuck Points generally to the more specific items on their Stuck Point logs. The benefit of addressing broadly applicable Stuck Points in groups also enables participants to support and engage in Socratic dialogue with other group members to further facilitate learning. Once the broad stuck point for group discussion is identified, leaders teach and discuss CPT skills by completing ABC sheets, Exploring Questions (previously called

Challenging Questions), Thinking Patterns (previously Problematic Patterns), or Alternative Thoughts (previously Challenging Beliefs) Worksheets as a group on a whiteboard, smartboard, or web screen. Participants are encouraged to take notes and simultaneously complete the discussed worksheet during group sessions; this recommendation facilitates learning CPT concepts and provides opportunities for all participants to challenge Stuck Points germane to their own cognitions.

After focusing on trauma-related (i.e., assimilated) Stuck Points earlier in treatment, group leaders help clients focus on Stuck Points that have overgeneralized from their trauma experiences in the latter portion of treatment. The overgeneralized beliefs are termed overaccommodated Stuck Points, which occur when individuals alter their beliefs about themselves, others, and the world to extremes in order to accommodate the trauma (Resick et al., 2024). For example, individuals may commonly apply beliefs to whole groups or classes of individuals (e.g., "All men will hurt me"). Similar to assimilated Stuck Points, facilitators begin group sessions by asking group members to volunteer examples of Stuck Points, especially as they relate to a module focus in CPT (e.g., trust). Next, the group collaboratively identifies an overaccommodated belief that is generally relatable for participants (e.g., "I can't trust people"). Then group members collectively use CPT skills (e.g., Alternative Thoughts Worksheet) to address the stuck point on a whiteboard, smartboard, or web screen. This collaborative and group-oriented focus on exploring and challenging Stuck Points allows all group members to learn CPT skills and develop flexibility for unhelpful cognitions.

Group Cohesiveness

When delivering CPT in a group format, as with many group treatment modalities, group cohesion and conflict are natural parts of the process and can be expected to varying degrees. When a group is learning CPT together, there can be a general baseline understanding that they are engaged in the therapy to recover from PTSD. In this process, a cohesive group can be instrumental in each individual's recovery such as receiving support as needed, engaging in discussions that require vulnerability and thus deepening emotional connections, receiving validation for one's experiences ("I'm not alone"), and overall encouragement throughout the therapy. When other group members can share perspectives that are cognitively flexible in pointing out evidence against Stuck Points, it may help those who are stuck in more rigid beliefs see that it is possible to see their Stuck Points differently. This may be particularly true for groups with a common experience or aspect of identity (e.g., military veterans, sexual assault survivors, etc.). Group rules established in the first session (e.g., show one another respect, no cross-talking, use "I" statements, etc.) can provide facilitators with the structure to address group conflict among members down the line. Many times, Stuck Points will play a role in the cohesiveness of the group. For example, Stuck Points related to trust (e.g., "I can't trust anyone") may lead some individuals to present as guarded and could contribute to how connected or cohesive the group becomes. Stuck Points related to power and control may also contribute to any potential conflict. For many individuals, avoidance tactics can surface when presented with the evidence that their foundational beliefs about trauma, themselves, others, and/or the world are not completely accurate. Avoidance can be seen in group members criticizing the therapy or other group members' beliefs and getting into arguments unrelated to the actual content, to name a few. This may be a way for some individuals to avoid reflecting on their own stuck points and sitting with the uncertainty that can come with challenging them. It is also noteworthy that group conflict can actually move a group forward in the process of changing beliefs.

When group conflict arises, facilitators have the task of striking a balance between addressing the conflict directly and maintaining fidelity to the protocol in delivering group material. Interventions that tailor to both tasks include using CPT skills (e.g., ABC sheets) and Socratic dialogue to address the conflict by determining which stuck points are being activated by group members. Depending on which session of the protocol the group is on at that time, group members may be more able to identify and explore these stuck points and get back on track in group. If group conflict is directed toward facilitators, it can be most effective to engage in more Socratic dialogue rather than engaging in a power struggle with the group. By shifting the power to the group and emphasizing that they have power and control over being in the group and engaging in the process of changing thoughts, many situations can be de-escalated. This process may also unearth additional stuck points along the way. Additionally, if there are certain group members who consistently interrupt group cohesion with conflict, it may be prudent for facilitators to meet with the individual outside of group sessions to determine whether additional work is needed on certain stuck points, and ultimately, if the group is a good fit for that person.

Homework Adherence

Part of setting the stage for conducting group CPT is to address homework noncompliance from the beginning to ensure that everyone is aware of the conditions of participating in the group. Between session assignments in CPT assist in extending the elements of the therapy beyond sessions and allow individuals to consolidate the content learned in session (Galovski et al., 2020). When some group members complete assignments and others do not, the group's progress can be disrupted as others may be further along in skill development and practice. At the same time, it may be helpful for more hesitant group members to see that those who are completing assignments are feeling better and have a better grasp of the material. Additionally, a significant portion of time in group CPT is spent reviewing worksheets from multiple group members, so it is important for facilitators to have homework to review. If there are Stuck Points interfering with homework completion (e.g., "Treatment won't work," "I don't have time for homework"), facilitators should identify and address these cognitions early on to increase homework compliance for the remainder of the treatment.

CPT+A Considerations

CPT flexibly provides options to implement treatment either with (i.e., CPT+A; Resick et al., 2024) or without (i.e., CPT) written trauma accounts. Dismantling research has underscored the effectiveness of both CPT and CPT+A (e.g., Resick et al., 2008), so clinics or programs may appropriately implement either treatment option in group formats. However, given that sharing trauma accounts in groups is not recommended in the CPT manual (Resick et al., 2024), would be time-intensive, possibly aversive to some group members, and potentially triggering for participants, incorporating trauma accounts in group CPT+A treatment requires special consideration and planning. Further, logistical options differ for CPT+A offered exclusively in group formats compared to CPT+A administered with group therapy in conjunction with individual therapy.

For CPT+A groups, participants may require individual support in order to process the written trauma accounts. As noted previously, it is not recommended for participants to share trauma accounts with other group members. Further, it can be more difficult to conduct CPT+A in an exclusively group-only format as participants may want to share the accounts they wrote for practice with other members in the group sessions. Thus, therapists might find it easier to conduct group and individual CPT+A treatment in certain circumstances, such as for group members with a high need to disclose or high levels of dissociative symptoms (Resick et al., 2012).

When combining individual and group formats simultaneously, practice assignments, including trauma accounts in CPT+A, are completed for individual sessions for participants to read and process with individual therapists. Group sessions are then used to process participants' experiences and reactions to writing trauma accounts, rather than sharing detailed narratives in group. Group members are encouraged to provide support and validation for one another during this emotionally challenging portion of treatment. This combined CPT+A format enables group members to process traumas within supportive and previously established therapeutic relationships, while also promoting approach behaviors by reading and processing the accounts with providers.

In addition, there are two other strategies to integrate a small number of individual sessions to accommodate trauma account processing. First, group facilitators, whether one provider or multiple providers, may schedule individual sessions with each participant during the weeks when trauma accounts are written and processed. In the case of multiple group leaders, they may divide up group members amongst themselves for scheduling individual therapy sessions. Alternatively, if clinics or programs have multiple clinicians trained in CPT, these clinicians may see group members for individual sessions just for the purpose of processing trauma accounts. Thus, participants would be seen individually for therapy just once or twice. However, this second strategy has multiple downsides, including lack of therapeutic rapport or alliance between participants and new individual providers. Further, it is unlikely that programs offering group-only CPT+A have multiple providers competently trained in CPT who are available to provide individual therapy for a small portion of the overall treatment. Therefore, it may be preferable for only the group facilitators to meet with group members individually for the purpose of processing trauma accounts; these therapists have already established rapport with group members, which is particularly important for compliance and comfort during such an emotionally intensive and personal component of treatment.

It is worth noting that avoidance is important to discuss and mitigate in both group-only and combined group and individual formats of CPT+A. Preemptively, participants' desires to avoid writing trauma accounts should be addressed in group when the trauma accounts are assigned. Group leaders may find it particularly useful to incorporate group members' reactions to writing trauma accounts by collectively completing an ABC worksheet as a group. In particular, an ABC worksheet may be completed on a whiteboard with the assignment of the written trauma account as the "Activating Event"; group members are always encouraged to simultaneously complete worksheets on their own paper worksheets to foster attention and retention of skills and content. During this particular group session, group members can be asked to identify their immediate thoughts (e.g., "This will never work," "I will not be able to handle writing about the trauma," "This will only make me worse") and emotions (e.g., anxiety, dread, anger) in reaction to the assignment to write the trauma account. Next, they should be encouraged to collectively identify alternative or more helpful cognitions that may attenuate avoidance (e.g., "Maybe writing this account will be helpful for me," "Telling my story will give me control over the trauma memory," "I am strong and capable to cope with facing my trauma's details"), with therapeutic support as necessary. Following completion of written trauma accounts, both types of group CPT+A modalities should discuss group members' experiences of writing the trauma accounts during group sessions, including thoughts and feelings about the assignment, rather than disclosing content from the written accounts. Participants are also encouraged to share their experiences and challenges writing the trauma accounts with other members in group sessions, supporting and encouraging each other in the process.

CPT Individual + Group

As previously described, combined group and individual CPT may be the most resource-intensive format for treatment, given the need for multiple therapists trained and competent in CPT. Individuals participating in this treatment format are also required to attend more sessions of therapy, compared to individual-only or group-only CPT, which may be challenging for participants with busy schedules. Nonetheless, the combined format addresses logistical challenges of group CPT+A and provides opportunities for multiple perspectives in treatment, including from other group members, group facilitators, and individual therapists. Although this level of care is unlikely to be necessary or even feasible for many of those seeking treatment for PTSD, especially given extensive evidence on the benefits of individual CPT (Lamp et al., 2019; Resick et al., 2017), this combined option may be beneficial and appealing for many individuals diagnosed with PTSD who are seeking more intensive treatment. Individuals with more severe psychopathology may benefit from or be more likely to choose this more intensive approach, but more research is needed in this area.

The combined group and individual CPT format presents several practical considerations. For instance, clinics offering the combined CPT modality need to determine schedules for individual and group sessions, including the timing or spacing of sessions. Residential programs in the VA commonly provide individual and group sessions that both occur twice a week (e.g., Walter et al., 2014), spaced at least two days apart to enhance practice and retention of content (Resick et al., 2024). With combined group and individual CPT, individual sessions should begin first and are staggered with group sessions, such that group and individual sessions alternate in the schedule. Group sessions are often designed to teach new material and process completion of prior assignments, and individual sessions are focused on review of individuals' worksheets and skills. Additionally, programs offering combined CPT should determine the allocation of therapists with individual clients. Group leaders may concurrently serve as individual therapists to some or all group members, depending on availability of CPT-trained providers. Therapists who are uninvolved in CPT group facilitation may also provide individual therapy for the program. In fact, it may be beneficial for participants to discuss CPT skills with a variety of providers in order to generalize knowledge or learn from multiple therapeutic styles; nonetheless, more research is needed in this area. More information on the implementation and session-by-session structure of combined group and individual CPT is in the published group manual (Chard et al., 2014).

Massed Delivery of Group CPT

Cognitive processing therapy has also been adapted for delivery in a condensed or massed format. Some of the advantages of this type of treatment delivery include a potentially faster recovery, less opportunity for avoidance, and greater rates of treatment completion; however, there may be less time and opportunity to practice assignments in between sessions (e.g., Wright et al., 2022). Much of the current literature has examined massed delivery of CPT in an individual format (i.e., Held et al., 2023; Galovski et al., 2022) with success in reducing PTSD symptoms; however, there have been studies examining a combined group and individual format (Wachen et al., 2024). Morris et al. (2022) examined CPT delivered over a 5-day period in a case study of active-duty service members in a combined group and individual therapy format. PTSD symptomatology decreased for most participants involved in this study, again highlighting the utility of a flexible approach to treatment delivery. As research continues to examine this type of short-term, intensive implementation, this may allow for more individuals to engage in an effective dosage of CPT in a shorter period of time. See Chap. 14 for more information about massed delivery of CPT.

Case Example

To illustrate the delivery of CPT in a group format, the following case example will demonstrate the use of an Exploring Questions Worksheet to challenge a common assimilated Stuck Point. Assimilated Stuck Points such as, "It was my fault" and "I should've known this would happen," often surface as ways the individual has made sense of why the trauma has happened to them. In a group format, particularly when trauma details are not discussed, it is important to engage the group in the process of looking at the belief differently as opposed to eliciting specific details about traumas. This case example occurs in a group of veterans in a residential treatment program. For the purposes of this example, the following discussion occurs after check-in and homework review.

Facilitator: *Now we're going to move on to another tool to help in determining if a stuck point is realistic or not. The ABC sheets helped in separating thoughts and emotions, and now we will take a closer look at your thoughts in a systematic way—almost like putting them under the microscope to see if they hold up to the test. Could folks open up their CPT session packet to the first page that says "Exploring Questions Sheet" at the top? Great. We will use a stuck point that most of the group can identify with as an example, and we will ask each one of these questions about that specific stuck point. What are some Stuck Points (without going into specific trauma details) that you all see on your stuck point log about why the trauma happened?*

Participant 1: *Do you mean something like, "I should've seen it coming"?*

Participant 2: *Yea, I have one like that. What about, "It happened because I was drunk"?*

Facilitator: *Yes, these are all great examples. Any others?*

Participant 3: *I basically just think the whole thing was my fault and that I deserved it. This stuff always happens to me.*

Facilitator: *Okay, so there seems to be a theme along the lines of "the trauma was my fault." Does that seem to fit for most of the group?*

Participants 1 and 3: *Yep.*

Participant 2: *Definitely.*

Facilitator: *Again, this is just an example to use for today's worksheet, so if this stuck point applies to you, feel free to write in more specific details on your individual sheet as we go along at the board. If this doesn't apply to you, that's okay too—you may be able to help the group explore the questions even better! This is* *just a chance to see how to go through this process to really examine your Stuck Points.*

Facilitator: *Alright, so if you can all write in that very top line next to Belief/Stuck point, "It was my fault." You're always going to put a Stuck Point from your Stuck Point log at the very top of this sheet, and each question will be about that Stuck Point. Looking at that first question, can someone read it for me?*

Participant 2: *What is the evidence against this Stuck Point?*

Facilitator: *Here is where I want you to list out specific pieces of evidence against your Stuck Point. Evidence being the cold, hard facts; not an opinion or a feeling. Think of evidence that would stand up in court. So, is there any evidence against the Stuck Point, "It was my fault"?*

Participant 4: *Well, the trauma happened. I know it did. That's the evidence I have.*

Facilitator: *Yes, absolutely the trauma happened. We are not challenging that here and would not ever challenge that. We are looking for evidence against the belief it was your fault that it did happen. Make sense?*

Participant 4: *Okay, then I'd say I was there, I trusted that person and they hurt me.*

Participant 1: *I think that too. I think that if I trusted someone, then I'm to blame for it happening. I just shouldn't have done that.*

Facilitator: *Does trusting a person mean that it was your fault? Let's think about it this way, going back to our conversation about levels of responsibility. What was your intent in trusting the person?*

Participant 2: *I guess not necessarily...I mean, I've trusted a lot of people and haven't been hurt like that. I obviously didn't go into the situation intending for it to happen.*

***Facilitator*:** *Ah, so this is actually really good evidence against. Why don't we put what you just said in the "evidence against" section: I've trusted people before and haven't been hurt; I did not intend for this to happen. Good points.*

***Facilitator*:** *Are there other pieces of evidence against we should list here?*

***Participant 4*:** *Going back to what we said earlier, the other person was the one that chose to hurt me.*

Facilitator: *Exactly! Let's get that up here too. Again, if there are specific pieces about your traumas you want to include, go ahead and jot those down on your sheet.*

***Facilitator*:** *Okay, onto the next question—What information are you not including? Especially when you say "It is my fault"?*

Participant 1: *So like, what other people were doing or wanted from that night?*

Facilitator: *Yes! Would you say "It was my fault" is a fact, 100% true? If not, then we need to consider who else had a role in what happened or wanted things to turn out the way they did.*

Participant 1: *I get that. So thinking about other people's choices that day?*

Facilitator: *Yes.*

The facilitator continued with the rest of the Exploring Questions and engaged the group in discussing how to use the questions to examine the accuracy of the

Stuck Point. The group members engaged in discussion of the questions and followed along using their own worksheets to explore their similar Stuck Points.

Future Directions

Research on group CPT has highlighted promising avenues for group interventions for PTSD, but more studies are needed. In particular, more research is needed on implementation approaches that reduce barriers for treatment, along with identifying for whom different components or modalities of treatment way work best. For example, massed treatment has been an emerging area of the field (e.g., Held et al., 2023, Wachen et al., 2024), and this concentrated dose of treatment may provide brief, condensed options for individuals who are unable to dedicate long periods of time to therapy or want to pursue a faster recovery process. Additionally, more research is needed to assess potential moderators of group CPT. Specifically, it would be useful to identify for whom group versus individual treatment is most effective, such that group or individual treatment may be better suited for some individuals (e.g., severity of symptoms; history of head injury) than others. Some individuals may benefit more from individual treatment, while others may be best supported through group CPT, but more literature is required to address these research questions and uniquely tailor treatment to each individual's context. Further, few studies examined the combined format of individual and group CPT. Some research has demonstrated that treatment benefits in combined individual and group CPT may be less than individual-only outpatient treatment, but these results may be better explained by differences in symptom severities or other demographic differences among those who chose each type of treatment modality (Walter et al., 2014). However, research on this combined format is limited, and more studies are needed to disentangle potential differences in symptom severity, demographics, and treatment gains across treatment modalities. Overall, long-term, research should help identify opportunities to tailor treatment type to the clinical and practical needs of each individual pursuing PTSD treatment.

Summary

CPT was originally developed as a group treatment, and over the past 30 years research has shown that it is not only effective presented in group formats, but also in individual or combined individual and group delivery. Although many clients prefer individual therapy, there are decided benefits to group therapy that fit well with CPT, including normalizing emotions, collective learning, and the ability to challenge and support each other in change. In addition, group CPT offers a cost benefit to clients as it is frequently offered at lower cost, and it allows clinicians the ability to see more clients at once, therefore reducing waitlists and increasing access to evidence-based care.

Competing Interests Dr. Chard is co-author of the Cognitive Processing Therapy treatment manual and receives royalties from Guilford Press.

References

Alvarez, J., McLean, C., Harris, A. H., Rosen, C. S., Ruzek, J. I., & Kimerling, R. (2011). The comparative effectiveness of cognitive processing therapy for male veterans treated in a VHA posttraumatic stress disorder residential rehabilitation program. *Journal of Consulting and Clinical Psychology, 79*(5), 590.

American Psychological Association. (2017, February 24). *Clinical practice guidelines for the treatment of posttraumatic stress disorder (PTSD) in adults*. https://www.apa.org/ptsd-guideline/ptsd.pdf

Brown, L. A., Belli, G. M., Asnaani, A., & Foa, E. B. (2019). A review of the role of negative cognitions about oneself, others, and the world in the treatment of PTSD. *Cognitive Therapy and Research, 43*, 143–173.

Chard, K. M. (2005). An evaluation of cognitive processing therapy for the treatment of posttraumatic stress disorder related to childhood sexual abuse. *Journal of Consulting and Clinical Psychology, 73*(5), 965–971. https://doi.org/10.1037/0022-006X.73.5.965

Chard, K. M., Resick, P. A., Monson, C. M., & Kattar, K. A. (2014). *Cognitive processing therapy therapist group manual: Veteran/military version*. Department of Veterans' Affairs.

Cloitre, M., Stovall-McClough, K. C., Nooner, K., Zorbas, P., Cherry, S., Jackson, C. L., Gan, W., & Petkova, E. (2010). Treatment for PTSD related to childhood abuse: A randomized controlled trial. *American Journal of Psychiatry, 167*(8), 915–924.

Dekel, S., Peleg, T., & Solomon, Z. (2013). The relationship of PTSD to negative cognitions: A 17-year longitudinal study. *Psychiatry, 76*(3), 241–255.

Department of Veterans Affairs & Department of Defense. (2023). *VA/DoD clinical practice guideline for the management of posttraumatic stress disorder and acute stress disorder* (Version 4.0). https://www.healthquality.va.gov/guidelines/MH/ptsd/VA-DoD-CPG-PTSD-Full-CPGAug242023.pdf

Dondanville, K. A., Wachen, J. S., Hale, W. J., Mintz, J., Roache, J. D., Car-son, C., Litz, B. T., Yarvis, J. S., Young-McCaughan, S., Peterson, A. L., Resick, P. A., & for the STRONG STAR Consortium. (2019). Examination of treatment effects on hazardous drinking among service members with PTSD. *Journal of Traumatic Stress, 32*(2), 310–316. https://doi.org/10.1002/jts.22393

Galovski, T. E., Nixon, R. D., & Kaysen, D. (2020). *Flexible applications of cognitive processing therapy: Evidence-based treatment method*. Elsevier Academic Press.

Galovski, T. E., Werner, K. B., Weaver, T. L., Morris, K. L., Dondanville, K. A., Nanney, J., Wamser-Nanney, R., McGlinchey, G., Fortier, C. B., & Iverson, K. M. (2022). Massed cognitive processing therapy for posttraumatic stress disorder in women survivors of intimate partner violence. *Psychological Trauma: Theory, Research, Practice, and Policy, 14*(5), 769–779. https://doi.org/10.1037/tra0001100

Held, P., Smith, D. L., Pridgen, S., Coleman, J. A., & Klassen, B. J. (2023). More is not always better: 2 weeks of intensive cognitive processing therapy-based treatment are noninferior to 3 weeks. *Psychological Trauma: Theory, Research, Practice, & Policy, 15*(1), 100–109. https://doi.org/10.1037/tra0001257

Holder, N., Shiner, B., Li, Y., Madden, E., Neylan, T. C., Seal, K. H., et al. (2020). Cognitive processing therapy for veterans with posttraumatic stress disorder: What is the median effective dose? *Journal of Affective Disorders, 273*, 425–433.

Jeffreys, M. D., Reinfeld, C., Nair, P. V., Garcia, H. A., Mata-Galan, E., & Rentz, T. O. (2014). Evaluating treatment of posttraumatic stress disorder with cognitive processing therapy and prolonged exposure therapy in a VHA specialty clinic. *Journal of Anxiety Disorders, 28*(1), 108–114.

Lamp, K. E., Avallone, K. M., Maieritsch, K. P., Buchholz, K. R., & Rauch, S. A. (2019). Individual and group cognitive processing therapy: Effectiveness across two veterans affairs posttraumatic stress disorder treatment clinics. *Psychological Trauma: Theory, Research, Practice, and Policy, 11*(2), 197.

McDowell, J., & Rodriguez, J. (2013). Does substance abuse affect outcomes for trauma-focused treatment of combat-related PTSD? *Addiction Research and Theory, 21*(5), 357–364. https://doi.org/10.3109/16066359.2012.746316

Monson, C. M., Schnurr, P. P., Resick, P. A., Friedman, M. J., Young-Xu, Y., & Stevens, S. P. (2006). Cognitive processing therapy for veterans with military-related posttraumatic stress disorder. *Journal of Consulting and Clinical Psychology, 74*(5), 898.

Morland, L. A., Hynes, A. K., Mackintosh, M., Resick, P. A., & Chard, K. M. (2011). Group cognitive processing therapy for PTSD delivered to rural combat veterans via telemental health: Lessons learned from a pilot cohort. *Journal of Traumatic Stress, 24*(4), 465–469.

Morland, L. A., Mackintosh, M. A., Greene, C. J., Rosen, C. S., Chard, K. M., Resick, P., & Frueh, C. (2014). Cognitive processing therapy for posttraumatic stress disorder delivered to rural veterans via telemental health: A randomized noninferiority clinical trial. *Journal of Clinical Psychiatry, 75*(5), 470–476.

Morris, K. L., Schwartz, C., Galovski, T. E., Dondanville, K. A., & Wachen, J. S. (2022). Massed cognitive processing therapy in active-duty military: A case series. *Cognitive and Behavioral Practice, 30*(3), 326–340. https://doi.org/10.1016/j.cbpra.2022.04.004

Pietrzak, R. H., Goldstein, R. B., Southwick, S. M., & Grant, B. F. (2011). Prevalence and Axis I comorbidity of full and partial posttraumatic stress disorder in the United States: Results from wave 2 of the national epidemiologic survey on alcohol and related concerns. *Journal of Anxiety Disorders, 25*(3), 456–465.

Resick, P. A., & Schnicke, M. K. (1993). *Cognitive processing therapy for rape victims: A treatment manual*. Sage.

Resick, P. A., Galovski, T. E., Uhlmansiek, M. O., Scher, C. D., Clum, G. A., & Young-Xu, Y. (2008). A randomized clinical trial to dismantle components of cognitive processing therapy for posttraumatic stress disorder in female victims of interpersonal violence. *Journal of Consulting and Clinical Psychology, 76*(2), 243–258. https://doi.org/10.1037/0022-006X.76.2.243

Resick, P. A., Suvak, M. K., Johnides, B. D., Mitchell, K. S., & Iverson, K. M. (2012). The impact of dissociation on PTSD treatment with cognitive processing therapy. *Depression and Anxiety, 29*(8), 718–730.

Resick, P. A., Wachen, J. S., Mintz, J., Young-McCaughan, S., Roache, J. D., Borah, A. M., et al. (2015). A randomized clinical trial of group cognitive processing therapy compared with group present-centered therapy for PTSD among active duty military personnel. *Journal of Consulting and Clinical Psychology, 83*(6), 1058.

Resick, P. A., Wachen, J. S., Dondanville, K. A., Pruiksma, K. E., Yarvis, J. S., Peterson, A. L., et al. (2017). Effect of group vs individual cognitive processing therapy in active-duty military seeking treatment for posttraumatic stress disorder: A randomized clinical trial. *JAMA Psychiatry, 74*(1), 28–36.

Resick, P. A., Monson, C. M., & Chard, K. M. (2024). *Cognitive processing therapy for PTSD: A comprehensive manual* (2nd ed.). Guilford Press.

Schnaider, P., Boyd, J. E., Cameron, D. H., & McCabe, R. E. (2022). The relationship between emotion regulation difficulties and PTSD outcomes during group cognitive processing therapy for PTSD. *Psychological Services, 19*(4), 751–759. https://doi.org/10.1037/ser0000546

Schnurr, P. P., Chard, K. M., Ruzek, J. I., Chow, B. K., Resick, P. A., Foa, E. B., et al. (2022). Comparison of prolonged exposure vs cognitive processing therapy for treatment of posttraumatic stress disorder among US veterans: A randomized clinical trial. *JAMA Network Open, 5*(1), e2136921–e2136921.

Spiller, T. R., Duek, O., Buta, E., Gross, G., Smith, N. B., & Harpaz-Rotem, I. (2022). Comparative effectiveness of group v individual trauma-focused treatment for posttraumatic stress disorder in veterans. *Psychological Medicine, 53*(10), 4561–4568. https://doi.org/10.1017/S0033291722001441

Straud, C. L., et al. (2021). The impact of hazardous drinking among active-duty military with PTSD: Does CPT format matter? *Journal of Traumatic Stress, 34*, 210–220.

Wachen, J. S., Mintz, J., LoSavio, S. T., Kennedy, J. E., Hale, W. J., & Straud, C. L. . (2022). The impact of prior head injury on outcomes following group and individual cognitive processing therapy among military personnel. *Journal of Traumatic Stress, 35*(6), 1684–1695.STRONG STAR Consortium

Wachen, J. S., Morris, K. L., Galovski, T. E., Dondanville, K. A., Resick, P. A., & Schwartz, C. (2024). Massed cognitive processing therapy for combat-related posttraumatic stress disorder: Study design and methodology of a non-inferiority randomized controlled trial. *Contemporary Clinical Trials, 136*, 107405.

Walter, K. H., Varkovitzky, R. L., Owens, G. P., Lewis, J., & Chard, K. M. (2014). Cognitive processing therapy for veterans with posttraumatic stress disorder: A comparison between outpatient and residential treatment. *Journal of Consulting and Clinical Psychology, 82*(4), 551–561. https://doi.org/10.1037/a0037075

Wright, E. C., Wachen, J. S., Yamokowski, C., Galovski, T., Morris, K., Goetter, E. M., et al. (2022). Clinical and administrative insights from delivering massed trauma focused therapy to service members and veterans. *Cognitive and Behavioral Practice*. Advanced online publication.

Zielinski, M. J., Allison, M. K., Smith, M. K. S., Curran, G., Kaysen, D., & Kirchner, J. E. (2023). Implementation of group cognitive processing therapy in correction centers: Anticipated determinants from formative evaluation. *Journal of Traumatic Stress, 36*(1), 193–204. https://doi.org/10.1002/jts.22898

Chapter 14
Implementing CPT in a Massed Delivery Format

Philip Held and Brian J. Klassen

Scope of Problem

The once-weekly delivery model for psychotherapy sessions has evolved as a standard practice in our field. This norm pervades not only institutional expectations and training models, but also extends to payers, which are accustomed to billing based on weekly sessions. Moreover, much of the research supporting the effectiveness of psychotherapy is the result of clinical trials and other research where therapists deliver psychotherapy via once or twice weekly sessions. In the case of posttraumatic stress disorder (PTSD), interventions such as Cognitive Processing Therapy (CPT; Resick et al., 2024) are well-known to produce large and lasting symptom reductions alongside improvements in functioning (Asmundson et al., 2019). CPT was originally designed as a 12-session protocol, and although original clinical trials to evaluate its effectiveness were conducted using twice weekly sessions (e.g., Resick et al., 2002), the norm in practice is to provide care to individuals once per week (Held et al., 2019; Resick et al., 2024; Schleider et al., 2020). In other words, to complete a full course of 12 weekly CPT sessions, an individual would be in treatment for approximately 3–4 months, assuming regular attendance. Untreated PTSD increases the risk for different problems, including suicidal ideation (Akbar et al., 2023), alcohol and substance use (Dell'Aquila & Berle, 2023), as well as overall mortality (Nilaweera et al., 2023). Furthermore, PTSD can interfere with individuals' abilities to fulfill important functions in their relationships, at school, or at work (Jellestad et al., 2021), resulting in significant relational and societal impacts. Therefore, it is imperative to not only treat PTSD with effective

P. Held (✉) · B. J. Klassen
Department of Psychiatry and Behavioral Sciences, Rush University Medical Center, Chicago, IL, USA
e-mail: Philip_Held@rush.edu; Brian_Klassen@rush.edu

J. S. Wachen, T. E. Galovski (eds.), *Cognitive Processing Therapy for Complex Cases*, CBT: Science Into Practice,
https://doi.org/10.1007/978-3-031-87356-0_14

interventions (Department of Veterans Affairs, 2023), such as CPT, but to treat PTSD expediently to reduce the impact of the disorder on functioning.

With an understanding of the deleterious impacts of untreated PTSD, researchers and clinicians began to explore the effects of accelerating the delivery of evidence-based psychotherapies for PTSD, such that sessions were delivered more frequently than once or twice per week. It was critical to examine the safety and feasibility of accelerating trauma-focused evidence-based psychotherapies for PTSD raised questions about the safety and feasibility, as well as whether such models would obtain similar outcomes as treatment delivered once or twice per week. Moreover, as PTSD commonly co-occurs with other mental health conditions, it was necessary to explore whether symptom improvements achieved when treatment was accelerated could extend to other co-occurring conditions. Over the last decade, researchers have systematically studied these accelerated delivery formats that are now collectively referred to as "massed" treatment (although other terms, such as "accelerated" or "intensive" are used interchangeably; see Sciarrino et al. (2020) and Wachen et al. (2019) for reviews). In massed treatment, session frequency is increased to multiple sessions per week. Treatments are commonly considered to be delivered in massed format if individuals receive three or more sessions per week (Held & Wachen, 2023), which allows them to complete a full course of CPT in 1 month or less. Some forms of massed CPT have offered as many as three sessions per day, resulting in treatment completion in just 1 week (Galovski et al., 2022; Held et al., 2019, 2022a; Wachen et al., 2024).

We recognize that the thought of treating PTSD in as little as 1–3 weeks may be perplexing to some patients as well as providers. This may be especially true when working with individuals who have lived with their PTSD for many years or even decades. For example, providers may be concerned that delivering CPT on a daily basis might be too overwhelming for individuals, that patients would not have sufficient time to process information learned in session, or that the time to practice newly acquired skills would be too short to have any long-term success, among many other concerns (Wright et al., 2022). Admittedly, we shared some of these concerns, but viewed them as empirical questions. We now encourage both patients and providers who are hesitant about massed CPT to use their curiosity about what may and may not be possible, as the field has amassed substantial evidence that supports the delivery of CPT in a massed format.

Research Overview

Just like its traditional once or twice weekly counterpart (Asmundson et al., 2019), massed CPT has been delivered individually, in group format, and with a combination of these two delivery methods (Bryan et al., 2022; Galovski et al., 2022; Wachen et al., 2024; Zalta et al., 2018). Massed CPT may also be delivered in conjunction with other interventions or recreational activities as part of intensive treatment programs (Bryan et al., 2018; Held et al., 2020a). For the latter approach, individuals may travel to a treatment center where they reside for the duration of treatment. This has been hypothesized to be beneficial for reducing symptoms of avoidance, while facilitating an individual's focus on the treatment protocol (Harvey et al., 2017; Held et al., 2019). Examples of interventions with which massed CPT has been combined in these settings include psychoeducation or wellness approaches (Harvey et al., 2017), mindfulness or yoga (Miller et al., 2020), or dialectical behavior therapy skills groups (Lofgreen et al., 2020). Adjunctive treatments are often included because they are thought to increase patient engagement, help address common comorbidities associated with PTSD, or result in PTSD symptom improvement in their own right (Harvey et al., 2017). The session frequency across these delivery methods has varied greatly, resulting in treatments ranging in duration from 1 to 3 weeks. Despite variation in treatment delivery formats, published studies of massed CPT have all offered adequate doses (i.e., eight or more sessions) of either individual or group CPT. Completing an adequate amount of CPT may help individuals to derive symptom reductions and functional improvement from treatment.

Massed CPT as a stand-alone intervention has been compared to massed CPT in conjunction with recreational activities (Bryan et al., 2022). These studies have not supported the notion that adjunctive services improve outcomes beyond massed CPT as a stand-alone treatment (Sciarrino et al., 2020). The findings across these studies suggest that CPT, rather than its combination with adjunctive services, drives change in most individuals. Specifically, massed CPT as a stand-alone intervention outperformed massed CPT combined with recreational activities with regard to PTSD symptom reductions (Bryan et al., 2022). Similarly, Held et al. (2022b) compared two massed treatment programs, and found that reducing the amount of adjunctive services, such as psychoeducation, yoga, and even group therapy by approximately 40 total hours while keeping a similar number of individual CPT sessions resulted in comparable reductions in PTSD symptoms. Moreover, reducing the overall treatment duration and amount of adjunctive services did not appear to impact individuals' abilities to maintain their treatment gains; the shorter program was found to produce comparably large PTSD symptom reduction up to 1 year following treatment completion (Held et al., 2024a). While the reasons for the apparent lack of increased patient engagement or improved clinical outcomes relative to stand-alone massed CPT are not clear, it may be that adjunctive treatments leave less time for out-of-session practice of CPT skills, or may result in some confusion for patient's regarding how to understand their problems and the treatment approach (e.g., "*should I address my PTSD symptoms through changing inaccurate beliefs about my trauma or by getting more physically active?*"). Lastly, it is possible that because adjunctive activities are generally less emotionally salient and explicitly not trauma-focused, they may become avenues for avoidance (Bryan et al., 2022). These findings have implications for clinicians and administrators who may be considering the development of massed CPT treatment programs. Specifically, developers may strive to create treatment schedules that maximize focus on CPT. This is especially important when these programs are short in duration, as it may be prudent to focus on a single presenting problem (i.e., PTSD) in the allotted time.

Studies examining massed CPT have shown that the treatment provides large and lasting improvements in both PTSD (Galovski et al., 2022; Held et al., 2022b, 2024a; Yamokoski et al., 2022) as well as associated symptoms and functioning (Smith et al., 2022) across a variety of trauma types and populations, including civilians, service members, and veterans (Held et al., 2019; Ragsdale et al., 2020; Sciarrino et al., 2020; Wachen et al., 2019). Importantly, massed CPT has not been associated with symptom exacerbation or adverse events in published studies. Thus, although it may appear as if the treatment is more intensive due to the increased session frequency, massed CPT has been found to be well-tolerated and safe. In a pilot, randomized controlled clinical trial in civilians, massed CPT delivered over the course of a single week showed that individuals who completed treatment were likely to experience similarly large PTSD symptom reductions as those who received weekly CPT (Galovski et al., 2022). As mentioned earlier in this chapter, the key difference is that massed CPT allows individuals to experience these improvements in a matter of days. To put this into perspective, our prior research has shown that meaningful PTSD symptom improvements (i.e., 10 or more points on the PCL-5) occurred around the sixth CPT session in massed CPT (Held et al., 2022a). Whereas the sixth session occurs approximately 1.5 months into treatment in once weekly CPT, the sixth session is reached after just 3 days in 1-week massed CPT where individuals receive at least two sessions of the intervention per day (Galovski et al., 2022; Held et al., 2022a; Wachen et al., 2024).

An adequate dose of CPT, regardless of the time frame in which it is administered, may provide individuals with the necessary skills to manage their symptoms long-term. Despite the short duration of time in therapy, studies found that symptom improvements during massed CPT can generally be maintained for at least 12 months after the completion of treatment (Held et al., 2020b, 2024a). These improvements may be able to be maintained for much longer as is the case for more traditional CPT which has been shown to provide lasting effects for up to ten years (Resick et al., 2012), but there is currently no research that has examined massed CPT outcomes beyond the 12-month time frame. Longer-term follow-up studies to track maintenance of treatment gains following massed delivery of CPT are needed to fully understand the maintenance of treatment gains and the impact on psychosocial functioning across important life domains.

Massed CPT has repeatedly been shown to be associated with high treatment completion rates of around 90%, whether delivered stand-alone or as part of intensive treatment programs (Bryan et al., 2018; Held et al., 2022a, 2022b; Wright et al., 2022; Yamokoski et al., 2022). This compares favorably to once weekly CPT delivered in clinical settings where completion rates are around 60% (Kehle-Forbes et al., 2016). There may be several possible explanations for the high completion rates in massed CPT. First, individuals often travel to intensive treatment programs and are temporarily housed nearby (Held et al., 2020a). This may increase retention as it is more challenging for individuals to avoid treatment or leave all together—although it is not impossible. However, similarly high completion rates have also been noted when massed CPT was delivered on an outpatient basis (Galovski et al., 2022), or even when delivered virtually from individuals' homes where they could have opted to not attend sessions (Held et al., 2021a, 2022a). Another factor is the clear treatment structure. Clearing one's schedule for 1 to 3 weeks for treatment is likely more straightforward than arranging one's schedule each week for 3 to 4 months, where individuals may face an increased chance for unexpected interfering events to occur. Although this hypothesis needs to be tested, it is possible that the abbreviated time frame in which symptom remit in massed CPT functions as an additional motivator for individuals to complete treatment. Individuals may become curious or enthusiastic about how much more improvement they can experience throughout the remainder of treatment given their significant progress in a matter of a few treatment days.

Although starting massed CPT may increase the chance of receiving a full course of treatment, treatment attendance can also be a barrier. For many individuals, traveling to an intensive treatment program or attending massed CPT in person every day or even multiple times per day may not be feasible, especially when they are required to balance multiple responsibilities on top of managing their PTSD. Fortunately, in-person attendance is not required in order for massed CPT to be effective. Both research trials and data from specialty clinics have now shown that virtually delivered massed CPT is likely as effective as in-person treatment (Held et al., 2021a, 2022a). These findings should not be surprising given the robust literature on the effectiveness of traditional models of CPT delivered virtually (e.g., Morland et al., 2015, 2020). Like in-person treatment, virtual massed CPT was associated with minimal dropout and large symptom reductions. Although longer-term follow-up data for virtual massed CPT has not yet been published, preliminary data show that individuals were able to maintain improvements 3 months following the completion of their virtual treatment (Held et al., 2022a). Moreover, despite being available to individuals, only 25% opted to receive booster sessions following 1-week virtual massed CPT (Held et al., 2022a). Overall, virtual massed CPT has been well-received by individuals who have commented that the virtual treatment format made it possible for them to receive treatment while continuing to fulfill family, school, or work responsibilities (Kovacevic et al., 2023). For this reason, together with the strong outcome data, virtual massed CPT should be considered when individuals may express hesitation about being able to attend in-person treatment. See Chap. 16 for more detail on delivering CPT via telehealth.

A common misconception held by clinicians who initially learn about massed CPT is that the treatment format is only effective for individuals without co-occurring conditions. There have now been numerous studies on a variety of co-occurring concerns, all of which have clearly demonstrated the effectiveness of massed CPT (Held et al., 2021b, 2021c; Lofgreen et al., 2020; Post et al., 2021; Smith et al., 2023; Zalta et al., 2020). In other words, the approach is not only helpful for individuals with "straightforward" presentations of PTSD, but may be especially important in cases where untreated PTSD exacerbates co-occurring concerns. For example, individuals who reported hazardous drinking behaviors endorsed higher PTSD symptoms at the start of a massed CPT program, and still achieved comparable overall PTSD symptom reductions, suggesting that treatment was effective for these individuals (Held et al., 2021c). Massed CPT has also been shown to reduce suicidal ideation (Post et al., 2021; Smith et al., 2023). In fact, the reduction of PTSD symptoms during massed CPT predicted reduced suicidal ideation in the short-term (Post et al., 2021) and up to 3 months following treatment completion (Smith et al., 2023). The receipt of massed CPT appears to reduce the amount pain interferes with individuals' lives, even when pain or pain-related cognitions are not the focus of treatment (Kovacevic et al., 2024). Subsequent research has shown that reductions in pain intensity follow initial reductions in PTSD severity during massed CPT (Held et al., 2024b). Finally, research on massed CPT has shown that individuals experience the same benefit regardless of the amount of time they have lived with their PTSD (Splaine et al., 2022).

As we alluded to above, trauma type has not been shown to impact massed CPT outcomes. In studies examining the impact of massed CPT programs comparing combat and military sexual traumas, massed CPT has been shown to produce equivalent PTSD and depression symptom reductions (Held et al., 2022b; Lofgreen et al., 2020). Massed CPT has also been examined in the context of multiple sexual victimizations (Tirone et al., 2020), which are sometimes viewed as making treatment more challenging due to the multiple contextual layers associated with these traumas. In both cases, massed CPT has been shown to be effective for individuals who fall into these groups, producing the same symptom improvements for those with and without these experiences. Similar findings have been shown for other inter- and intrapersonal experiences, such as the experience of morally injurious events. Massed CPT was found to be effective for individuals regardless of whether they worked on a morally injurious index trauma or not, or the extent to which they self-reported morally injurious experiences (Held et al., 2021b).

In summary, the aforementioned research on the effectiveness of massed CPT in individuals who present with various co-occurring concerns highlights the robustness of the treatment approach. One possible explanation for these results might be that the condensed nature of treatment prevents the co-occurring conditions from interfering with treatment. Another possible explanation could be that the limited amount of time and the associated "positive pressure"—a sense of being in the same boat—may result in patients and their providers remaining keenly focused on treating the primary problem at hand (i.e., PTSD). This hypothesis is supported by research that has examined the working alliance during massed CPT. A study examining patient perceived working alliance with their massed CPT therapist found that the perceived working alliance grew rapidly over the course of 3-week massed CPT treatment program. The results suggested that perceived agreement on the tasks to be addressed in therapy was the strongest predictor of PTSD symptom reductions (Held et al., 2022c). Talking about sensitive topics, such as one's traumatic experiences, up to multiple times per day with a new provider may rapidly facilitate the kind of affective bond that may be necessary to restructure one's beliefs about themselves, others, and the world. Regardless of the exact mechanism through which strong relationships are formed during massed CPT, it is important for providers to bear in mind that the sheer brevity of treatment does not appear to negatively impact the ability to form strong relationships with patients. Similar to research on once weekly CPT, individuals report that the perceived working alliance with their providers grows throughout massed CPT (Held et al., 2022c).

Clinical Application

In the following section, we describe the clinical application of massed CPT delivered virtually. We focus on different aspects of the treatment delivery, including clinician factors, treatment techniques, and patient factors, as well as different program variations. We conclude this section with a case example of Thomas, who has undergone 1-week massed CPT.

Clinician factors The experience of delivering massed CPT for clinicians themselves is relatively understudied. On an individual-therapist level, some therapists may thrive in delivering massed CPT, while others seem to struggle (Wright et al., 2022). This observation suggests that the therapist's experience of traditional weekly treatment and delivering massed CPT are not the same. These differences should be considered when designing programs and providing supervision. The presence of therapist stuck points (LoSavio et al., 2019; Resick et al., 2024), specifically regarding the delivery of massed CPT, should be considered. Examples may include "*my patient is too complex to benefit from massed CPT*" or "*shorter treatments are not effective for trauma that happened a long time ago*." Positively, therapists who routinely deliver massed CPT have anecdotally observed increases in their self-efficacy, quite possibly because of the rapid clinical improvements and reduced premature therapy termination associated with the massed delivery format (Wright et al., 2022). Conversely, the unique emotional burdens of working intensely with fewer patients in a context that may be perceived as more high-stakes can be a drawback for some therapists (Wright et al., 2022). Branson (2019), in reviewing the literature on clinician burn-out, has suggested that ongoing supervision, peer consultation, taking time to reflect on the meaning of one's work, and adhering to predetermined work–rest cycles are considered best practices, which can also be applied to the routine delivery of massed CPT.

Techniques Most of the existing massed CPT formats adhere to the standard CPT protocol (Resick et al., 2024). One key reason for the decision to keep the protocol mostly unchanged is that providers who are already familiar with CPT can easily deliver the massed intervention while maintaining the fidelity of the treatment, without needing to learn another protocol or engage in numerous, specific adaptations. Furthermore, the general clinical approach is similar to traditional CPT; we focus as early as possible on assimilated stuck points, which has been shown to be associated with improved clinical outcomes (Farmer et al., 2017). There are some points that are worth highlighting as differences between traditional and massed CPT as they can meaningfully impact treatment delivery. Whenever possible we do not use general, non-trauma examples in teaching the cognitive model to patients.

Instead, we attempt to explain how assimilated beliefs might form after a trauma similar to the patient's experience, ideally using their own examples which they may have provided when discussing their experience of PTSD. We also have the routine practice of emphasizing assimilated beliefs when assigning homework, even as early as the first A-B-C sheets, where we instruct the patient to consider column A as their index trauma. Massed CPT is sometimes delivered via 10 sessions (i.e., daily for two 5-day workweeks, rather than 12 sessions in the original CPT protocol). The 10-session format allows individuals to have two sessions per day and complete treatment in a single week. Early conversations with patients suggested that this format may be more feasible from a scheduling perspective as it allows them to schedule their two daily sessions at consistent times each day rather than trying to remember additional sessions on some days. Moreover, having two daily sessions provides them with enough time during the day to complete other tasks. Patients also suggested that it would be inconvenient to also schedule sessions on weekends or into the following week. In this delivery model, we have found it helpful to decide with the patient which two or three of the five themes are most relevant. The identified themes will be focused on during session whereas the others may be assigned as homework (see case example below).

Although homework completion has not been systematically studied in the context of massed CPT, administrators of massed programs have noticed that homework completion in massed CPT appears to be better compared to what is commonly observed in once or twice weekly treatment (Wright et al., 2022). Possible reasons for high homework compliance may be that patients have limited time in between massed CPT sessions, which leads them to consider homework completion a priority. Indeed, some programs have scheduled time in the treatment day for homework completion. Additionally, having a specific upcoming deadline for the homework assignment and a designated time frame to complete the homework (e.g., knowing that homework needs to be completed this afternoon ahead of tomorrow morning's session) might also help reduce procrastination or avoidance. Once homework is completed, therapists can quickly review and provide corrective feedback if needed. This might prevent individuals from completing homework assignments and practicing the skills incorrectly for a longer time (which may ultimately require additional time to unlearn), and this provides an opportunity for therapists to reinforce skill development. Furthermore, receiving therapist feedback in a timely manner may increase patient's motivation and the sense that homework completion is an important part of their progress in treatment (Woolley et al., 2023). Research on twice weekly CPT has highlighted the importance of homework completion for improved outcomes (Stirman et al., 2018). Although less is known about the importance of completing homework correctly or receiving corrective feedback quickly, research on CPT suggests that patients' understanding of the importance of homework contributes to the completion of assignments and ultimately treatment success (Woolley et al., 2023). Better understanding the process of homework completion in massed CPT may further shed light on the model's specific benefits.

Traditional supervision and consultation models need to be adapted to the massed format as well. For example, the standard once weekly supervision model would result in entire cases being complete between supervision session in formats, such as 1-week CPT (Galovski et al., 2022; Held et al., 2022a). To provide therapists with support during treatment, some programs have incorporated brief daily 15-min huddles for the team to exchange information about patients (Yamokoski et al., 2022). In our clinical settings, we have found that briefer and more frequent supervision meetings (e.g., daily 30-min supervisions for every two CPT sessions), that also use session recordings, have been helpful when trainees provide massed CPT. We have found that training providers using massed CPT instead can potentially speed up the overall training process. By taking on massed CPT cases for training purposes, trainees are often able to complete several cases in the first month after their CPT training. Moreover, the high completion rate associated with massed CPT appears to also increase the likelihood for trainees to complete the CPT protocol with the majority of their training cases. This may also provide an opportunity for high degrees of skill attainment and specialization, the longer clinicians practice CPT. The same principles of massed learning and massed practice that we described above in the context of individuals learning CPT skills may also apply to providers. By delivering CPT more frequently, providers may also quickly become adept at providing the intervention. Like in language immersion programs, providers can become relatively "fluent" in CPT in a few weeks, but more studies specifically examining training in massed CPT are needed.

Patient factors Patient motivation and ability to engage in treatment are often central considerations in judging a patient's suitability for massed CPT. Although the transtheoretical stages of change model (Krebs et al., 2018) has not been systematically studied regarding patient outcomes in massed CPT, we have found it to be a helpful concept in understanding why patients would elect massed treatment when offered. It may appear self-evident that an emotionally demanding and fast-paced treatment like massed CPT may only be appropriate for those in the action stage; however, we would caution that this may not always be the case. The relationship between massed treatment and motivation is complex, as patients' motivation may increase early in treatment after rapid decreases in symptoms (Kovacevic et al., 2023; Wright et al., 2022). This hypothesis needs further study, however.

Despite the advantages of massed CPT, the model can present some practical concerns for patients and their significant others that should be addressed before proceeding. Some patients may find the increased treatment schedule too demanding, while juggling other responsibilities. We have found the use of telehealth to address some of these barriers, while also providing good clinical outcomes (Held et al., 2021a; 2022a). In the case described below, the patient actively engaged in treatment for 4 h a day (2 h in session, plus 2 h of homework time), which left time for other responsibilities. He was also offered massed CPT via telehealth, which further reduced his time commitment to only the most essential elements of treatment. It may be important to engage the patient's significant others in the massed treatment process as well, to help set realistic expectations about the time commitment as well as to facilitate their support. Although the case described below had positive influence from his girlfriend, this will not always be the case for every patient, so it is useful to consider the patient's social context when considering massed treatment. Talking with employers or schools about temporary leave for the patient while they complete treatment may also alleviate some barriers—but, as described earlier, some patients have been able to work around existing obligations, such as by completing an initial session before work and another either during their lunch breaks or after work, for example (Kovacevic et al., 2023). Lastly, we have found it helpful to have referrals for organizations that provide financial assistance if patients are concerned about lost income due to their engagement in a massed treatment protocol.

Case Example

This case example focuses on Thomas, a combat veteran in his 30s, who self-referred for PTSD treatment. He had experienced increased alienation from his girlfriend, which was distressing to him. Intake procedures included a semi-structured psychosocial interview, administration of symptom measures, and a review of his medical records. Administration of structured diagnostic interviews confirmed diagnoses of PTSD, Persistent Depressive Disorder, Alcohol Use Disorder in full remission, and Cannabis Use Disorder in full remission. Although Thomas endorsed exposure to a wide variety of traumas, including combat, the sudden and violent loss of peers, and exposure to natural disasters in childhood, he identified severe childhood physical abuse from his father as the index trauma. Thomas had a significant history of prior mental health treatment, including command-directed counseling for alcohol use disorder while serving in the Marines. After separating from the Marines, Thomas was hospitalized twice for suicidal ideation. Thomas also initiated, but did not complete, three separate residential programs for PTSD because he felt like the treatment was too slow and residential treatment felt too restrictive. Thomas also noted that, despite being referred several times, he had not established consistent outpatient therapy. At the start of treatment, Thomas' self-report PTSD and depression symptom scores were suggestive of a PTSD diagnosis as well as Depression symptoms in the Moderate range of severity. Specifically, he scored a 56 on the PTSD Checklist for DSM-5 (PCL-5; total possible score: 80), which are considered moderate to severe PTSD symptoms, and a 12 on the Patient Health Questionnaire (PHQ-9; total possible score: 27), which are considered moderate depressive symptoms.

Treatment Process Thomas was offered a course of 1-week virtual massed CPT that included ten sessions over the course of Monday through Friday, or one work week. Virtual treatment via telehealth was offered because Thomas lived several hours drive from the clinic. CPT sessions were scheduled twice per day (Monday–Friday) with approximately 1-h in-between sessions, during which time Thomas was expected to complete assigned homework. Given the virtual nature, when not in treatment, Thomas was free to engage in whatever other activities he wished.

Although he was also offered a more comprehensive 2-week massed CPT program that was held in-person and included adjunctive services, he remarked: "*just give me the lean version. I don't really want extra fluff... plus, I can't spare the time off work.*" The accelerated and focused nature of the treatment appealed to Thomas. He stated: "*Yeah, I mean, if I can start feeling better in a week, why wait three months? That's a no-brainer to me. I'm ready to go—let's just knock this out.*" At the time, Thomas was working in the construction industry and had arranged with his employer to have 1 week off from work so that he could attend treatment.

Although Thomas was interested in the practical aspects of the massed CPT model, he expressed some initial skepticism in the first session about how much he could expect to benefit given the limited treatment duration. In addressing Thomas' concern, the therapist was careful, through Socratic dialogue, to address how massed CPT might differ from previous rounds of treatment:

Thomas: *So, listen, I want you to know that I'm bought in, and I'm here to work through some things. My girlfriend also wants me here, but a week seems so short. I mean, I've been having issues for a long time.*

Therapist: *Yes, I agree that a week isn't a long time. We talked before about how this is a new approach, but we have some examples of where it's really helped people with similar experiences to yours see themselves and their traumas differently. When you think about your past attempts at treatment, how does this one sound?*

Thomas: *Well, it sounds a lot more intense. I remember you telling me that we'd talk about my trauma at least a little bit every session.*

Therapist: *Yeah, exactly. How does that compare to other programs you did in the past?*

Thomas: *I don't think my abuse or relationship with my dad ever came up. Plus, we spent so much time in group therapy, and I already felt like I didn't belong there, that I wouldn't have brought it up.*

Therapist: *Perhaps a different approach means different results?*

Thomas: *Yes, I see what you mean. Like I said, I'm willing to try.*

As in traditionally delivered CPT (Farmer et al., 2017; Resick et al., 2024), treatment started by identifying several key assimilated stuck points associated with his index trauma, such as "*I should have been more careful not to anger my dad,*" "*I should have told someone,*" and "*I should have stayed out of the way.*" Given that Thomas had an hour between sessions, he was expected to complete at least three worksheets following each session, and to complete more if he could. In addition to scheduling the massed CPT sessions, Thomas was also encouraged and agreed to schedule homework completion time as "appointments" in his calendar.

Using CPT worksheets and Socratic dialogue, Thomas was able to see that some of his current low self-concept may have been related to unwarranted feelings of guilt and shame that the abuse he suffered was his fault. Within 2 days, Thomas had reached CPT session 4, and had built broader contextual awareness about his father's (vs. his own) responsibility for the abuse. Thomas arrived at the conclusion that he would sometimes purposely provoke his father and take beatings so that his younger siblings would be spared, and he began to consider his father's own history of trauma. Thomas generally followed the recommendation of completing three worksheets prior to the next session. Through the use of ABC worksheets, Thomas had built increased awareness of how his beliefs affected his emotions—especially, how beliefs like "*I should have told someone*" left him feeling guilty for his own abuse. By the end of CPT session 4, Thomas had already reduced his belief in some key stuck points. In line with the standard CPT protocol (Resick et al., 2024), Challenging Questions worksheets were introduced in CPT session 4, along with additional Socratic dialogue around his key assimilated stuck points.

At the beginning of session 5 which occurred on Wednesday morning, Thomas and his therapist had an exchange that highlights the (sometimes surprising) speed with which patients can challenge and reframe stuck points, and the emotional relief that can result:

Therapist: *Ok—before we review the homework you completed yesterday, I wanted to show you something. (*Therapist shares screen, showing a Microsoft Excel with daily self-report symptom scores. Thomas had already achieved clinically significant reductions in PTSD and depression symptoms. Specifically, PCL-5 score had reduced by 12 points and his PHQ-9 score had reduced by 3 points*). Remember how I said we'd be tracking your symptoms of PTSD and depression each day with those questionnaires I ask you to fill out? Well, we're seeing some big drops in your scores today, meaning that you're feeling less bothered and upset by your symptoms. How does that track with how you're feeling?*

Thomas: *Yeah, I mean… since I've been opening up… you have to understand, I never really went into my childhood in this much detail with anybody before. It has been hard—but I thought it would be a lot harder. I have to say, I really am feeling better.*

Therapist: *Huh… ok. Like we are breaking new ground here?*

Thomas: *I really think so. I'm looking at things more realistically. For a long time, I just tried to see myself as perfect, or tried to hold myself to this impossible standard—like, I couldn't have had those things done to me. I guess I just realized that I'm human and I need to cut myself a little more slack.*

Therapist: *That's great. So, I really don't want to make a huge deal out of these numbers because it's just one way to measure progress. What matters most are the changes you notice in your life and how you think about yourself and your trauma.*

Thomas: *Yeah, I get that. Those worksheets I filled out last night really helped me dial back feeling like I should have told somebody about what was happening to me. The question about emotions impacting my thoughts and seeing situations as black-or-white really got me. I realized that I wasn't seeing the situation logically… which was hard because I see myself as a logical person. This will sound* *weird, but I called my girlfriend to fill her in and she got so excited. She said I sounded different.*

Therapist: *Maybe you've thought about this already, but have you considered that we're now about half-way done with treatment?*

Thomas: *(shakes his head)... I had started to wonder if maybe too much stuff has happened to me... like... maybe my brain was just broken. This therapy is really helping. I feel like I could quit now and be OK, but I'm glad we can keep working... Ok, what's next?*

After his assimilated stuck points were thoroughly addressed by CPT session 6, therapy transitioned to the five themes of Safety, Trust, Power/Control, Intimacy, and Esteem. Thomas was provided all remaining CPT handouts at session 7 and given a brief overview of each theme. At this point, three CPT sessions remained, and Thomas was encouraged to focus on the themes that were most impacted by the trauma. Given that he struggled with low self-concept and commitment to his girlfriend, Thomas chose to emphasize Esteem, Intimacy, and Trust. He agreed to complete Safety, and Power/Control for homework outside of session. CPT Sessions 7, 8, and 9 were spent on identifying and address overaccommodated stuck points such as "*I'm no good,*" "*I have nothing to offer my girlfriend,*" and "*If I let someone in, they'll betray me.*" During CPT session 10, the final session in this particular 1-week CPT protocol, Thomas was asked to read his final impact statement and reflect with his therapist about how his thinking had changed. This exchange highlights the genuine change that Thomas saw occur in his thinking, despite the brevity of the treatment. He identified the trauma-focused and time-limited nature of the treatment as major contributors to his good outcome.

Thomas: [looking at his initial impact statement and his re-written impact statement side-by-side on the screen] *This is amazing... it's like someone else wrote this.*

Therapist: *I agree. You've really worked hard and used this time well. What has changed the most over the past week?*

Thomas: *Like I said a few sessions ago, I realized how hard I was being on myself for not telling anyone about the beatings I'd get from my dad. Part of me knew that didn't make sense, but like talking it out with you, and taking some more time to write about for homework, showed me that blaming myself created so much guilt that affected so much of my life.*

Therapist: *Yes, I think so too. And it happened so quickly!*

Thomas: *Well, I knew I only had a week, so I had to put the work in. This therapy was laser-focused on the right stuff and taught me how to think about things on my own. It was helpful to bypass a lot of the fluff and get straight to the root causes.*

For continued practice, Thomas was also assigned termination-related stuck points, such as "*Once I end therapy, all my progress will go away.*" One week after therapy termination, Thomas came in for a scheduled check-in. At this time, Thomas reported total scores of 22 and 7 on the PCL-5 and PHQ-9, respectively. These scores indicated a good therapy end state, as well as clinically meaningful reductions in PTSD and Depression symptoms, although it is possible that Thomas could have had even further symptom reductions had he received all 12 CPT sessions.

For aftercare, Thomas elected to schedule a follow-up session 1 month after termination to assess his status and determine if more treatment was needed. We recommend waiting for at least 1 month following massed CPT completion to provide individuals with the opportunity to practice the skills they have learned and better understand what areas they may still be struggling with and could use additional support. During the follow-up session, Thomas remarked that he was "*back at work and doing fine*" and that "*my buddies have noticed that I've mellowed out.*" Despite some arguments with his girlfriend, he stated: "*it's like we're more able to talk about the real issues in our relationship instead of my flying off the handle and assuming she would walk out on me.*" His symptoms remained unchanged from termination, and Thomas stated: "*I'm not feeling perfect, but I am feeling better.*"

Future Directions

Although there are a number of clear benefits to delivering CPT in a massed format, increasing the session frequency also has downsides. As we touched on above, adding additional sessions per week can create additional burdens for some individuals, especially those who are also balancing work, school, or family responsibilities. In these cases, adding sessions may end up feeling like an additional stressor. A key limitation of the current research is that existing studies and clinical programs do not tend to offer a choice of the specific session frequency. As a result, many studies may be flawed as a result of selection bias in that only individuals who are interested in massed CPT sign up for the studies, which precludes us from understanding which individuals tend to choose massed treatment formats, and for whom massed CPT is particularly effective. Relatedly, we do not yet know which session frequency is optimal for any given individual. Based on the current research, it appears that the more frequently CPT sessions can be scheduled, the more likely individuals will be to complete it and ultimately have increased chances at experiencing meaningful symptom reductions. However, these types of decisions need to be made collaboratively with patients. In this vein, there is an urgent need for studies that use shared decision making and take patient preferences around session frequency into account as well as studies that determine for whom massed CPT may work particularly well.

Increasing the session frequency may not only be challenging for patients, but also require some flexibility on the provider. For example, providers who are used to scheduling individuals on a once per week basis may have difficulties finding room for massed CPT cases in their schedules. Assuming individuals with PTSD and their providers agree to complete a course of massed CPT with a session frequency of two sessions per day over the course of a single week, another challenge is dropout. Although dropout rates for massed CPT are generally lower than what is commonly reported for once weekly CPT, it may have bigger impacts on the practice. For example, with 10–12 CPT sessions pre-scheduled, should an individual discontinue after the first or second session, it would likely be challenging, if not impossible to fill the now vacant therapy slots within the week on such short notice. Similarly, should an individual need to miss one or two sessions, the course of therapy might need to be extended into the following week or into days that were not previously planned. Such unforeseen changes can result in potential scheduling complications. While this might work in specialty clinic settings that primarily provide massed treatment, it can create additional administrative burdens on the provider, and may suggest limited feasibility in other settings.

To date, massed CPT has primarily been studied in clinical trials and in specialty clinic settings that focus on the delivery of CPT to various populations in massed format. Indeed, much of the published research to date is drawn from data from specific military/veteran treatment programs. Further research with other populations and treatment settings will be important to build support for the efficacy of this treatment model in reducing symptoms of PTSD and promoting longer term functional improvements. Further, it also will be important to systematically assess for which settings massed CPT is most well-suited. For example, while it may be more easily adopted by specialty clinics, it is unclear to what extent massed CPT can be adopted in private practice or community settings. To address these questions, studies examining whether and which adaptations to massed CPT may be necessary to fit with these other practice settings will be important. Relatedly, it will also be critical to study what strategies may facilitate its implementation, including those focused on evaluating appropriate training, supervision, and consultation strategies for massed CPT.

Another challenge to increased availability of massed CPT in community settings is the barrier that insurance reimbursement may present. Many current billing models consider weekly therapy to be the industry standard, with more frequent billing being allowed in partial hospitalization or intensive outpatient programs. Thus, if providers are attempting to bill for multiple individual CPT sessions per day as part of a massed treatment course, they may face issues with reimbursement depending on the payer. This is a clear issue relating to feasibility. Unless this can get addressed at a policy level, it is unlikely that massed CPT will be adopted widely across providers outside of specialty settings that may have different avenues to fund services. The rapidly mounting research on the effectiveness of massed CPT will hopefully be beneficial in making a strong case for this treatment delivery format as a viable alternative to the traditional once weekly treatment cadence.

Summary

Given the promising results to date, interest in massed CPT has rapidly grown in recent years. It is now apparent that massed CPT can be highly effective even for individuals with long-standing PTSD and co-occurring concerns. It is our hope that this chapter helped increase providers' curiosity about massed CPT, and that providers are increasingly open to trying out the massed treatment delivery format with patients who have expressed interest. Given that research has shown that different massed CPT schedules appear to provide similar benefit, providers should feel assured that any additional sessions beyond the traditional once or twice weekly cadence will increase the chance of both treatment completion and symptom reduction. In our experience, it has been easier to reduce the session frequency should a patient not respond as well as they hoped than it is to scale up the frequency from once weekly to more frequent. We enjoy learning about therapists' experiences delivering massed CPT and are excited to see how the field of massed treatment delivery develops in the coming decade and beyond.

Competing Interests Philip Held has received research grants from the Department of Defense (W81XWH-22-1-0739; TP230421; TP230385), Wounded Warrior Project®, United Services Automobile Association (USAA)/Face the Fight, and the Crown Family Foundation. Brian J. Klassen has received research grants from Wounded Warrior Project®, the Robert R. McCormick Foundation, the Lundbeck U.S. Charitable Trust, and Bears Care.

The content is solely the responsibility of the authors and does not necessarily represent the official views of the Department of Defense, Wounded Warrior Project®, USAA, or any other funding agency.

References

Akbar, R., Arya, V., Conroy, E., Wilcox, H. C., & Page, A. (2023). Posttraumatic stress disorder and risk of suicidal behavior: A systematic review and meta-analysis. *Suicide and Life-Threatening Behavior, 53*(1), 163–184. https://doi.org/10.1111/sltb.12931

Asmundson, G. J. G., Thorisdottir, A. S., Roden-Foreman, J. W., Baird, S. O., Witcraft, S. M., Stein, A. T., Smits, J. A. J., & Powers, M. B. (2019). A meta-analytic review of cognitive processing therapy for adults with posttraumatic stress disorder. *Cognitive Behaviour Therapy, 48*(1), 1–14. https://doi.org/10.1080/16506073.2018.1522371

Branson, D. C. (2019). Vicarious trauma, themes in research, and terminology: A review of literature. *Traumatology, 25*(1), 2–10. https://doi.org/10.1037/trm0000161

Bryan, C. J., Leifker, F. R., Rozek, D. C., Bryan, A. O., Reynolds, M. L., Oakey, D. N., & Roberge, E. (2018). Examining the effectiveness of an intensive, 2-week treatment program for military personnel and veterans with PTSD: Results of a pilot, open-label, prospective cohort trial. *Journal of Clinical Psychology, 74*(12), 2070–2081. https://doi.org/10.1002/jclp.22651

Bryan, C. J., Russell, H. A., Bryan, A. O., Rozek, D. C., Leifker, F. R., Rugo, K. F., Baker, J. C., Khazem, L. R., Roberge, E. M., Shirley, D. M., & Asnaani, A. (2022). Impact of treatment setting and format on symptom severity following cognitive processing therapy for posttraumatic stress disorder. *Behavior Therapy, 53*(4), 673–685. https://doi.org/10.1016/j.beth.2022.01.014

Dell'Aquila, A., & Berle, D. (2023). Predictors of alcohol and substance use among people with post-traumatic stress disorder (PTSD): Findings from the NESARC-III study. *Social Psychiatry and Psychiatric Epidemiology, 58*(10), 1509–1522. https://doi.org/10.1007/s00127-023-02472-6

Department of Veterans Affairs. (2023). *VA/DOD clinical practice guideline for the management of posttraumatic stress disorder and acute stress disorder.*

Farmer, C. C., Mitchell, K. S., Parker-Guilbert, K., & Galovski, T. E. (2017). Fidelity to the cognitive processing therapy protocol: Evaluation of critical elements. *Behavior Therapy, 48*(2), 195–206. https://doi.org/10.1016/j.beth.2016.02.009

Galovski, T. E., Werner, K. B., Weaver, T. L., Morris, K. L., Dondanville, K. A., Nanney, J., Wamser-Nanney, R., McGlinchey, G., Fortier, C. B., & Iverson, K. M. (2022). Massed cognitive processing therapy for posttraumatic stress disorder in women survivors of intimate partner violence. *Psychological Trauma: Theory, Research, Practice, and Policy, 14*(5), 769–779. https://doi.org/10.1037/tra0001100

Harvey, M. M., Rauch, S. A. M., Zalta, A. K., Sornborger, J., Pollack, M. H., Rothbaum, B. O., Laifer, L. M., & Simon, N. M. (2017). Intensive treatment models to address posttraumatic stress among post-9/11 warriors: The warrior care network. *FOCUS, 15*(4), 378–383. https://doi.org/10.1176/appi.focus.20170022

Held, P., Bagley, J. M., Klassen, B. J., & Pollack, M. H. (2019). Intensively delivered cognitive-behavioral therapies: An overview of a promising treatment delivery format for PTSD and other mental health disorders. *Psychiatric Annals, 49*(8), 339–342. https://doi.org/10.3928/00485713-20190711-01

Held, P., Klassen, B. J., Boley, R. A., Wiltsey Stirman, S., Smith, D. L., Brennan, M. B., Van Horn, R., Pollack, M. H., Karnik, N. S., & Zalta, A. K. (2020a). Feasibility of a 3-week intensive treatment program for service members and veterans with PTSD. *Psychological Trauma: Theory, Research, Practice, and Policy, 12*(4), 422–430. https://doi.org/10.1037/tra0000485

Held, P., Zalta, A. K., Smith, D. L., Bagley, J. M., Steigerwald, V. L., Boley, R. A., Miller, M., Brennan, M. B., Van Horn, R., & Pollack, M. H. (2020b). Maintenance of treatment gains up to 12-months following a three-week cognitive processing therapy-based intensive PTSD treatment programme for veterans. *European Journal of Psychotraumatology, 11*(1), 1789324. https://doi.org/10.1080/20008198.2020.1789324

Held, P., Coleman, J. A., Petrey, K., Klassen, B. J., Pridgen, S., Bravo, K., Smith, D. L., & Van Horn, R. (2021a). A case series examining PTSD and depression symptom reductions over the course of a 2-week virtual intensive PTSD treatment program for veterans. *Psychological Trauma: Theory, Research, Practice, and Policy*. https://doi.org/10.1037/tra0001106

Held, P., Klassen, B. J., Steigerwald, V. L., Smith, D. L., Bravo, K., Rozek, D. C., Van Horn, R., & Zalta, A. (2021b). Do morally injurious experiences and index events negatively impact intensive PTSD treatment outcomes among combat veterans? *European Journal of Psychotraumatology, 12*(1), 1877026. https://doi.org/10.1080/20008198.2021.1877026

Held, P., Steigerwald, V. L., Smith, D. L., Kaysen, D., Van Horn, R., & Karnik, N. S. (2021c). Impact of hazardous alcohol use on intensive PTSD treatment outcomes among veterans. *European Journal of Psychotraumatology, 12*(1), 1888541. https://doi.org/10.1080/20008198.2021.1888541

Held, P., Kovacevic, M., Petrey, K., Meade, E. A., Pridgen, S., Montes, M., Werner, B., Miller, M. L., Smith, D. L., Kaysen, D., & Karnik, N. S. (2022a). Treating posttraumatic stress disorder at home in a single week using 1-week virtual massed cognitive processing therapy. *Journal of Traumatic Stress, 35*(4), Article 4. https://doi.org/10.1002/jts.22831

Held, P., Smith, D. L., Pridgen, S., Coleman, J. A., & Klassen, B. J. (2022b). More is not always better: 2 weeks of intensive cognitive processing therapy-based treatment are noninferior to 3 weeks. *Psychological Trauma: Theory, Research, Practice, and Policy*. https://doi.org/10.1037/tra0001257

Held, P., Meade, E. A., Kovacevic, M., Smith, D. L., Pridgen, S., Coleman, J. A., & Klassen, B. J. (2022c). Building strong therapeutic relationships quickly: The effect of the perceived working alliance on veterans' intensive PTSD treatment outcomes. *Psychotherapy, 59*(3), 470–480. https://doi.org/10.1037/pst0000447

Held, P., & Wachen, J. (2023). Concluding comment: Posing key questions to shape future research, enhance patient outcomes, and facilitate the implementation of intensive treatments. *Cognitive and Behavioral Practice*, S1077722923000548. https://doi.org/10.1016/j.cbpra.2023.05.001

Held, P., Smith, L. J., Parmar, A. M., Pridgen, S. A., Smith, D. L., & Klassen, B. (2024a). Veterans' 12-month PTSD and depression outcomes following 2- and 3-week intensive cognitive processing therapy-based treatment. *European Journal of Psychotraumatology, 15*(1), 2350908. https://doi.org/10.1080/20008066.2024.2350908

Held, P., Mundle, R. S., Pridgen, S., Smith, D. L., Coleman, J. A., Klassen, B. J., & Burns, J. W. (2024b). Reductions in PTSD severity precede reductions in pain intensity among veterans receiving intensive treatment. *Psychological Trauma: Theory, Research, Practice, and Policy*. https://doi.org/10.1037/tra0001761

Jellestad, L., Vital, N. A., Malamud, J., Taeymans, J., & Mueller-Pfeiffer, C. (2021). Functional impairment in Posttraumatic Stress Disorder: A systematic review and meta-analysis. *Journal of Psychiatric Research, 136*, 14–22. https://doi.org/10.1016/j.jpsychires.2021.01.039

Kehle-Forbes, S. M., Meis, L. A., Spoont, M. R., & Polusny, M. A. (2016). Treatment initiation and dropout from prolonged exposure and cognitive processing therapy in a VA outpatient clinic. *Psychological Trauma: Theory, Research, Practice, and Policy, 8*(1), 107–114. https://doi.org/10.1037/tra0000065

Kovacevic, M., Montes, M., Tirone, V., Pridgen, S., Smith, D. L., Burns, J. W., & Held, P. (2024). Treating a common comorbidity: Pain outcomes following a 3-week cognitive processing therapy–based intensive treatment for posttraumatic stress disorder address. *Journal of Traumatic Stress, 37*(1), 47–56. https://doi.org/10.1002/jts.22979

Kovacevic, M., Tharaud, J. B., Montes, M., Mundle, R. S., Splaine, C. C., Silverberg, J., Pridgen, S. A., Werner, B., & Held, P. (2023). 'Undoing a knot': A qualitative study of massed 1-week Cognitive Processing Therapy. *European Journal of Psychotraumatology, 14*(2), 2205126. https://doi.org/10.1080/20008066.2023.2205126

Krebs, P., Norcross, J. C., Nicholson, J. M., & Prochaska, J. O. (2018). Stages of change and psychotherapy outcomes: A review and meta-analysis. *Journal of Clinical Psychology, 74*(11), 1964–1979. https://doi.org/10.1002/jclp.22683

Lofgreen, A. M., Tirone, V., Carroll, K. K., Rufa, A. K., Smith, D. L., Bagley, J., Zalta, A. K., Brennan, M. B., Van Horn, R., Pollack, M. H., & Held, P. (2020). Improving outcomes for a 3-week intensive treatment program for posttraumatic stress disorder in survivors of military sexual trauma. *Journal of Affective Disorders, 269*, 134–140. https://doi.org/10.1016/j.jad.2020.03.036

LoSavio, S. T., Dillon, K. H., Murphy, R. A., & Resick, P. A. (2019). Therapist stuck points during training in cognitive processing therapy: Changes over time and associations with training outcomes. *Professional Psychology: Research and Practice, 50*(4), 255–263. https://doi.org/10.1037/pro0000224

Miller, M. L., Bagley, J. M., Normand, P., Brennan, M. B., Van Horn, R., Pollack, M. H., & Held, P. (2020). Increasing mindfulness skills of veterans with PTSD through daily mindfulness training incorporated into an intensive treatment program. *Mindfulness, 11*(4), 964–974. https://doi.org/10.1007/s12671-020-01326-5

Morland, L. A., Mackintosh, M.-A., Rosen, C. S., Willis, E., Resick, P., Chard, K., & Frueh, B. C. (2015). Telemedicine versus in-person delivery of cognitive processing therapy for women with posttraumatic stress disorder: A randomized noninferiority trial. *Depression and Anxiety, 32*(11), 811–820. https://doi.org/10.1002/da.22397

Morland, L. A., Wells, S. Y., Glassman, L. H., Greene, C. J., Hoffman, J. E., & Rosen, C. S. (2020). Advances in PTSD treatment delivery: Review of findings and clinical considerations for the use of telehealth interventions for PTSD. *Current Treatment Options in Psychiatry*, 1–21. https://doi.org/10.1007/s40501-020-00215-x

Nilaweera, D., Phyo, A. Z. Z., Teshale, A. B., Htun, H. L., Wrigglesworth, J., Gurvich, C., Freak-Poli, R., & Ryan, J. (2023). Lifetime posttraumatic stress disorder as a predictor of mortality: A systematic review and meta-analysis. *BMC Psychiatry, 23*(1), 229. https://doi.org/10.1186/s12888-023-04716-w

Post, L. M., Held, P., Smith, D. L., Black, K., Van Horn, R., Pollack, M. H., Rothbaum, B. O., & Rauch, S. A. M. (2021). Impact of intensive treatment programs for posttraumatic stress disorder on suicidal ideation in veterans and service members. *Psychological Services, 18*(4), 671–678. https://doi.org/10.1037/ser0000518

Ragsdale, K. A., Watkins, L. E., Sherrill, A. M., Zwiebach, L., & Rothbaum, B. O. (2020). Advances in PTSD treatment delivery: Evidence base and future directions for intensive outpatient programs. *Current Treatment Options in Psychiatry, 7*(3), 291–300. https://doi.org/10.1007/s40501-020-00219-7

Resick, P. A., Monson, C. M., & Chard, K. M. (2024). *Cognitive processing therapy for PTSD: A comprehensive therapist manual* (2nd ed.). The Guilford Press.

Resick, P. A., Nishith, P., Weaver, T. L., Astin, M. C., & Feuer, C. A. (2002). A comparison of cognitive-processing therapy with prolonged exposure and a waiting condition for the treatment of chronic posttraumatic stress disorder in female rape victims. *Journal of Consulting and Clinical Psychology, 70*(4), 867–879. https://doi.org/10.1037/0022-006x.70.4.867

Resick, P. A., Williams, L. F., Suvak, M. K., Monson, C. M., & Gradus, J. L. (2012). Long-term outcomes of cognitive-behavioral treatments for posttraumatic stress disorder among female rape survivors. *Journal of Consulting and Clinical Psychology, 80*(2), 201–210. https://doi.org/10.1037/a0026602

Schleider, J. L., Dobias, M. L., Mullarkey, M. C., & Ollendick, T. (2020). Retiring, rethinking, and reconstructing the norm of once-weekly psychotherapy. *Administration and Policy in Mental Health and Mental Health Services Research*. https://doi.org/10.1007/s10488-020-01090-7

Sciarrino, N. A., Warnecke, A. J., & Teng, E. J. (2020). A systematic review of intensive empirically supported treatments for posttraumatic stress disorder. *Journal of Traumatic Stress, 33*(4), 443–454. https://doi.org/10.1002/jts.22556

Smith, D. L., Kovacevic, M., Montes, M., Pridgen, S., & Held, P. (2022). Improving mental, physical, and social functioning through participation in a 3-week cognitive processing therapy-based intensive PTSD treatment. *Journal of Anxiety Disorders, 102560*. https://doi.org/10.1016/j.janxdis.2022.102560

Smith, D. L., Tharaud, J. B., Pridgen, S. A., & Held, P. (2023). Predicting suicidal ideation 3 months following intensive posttraumatic stress disorder treatment. *Psychological Trauma: Theory, Research, Practice, and Policy*. https://doi.org/10.1037/tra0001614

Splaine, C., Smith, D. L., & Held, P. (2022). The role of time since trauma on treatment outcomes of veterans in two intensive posttraumatic stress disorder treatment programs. *Journal of Traumatic Stress*, jts.22881. https://doi.org/10.1002/jts.22881

Stirman, S. W., Gutner, C. A., Suvak, M. K., Adler, A., Calloway, A., & Resick, P. A. (2018). Homework completion, patient characteristics, and symptom change in cognitive processing therapy for PTSD. *Behavior Therapy, 49*(5), 741–755. https://doi.org/10.1016/j.beth.2017.12.001

Tirone, V., Smith, D., Steigerwald, V. L., Bagley, J. M., Brennan, M., Van Horn, R., Pollack, M., & Held, P. (2020). Examining the impact of sexual revictimization in a sample of veterans undergoing intensive PTSD treatment. *Journal of Interpersonal Violence*, 886260519897333. https://doi.org/10.1177/0886260519897333

Wachen, J. S., Dondanville, K. A., Evans, W. R., Morris, K., & Cole, A. (2019). Adjusting the timeframe of evidence-based therapies for PTSD-massed treatments. *Current Treatment Options in Psychiatry, 6*(2), 107–118. https://doi.org/10.1007/s40501-019-00169-9

Wachen, J. S., Morris, K. L., Galovski, T. E., Dondanville, K. A., Resick, P. A., & Schwartz, C. (2024). Massed cognitive processing therapy for combat-related posttraumatic stress disorder: Study design and methodology of a non-inferiority randomized controlled trial. *Contemporary Clinical Trials, 136*, 107405. https://doi.org/10.1016/j.cct.2023.107405

Woolley, M. G., Smith, B. N., Micol, R. L., Farmer, C. C., & Galovski, T. E. (2023). Evaluating the relative contribution of patient effort and therapist skill in integrating homework into treatment for posttraumatic stress disorder. *Psychological Trauma: Theory, Research, Practice, and Policy*. https://doi.org/10.1037/tra0001459

Wright, E. C., Wachen, J. S., Yamokoski, C., Galovski, T., Morris, K., Goetter, E. M., Klassen, B., Jacoby, V., Zwiebach, L., Sornborger, J., Dondanville, K. A., Fina, B. A., & Rauch,

S. A. M. (2022). Clinical and administrative insights from delivering massed trauma-focused therapy to service members and veterans. *Cognitive and Behavioral Practice*, S1077722922001109. https://doi.org/10.1016/j.cbpra.2022.06.005

Yamokoski, C., Flores, H., Facemire, V., Maieritsch, K., Perez, S., & Fedynich, A. (2022). Feasibility of an intensive outpatient treatment program for posttraumatic stress disorder within the veterans health care administration. *Psychological Services*. https://doi.org/10.1037/ser0000628

Zalta, A. K., Held, P., Smith, D. L., Klassen, B. J., Lofgreen, A. M., Normand, P. S., Brennan, M. B., Rydberg, T. S., Boley, R. A., Pollack, M. H., & Karnik, N. S. (2018). Evaluating patterns and predictors of symptom change during a three-week intensive outpatient treatment for veterans with PTSD. *BMC Psychiatry, 18*(1), 242. https://doi.org/10.1186/s12888-018-1816-6

Zalta, A. K., Pinkerton, L. M., Valdespino-Hayden, Z., Smith, D. L., Burgess, H. J., Held, P., Boley, R. A., Karnik, N. S., & Pollack, M. H. (2020). Examining insomnia during intensive treatment for veterans with posttraumatic stress disorder: Does it improve and does it predict treatment outcomes? *Journal of Traumatic Stress, 33*(4), 521–527. https://doi.org/10.1002/jts.22505

Chapter 15
Incorporating Case Formulation into the Delivery of Cognitive Processing Therapy

Tara E. Galovski, Lauren B. McSweeney, and Saige E. Galovski

Scope of Problem

Over the last three decades, research on psychotherapies for PTSD has burgeoned. The empirical support for Cognitive Processing Therapy (CPT) alone has proliferated as evidenced by this book. Despite over 45 published randomized controlled clinical trials, volumes of effectiveness studies, and hundreds of papers examining secondary outcomes (Resick et al., 2024; Galovski et al., 2020), attrition and non-response rates for CPT (and other) first line treatments for PTSD (American Psychological Association, 2017; International Society for Traumatic Stress Studies, 2018; Department of Veterans Affairs & Department of Defense, 2023) remain high, suggesting room for improvement (Steenkamp et al., 2015; Watts et al., 2013). The evolution of CPT has included substantial efforts to modify the protocol through enhancements and/or expansions of the original 12-session format (Galovski et al., 2024b). Given the complexity of PTSD, the high likelihood of comorbid conditions, and the demonstrable and significant impairment in functioning associated with the disorder, the growing body of CPT research provides guidance for intervening with clinically complex patients—essentially the vast majority of patients who suffer from PTSD. Despite the accumulation of empirical support demonstrating the robustness of CPT and other trauma-focused treatments, these single-disorder

T. E. Galovski (✉) · L. B. McSweeney
Women's Health Sciences Division, National Center for PTSD, VA Boston Healthcare System and Boston University Chobanian and Avedesian School of Medicine, Boston, MA, USA
e-mail: Tara.Galovski@va.gov; Lauren.Mcsweeney@va.gov

S. E. Galovski
University of Vermont, Burlington, VT, USA

J. S. Wachen, T. E. Galovski (eds.), *Cognitive Processing Therapy for Complex Cases*, CBT: Science Into Practice,
https://doi.org/10.1007/978-3-031-87356-0_15

protocols have not been widely adopted by clinicians in routine clinical care perhaps due to the complexity of trauma survivors' clinical presentations (Galovski et al., 2024a).

Transporting these protocols developed in academia to clinical care settings has long been challenging for a number of reasons (see Galovski et al., 2024b for a conceptual review). After completion of training in evidence-based practices, clinicians must deliver the treatment with fidelity across patients with a plethora of possible competing symptoms, conditions, and life stressors that can interfere with the administration of the protocol. Indeed, clinicians are often left wondering if they are seemingly trying to fit a square peg into a round hole as they attempt to implement the protocols, including CPT, in clinical practice across various healthcare settings. There is little guidance within the treatment protocols for managing the universe of possible challenges to optimal therapy outcomes that may arise over the course of therapy. When turning to the literature to guide treatment decisions with clinically complex patients, therapists are tasked with synthesizing the enormous amounts of available data and applying the research in real time in clinical care—a task which is challenging at best. As a result of grappling with clinical complexities, therapists and patients alike may get disheartened and worry that the therapy is "not working." These types of concerns may influence the decision to prematurely abandon the therapy protocol and, in doing so, perhaps deny the patient the proper dose of the very intervention that has the highest likelihood of providing the patient relief (Kehle-Forbes et al., 2023; Nixon et al., 2021).

Further complicating the clinical care of PTSD, impairments in psychosocial functioning are profound, especially as the length of time increases during which survivors of trauma suffer from the disorder. Indeed, living with PTSD exacts a significant toll on many aspects of well-being and quality of life even decades after the trauma exposure (Bonfils et al., 2022; Schnurr et al., 2009; Vogt et al., 2017; Vogt et al., 2021). Trauma-focused therapies tend to focus first and foremost on reducing the 20 core symptoms of PTSD, with less attention paid to improvements in important areas of psychosocial functioning. The common conceptualization in administering short-term treatments for PTSD is that as the core PTSD symptoms decrease, improvements in functioning will follow. However, we know that it is quite often the impairments in functioning (e.g. relationship problems, occupational or legal difficulties, etc.) that drive patients to seek treatment, perhaps more so than the core symptoms (Schnurr & Lunney, 2016; Reich et al., 2019). Incorporating the intentional and direct targeting of impairments in functioning might, in fact, optimize the patients' likelihood of going on to live their best lives after their trauma therapy journey is completed. Because no two patients will ever present to therapy with exactly the same trauma experience, the same clinical complexities, or the same challenges in psychosocial functioning, we believe that a *personalized approach* to delivering manual-based therapies like CPT has the ability to optimize outcomes.

Research Overview

As noted throughout this book, the core CPT protocol has been enhanced in several important ways over the years. Originally developed as a 12-session protocol (Resick & Schnicke, 1996), Galovski et al., (2012) tested the concept of a variable length of treatment in which patient progress determined the end of therapy. This idea was developed as Dr. Galovski saw her patients making great strides over the course of CPT but observed that some patients still had room to improve at the end of the 12-session treatment. If patients were improving over the course of the protocol, why not keep going and determine if additional sessions could move the needle further to recovery for more patients? Indeed, by allowing extra sessions, Galovski discovered that seemingly "refractory" patients could not only lose their PTSD diagnosis, but also achieve the more stringent outcome criteria of good end-state functioning (defined as scores in the mild range on self-reported PTSD and depression scales) with the addition of only three more sessions on average. Extending therapy duration resulted in significantly fewer patients (8% compared to 20–30% in previous CPT trials) remaining PTSD positive by the end of the 18th session (the maximum allowable number of sessions in the trial). Interestingly, about 60% of patients met good end-state functioning and lost their PTSD diagnosis *sooner* than 12 sessions (on average 9 sessions), and these treatment gains were maintained in the long-term follow-up. This trial also allowed for the addition of emergency sessions in the event that a crisis occurred in patients' lives while in therapy. Although it is important to stay trauma-focused and not collude with avoidance, we learned that, when clinically indicated, providing non-protocol support through a crisis did not disrupt treatment progress.

Over the years, researchers have successfully tested additional modifications to the protocol, including many which are reviewed in various chapters in this book. For example, we have modified the worksheets to accommodate learning and cognitive needs (Chard et al., 2011) and even eliminated the worksheets entirely to meet the needs of largely illiterate populations (Bass et al., 2013). We have adapted the protocol to better meet the needs of different cultures (e.g. Bass et al., 2013; Bolton et al., 2014; Ito et al., 2017; Kaysen et al., 2013; Schulz et al., 2006; Weiss et al., 2015) and ages (Rosner et al., 2019) and translated the protocol into 13 languages. Fortunately, when the global COVID-19 pandemic struck, several clinical trials had already been published examining the efficacy of CPT delivered via telehealth compared to in-person and found no differences (as reviewed in Moring et al., 2020). Clinicians were able to quickly pivot to this modality and to continue services for many in need. Telehealth continues to be a viable option for many who choose not to (or cannot) receive therapy in person. Recent and ongoing studies have demonstrated support for implementing the entire CPT protocol in a "massed" format, meaning that all sessions are provided across a week or two (Galovski et al., 2022; Wachen et al., 2024). This treatment format may be particularly optimal for those who cannot attend sessions once per week over months (such as college students on break from school, people with impending medical needs such as a surgery or pregnancy, active duty service members with pending deployments, etc.). Stepped down approaches to clinical care have also begun to emerge with the goal of assisting patients in titrating back from regular therapy sessions to self-management (Kehle-Forbes et al., 2023). Finally, a CPT self-help manual was recently published and may increase access to self-guided trauma-focused work for many survivors who may prefer this route (Resick et al., 2023).

In addition to the *enhancements* to the CPT protocol, other studies have also *expanded* CPT with interventions designed to treat comorbid conditions that may challenge optimal outcomes. The first of these studies was conducted by Galovski and colleagues and was designed to improve sleep impairment in the context of PTSD (Galovski et al., 2016). In her clinical work, Galovski repeatedly noted that many of her CPT patients were exhausted in session. She hypothesized that improved sleep might not only be restorative and palliative for physical health reasons, but it may also increase the patient's ability to engage in the process of CPT treatment, thereby increasing its effectiveness. Sleep-directed hypnosis was chosen as an augmentation to CPT because there was existing empirical support for hypnosis to remediate sleep and because it is script-driven and does not require a great deal of additional training for therapists. Interestingly, the sleep intervention did significantly improve sleep for patients, but improved sleep did not have an effect on the course of PTSD recovery.

Additionally, while improved sleep was associated with decreases in comorbid depression, drop-out rates were quite high in this study. We wondered if these high attrition rates might be, in part, attributable to the delay in beginning the trauma-focused work as the participants completed either the three weeks of the sleep-directed hypnosis or the three-week waitlist control. If so, striking while the iron is hot and the patient is motivated to begin trauma-focused work might be key in treating PTSD. Delaying treatment to target other conditions or symptoms might increase the risk for dropout. Also noteworthy, to be included in the study, every participant needed to endorse clinically significant sleep impairment on the Clinician-administered PTSD Scale (CAPS; Blake et al., 1995). However, participants varied in the severity of their sleep impairment. It might be the case that not everyone with sleep impairment (particularly those with more moderate levels of impairment) may have needed an added intervention. In other words, augmenting trauma-focused treatment with another therapy targeting a comorbid condition might only be warranted for those patients for whom the comorbid symptoms are clearly and demonstrably interfering with the progress of treatment.

This concept may be true for other trials that tested augmentations to CPT (e.g. behavioral activation for depression, see Angelakis et al., 2020; Walters et al., 2023 and Transcranial Magnetic Stimulation [TMS], see Kozel et al., 2018). The randomization necessary for a methodologically rigorous trial may have, in fact, masked the effects of the augmentation for those participants who needed it most. It is possible that some of the participants in the augmentation trials did not need the added intervention (sleep, behavioral activation, TMS, etc.) despite presenting with clinically significant co-occurring symptoms in these domains. Randomized clinical trials may have artificially forced patients into receiving clinical care that may not have been prioritized in real-world CPT delivery. In other words, the randomization itself by definition does not consider for whom it might be clinically wise to implement an added, targeted intervention for a specific comorbid condition known to be a risk factor for poor outcomes. Only a *personalized* approach to care can determine the individual need for expansions and enhancements of the core protocol for the individual patient suffering from PTSD. Taken together, these types of enhancements and expansions of CPT have greatly increased our knowledge about effectively treating patients with complex clinical presentations in a flexible manner. However, applying these findings to the individual receiving clinical care in real time is more challenging.

Clinical Application

Despite the wealth of knowledge that the substantial body of literature yields, clinicians continue to face significant challenges in implementing CPT and other manualized treatments for PTSD. As we described, PTSD is a highly comorbid disorder—in fact it rarely occurs in isolation. In order to effectively treat PTSD and co-occurring conditions, must clinicians gain additional expertise in the full range of empirically supported expansions (e.g. CBT-I or sleep-directed hypnosis for sleep impairment, behavioral activation for comorbid depression, TMS for comorbid depressive symptoms and cognitive function impairments)? Is it even possible to stay abreast of all the recent publications and advances in treatment outcome research while in clinical practice, particularly if one does not specialize in PTSD treatment? Further, despite all of the advances in treatment outcomes research, there are many clinical complexities that occur in the context of standard care that have not yet been the focus of clinical trials (Reich et al., 2019; Bonfils et al., 2022; Radstaak et al., 2022). Indeed, it is unlikely that the field will ever be saturated with enough completed clinical trials to provide an empirically tested solution to every eventuality that can occur during the treatment of PTSD. This may be especially true for co-occurring conditions and symptoms that do not constitute a comorbid condition such as functional impairments or distress from complicating major life stressors. Indeed, while the overall outcomes of studies provide excellent general guidance for clinicians, the results of the studies do not necessarily apply to the idiosyncratic needs of the individual presenting to therapy (Galovski et al., 2024b). We propose that the next step in the evolution of psychotherapy is the *personalization* of our clinical approach to treating PTSD.

Personalized Approach to Therapy

We have recently developed a model of care that incorporates case formulation into CPT called Personalized Approach to Therapy (PATh) (Galovski et al., 2024a). Case formulation is not a new or original concept, but its application has become increasingly refined to enhance individualized treatment, particularly in cases like PTSD. Dr. Persons' case formulation approach to cognitive therapy (Persons, 2012) broadly suggests a two-level model to explain psychological problems. Level one consists of the specific, overt problems that the patient and therapist observe and that often are the reason for seeking treatment. In the case of PTSD, these are often the core symptoms of PTSD but might also include comorbid issues and conditions such as anger, depression, and relationship problems. Level two of Person's model considers the underlying psychological mechanism that is likely driving the observed presentation. From a cognitive theory perspective, these mechanisms are often core beliefs. The underlying core belief (e.g. "I am not worthy of love"), perhaps developed during childhood physical abuse, may contribute to current relationship difficulties, excessive drinking, and/or depression. The application of case formulation in any therapy requires thorough assessment, continued monitoring, real time treatment decision-making based on the information gathered through monitoring, and the flexibility to modify and resume as needed.

Prior research on incorporating case formulation into CPT highlights its potential to improve treatment outcomes, particularly for patients with complex presentations. Including case formulation provides a systematic way for therapists to identify and address Challenges to Optimal Therapy Outcomes (COTOs), such as comorbid conditions, avoidance behaviors, or motivational challenges (Galovski et al., 2024a; Nixon & Bralo, 2019). Nixon and Bralo (2019) investigated the use of explicit case formulation within CPT and found that it facilitated flexible adjustments to the treatment protocol without compromising the core therapeutic elements. For example, therapists were able to incorporate additional evidence-based strategies, such as motivational interviewing or techniques to address substance use, when therapy progress was stalled. This approach was associated with significant reductions in PTSD and depression severity, with 93% of participants who completed follow-up assessments no longer meeting PTSD diagnostic criteria (Nixon & Bralo, 2019). Additionally, case formulation helped strengthen the therapeutic alliance by involving patients collaboratively in the treatment process, which has been linked to improved retention and engagement (Nixon & Bralo, 2019). These findings led to further study testing personalized approaches by integrating case formulation designed to enable clinicians to tailor interventions to individual needs, improving both symptom reduction and functional recovery (Galovski et al., 2024a). The integration of case formulation into CPT demonstrates that balancing fidelity to the protocol with flexibility in addressing individual challenges can enhance outcomes and increase treatment acceptability among diverse populations (Nixon & Bralo, 2019; Resick et al., 2024).

Building on this evidence, the PATh model incorporates case formulation into CPT to systematically optimize treatment outcomes. Starting from the premise that both patient and therapist agree that the patient is suffering from PTSD and that CPT is an appropriate intervention to target the disorder (similar to the start of any course of CPT), the PATh model emphasizes a comprehensive understanding of the patient's presenting problems beyond the core symptoms of PTSD. Unlike traditional applications, this approach integrates individualized assessments into the structure of CPT to identify COTOs and tailor the intervention to address them effectively. The overarching goal of this approach is not to decrease fidelity to the CPT protocol but to best meet the individual patient's needs without compromising CPT's efficacy. To accomplish this goal, we have developed the PATh manual which provides clinical guidance and parameters around incorporating flexibility into clinical care without compromising efficacy.

PATh Model: Getting Started

The application of the PATh model begins with session 1 of CPT and the assessment of the entirety of the presenting problems. To accomplish this first goal, the PATh model employs the "Roadmap to Case Formulation." The Roadmap to Case Formulation is incorporated into session 1 of CPT. Because the inclusion of this more nuanced assessment of clinical need can require additional time, we encourage therapists to take two sessions to complete CPT session 1 material if necessary. The Roadmap is a one-page tool that prompts the clinician to first identify the patient's strengths, then identify potential challenges or issues that might interfere with recovery. To aid in this process, we suggest that therapists broadly query potential challenges within five major categories: Avoidance, Engagement, Emotional Regulation, Comorbid Difficulties, and Current Major Stressors. Finally, we ask the patient to specify their well-being goals. This entire process is intended to be broad and dynamic and easily incorporated throughout CPT session 1, but specific questions and examples are provided in the PATh manual. We provide an abbreviated example of the administration of the Roadmap in CPT Session 1 as follows:

Case Example

Mike is a 23-year-old, biracial, cisgender, heterosexual man who is referred to our clinic through a jail-diversion program that is designed to divert people with mental health challenges from the justice system to receive appropriate treatment. Mike had recently been arrested for disorderly conduct at a local bar. The charges had been reduced contingent on his participation in mental health services. A psychiatric assessment revealed a diagnosis of severe PTSD secondary to his friend's death that had occurred approximately 1 year prior. During the course of the assessment,

Mike described an extensive trauma history including physical abuse in the home by his father and older brother throughout his childhood. Mike's father and brother were members of a local gang as were many members of Mike's community. Mike himself became involved in the gang at age 12. Over the next 7 years, he both experienced and perpetrated violence against others. Mike refused to share the details of any specific events during that time but described himself as being deeply involved in gang activities between the ages of 12–19. At age 19, Mike's longtime girlfriend (and current partner, Rachel) became pregnant with their son. Shortly after his son, Tyson, was born, a small child in his neighborhood was killed in a gang-related drive-by shooting. In order to protect Tyson and Rachel, Mike made the decision to separate from his gang and became gainfully employed as a construction worker. Mike cut off ties with the gang (including his family members) except for his friendship with his lifelong best friend (Jake), who remained an active member. Three years after Mike's separation from this lifestyle, Mike and Jake met at a local bar to have a couple of beers. They had a great night catching up, but as they were leaving, a car slowed down and shots were fired. Mike was hit in the arm and leg. Jake was fatally shot. In the year since, Mike reported vivid nightmares and other symptoms of PTSD, increased drinking, increased isolation, and has had multiple angry outbursts at work and home.

Session 1

We advise completing the Roadmap portion of the case formulation throughout session 1 of CPT in a very natural and organic way. For example, therapists can integrate portions of the Roadmap into the traditional session 1 content or can conduct the entire Roadmap assessment at the end of the session.

Therapist: *Mike, you have done a really good job of describing the events throughout your life and especially Jake's death, that have led you to this visit. As we discussed, you meet criteria for PTSD. I know losing Jake has had an enormous impact on your life even beyond these symptoms of PTSD that you are experiencing. I think CPT will be very helpful to you in beginning to move through some of the distress and the challenges that you are describing. I also hear that you have some pretty remarkable personal strengths and supports in your corner. When things feel particularly tough, what are some of the strengths and resources that help you get through the day?*

Mike (dressed in dark jeans, a black hoodie, and a baseball cap pulled low on his forehead): *Not a hell of a lot. The person who always had my back was Jake. He's gone and he's not coming back. Things used to be great with Rachel, but she doesn't get it. She's just pissed off at me all the time. My family sucks. My mom died was I was little—never knew her. My dad and brother are what got me into this crap in the first place. I swear, if it weren't for my kid—I'd blow out of this town.*

Therapist (validating Mike's account of his situation and helping him to expand on what sounds like it might be a strength)**:** *It sounds like things can sometimes feel overwhelming. That makes sense given everything that you've survived. Tell me more about your kid—sounds like you two are close?*

Mike: (tiny bit of a smile) *Tyson is all right! Little man just turned 4. We're pretty tight.*

Therapist: *That's awesome. I'm glad you are close—you must be a pretty good dad!*

Mike: *I don't know about that. I'd do anything for that kid though—he loves to pretend he's in construction like his dad.*

Therapist: *That's great! Are you still working with the same construction company?*

Mike: *Yup—they gave me a shot when I separated from the gang four years ago and didn't have many options. They've been good to me even though I can be a real punk, especially lately.*

Therapist: *So, listening to you—it sounds like even though the last year has been really rough, you have some good support and resources in your corner. I'm going to add your son, being a great dad, and solid support at work to your strengths here on the Roadmap. Did I miss anything?*

Mike: *Maybe add Rachel—it's been rough lately, but she sticks around.*

Therapist and patient go on to identify Mike's challenges across the five major domains on the Roadmap. With some conversation, they identify many areas in the "Avoidance" domain, especially around anything that reminds Mike of Jake. Most of the avoidance (not talking about him, not going to places that they would frequent, avoiding the street that the bar was on, etc.) is consistent with typical PTSD symptoms and will be targeted through the CPT protocol. With respect to identifying COTOs in the "Engagement" domain, Mike and therapist noted that while therapy is not court mandated, his sentence reduction is contingent on his attendance and might impact his genuine participation in the therapeutic process if he continues to believe that he is "forced" to engage in CPT. Within the "Emotion Regulation" domain, Mike and his therapist noted significant problems with anger and angry outbursts, including the fight in the bar that ended in his arrest, escalating tensions and fights with Rachel (no physical abuse), and recent feedback from work that his "attitude needs to change." Mike did not endorse symptoms consistent with another mental or physical illness in "Comorbidity" domain, but did note that his drinking had significantly increased over the course of the last year and complicated his anger. "Current Major Stressors" included ongoing financial concerns and the upcoming anniversary of Jake's death. When Mike was asked what his overall well-being goals were, he replied "getting done with this therapy and getting people off my back." He did note that he wished that he and Rachel and Tyson could get back to where as a family they were before Jake died. He recalled that those were "good times."

In the PATh model, once the information is gathered and the full clinical picture emerges via the Roadmap, the patient and therapist collaboratively decide which of the patient's life challenges are most prominent and have the most potential to interfere with holistic outcomes. In the PATh model of care, we call these "Challenges to Optimal Therapy Outcomes" (COTOs). Together, the patient and therapist decide on the most prominent COTOs, and the therapist asks the patient to begin to track them on daily diaries. The patient adds COTOs (typically 2–4) to the diary. The therapist instructs the patient to simply rate the intensity and frequency of the COTO at the end of each day on the Likert scale provided on the diary (0 = not at all upsetting/did not happen at all to 5 = debilitating or unable to function/continuously happened). Additionally, the therapist and patient collaboratively create idiosyncratic parameters around each COTO. These parameters operationalize the severity of each COTO so that, session by session, the therapist and patient can quickly evaluate any escalations in COTOs and modify treatment accordingly. We provide an example of developing the COTO diaries here:

Session 1a

At the end of session 1a of CPT, the therapist and patient construct the daily diaries.

Therapist: *Really nice job, Mike. I have a really good overall picture of your various life challenges in addition to your PTSD symptoms. I want to take a minute and think about which of these challenges that we've identified on the Roadmap might get in the way of you digging into this therapy and beginning the process of recovering from PTSD?*

Mike: *Even just hearing you talk about this is starting to piss me off. Nothing is going to bring Jake back, so I'm not sure what there is to "recover from." And I am kind of being forced to be here, so why don't you just tell me what I need to do, and we'll call it a day.*

Therapist: *Yeah—I can see you getting pissed off. It's interesting that you also noted getting pissed off as one of your challenges in our conversation earlier. Sounds like anger is popping up in other ways (with Rachel, at the bar, at work) as well. I wonder if that might be worth keeping track of going forward?*

Mike: *Yeah, I'm angry. My friend died. I'm angry about it. He is always going to be dead and I'm always going to be angry. And you not understanding that and trying to "fix my anger" just means that you don't understand me at all.*

Therapist: *Nothing you said is wrong there. You have every right to be angry—an incredible injustice was done, and it can never be undone. The part that can be changed is you having PTSD (like your nightmares, flashbacks, inability to experience joy with your son like you used to, inability to do the things that you used to love). I know we can treat PTSD with CPT. But if anger gets too big (for example, lands you in jail), it can get in the way of not only recovering from PTSD, but also of you living your best life with Rachel, Tyson and anyone else who comes along down the road. I think it is worth just keeping track of your feelings of anger for now. Would you be willing to give it a try?*

Mike: (begrudgingly and skeptically): *Sure.*

Through the same process, the therapist and Mike also identify problematic drinking as another potential COTO to track as well as Mike's potential resistance to engaging in therapy. The next step was to set individualized parameters around each of the identified COTOs so that the severity of any escalations in COTOs could be best understood to inform Mike's idiosyncratic treatment needs.

Therapist: *As a final step in tracking these COTOs, we want to personalize the scale that you are going to use to track your COTOs. Let's start with anger. A zero on the scale means that this was not at all upsetting—can you think of what a zero would look like for you?*

Mike: *Like what it means for me personally to be not feeling angry?* [Therapist nods.] *I can think of lots of times before Jake died that I was pretty relaxed. Watching football games with Tyson on Sundays was always great.*

Therapist: *Perfect—that is a good way to think about what a zero means to you when you are tracking your anger. How about the opposite—what does a 5 or "extremely angry" look like for you?*

Mike: *I mean—probably most recently when I got arrested for beating that guy up at the bar. It all happened so fast. I lost control—just didn't care and felt like I was going to explode.*

Therapist: *That's a great example of a 5 on this scale for you. Where would you say you are on the scale now?*

Mike: *I'm not going to lie. This hasn't been the best hour—let's give it a 2.*

The therapist and patient repeat the process of personalizing the anchors for the other two COTOs. Therapist asks the patient to track each of the three identified COTOs on the daily diaries, rating each one using the Likert scale at the end of the day between now and next session. Therapist assigns the Impact Statement which (as per the PATh model) includes an instruction to also describe the way that the trauma has impacted any of the COTOs (in addition to the traditional CPT instruction for this assignment). CPT proceeds as usual with the patient bringing in the diaries every week to be checked by the therapist. The therapist looks for any significant elevations in COTOs that might warrant more immediate clinical attention (e.g. a rating of "5" over the last week or a 2-or-more point increase from the baseline score—in Mike's case, a 4 or 5 would be an alert to the therapist to discuss the increase further).

The PATh model has expanded CPT to incorporate attention to these COTOs in each of the weekly practice assignments with the goal of intentionally generalizing these skills to impairments and challenges in other aspects of the patients' lives that are not necessarily specifically trauma focused. Therapists may or may not allocate session time to less trauma-focused worksheets depending on where the patient is in their protocol and recovery. For example, it is unlikely that therapists would attend to non-trauma, COTO-related stuck points in the first half of therapy when the focus is largely on assimilated stuck points. But as the therapy progresses, there may be more opportunity to incorporate some of those COTO-related stuck points into session, if need be. Regardless, by specifically including instructions to utilize the worksheets for COTO-related stuck points, therapists are giving the clear message that the patient's additional struggles and challenges are heard AND that the patient holds the skills in their hands to cognitively process the thoughts that are driving their distress. By intentionally and specifically expanding the topic areas that the CPT worksheets cover, we hope to expand the generalizability of the intervention and achieve more holistic outcomes.

As the therapy progresses, examination of the diaries and/or self-report of the patient may indicate increases or amplifications of COTOs. Using the case formulation approach, the PATh manual guides the therapist in making clinical decisions in real time. Decisions include staying the course (e.g. the amplification can be handled within the context of straightforward CPT) or diverging from therapy. Diverging from therapy may include any number of interventions including but not limited to hospitalization, increasing resources outside of therapy (referrals, etc.), or pausing CPT and including additional, non-CPT therapy to stabilize the COTO. We provide an example of the implementation of case formulation mid-therapy in the PATh approach to CPT here.

Case Example Continued

Therapist and patient move through sessions 2 and 3 of CPT. Although continuing to show some significant resistance in engaging in the cognitive processing, the usual CPT techniques of increasing motivation and engagement (identifying relevant stuck points, psychoeducation, reiterating the treatment rationale) are effective in increasing his engagement. Together, they identify several critical assimilated stuck points. Specifically, Mike believes that Jake's death is his fault because: "We never should have gone to that bar in that neighborhood." "I should have worked harder to get him out of that lifestyle." "I should never have left the gang without Jake. I should have stayed." "If I had stayed, I could have stopped this." Although Mike identified these stuck points and understood all the evidence against these beliefs, his PTSD symptoms did not abate, and his anger was worsening outside of sessions.

Session 4

Mike comes into session looking exhausted and defeated.

Therapist: *Hi Mike—how are you?*
Mike (passes over his diaries and sheets): *Not great. This has not been the best week.*
Therapist (glancing through diaries): *Let's take a minute and talk through it. Looks like you were feeling pretty angry last week. Can you tell me more?*

Mike (angrily): *Yeah—I am sleeping on the couch—Rachel can barely look at me. Tyson looks sad and confused all the time. I feel so wound up and just need to be alone and cool down. I think I'm getting worse.*

Therapist (wanting to get more specific about this COTO): *Looks like Wednesday was a particularly bad day. What happened then?*

Mike: *Yeah—Wednesday sucked. This idiot at work keeps getting in my space and moved all my stuff in the breakroom and one of my work gloves was missing. Which then makes me late. I ended up getting in his face and when he just laughed it off as if it was no big deal, I kicked a chair across the room on my way out. Apparently, it scared one of the women in the breakroom. Now I am on probation and will lose my job if I mess up one more time. I just feel like it is coming from all angles. Then I have to come here and talk about Jake. If he were still here, none of this would have happened, and talking about something that can't be changed is only making it worse.*

Therapist: *I hear that. It sounds like your anger is growing the more you talk about Jake's death. In some ways, I think this might mean that we are getting closer to the heart of what is keeping you stuck in PTSD. Have you ever noticed that anger increases when you feel stressed, upset, or sad in the past, even before Jake's death?*

Mike: *Yeah—when I used to be in the gang and things got rough, I would explode. You need to be the tough guy—it's not an option to run away. No one messes with crazy.*

Therapist: *That makes a lot of sense, and it sounds like your anger protected you in dangerous or volatile situations in the past. When your anger escalates now, as you start to move through your PTSD and the memory of the trauma of Jake's death, I wonder if, in some ways, you might be also protecting yourself from feeling the pain of Jake's death?* (Therapist uses this opportunity to insert some psychoeducation about the function that anger can serve.) *But, being angry can also be a way to avoid thinking or feeling about this memory. As we talked about, avoiding these memories keeps you stuck in that pain. All of that said, I also hear that your job is in jeopardy and your relationship with Rachel is really struggling as well. How about this? Why don't we take a pause from CPT for three sessions. We can continue weekly or meet two times per week. We can focus on getting you some skills that you can use in real time to manage your anger. I am confident that you can continue the good work that you are doing in CPT as soon as we get your anger stabilized. What do you think?*

Mike: *I can't lose my job. If there is anything you can do to help me keep my temper under control, that would be great.*

In order to capture the rationale for the divergence, the nature and length of the divergence, and the desired outcome of the divergence, the PATh model includes a "Decision to Diverge" plan that is completed collaboratively in session. Most importantly, to the extent possible, the plan includes a precise date at which the patient will resume CPT. We know that too often, a patient and therapist hit a road bump (or experience an amplification in a COTO) and may conclude that the therapy is not working and terminate prematurely. Early work on applying this case formulation approach to CPT suggests that the need to diverge occurred in about 25–30% of cases. The PATh manual provides support and guidance in formulating clinical decisions to stay the course or diverge form the protocol for a specified period of time and then return to CPT.

Divergence

Mike and therapist completed the Decision to Diverge plan together and commit to three sessions of anger management with a planned and scheduled return to CPT. Anger management sessions consist of both cognitive and behavioral techniques designed to help the patient reduce anger in real time. While the cognitive technique (identifying and challenging the belief that is causing anger) is consistent in theory with CPT, the content is not trauma-focused and, as such, represents a departure from the CPT protocol. For example, Mike noted that the belief causing his anger at work was "I'm being disrespected." Underlying that belief was the core belief of "I'm not worthy of respect." In traditional CPT, this likely would have been considered an over-accommodated belief and challenged later in the protocol. But, because his anger had escalated to the extent that it was presenting a significant challenge to optimal outcomes (in this case, a serious risk to occupational and relationship functioning and the potential for additional legal and financial complications), we diverted to prioritizing anger-related, non-trauma beliefs even though his assimilated beliefs had not been resolved. We complemented this cognitive work with relaxation training and the development of distraction and affect regulation strategies—also departures from the CPT protocol. These strategies were successful in stabilizing Mike's anger and related behaviors, and he reported feeling calmer, less agitated and irritable, and much more in control of his reactions to annoyances. Interestingly, he also no longer believed that he did not deserve respect (as a result of his cognitive work on this stuck point during anger management sessions). He now recognized that others' behaviors that he had previously believed to be disregarding and disrespectful were more likely just thoughtless or careless (like his co-worker losing his work glove). Even if someone was genuinely and intentionally disrespecting him, he realized that this did not mean he was not worthy of respect. Sometimes other people's bad behavior was not about him. CPT session 5 resumed as scheduled.

Return to CPT

When therapist and Mike resume CPT, the therapist notes (via the diaries) that the anger remained stable since the last session, and she reviews where they had left off in the CPT protocol before they diverged.

Therapist: *I'm glad things seem better at home and work. I want to turn our attention back to thinking through some of your stuck points that we had identified about Jake's death. Are you ready to turn your attention back to PTSD? Any concerns?*

Matt (sighs): *Yup—that was the deal, right? I don't have concerns that I can't handle talking about Jake. I just don't think it will help—because it will never change the fact that he is gone. I do feel better though. I don't feel like I'm going to explode all the time. I didn't have to force myself to come here today even knowing that we were going to do trauma stuff. I'll try to get back to it, but I still don't really see the point.*

Therapist: *I appreciate that, and I wish that we could change the outcome and that Jake was still here. Let's retrace our steps a bit and see where we left off. Remember to let me know if, at any time, you feel yourself getting pissed off* (Mike's words). *Let's see if we can put these pieces of the puzzle together. Does that work?*

Mike (looking both resigned and doubtful): *Yup.*

Therapist (reviews where they had left off)**:** *Ok—thinking back a few sessions, I recall that you had identified some important stuck points and that we had begun to unpack those a bit and found that some of them really didn't hold that much water. But these beliefs were still causing you some significant amount of emotion. For example, when we talked through the idea that you should have made Jake leave the gang, we realized that you had tried your hardest to convince him to get out for years. You recalled that he had even left for a short time and slept on your couch for a couple of months. You had gotten him a job at your construction company, right?*

Mike (pulls his hat lower over his eyes, looking down): *Yeah. But then he went back. It's tough. He felt like he belonged there more than anywhere else. He respected my choice and said he needed me to respect his.*

Therapist: *Respect is so important, right?*

Mike (nodding): *For a lot of us, that's all we got.*

Therapist: *So sometimes respecting someone's right to make their own decisions is important even when you don't agree with those decisions?*

Mike: *We'd argue about it, and he'd just ask me to let it go. And I did, until the next argument. I had so much respect for him, and he always had my back. Even if I didn't respect his decisions, I could never make him do anything he didn't want to do. He was a stubborn SOB.*

Therapist: *That's really important—sounds like you both respected each other's choices. It also sounds like you realize that the choice was his to make, not yours. So, would you say that the belief that you should have made him leave the gang earlier is not realistic? That his choice in staying or leaving was not up to you?*

Mike: *I do see that. But he was more than a friend. He was more of a brother than my own brother. I let him down.*

Therapist [recognizing that now we have another stuck point, asks a clarifying question]**:** *How so?*

Mike: *If he wouldn't leave, I should have stayed. I could have protected him. And I know we talked about this. I know we thought of all the reasons that I left the gang. Jake loved my son. He got why I had to leave. He knew Rachel wanted me out. I know I left for the right reasons. I know if I had stayed, it might not have changed the fact that they came after him that day or any other day. But I…* [Puts his head down and clenches fists. The therapist can see that Mike is getting visibly agitated).

Therapist (gives Mike a moment to sit with this emotion. She sees him taking deep breaths and calming himself. After a couple of minutes, she resumes the Socratic questioning): *In hearing you talk through all of this, I can see how you are thinking through each of these beliefs and really considering if there are facts to support them. I hear you changing your mind about whether or not you should have (or could have) forced Jake to leave the gang. And thinking through your choice to get out. But I don't get the sense that you are feeling any differently? Almost like you are hearing the change in these beliefs in your head, but not feeling them in your heart?*

Mike just stares at the therapist.

Therapist: *What would it mean to you if it wasn't your fault that Jake died?*

Mike (pauses for a long time): *So, I am supposed to just let go? Just be ok with this? He's the closest thing to family that I ever had. That matters. I'm not going to just forget.*

Therapist (hearing the stuck point that is likely preventing Mike from letting go of his self-blame and moving toward recovery): *I wonder if there is a stuck point in there? If I don't blame myself for Jake's death, then….?*

Mike: *What if I forget? He can't just fade away like he meant nothing. That happens to so many of us—not Jake. He deserves more.*

Therapist: *It really sounds like it. Let me ask you—do you think you could ever forget him?*

Mike (angrily): *No!*

Therapist: *I agree. Are there other ways to remember him other than beating yourself up about what you could have done differently—especially since you know there weren't really any options? I know Jake's death was horrific and those memories are large and painful. What other memories do you have?*

Mike relaxes a little and spends some time recounting some of his best memories of Jake. He's even chuckling at points.

Therapist: *He really does sound like a great guy! Knowing all of this about him, I want to come back to this stuck point of "If I don't beat myself up about Jake's death, he will fade away and no longer matter." It almost sounds like you are thinking that you need to hold onto this pain to keep his memory alive and strong?* (Mike slowly nods.) *Let me ask you—do you think, even if you wanted to, that you could ever forget Jake?* (Mike shakes his head no). *It doesn't sound like it to me either. The way you describe him—it seems like you will hold him in your heart forever* (Mike puts his face in his hands, covering his eyes. Therapist lets him sit with that for a second). *In thinking about this a bit more, you clearly knew Jake best. How do you think he would rather you remembered and honored him?*

Mike (looks up): *He'd want me to live. That's what he would say. Go live and, every once in a while, have a beer and tell Tyson about all the crazy crap we did* (For the first time, the therapist sees glimpses of real sadness as Mike swallows hard and his eyes moisten). *It's just hard, you know? Living is not the same without him. I just really miss him.*

Therapist: *I hear that. I think it really is about making your world big enough to hold his memory, honor him, and live.*

Mike's PTSD decreased steadily after Session 5. He started to communicate better with Rachel and began to re-engage in their family life and parenting. The idea that he somehow should have prevented Jake's death and that moving on with his life was disrespectful to Jake had prevented him from allowing himself to derive any happiness in his relationships or enjoyment in activities. He now saw that experiencing enjoyment (watching the game with Rachel and Tyson on Sundays) and happiness (laughing when Tyson did something funny, experiencing loving feelings with Rachel) was possible even though Jake was gone. When he felt guilty that he was experiencing happiness and Jake could not, he reminded himself that, of all people, Jake would *want* him to be happy. He recognized that if the situation was reversed and he had been killed that night, he would absolutely want Jake to "live."

Over the course of the next sessions, Jake's PTSD continued to decrease. Interestingly, when he got to the modules (sessions 8–12), many of his over-accommodated stuck points related to the themes were already, or easily, resolved given the cognitive work he had done during his anger management sessions. His work on respect overlapped considerably with the topics discussed in CPT. In addition to continuing to work on any assimilated stuck points (which, in his case were largely resolved after session 5), and challenging over-accommodated stuck points in each of the trauma themes, the PATh model also asks the patient to use the worksheets to challenge any stuck points related to their COTOs and any impairments in psychosocial functioning that they might be experiencing. Mike occasionally challenged stuck points throughout therapy related to anger, alcohol use, and even around his resistance to coming into therapy. In the latter half of the therapy, he identified stuck points about his relationship with Rachel, his self-blame about his perceived poor parenting of Tyson over the past year, and about interactions with colleagues at work. During the sessions, the therapist relied on the core principles of CPT in deciding what topic to prioritize at different points of the therapy. Assimilation always took priority over over-accommodated stuck points. Trauma-related over-accommodated stuck points (e.g. "The world is unsafe.") took priority over non-trauma-related beliefs (e.g. "My co-workers are punks."). Mike's PCL score had started at a 52 and was down to a 11 by CPT session 7. Mike could have stopped therapy then (technically he was an early completer) but given his difficulties with his relationship with Rachel and some lingering issues with work, he (and Rachel!) wanted to continue therapy for a few sessions.

Despite the significant reduction in PTSD scores by CPT 7, Mike was often quiet and looked tired in session. At Session 9, the therapist and Mike talked about his mood, and Mike described feeling very heavy and sad. Utilizing the case formulation approach, the therapist and Mike understood that as his PTSD symptoms had decreased, his grief had surfaced. Mike had not really had the chance to fully grieve this tremendous loss. They considered another divergence from the protocol to do some grief work but realized that this work could be readily absorbed into the CPT protocol. Several related stuck points were identified such as "If I cry [especially in front of Rachel and Tyson], I'm a punk." and "If I start letting myself feel all that is bottled up in me, I will lose control and lose all my progress." Challenging these stuck points helped Mike create space in his life to safely and effectively mourn his loss. Together, they decided that there was no need to add divergent sessions and continued to address grief-related stuck points in the context of the protocol. The therapist gave Mike some suggestions for additional reading about the grief process and some resources such as a support group. Mike did not take her up on these suggestions.

In ending CPT with a case formulation approach using the PATh model, therapists are not only considering PTSD symptom reduction, but also considering the effect that the cognitive processing has had on the COTO-related stuck points. Therapists have the latitude to continue CPT for extra sessions if the patient will continue to benefit from additional attention on COTOs that may be less central to PTSD. The goal is to achieve more holistic outcomes, not to retain patients in CPT longer than is clinically indicated.

Case Example Continued

Although CPT is conducted in a variable format and he could have ended early or taken additional sessions at the end of the protocol, Mike's therapy came to a natural conclusion at the end of protocol session 12. His PCL remained low (ended with a 9), he reported significant improvement in his family relationships and was taken off probation at work. He even reported that his boss specifically noted a big change in him. At session 12, Mike presented to therapy in a white T shirt and jeans with no hat. This is the first time he had come into the clinic without a hoodie and hat. Although he had completed minimal worksheets throughout therapy, he wrote a short but poignant final Impact Statement. He fully recognized that he could not have done anything to prevent Jake's death that night. He acknowledged that Jake would be "giving him hell" if he'd seen how he'd been "falling apart" this past year. He described himself as picking up the pieces of his life again and, for the first time, enjoying some parts of it. Mike spontaneously described several rituals he had begun to engage in to keep Jake's memory close and "get with his feelings" (e.g. spending time on the beach they used to go to when they were young, writing a letter to him on the anniversary of his death, and regularly telling Tyson funny "Jake stories" at bedtime.) Mike also talked about respect in his Impact Statement and recognized how important it was to him. He seemingly had a broader view of the concept and mentioned that he no longer constantly felt disrespected and like he was "about to explode." Specifically, he said, "Sometimes people's punk behavior doesn't have anything to do with me and isn't about respect. I know I got respect. I gotta teach my son that other people don't define you. You got to know it in here. [points to his heart]."

In summary, fidelity to the CPT manual is very important. We don't know what would have happened if Mike had not completed the Roadmap (which added an additional session) and the therapist had not been monitoring the escalating anger. This information may have come out in other ways in traditional CPT. We do not know what would have happened if they had not diverged to address the anger. It is possible that if they had persisted in the protocol, they would have gotten to the same place sooner (the anger management work added three sessions). It is also possible that the anger would have escalated, preventing engagement with the trauma-related cognitive processing and resulting in significantly worsened psychosocial impairments. The challenge is balancing fidelity with flexibility. If we move too far astray of the protocol, we run the risk of denying the patient the efficacious content of an evidence-based psychotherapy at the dose that they need to recover. However, we have learned from past research that flexible applications of the protocol improve the therapy (Galovski et al., 2020, 2024b). Adding emergency sessions, administering therapy with a varying length or in a massed format, and administering in different cultures with adapted materials are some of the examples of significant modifications of the original protocol (reviewed in detail throughout this book) that moved the needle further toward recovery for more people (Resick et al., 2024). The burning question remains: How far can we flex the protocol before we risk the efficacy? The PATh model seeks to provide much-needed guidance in making these clinical decisions in real time.

In the case of Mike, his anger was escalating to severe levels and may have had many potential negative outcomes and posed a risk for early dropout or termination by the clinician. Too often when COTOs emerge during the course of therapy, patients and clinicians alike come to the conclusion that "this therapy is not working" or "this is not the right time to do trauma work—the patient is too fragile or not ready." In providing guidance about integrating a case formulation approach into therapy, the PATh model allows for other options including taking discrete breaks from the protocol to stabilize the COTO and then return to trauma work. In this case example, this model supported Mike in moving through PTSD, significant anger problems, major psychosocial impairments, and grief. In sum, the ultimate therapy goal of helping our patients to resume living their best lives was met.

Future Directions

The PATh model is one potential avenue toward personalizing care for PTSD. The use of this approach is not circumspect to CPT. The challenge in implementing this type of flexibility into evidence-based protocols is modifying the protocol to the extent that it is no longer recognizable and, in doing so, comprising the efficacy. We continuously urge therapists to adhere to the protocol as much as possible and increase their competence in delivering it as much as possible. That said, we recognize that far too often, therapy is terminated prematurely when minor tweaks in our manuals might retain more survivors needing care and move the needle further toward recovery.

Competing Interests: Tara Galovski has received a research grant RX003369 funded by VA RR&D to support the PATh model described in this chapter. She also occasionally receives compensation for CPT trainings and consultation for clinicians. Lauren McSweeney and Saige Galovski have no conflicts of interest that are relevant to this chapter.

References

American Psychological Association. (2017). *Clinical practice guideline for the treatment of posttraumatic stress disorder (PTSD) in adults.* https://www.apa.org/ptsd-guideline/ptsd.pdf.

Angelakis, S., Weber, N., & Nixon, R. D. (2020). Comorbid posttraumatic stress disorder and major depressive disorder: The usefulness of a sequential treatment approach within a randomised design. *Journal of Anxiety Disorders, 76*, 102324. https://doi.org/10.1016/j.janxdis.2020.102324

Bass, J. K., Annan, J., McIvor Murray, S., Kaysen, D., Griffiths, S., Cetinoglu, T., Wachter, K., Murray, L. K., & Bolton, P. A. (2013). Controlled trial of psychotherapy for Congolese survivors of sexual violence. *New England Journal of Medicine, 368*(23), 2182–2191. https://doi.org/10.1056/NEJMoa1211853

Blake, D. D., Weathers, F. W., Nagy, L. M., Kaloupek, D. G., Gusman, F. D., Charney, D. S., & Keane, T. M. (1995). The development of a Clinician-Administered PTSD Scale. *Journal of Traumatic Stress, 8*(1), 75–90. https://doi.org/10.1007/BF02105408

Bolton, P., Bass, J., Zangana, G. A. S., Kamal, T., Murray, S. M., Kaysen, D., et al. (2014). A randomized controlled trial of mental health interventions for survivors of systematic violence in Kurdistan, Northern Iraq. *BMC Psychiatry, 14*(1), 1–15. https://doi.org/10.1186/s12888-014-0360-2

Bonfils, K. A., Tennity, C. L., Congedo, B. A., Dolowich, B. A., Hammer, L. A., & Haas, G. L. (2022). Functional outcomes from psychotherapy for people with posttraumatic stress disorder: A meta-analysis. *Journal of Anxiety Disorders, 89*, 102576. https://doi.org/10.1016/j.janxdis.2022.102576

Chard, K. M., Schumm, J. A., McIlvain, S. M., Bailey, G. W., & Parkinson, R. B. (2011). Exploring the efficacy of a residential treatment program incorporating cognitive processing therapy-cognitive for veterans with PTSD and traumatic brain injury. *Journal of Traumatic Stress, 24*(3), 347–351. https://doi.org/10.1002/jts.20644

Department of Veterans Affairs & Department of Defense. (2023). *VA/DOD clinical practice guidelines for the management of posttraumatic stress disorder and acute stress disorder.* https://www.healthquality.va.gov/guidelines/MH/ptsd/VA-DoD-CPG-PTSD-Full-CPG.pdf

Galovski, T. E., Blain, L. M., Mott, J. M., Elwood, L., & Houle, T. (2012). Manualized therapy for PTSD: Flexing the structure of cognitive processing therapy. *Journal of Consulting and Clinical Psychology, 80*(6), 968–981. https://doi.org/10.1037/a0030600

Galovski, T. E., Harik, J. M., Blain, L. M., Elwood, L., Gloth, C., & Fletcher, T. D. (2016). Augmenting cognitive processing therapy to improve sleep impairment in PTSD: A randomized controlled trial. *Journal of Consulting and Clinical Psychology, 84*(2), 167–178. https://doi.org/10.1037/ccp0000059

Galovski, T. E., Nixon, R., & Kaysen, D. (2020). *Flexible applications of cognitive processing therapy: Evidence-based treatment methods*. Academic Press.

Galovski, T. E., Werner, K. B., Weaver, T. L., Morris, K. L., Dondanville, K. A., Nanney, J., et al. (2022). Massed cognitive processing therapy for posttraumatic stress disorder in women survivors of intimate partner violence. *Psychological Trauma: Theory, Research, Practice, and Policy, 14*(5), 769–781. https://doi.org/10.1037/tra0001100

Galovski, T. E., McSweeney, L. B., Nixon, R. D. V., Wachen, J. S., Smith, B. N., Noorbaloochi, S., et al. (2024a). Personalizing cognitive processing therapy with a case formulation approach to intentionally target impairment in psychosocial functioning associated with PTSD. *Contemporary Clinical Trials Communications*, 101385. https://doi.org/10.1016/j.conctc.2024.101385

Galovski, T. E., Nixon, R. D., & Kehle-Forbes, S. (2024b). Walking the line between fidelity and flexibility: A conceptual review of personalized approaches to manualized treatments for posttraumatic stress disorder. *Journal of Traumatic Stress, 37*(5), 768–774. https://doi.org/10.1002/jts.23073

International Society for Traumatic Stress Studies (ISTSS). (2018). *ISTSS PTSD prevention and treatment guidelines: Methodology and recommendations*. www.istss.org/getattachment/Treating-Trauma/New-ISTSS-Prevention-andTreatmentGuidelines/ISTSS_PreventionTreatmentGuidelines_FNL.pdf.aspx

Ito, M., Horikoshi, M., Resick, P. A., Katayanagi, A., Miyamae, M., Takagishi, Y., et al. (2017). Study protocol for a randomised controlled trial of cognitive processing therapy for posttraumatic stress disorder among Japanese patients: The Safety, Power, Intimacy, Esteem, Trust (SPINET) study. *BMJ Open, 7*(6), e014292. https://doi.org/10.1136/bmjopen-2016-014292

Kehle-Forbes, S. M., Galovski, T., Polusny, M. A., Possemato, K., Nugent, S., McManus, E., & Baier, A. L. (2023). Development and pilot test of a therapist-assisted self-management program for completers of trauma-focused therapy for posttraumatic stress disorder. *Cognitive and Behavioral Practice*. https://doi.org/10.1016/j.cbpra.2023.08.002

Kozel, F. A., Motes, M. A., Didehbani, N., DeLaRosa, B., Bass, C., Schraufnagel, C. D., et al. (2018). Repetitive TMS to augment cognitive processing therapy in combat veterans of recent conflicts with PTSD: A randomized clinical trial. *Journal of Affective Disorders, 229*, 506–514. https://doi.org/10.1016/j.jad.2017.12.046

Kaysen, D., Lindgren, K., Zangana, G. A. S., Murray, L., Bass, J., & Bolton, P. (2013). Adaptation of cognitive processing therapy for treatment of torture victims: Experience in Kurdistan, Iraq. *Psychological Trauma: Theory, Research, Practice, and Policy, 5*(2), 184–192. https://doi.org/10.1037/a0026053

Moring, J. C., Dondanville, K. A., Fina, B. A., Hassija, C., Chard, K., Monson, C., et al. (2020). Cognitive processing therapy for posttraumatic stress disorder via telehealth: Practical considerations during the COVID-19 pandemic. *Journal of Traumatic Stress, 33*(4), 371–379. https://doi.org/10.1002/jts.22544

Nixon, R. D., & Bralo, D. (2019). Using explicit case formulation to improve cognitive processing therapy for PTSD. *Behavior Therapy, 50*(1), 155–164. https://doi.org/10.1016/j.beth.2018.04.003

Nixon, R. D., King, M. W., Smith, B. N., Gradus, J. L., Resick, P. A., & Galovski, T. E. (2021). Predicting response to cognitive processing therapy for PTSD: A machine-learning approach. *Behaviour Research and Therapy, 144*, 103920. https://doi.org/10.1016/j.brat.2021.103920

Persons, J. B. (2012). *The case formulation approach to cognitive-behavior therapy*. Guilford Press.

Radstaak, M., Hüning, L., Lamers, S., & Bohlmeijer, E. T. (2022). Examining well-being in posttraumatic stress disorder treatment: An explorative study. *Journal of Traumatic Stress, 35*(3), 914–925. https://doi.org/10.1002/jts.22798

Reich, K., Nemeth, L., & Acierno, R. (2019). Evidence-based psychotherapy interventions to improve psychosocial functioning in veterans with PTSD: An integrative review. *Journal of Psychosocial Nursing and Mental Health Services, 57*(10), 24–33. https://doi.org/10.3928/02793695-20190531-04

Resick, P. A., & Schnicke, M. (1996). *Cognitive processing therapy for rape victims: A treatment manual*. Sage Publications.

Resick, P. A., LoSavio, S. T., Monson, C. M., Kaysen, D. L., Wachen, J. S., Galovski, T. E., et al. (2024). State of the science of cognitive processing therapy. *Behavior Therapy*. https://doi.org/10.1016/j.beth.2024.04.003

Resick, P. A., Stirman, S. W., & LoSavio, S. T. (2023). *Getting unstuck from PTSD: Using cognitive processing therapy to guide your recovery*. Guilford Publications.

Rosner, R., Rimane, E., Frick, U., Gutermann, J., Hagl, M., Renneberg, B., et al. (2019). Effect of developmentally adapted cognitive processing therapy for youth with symptoms of posttraumatic stress disorder after childhood sexual and physical abuse: A randomized clinical trial. *JAMA Psychiatry, 76*(5), 484–491. https://doi.org/10.1001/jamapsychiatry.2018.4349

Schnurr, P. P., Lunney, C. A., Bovin, M. J., & Marx, B. P. (2009). Posttraumatic stress disorder and quality of life: Extension of findings to veterans of the wars in Iraq and Afghanistan. *Clinical Psychology Review, 29*(8), 727–735. https://doi.org/10.1016/j.cpr.2009.08.006

Schnurr, P. P., & Lunney, C. A. (2016). Symptom benchmarks of improved quality of life in PTSD. *Depression and Anxiety, 33*(3), 247–255. https://doi.org/10.1002/da.22477

Schulz, P. M., Marovic-Johnson, D., & Huber, L. C. (2006). Cognitive-behavioral treatment of rape-and war-related posttraumatic stress disorder with a female, Bosnian refugee. *Clinical Case Studies, 5*(3), 191–208. https://doi.org/10.1177/1534650103262401

Steenkamp, M. M., Litz, B. T., Hoge, C. W., & Marmar, C. R. (2015). Psychotherapy for military-related PTSD: A review of randomized clinical trials. *JAMA, 314*(5), 489–500. https://doi.org/10.1001/jama.2015.8370

Vogt, D., King, M. W., Borowski, S., Finley, E. P., Perkins, D. F., & Copeland, L. A. (2021). Identifying factors that contribute to military veterans' post-military well-being. *Applied Psychology: Health and Well-Being, 13*(2), 341–356. https://doi.org/10.1111/aphw.12252

Vogt, D., Smith, B. N., Fox, A. B., Amoroso, T., Taverna, E., & Schnurr, P. P. (2017). Consequences of PTSD for the work and family quality of life of female and male U.S. Afghanistan and Iraq War veterans. *Social Psychiatry and Psychiatric Epidemiology, 52*(3), 341–352. https://doi.org/10.1007/s00127-016-1321-5

Wachen, J. S., Morris, K. L., Galovski, T. E., Dondanville, K. A., Resick, P. A., & Schwartz, C. (2024). Massed cognitive processing therapy for combat-related posttraumatic stress disorder: Study design and methodology of a non-inferiority randomized controlled trial. *Contemporary Clinical Trials, 136*, 107405. https://doi.org/10.1016/j.cct.2023.107405

Walters, K. H., Hunt, W. M., Otis, N. P., Kline, A. C., Miggantz, E. L., Thomsen, C. J., & Glassman, L. H. (2023). Comparison of behavioral activation-enhanced cognitive processing therapy and cognitive processing therapy among U.S. service members: A randomized clinical trial. *Psychiatry Research, 326*, 115330. https://doi.org/10.1016/j.psychres.2023.115330

Watts, B. V., Schnurr, P. P., Mayo, L., Young-Xu, Y., Weeks, W. B., & Friedman, M. J. (2013). Meta-analysis of the efficacy of treatments for posttraumatic stress disorder. *The Journal of Clinical Psychiatry, 74*(6), e1170. https://doi.org/10.4088/JCP.12r08225

Weiss, W. M., Murray, L. K., Zangana, G. A. S., Mahmooth, Z., Kaysen, D., Dorsey, S., et al. (2015). Community-based mental health treatments for survivors of torture and militant attacks in Southern Iraq: A randomized control trial. *BMC Psychiatry, 15*, 1–16. https://doi.org/10.1186/s12888-015-0622-7

Chapter 16
Delivering CPT Using Telehealth

Leslie A. Morland, Lisa Glassman, Tamara R. Wachsman, and John C. Moring

Scope of the Problem

Cognitive processing therapy (CPT), like many psychotherapy protocols, has traditionally been delivered in person. Traditionally, when searching for a therapist, patients must consider how far they would be willing to travel, limiting trained provider options to those available in their immediate area. There are also certain expectations about what in-person psychotherapy involves. Although the content of therapy may differ between providers, a patient could expect a carefully curated, quiet, well-controlled environment. The therapists, too, have many traditional expectations about what therapy should be like, and therapists are often trained to create a physical and emotional therapeutic environment that promotes trust, insight, and healing for individuals with trauma histories. The unspoken expectations of CPT, such as using paper worksheets collaboratively, providing handouts, and reading trauma accounts together can be more easily navigated when delivered in-person. However, there is undoubted value in the ability to reach individuals that

L. A. Morland (✉)
National Center for PTSD, Women's Health Science Division, Boston, VA, USA
e-mail: Leslie.morland@va.gov

L. Glassman
Naval Health Research Center, San Diego, CA, USA

T. R. Wachsman
VA San Diego Healthcare System, San Diego, CA, USA
e-mail: tamara.wachsman@va.gov

J. C. Moring
Department of Psychiatry and Behavioral Sciences, The University of Texas Health Science Center at San Antonio, San Antonio, TX, USA
e-mail: moringj@uthscsa.edu

J. S. Wachen, T. E. Galovski (eds.), *Cognitive Processing Therapy for Complex Cases*, CBT: Science Into Practice,
https://doi.org/10.1007/978-3-031-87356-0_16

would not otherwise be able or willing to receive in-person psychotherapy. Limitations and benefits of existing delivery formats of CPT will be explored, followed by the current state-of-the-science. Next, practical guidelines and case examples will be offered to assist clinicians who seek to deliver CPT without the need for traditional in-office visits.

Unfortunately, there are many limitations to the traditional methods of therapy delivery. Most importantly, there are disparities in access to CPT and other evidence-based treatments for posttraumatic stress disorder (PTSD; e.g., McClendon et al., 2020). Despite the existence of multiple gold standard PTSD interventions (Department of Veterans Affairs & Department of Defense, Clinical Practice Guidelines, 2023), not all individuals with PTSD have access to evidence-based treatment or ultimately receive an adequate dose of therapy (e.g., Lewis et al., 2020; McClendon et al., 2020). There are many barriers to traditional in-person care, including concerns related to privacy and stigma (e.g., Bonfils et al., 2018; Ouimette et al., 2011), logistical barriers (e.g., limited specialized local providers, childcare needs, work conflicts, transportation, cost; Kantor et al., 2017; Ouimette et al., 2011) and PTSD-related barriers (e.g., avoidance, anxiety, trust; Kazlauskas, 2017; Ouimette et al., 2011). Patients located in rural areas, those who have physical mobility issues, and individuals who work full time represent just some of the special populations who regularly find access to evidence-based PTSD care even further out of reach (e.g., S. Rep. No. 108-405, 2004). A "one size fits all" approach to therapy, reflected by reliance on a single modality, ignores patient preferences for how they obtain their mental health treatment and undermines efforts to provide individualized, client-centered care.

There are also several limitations to traditional in-person PTSD treatment for providers. Obtaining training in CPT and other evidence-based interventions is time consuming and expensive; it also often requires in-person training. This is restrictive for many providers, including those with family responsibilities or financial limitations. These barriers can be especially challenging for providers with mobility challenges or who live in rural areas. Providers also have logistical barriers, including commute time/cost and childcare. Many providers struggle with their own challenges to providing the quality of care they desire. Taken together, these factors may contribute to stress and burnout. Ultimately, the "one size fits all" approach to the delivery of therapy does not work for many patients and providers, and may contribute to treatment dropout, low access to care, and provider burn out.

Recent advances in telehealth technology, in combination with a rapid increase in demand for remote treatment during the COVID-19 pandemic, have completely changed the landscape of mental health care delivery. Telehealth is an umbrella term that describes several remote modalities for the delivery of mental health care. Clinical video teleconferencing (CVT), phone, texting, mobile apps, and internet-based therapy are some of the most common telehealth modalities typically used to deliver PTSD treatment, whether stand-alone, in combination with one another, or combined with in-person treatment. PTSD treatment delivered by telehealth modalities eliminates or reduces many of these barriers to care, while also respecting patient and provider preferences. Telehealth can increase access to, and equity of, care by increasing patient access to well-trained providers capable of delivering care via telehealth. The provision of therapy via telehealth allows providers to meet patients "where they're at" in terms of preference, symptoms, and logistical, medical, and psychiatric challenges. Matching patients with the modality they prefer and that works best for their life circumstances can increase access to and engagement in care.

Similarly, providers also benefit when incorporating telehealth into their practice. Reducing commuting time and the need to maintain office space for in-person therapy sessions saves time and money. Further, telehealth allows therapists more flexibility to design and implement a practice that works for them, including facilitating access to clients to whom they can provide specialized care. Flexibility in modality may improve provider mental health while reducing burnout, though this is an area with little research to date.

The benefits of telehealth are substantial, but there can be drawbacks to the use of telehealth for the delivery of CPT. Although telehealth increases access to providers, it doesn't necessarily mean access to *well-trained* providers. It may still be difficult for patients to find CPT-trained therapists, even when patients can connect to a wider variety of providers. Further, technological problems, real or anticipated, could impact the quality of therapy sessions, especially if patient and provider comfort and proficiency with telehealth is low. Troubleshooting can be challenging in-session, but willingness to flexibly move between telehealth modalities (e.g., switching from video to phone) can minimize the impact. Perhaps one of the major unintended consequences of a large adoption of telehealth across the field of mental health has been an emerging digital divide; not all individuals have equal access to phones, tablets, computers, high-speed internet, or comfort with the use of technology (e.g., Adepoju et al., 2022; Cortelyou-Ward et al., 2020). Thus, there are equity issues with telehealth that must be identified and eliminated.

There are challenges on the provider side as well. Providers delivering telehealth from their homes may find it difficult to set solid work/life boundaries. It may be difficult to provide a complete "blank slate" when delivering therapy from a home office, or to take proper vacations when most interactions with clients are remote. Telehealth can often be more casual, as patients may also be at home. Patients may be tempted to log in to a session with a family member in the room or while cleaning the house. It can be difficult to maintain a level of professionalism or privacy expected in therapy when the therapist has little control over the patient's environment during the session. Further, it can be challenging to change all therapy documentation (e.g., forms, licensing information, mailing information) to reflect remote work, and it may be even harder to adapt documentation to reflect multiple modalities.

Telehealth technologies are dynamic and continue to advance rapidly. What is common now may be antiquated by the time you read this chapter, and new modalities may have been invented. Nevertheless, telehealth has completely changed the delivery of PTSD treatment, eliminating barriers to the delivery of CPT to patients in need of care. Although telehealth isn't without its own limitations, increasing options available to patients to encourage the provision of patient-centered care can support equity in access to CPT and other evidence-based treatments.

Research Overview

In response to a sharp increase in telehealth over the last two decades, the effectiveness, feasibility, and acceptability of the telehealth modality has been increasingly explored through research. Virtual options for patients to connect with providers and access mental health care help mitigate a multitude of obstacles. However, it remains critical to determine whether telehealth is as effective as in-person psychotherapy to inform the decision of whether it should be offered for EBPs like CPT. The existing literature has explored the use of telehealth in general, as well as specifically for CPT.

As mentioned above, telehealth delivery of psychotherapy can occur in a variety of formats. The most common virtual options are video appointments that are either office-based (e.g., the patient uses a computer at a clinic/office that is closer to their location than where the provider is located) or home-based (e.g., the patient uses a computer to join the appointment from their home). CVT to deliver mental health services has been demonstrated to be effective. Randomized clinical trials examining both office-based and home-based CVT indicate that they are non-inferior to in-person options for evidence-based PTSD treatments. For example, Knowlton and Nelson (2021) compared treatment effects of CPT and prolonged exposure (PE; Foa et al., 2007) across three different modalities, including in-person, clinic-to-clinic telehealth, and home-based telehealth. Participants included veterans residing in rural areas who suffered from PTSD. Findings demonstrated no differences in symptom reduction across the three different delivery modalities, for those who completed full PE or CPT protocols. Other studies that have examined effects of CPT, specifically, have found no differences in PTSD symptom improvement when delivered in-person or via telehealth (Maieritsch et al., 2016; Morland et al., 2014, 2015). A more recent study examined differences in treatment delivery formats of CPT, including in-home in-person, home-based telehealth, and in-office in-person (Peterson et al., 2022). Across all three treatment arms, veterans and active duty service members experienced significant improvement in their PTSD symptoms at posttreatment. Those who received CPT via in-home or home-based telehealth experienced greater PTSD symptom reduction compared to those assigned the in-office in-person treatment arm. However, differences in treatment outcomes were non-existent at the 6-month follow-up assessment. Therefore, telehealth is an effective treatment delivery approach when implementing CPT.

Importantly, comfort with telehealth technologies has increased and expanded greatly within the last decade. Since the start of the COVID-19 pandemic, many individuals have become more comfortable with remote communication across professional, personal, and healthcare environments. Given that most of these studies were completed prior to 2020, they may not reflect current perspectives on telehealth. However, research findings generally support that telehealth interventions effectively reduce symptoms of PTSD, anxiety, and depression, and that telehealth delivery of CPT is an effective modality to address PTSD and related symptoms.

The majority of psychotherapy protocols were originally designed to be delivered in-person. However, while it is important to abide by treatment fidelity, it is necessary to also be adaptable to a variety of circumstances. Although aspects of a treatment may need to be changed for it to be provided via telehealth, the overall impact is usually minimal (Morland et al., 2011). The intervention structure is not compromised by the CVT modality; in general, findings regarding PTSD EBPs support adherence to the manual being maintained across modalities (Morland et al., 2020). Though additional preparation may be required on the part of the provider to allow for worksheets and assessments to be completed virtually, the telehealth modality does not interfere with the CPT protocol (Moring et al., 2020).

One of the major concerns providers have regarding telehealth options is the impact on therapeutic alliance. Using a virtual modality can create disconnect between the patient and provider and may feel more impersonal due to not being in the same room or being able to read body language (Ashwick et al., 2019). However, with CVT in particular, the patient and provider are able to closely see each other's faces. Rapport is still generated through verbal and nonverbal cues, similar to in-person therapy (Ashwick et al., 2019). Therapeutic alliance with telehealth therapy for PTSD has been shown to be comparable to when the treatment is provided in-person (Germain et al., 2010). Indeed, the provider's willingness to use a modality that takes into account the client's circumstances (e.g., inability to easily travel to a clinic for in-person sessions) may contribute to greater therapeutic alliance.

Both provider and client satisfaction with CVT are comparable to in-person care for PTSD (e.g., Gros et al., 2018). Peterson et al. (2022) found that participants were least likely to decline receiving CPT with a telehealth treatment condition compared to in-office and in-home modalities, supporting the acceptability of CVT. Additionally, group virtual delivery of CPT is satisfactory to patients (Morland et al., 2011). Experience with virtual CPT also contributes to a more positive outlook toward the modality. A sample of ethnically/racially diverse veterans completing CPT via CVT reported that telehealth was convenient, increased privacy/confidentiality, was less stressful, and facilitated timely access to care compared to in-person treatment, and participants completed the telehealth protocol with a stronger preference and willingness to recommend it to others (Whealin et al., 2017). Taken together, these studies suggest that patients indicate overall satisfaction with telehealth, with many preferring it to other treatment modality options.

Patients often report concerns regarding privacy when considering treatment via telehealth (Whealin et al., 2017). While CVT offers more flexibility and mitigates obstacles such as distance to a clinic, the onus is on the patient to identify and utilize a private space for their appointments. While this issue can be addressed through planning and taking advantage of non-traditional spaces (e.g., logging into the session from a parked car), patients may be less likely to participate fully in their therapy sessions if privacy is a concern. When determining whether to utilize CVT for CPT, the provider should discuss with the client what the expectations are for utilizing the modality as well as environmental limitations the client may have that could impact their ability to have private and distraction-free appointments.

One lingering gap in the research on the delivery of CPT—or any intervention—via telehealth regards how to best manage suicide risk virtually. Processes to assess suicide risk virtually are being developed and a key aspect is preparatory safety planning (McManus et al., 2022). However, managing suicide risk virtually remains an impediment to therapists feeling comfortable providing care remotely; further research on best practices is needed. Identifying emergency contacts at the start of treatment and confirming the patient's physical location at the beginning of each session can help a provider to ensure patient safety (Morland et al., 2020). Ensuring that high-risk patients have safe and equal access to CPT via telehealth is critical.

In sum, there is strong research support for the delivery of CPT via telehealth. The modality is efficacious, feasible, and acceptable (Moring et al., 2020) to providers and patients. Following the COVID-19 pandemic, telehealth delivery of PTSD EBPs has become more common and accepted. With many providers now being able to offer treatment both in-person or via CVT, factors including therapeutic alliance, client satisfaction, and safety with telehealth delivery of CPT should be further studied. Overall, research supports providing CPT with telehealth, though there are practical considerations, both logistical and clinical, that must be considered when utilizing the modality.

Clinical Application

Logistical Factors

The delivery of CPT via telehealth has grown exponentially and will continue to evolve with new technology, platforms, and increased access to high-speed internet. Providers practicing at outpatient community mental health programs, university-based clinics, private practices, and on clinical trials have provided valuable information on the specific strategies needed to successfully implement CPT using telehealth. However, before using telehealth, providers should take time to consider certain decision points related to a telehealth-inclusive practice, including whether to deliver care from one's own home office versus a separate office outside of the home, how to choose a virtual platform, obtaining referrals, and licensing issues.

Before incorporating telehealth practice, providers should first consider the environment in which they intend to deliver care. If providers choose to use a home office, they must have a dedicated space, free from everyday distractions (e.g., family members, pets). It is vital for providers to communicate with family members within the same living space to respect working hours and to not disturb the home office. A breach of confidentiality can easily occur if others access the home office during a therapy session. Even the illusion of a lack of privacy, like seeing clients from an open area in the house, may be enough to concern patients. These issues should be discussed as a part of informed consent prior to initiating telehealth (e.g., the therapist should tell the patient that they are using a private space).

Furthermore, therapists should consider their own level of comfort regarding their privacy and how to best maintain their own boundaries with their clients. Providers may wish not to share their background decorations, personal family photos, or artwork. Certain platforms now allow for individuals to "blur" their backgrounds, or to set their background as a photo or template to prevent possible patient intrusiveness. Providers may feel as though their own privacy or sense of control over the sessions is violated if their patients can hear their children crying outside the door of their home office or if their dog frequently barks loudly. Some patients may not mind these disruptions, while others may find this very distracting. Such considerations should factor into a provider's decision as to where and when they see patients via telehealth.

Providers should be aware of the isolative nature of telehealth, especially when delivered at a home office. Different from a community mental health setting or group private practice, other providers are not readily available for on-demand consultation needs. Therefore, there may be more barriers to receiving consultation. It is recommended that providers, especially those with an exclusively telehealth-based practice, identify several other providers willing to discuss aspects of cases for clarity and to help determine the best possible therapeutic route.

Since the COVID-19 pandemic, there has been a significant increase in the number of platforms available to conduct psychotherapy via telehealth. Moreover, platforms have evolved to incorporate additional integrative features that make for a user-friendly, HIPAA compliant experience. Providers should consider the cost of the platform and the features that are preferred, versus essential. For example, some software programs incorporate the informed consent process, electronic medical record (EMR)/electronic health record (EHR) systems, medical billing, programming for initial assessments, and appointment scheduling. The most essential aspect when considering a specific telehealth platform is the assurance that all aspects of the platform are secure and compliant with all relevant regulations set forth by the Health Insurance Portability and Accountability Act (HIPAA). Security infrastructure includes secure and encrypted online access with two-factor authentication, as well as secure servers for data privacy, health information, and encrypted videoconferencing technology.

The consent process for telehealth is slightly different than in-person delivery of psychotherapy. Prior to the consent discussion, providers should either mail the consent form to their clients, or alternatively, send the form through their established patient portal. The form should use easy-to-understand language, and providers can use the consent form as a checklist throughout the consent process. It is important to review the basics of telehealth, the benefits and risks of telehealth, any possible alternative options such as office visits, the ability to withdraw consent, and costs of telehealth sessions. The consent form should detail policies regarding how many no-shows are acceptable prior to termination of services, as well as the cost of no-shows. The teach-back method is a preferred way to review the consent form and ensure clients' understanding. This process involves reviewing small segments of the form, clarifying and checking, and asking clients to repeat their understanding of each segment. Providers should document clients' verbal and signed consent, and mail or email a copy of the consent form for clients to retain. If a portal is not used, clients can be mailed two consent forms and a return envelope. One form is for the client to keep, and the other to sign and mail back to their therapist.

Assessment Considerations

The identification of clients who may meet criteria for PTSD and are appropriate for CPT delivered using telehealth remains similar to in-person processes. The provider should still utilize assessments like the Primary Care PTSD Screener (PC-PTSD; Prins et al., 2015) and the PTSD Checklist for DSM-5 (PCL-5; Weathers et al., 2013) to assess for PTSD diagnosis and symptom severity. These assessments can be used at the start of treatment to establish diagnosis and throughout treatment to evaluate symptom change over time. The primary difference to in-person CPT screening procedures is that the assessments may be administered over the phone, CVT, or even with a fillable PDF or survey sent to the client.

When conducting CPT with telehealth, it may be more important to spend time on safety planning in advance of the initial session than when meeting with the client in-person. Additional and routine assessments for the development of a comprehensive case conceptualization may reveal other co-occurring conditions that may prevent patients benefiting from CPT. For example, patients with severe suicidality require different and immediate interventions to ensure safety of the patient and/or others. For individuals with less severe suicidality, interventions such as crisis response planning for suicidality (CRP; Bryan et al., 2017; Rudd et al., 2006) is typically conducted in one session, can be integrated into CPT, and does not reduce fidelity to the protocol (Rozek & Bryan, 2020). Moreover, the flexibility of CRP allows the intervention to be delivered in response to other problematic behaviors, including self-harm and substance misuse. See Chaps. 3 and 11 for more details on crisis response planning. Other comorbid conditions that warrant immediate attention or may deem individuals inappropriate for CPT, particularly when provided via telehealth, include dangerous living situations, active psychosis, severe cognitive impairment, or any other medical or psychological condition that would prevent individuals from processing the traumatic event.

Professional Practice Considerations

Prior to initiating CPT, providers must also consider options for consultation if there are any questions about appropriateness of utilizing CPT for certain patients, questions concerning implementation of the protocol, or how to challenge specific stuck points. When providers primarily utilize telehealth, particularly if they work from home, there may be a disconnect from colleagues who could offer consultation. Online resources can help to mitigate this disconnect. If providers work with veterans in the community or VA, the National Center for PTSD (www.ptsd.va.gov) is a great resource and offers expert guidance on assessment, clinical management, and implementation of evidence-based treatments, such as CPT. Other training resources are available through the STRONG STAR Training Initiative (SSTI; strongstartraining.org), and the Medical University of South Carolina CPTWeb 2.0 (cpt2.musc.edu). Utilizing these resources is of particular use when adapting CPT to a virtual modality, and the decisions about necessary changes that must be made when doing so.

Providers must also remain up to date regarding specific state licensing board rules, regulations, and statutes as they pertain to the delivery of therapy via telehealth. For example, there are differences in state regulations regarding whether a provider can deliver therapy across jurisdictional lines if the provider or client travels out of state. Clinicians may wish to determine whether their licensing state participates in the Psychology Interjurisdictional Compact (PSYPACT®), which is designed to help facilitate the practice of telepsychology across state boundaries. Providers may obtain licensure in more than one state, but must be careful to follow the specific laws, codes, and licensing requirements of each state in which they are licensed.

Whether the client resides in the state of the provider in which they are licensed, in a participating PSYPACT® state, or in a separate state the provider is licensed in, it is important to obtain and document the client's location at each visit in case of any medical or mental health emergency situations. An added layer of protection that is recommended is to obtain the name of a trusted individual to be contacted if the client was to be in an emergency situation. If the client is willing, information regarding this "patient-support person" should include their name and telephone number, and they should be contacted by the client to inform them of their role. This individual should also be able to arrive at the client's house to perform a wellness check in a relatively short amount of time. Proper releases of information should be gathered to document the patient-support person. The provider should also obtain information about the client's local emergency services and their telephone numbers, to include hospitals, police department, and shelters. The purpose of collecting this information, and when it may be used, should be properly documented and discussed during the informed consent process.

Client Logistics

The exchange of information, including measures, handouts, and worksheets, is integral for the implementation of CPT and to track client progress. Certain telehealth platforms allow for an easy, secure, and flexible transmission of documents. Measures, such as the previously discussed PCL-5 for PTSD assessment, and the

Patient Health Questionnaire-9 (PHQ-9; Kroenke et al., 2001) are efficient strategies to assess for weekly patient progress throughout the duration of CPT. These measures can be accessed on telehealth platforms and completed by the patient, prior to meeting with the mental health provider. If the selected telehealth platform does not allow for easy exchange of documents, providers may choose to rely on a HIPAA compliant file-sharing platform that offers several layers of security. Conventional email platforms are not recommended due to the lack of adequate security; however, this method may be feasible and acceptable with appropriate client consent and password protection, if necessary. Providers without the capability of automatic reminders and fillable measures within their platform-of-choice should send measures via file-sharing platforms or email, to allow patients enough time to complete and return them prior to the beginning of therapy sessions. Patients can also be instructed to retain a blank electronic file of selected measures, to be completed prior to session, saved with a different filename (e.g., PCL_Month_Day_Year; PHQ_Month_Day_Year), and sent prior to each session.

Many clients will not have much experience working within a telehealth platform, and it is important to establish expectations, boundaries, and guidelines. It is helpful if these guidelines are provided to the client in written format and delivered via methods previously discussed. It is also recommended to verbally review the expectations of the client during the first telehealth session. These steps are usually conducted after the client has provided consent and the therapeutic relationship has been established.

Clients should be instructed to receive therapy in a location that is private and without distraction. To establish privacy and to facilitate concentration throughout sessions, clients may need to inform family members or roommates to respect the need for privacy. These parameters may not be feasible for some clients, and therefore, it may be necessary to conduct therapy while they are parked in their car, work-approved office, or other settings that can guarantee privacy. It is also possible that electronic devices in which the therapy is delivered (e.g., mobile phones, desktop computers, or laptops) are communal resources. In these circumstances, clients must be reminded to completely log off programs to protect login credentials, passwords, and personal information. Additionally, electronic worksheets and handouts may need to be password protected if stored on communal devices.

Other practical guidelines for clients include minimization of distractions and household activities while in session. Distractions could include accessing the web browser, completing household chores or homework, eating, or smoking; these distractions may serve as avoidance behaviors as well. Clients should be instructed to treat a telehealth session as a traditional in-office appointment, which entails being on time for the appointments, dressing appropriately, and being attentive and engaged, to maximize therapeutic engagement. Therefore, clients should be sitting upright, with the camera turned on, and the device placed in a "hands-free" way so the client can focus and write on the worksheets. Additional expectations for the client, consistent with in-office settings, is the notification of cancellation of an appointment that is consistent with provider policy, sending any documents (e.g., measures, practice assignments) on time and prior to the appointment, and to have all devices ready and turned on to facilitate on-time appointments. Clients should also be instructed to provide a back-up communication technology plan, including a silenced mobile phone near the client, to be readily available in case of equipment or technology failure.

Strategies for Delivering CPT via Telehealth

There are certainly many factors to consider prior to initiating remote CPT with a client, including client characteristics, licensing issues, and decisions regarding telehealth platforms and the exchange of documents. Once the client is established and is aware of therapy expectations, CPT can be initiated. The content of the sessions should not be altered, but there is plenty of room for flexibility regarding how to best deliver the content and maintain fidelity to the protocol. CPT involves the explanation of certain concepts using handouts. Clients should be referred to their Patient Workbook to follow along with the relevant materials and concepts explained by the therapist. For example, the therapist may suggest, "Let's look at your materials that are in your electronic Patient Workbook and find the handout titled, 5.1: Recovery or Nonrecovery From PTSD Symptoms Following Traumatic Events." The provider can hold up the referenced handout, or electronically display the handout, to make it easier for the client to find. When referring to practice assignments, providers can direct their patients to the relevant practice assignment instructions and read the instructions verbatim to the client.

There are additional options for sharing patient practice assignment documents. The CPT therapist manual and client materials can be downloaded after the purchase of the CPT manual through Guilford Press (Resick et al., 2024). Providers who have Adobe® Acrobat® Pro may transform the CPT materials into fillable worksheets so that patients can type their practice and send the forms electronically to their provider. Another aspect to consider is whether to send materials in a session-by-session format, or to provide patients with the entire Patient Workbook at the beginning of therapy. Providers can work with their patients' preferences, and their own comfort level, regarding the additional time commitment that may involve sending session-by-session practice handouts and worksheets. A hard-copy version of the Patient Workbook may be provided at an initial in-person meeting or delivered via ground shipping. If a hard-copy Patient Workbook is assembled, providers should consider separating the assignments/sessions with tabs, to help patients track and organize their sessions accordingly. Clients may be able to take photos of handwritten practice assignments to be shared via the telehealth platform, file-sharing system, approved email, or by using a screen-share option. Alternatively, clients can hold documents up to the camera to allow providers to take a snapshot of the practice worksheets. During sessions, it can be helpful if patients are able to share their screen while collaboratively working with their provider regarding specific stuck points. When teaching a new skill and introducing the relevant new worksheet, it is helpful for providers to share their screen with their patients.

There are interactive exercises throughout CPT that can be effectively taught and demonstrated through telehealth platforms. For example, during Session 8 of CPT, likelihood estimates are calculated to challenge safety-related beliefs, such as, "I will be raped again." Providers can choose to use virtual whiteboards, if available, to draw and write the statistical calculations with respect to the likelihood of being raped, based on the client's own personal experiences. Providers can also use a blank piece of paper and instruct the client to follow-along in writing down the information. The clinicians can then periodically hold up the paper to the camera to ensure the client follows along and understands the exercise.

All components of CPT can be effectively delivered via telehealth. However, the format and style of which CPT is delivered may be dependent upon the telehealth platform, clients' broadband internet capabilities, the way in which clients troubleshoot technological problems, and handling client-specific factors, such as crises and non-compliance with practice assignments. There may be times when streaming video is unreliable or unstable, due to fluctuations in broadband capabilities. During times in which video usage is not possible because of poor connectivity, it is acceptable to continue the session via telephone. Preliminary evidence suggests that telephone-based care may be as acceptable as other treatment delivery modalities (Cuijpers et al., 2019). Individuals in rural areas may still not have the access to suitable high-speed broadband internet, required for streaming video. In these circumstances, it is necessary to engage in a collaborative decision-making process and use clinical judgment to determine whether it is most appropriate to conduct CPT via telephone.

Other challenges can occur when delivering CPT via telehealth, including difficulty to identify whether clients may be high or intoxicated without immediate cues that are more apparent when meeting in-person (Gros et al., 2013). Providers may need to be attentive to other cues, such as slurred speech, distractibility, or tangential speech content. CPT may need to be adapted to address substance use concerns in some cases, and clients should understand the importance of abstaining from drug and alcohol use both before sessions and when they are actively engaged in their practice assignments.

Clients may also present to their therapy session in crisis. The same approaches used for in-person CPT sessions are recommended for telehealth modalities. First, it is important to determine the nature of the crisis, and whether the crisis warrants more immediate attention. For instance, if a client indicates suicidality, clinicians should conduct a full risk assessment and proceed with appropriate interventions. If more immediate attention and increased care is warranted, providers should remain on the telehealth platform until additional support arrives. Other times, clients may wish to discuss other stressful events that have occurred throughout the time in between sessions. These issues can distract from the focus of therapy and serve as avoidance of talking about the traumatic event and the stuck points that contribute to clients' PTSD symptoms. Like in-person CPT, providers should discern between stressful situations and crises. It is suggested to reserve 5 or 10 min at the end of CPT sessions if there are important stressors that the client would like to discuss.

As with in-person CPT, providers will inevitably encounter clients who demonstrate treatment interfering behaviors and stuck points that limit therapy engagement. Clients may not be engaged in their practice assignments, outside of session. As the evidence suggests, treatment adherence (Stirman et al., 2018) and consistency (Gutner et al., 2016) are the main factors that drive treatment outcomes. Therefore, motivational interviewing (MI; Miller & Rollnick, 2013) may be helpful for clients to resolve ambivalence about behavior change, integrate practice within their everyday lives, attend therapy sessions consistently, and limit avoidance.

Providers may also consider adjunct tools to facilitate PTSD symptom reduction and assist in practice completion and stress reduction. CPT Coach is a mobile application that clients can download and use while receiving CPT. The app contains all the support materials needed for clients that are found within the CPT manual, including the handouts, modules, and practice worksheets. Clients can choose to use the CPT Coach, rather than the hard-copy versions or the electronic versions. The Virtual Hope Box is a different mobile app designed to provide easily accessible methods for clients to engage in relaxation, distraction, inspirational quotes, pictures, games, and mindfulness exercises, and can be particularly helpful during moments of acute stress. The application may be placed on a safety plan to remind clients of this resource.

Case Example

Regina was a 45-year-old veteran female, self-identified as a Hispanic lesbian, and resided in a rural area of Texas. She enlisted in the Air Force when she was 18 years old and was deployed to Afghanistan in service of Operation Enduring Freedom (OEF) in 2005 and 2006. During her service, a superior officer raped her and told her that her career would be in jeopardy if she reported it. She met her current wife while she was enlisted in the Air Force and became concerned about the consequences if her Command became aware of the relationship. She soon separated from the military and found employment as a clerk at a grocery store in the town in which she and her wife resided. Regina began feeling angry and irritable, had trouble concentrating, started isolating from friends, and felt a lack of motivation to engage in hobbies. She noticed these symptoms were interfering with her relationship with her wife and coworkers.

Due to these concerns, she searched for providers online, and was surprised that many clinicians offered telehealth services. Given her busy work schedule, her residence in a rural part of the state, and limited income, telehealth was ideal. Regina did not have to worry about travel expenses, the travel time to the location of the therapist's office, or the possibility of needing to take time off work to attend therapy sessions. She found a therapist, Dr. Martinez, and reviewed her professional website. After reviewing her credentials and biography, Regina felt comfortable submitting a referral request on the provider's website.

Regina was contacted via telephone to schedule an initial appointment. Dr. Martinez provided the necessary instructions, via email, to access the online telehealth platform and set up an account. Dr. Martinez explained that the consent form would be available for her review, prior to the first session, and that the consent form would be discussed more thoroughly during the initial session. The consent document was reviewed during the first visit, while Regina followed along with the document provided via the online portal. Dr. Martinez used the teach-back method throughout the explanation, and Regina was able to describe back to Dr. Martinez about her understanding of each section, including policies regarding payment and no-shows. She was able to re-state that payments were due no later than 1-week after each session, by debit or credit card via the online portal, and that otherwise a late fee would be applied to her account. Regina verbally consented to treatment, was instructed to digitally sign the consent form in the client portal. Dr. Martinez documented both the verbal and written consent in Regina's record.

The platform also notified Regina of the screeners she would need to complete prior to the first session, including the PC-PTSD Screener (Prins et al., 2015) and the PHQ-9 (Kroenke et al., 2001). Dr. Martinez conducted a standard biopsychosocial interview to initially start to develop her case conceptualization of Regina, and obtained information for an emergency contact, which Regina chose to be her wife. Dr. Martinez noticed that Regina scored a "5" on the PC-PTSD Screener, which warranted further assessment for PTSD. Throughout the next several sessions, Dr. Martinez focused on the assessment of PTSD, which involved identifying a potential Criterion-A event that could explain Regina's current symptoms and presenting complaints. Regina completed the Life Events Checklist and indicated that the worst event that she experienced was her military sexual trauma (MST). Dr. Martinez worked with Regina to complete the PCL-5, anchored to the rape. Regina scored a 56 on the PCL-5, which is indicative of a reliable diagnosis of PTSD. She also scored a 16 on the PHQ-9, indicating moderately severe depression, with no indication of suicidality.

After the assessment for PTSD, Dr. Martinez explained to Regina that she met criteria for PTSD and provided psychoeducation regarding PTSD and its treatment. She also explained that she was trained in CPT and gave the rationale for the intervention. Regina and Dr. Martinez worked collaboratively to engage in shared decision making to determine the best approach. Regina agreed that CPT was an appropriate choice to address her PTSD. Expectations and policies were reviewed, and Regina agreed that she would (1) attend regular therapy sessions, (2) complete the assigned practice, and (3) use the telehealth platform to send her practice and PTSD and depression measures the day before her sessions. All other clinic policies were reviewed.

Session 1 of CPT was scheduled for the following week on Regina's day off from work. Regina completed her online assessments and was on time for the appointment. After the first session, she agreed to write her Impact Statement to be sent electronically through the secure portal and 1 day prior to CPT Session 2. Regina remembered to complete her online PCL-5 and PHQ-9 assessments, but Dr. Martinez did not receive Regina's impact statement. Dr. Martinez contacted Regina to ask about the practice assignment, and Regina explained that she forgot to send it. Dr. Martinez explained the importance of sending assignments prior to the session and instructed Regina to take the time to send the document, prior to beginning Session 2. Regina understood and was able to send the document. Sessions 2 and 3 were completed without any concerns; however, the last 10 min of Session 3 needed to be conducted via telephone due to audio and visual problems, most likely due to slowed internet speeds.

The same issue of audio and video lag occurred in Session 4, so the session was completed via telephone. Dr. Martinez and Regina wondered whether their typical sessions were scheduled at a particularly high-traffic time of day for broadband internet. To circumvent this issue, an earlier time of day was agreed upon, when there is likely less internet traffic. Rescheduling the session time helped with audio and video lags for the subsequent sessions.

Several times throughout therapy, technical problems were experienced related to sending and receiving documents via the telehealth platform. Regina uploaded her practice assignments, which sometimes resulted in an error message on Dr. Martinez's computer. Dr. Martinez received the message that the file could not be opened, so she instructed Regina to hold her assignments to the camera, as they were discussing each worksheet. The same strategies were used when Regina reached Session 8, and safety-related concepts were discussed, and the statistical likelihood of safety-related stuck points was explained. Regina followed along with the exercise, and both Dr. Martinez and Regina held documents to the camera to ensure that Regina fully understood the concepts. During Session 8, Regina expressed concerns about her relationship, and conveyed that she was bothered by her wife's interest in obtaining a second job. The discussion was reserved for the end of the session, as to not distract from challenging safety-related stuck points.

Prior to Session 9 of CPT, Dr. Martinez noticed that Regina had not attempted to send her practice assignments, nor did she complete her online PTSD and depression assessments. Regina was on time for the session, and Dr. Martinez immediately inquired about her practice and why she had not completed the assessments. Regina stated that she had been upset after a recent verbal altercation with her wife, when her wife mentioned the possibility of divorce. She also explained that while she was not intoxicated at the time of the session, she was drinking excessively throughout the last 3 days and had been feeling very angry and anxious.

Dr. Martinez decided to pause CPT to discuss this altercation and the excessive drinking. Dr. Martinez assessed for any suicidal ideation, to which Regina denied, and the amount and duration of her drinking. A crisis response plan (CRP; Bryan et al., 2017; Rudd et al., 2006) was created for moments in which Regina may experience heightened levels of distress and engage in dangerous levels of drinking. Although originally developed for the management of suicidality, development of a CRP is beneficial for a variety of behaviors. Had Regina expressed concerns of suicide, implementation of CRP would be appropriate, as well. The safety plan included warning signs that she was "going down a bad path," which included anxiety, thoughts that she was not loved, and increased heart rate. She identified ways to manage the distress on her own, including going for a walk around the block, solving jigsaw puzzles, and watching her favorite gameshow. She also identified reasons for not drinking, her social support, and professional support. Motivational interviewing (MI; Miller & Rollnick, 2013) techniques were also helpful to empower Regina to decrease the extent of her drinking. Regina was also encouraged to engage in her practice as often as possible. Dr. Martinez explained that therapy will be more effective if Regina is able to examine her thoughts, especially in moments that she is emotionally distressed. Regina agreed to this plan and understood the rationale. Though the CPT session was paused to discuss Regina's level of distress, the format and style of the appointment was consistent with CPT. Regina and Dr. Martinez collaboratively explored underlying stuck points in relation to the verbal fight. Regina was able to recognize that she had thoughts, "If my wife makes more money, she will eventually leave me," and, "If I'm not in control financially, I have no control in the relationship." She also identified other stuck points related to drinking, including, "Drinking will help me forget about my problems." Several of these stuck points were able to be challenged within this session, while other stuck points were assigned for practice. Consistent with the previous Session 8, Regina was also instructed to focus on trust-related stuck points.

Regina uploaded her practice assignments and completed her measurements prior to Session 9. She arrived on time and appeared relaxed. She stated that she was very proud of herself for working through stuck points related to her excessive drinking. Her alcohol use was assessed, and Regina denied drinking throughout the past week. She was able to complete worksheets related to urges to drink and identified that her drinking was also related to her desire to relax and manage her distress. Regina recognized that her drinking was previously reinforced by friends and family members that used alcohol as a tool to decompress. She recognized that there are other, more healthy, ways to regulate her emotions and relax, and that the behavior has been a habit that can be challenged. While reviewing other practice Challenging Beliefs Worksheets (CBWs, now called Alternative Thoughts Worksheet), she explained that she was also able to address stuck points that negatively impacted her relationship, and moreover, apologized to her wife for her reactions. Dr. Martinez praised Regina for her hard work and encouraged her to continue to identify additional stuck points that may interfere with the quality of her relationship. Regina continued to remain compliant with her practice assignments.

At Session 12, Regina submitted her final Impact Statement. Her PCL-5 score was 19, and her PHQ-9 score was four. She demonstrated significant improvement in her symptoms, and no longer met criteria for PTSD. Dr. Martinez emphasized that her improvement was based on Regina's hard work throughout therapy, and her commitment to get better. Dr. Martinez and Regina discussed plans moving forward, and it was agreed that monthly booster sessions would be beneficial. Dr. Martinez explained that future sessions would have the same format, in which Regina would be expected to submit her practice CBWs, to be reviewed and explored further in session. Regina agreed to this approach.

This case example demonstrates how CPT can be modified for telehealth delivery. Connection issues were circumvented by completing the sessions by telephone, when needed. Alternative times of the day were identified, to avoid high internet traffic that caused video and audio lags. CPT was also paused to allow for a crisis session and to discuss significant and distressing relationship problems. Clinicians who utilize telehealth are encouraged to be flexible in their approach, in the management of file sharing and obtaining measures, while still adhering to the protocol and implementing the necessary components of CPT.

Future Directions

CPT is an established, evidence-based intervention for PTSD with significant research supporting its efficacy when delivered through in-person and via remote modalities. Providing CPT via telehealth greatly increases access to evidence-based interventions for PTSD, allowing patients more autonomy in choosing how and when they receive treatment. However, there are still limitations to the efficient, broad delivery of CPT via telehealth that guide future research.

Importantly, there are still several populations where the efficacy of CPT delivered via telehealth has yet to be established. For example, there is limited research available on the utility of telehealth for individuals with disabilities (e.g., hearing loss, vision disturbances, physical limitations) or for those who are deemed "high risk" (e.g., suicidality, substance use disorders). These individuals need effective interventions with few barriers to obtaining care. Unfortunately, there is little information on treatment modality preferences, CPT treatment outcomes, or unique barriers to receiving telehealth within these groups. Future research should explore how telehealth services can be adapted to improve CPT delivery for these important populations, and to provide guidelines for practitioners who should be prepared for any adaptations necessary.

Older adults represent another group that is traditionally underserved by telehealth research. Many providers assume that older adults may not want remote, tech-heavy treatment modalities, even though this is not supported by the literature (Batsis et al., 2019). Given that PTSD may be present in later life, additional research is needed on treatment preferences and unique barriers and facilitators to telehealth for older adults. Overall, more research is needed on the delivery of CPT across more diverse and unique populations to ensure equity of access to first line PTSD treatments, independent of age, ability, symptom severity, and location.

Many providers and patients still struggle with technological illiteracy. In response to the COVID-19 pandemic, many were forced to adopt telehealth modalities quickly and without preparation. However, telehealth technology is a rapidly evolving domain, and comfort with this dynamic landscape may not be easy to maintain. Further, delivering treatment over remote technology has unique ethical and legal guidelines and risks, requiring extra attention and sometimes extra work (e.g., noting the location of the patient at each session) for patients and providers (Lustgarten & Elhai, 2018). Historically, there has been a deficiency in remote modality training among mental health practitioners, and educational core competencies rarely include telehealth delivery objectives (e.g., Dopp et al., 2021).

Increasing training opportunities early in the formal educational training of mental health care providers will increase comfort, confidence, and competence in the flexible delivery of evidence-based therapies, including CPT. Licensing boards may consider requiring telehealth training in order to obtain or renew licenses to ensure that practitioners are aware of legal, ethical, and practical issues in the delivery of telehealth to improve competency and to demystify the delivery of remote interventions.

Regarding the delivery of CPT, there has been recent interest in developing additional technological products to support the efficacy of, and engagement in, CPT. Virtual reality has been used to enhance exposure-based interventions for PTSD (e.g., Beidel et al., 2019), but may also be useful in CPT during the development of the trauma account or in testing biased thinking. Similarly, mobile applications may support engagement in CPT in between weekly sessions. CPT Coach was developed to help support clients receiving CPT, and contains electronic versions of worksheets, educational materials, and other tools that can be delivered under the supervision of a mental health care provider. However, research on the usability and efficacy of CPT Coach in enhancing outcomes and engagement is limited (e.g., Armstrong et al., 2017). Other synchronous (e.g., video therapist support) and asynchronous (e.g., text; Stirman et al., 2021) adjunctive modalities may be useful in increasing engagement in therapy, and may help providers deliver individualized, preference-based care to their clients. Unfortunately, research on the utility and efficacy of these supplemental, technology-based tools are limited (Armstrong et al., 2017; Rodriguez-Paras et al., 2017).

Regrettably, many providers who deliver therapy for PTSD are not trained in evidence-based interventions, including CPT. There are many barriers to providers themselves obtaining training in evidence-based trauma-informed care (Finch et al., 2020). Increasing access to affordable and accessible training opportunities for providers, while also improving opportunities for providers to deliver care remotely, when necessary (e.g., disaster response, inter-country), will inherently increase the availability of CPT to trauma survivors across the world.

Summary

The incorporation of telehealth in the provision of mental health care has changed the landscape for how we provide trauma-informed care to survivors. Research on CVT for the delivery of CPT suggests that this modality is not only feasible and non-inferior to traditional in-person care, but in many cases is preferable to in-person treatment. Providers can maintain the credibility and effectiveness of CPT when using telehealth with few modifications. The substantial increase in the uptake of telehealth modalities has ensured that patients have flexible access to CPT, including individuals who may otherwise struggle to access effective PTSD treatment. However, it is the responsibility of providers to ensure that patients receive high quality, effective, and reliable care independent of the modality used to deliver CPT.

Competing Interests The authors have no conflicts of interest to declare that are relevant to the content of this chapter.

References

Adepoju, O. E., Chae, M., Ojinnaka, C. O., Shetty, S., & Angelocci, T. (2022). Utilization gaps during the COVID-19 pandemic: Racial and ethnic disparities in telemedicine uptake in federally qualified health center clinics. *Journal of General Internal Medicine, 37*(5), 1191–1197. https://doi.org/10.1007/s11606-021-07304-4

Armstrong, C. M., Hoyt, T., Kinn, J. T., Ciulla, R. P., & Bush, N. E. (2017). Mobile behavioral health applications for the military community: Evaluating the emerging evidence base. *Best Practices in Mental Health: An International Journal, 13*(1), 106–119.

Ashwick, R., Turgoose, D., & Murphy, D. (2019). Exploring the acceptability of delivering Cognitive Processing Therapy (CPT) to UK veterans with PTSD over Skype: A qualitative study. *European Journal of Psychotraumatology, 10*(1), 1573128. https://doi.org/10.1080/20008198.2019

Batsis, J. A., DiMilia, P. R., Seo, L. M., Fortuna, K. L., Kennedy, M. A., Blunt, H. B., Bagley, P. J., Brooks, J., Brooks, E., Kim, S. Y., Masutani, R. K., Bruce, M. L., & Bartels, S. J. (2019). Effectiveness of ambulatory telemedicine care in older adults: A Systematic Review. *Journal of the American Geriatrics Society, 67*(8), 1737–1749. https://doi.org/10.1111/jgs.15959

Beidel, D. C., Frueh, B. C., Neer, S. M., Bowers, C. A., Trachik, B., Uhde, T. W., & Grubaugh, A. (2019). Trauma management therapy with virtual-reality augmented exposure therapy for combat-related PTSD: A randomized controlled trial. *Journal of Anxiety Disorders, 61*, 64–74. https://doi.org/10.1016/j.janxdis.2017.08.005

Bonfils, K. A., Lysaker, P. H., Yanos, P. T., Siegel, A., Leonhardt, B. L., James, A. V., Brustuen, B., Luedtke, B., & Davis, L. W. (2018). Self-stigma in PTSD: Prevalence and correlates. *Psychiatry Research, 265*, 7–12. https://doi.org/10.1016/j.psychres.2018.04.004

Bryan, C. J., Mintz, J., Clemans, T. A., Leeson, B., Burch, T. S., Williams, S. R., Maney, E., & Rudd, M. D. (2017). Effect of crisis response planning vs. contracts for safety on suicide risk in US Army soldiers: A randomized clinical trial. *Journal of Affective Disorders, 212*, 64–72. https://doi.org/10.1016/j.jad.2017.01.028

Cortelyou-Ward, K., Atkins, D. N., Noblin, A., Rotarius, T., White, P., & Carey, C. (2020). Navigating the digital divide: Barriers to telehealth in rural areas. *Journal of Health Care for the Poor and Underserved, 31*(4), 1546–1556. https://doi.org/10.1353/hpu.2020.0116

Cuijpers, P., Noma, H., Karyotaki, E., Cipriani, A., & Furukawa, T. A. (2019). Effectiveness and acceptability of cognitive behavior therapy delivery formats in adults with depression: A network meta-analysis. *JAMA Psychiatry, 76*(7), 700–707. https://doi.org/10.1001/jamapsychiatry.2019.0268

Department of Veterans Affairs, & Department of Defense. (2023). *VA/DoD clinical practice guideline for management of posttraumatic stress disorder and acute stress disorder, version 4.0.* https://www.healthquality.va.gov/guidelines/MH/ptsd/VA-DoD-CPG-PTSD-Full-CPG.pdf

Dopp, A. R., Mapes, A. R., Wolkowicz, N. R., McCord, C. E., & Feldner, M. T. (2021). Incorporating telehealth into health service psychology training: A mixed-method study of student perspectives. *Digital Health, 7*. https://doi.org/10.1177/2055207620980222

Finch, J., Ford, C., Grainger, L., & Meiser-Stedman, R. (2020). A systematic review of the clinician related barriers and facilitators to the use of evidence-informed interventions for posttraumatic stress. *Journal of Affective Disorders, 263*, 175–186. https://doi.org/10.1016/j.jad.2019.11.143

Foa, E. B., Hembree, E. A., & Rothbaum, B. O. (2007). *Prolonged exposure therapy for PTSD: Emotional processing of traumatic experiences: Therapist guide*. Oxford University Press.

Germain, V., Marchand, A., Bouchard, S., Guay, S., & Drouin, M. S. (2010). Assessment of the therapeutic alliance in face-to-face or videoconference treatment for posttraumatic stress disorder. *Cyberpsychology, Behavior, and Social Networking, 13*(1), 29–35. https://doi.org/10.1089/cyber.2009.0139

Gros, D. F., Lancaster, C. L., López, C. M., & Acierno, R. (2018). Treatment satisfaction of home-based telehealth versus in-person delivery of prolonged exposure for combat-related PTSD in veterans. *Journal of Telemedicine and Telecare, 24*(1), 51–55. https://doi.org/10.1177/1357633X16671096

Gros, D. F., Morland, L. A., Greene, C. J., Acierno, R., Strachan, M., Egede, L. E., Tuerk, P. W., Myrick, H., & Frueh, B. C. (2013). Delivery of evidence-based psychotherapy via video telehealth. *Journal of Psychopathology and Behavioral Assessment, 35*(4), 506–521. https://doi.org/10.1007/s10862-013-9363-4

Gutner, C. A., Suvak, M. K., Sloan, D. M., & Resick, P. A. (2016). Does timing matter? Examining the impact of session timing on outcome. *Journal of Consulting and Clinical Psychology, 84*(12), 1108. https://doi.org/10.1037/ccp0000120

Kantor, V., Knefel, M., & Lueger-Schuster, B. (2017). Perceived barriers and facilitators of mental health service utilization in adult trauma survivors: A systematic review. *Clinical Psychology Review, 52*, 52–68. https://doi.org/10.1016/j.cpr.2016.12.001

Kazlauskas, E. (2017). Challenges for providing health care in traumatized populations: Barriers for PTSD treatments and the need for new developments. *Global Health Action, 10*(1), Article 1322399. https://doi.org/10.1080/16549716.2017.1322399

Knowlton, C. N., & Nelson, K. G. (2021). PTSD telehealth treatments for veterans: Comparing outcomes from in-person, clinic-to-clinic, and home-based telehealth therapies. *Journal of Rural Mental Health, 45*(4), 243–255. https://doi.org/10.1037/rmh0000190

Kroenke, K., Spitzer, R. L., & Williams, J. B. (2001). The PHQ-9: Validity of a brief depression severity measure. *Journal of General Internal Medicine, 16*(9), 606–613. https://doi.org/10.1046/j.1525-1497.2001.016009606.x

Lewis, C., Roberts, N. P., Gibson, S., & Bisson, J. I. (2020). Dropout from psychological therapies for post-traumatic stress disorder (PTSD) in adults: Systematic review and meta-analysis. *European Journal of Psychotraumatology, 11*(1), Article 1709709. https://doi.org/10.1080/20008198.2019.1709709

Lustgarten, S. D., & Elhai, J. D. (2018). Technology use in mental health practice and research: Legal and ethical risks. *Clinical Psychology: Science and Practice, 25*(2), e12234. https://doi.org/10.1111/cpsp.12234

Maieritsch, K. P., Smith, T. L., Hessinger, J. D., Ahearn, E. P., Eickhoff, J. C., & Zhao, Q. (2016). Randomized controlled equivalence trial comparing videoconference and in person delivery of cognitive processing therapy for PTSD. *Journal of Telemedicine and Telecare, 22*(4), 238–243. https://doi.org/10.1177/1357633X15596109

McClendon, J., Dean, K. E., & Galovski, T. (2020). Addressing diversity in PTSD treatment: Disparities in treatment engagement and outcome among patients of color. *Current Treatment Options in Psychiatry, 7*, 275–290. https://doi.org/10.1007/s40501-020-002120

McManus, K., Cray, H., Hsu, C., Longsjo, E., Patrick, R., & Vahia, I. (2022). Developing a new suicide risk assessment for virtual encounters with non-clinicians. *The American Journal of Geriatric Psychiatry, 30*(4), S100–S101.

Miller, W. R., & Rollnick, S. (2013). *Motivational interviewing: Helping people change* (3rd ed.). Guilford Press.

Moring, J. C., Dondanville, K. A., Fina, B. A., Hassija, C., Chard, K., Monson, C., LoSavio, S. T., Wells, S. Y., Morland, L. A., Kaysen, D., Galovski, T. E., & Resick, P. A. (2020). Cognitive processing therapy for posttraumatic stress disorder via telehealth: Practical considerations during the COVID-19 pandemic. *Journal of Traumatic Stress, 33*(4), 371–379. https://doi.org/10.1002/jts.22544

Morland, L. A., Hynes, A. K., Mackintosh, M.-A., Resick, P. A., & Chard, K. M. (2011). Group cognitive processing therapy delivered to veterans via telehealth: A pilot cohort. *Journal of Traumatic Stress, 24*(4), 465–469. https://doi.org/10.1002/jts.20661

Morland, L. A., Mackintosh, M. A., Greene, C. J., Rosen, C. S., Chard, K. M., Resick, P., & Frueh, B. C. (2014). Cognitive processing therapy for posttraumatic stress disorder delivered to rural veterans via telemental health: A randomized noninferiority clinical trial. *The Journal of Clinical Psychiatry, 75*(5), 470–476. https://doi.org/10.4088/JCP.13m08842

Morland, L. A., Mackintosh, M. A., Rosen, C. S., Willis, E., Resick, P., Chard, K., & Frueh, B. C. (2015). Telemedicine versus in-person delivery of cognitive processing therapy for women with posttraumatic stress disorder: A randomized noninferiority trial. *Depression and Anxiety, 32*(11), 811–820. https://doi.org/10.1002/da.22397

Morland, L. A., Wells, S. Y., Glassman, L. H., Greene, C. J., Hoffman, J. E., & Rosen, C. S. (2020). Advances in PTSD treatment delivery: Review of findings and clinical considerations for the use of telehealth interventions for PTSD. *Current Treatment Options in Psychiatry, 7*, 221–241. https://doi.org/10.1007/s40501-020-00215-x

Ouimette, P., Vogt, D., Wade, M., Tirone, V., Greenbaum, M. A., Kimerling, R., Laffaye, C., Fitt, J. E., & Rosen, C. S. (2011). Perceived barriers to care among veterans health administration patients with posttraumatic stress disorder. *Psychological Services, 8*(3), 212. https://doi.org/10.1037/a0024360

Peterson, A. L., Mintz, J., Moring, J. C., Straud, C. L., Young-McCaughan, S., McGeary, C. A., McGeary, D. D., Litz, B. T., Velligan, D. I., Macdonald, A., Mata-Galan, E., Holliday, S. L., Dillon, K. H., Roache, J. D., Bira, L. M., Nabity, P. S., Medellin, E. M., Hale, W. J., & Resick, P. A. (2022). In-office, in-home, and telehealth cognitive processing therapy for posttraumatic stress disorder in veterans: A randomized clinical trial. *BMC Psychiatry, 22*(1), 41. https://doi.org/10.1186/s12888-022-03699-4

Prins, A., Bovin, M. J., Kimerling, R., Kaloupek, D. G., Marx, B. P., Pless Kaiser, A., & Schnurr, P. P. (2015). *The primary care PTSD screen for DSM-5 (PC-PTSD-5)*. https://www.ptsd.va.gov/professional/assessment/screens/pc-ptsd.asp

Resick, P. A., Monson, C. M., & Chard, K. M. (2024). *Cognitive processing therapy for PTSD: A comprehensive manual.* .

Rodriguez-Paras, C., Tippey, K., Brown, E., Sasangohar, F., Creech, S., Kum, H. C., Lawley, M., & Benzer, J. K. (2017). Posttraumatic stress disorder and mobile health: App investigation and scoping literature review. *JMIR mHealth and uHealth, 5*(10), e156. https://doi.org/10.2196/mhealth.7318

Rozek, D. C., & Bryan, C. J. (2020). Integrating crisis response planning for suicide prevention into trauma-focused treatments: A military case example. *Journal of Clinical Psychology, 76*(5), 852–864. https://doi.org/10.1002/jclp.22920

Rudd, M. D., Mandrusiak, M., & Joiner, T. E., Jr. (2006). The case against no-suicide contracts: The commitment to treatment statement as a practice alternative. *Journal of Clinical Psychology, 62*(2), 243–251. https://doi.org/10.1002/jclp.20227

S. Rep. No. 108-405. (2004). https://www.govinfo.gov/content/pkg/CHRG-108shrg90515/pdf/CHRG-108shrg90515.pdf

Stirman, S. W., Gutner, C. A., Suvak, M. K., Adler, A., Calloway, A., & Resick, P. (2018). Homework completion, patient characteristics, and symptom change in cognitive processing therapy for PTSD. *Behavior Therapy, 49*(5), 741–755. https://doi.org/10.1016/j.beth.2017.12.001

Stirman, S. W., Song, J., Hull, T. D., & Resick, P. A. (2021). Open trial of an adaptation of cognitive processing therapy for message-based delivery. *Technology, Mind, and Behavior, 2*(1). https://doi.org/10.1037/tmb0000016

Weathers, F. W., Litz, B. T., Keane, T. M., Palmieri, P. A., Marx, B. P., & Schnurr, P. P. (2013). *The PTSD checklist for DSM-5 (PCL-5)*. https://www.ptsd.va.gov/professional/assessment/adult-sr/ptsd-checklist.asp

Whealin, J. M., King, L., Shore, P., & Spira, J. L. (2017). Diverse veterans' pre-and post-intervention perceptions of home telemental health for posttraumatic stress disorder delivered via tablet. *The International Journal of Psychiatry in Medicine, 52*(1), 3–20. https://doi.org/10.1177/0091217417703291

Part V
Dissemination of CPT

Chapter 17
Dissemination and Implementation Efforts in Large Healthcare Settings

Kelly P. Maieritsch, Ellen T. Healy, and Kathleen M. Chard

Dissemination and Implementation Efforts in Large Healthcare Settings

Over the past 20 years, there has been a dramatic increase in efforts to disseminate evidence-based treatments throughout much of the world to increase the limited access most of the population has to quality mental health care (Clark, 2018). In the United States, estimates suggest that one-third of adults with a mental health disorder receive care, and in developing countries those rates can be as low as 2% (McHugh & Barlow, 2012). This chapter will briefly review some of the larger dissemination studies and will then focus on efforts related to implementation of Cognitive Processing Therapy (CPT) within a specific health care setting (the United States Veterans Health Administration), including key components and lessons learned.

One of the largest dissemination programs for mental health treatment has occurred in Great Britain with the English Improving Access to Psychological

K. P. Maieritsch (✉)
National Center for PTSD, Executive Division, White River, VT, USA
e-mail: Kelly.Maieritsch@va.gov

E. T. Healy
Office of Mental Health, VA Central Office, Washington, DC, USA

Department of Psychiatry, Boston University Chobanian & Avedisian School of Medicine, Boston, MA, USA

K. M. Chard
Cincinnati VA Medical Center, Cincinnati, OH, USA

Department of Psychiatry & Behavioral Neuroscience, University of Cincinnati School of Medicine, Cincinnati, OH, USA
e-mail: Kathleen.Chard@va.gov

J. S. Wachen, T. E. Galovski (eds.), *Cognitive Processing Therapy for Complex Cases*, CBT: Science Into Practice,
https://doi.org/10.1007/978-3-031-87356-0_17

Therapies (IAPT) program. IAPT was designed to bring research and training together for practitioners by training them in evidence-based treatments for depression and anxiety (Clark, 2011, 2018). The initiative has relied on the treatment guidelines published by the National Institute for Health and Care Excellence (NICE, 2011) that provide a review of the evidence for mental health treatments and offer summary recommendations for treatments for various mood disorders. Important in the creation of the program was inclusion of key stakeholders who could offer valuable insights as to the most effective ways to obtain buy-in from administrators, clinicians, and patients. In addition, they created a plan for the dissemination that started with three pilot sites and then expanded with changes based on information from the original locations (Clark, 2009). The goal of the program was to train 10,500 new therapists by 2021, and in the update published in 2017, they reported having trained 7000 new clinicians, seeing over 960,000 patients a year, with 560,000 receiving a course of treatment, and 51% showing recovery at the end of treatment. Findings from the initiative suggest that it is possible to create large scale dissemination while maintaining average clinical outcomes that are in keeping with the results of the original research studies (Clark, 2018). Some important takeaways to date have included the following: shorter wait times between assessment and treatment initiation led to better treatment outcomes, the optimal number of sessions appeared to be nine to ten, and services with higher rates of missed appointments had worse overall outcomes. Limitations of the IAPT include the need for expansion of the program, especially in the area of older adults, as well as the use of assessment tools that have been variable, which leads to problems of diagnosis, integration into therapy, and outcomes tracking.

Another large, ongoing dissemination program in the United States Veterans Health Administration (VHA) focuses on training clinicians in evidence-based psychotherapies, including cognitive processing therapy (CPT) and prolonged exposure (PE) to treat posttraumatic stress disorder (PTSD; Karlin et al., 2010). Given the documented effectiveness of evidence-based psychotherapies for PTSD, this initiative sought to increase the dissemination of these therapies within VHA at a time that the nation was at war and there was a dramatic increase in the number of veterans seeking care from the VHA for PTSD and other mental health conditions. In addition, in the early 2000s, the VHA recognized that although many psychotherapies, including CPT, have a strong evidence base and are recommended as first-line treatments in clinical practice guidelines, e.g., Department of Veterans Affairs/Department of Defense Clinical Practice Guidelines for PTSD (VA/DoD CPG for PTSD, 2023), the broad availability of these treatments in clinical settings was limited. For example, Rosen et al. (2004) reported on a survey of six VA medical centers which found manualized trauma-focused therapies were infrequently provided prior to the initiation of these dissemination efforts. Starting in 2005, VHA undertook a dissemination and implementation initiative to transform mental health care to be evidence-based and recovery-oriented. As Karlin and Cross (2014) outlined, VHA developed a multidimensional model for disseminating and implementing evidenced based psychotherapies (EBPs) that employed specific strategies at policy, provider, local systems, patient, and accountability levels. There was recognition that the low levels of EBP delivery reflected a limited availability of intensive, competency-based training in EBPs that went beyond education and exposure to these interventions.

CPT was the first intervention selected to be widely disseminated in VHA, soon to be joined by approximately 15 other EBP training programs. CPT and PE were chosen specifically for PTSD due to the accumulation of empirical support from randomized controlled studies evaluating their effectiveness and the VA/DoD Clinical Practice Guideline for PTSD at the time (U.S. Department of Veterans Affairs/Department of Defense, 2004) offering "a strong recommendation that the interventions were always indicated and acceptable."

By intervening on various levels and anticipating barriers to implementation, the VHA's model intended to facilitate ongoing sustainability. To that end, a number of top-down and bottom-up strategies within VHA assisted with both dissemination and implementation of EBPs to maximize the likelihood of success. One strategy included the development of policy aligning with the provision of specific EBPs, suggesting standardized offerings across the health care system. Additionally, several programs including the EBP Coordinator program and the PTSD Mentoring & Implementation Program were developed, along with a robust training program, to support implementation efforts through local advocacy for EBP training and evidence-based practice and national and regional promotion of best practices for implementation of EBPs in specialty clinical settings. Changes were made to the VHA CPT Training Program over the course of the dissemination to further support the initiative. The process of the development and implementation of the VHA CPT Training Program and related VHA initiatives are described in detail below and may serve as a model for the dissemination of EBPs in large healthcare systems.

Dissemination: CPT Training and Consultation in VHA

The VHA CPT Training Program was first developed with an active collaboration between Dr. Patricia Resick, the original developer of CPT, and national leadership in the VHA Office of Mental Health Services (now called Office of Mental Health) and the National Center for PTSD (VHA Center of Excellence). The first efforts focused on creating an adapted therapist manual (e.g., Resick et al., 2014a) and a patient materials manual (e.g., Resick et al., 2014b), which included example worksheets for military-related trauma, as well as extensive training materials including slide presentations and training videos. Manuals were also developed (and later revised) for trainers (e.g., Resick et al., 2023) and consultants (e.g., Resick et al., 2024), with an emphasis on standardizing learning objectives and providing consultants session-by-session consultative suggestions and checklists of standard elements. A VHA intranet site was developed that allowed all clinicians access to therapy materials, literature, and training resources. A core team of 'national trainers' was cultivated with an initial train-the-trainer workshop hosted by the CPT treatment authors. Together, this newly built team of CPT trainers and experts worked collaboratively to review and update the materials necessary to facilitate wide-scale training, specifically providing input and feedback to for continuous improvement of training materials. As CPT training got underway, the multidimensional model for disseminating and implementing EBPs supported these training efforts, with focus on policy, provider, local systems, patient, and accountability levels.

With respect to national policy, the original version of the VHA Handbook 1160.01, *Uniform Mental Health Services in VA Medical Centers and Clinics* (U.S. Department of Veterans Affairs, 2008) established that specific evidence-based interventions, including CPT, should be available to all Veterans who have a diagnosis of PTSD. Further, the policy emphasized the importance of treatment fidelity by outlining that VHA medical centers must have appropriate staff capacity to be delivered "as designed and shown to be effective" (p. 31). Current version of this policy continues to reflect the expectation regarding of provision of evidence-based treatments (U.S. Department of Veterans Affairs, 2023).

To target the provider level of implementation, the VHA CPT Training Program included two key components, an in-person experiential workshop followed by ongoing weekly consultation. The CPT Training program did not start with a consistent consultant for each call. However, this was quickly changed as the importance of discussing cases on a consistent bases with the same consultant each week became apparent. The VHA CPT Training Program also worked to establish additional means of support for clinicians after completing training, including offering ad hoc consultation with a CPT expert and 1-h webinars on advanced CPT topics which are recorded and serve as an enduring resource. The PTSD Consultation Program, initiated a few years after the initiation of the VHA CPT Training Program, is another consultative program from the National Center for PTSD that is available to all VHA clinicians and veteran-serving community providers to ask questions about PTSD assessment and treatment, including CPT, to enhance provider implementation.

Addressing local-level systems and organizational factors are critical to EBP implementation. VHA is a large healthcare system with multiple priorities and needs, and considerations like clinic structures, provider workload, and cultural support for short-term evidence-based treatment impact the success of implementation. To facilitate support locally, VHA created an EBP Coordinator position at every medical center. The EBP Coordinators serve to educate leadership and staff about EBPs and work with mental health leadership and other stakeholders, such as clinic schedulers, to ensure the clinic infrastructure is supportive of EBP delivery (e.g., weekly hour-long appointments can be scheduled). EBP Coordinators also track EBP delivery, help connect clinicians to training opportunities, and advocate for providers. These resources are important to ensure that trained providers are working within a system where CPT implementation is feasible.

In order to ensure EBPs reach the intended recipients, it is important to attend to patient-level factors to promote implementation. Patients need to understand what therapy options are available to them and believe that therapy will be helpful for them. To that end, the VHA CPT Training Program has worked to create accessible patient-facing materials including a brochure describing the treatment components and rationale as well as an introductory video that includes Veterans discussing their experiences with CPT. Additionally, the National Center for PTSD has created materials to help patients understand their treatment options including brief white-board videos explaining EBPs, *AboutFace* videos with Veterans sharing their stories and experience with treatment, and the *PTSD Treatment Decision Aid* tool that walks patients through effective treatment options. The National Center for PTSD has also created a treatment companion app called *CPT Coach* which is a tool patients may use to engage in the therapy, as it includes mobile versions of practice assignments as well as psychoeducation materials and tools to track progress and set reminders. Additionally, VHA has created patient-facing resources online with information about the VA/DOD Clinical Practice Guidelines (U.S. Department of Veterans Affairs, 2024b) and information about evidence-based therapies (U.S. Department of Veterans Affairs, 2024a).

The final component of the VHA multilevel model of dissemination and implementation is a focus on accountability by monitoring and evaluating progress (Karlin & Cross, 2014). The evaluation of the VHA CPT Training Program is an important component of accountability. From the early days of the dissemination process, program evaluation has been integral in informing and refining the training processes (Chard et al., 2012). Program evaluation data is collected at both the clinician and patient level. Clinician data includes faculty evaluations at workshops, pre- and post-workshop self-efficacy ratings, and training completion information. Additionally, provider surveys are conducted after clinicians complete training to better understand ongoing use of CPT and barriers to implementation. Through the years of the VHA CPT Training Program, these measures informed refinements to the training program that incorporated both administrative changes and training content enhancement. Given how many providers identified barriers to implementing CPT in their setting, the application for training was strengthened to clarify the requirements and commitment for clinicians and to ensure their supervisor's support. The VHA CPT Training Program's approach to consultation was also changed based on early program experiences.

What Does CPT Training in VHA Look like?

The VHA CPT Training Program entails attending a 2-day workshop focused on implementing CPT delivered individually along with an optional third workshop day focused on CPT delivered in a group format. CPT workshops combine didactics, video demonstrations, and experiential learning with role plays to practice the CPT skills. The didactic aspect of the workshop involves reviewing the research evidence for CPT, explaining the rationale and theory underlying the treatment, and providing a step-by-step walk-through of what each CPT session entails. The workshop is designed to be interactive, with discussions of barriers to implementation, exercises to solidify understanding, and opportunities for questions and discussion.

After attending the workshop, clinicians are provided 6 months of weekly CPT consultation with a CPT expert. For those who actively participate in at least 75% of 6 months of consultation calls and successfully complete at least two CPT cases that were discussed and reviewed with their consultant, clinicians can apply to be designated as a "CPT Provider." The VHA built a CPT provider roster that recognizes all the VHA clinicians who have successfully completed CPT training. This roster is posted on an internal VHA SharePoint site and is available for any clinician to find CPT providers.

Consultation as an Integral Part of CPT Training

Consultation is a critical aspect of training in evidence-based psychotherapy. Research has demonstrated that didactic training alone does not adequately promote sustained implementation of an intervention with fidelity (Frank et al., 2020; Herschell et al., 2010). Consultation after didactic training is thought to facilitate further learning. It consolidates knowledge and allows clinicians to get feedback and adjust their practice as they are working with clients. In particular, the discussion of the application of specific CPT strategies to individual clients during consultation has been shown to be associated with improvements in client PTSD symptoms (Mallard Swanson et al., 2021).

Initially, the VHA CPT Training Program offered consultation as an encouraged, but optional, aspect of the training process. Consultation calls were drop-in structure and clinicians were asked to attend regularly as they worked on their CPT cases over the course of 6 months. However, for busy clinicians, drop-in consultation was frequently interrupted, and attendance was often sporadic. It was clear that consistency of the training experience was lacking. Consequently, the VHA CPT Training Program instituted consultation group assignments where clinicians were assigned to one consultant and met for a 1-h group each week at the same time. As part of this change, 6 months of weekly consultation became a required part of attending a CPT workshop in VHA. Because it is necessary to firm up the commitment to the training process before accepting clinicians to attend the training, the application for training explicitly lists the requirements of training and consultation and both the clinician and their supervisor sign a statement of commitment.

Decentralizing: From National to Regional Trainings

The VHA CPT Training Program began as a nationally centralized training program, in which trainings were funded and coordinated at a national level. Workshops were held in various locations around the country and clinicians traveled to attend in-person workshops. A small core team of CPT trainers facilitated the trainings, ensuring the provision of consistent and high-quality trainings. This model allowed many clinicians to be trained, but the high travel costs made this model unsustainable over the long-term. Alternative training models were considered with the goals to increase training availability and improve cost effectiveness while maintaining the quality of the training experience. Surveys of VHA stakeholders (e.g., regional Mental Health Leads, hospital Mental Health Chiefs, local EBP Coordinators) indicated that regional training models received the highest acceptability ratings among the alternative EBP training models including blended learning, online training, and video teleconferencing (Smith et al., 2017). In 2010, the VHA CPT Training Program began to decentralize by training regional trainers who could lead CPT trainings locally in their region. Between 2010 and 2015, the VHA CPT Training Program continued to hold national workshops, but began to scale down the number of workshops while building regional training capacity by training new regional trainers throughout the VHA. Also, during this period, there were increased federal restrictions on conference travel which further emphasized the need to decentralize the training model (Smith et al., 2017).

The 'train-the-trainer' model to disseminate training more broadly on a local level has shown promise across many mental health conditions (Frank et al., 2020). VHA employed this model to create a system of CPT regional trainers who serve as trainers and consultants to MH clinicians locally. Potential candidates for the CPT Train-the-Trainer workshops are VHA MH providers who have completed CPT training and have extensive clinical experience with CPT. At the Train-the-Trainer workshops, experienced CPT clinicians are trained how to teach others how to provide CPT, with an emphasis on cultivating public speaking skill and developing a strong understanding of the evidence and rationale for the treatment. Fidelity to the CPT model is strongly emphasized at the Train-the-Trainer workshop in an attempt to minimize drift amongst CPT trainers when they lead their own workshops. To select candidates for the Train-the-Trainer, the applications include the submission of (1) an audio recording of the first CPT session where CPT rationale is explained, and (2) a video recording of a presentation with a live audience. These recordings are valuable to assess potential trainers' ability to explain the rationale of CPT and their public speaking skill. Starting in 2016, the VHA CPT Training Program relied on a fully decentralized regional training model, and since that time, there has been an average of 70 CPT regional trainers in the VHA system who train more than 500 providers per year. Veteran symptom outcomes are comparable between those treated by clinicians trained nationally versus those treated by clinicians trained by a regional trainer (Smith et al., 2017). Furthermore, compared to those who attended national workshops, regional CPT training attendees reported similarly high satisfaction with the workshop and endorsed that they learned new knowledge and skills and can apply these knowledge and skills to improve job performance (Smith et al., 2017).

Once trained to be CPT regional trainers, these VHA mental health clinicians serve as both CPT trainers and CPT consultants for their region with their leadership support to spend work hours to serve in the role. The VHA CPT Training Program team provides guidance for setting up workshops, training materials and processes, support for accreditation, logistical background support for virtual trainings, and tracking of trainee participation. In turn, the CPT regional trainers are tasked with planning and setting up their own workshops (which may be held in-person or virtually), sending out training announcements, reviewing applications, and making acceptance decisions. Since consultation is a required part of training, CPT regional trainers are responsible for providing consultation to all clinicians they train. Thus, the size of their workshop is determined in part by calculating the consultation capacity that they can provide. Since consultation calls may have up to eight participants on a call, this is often the limiting factor for workshop size. By delegating the planning and administrative tasks (such as reviewing and selecting applicants) to regional trainers, the small number of national VHA CPT Training Program office staff have been able to support large numbers of CPT trainings annually.

What Does CPT Consultation Look like?

Consultees are asked to come prepared to discuss their cases and ask questions. Given that 1-h consultation groups may have up to eight clinicians in attendance, it is important that the time is structured and paced to allow everyone time to participate. Consultation was initially held by conference telephone calls, but with the rise of internet video conference platforms in recent years, using a video platform became preferable given that it enhances the engagement and accountability to have everyone participating on screen. Discussion of any clinical emergencies in the context of CPT are prioritized. To collect information efficiently, clinicians are asked to present cases by identifying the CPT session number, basic brief demographics about the case (e.g., age, gender, trauma), most recent PTSD Checklist score (collected each session for measurement-based care), and then specific questions that they may have. Consultation discussion pertains to both managing patient concerns and cultivating clinician skill. Common patient concerns include how to handle patient avoidance and missed sessions, managing homework compliance, and ensuring patient understanding and engagement. Consultants work with clinicians to ensure their understanding and ability to explain the treatment rationale, develop Socratic questioning skill, solidify the ability to identify and categorize stuck points, and recognize where therapist beliefs (stuck points) may interfere with the therapy fidelity.

Below are two vignettes that illustrate how a consultant might address issues raised in CPT consultation. The first is an example of how a clinician gathers information about how the case is going and then focuses in on reviewing and explaining some concepts as it applies to the client in order to build the clinician's CPT skill.

Clinician: *This week I held session 4 and my patient's PCL still hasn't improved—it is still a 64. I am feeling stuck.*

Consultant: *Ok, does the patient's self-report also seem to indicate not much change?*

Clinician: *I think so. He is still blaming himself quite a bit and is easily upset. He is still avoidant of talking about his trauma.*

Consultant: *So, it sounds like the PCL measurement is accurately capturing his current level of symptoms. What is one of the assimilated stuck points you are working on?*

Clinician: *Well, last session we worked on "I can't trust anyone." He has major trust issues since the trauma, that's the main concern he has identified and what he wants to talk about.*

Consultant: *I remember you mentioned his stuck points about trust, but given that his PCL is still quite high, that makes me think that we need to target his stuck points about the trauma specifically first. Remember, assimilated stuck points are beliefs about the trauma itself, thoughts about why the trauma happened. And we want to prioritize assimilated stuck points first, as these beliefs can serve as evidence to support over-accommodated stuck points. Over-accommodated stuck points are beliefs that are often over-generalized conclusions based on the trauma experience that apply to how a patient sees their world now. So, the stuck point, "I can't trust anyone" is what kind of stuck point?*

Clinician: *Oh, I see, "I can't trust anyone" is an over-accommodated stuck point. I always get confused about that.*

Consultant: *That's right. Now, you mentioned the patient has some self-blame related to the trauma, what are some things he is saying?*

Clinician: *Well, he says that it's his fault the trauma happened and that he should have spoken up to leadership when he had a gut feeling that something was going to go wrong.*

Consultant: *Excellent, those are two good assimilated stuck points to prioritize—"It is my fault that the trauma happened" and "I should have spoken up to leadership." Do you see why we want to start here first before focusing on over-accommodated stuck points like "I can't trust anyone"? Do you think you can work on one of these stuck points on the Challenging Questions Worksheet in the next session?*

Clinician: *Yes, I do—that helps a lot.*

In this case example, the consultant gathers information by asking questions about the case to understand the case progress. By asking specifically about assimilated stuck points, the consultant targets the conversation and identifies that the clinician still had some confusion about these concepts. Then, in the context of the specific case, the consultant provides an opportunity to clarify the concept and apply it in a concrete manner. This discussion in consultation helps the clinician know what to focus on in the next session. Consultation allows the consultee to get input that both consolidates their own learning and ensures that quality care is provided during the learning process.

There are times during consultation when clinicians seek to include strategies from other therapeutic approaches or treatment protocols to address the client's presenting concerns in a given session. It's important in consultation to both respect the experience the clinician brings to their clinical work, while also helping them understand the value of fidelity to the CPT protocol that is grounded in the cognitive theory underlying the treatment model. This includes educating on how to utilize the resources within the protocol to address the presenting concern.

Clinician: *I completed session 4 this week and it mostly went well.*

Consultant: *Mostly?*

Clinician: *Yes, the client did bring in a few ABC worksheets, but seemed to be experiencing a lot of distress when talking about the events in her column A (activating event). I tried to go over the worksheet, but it was pretty challenging with the amount of distress, so we took some time to work on emotion regulation.*

Consultant: *What specifically did you do to work on emotion regulation?*

Clinician: *I had her {the client] put down the worksheet and do some counted breathing and then mindfulness of her current surrounding to help with grounding.*

Consultant: *Hmm, did that seem to work... how long did that take?*

Clinician: *It did seem to help eventually, not entirely sure how long it took.*

Consultant: *Ok, I'm curious if we can go back to what led to the distress. It seemed to be related to the event on the ABC worksheet.*

Clinician: *I think but it's hard to tell, she started reading the situation and was almost immediately upset.*

Consultant: *Got it, so what was the event?*

Clinician: *She had written down more, but basically, she and her boyfriend had a fight about going out, she didn't want to, and he stormed out.*

Consultant: *What had she written down for her thoughts and emotional reaction on the worksheet?*

Clinician: *Nothing in the thought column, but "terrified" in the emotional reaction.*

Consultant: *Did that seem to be what she was feeling in terms of distress in the moment?*

Clinician: *Yes, I guess that does fit with how she was reacting in the moment.*

Consultant: *I wonder what types of thoughts your client might have in response to this situation that would lead to feeling terrified. And, terrified of what? Is there anything on her stuck point log that might have been an automatic thought here?*

Clinician: *Let me look. I could see maybe "People will always leave me" or maybe "I lose everyone I love".*

Consultant: *Those both sound like they could be stuck points that played a role in her making sense of this situation. Did you get a chance to ask her about her thoughts and stuck points?*

Clinician: *Not really, the mindfulness took a bit and then we really had to get to the challenging questions, or I wouldn't have been able to go over them.*

Consultant: *Hmmm, while I can understand why breathing and mindfulness made sense to do in that moment, I'm wondering if there was any way to utilize the ABC sheet to accomplish the same goal of emotion regulation while staying consistent with the cognitive model? That way you have time to completely review the ABC concept while also addressing the emotional reaction.*

Clinician: *I'm not sure what you mean?*

Consultant: *Well, it certainly wouldn't be uncommon for someone to have an emotional reaction in session. With CPT, we would want to utilize the ABC model to facilitate mindful awareness of what they are both feeling and thinking, and then explore how the thoughts or stuck points are possibly contributing to the presence and/or strength of the emotional reaction.*

Clinician: *Ok, but it's hard to focus on a worksheet when she is upset.*

Consultant: *So, one way to do that would be to consistently model the ABC relationship in your dialogue when discussing her distress; this doesn't have to happen yet on paper. So, for example, when she began describing the situation, you basically ask about the related thoughts and feelings. Have you tried just talking through the ABC model in your discussion without necessarily focus on the worksheet itself?*

Clinician: *Well maybe?*

Consultant: *It's another way you can model the practice of identifying the thoughts and feelings when someone is distressed without feeling like you are ignoring it to focus on a worksheet. You can probe about how she is feeling, getting her to label the emotion in session. This would help clarify if she was reacting to the situation and if she is currently having the same reaction as what was on the sheet. You can certainly ask her to take a breath if that has worked for her in the past, and continue with having her label the emotions even as she is possibly having them, and to ground you can utilize past tense when describing them back. "Ok, so you were feeling terrified when this happened last week, so let's talk about what led to your feeling terrified and maybe we can help you feel less fearful now." Then follow her labeling of the emotional reaction with some clarification questions to get at the thoughts, something like "Ok so you felt terrified when this happened, what in this situation led to you feeling terrified? Was it something during the fight? Or perhaps was it when he left?" These questions help engage her cognitively and bring it back to understanding what happened and ultimately how she was interpreting what happened. Something like, "Ok, so you really felt terrified when he left, what did it mean to you that he left?" In this case I would be probing to see if her interpretation was consistent with a stuck point.*

Clinician: *I could try that.*

Consultant: *Ok, and while I can understand and appreciate you wanting to bring other strategies into CPT, it's really important to make sure to try the model first to consistently stick to the theory and approach you agreed to take with your client at session 1. There are clearly lots of ways to help regulate emotion. In CPT we do so by helping get to the thoughts fueling that emotion. Once we know the stuck point, we can discuss alternative thoughts that lead to less intense reactions.*

In this case example, the consultant gently provided feedback to help the consultee understand how to handle patient distress while also maintaining fidelity to the CPT model. Often, clinicians revert to clinical strategies that they are most familiar or comfortable with when they are unsure what to do within CPT. Consultation provides the opportunity to provide corrective feedback and facilitate nuanced learning to optimize skilled CPT delivery and enhance patient outcomes.

The VHA CPT Training program seeks to educate clinicians to provide CPT in a skilled, adherent way through experiential learning at the initial workshop and the follow-up consultation while they start to implement the treatment. While providing quality training is an important first step to therapy implementation in a large health care system, broader organizational supports are necessary for implementation to be sustainable over the long-term. The VHA CPT Training Program advocates for systemic support through contact with clinicians and supervisors, but to fully facilitate implementation, top-down policies and clinic facilitation efforts support organizational factors and clinic structures.

Implementation: Supporting Sustainability within Large Health Care Settings

Implementation is a constellation of processes intended to get an intervention, such as CPT, into use within an organizational setting (Damschroder, 2009). This is a process that helps transition a healthcare system from the point of deciding to adopt a new intervention into their practice setting, to routine use of that intervention. Implementation of evidence-based practice in large health care settings can be a complex process and requires consideration of multiple system level challenges and the resources needed to address potential barriers, as well as identification and reinforcement of system level efforts that facilitate implementation. In other words, for dissemination of CPT in a large health care setting to be successfully integrated, efforts should include plans for implementation in the practice setting that consider factors ensuring not only initial uptake but sustainability of the practice. The field of implementation science has yielded a growing body of literature studying methods and strategies that facilitate the uptake of evidence-based practice into practice settings, which includes the identification of and methods to address barriers to routine use (Bauer & Kirchner, 2020). Both barriers and facilitators supporting the provision of an evidenced based practice may arise at different levels within the healthcare system, including patient level, provider level, organizational level, and or policy level (Damschroder, 2009). One of the challenges of ensuring that implementation is successful and sustained over time is increasing awareness of not only key dimensions and strategies to support utilization, but also knowledge that these are likely to change over time. The sustainability of providing CPT within a larger health care setting must provide support for resources to attend to not only the patient and provider levels (i.e., training and consultation) but also to address unique organizational factors and setting characteristics. As the size of the system increases, so does the likelihood of the need for multiple programmatic resources to support dissemination and implementation. Further, organizational structure can also influence the fit between specific practices and the organization (Aarons et al., 2011).

We'll focus on describing in more detail one of the many programs that was developed to facilitate the organizational change needed in VHA to support provision of CPT, and its role in sustainability and collaboration with the VHA CPT Training Program.

PTSD Mentoring and Implementation Program

Larger health care settings often have broader service contexts and settings, as is the case with the VHA. Mental health services are considered a specialty service, and within mental health there is a comprehensive continuum of care including services provided in primary care, generalized and specialized outpatient clinics (e.g., PTSD specialty care), residential treatment programs, and intensive inpatient programs (OMSHP CoC workgroup, 2017). As part of the larger VHA health care system transformation to evidence-based care, there was identification of the need to develop specific resources to support the system changes required for successful implementation within the clinical settings designed to provide outpatient PTSD specialty care (Department of Veteran Affairs, 2012).

The VHA National Center for PTSD was tasked with designing and implementing a mentoring program for directors of outpatient specialized PTSD programs across the full VHA enterprise. In early 2008, the PTSD Mentoring Program (later named PTSD Mentoring and Implementation Program) was launched with the mission of ensuring the provision and improvement of the best clinical services for Veterans seeking care for PTSD and to help foster change in the PTSD treatment culture to an evidence-based, recovery-oriented model of care (Karlin & Cross, 2014). The program sought to accomplish this task by focusing on sharing best practices and effective clinic management practices within the network of PTSD specialty clinic leadership (Bernardy et al., 2011). The program was designed consistently within the structure of the organization. Specifically, the program established two PTSD mentors within each of the VHA's 18 regions called Veterans Integrated Service Networks (VISNs). By establishing the mentors at the VISN level, they were able to serve as regional champions of evidence-based practice and support utilization through collaborative problem-solving of local and regional barriers. The initial scope of the program included a variety of activities to engage program participants, disseminate information needed to inform program management and facilitate peer-to-peer sharing of innovations and solutions, and facilitate mutual instrumental and emotional support (Rosen et al., 2012). The target participants for the program were leads at the specialty clinic level of the mental health service line leadership, with additional participants included based on needs (e.g., PTSD residential program leadership). In fact, establishing and maintaining this network of frontline program leadership was critical to ensure ongoing quality improvement and implementation, as well as to guarantee that when staff and/or leadership transitions happen there is continuity in the implementation of best practices. Core program activities included national and regional conference calls, bimonthly VISN Mentor conference calls, email listserv, intranet site, and ongoing contacts with the national program manager who served an external facilitator to the VISN Mentors. Routine in-person meetings of the full program participants and smaller meetings for VISN Mentors only, are considered essential and occurred as funding allowed during the early years of the program.

Another key factor specific to organizational implementation and sustainment is the policies in place to support the system change. As already noted, coinciding with the launch of the VHA CPT Training and PTSD Mentoring Programs was the publication of Uniform Mental Health Services Handbook (U.S, Dept. VA, 2008; U.S, Dept. VA, 2024a, 2024b). The UMHS handbook established new standard requirements for VHA mental health services nationwide, specifying services that must be required at each medical center and associated community-based outpatient clinics (CBOC). The handbook included requirements ensuring access for all veterans to either CPT or PE for PTSD. This was the first time VHA policy explicitly outlined that services *must be provided standardly across the health care system* and identified specific evidence-based treatments for PTSD that must be offered. Given the importance of organizational policy for implementation efforts, this represented a significant shift in the strategic plan for mental health care. Taken together, the VHA CPT Training and PTSD Mentoring programs, aided by policy, were designed to play a significant role in the organization's transition from a pathology approach to care to one of recovery for Veterans with PTSD (Bernardy et al., 2011).

An early evaluation of the PTSD Mentoring program in 2010 (Rosen et al., 2012) demonstrated support that the original programmatic goals were being met. Program participants were surveyed on several items including how often they engaged in 14 specific program activities in the past 6 months, how much the program helped them achieve 15 specific benefits, the extent to which several factors served as barriers to program participation (i.e., lack of time, lack of leadership support, calls conflicting with other duties, and lack of benefit), and agreement with positive and negative qualities of their VISN Mentors. Additionally, the survey respondents were asked about changes they made to their clinics and the degree to which the program helped with those changes. The results indicated that participation was positively associated with quality of their VISN Mentor and negatively associated with lack of time. The majority indicated the program helped them feel more connected to the network of program directors and feel more supported, and a large proportion indicated they made substantial changes in their programs to implement evidence-based treatments. Further, 40–50% indicated the program helped them implement the UMHS Handbook mandates and other VHA policies in their programs, enhance the quality of the care they provided, solve practical problems, and facilitate access to training.

The PTSD Mentoring program has developed significantly over the past 15 years since the initial launch and 2010 evaluation, and while many of the original goals and program structure remain foundational, several other organizational changes have impacted the program's necessity and ability to expand the scope of support provided to the field. Many aspects of this evolution of the program mirror the systematic changes that were already discussed for the VHA CPT Training Program. One of the most significant organizational changes impacting all efforts toward implementation of EBPs was the launch of documentation templates with the VHA electronic health record (EHR). These templates were designed for specific EBPS including CPT and were tailored for each session's content. The templates also included data elements called health factors, that within the VHA EHR could be extracted to provide data on session-level provision of CPT. Those templates were launched in 2014–2015, and while they provided the map for monitoring CPT provision, it took significant support and education from the VHA CPT Training and PTSD Mentoring programs to encourage consistent utilization for the PTSD templates specifically. It wasn't, however, until 2019 that researchers were able to demonstrate that the templates were utilized successfully in practice (Shines et al., 2021). Utilizing natural language processing, they were able to identify provision of CPT and PE from unstructured or semi-structured free text in the EHR to classify if the documentation described provision of the EBP and calculated the agreement between the NLP results and the EBP templates data annually from 2014–2019. They found that by 2019, almost 90% of EBP for PTSD visit days were captured using the EBP templates. The utilization of the EBP templates in practice was further aided by inclusion of extra credit on certain national performance metrics for psychotherapy, if the sessions monitored demonstrated EPB provision by use of the templates. These metrics are intended to monitor national, regional, and facility level compliance with policies supporting the prioritization of EBP provision in mental health.

Around the time the templates reached their clear utilization, the Mentoring Program was able to launch two different monitoring efforts using the health factor data from the EBP templates to determine the reach of EBPs in PTSD specialty care. Intervention reach can be considered in terms of the percent and representativeness of individuals in a defined population (e.g., Veterans receiving care in VHA) who receive the treatment (Sayer et al., 2017). The primary monitoring efforts were based on EBP reach, defined as the proportion of Veterans with PTSD accessing care who initiate the treatment (i.e., at least 1 templated session of CPT or PE). The first programmatic data monitoring effort was the development of data reports in collaboration with Dr. Nina Sayer, and her work group, who designed the multi-project program to promote access to EBPs for PTSD and support the sustainability of their provision (Promoting Effective, Routine, and Sustained Implementation of Stress Treatments: PERSIST). The initial PERSIST project identified PTSD specialty programs (called PTSD Clinical Teams or PCTs in VHA) and organizational factors associated with high vs. low reach of CPT and PE to patients with PTSD (Sayer et al., 2017). The next project piloted an intervention (Implementation facilitation: IF) to help low EBP reach PCTs transition to high EBP reach, and results demonstrated sites receiving IF showed a much larger increase in EBP reach than matched controls (Sayer et al., 2021). In both projects, EBP reach was the primary data monitored. This led to the most recent project, which focused on scaling the strategies learned from the first projects through the PTSD Mentoring Program. A central strategy was not only the monitoring of EBP reach, but the targeted distribution of that data in the field to local and VISN leadership through the PTSD Mentoring Program network of VISN Mentors. These reports summarized quarterly EBP reach at the VISN and facility level, and allowed for a data feedback process for sites who were now aware of their EBP reach and could track their own progress toward higher reach and seek support to facilitate programmatic changes. The PERSIST data reports provided EBP reach for Veterans with PTSD across the continuum of mental health settings where Veterans with PTSD received psychotherapy (I.e., General Mental Health, PCT, PTSD Residential, Primary Care Mental Health Integration). This also allowed for evaluation of area of greatest EBP provision, which consistently demonstrated the unique role of PTSD specialty care in providing the largest proportion of PTSD EBPs across the enterprise.

The second programmatic data monitoring effort involved developing a program manager data dashboard that could provide tracking of key administrative data for PCTs only. This dashboard was designed as a tool where PCT leadership could access their site's data, which included simple summary widgets, graphs, and tables with exportable data that could be analyzed. This dashboard provided an EBP reach proportion as well; however, it differed slightly from the PERSIST definition as all Veterans in the PCT were included, not just those with a primary diagnosis of PTSD. Both tools, the PERSIST reports and the program manager dashboard, provided the data feedback needed to promote a significant shift in the transformation of outpatient PTSD specialty care. This shifted included increased provision of EBPs and adoption of similar principles of PTSD specialty care that facilitated best administrative practices.

Another key initiative supported by the PTSD Mentoring program was the effort to implement more systematic tracking of the effectiveness of EBP provision through measurement-based care (MBC). The Measurement-Based Care in Mental Health Initiative within the VHA Office of Mental Health sought to implement measurement-based care across all VHA mental health programs and make MBC a standard of care. Through different phases of the national initiative, they piloted a variety of implementation strategies and supported specific programs (Resnick & Hoff, 2020). The most recent phase of the initiative (Phase 3) launched in 2020, centered specifically on outpatient PTSD specialty care. Through partnership between the MBC initiative and the PTSD Mentoring Program, a field-based interdisciplinary group of providers and leadership in PTSD specialty care developed best practice guidelines for the implementation of MBC in PCTs (Singh et al., 2022). This work informed organizational policy updates requiring MBC as a principle of care in PCTs. Again, to support implementation of this requirement, the PTSD Mentoring Program played a key role in providing the MBC data monitoring and feedback to the field. An initial minimum threshold was established (i.e., Veterans receiving two or more PCL-5 s completed in the EHR) and data could be extracted to provide proportions of Veterans seen at least twice who met the MBC threshold for collection. The MBC collection data was distributed to sites and eventually included with the PERSIST EBP VISN and facility data into a single *PTSD Specialty Program Quarterly Data Report*. While there has yet to be an established target for MBC implementation, national quarterly distributions of MBC collection data have demonstrated steady median implementation increases from 2021 to

2023, suggesting a positive impact of the collaboration, data feedback and programmatic supports.

The utilization of audit and data feedback has become one of the central features of the program and the 2023 rebranding to the PTSD Mentoring and Implementation Program. The program aims to support and maintain the network of frontline leadership through quality improvement and implementation efforts. The program design and tools allow for development, implementation, and sustainment of ongoing healthcare system initiatives.

Collaborations Between VHA CPT Training and PTSD Mentoring Programs

As the VHA CPT Training and PTSD Mentoring Programs have evolved in parallel to adapt to the needs of the organization, they have also steadily increased collaboration efforts to support EBP implementation more seamlessly from training to sustainable practice in the clinic setting. As noted earlier, the PTSD Mentoring Program worked to help PTSD specialty care staff obtain access to training. By identifying PTSD clinic staff that are a high priority to receive training, the PTSD Mentoring Program helps the VHA CPT Training Program ensure that training resources are directed where needs are the highest. As the VHA CPT Training Program transitioned to a regional training model, access to training opportunities increased significantly, and as a result the PTSD Mentoring program could routinely coordinate with the VHA CPT Training Program to facilitate timely access to CPT training for new hires to PTSD Specialty programs. With the introduction of virtual online CPT workshops in 2020, it became even more feasible to find training slots because it was no longer limited by locality and travel resources. The PTSD Mentoring Program also provided support and promotion of the VHA CPT Training Program and resources via the Mentoring Program's SharePoint, as well as announcements via their email distribution group. Finally, the programs have worked together to continue to promote implementation of MBC when providing CPT and have conducted a joint webinar on using measurement to inform CPT. The PTSD Mentoring program will continue to partner with the VHA CPT Training Program and will provide ongoing support and consultation regarding needs identified with the network of PTSD specialty care.

Summary

The efficacy of the disseminations of treatments for a variety of mental health diagnoses in various parts of the world has been borne out in the documented increases in access to treatment, often in populations that do not have access to mental health care, particularly with

treatments that are evidence based. The dissemination and implementation of CPT in the VHA may serve as an example for efforts in other large health care settings. The multilevel approach focusing on the patient, provider, organization, and policy levels allows for targeted efforts to ensure successful uptake of an innovation. A robust training program includes training and consultation and is adaptable to organizational changes and needs. In the case of the VHA CPT Training Program, the initial centralization allowed for the refinement of the program and the subsequent decentralization ensured sustainability and cost effectiveness. Larger health care systems will likely need additional organizational programs targeting implementation and sustainment to support training efforts. The VHA effort included several, and the PTSD Mentoring and Implementation program serves as an example of a program targeting organizational level-issues and demonstrates the importance of monitoring and data feedback. By learning from these multidimensional dissemination and implementation models, future efforts can more successfully improve access to evidence-based care, and in particular maximize implementation of CPT throughout other large healthcare systems.Competing InterestsKathleen M. Chard is co-author of the Cognitive Processing Therapy Treatment Manual and receives royalties from Guilford Press.

Ellen T. Healy and Kelly P. Maieritsch do not have any competing interests to disclose. The authors' comments are their own and they are speaking on their own behalf and not on behalf of VHA.

References

Aarons, G. A., Hurlburt, M., & Horwitz, S. M. (2011). Advancing a conceptual model of evidence-based practice implementation in public service sectors. *Administrative Policy Mental Health, 38*, 4–23. https://doi.org/10.1007/s10488-010-0327-7

Bauer, M. S., & Kirchner, J. (2020). Implementation science: What is it and why should I care? *Psychiatry Research, 283*, 112376. https://doi.org/10.1016/j.psychres.2019.06.036

Bernardy, N. C., Hamblen, J. L., Friedman, M. J., Ruzek, J. I., & McFall, M. E. (2011). Implementation of a posttraumatic stress disorder mentoring program to improve treatment services. *Psychological Trauma, Theory, Research, Practice and Policy, 3*(3), 292–299. https://doi.org/10.1037/a0024847

Chard, K. M., Ricksecker, E. G., Healy, E. T., Karlin, B. E., & Resick, P. A. (2012). Dissemination and experience with cognitive processing therapy. *Journal of Rehabilitation Research & Development, 49*(5), 667–678. https://doi.org/10.1682/JRRD.2011.10.0198

Clark, D. M. (2009). Improving access to psychological therapy: Initial evaluation of two UK demonstration sites. *Behavior Research and Therapy, 47*, 910–920. https://doi.org/10.1016/j.brat.2009.07.010

Clark, D. M. (2011). Implementing NICE guidelines for the psychological treatment of depression and anxiety disorders: The IAPT experience. *International Review of Psychiatry, 23*(4), 318–327. https://doi.org/10.3109/09540261.2011.606803

Clark, D. M. (2018). Realizing the mass public benefit of evidence-based psychological therapies: The IAPT program. *Annual Review of Clinical Psychology, 14*, 159–183. https://doi.org/10.1146/annurev-clinpsy-0508170084833

Damschroder, L. J. (2009). Clarity out of chaos: Use of theory in implementation research. *Psychiatry Research, 283*, 112461. https://doi.org/10.1016/j.psychres.2019.06.036

Department of Veterans Affairs. (2012). *FY 2012 Report of the VA special committee on posttraumatic stress disorder*. Special Committee on PTSD: Author.

Frank, H. E., Becker-Haimes, E. M., & Kendall, P. C. (2020). Therapist training in evidence-based interventions for mental health: A systematic review of training approaches and outcomes. *Clinical Psychology: Science and Practice, 27*(3), e12330. https://doi.org/10.1111/cpsp.12330

Herschell, A. D., Kolko, D. J., Baumann, B. L., & Davis, A. C. (2010). The role of therapist training in the implementation of psychosocial treatments: A review and critique with recommendations. *Clinical Psychology Review, 30*(4), 448–466. https://doi.org/10.1016/j.cpr.2010.02.005

Karlin, B. E., & Cross, G. (2014). From the laboratory to the therapy room: National dissemination and implementation of evidence-based psychotherapies in the US Department of Veterans Affairs Health Care System. *American Psychologist, 69*(1), 19. https://doi.org/10.1037/a0033888

Karlin, B. E., Ruzek, J. I., Chard, K. M., Eftekhari, A., Monson, C. M., Hembree, E. A., Resick, P. A., & Foa, E. B. (2010). Dissemination of evidence-based psychological treatments for posttraumatic stress disorder in the Veterans Health Administration. *Journal of Traumatic Stress, 23*(6), 663–673. https://doi.org/10.1002/jts.20588

Mallard Swanson, K., Song, J., Beristianos, M., Aajmain, S., Lane, J. E. M., Landy, M. S. H., Suvak, M. K., Shields, N., Monson, C. M., & Stirman, S. W. (2021). A glimpse into the "black box": Which elements of consultation in an EBP are associated with client symptom change and therapist fidelity? *Implementation Research and Practice, 2*. https://doi.org/10.1177/26334895211051791

McHugh, K., & Barlow, D. (2012). Dissemination and implementation of evidence-based psychological interventions: Current status and future directions. In K. McHugh & D. Barlow (Eds.), *Dissemination and implementation of evidence-based psychological interventions*. Oxford Press.

NICE. (2011). Common mental health disorders: Identification and pathways to care. In *Clinical guidelines 123*. National Institute of Clinical Excellence.

Office of Mental Health and Suicide Prevention Continuum of Care Workgroup. (2017). *Defining the 'future state' continuum of mental health services in Veterans Health Administration.*

Resick, P. A., Monson, C. M., & Chard, K. M. (2014a). *Cognitive processing therapy: Veteran/military version: Therapist's manual*. Department of Veterans Affairs.

Resick, P. A., Monson, C. M., & Chard, K. M. (2014b). *Cognitive processing therapy: Veteran/military version: Therapist and patient materials manual*. Department of Veterans Affairs.

Resick, P. A., Monson, C. M., Galovski, T. E., Chard, K. M., Kattar, K. A., & Healy, E. T. (2024). *Cognitive processing therapy consultant's manual: Veteran/military version*. Department of Veterans' Affairs.

Resick, P. A., Monson, C. M., Price, J. L., Chard, K. M., Kattar, K. A., & Healy, E. T. (2023). *Cognitive processing therapy trainer's manual: Veteran/military version*. Department of Veterans' Affairs.

Resnick, S. G., & Hoff, R. A. (2020). Observations from the national implementation of measurement based care in mental health in the department of veterans affairs. *Psychological Services, 17*(3), 238–246. https://doi.org/10.1037/ser0000351

Rosen, C. S., Chow, H. C., Finney, J. F., Greenbaum, M. A., Moos, R. H., Sheikh, J. I., & Yesavage, J. A. (2004). VA practice patterns and practice guidelines for treating posttraumatic stress disorder. *Journal of Traumatic Stress, 17*(3), 213–222. https://doi.org/10.1023/B:JOTS.0000029264.23878.53

Rosen, C. S., Nguyen, T., Bernardy, C. N., Hamblen, J. L., Ruzek, J. I., & Friedman, M. J. (2012). Evaluation of a mentoring program for PTSD clinic managers in the U.S. Department of Veterans Affairs. *Psychiatric Services, 63*(10), 1047–1050. https://doi.org/10.1176/appi.ps.201100446

Sayer, N. A., Bernardy, N. C., Yoder, M., Hamblen, J. L., Rosen, C. S., Ackland, P. E., Kehle-Forbes, S. M., Clothier, B. A., Schnurr, P. P., Orazem, R. J., & Noorbaloochi, S. (2021). Evaluation of an implementation intervention to increase reach of evidence-based psychotherapies for PTSD in US Veterans Health Administration PTSD clinics. *Administrative and Policy in Mental Health Services Research, 48*, 450–463. https://doi.org/10.1007/s10488-020-01086-3

Sayer, N. A., Rosen, C. S., Bernardy, N. C., Cook, J. M., Orazem, R. J., Chard, K. M., Mohr, D. C., Kehle-Forbes, S. M., Eftekhari, A., Crowley, J., Ruzek, J. I., Smith, B. N., & Schnurr, P. P. (2017). Context matters: Team and organizational factors associated with reach of evidence-based psychotherapies for PTSD in the Veterans Health Administration. *Administrative and Policy in Mental Health Services Research, 44*, 904–918. https://doi.org/10.1007/s10488-017-0809-y

Shines, B., Levis, M., Dufort, V. M., Patterson, O. V., Watts, B. V., Duvall, S. L., Russ, C. L., & Maguen, S. (2021). Improvements to PTSD quality metrics with natural language processing. *Journal of Evaluation in Clinical Practice, 28*, 1–11. https://doi.org/10.1111/jep.13587

Singh, R. S., Landes, S. J., Resnick, S. G., Abraham, T. H., Maieritsch, K. P., Pollack, S. J., & Kirchner, J. E. (2022). Engaging frontline workers in policy development to support the implementation of measurement-based care: Lessons learned from a field-based workgroup. *Frontiers in Health Services, 55*, 1–10. https://doi.org/10.3389/frhs.2022.929438

Smith, T. L., Landes, S. J., Lester-Williams, K., Day, K. T., Batdorf, W., Brown, G. K., et al. (2017). Developing alternative training delivery methods to improve psychotherapy implementation in the US Department of Veterans Affairs. *Training and Education in Professional Psychology, 11*(4), 266. https://doi.org/10.1037/tep0000156

U. S. Department of Veterans Affairs. (2024a, May). *Evidence-based therapy*. https://www.mentalhealth.va.gov/get-help/treatment/ebt.asp

U. S. Department of Veterans Affairs. (2024b, September). *VA/DOD clinical practice guidelines*. https://www.healthquality.va.gov/

U.S. Department of Veterans Affairs. (2008). *Uniform mental health services in VA medical centers and clinics (VHA handbook 1160.01)*. Author.

U.S. Department of Veterans Affairs. (2023). *Uniform mental health services in VHA medical points of service (VHA handbook 1160.01)*. Author.

U.S. Department of Veterans Affairs/Department of Defense. (2004). *Clinical practice guidelines for the management of posttraumatic stress (version 1.0)*. Author.

Chapter 18
CPT Dissemination in Community Settings

Amy M. Williams and Stefanie T. LoSavio

CPT Dissemination in Community Settings

Cognitive processing therapy (CPT; Resick et al., 2017) is recommended as a front-line treatment in clinical practice guidelines for posttraumatic stress disorder (PTSD) including those of the American Psychological Association (APA, 2017a), International Society for Traumatic Stress Studies (ISTSS; Forbes et al., 2020), and U.S. Departments of Veterans Affairs (VA) and Defense (VA/DoD, 2023). Thirty years after the publication of the first manual, CPT has been refined, adapted cross-culturally, and translated into numerous languages (Resick et al., 2024). While continued research on interventions for PTSD is imperative, an urgent, ongoing challenge is making sure that those suffering from PTSD have access to evidence-based psychotherapies (EBPs) for PTSD such as CPT (Finley et al., 2018; Kazdin, 2017; Lu et al., 2016).

Early research and training in CPT focused primarily on civilian populations with interpersonal traumas such as sexual abuse, sexual assault, and intimate partner violence (for a summary, see Resick et al., 2024). Training of clinicians was provided by the treatment developers and was geared mostly toward clinicians who were involved in research, receiving both group and individual consultation, and undergoing regular fidelity review of their sessions. In 2006, the VA spearheaded the first nationwide CPT dissemination effort. Since that time, the VA has trained thousands of therapists in CPT. The VA training program has adopted a

A. M. Williams (✉)
The Headstrong Project, New York, NY, USA
e-mail: awilliams@theheadstrongproject.org

S. T. LoSavio
Department of Psychiatry and Behavioral Sciences, University of Texas Health Science Center at San Antonio, San Antonio, TX, USA

J. S. Wachen, T. E. Galovski (eds.), *Cognitive Processing Therapy for Complex Cases*, CBT: Science Into Practice,
https://doi.org/10.1007/978-3-031-87356-0_18

"train-the-trainer" model with regional trainers and consultants (Chard et al., 2012; Karlin et al., 2010; Rosen et al., 2017). Outside of the VA, however, available training opportunities have been more limited.

Needs assessments for CPT training have been conducted in both the VA and community and have primarily concentrated on military-connected populations (Koblinsky et al., 2014; Tanielian et al., 2014); however, the majority of the estimated 13 million adults annually suffering from PTSD are not veterans (VA National Center for PTSD, 2023). In fact, a recent survey of individuals across 17 states reported more patients seeking health care through private insurance than through Medicare, Medicaid, and VA or military coverage (Wray et al., 2021). Combined with data showing that up to half of eligible veterans receive care outside the VA (Farmer et al., 2016), this suggests that a large percentage of both veteran and civilian patients receive PTSD treatment in the community.

Many community providers report a lack of knowledge for best practices in treating PTSD and may not be aware of clinical practice guidelines for its treatment (Finley et al., 2019; Kilpatrick et al., 2011; Koblinsky et al., 2014; Tanielian et al., 2014). Although it is difficult to ascertain the number of community clinicians utilizing CPT, one recent study suggested that rates are higher among psychologists than Masters level clinicians and that some clinicians utilizing CPT may not have received any type of specific supervision or advanced training (Finley et al., 2019). While there appears to be interest in receiving training in PTSD ESTs, there are barriers to implementation in both public health and private practice settings (Milgram et al., 2022).

In this chapter, we will discuss (1) dissemination and implementation (D&I) concepts relevant to CPT, (2) current didactic and competence training approaches for CPT, (3) reach of CPT, (4) training models that have been used to disseminate CPT in the community, (5) challenges associated with implementing CPT and strategies for enhancing implementation, and (6) future directions.

Dissemination and Implementation: Relevant Processes and Outcomes

While a thorough introduction of D&I science is beyond the scope of this chapter, reviewing certain shared terminology may be helpful. *Adoption* is the decision by a clinician or clinical system to learn and implement an intervention. *Dissemination* is the active approach of facilitating initial adoption or spreading an evidence-based intervention to a target audience (e.g., providers). *Implementation* is the process of putting evidence-based interventions to use within a specific setting. Thus, there is an overlap between dissemination and implementation. *Fidelity* is adherence to prescribed elements of treatment and competence in its delivery. *Reach* is the uptake of an evidence-based intervention, calculated as the percentage of patients who receive a given intervention. *Sustainability* is the extent to which an evidence-based intervention can deliver its intended benefits over time after external support has ended (Glasgow et al., 1999; McHugh & Barlow, 2010; Rabin et al., 2008; Sayer et al., 2021).

Training clinicians to competently administer an EBP requires both *didactic training*, including methods for transferring information, such as manuals and workshops, and *competence training*, which involves the acquiring of skills necessary to administer a treatment skillfully and with fidelity (McHugh & Barlow, 2010).

Didactic and Competence Training in CPT

Professional ethical guidelines address practicing within one's boundaries of competence based on education, training, consultation, study, and professional experience (APA, 2017b; National Association of Social Workers [NASW], 2017). For therapists delivering CPT, there are multiple pathways of training and reaching such competence. The CPT treatment manual provides the core essentials of the CPT protocol (Resick et al., 2024). The current standard for disseminating ESTs, including CPT, is a combination of *workshop plus consultation* (Beidas & Kendall, 2010). Broadly speaking, the CPT workshop is primarily didactic in nature and consultation is primarily driven toward establishing competence. Both attendance at the workshop and completion of a course of clinical consultation are required to be officially rostered as an approved CPT provider.

In addition to the workshop, there are a variety of basic and advanced learning materials that can be found in multiple formats including web-based trainings, online resources, and textbooks.

Clinical case consultation is provided by an approved CPT trainer or master clinician in either an individual or group format, typically for 1-hour per week over the course of approximately 6 months, during which time clinicians treat trauma survivors with PTSD with CPT. In consultation, expert consultants support providers to deliver CPT to their specific patients including addressing questions regarding administration of the protocol and barriers to delivering CPT with fidelity. Some training programs offer consultation as part of their training program. Clinicians can also request consultations through the CPT website (https://cptforptsd.com/consultation/). Less formally, the National Center for PTSD offers free, on-demand consultation to healthcare providers who treat veterans in the community or VA (https://www.ptsd.va.gov/professional/consult).

CPT Training Resources

- CPT Manual (Resick et al., 2024): The manual contains background on the research supporting CPT, treatment considerations, session-by-session guidance, and relevant patient-facing handouts and worksheets.

- CPT Live Workshop: A 2-day, experiential workshop is provided by an approved CPT trainer. The workshop includes a combination of lecture, video examples, and role plays to learn how to deliver CPT. A third day is sometimes offered to learn group-administered CPT.
- Web-based training: CPT Web2.0 (https://cpt2.musc.edu) is a 13 credit-hour asynchronous online training course. The course includes videos as well as additional clinical materials and resources.
- CPT Website: The CPT administration website (www.CPTforPTSD.com) provides information about in-person or videoconference workshop trainings and consultation from approved CPT trainers and a variety of CPT resources including client- and therapist-facing videos.
- Center for Deployment Psychology (www.deploymentpsych.org) has a mission to train military and civilian behavioral health professionals to offer treatment to military personnel, veterans and their families. In addition to workshops, their website includes CPT resources including videos and a CPT metaphor bank and FAQ section.
- The STRONG STAR Training Initiative (https://www.strongstartraining.org) provides a learning community for veteran- and civilian-serving providers to learn evidence-based treatments for PTSD including CPT. Training includes workshop, consultation, and access to training resources and other advanced trainings.
- VA National Center for PTSD Consultation Program (www.ptsd.va.gov/professional/consult): The PTSD Consultation Program provides free consultation services for veteran-serving providers within the VA and in the community. The program hosts a monthly lecture series on topics related to PTSD treatment (many of which are CPT-specific) and provide no-cost CEUs.
- *Flexible Applications of Cognitive Processing Therapy* (Galovski et al., 2020) offers advanced topics and application suggestions for CPT.

As part of the initial VA CPT rollout, Resick et al. (2007) authored a consultant's manual to equip consultants with materials and resources for providing effective consultation. While CPT consultation is inherently flexible, the manual outlined specific processes and parameters in a session-by-session format. This standardization marked an important first step in developing an evidence-based consultation practice. The consultant manual was later updated based on feedback from therapists and consultants (Resick et al., 2010).

Both workshops and consultation appear effective in increasing knowledge regarding CPT, although those receiving consultation are more likely to implement and complete CPT with clients (Charney et al., 2019). The importance of attending post-workshop consultation to implementation and, in some cases, better clinical outcomes has been demonstrated in numerous studies (Charney et al., 2019; Frank et al., 2022; Mallard et al., 2021; Monson et al., 2018). In addition to increasing knowledge, consultation improves therapists' confidence with administering CPT. Among therapists with low self-efficacy related to CPT treatment fidelity and outcomes, those who did not receive consultation had poorer outcomes than those who participated in consultation (Pace et al., 2021).

Beyond consultation attendance, researchers have begun to identify specific consultation strategies that most effectively contribute to increased treatment fidelity and improved clinical outcomes (Landy et al., 2023; Mallard et al., 2021). By coding consultation calls, Landy et al. (2023) organized the elements of case consultation into six themes: Organization, Knowledge Consolidation (e.g., review of information, continued training), Case Conceptualization (e.g., case material, conceptualizing comorbidities), Directive Instruction (specific steps for clinicians to take, modeling), Nondirective Instruction (e.g., encouraging clinician reflection, sharing personal experience), and Provision of Feedback (e.g., correction and praise). Therapist competence for elements of Case Conceptualization and Directive Instruction, which emphasize applying specific CPT strategies to individual cases, were associated with a reduction in PTSD symptoms (Mallard et al., 2021).

Reach of CPT

Existing training models have had varying levels of success in dissemination and implementation of CPT. Lessons learned in the early years of the VA rollout led to changes at both the VA and community levels in consultation (e.g., from a drop-in telephone calls to assigned consultants), inclusion of training agreements, standardization of workshops, decentralization of training processes (e.g., from national trainers to regional trainers and consultants). Additionally, numerous clinical education resources were developed, including manuals, help sheet guides, video vignettes, tutorials, and an interactive web-based course/resources (Chard et al., 2012).

Reach of an intervention is impacted by factors occurring at the organizational (e.g., attitudes regarding EBPs), provider (e.g., decision to implement, perceived competence), and patient (e.g., selecting the treatment) levels. Competency-based training in CPT typically increases the likelihood that providers will offer CPT (Dondanville, Fina, Steigerwald, et al., 2021). However, even in the VA where training is mandated, incentivized, and readily available, reach of CPT and Prolonged Exposure (PE) is variable, ranging from as low as 6% (Shiner et al., 2013) to as high as 52% (Hundt et al., 2017). Across PTSD programs in the VA, "low reach" clinics reached less than 20% of patients whereas "high reach" clinics reached more than 33% of patients (Sayer et al., 2017). Undoubtedly, reach is substantially lower in the community, where broad directives for training and treatment delivery do not exist. Over time, if not properly supported, many settings may experience a decline in reach and fidelity (Finley et al., 2015; Rosen et al., 2017).

In a review of implementation studies for a variety of EBPs in the VA, organizational characteristics such as prioritization of EBPs and a growing culture supporting the use of EBPs consistently emerged as important factors contributing to higher reach (Rosen et al., 2016). To increase implementation of EBPs for PTSD in the VA,

Sayer et al. (2021) used an external facilitator (an implementation expert with clinical and consultation experience) guided by a toolkit to target two VA PTSD specialty clinics with low reach of CPT and PE. Using strategies such as creating mission statements centered around delivery of EBPs, engaging leadership and staff, developing clinic procedures that facilitate delivery, and fostering positive perceptions of the mission, an external expert worked closely with a local champion to support the changes. EBP reach more than doubled over a 1-year period of time. This approach, which combines external facilitation with targeted strategies and local engagement, demonstrates a potentially valuable model for enhancing the implementation of EBPs in settings where there are challenges with reach.

Community-Based Training Models

Outside of the VA, there are many examples of the "workshop plus consultation" model with varying degrees of additional support at the system or organizational/clinic level. For example, in 2010, the state of Texas community mental health system launched an initiative to implement CPT statewide through a grant aimed at assisting veterans who might not be eligible for VA services. This effort involved collaboration with various county and state government stakeholders to integrate CPT into the existing community mental health system. Through state-wide informative webinars to organizational leadership and state legislative efforts, the training was incorporated into the Texas Health and Human Services Commission's (HHSC) training infrastructure, expanding its focus to include both veteran and non-veteran clients with PTSD. Similar to the VA's dissemination efforts, challenges emerged, such as educating clinic staff about EBPs and modifying health record templates for proper coding of PTSD interventions. These challenges necessitated action at both the provider and leadership levels. Over time, Texas HHSC has developed a roster of CPT approved providers specific to the state's community mental health system and has trained over 500 providers to date.

In an attempt to enhance implementation in community mental health settings, LoSavio, Dillon, Murphy, Goetz, et al. (2019) designed and launched a series of Learning Collaboratives across multiple agencies in the state of North Carolina. The Learning Collaborative model is a more intensive training approach that focuses not only on clinician-level training—with additional training elements to support clinical proficiency—but also engages the organization in the training process, with a focus on supporting implementation of the intervention and fostering sustainability. The model employs a team-based approach, where clinicians participate with other members of their organization and with the involvement of a senior leader—someone within the organization with administrative authority who can help build organizational capacity for the intervention. There are multiple learning sessions, which provide opportunities for advanced clinical training and implementation support following the foundational workshop. These sessions are interspersed with action periods during which clinicians apply the model, while receiving consultation, and work to integrate the intervention into their practice setting. The organization's senior leaders also develop implementation plans and submit monthly metrics on the implementation and reach of the intervention that are discussed during monthly implementation calls. Thus, this comprehensive approach targets both clinical competence and implementation outcomes such as sustainability. The effectiveness of the Learning Collaborative model has been reflected in high rates of reach (informing and enrolling patients in CPT), proportion of clients completing treatment with clinically significant improvement, and sustainability, with 95% of fully-trained clinicians still using CPT 6 months after the training program ended (LoSavio, Dillon, Murphy, & Resick, 2019).

Another training model that incorporates some elements of the Learning Collaborative model is the Learning Community model. As an example of this model, the STRONG STAR Training Initiative, provides training in CPT to community-based clinicians (Dondanville, Fina, Straud, et al., 2021). In addition to the workshop plus consultation, organizational consultation is available, and clinicians have access to a provider portal including treatment delivery and training resources, as well as advanced trainings. Patients treated by clinicians enrolled in the STRONG STAR Training Initiative have evidenced large reductions in PTSD and depression, comparable to those reported by VA providers (Dondanville et al., 2022). Moreover, use of CPT by providers trained in this model was sustained: 95% reported using CPT 6 months post-training and 87% at 1-year post-training (Dondanville et al., 2022).

Implementing CPT: Challenges and Suggestions

There are a variety of barriers to implementing CPT at the patient, therapist, and organizational levels. For example, patient characteristics often influence a therapist's choice about whether to offer CPT. In studies with veteran/military populations, therapists have reported being less likely to initiate CPT when patients appear to lack motivation or willingness to engage in trauma-focused therapy, have psychiatric comorbidities including substance use disorders, and possess cognitive limitations (Cook et al., 2020; Loskot et al., 2023; Osei-Bonsu et al., 2017). Community mental health providers report similar themes, being more likely to implement CPT when patients are motivated, stable, have higher education and less likely to engage based on complexity like psychosocial challenges and significant comorbidities (Thomas et al., 2023). However, research shows that CPT is safe and effective for a wide range of patients, including those with more complex trauma histories and psychiatric comorbidities (LoSavio et al., 2024). Thus, CPT may not be offered widely enough to reach patients that could benefit from it.

Therapist beliefs surrounding CPT's effectiveness are one of the most consistent predictors for implementation of CPT (Cook et al., 2020; Rosen et al., 2016). Even though much work has been conducted regarding the flexibility of CPT (Galovski et al., 2020), clinicians often express concern about using manualized approaches, citing a lack of personalization or losing the "art" of therapy (Milgram et al., 2022). Specific to CPT, LoSavio, Dillon, Murphy, and Resick (2019) identified the following common "therapist stuck points": "I need to implement the CPT therapy components perfectly for treatment to work"; "My clients would improve more if they worked with a more experienced CPT provider than me"; "Clients need preparatory treatment before they are ready to deal with their trauma"; and "Clients won't be able/willing to do the amount of homework involved in CPT." Although such therapist concerns were reduced during consultation, less reduction over the course of training predicted less competence with CPT as well as a lower likelihood of completing training and being rostered in the therapy. The therapists who had the most change in therapy-inconsistent beliefs were those who had greater engagement in consultation (LoSavio, Dillon, Murphy, & Resick, 2019).

Organizational barriers to CPT implementation include factors related to support of training and ongoing supervision, clinical operations involving patient selection and preparation, and leadership engagement (Sayer et al., 2017). As noted, most dissemination of CPT has occurred in VA, and even many community-based training programs have focused on veteran-serving agencies (Chard et al., 2012; Dondanville, Fina, Steigerwald, et al., 2021; Dondanville, Fina, Straud, et al., 2021; LoSavio, Dillon, Murphy, Goetz, et al., 2019; Williams & Dietch, 2018). Comparatively, less is known regarding successful implementation strategies specifically for community-based clinicians. Public or community mental health settings, often constrained by limited resources, may underestimate the number of patients with PTSD who could benefit from an EBP. This underestimation can result in a lack of prioritization for specialized PTSD training programs. Moreover, engaging leadership in these settings can be challenging due to competing demands on their time and resources. Large caseloads can create a burden on clinicians attempting to learn a new treatment. High employee turnover can also impact training and ongoing supervision over time, with some clinicians starting but not completing the consultation process. Conversely, clinicians in private practice are less likely to have access to formalized training programs such as those offered in public health settings (Frank et al., 2022; Thomas et al., 2023). Thus, community-based clinicians may face challenges in finding available CPT training including consultation. In addition, private practice providers may not feel incentivized to attend training because there is an expense both for the training while simultaneously losing income by not seeing patients when they are in workshops and consultation (Thomas et al., 2023). Nevertheless, certain strategies may prove helpful for implementing CPT in private practice. These include:

CPT Implementation Tips for Private Practice Therapists

- Align your "mission" with the use of EBPs like CPT. For example, "As a trauma therapy specialist, I am trained in treatment protocols for treating PTSD that have been shown to be effective."

- Consider providing links or directing clients to consumer-facing websites about CPT such as the VA National Center for PTSD's page on treatment options (https://ptsd.va.gov/understand_tx).
- Use practice management software that simplifies the process of continuous assessment necessary in CPT. Most current packages can automate assessments and, because the PTSD Checklist (PCL-5) and Patient Health Questionnaire (PHQ-9) are free of cost, they are usually included in the suite of self-report measures.
- Increase efficient clinical practice with CPT by organizing materials in advance such as session handouts, fillable PDFs, and progress note templates, as well as familiarity with the CPT Coach Mobile App. These are available through many of the resources above and also through a CPT trainer or consultant.
- Get involved in a CPT community of practitioners. Finding therapists who are also using CPT helps sustain your practice and keeps your skills current. Professional organizations such as the International Society for Traumatic Stress Studies (https://istss.org) are invaluable for keeping abreast of innovation and connecting with others at annual meetings. The online provider roster at the official www.CPTforPTSD.com website can also help locate therapists in your community.

Future Directions

Additional research is needed to identify optimal strategies for training clinicians in evidence-based, trauma-focused treatments like CPT, particularly as the mental health landscape evolves. Ensuring the long-term sustainability of these interventions is equally critical. Understanding therapist effects on patient engagement (Sayer et al., 2022) could provide valuable insights into key areas for consultation emphasis. Furthermore, understanding which training and implementation strategies are most effective for different types of providers, settings, and conditions remains a largely unaddressed area of study. Emerging innovations, such as the use of generative artificial intelligence (AI) also hold promise for expanding access to effective PTSD treatment training.

While not a training initiative per se, advances in research on alternative formats for direct delivery of CPT to individuals may also advance dissemination of the intervention. For example, researchers have examined an asynchronous text-based delivery of CPT (Stirman et al., 2021) and a self-help book version of CPT has been published (Resick et al., 2023). Web-based versions of treatment have been developed for other models (McLean et al., 2021) and are under development for CPT as well. Innovative approaches like these may circumvent some of the barriers preventing the availability of CPT.

Summary

Despite widespread efforts to disseminate CPT, CPT and other evidence-based PTSD treatments remain underutilized. Barriers exist at multiple levels, such as the organizational level—with clinic culture and leadership playing an important role—and the clinician level—with therapist treatment attitudes and fidelity to the protocol being influential. In the community, lack of policy and fewer training resources contribute to what is almost certainly lower rates of CPT delivery than the VA. Overall, continued efforts are needed to ensure evidence-based treatments like CPT are available on the front lines of mental healthcare.**Competing InterestsDr. Williams receives honoraria for training and consulting in CPT from the Patient-Centered Outcomes Research Institute, Department of Veterans Affairs, and Texas Health and Human Services. Dr. LoSavio receives royalties from the CPT self-help book, training and consulting fees for CPT training, and salary support and consulting fees for CPT research studies including from the National Institutes of Health, Patient-Centered Outcomes Research Institute, Department of Veterans Affairs, and Department of Defense.**

References

American Psychological Association. (2017a). *Clinical practice guidelines for treatment of posttraumatic stress disorder (PTSD) in adults*. http://www.apa.org/ptsd-guideline/ptsd.pdf

American Psychological Association. (2017b). *Ethical principles of psychologists and code of conduct* (2002, amended effective June 1, 2010, and January 1, 2017). https://www.apa.org/ethics/code/

Beidas, R. S., & Kendall, P. C. (2010). Training therapists in evidence-based practice: A critical review of studies from a systems-contextual perspective. *Clinical Psychology (New York, N.Y.), 17*(1), 1–30. https://doi.org/10.1111/j.1468-2850.2009.01187.x

Chard, K. M., Ricksecker, M. A., Healy, E. T., Karlin, B. E., & Resick, P. A. (2012). Dissemination and experience with cognitive processing therapy. *Journal of Rehabilitation Research and Development, 49*(5), 667–678. https://doi.org/10.1682/jrrd.2011.10.0198

Charney, M. E., Chow, L., Jakubovic, R. J., Federico, L. E., Goetter, E. M., Baier, A. L., Riggs, D., Phillips, J., Bui, E., & Simon, N. M. (2019). Training community providers in evidence-based treatment for PTSD: Outcomes of a novel consultation program. *Psychological Trauma, 11*(7), 793–801. https://doi.org/10.1037/tra0000427

Cook, J. M., Thompson, R., Simiola, V., Wiltsey Stirman, S., & Schnurr, P. P. (2020). Provider general attitudes versus specific perceptions of evidence-based psychotherapies for PTSD. *Psychological Services, 17*(1), 46–53. https://doi.org/10.1037/ser0000280

Dondanville, K. A., Fina, B. A., Steigerwald, V. L., McCarthy, K. D., Worley, C., Straud, C. L., Moring, J. C., & Rozek, D. C. (2021). How often do community-based mental health providers educate and initiate PTSD treatment following training? Answering the question of reach. *Implementation Research and Practice, 2*. https://doi.org/10.1177/26334895211011771

Dondanville, K. A., Fina, B. A., Straud, C. L., Finley, E. P., Tyler, H., Jacoby, V., Blount, T. H., Moring, J. C., Pruiksma, K. E., Blankenship, A. E., Evans, W. R., & Zaturenskaya, M. (2021). Launching a competency-based training program in evidence-based treatments for PTSD: Supporting veteran-serving mental health providers in Texas. *Community Mental Health Journal, 57*(5), 910–919. https://doi.org/10.1007/s10597-020-00676-7

Dondanville, K. A., Fina, B. A., Straud, C. L., Tyler, H., Jacoby, V., Blount, T. H., Moring, J. C., Blankenship, A. E., & Finley, E. P. (2022). Evaluating a community-based training program for evidence-based treatments for PTSD using the RE-AIM framework. *Psychological Services, 19*(4), 740–750. https://doi.org/10.1037/ser0000567

Farmer, C. M., Hosek, S. D., & Adamson, D. M. (2016). *Balancing demand and supply for veterans' health care: A summary of three RAND assessments conducted under the Veterans Choice Act*. RAND Corporation. https://www.rand.org/pubs/research_reports/RR1165z4.html

Finley, E. P., Garcia, H. A., Ketchum, N. S., McGeary, D. D., McGeary, C. A., Stirman, S. W., & Peterson, A. L. (2015). Utilization of evidence-based psychotherapies in Veterans Affairs posttraumatic stress disorder outpatient clinics. *Psychological Services, 12*(1), 73–82. https://doi.org/10.1037/ser0000014

Finley, E. P., Mader, M., Haro, E. K., Noël, P. H., Bernardy, N., Rosen, C. S., Bollinger, M., Garcia, H. A., Sherrieb, K., & Pugh, M. J. V. (2019). Use of guideline-recommended treatments for PTSD among community-based providers in Texas and Vermont: Implications for the Veterans Choice Program. *The Journal of Behavioral Health Services & Research, 46*(2), 217–233. https://doi.org/10.1007/s11414-018-9613-z

Finley, E. P., Noël, P. H., Lee, S., Haro, E., Garcia, H., Rosen, C., Bernardy, N., Pugh, M. J., & Pugh, J. A. (2018). Psychotherapy practices for veterans with PTSD among community-based providers in Texas. *Psychological Services, 15*(4), 442–452. https://doi.org/10.1037/ser0000143

Forbes, D., Bisson, J. I., Monson, C. M., & Berliner, L. (Eds.). (2020). *Effective treatments for PTSD: Practice guidelines from the International Society for Traumatic Stress Studies* (3rd ed.). The Guilford Press.

Frank, H. E., Milgram, L., Freeman, J. B., & Benito, K. G. (2022). Expanding the reach of evidence-based mental health interventions to private practice: Qualitative assessment using a policy ecology framework. *Frontiers in Health Services, 2*, 892294. https://doi.org/10.3389/frhs.2022.892294

Galovski, T. E., Nixon, R. D. V., & Kaysen, D. (2020). *Flexible applications of cognitive processing therapy: Evidence-based treatment methods*. Elsevier Science & Technology.

Glasgow, R. E., Vogt, T. M., & Boles, S. M. (1999). Evaluating the public health impact of health promotion interventions: The REAIM framework. *American Journal of Public Health, 89*, 1322–1327. https://doi.org/10.2105/AJPH.89.9.1322

Hundt, N. E., Harik, J. M., Thompson, K. E., Barrera, T. L., & Miles, S. R. (2017). Increased utilization of PE and CPT over time: A case example from a large Veterans Affairs PTSD Clinic. *Psychological Services, 15*(4), 429–436. https://doi.org/10.1037/ser0000138

Karlin, B. E., Ruzek, J. I., Chard, K. M., Eftekhari, A., Monson, C. M., Hembree, E. A., Resick, P. A., & Foa, E. B. (2010). Dissemination of evidence-based psychological treatments for posttraumatic stress disorder in the Veterans Health Administration. *Journal of Traumatic Stress, 23*(6), 663–673. https://doi.org/10.1002/jts.20588

Kazdin, A. E. (2017). Addressing the treatment gap: A key challenge for extending evidence-based psychosocial interventions. *Behaviour Research and Therapy, 88*, 7–18. https://doi.org/10.1016/j.brat.2016.06.004

Kilpatrick, D. G., Best, C. L., Smith, D. W., Kudler, H., & Cornelison-Grant, V. (2011). *Serving those who have served: Educational needs of health care providers working with military members, veterans, and their families*. Medical University of South Carolina Department of Psychiatry, National Crime Victims Research & Treatment Center.

Koblinsky, S. A., Leslie, L. A., & Cook, E. T. (2014). Treating behavioral health conditions of OEF/OIF veterans and their families: A state needs assessment of civilian providers. *Military Behavioral Health, 2*(2), 162–172. https://doi.org/10.1080/21635781.2014.890884

Landy, M. S. H., Vezer, E., Bance, S., Loskot, T., Ip, J., Zeifman, A. P., Mutschler, C., Thomas, F. C., McShane, K., Monson, C. M., & Stirman, S. W. (2023). Elucidating the elements of clinical case consultation in cognitive processing therapy. *The Counseling Psychologist, 51*(5), 626–654. https://doi.org/10.1177/00110000231166103

LoSavio, S. T., Dillon, K. H., Murphy, R. A., Goetz, K., Houston, F., & Resick, P. A. (2019). Using a learning collaborative model to disseminate cognitive processing therapy to community-based agencies. *Behavior Therapy, 50*(1), 36–49. https://doi.org/10.1016/j.beth.2018.03.007

LoSavio, S. T., Dillon, K. H., Murphy, R. A., & Resick, P. A. (2019). Therapist stuck points during training in cognitive processing therapy: Changes over time and associations with training outcomes. *Professional Psychology, Research and Practice, 50*(4), 255–263. https://doi.org/10.1037/pro0000224

LoSavio, S. T., Holder, N., Wells, S. Y., & Resick, P. A. (2024). Clinician concerns about cognitive processing therapy: A review of the evidence. *Cognitive and Behavioral Practice, 31*(2), 152–175. https://doi.org/10.1016/j.cbpra.2022.08.005

Loskot, T., Lagdamen, J., Mutschler, C., Thomas, F., Kannan, K., Beristianos, M., Cook, J., Finley, E., Monson, C., & Wiltsey-Stirman, S. (2023). Multilevel factors in providers' decisions to utilize CPT in military- and veteran-serving treatment settings. *Psychological Services, 20*(4), 798–808. https://doi.org/10.1037/ser0000715

Lu, M. W., Plagge, J. M., Marsiglio, M. C., & Dobscha, S. K. (2016). Clinician documentation on receipt of trauma-focused evidence-based psychotherapies in a VA PTSD clinic. *The Journal of Behavioral Health Services & Research, 43*, 71–87. https://doi.org/10.1007/s11414-013-9372-9

Mallard, S. K., Song, J., Beristianos, M., Aajmain, S., Lane, J. E. M., Landy, M. S. H., Suvak, M. K., Shields, N., Monson, C. M., & Stirman, S. W. (2021). A glimpse into the "Black Box": Which elements of consultation in an EBP are associated with client symptom change and therapist fidelity? *Implementation Research and Practice, 2*. https://doi.org/10.1177/26334895211051791

McHugh, R. K., & Barlow, D. H. (2010). The dissemination and implementation of evidence-based psychological treatments: A review of current efforts. *The American Psychologist, 65*(2), 73–84. https://doi.org/10.1037/a0018121

McLean, C. P., Foa, E. B., Dondanville, K. A., Haddock, C. K., Miller, M. L., Rauch, S. A., et al. (2021). The effects of web-prolonged exposure among military personnel and veterans with posttraumatic stress disorder. *Psychological Trauma: Theory, Research, Practice, and Policy, 13*(6), 621.

Milgram, L., Freeman, J. B., Benito, K. G., Elwy, A. R., & Frank, H. E. (2022). Clinician-reported determinants of evidence-based practice use in private practice mental health. *Journal of Contemporary Psychotherapy, 52*, 337–346. https://doi.org/10.1007/s10879-022-09551-w

Monson, C. M., Shields, N., Suvak, M. K., Lane, J. E. M., Shnaider, P., Landy, M. S. H., Wagner, A. C., Sijercic, I., Masina, T., Wanklyn, S. G., & Stirman, S. W. (2018). A randomized controlled effectiveness trial of training strategies in cognitive processing therapy for posttraumatic stress disorder: Impact on patient outcomes. *Behaviour Research and Therapy, 110*, 31–40. https://doi.org/10.1016/j.brat.2018.08.007

National Association of Social Workers. (2017). *NASW code of ethics*. Retrieved August 9, 2023, from https://www.socialworkers.org/About/Ethics/Code-of-Ethics/Code-of-Ethics-English

Osei-Bonsu, P. E., Bolton, R. E., Wiltsey Stirman, S., Eisen, S. V., Herz, L., & Pellowe, M. E. (2017). Mental health providers' decision-making around the implementation of evidence-based treatment for PTSD. *The Journal of Behavioral Health Services & Research, 44*(2), 213–223. https://doi.org/10.1007/s11414-015-9489-0

Pace, B. T., Song, J., Suvak, M. K., Shields, N., Monson, C. M., & Stirman, S. W. (2021). Therapist self-efficacy in delivering cognitive processing therapy in a randomized controlled implementation trial. *Cognitive and Behavioral Practice, 28*(3), 327–335.

Rabin, B. A., Brownson, R. C., Haire-Joshu, D., Kreuter, M. W., & Weaver, N. L. (2008). A glossary for dissemination and implementation research in health. *Journal of Public Health Management and Practice, 14*(2), 117–123. https://doi.org/10.1097/01.PHH.0000311888.06252.bb

Resick, P. A., Monson, C. M., & Chard, K. M. (2017). *Cognitive processing therapy for PTSD: A comprehensive manual*. The Guilford Press.

Resick, P. A., Monson, C. M., & Chard, K. M. (2024). *Cognitive processing therapy for PTSD: A comprehensive manual* (2nd ed.). Guilford Press.

Resick, P. A., Monson, C. M., & Galovski, T. E. (2007). *Cognitive processing therapy veteran/military version: A consultant's manual*. Veterans Administration.

Resick, P. A., Monson, C. M., Galovski, T. E., Chard, K., & Kattar, K. (2010). *Cognitive processing therapy veteran/military version: A consultant's manual*. 2nd ed..

Resick, P. A., Stirman, S. W., & LoSavio, S. T. (2023). *Getting unstuck from PTSD: Using cognitive processing therapy to guide your recovery*. The Guilford Press.

Rosen, C. S., Matthieu, M. M., Wiltsey Stirman, S., Cook, J. M., Landes, S., Bernardy, N. C., Chard, K. M., Crowley, J., Eftekhari, A., Finley, E. P., Hamblen, J. L., Harik, J. M., Kehle-Forbes, S. M., Meis, L. A., Osei-Bonsu, P. E., Rodriguez, A. L., Ruggiero, K. J., Ruzek, J. I., Smith, B. N., et al. (2016). A review of studies on the system-wide implementation of evidence-based psychotherapies for posttraumatic stress disorder in the Veterans Health Administration. *Administration and Policy in Mental Health and Mental Health Services Research, 43*(6), 957–977. https://doi.org/10.1007/s10488-016-0755-0

Rosen, R. C., Ruzek, J. I., & Karlin, B. E. (2017). Evidence-based training in the era of evidence-based practice: Challenges and opportunities for training of PTSD providers. *Behaviour Research and Therapy, 88*, 37–48. https://doi.org/10.1016/j.brat.2016.07.009

Sayer, N. A., Bernardy, N. C., Yoder, M., Hamblen, J. L., Rosen, C. S., Ackland, P. E., Kehle-Forbes, S. M., Clothier, B. A., Schnurr, P. P., Orazem, R. J., & Noorbaloochi, S. (2021). Evaluation of an implementation intervention to increase reach of evidence-based psychotherapies for PTSD in US Veterans Health Administration PTSD clinics. *Administration and Policy in Mental Health and Mental Health Services Research, 48*(3), 450–463. https://doi.org/10.1007/s10488-020-01086-3

Sayer, N. A., Rosen, C. S., Bernardy, N. C., Cook, J. M., Orazem, R. J., Chard, K. M., et al. (2017). Context matters: Team and organizational factors associated with reach of evidence-based psychotherapies for PTSD in the Veterans Health Administration. *Administration and Policy in Mental Health and Mental Health Services Research, 44*(6), 904–918. https://doi.org/10.1007/s10488-017-0809-y

Sayer, N. A., Wiltsey-Stirman, S., Rosen, C. S., Bernardy, N. C., Spoont, M. R., Kehle-Forbes, S. M., Eftekhari, A., Chard, K. M., & Nelson, D. B. (2022). Investigation of therapist effects on patient engagement in evidence-based psychotherapies for posttraumatic stress disorder in the Veterans Health Administration. *Journal of Traumatic Stress, 35*(1), 66–77. https://doi.org/10.1002/jts.22679

Shiner, B., D'Avolio, L. W., Nguyen, T. M., Zayed, M. H., Young-Xu, Y., Desai, R. A., Schnurr, P. P., Fiore, L. D., & Watts, B. V. (2013). Measuring use of evidence based psychotherapy for posttraumatic stress disorder. *Administration and Policy in Mental Health and Mental Health Services Research, 40*(4), 311–318. https://doi.org/10.1007/s10488-012-0421-0

Stirman, S. W., Song, J., Hull, T. D., & Resick, P. A. (2021). Open trial of an adaptation of cognitive processing therapy for message-based delivery. *Technology, Mind, and Behavior, 2*(1) https://psycnet.apa.org/doi/10.1037/tmb0000016

Tanielian, T., Farris, C., Epley, C., Farmer, C. M., Robinson, E., Engel, C. C., Robbins, M. W., & Jaycox, L. H. (2014). *Ready to serve: Community-based provider capacity to deliver culturally competent, quality mental health care to veterans and their families*. RAND Corporation. http://www.jstor.org/stable/10.7249/j.ctt14bs1qk

Thomas, F. C., Loskot, T., Mutschler, C., Burdo, J., Lagdamen, J., Sijercic, I., Lane, J. E. M., Liebman, R. E., Finley, E. P., Monson, C. M., & Wiltsey-Stirman, S. (2023). Initiating cognitive processing therapy (CPT) in community settings: A qualitative investigation of therapist decision-making. *Administration and Policy in Mental Health and Mental Health Services Research, 50*(1), 137–150. https://doi.org/10.1007/s10488-022-01229-8

VA National Center for PTSD. (2023). https://www.ptsd.va.gov/

VA/DoD Clinical Practice Guideline. (2023). *Management of posttraumatic stress disorder and acute stress disorder work group*. U.S. Government Printing Office.

Williams, A.M. & Dietch, J.R. (2018, November). CPT in community mental health: Front-line application with co-occurring psychosis. In *Poster presentation at the 34th ISTSS annual meeting, Washington, DC*.

Wray, C. M., Khare, M., & Keyhani, S. (2021). Access to care, cost of care, and satisfaction with care among adults with private and public health insurance in the US. *JAMA Network Open, 4*(6), e2110275. https://doi.org/10.1001/jamanetworkopen.2021.10275

Part VI
Future Directions in CPT

Chapter 19
Looking Ahead: Future Directions in CPT

Tara E. Galovski and Jennifer S. Wachen

There is little question that engaging in treatment for PTSD can be very challenging for those suffering from this chronic and enduring disorder. The core 20 symptoms of PTSD are further complicated by the host of mental and physical health conditions that commonly co-occur and complicate recovery. Indeed, taking the courageous step to engage in trauma-focused therapy requires patients to do the very thing that they absolutely do not want to do—engage in the memory of the worst thing that has ever happened to them. On paper, avoiding the memory of one's worst experience seems like a good idea, but, as we well know, that avoidance keeps survivors locked in PTSD and perpetuates pain and suffering. The fundamental and substantial challenge of reducing avoidance in treating PTSD is further complicated by the significant psychosocial impairments that develop with PTSD and appear to worsen over time in the absence of treatment. Indeed, we see trauma survivors suffering from PTSD experience their worlds growing smaller and smaller as time passes, and disruptions in social, occupational, recreational, and relational impairments pile up. As therapists, we are called to help our patients restore their world despite their lived experiences. Therapists know all too well that we can't alter the past, but we can help survivors with PTSD build their worlds large enough to hold the memory of the trauma and still live their best lives.

The mission of recovery is lofty and, as authors have reviewed throughout this book, the path is complicated. As we step back and absorb the breadth and scope of the research captured and summarized in this volume, it becomes readily apparent that, as a result of these research efforts, the needle has moved tremendously in the

T. E. Galovski (✉) · J. S. Wachen
Women's Health Sciences Division, National Center for PTSD, VA Boston Healthcare System and Boston University Chobanian and Avedesian School of Medicine, Boston, MA, USA
e-mail: Tara.Galovski@va.gov

J. S. Wachen, T. E. Galovski (eds.), *Cognitive Processing Therapy for Complex Cases*, CBT: Science Into Practice,
https://doi.org/10.1007/978-3-031-87356-0_19

direction of recovery for trauma survivors from all walks of life, across trauma types, and from across the globe. Beyond a summary of research, the care that each of the expert authors took to provide detailed descriptions of the clinical applications of the fruits of their research makes this volume an invaluable resource for providers grappling with the complexity of PTSD clinical presentations. We cannot thank our colleagues enough for their outstanding contributions!

This volume is an excellent example of the evolution of a therapy born in an office on an academic hall on a midwestern university campus over three decades ago. Notably, CPT was developed during a time when research on sexual trauma and its sequelae was in its infancy. Dr. Resick is not only a pioneer in developing this intervention, but also a pioneer in bringing attention to the impact of sexual violence and gender-based violence more broadly. CPT was also developed during an era of a significant upheaval within the field of psychology around the movement to "bridge the scientist-practitioner gap." This era was not without contention and significant pushback by leaders in the field against the idea of the establishment of clinical practice guidelines and the identification of evidence-based treatments (originally termed "empirically validated treatments"), and great debate ensued (reviewed in Galovski, McSweeney, et al., 2024).

Broadly, the idea that any manual-based therapy can accumulate enough scientific evidence to reach the status of "top-tier" or "frontline" treatment was hotly debated (Nathan, 1998). Concerns included the rigidity of manualized therapy, the lack of focus of manualized therapy on patient needs beyond core symptoms, and the lack of attention to nonspecific factors that also contribute to recovery (Garfield, 1998; Goldfried & Wolfe, 1996). Criticisms resounded about the narrow scope of manuals and lack of attention to the full range of aspects of the patients' clinical complexities. Criticisms also extended to the research designs (e.g. inadequate measurement, lack of complexity of study participants) of clinical trials conducted in academia's ivory towers. Pioneers such as Dr. Resick fearlessly led the charge in persisting in conducting state-of-the-art clinical trials with the most complex PTSD cases (Resick et al., 2002; Resick et al., 2008). The success of these early trials with clinically complicated participants with severe PTSD speaks to the robust nature of the core CPT protocol which has been largely retained to this day.

From these early days, the CPT family of investigators and providers grew quickly—now numbering in the thousands worldwide. Many family members contributed to this book! Over the years, efficacy, effectiveness, predictors, and secondary outcomes studies and publications have proliferated (Galovski et al., 2020; Resick et al., 2024) as investigators engaged in enhancements, expansions and, more recently, personalization of the original manual (Galovski, Nixon, & Kehle-Forbes, 2024). The fruits of this labor are captured in this volume and the clinical application of this empirical knowledge is explicated throughout by leading experts in each topic area. In conducting this work, these contributors have faithfully walked the fine line between flexing and improving the core manual to better meet more patients' needs and maintaining fidelity to the principles of the protocol. This clinical wisdom and guidance are imparted to the reader in every chapter. Authors consistently highlight the need to stay true to the underlying tenets of the therapy, lest CPT become unrecognizable and its efficacy diluted.

Turning our eyes to the future, it is clear that there is much work to be done (Bradley et al., 2005; Steenkamp et al., 2015; Truijens et al., 2019). For example, we know that far too many of our patients treated with CPT and other trauma-focused EBPs have suboptimal response rates. Poor response is highly related to the high drop-out rates that we consistently observe in both clinical trials and in practice. We likewise observe different effect sizes for different patient populations, indicating the need for additional modifications to better meet needs equitably. And we know that training options for many care providers are scant and barriers to accessing training are significant (Finch et al., 2020). As a result, community providers adopt CPT and other EBPs in clinical practice at very low rates which, of course, has substantial implications for providing care for so many in need in the midst of the ongoing, global mental health crisis (Gallo & Barlow, 2012; Hepner et al., 2018).

To meet these overarching needs, authors have offered numerous suggestions for future directions for additional research. These suggestions are multi-faceted and varied in scope and breadth. Drs. Nixon, Kehle-Forbes, Held, Werner, and Scheid along with their co-authors suggest turning attention to answering the question "what works best for whom?" For example, we have data to suggest that group therapy may be particularly suited to those also suffering from substance use disorders. Dr. Walter further notes the importance of understanding which of our available modifications might move the needle further for members of the military population for whom effects have consistently been less robust. Patient matching research is a lofty goal and several authors cite the need for more reliance on technological advances to help in accomplishing this level of science. Multiple authors suggest increased reliance on advanced technological tools and statistical techniques to better evaluate and understand the complex relationships between PTSD and comorbid conditions and the underlying mechanisms that drive treatment effects. Drs. Nixon, Saks, Morland, and Werner are among those who suggest the inclusion of ecological momentary assessment, wearables, devices for better monitoring improvement, and other technologies to aid these empirical efforts.

While the research on CPT has broadly proliferated in leaps and bounds over the last three decades, authors noted particularly vulnerable populations that remain under-studied. Authors universally spoke to their commitment to testing CPT's effectiveness with under-served and under-represented patient populations. In order to better meet the diverse nature of patient needs, Drs. Collazo, Kaysen, Walter and others put forth a clear call to expand manual guidance and content to include culturally relevant material and to build in flexibility to ensure the most robust possible protocol is implemented, increasing the likelihood of more holistic outcomes. Dr. Sacks' work in implementing CPT in patient populations suffering from comorbid serious mental illness and Dr. Jak's work describing delivery of CPT for those also suffering from a range of health complications which often take priority during treatment are great examples of the necessity of further research to better meet the unique needs of vulnerable populations. Drs. Holder, Holliday, and Nanney echo this sentiment with their work and guidance in incorporating the ability to flex the scaffolding of CPT for high risk and emotionally dysregulated patients. This guidance is critical for therapists grappling with administering trauma-focused care while diligently making every effort to ensure their patients' safety.

Throughout the literature reviews and clinical examples presented in the chapters, authors resoundingly and repeatedly spoke to, and relied on, the importance of the heart and soul of CPT, Socratic Questions. We hope that the examples provided guidance to crystallize this rather elusive skill for clinicians. The gentle, empathic, and collaborative nature of this key element of CPT empowers patients to question trauma-related, deeply hurtful, and woefully inaccurate beliefs based on real evidence and to change their minds. As CPT clinicians, we have all had the honor and privilege of watching that process unfurl and have borne witness to the remarkable change that can take place in our patients' mental health and in their lives. Reliance on this core skill (*asking* the question and *resisting telling* the patient their truth) is the key factor in this treatment's success. Continuing to exert efforts in improving this skill for all therapists is essential.

Finally, authors note the need for improved training materials that include the clinical guidance provided in this book, increased access to training for more clinicians, and reduction of barriers to implementation of therapy. Questions remain about how to successfully implement intensive or massed interventions across healthcare systems and in private practice, how and when to best conduct group therapy, and how to increase access to continuing education for clinicians so that they may be knowledgeable about protocol modifications and advancements. As Dr. Wamser notes, these needs and barriers extend to prevention and early intervention for trauma survivors. Drs. Maieritsch, Healy, and Williams and their co-authors describe herculean efforts in the training of CPT thus far. They further note that the numbers of trained clinicians and the uptake of that training is far too low, especially given the substantial global need. Developing empirically supported methods to significantly enhance training is ever more apparent given the enormity of the research captured in this book. It is imperative to continue to make every effort to bridge the scientist-practitioner gap.

In summary, we offer several broad suggestions for the continued evolution of CPT. First, packaging the fruits of the research summarized in this book and personalizing CPT to best meet the patients' needs is critical (Galovski, Nixon, & Kehle-Forbes, 2024). Further, CPT therapists must consider patient needs more holistically. Intentionally considering outcomes beyond the core symptoms of PTSD to include functioning and well-being will move the needle further toward holistic recovery and prevent relapse (Bonfils et al., 2022; Galovski, Nixon, & Kehle-Forbes, 2024). Second, increasing access to CPT requires efforts beyond increasing training for more clinicians. The recent self-help CPT book (Resick et al., 2023) is a great example of a more scalable model of care. Research is needed to understand its effect as well as its ability to serve as a conduit to higher levels of care when warranted. Another example of a scalable strategy currently under development by our research team is a self-directed, internet-based version of CPT, in which individuals engage in an interactive program to learn and practice the skills of CPT at their own pace. If some people are effectively able to utilize CPT in this way without the need for the involvement of a trained therapist, this would greatly increase the reach of the intervention and the number of people who could benefit. Titrating care delivery following completion of CPT to enhance benefits, increase

holistic outcomes, and increase continued self-directed care is also a promising area of continued research (Kehle-Forbes et al., 2023). Finally, increased integration of CPT delivery into larger patient ecosystems may directly impact both retention and non-response rates. Given the consistent research showing the importance of social support in recovery from PTSD (Cacioppo et al., 2015; Lord et al., 2020), understanding the impact of enhancements to care via support from partners or families (Howard et al., 2022) or peer support (Galovski et al., 2022; Galovski, Street, et al., 2024) might increase the likelihood of completion and optimal outcomes. We can't wait to see what the future holds in the continued evolution of CPT.Competing InterestsTara Galovski has received research grants to study cognitive processing therapy from the U.S. Department of Defense, National Institutes of Health, Veterans Health Administration, Substance Abuse and Mental Health Service Administration, and foundation support and receives honoraria for training and consulting in CPT. Jennifer Wachen has received research grants to study cognitive processing therapy from the U.S. Department of Defense and receives honoraria for training and consulting in CPT.

References

Bonfils, K. A., Tennity, C. L., Congedo, B. A., Dolowich, B. A., Hammer, L. A., & Haas, G. L. (2022). Functional outcomes from psychotherapy for people with posttraumatic stress disorder: A meta-analysis. *Journal of Anxiety Disorders, 89*, 102576. https://doi.org/10.1016/j.janxdis.2022.102576

Bradley, R., Greene, J., Russ, E., Dutra, L., & Westen, D. (2005). A multidimensional meta-analysis of psychotherapy for PTSD. *American Journal of Psychiatry, 162*(2), 214–227. https://doi.org/10.1176/appi.ajp.162.2.214

Cacioppo, S., Grippo, A. J., London, S., Goossens, L., & Cacioppo, J. T. (2015). Loneliness: Clinical import and interventions. *Perspectives on Psychological Science, 10*(2), 238–249.

Finch, J., Ford, C., Grainger, L., & Meiser-Stedman, R. (2020). A systematic review of the clinician related barriers and facilitators to the use of evidence-informed interventions for posttraumatic stress. *Journal of Affective Disorders, 263*, 175–186. https://doi.org/10.1016/j.jad.2019.11.143

Gallo, K. P., & Barlow, D. H. (2012). Factors involved in clinician adoption and nonadoption of evidence-based interventions in mental health. *Clinical Psychology: Science and Practice, 19*(1), 93–106. https://doi.org/10.1111/j.1468-2850.2012.01276.x

Galovski, T. E., McSweeney, L., Nixon, R. D. V., Wachen, J. S., Smith, B. N., Noorbaloochi, S., Vogt, D., Niles, B., & Kehle-Forbes, S. M. (2024). Personalizing cognitive processing therapy with a case formulation approach to intentionally target impairment associated with psychosocial functioning associated with PTSD. *Contemporary Clinical Trials, 42*, 101385. https://doi.org/10.1016/j.conctc.2024.101385

Galovski, T. E., Nixon, R., & Kaysen, D. (2020). *Flexible applications of cognitive processing therapy: Evidence-based treatment methods*. Academic Press.

Galovski, T. E., Nixon, R. D. V., & Kehle-Forbes, S. M. (2024). Walking the fine line between fidelity and flexibility: A conceptual review of personalized approaches to manualized treatments for PTSD. *Journal of Traumatic Stress, 37*(5), 768–774. https://doi.org/10.1002/jts.23073

Galovski, T. E., Street, A. E., Cooney, C., & Winters, M. R. (2024). Evaluating the impact of a peer support program on participants' well-being: Finding belongingness through the Women Veterans Network (WoVeN). *Medical Care, 62*(12 Suppl 1), S43–S49. https://doi.org/10.1097/MLR.0000000000002039

Galovski, T. E., Street, A. E., McCaughey, V. K., Archibald, E. A., Wachen, J. S., & Chan, A. C. (2022). WoVeN: The women veterans network: An innovative peer support network for women veterans. *Journal of General Internal Medicine, 37*, 842. https://doi.org/10.1007/s11606-022-07579-1

Garfield, S. L. (1998). Some comments on empirically supported treatments. *Journal of Consulting and Clinical Psychology, 66*(1), 121–125. https://doi.org/10.1037/0022-006X.66.1.121

Goldfried, M. R., & Wolfe, B. E. (1996). Psychotherapy practice and research: Repairing a strained alliance. *American Psychologist, 51*(10), 1007–1016. https://doi.org/10.1037/0003-066X.51.10.1007

Hepner, K. A., Farris, C., Farmer, C. M., Iyiewuare, P. O., Tanielian, T., Wilks, A., Robbins, M., Paddock, S. M., & Pincus, H. A. (2018). Delivering clinical practice guideline-concordant care for PTSD and major depression in military treatment facilities. *Rand Health Quarterly, 7*(3), 3.

Howard, K. P., Spoont, M. R., Polusny, M. A., Eftekhari, A., Rosen, C. S., & Meis, L. A. (2022). The role of symptom accommodation in trauma-focused treatment engagement and response. *Journal of Traumatic Stress, 36*, 1–13. https://doi.org/10.1002/jts.22912

Kehle-Forbes, S. M., Galovski, T. E., Polusny, M. A., Possemato, K., Nugent, S., McManus, E., & Baier, A. L. (2023). Development and pilot test of a therapist-assisted self-management program for completers of trauma-focused therapy for posttraumatic stress disorder. *Cognitive and Behavioral Practice.* https://doi.org/10.1016/j.cbpra.2023.08.002

Lord, K. A., Suvak, M. K., Holmes, S., et al. (2020). Bidirectional relationships between posttraumatic stress disorder and social functioning during cognitive processing therapy. *Behavior Therapy, 51*(3), 447–460.

Nathan, P. E. (1998). Practice guidelines: Not yet ideal. *American Psychologist, 53*(3), 290–299. https://doi.org/10.1037/0003-066X.53.3.290

Resick, P. A., Galovski, T. E., Uhlmansiek, M. O. B., Scher, C. D., Clum, G. A., & Young-Xu, Y. (2008). A randomized clinical trial to dismantle components of cognitive processing therapy for posttraumatic stress disorder in female victims of interpersonal violence. *Journal of Consulting and Clinical Psychology, 76*(2), 243–258. https://doi.org/10.1037/0022-006X.76.2.243

Resick, P. A., LoSavio, S. T., Monson, C., Kaysen, D. L., Wachen, J. S., Galovski, T. E., Wiltsey Stirman, S., Nixon, R. D. V., & Chard, K. (2024). State of the science of cognitive processing therapy. *Behavior Therapy, 55*, 1205–1221.

Resick, P. A., Nishith, P., Weaver, T. L., Astin, M. C., & Feuer, C. A. (2002). A comparison of cognitive-processing therapy with prolonged exposure and a waiting condition for the treatment of chronic posttraumatic stress disorder in female rape victims. *Journal of Consulting and Clinical Psychology, 70*(4), 867–879. https://doi.org/10.1037/0022-006X.70.4.867

Resick, P. A., Stirman, S. W., & LoSavio, S. T. (2023). *Getting unstuck from PTSD: Using cognitive processing therapy to guide your recovery*. The Guilford Press.

Steenkamp, M. M., Litz, B. T., Hoge, C. W., & Marmar, C. R. (2015). Psychotherapy for military-related PTSD: A review of randomized clinical trials. *JAMA, 314*(5), 489–500. https://doi.org/10.1001/jama.2015.8370

Truijens, F., Zühlke-van Hulzen, L., & Vanheule, S. (2019). To manualize, or not to manualize: Is that still the question? A systematic review of empirical evidence for manual superiority in psychological treatment. *Journal of Clinical Psychology, 75*(3), 329–343. https://doi.org/10.1002/jclp.22712

Index

J. S. Wachen, T. E. Galovski (eds.), *Cognitive Processing Therapy for Complex Cases*, CBT: Science Into Practice,
https://doi.org/10.1007/978-3-031-87356-0

MIX
Papier aus verantwortungsvollen Quellen
Paper from responsible sources
FSC® C105338

If you have any concerns about our products,
you can contact us on
ProductSafety@springernature.com

In case Publisher is established outside the EU,
the EU authorized representative is:
Springer Nature Customer Service Center GmbH
Europaplatz 3, 69115 Heidelberg, Germany

Printed by Libri Plureos GmbH
in Hamburg, Germany